Economic Development

Economic Development

PRINCIPLES, PROBLEMS, AND POLICIES

Benjamin Higgins, M.Sc., Ph.D.

Professor of Economics, University of Texas.
Visiting Professor of Economics and Director of the Indonesia Project, Massachusetts Institute of Technology.

W · W · NORTON & COMPANY · INC · *New York*

Library of Congress Catalog Card No. 59-6085

PRINTED IN THE UNITED STATES OF AMERICA
FOR THE PUBLISHERS BY THE VAIL-BALLOU PRESS
4 5 6 7 8 9

TO THOSE WHO TAUGHT ME MOST

Alvin Hansen

Herbert Heaton   Lionel Robbins

Arthur Marget   Paul Rosenstein-Rodan

Contents

PART 3

Principles: Lessons of History

PART 4

Principles: Theories of Underdevelopment

PART 5
Policies

Preface

As ordinarily conceived, a textbook is mainly concerned with presenting "received doctrine"; it only hints at the controversies raging on the frontiers of knowledge. It is also expected to be understandable to students and intelligent laymen without previous training in the field.

At this point in the history of economic thought, no such textbook can be written on economic development. Compared to fields like general economic theory, money and banking, public finance, international trade, or even economic fluctuations, the range of agreement on economic development is extremely narrow. In the case of the underdeveloped areas, economists are particularly aware of deficient knowledge. Is the problem of poverty and stagnation in those countries essentially economic, or is it basically technological, psychological, sociological, or political? No one is altogether sure.

Since World War II, however, economic development has become a major consideration of policy, whatever the state of economic theory concerning it. People in advanced countries have been more insistent than ever before that national incomes should rise steadily, and the development of underdeveloped countries has been a matter of world-wide concern. The pressure to discover effective means of launching economic growth is compelling economists to reconsider their concepts of the scope and method of economics. Economists are being forced into a whole galaxy of peripheral fields in which they are somewhat unsure of their footing. Not since the crash of 1929 have professional economists faced more urgent demand for answers to pressing policy questions; and not since the crash have they been so inadequately equipped to answer the questions put to them. So we must try to meet the demand for policies—and for textbooks—before we are altogether ready.

For these reasons, this "textbook" has some of the characteristics of a "treatise." It reflects the conclusions of the author rather than those of other writers in the field and is less of a digest of the literature than most textbooks.

I have, of course, reviewed *some* of the writings in the field. For although the present state of knowledge is unsatisfactory as a basis for policy, there is a swelling literature and a growing area of agreement. The problem of economic growth was the first main interest of economists, and it remained their interest for nearly a century after the publication of Adam Smith's *Wealth of Nations* in 1776. Only in the late nineteenth century—possibly because Europe, America, and Australia were developing rapidly and few people were then concerned with raising incomes of Africans and Asians—did interest shift to theories of value and distribution, and later to theories of economic fluctuations. We are thus returning to the original concern of economics, rather than opening a field which is entirely new. When tackling any policy problem, it is always useful to see what the available literature offers in the way of analysis and solutions. I have, therefore, reviewed briefly the Classical model of economic growth as well as models offered by Marx, Schumpeter, Harrod, and Hansen.

Today however, neither in advanced nor in underdeveloped countries do conditions reproduce those of Europe between 1750 and 1913. The analyses of the process of growth made by earlier generations of economists, valuable as they are, are far from complete. I have therefore selected from the writings of contemporary economists what appears useful. But I have not tried to be comprehensive; it has not seemed wise to distract the reader by summarizing *every* view which the literature presents. I consider here only two kinds of publications: those which contain material which must be included in any satisfactory general theory of economic development; and those which I consider both dangerously wrong and widely held, so that refutation is important.

Within these limits, I have tried to make this as much of a textbook as possible. It is directed to the student and the intelligent layman, rather than to an exclusive audience of professional "development economists." Formal training in economics, beyond what is provided in a good introductory course, is not assumed. Indeed, I hope the book will be intelligible even to people with no previous training in economics. At the same time, I hope that the presentation offers novelty enough to make the book of some interest to economists as well.

I have tried to write so that any difficulties the reader encounters will be those arising inevitably from the complexity of the subject and our inadequate knowledge of it, rather than those resulting from use of technical jargon or highly specialized analytical tools. I have borne in mind, however, that to some people a simple diagrammatic or mathematical formulation is a help rather than a hindrance. Accordingly, I have tried to present major propositions in three ways: in words, in diagrams, and in equations. Those who dislike diagrams and equations should be able to follow the main argument from words alone, but those who are helped by diagrams and equations will find illustrations in these forms.

The latter half of the book deals with policy. I do not claim to have perfected a theory of development, but sensible and useful policy recommendations can be made without a perfected and thoroughly refined theory. And that is fortunate, for whether we like it or not, we are faced with the need to formulate policies for economic growth—we cannot await perfection of our theories. But the policies must at least be as good as our knowledge permits. Widespread understanding of the policy issues, both in underdeveloped and in advanced countries, is of the utmost importance for maintaining peace and prosperity.

The book has benefited enormously from having been written at the M.I.T. Center for International Studies, where so much work on economic development has been going on around me. Not only have I been able to use research materials prepared by my colleagues before formal publication; even more important perhaps has been the general stimulus from continuous discussion with them over the past four and a half years. It would be misleading to single out any of them for special thanks; it is the "atmosphere" they have created jointly that has been most helpful. References to their individual work are made in the text. The book has also benefited, of course, by my having been privileged to undertake four missions to underdeveloped countries, one for the Center and three for the United Nations. Finally, the presentation has been much improved by my wife's blue pencil.

Acknowledgements

Acknowledgements are due to the following publishers and journals for permission to utilize or draw upon earlier publications by the author: *The American Economic Review; The Canadian Journal of Economics and Political Science; The Economic Journal; The Economic Record; Ekonomi dan Keuangan Indonesia; Economic Development and Cultural Change;* the Institute of Pacific Relations; *Land Economics;* the Melbourne University Press; *Social Research;* the United Nations; and *World Politics.*

Acknowledgements are due to the following authors and publishers for permission to quote: G. C. Allen and A. G. Donnithorne, *Western Enterprise in Indonesia and Malaya*, Macmillan & Co., Ltd.; M. K. Atallah, *The Long-term Movement of the Terms of Trade between Agricultural and Industrial Products*, Netherlands Economics Institute; P. Bauer and B. S. Yamey, *The Economics of Underdeveloped Countries*, University of Chicago Press; J. H. Boeke, *Economics and Economic Policy of Dual Societies*, Institute of Pacific Relations; R. V. Clemence and F. S. Doody, *The Schumpeterian System*, Addison-Wesley Press; S. H. Frankel, *The Economic Impact on Underdeveloped Societies*, Oxford University Press; A. O. Hirschman, *The Strategy of Economic Development*, Yale University Press; B. F. Hoselitz (ed.), *The Progress of Underdeveloped Areas*, University of Chicago Press; D. H. K. Lee, *Climate and Economic Development in the Tropics*, Harper & Brothers; R. Lekachman (ed.), *National Policy for Economic Welfare at Home and Abroad*, Doubleday & Company, Inc.; H. Leibenstein, *Economic Backwardness and Economic Growth*, University of California Press and John Wiley & Sons, Inc.; W. A. Lewis, *The Theory of Economic Growth*, Richard D. Irwin, Inc.; W. Malenbaum, *East and West in India's*

Development, National Planning Association; R. Malthus, *Principles of Political Economy*, Augustus Kelly; G. M. Meier and R. E. Baldwin, *Economic Development: Theory, History, and Policy*, John Wiley & Sons, Inc.; J. Schumpeter, *Business Cycles*, McGraw-Hill Book Company, Inc.; J. J. Spengler and O. D. Duncan, *Demographic Analysis* and *Population Theory and Policy*, Richard D. Irwin, Inc.; H. F. Williamson and J. A. Buttrick, *Economic Development: Principles and Patterns*, Prentice-Hall, Inc.; W. S. Woytinsky and E. S. Woytinsky, *World Population and Production*, The Twentieth Century Fund, Inc.

Acknowledgements are also due to the following journals and authors for permission to quote: *The American Economic Review*, R. Eckaus, R. R. Nelson, H. Singer; *Economic Development and Cultural Change*, Phyllis Deane; *The Economic Journal*, H. Myint; *Journal of Economic History*, A. Gerschenkron; *The Manchester School of Economic and Social Studies*, W. A. Lewis; *Oxford Economic Papers*, H. Myint; *The Quarterly Journal of Economics*, R. Solow.

PART 1 Introduction: The Problem of Economic Development

1 The General Nature of the Development Problem

If it were possible to chart per capita income for all the countries now belonging to the United Nations, starting with the beginning of human history and ending with World War II, the charts would show long periods of dreary stagnation, interrupted by short spurts of economic progress in a few countries. The rapid and essentially continuous rise in per capita income in Europe, North America, and Australasia during the past two and a half centuries, which many of us in the Western world have come to regard as "normal," would appear as a phenomenon unique in history. Perhaps, as some economic historians insist, this remarkable rise in productivity, confined to so small a share of world population for so short a period, was "more than industrial and less than revolution"; but certainly the difference in *degree* between the rise in general living standards in those countries at that time, and any economic development that has occurred elsewhere, before or since, is so great as to constitute a difference in kind. Stagnation is the rule; economic development is the exception that requires special explanation.

Since the end of World War II, however, governments in other parts of the world—Latin America, Africa, the Middle East, Asia, and some European countries as well—have become increasingly "development-minded." A good many of these countries have embarked on the preparation and execution of economic plans. The Western world has demonstrated its interest in these development plans by providing technical and capital assistance in a manner novel in history. Indeed, the prospect of converting poor and stagnant economies into prosperous and progressive ones, through a joint effort of advanced and underdeveloped countries, is the most impressive item on the asset side of the postwar international relations ledger.

Since World War II, a whole battery of institutions has come into being to help underdeveloped areas with their development programs. The International Bank for Reconstruction and Development, a Specialized Agency of the United Nations, provides loan capital to the governments of underdeveloped countries. More recently, the International Finance Corporation has been established as a complement of the Bank, to provide funds for private investment in underdeveloped areas. The Technical Assistance Administration, the Food and Agriculture Organization, the International Labor Organization, the World Health Organization, UNESCO, other UN Specialized Agencies, and the Ford Foundation provide technical assistance. The United States has its own program of technical and capital assistance under the International Cooperation Administration and its subsidiary, the Development Loan Fund. The United States Export-Import Bank, although originally established for other purposes, has in recent years allocated the bulk of its funds for loans to underdeveloped areas. Australia, Canada, and Great Britain are providing capital and technical assistance to Commonwealth countries, and to some others as well, through the Colombo Plan Organization. Some West European countries also have bilateral aid programs.[1]

Since 1956, Russia has become an increasingly strong competitor of the Western countries in providing technical and capital assistance. Russian assistance has been concentrated in the "uncommitted" countries of Africa, Asia, and the Middle East. As a consequence, economic aid to these countries has become a major instrument in the Cold War.

But while the foreign aid programs have become entrenched as part of the foreign policy of Western countries, they are at the same time the subject of considerable controversy. In the United States, the Administration's annual effort to obtain increased sums for economic assistance, to have aid put on a long-run basis, without political strings, has encountered strong opposition, both within Congress and outside it. The whole concept of economic assistance has been attacked from some quarters as a "giveaway

[1] See Chap. 26 below and the tabulations presented there.

program." Even those who are convinced that furthering the economic development of underdeveloped countries is necessary to our security raise questions about the proper scale and scope of this assistance. How much capital do underdeveloped countries really need for a take-off into sustained growth? How much can they spend efficiently at the present time? How can one determine the most efficient allocation of the resources available for development? Is capital their main requirement for growth, or are such factors as management, technical skills, labor skills, more important? Would aid on any scale or of any type assure economic growth? Is there really any hope of achieving higher living standards in these countries without fundamental changes in their social institutions, psychological attitudes, perhaps even in their ideologies or religions? Answering these questions requires some understanding of the whole process of economic growth.

Nor is it only in the economically advanced countries that doubts exist about economic development and the role of foreign aid and investment in it. In many underdeveloped countries, too, serious questions are being asked. Countries recently released from colonial rule raise questions like these: "Will we endanger our hard-won independence and our way of life by accepting aid from Western capitalist countries? May not new style economic imperialism prove just as injurious as old style political imperialism?" In countries with more experience with, or insight into, the problems of dealing with the Sino-Soviet bloc, people ask, "Can we really hope to remain non-Communist if we accept large-scale aid from Russia or China?" Neutralist countries like India, Indonesia, and Burma, which attach great importance to their religious life and to a social philosophy stressing mutual welfare, are inclined to ask, "Is not the crass materialism of *both* the capitalist and communist systems a threat to our superior spiritual values? Is it safe to allow either the Communist bloc or the West a major role in our economic development? How much trade and aid can we take from godless Russia without any injurious impact on our own system of values? May not our society deteriorate if we depend too much on a moneygrubbing, ruthlessly exploitative, ferociously competitive, neurotic society like the United States?" The fact that some of these questions reflect a false image of Western society makes them no less influential at the moment.

Certainly understanding of the economics and politics of development must be more widespread in both underdeveloped and advanced countries if we are to realize our brave hopes of wiping poverty off the face of the earth. This book attempts to make a small contribution to extension of such knowledge.

The Meaning of "Underdeveloped"

In the first chapter of its report on *Measures for the Economic Development of Underdeveloped Countries*, the group of experts appointed by the UN Secretary-General says:

> We have had some difficulty in interpreting the term underdeveloped countries. We use it to mean countries in which per capita real income is low when compared with the per capita real incomes of the United States of America, Canada, Australia, and Western Europe. In this sense, an adequate synonym would be "poor countries."

In general, underdeveloped countries in this sense are those with per capita incomes less than one-quarter those of the United States—or, roughly, less than $500 per year. (See Table 1-1.) Of course, national averages can be misleading; there is a difference between underdeveloped *countries* and underdeveloped *areas*. In some countries with quite high average incomes large regions have very low per capita income. Striking examples of this are Italy, with its "developed" north and its "underdeveloped" south; Venezuela and Iran, with a rich petroleum industry superimposed on an otherwise little developed economy; Malaya, with its trade-rich Singapore and its relatively poor Malayan peasants. Yet even in such countries as Canada and the United States, one can find regions in which per capita income is low enough to warrant the use of the term "underdeveloped."

One might label a country underdeveloped if its government considers development a "problem" in a way which calls for positive policy. In this sense, Canada would have been an underdeveloped country throughout the nineteenth century. It might even be considered so today, despite its high per capita income and its high current rate of economic growth; Canada has a "Royal Commission on Economic Prospects" rather than a Planning Commission, but a Canadian Commission by any other name still smacks of development. However, we shall adopt the common definition of underdeveloped, which makes it synonymous with poor.

The term has come into wide usage with the organization of programs for technical and capital assistance since World War II. A country is added to the active list of countries under consideration for aid by the agencies administering these programs when its government becomes sufficiently interested in development to apply for assistance, and if it is regarded as a potential candidate for such aid by the agency. For policy purposes, we might even define an "underdeveloped country" as one with announced goals and policies for economic development which is regarded as a candidate for assistance through the foreign aid programs of the United States and other Western nations. Such a definition would scarcely serve for analytical purposes. We must be able to distinguish the countries with which we are concerned in some other fashion than referring to the files of applications in aid-administering agencies.

The expression underdeveloped is admittedly not a very happy one, and others have been suggested, such as preindustrialized and developing. The second of these is clearly a misnomer; the real problem is that some of these countries are not developing at all. If the term developing were taken literally, it would apply more clearly to the United States, Canada, and Australia than to Asian or African countries. The term preindustrialized, on the other hand, prejudges the policy conclusions. We ought not to decide that industrialization is tantamount to economic development until we have completed our analysis. In any case, the word underdeveloped has become a recognized technical term and is now in wide usage even by social scientists and politicians in the underdeveloped countries themselves. It seems better, therefore, to stick to it, remembering that it *is* a technical term, meaning only that per capita incomes are less than one-quarter that of the United States.

Being underdeveloped in this technical sense means nothing in terms of the level of civilization, culture, or spiritual values. It might be a good idea to organize a "reverse technical assistance program" with experts from the so-called underdeveloped countries being sent to the West to teach us some of their arts and skills. Mechanics in some Asian countries have much to teach those of the West, who can only replace damaged or worn parts with new ones and do not really know how to *fix* things as Asians do. We could benefit a great deal by acquiring some of the Asian's capacity for complete leisure—just doing nothing. We could also learn much about the value of contemplation. A team of Javanese and Balinese girls could teach our wives and daughters a good deal about how to stand, walk, sit, move, and otherwise go gracefully through daily life. Our social relations might be smoother if we adopted some of the face-saving devices of Asian societies, and we have a long way to go before art and religion mean as much in our daily lives as they do in Asian countries. But Asian, African, and some Latin American countries face poverty in a form that has largely disappeared in the United States, Canada, and some European nations. It is with the abolition of this poverty that economic development policy is concerned.

Problems of Measurement

The choice of "25 per cent of the United States level" as the per capita income dividing advanced from underdeveloped countries is, of course, somewhat arbitrary. It can be justified in terms of policy, but it is harder to defend in terms of pure analysis. The countries which in 1952–54 had per capita income above $500 were, for the most part, not countries with development "problems" of a sort which would be widely regarded as calling for joint action by the countries themselves in cooperation with advanced countries having foreign aid programs. On our definition Venezuela would not be included among underdeveloped countries. Venezuela has development plans and a great deal of poverty; but Venezuela would be considered by many people—both in Venezuela and in advanced countries—capable of financing its own development by "sowing its petroleum." On the other hand, many people would regard Israel and Argentina as underdeveloped, and therefore we cannot go much below $500 in choosing our dividing line.

More serious than the arbitrariness of the dividing line is the sheer difficulty of translating per capita incomes into United States dollars. Obviously, the Libyan figure of $25 cannot mean that the average standard of living was equivalent to what an American would suffer with an income of $25 per year. In the Introduction to the document presenting the figures in Table 1-1, the UN outlines some of the difficulties faced in making estimates of this kind: [2]

> In this connexion it is understandable that improvement in the quality of the estimates of national product has been generally more difficult and slower in the less developed countries than in the more widely industrialized countries of the world where as a rule, adequate statistical systems have evolved over the years. A problem of particular importance confronting the less developed countries in estimating their national product arises from the existence of a substantial non-monetized economy. Where only a part of the total output of goods

[2] United Nations, *Per-capita National Product of Fifty-five Countries: 1952–54,* Statistical Papers Series E, No. 4. (New York, 1957), p. 4.

and services of a country is traded at the market it is necessary for national income purposes to estimate that part which is produced outside the monetary sphere. This area of estimation is indeed subject to a wide margin of error since the extent of such activities is known in a very approximate manner only. . . . The use of exchange rates for expressing estimates of national product in a common currency unit is subject to a number of serious shortcomings, both theoretical and statistical, which have been described in various studies. The main criticism is directed at the fact that this method oversimplifies a complex problem of evaluating in a common currency unit the total output of goods and services of different countries. It is contended that approximately correct results can be obtained by this method only where there exists an equivalence between the prevailing exchange rates and the relationship of internal prices. This equivalence is unlikely to be achieved for most countries today in view of the prevalent use of exchange controls and quantitative restrictions on trade.

Recognizing that official rates of exchange are frequently a poor measure of comparative purchasing power, the UN sought to improve its estimates by using other conversion rates whenever there were multiple exchange rates or where price movements were large in comparison to price movements in the United States.

For European countries a more systematic attempt has been made to improve national income figures for comparative purposes by the OEEC.[3] In brief, the method utilized for increasing comparability consists of using relative price weight for "baskets" of commodities in various countries. The result is to reduce the discrepancies in per capita income, especially as between the United States and European countries. It seems likely that a similar procedure for underdeveloped countries would result in still greater reduction of gaps among per capita incomes.

Within broad categories, the figures in Table 1-1 are probably meaningful for relative levels of income. Thus it probably makes sense to say that average incomes in the Philippines are two and a half times as high as in India, or that incomes in the Argentine are a bit higher than in Ireland and that United States incomes are some 30 per cent higher than Canadian. On the other hand, to say that in the United States incomes are nearly forty times as high as in Burma has little real meaning.

[3] Milton Gilbert and Associates, *Comparative National Products and Price Levels* (Paris: OEEC, 1957).

TABLE 1-1.

Estimates of Per Capita Net National Product of 55 Countries Expressed in U.S. Dollars: Annual average 1952–54 (At factor cost)

Range in dollars	Africa: Country	Africa: Per capita	America: Country	America: Per capita	Asia: Country	Asia: Per capita	Europe: Country	Europe: Per capita	Oceania: Country	Oceania: Per capita
Over 1,000			United States	1,870			Switzerland	1,010		
			Canada	1,310						
750–1,000							Sweden	950	New Zealand	1,000
							Luxembourg	890	Australia	950
							Belgium	800		
							United Kingdom	780		
							Iceland	760		
							Denmark	750		
500–749			Venezuela *	540			France	740		
							Norway	740		
							Finland	670		
							Germany	510		
							Netherlands	500		
250–499	Union of South Africa	300	Argentina	460	Israel	470	Ireland	410		
			Puerto Rico	430	Malaya *	310	Austria	370		
			Chile	360	Lebanon	260	Italy	310		
			Cuba	310						
			Colombia	250						
			Panama	250						
Under 250	Egypt	120	Brazil	230	Turkey	210	Greece	220		
	Rhodesia and Nyasaland	100	Mexico	220	Japan	190	Portugal	200		
	Belgian Congo	70	Jamaica †	180	Philippines	150				
	Kenya	60	Dominican Republic	160	Ceylon	110				
	Uganda	50	Guatemala	160	Thailand *	80				
			Ecuador	150	Korea	70				
			Honduras	150	Pakistan	70				
			Paraguay	140	India	60				
			Peru	120	Burma	50				

* 1952 and 1953.
† 1952.
SOURCE: United Nations, *Per-capita National Product of Fifty-five Countries: 1952–54,* Statistical Papers Series E, No. 4 (New York, 1957).

Other Characteristics of Underdeveloped Countries

If poverty were always accompanied by other characteristics, we might hope to find in these characteristics a clue to the causes of poverty. Examination of statistics and descriptive information pertaining to underdeveloped countries reveals that there is indeed a correlation between national poverty and other features of the country's economic and social organization. It is difficult to improve on the list provided by Professor Harvey Leibenstein: [4]

X

Characteristics of Underdeveloped Areas

1. Economic
   (a) General
      (1) A very high proportion of the population in agriculture, usually some 70 to 90 per cent.
      (2) "Absolute over-population" in agriculture; that is, it would be possible to reduce the number of workers in agriculture and still obtain the same total output.
      (3) Evidence of considerable "disguised unemployment" and a lack of employment opportunities outside agriculture.
      (4) Very little capital per head.
      (5) Low income per head and, as a consequence, existence near the "subsistence" level.
      (6) Practically zero savings for the large mass of the people.
      (7) Whatever savings do exist are usually achieved by a landholding class whose values are not conducive to investment in industry or commerce.
      (8) The primary industries, that is, agriculture, forestry, and mining, are usually the residual employment categories.
      (9) The output in agriculture is made up mostly of cereals and primary raw materials, with relatively low output of protein foods. The reason for this is the conversion ratio between cereals and meat products; that is, if one acre of cereals produces a certain number of calories, it would take between five and seven acres to produce the same number of calories if meat products were produced.
      (10) Major proportion of expenditures on food and necessities.

[4] Harvey Leibenstein, *Economic Backwardness and Economic Growth* (New York, 1957), pp. 40–41. Some excellent descriptive material on underdeveloped countries is presented in Lyle W. Shannon, *Underdeveloped Areas* (New York, 1957).

(11) Export of foodstuffs and raw materials.
(12) Low volume of trade per capita.
(13) Poor credit facilities and poor marketing facilities.
(14) Poor housing.

(b) Basic characteristics in agriculture.

(1) Although there is low capitalization on the land, there is simultaneously an uneconomic use of whatever capital exists due to the small size of holdings and the existence of exceedingly small plots.
(2) The level of agrarian techniques is exceedingly low, and tools and equipment are limited and primitive in nature.
(3) Even where there are big landowners as, for instance, in certain parts of India, the openings for modernized agriculture production for sale are limited by difficulties of transport and the absence of an efficient demand in the local market. It is significant that in many backward countries a modernized type of agriculture is confined to production for sale in foreign markets.
(4) There is an inability of the small landholders and peasants to weather even a short-term crisis, and as a consequence, attempts are made to get the highest possible yields from the soil, which leads to soil depletion.
(5) There is a widespread prevalence of high indebtedness relative to assets and income.
(6) The methods of production for the domestic market are generally old-fashioned and inefficient, leaving little surplus for marketing. This is usually true irrespective of whether or not the cultivator owns the land, has tenancy rights, or is a sharecropper.
(7) A most pervasive aspect is a feeling of land hunger due to the exceedingly small size of holdings and small diversified plots. The reason for this is that holdings are continually subdivided as the population on the land increases.

2. Demographic

(1) High fertility rates, usually above 40 per thousand.
(2) High mortality rates and low expectation of life at birth.
(3) Inadequate nutrition and dietary deficiencies.
(4) Rudimentary hygiene, public health, and sanitation.
(5) Rural overcrowding.

3. Cultural and Political

(1) Rudimentary education and usually a high degree of illiteracy among most of the people.
(2) Extensive prevalence of child labor.
(3) General weakness or absence of the middle class.

(4) Inferiority of women's status and position.
(5) Traditionally determined behavior for the bulk of the populace.

4. Technological and Miscellaneous
(1) Low yields per acre.
(2) No training facilities or inadequate facilities for the training of technicians, engineers, etc.
(3) Inadequate and crude communication and transportation facilities, especially in the rural areas.
(4) Crude technology.

Leibenstein's "characteristics" are of three quite different kinds: statistical facts, general observations, and conclusions from analysis. The structure of employment, output, income, and consumption, amount of capital per head, per capita income, fertility and mortality rates, literacy, yields per acre—these are essentially statistical phenomena, even if the statistics for some countries may be inadequate. On the other hand, when Leibenstein speaks of "poor" credit and marketing facilities and "poor" housing, or of "low" levels of technique and "old-fashioned" methods, a "feeling of land hunger," or "inadequate transport facilities," he is making *observations*, in terms of some unstated criteria. Thus there is room for differences of opinion on these items, apart from the quality of the data. And when he talks of disguised unemployment in agriculture and in cities, or "conversion ratios" between meat and cereals, "uneconomic use of capital," and "dietary deficiencies," he is really presenting us with conclusions derived from somebody's analysis. Here the scope for quarrels is broader. For example, some economists would deny that there is much "disguised unemployment" in the agricultural sectors of most underdeveloped countries. They would argue that if "disguised unemployment" is rigorously defined to mean the numbers that could be wholly and permanently withdrawn from agriculture, with no change in technique and no drop in agricultural output, the figures would be rather low. We shall leave observation and analysis for their proper places in later chapters. Let us confine ourselves here to a quick look at some of the pertinent statistics.

Table 1-2 supports the statement that underdeveloped countries have a high proportion of their gainfully occupied population in agriculture. Among countries classified according to our definition of underdeveloped (having per capita incomes under $500 per year), there is a considerable range in this proportion, but a comparison with Table 1-1 shows a very high inverse correlation between per capita income and the proportion of the population engaged in agriculture. It is also worth noting that high-income countries sometimes thought of as agricultural, such as Canada, Australia, and New Zealand, are not really agricultural in terms of employment; their occupational structures are much the same as that of the United States.

TABLE 1-2.

Industrial Origin of Gross National Product in Various Countries

Country and year		Per cent in agriculture, forestry, fishing	Per cent in manufacturing
United States,	1955	4.3	28.6
Canada,	"	9.9	28.6
New Zealand,	1952	23.9	21.2
Italy,	1955	23.9	32.9
United Kingdom,	"	4.6	38.8
Brazil,	"	31.5	19.4
Colombia,	1954	40.6	16.7
India,	"	48.7	16.8
Indonesia,	1952	56.4	8.2
Japan,	1955	21.8	20.3
Nigeria,	1952	66.2	1.9
Egypt,	1954	35.8	10.7
Philippines,	1955	42.0	14.6

SOURCE: United Nations, *Statistical Yearbook on Income and Employment* (New York, 1957).

Underdeveloped countries also produce relatively large proportions of their national income in the agricultural sector (Table 1-3). The share of income in agriculture is less than the share of employment in agriculture, reflecting the relatively low productivity per man-year in the agricultural sector.

Direct evidence of this aspect of underdeveloped countries is provided in Tables 1-4 and 1-5. Here is one of the most discouraging characteristics of these countries; predominantly agricultural, they are nonetheless much less efficient in agriculture than the predominantly industrial countries. As J. K. Galbraith has put it, "a purely agricultural country is likely to be unprogressive even in its agriculture." And Gunnar Myrdal adds, "Industrialization creates technology which can then be applied to

TABLE 1-3.

Population Engaged in Agricultural Occupations in Specified Countries (both sexes)

Continent and country	Percentage in agriculture 1926–40	1941–65
Europe:		
France	36	27
Ireland	49	40
Italy	48	40
England and Wales	6	5
North and Central America:		
Canada	26	19
Costa Rica	63	55
El Salvador	75	63
Guatemala	71	....
Mexico	65	58
United States	19	12
South America:		
Argentina		25
Brazil	67	58
Chile	35	31
Colombia	72	72
Paraguay	....	56
Venezuela	50	41
Asia:		
Burma	68	....
Ceylon		53
Taiwan	....	63
India	66	71
Indonesia	66	
Israel (Jewish population)	....	11
Japan	48	47
Malaya, Federation of	61	64
Philippines	73	69
Africa:		
Egypt	71	65
Mauritius		45
Oceania:		
Australia	19	16
Hawaii	31	16
New Zealand	23	18

SOURCE: Food and Agriculture Organization, *Statistical Yearbook,* 1957.

TABLE 1-4.

Soybean and Tobacco Production (100 kilograms per hectare)

Country	Soybeans			Tobacco		
	1948–52	1954	1955	1934–38	1948–52	1955
Italy	14.0	14.9	14.8	13.0	13.4	14.9
United States	14.4	13.5	13.5	9.7	14.2	16.4
Canada	15.9	13.1	17.8	11.9	14.4	13.8
Brazil	14.3	14.4	14.9	9.0	7.6	7.6
Chile	......	......	......	20.8	20.3	21.0
China (mainland)	6.0	6.8	7.0	......	11.8	......
India	......	......	......	9.4	7.5	7.2
Indonesia:						
estatos	7.0	7.6	6.6	11.3	5.7	....
farms	8.9	8.1	6.5	4.5	......	....
Philippines	......	......	......	5.2	6.1	5.2
Japan	......	......	......	18.1	17.3	20.0

TABLE 1-5.

Rice Production (100 kilograms per hectare)

Country	1948–52	1954	1955
Italy	48.7	48.8	51.0
United States	25.6	28.2	34.3
Australia	48.6	61.8	45.9
Brazil	15.7	14.8	15.0
Burma	14.1	14.1	14.8
China (mainland)	21.6	24.7	......
India	11.1	12.2	12.6
Indonesia	15.7	17.4	16.5
Java and Madura	16.8	18.4	17.9
Japan	40.0	37.5	48.1
Thailand	13.1	12.6	14.3
Vietnam	....	12.5	12.3
Philippines	11.9	12.1	11.9

agriculture but not vice versa."[5]

Even in the production of major staples underdeveloped countries are frequently less efficient than advanced countries for which the same commodity is a minor export. Indeed, one of the most distressing shocks to the foreign economic adviser, when he

[5] Gunnar Myrdal. *Prospects for an International Economy* (New York, 1956), p. 464.

first goes on mission to an underdeveloped country, is the discovery that the most important local agricultural product is produced at very high cost and cannot compete in the free market with imports from advanced countries. Thus one finds Louisiana rice competing with native rice in the Philippines, imported dates underselling inferior home-grown dates in Libya, California oranges competing with the small, bitter native citrus fruits (*djeruk*) in the Riauw Archipelago of Indonesia. In many Asian countries rice is the staple food, and rice growing the occupation of the majority of the people. Yet of the Asian countries listed in Table 1-5, only Japan has yields as high as in Italy, Australia, and the United States. Vietnam, Thailand, and Burma all depend on rice exports for foreign exchange, yet their yields per hectare are low. Production in Australia and the United States takes the form of mechanized dry rice farming on very large holdings, running into hundreds or even thousands of acres. The typical holding of an Indian or Indonesian peasant family is closer to one acre and that acre is meticulously irrigated and intensively cultivated. Considering the difference in yields per hectare, the discrepancy in yields per man-year is enormous. A similar picture is obtained for soybeans, which one thinks of as an Asian product. Cassava and yams (or sweet potatoes) are foods to which Asians resort when rice is in short supply, but even here Asian yields are no higher than in Brazil or in some advanced countries.

Table 1-6 below and Table 28-2 present some demographic data. Here we find more variety. Underdeveloped countries in general cannot be said to be densely populated. Many of the countries listed in Table 1-6 have fewer people per square mile than the United States; most of them have densities lower than the United Kingdom. Of course, such aggregates tell us little about the degree of population pressure. Libya, with 1 person per square mile in 1956, had a more serious population problem than Burma with 29 people per square mile. Libya is mostly desert; Burma is fertile and has other resources. Again, the Indonesian average density was only 56 per square mile, lower than the Philippines; but Indonesia had one of the most complicated population problems in the world, since two-thirds of its 85 million people were concentrated on the relatively small island of Java, bringing densities on that island to the staggering figure of nearly 1,100 per square mile.

Rates of population growth show a similarly wide range. One cannot say that high rates of population growth are a distinguish-

TABLE 1-6.

Population Growth and Density

Area	Annual rate of increase, 1953–56	Population density, 1956 *
Africa:		
Egypt	2.3	24
Libya	1.2	1
Union of South Africa	1.8	11
Belgian Congo	1.8	5
Cape Verde Islands	3.3	44
Portuguese Guinea	3.4	15
Mauritius	3.3	305
Rhodesia	2.7	6
Nyasaland	3.1	14
Swaziland		
North America:		
Canada	2.7	2
United States	1.8	21
Central America:		
Costa Rica	3.9	19
El Salvador	3.4	113
Guatemala	3.1	31
Mexico	2.9	16
South America:		
Argentina	1.9	7
Colombia	2.2	11
Chile	2.6	9
Paraguay	2.9	4
Venezuela	3.1	7
Brazil	2.4	7
Asia:		
Burma	1.4	29
Ceylon	2.5	136
China	2.2	64
Taiwan	3.8	257
India	1.3	118
Indonesia	1.8	56
Israel	3.5	88
Japan	1.3	243
Malaya	3.1	48
Philippines	1.9	74

Area	Annual rate of increase, 1953–56	Population density, 1956
Europe:		
Italy	0.5	160
Ireland	0.5	41
France	0.8	79
United Kingdom	0.4	211
Australia	2.3	1

* Per square kilometer.
SOURCE: United Nations, *Demographic Yearbook, 1957* (New York, 1958).

ing mark of underdeveloped countries. In Central America and Africa, where densities are generally low, some countries do indeed have appalling rates of population growth. But in Asian countries with high densities, current rates of growth are, for the most part, lower than in Canada or Australia. Very few countries combine high densities and high growth rates.

Before the war, one could have said that underdeveloped countries are characterized by high birth rates and high death rates. Birth rates are still high in most underdeveloped countries, but death rates have fallen dramatically in many of them, as Table 28-2 shows. We shall have more to say about this phenomenon when we come to discuss population policy. The poor state of medical care and education is indicated in Table 1-7.

Finally, we see from Table 1-8 that underdeveloped countries may differ markedly in current rates of economic growth. Some, such as Chile, are virtually stagnant; others, such as Mexico and Brazil, are progressing very well indeed, so far as the ratio of national income to total population is concerned. These differences in rates of growth reflect differences in the proportion of national income channeled into investment, in the amount of increase in income that is achieved with a given amount of investment (incremental capital-output ratios, or ICOR), and in rates of population growth. Most underdeveloped countries, it is true, are investing less than 10 per cent of their national incomes; but there are notable exceptions, such as Burma and Mexico.

Thus whereas all the countries with incomes below $500 per year might be considered underdeveloped, in the sense that their future development is a matter on which policy decisions are being made both in those countries and in the advanced countries with aid programs, and although all such countries exhibit common characteristics, we see that there are important subdivisions

TABLE 1-7.

Indicators of Health and Education

Countries	Per cent of population, age 10 and over, illiterate (1945–54) *	Number of inhabitants per physician (1951–53) †
Rich:		
Australia	below 5	1,000
Canada	below 5	950
United Kingdom	below 5	1,200
United States	below 5	770
Poor:		
Brazil	51	3,000
Chile	24	1,800
Colombia	44	2,800
Egypt	75	3,600
India	82	5,700
Indonesia	92	71,000
Mexico	62	2,400
Venezuela	51	1,900

* United Nations, *Demographic Yearbook, 1955* (New York, 1955), Table 13.

† United Nations, *Statistical Yearbook, 1955* (New York, 1955), Table 172.

to be made among them. In the first place, of course, there is a marked difference between a country with a per capita income of $300 to $500 per year and one with $50 to $100 per year. The former might be considered to have future development within its own grasp, even if it is not currently growing. It is the latter group of countries that present the most appalling problems, particularly if they are stagnant as well as poverty-stricken.

Even rich and stagnant countries have troubles. The maintenance of full employment poses difficult policy questions in highly developed countries which cease to grow. When an "open society," in which opportunities for individual advancement accompany the growth of the economy as a whole, is transformed into a closed one where individual advancement is possible only at the expense of others, social and political problems are intensified as well. If per capita incomes are low but rising, if sustained growth seems assured, and if the gains in welfare are widely diffused, there is relatively little cause for concern. Such a society may well be less troubled than one that is rich but stagnant. Clearly, however, the economic problem is most serious in countries that are both stagnant and impoverished. Above all, therefore, *the* problem of economic development is launching a take-off into sustained growth in poor and stagnant countries. By "sustained growth" is meant a discernible rise in national and per capita real income, widely diffused throughout the population, that continues for two or more generations.

Categories of Underdeveloped Countries

At least four categories of underdeveloped countries can be distinguished:

1. First, there are countries which have per capita incomes low enough to put them into the underdeveloped category, but which have unutilized known resources, and which are currently undertaking enough industrialization and agricultural improvement to bring substantial increases in per capita income. Argentina, Brazil, Ceylon, Colombia, Mexico, Peru, the Philippines, Turkey, Italy, and Venezuela seem to be in this category. These countries, by definition, have sufficient domestic savings and taxes, plus assured foreign capital assistance, to finance the capital formation needed to raise incomes. At the same time, all these countries are confronted with bottlenecks—capital supply, skilled labor, managerial and technical skills—and with laggard sectors of the economy, which limit the rate of growth and make planning necessary. In most of them, growth is very unevenly distributed among social groups and among regions. The problem in these countries is one of sustaining growth, reducing open and disguised unemployment, and spreading the benefits of growth more widely.

2. Second, there are countries like Burma, China, Thailand, and perhaps Pakistan, whose per capita incomes are currently very low (under $100 per year), which do not appear to have abundant resources relative to the size of their populations, but where per capita income is currently rising. In these countries the rise in income must be accelerated, not just sustained.

3. Third, there are countries which are poor and stagnant, in the sense that per capita incomes show no rising trend, but which are relatively rich in resources. Indonesia provides an example in this category. Per capita income is higher than in India, Pakistan, or China—about $100 per year—but is not obviously rising and may even be falling as compared to 1939, 1929, or earlier. Yet Indonesia is a country with a wide variety of resources. In such

TABLE 1-8.

Per Capita Income, Rate of Growth of GNP, Investment, and Capital-Output Ratio: Selected countries, 1945–54

Area	Period (1)	Average rate of growth of real GNP or GDP * (2)	Gross fixed investment as per cent of GNP or GDP (3)	"Gross" incremental capital-output ratio,† column (3) ÷ column (2) (4)
Italy	1947–54	6.3	18.3	2.9
United Kingdom	1947–54	3.3	13.2	4.0
Canada	1947–54	3.8	21.0	5.5
United States ..	1947–54	3.3	16.4	5.0
Argentina	1945–53	3.2 (3.4)	16.9	5.3
Brazil	1945–53	6.7 (7.7)	14.6	2.2
Chile	1945–53	2.1 (3.1)	11.6	5.5
Colombia	1945–53	4.7 (6.5)	15.5	3.3
El Salvador	1945–52	3.5 (7.5) ‡	14.0	4.0
Mexico	1945–53	4.9 (4.7)	13.1	2.7
All Latin American countries .	1945–53	4.8 (5.4)	15.0	3.1
Burma	1947/48–52/53	2.2	11.3	5.1
Ceylon	1947–53	3.0	7.7	2.8
India	1948/49–53/54	2.9	9.2 ‖	3.2
Malaya	1947–53	3.9	8.8	2.3
Pakistan	1948/49–52/53	2.2	n.a.	n.a.
Thailand	1947–53	7.2	n.a.	n.a.

* The growth figures have been derived from gross product estimates which do not include the effects of changes in terms of trade. For the Latin American countries, rates of growth of gross income (including the effects of the terms of trade) are shown in parentheses. The estimates are for the gross national product in the case of the European countries, Canada, the United States, Honduras, and India, and for the gross domestic product for all other countries. The differences between GNP and GDP are so small for the countries for which GNP estimates are shown as to leave the growth rates virtually unaffected.

† The "gross incremental capital-output ratios" shown in column 4 differ from the normal concept of incremental capital-output ratios—which is also used in the text—because they have been computed by dividing gross investment rates by the annual rates of growth of the national (or domestic) product. Perhaps the simplest way to derive net rates would be to deduct a number of percentage points of GNP, or GDP (4? 5? 6?), from the gross investment rates. If such a "standard procedure" is used, the "net" capital-output ratios become somewhat smaller than the gross rates in the case of countries with high gross investment rates, and considerably smaller for countries with low gross investment rates. The magnitude of the continental capital-output ratios, for the OEEC countries and for Latin America, are influenced by the "abnormally" favorable rates (Germany,

countries, especially if the rate of population growth can be held within bounds, the hope for raising per capita income significantly would appear to be much better than in resource-poor countries. But where per capita income is stationary, or falling, or rising very slowly from a very low level, there is little hope that growth will become cumulative without a transformation of the economy. Here the task is not merely to sustain or direct growth already under way, but to *launch* a process of growth that can become cumulative at some level of per capita income.

4. Finally, there are countries which are very poor (with per capita incomes, say, below $100 per year), which are stagnant, and which are also poor in resources. Examples in this category are Libya, Jordan, and Yemen. Per capita income in Libya is estimated at about $30 per year. Outside the Italian colonization schemes, at least, there is no evidence that per capita income has risen in Libya for several centuries; there is some evidence that it has actually declined. Unfortunately, Libya provides little in the way of resources with which the development planner might work. Such countries need a special kind of plan, emphasizing improvement of existing economic undertakings more than structural change.

Such differences in basic economic situation obviously bring with them differences in the nature of the policies to be prescribed. In order to bring out more clearly the differences and similarities in the problems confronting various underdeveloped countries, we present some case studies in the next chapter.

Hen or Egg?

It is easy enough to list distinguishing characteristics of underdeveloped countries. Unfortunately, our hopes of isolating causal relationships in this way have not been fulfilled. For each of the characteristics has a hen-and-egg nature that makes it virtually impossible to separate causes from effects. The high proportion of population in agriculture is almost a definition, rather than a cause, of underdevelopment. It reflects the fact that the capital, technical and managerial skills, and the entrepreneurship needed

Austria) and the "abnormally" unfavorable rates (Argentina, Chile) alluded to in the text.

‡ 1946–52.

§ 1952.

|| Derived from estimates of net fixed investment (average for the period: 6 per cent of net national product).

n.a.: not available.

SOURCE: *Review of Economics and Statistics,* Vol. XXXVIII, 1956.

for industrialization have not been available to these countries. Similarly, overpopulation in agriculture results when population growth continues while little or no industrialization takes place. If population growth continues long enough without industrialization, there will be disguised unemployment in agriculture. The lack of capital is a cause of underdevelopment, but it is also a result of low levels of income, and thus a result of underdevelopment. The concentration of agricultural output in cereals and raw materials reflects low levels of technique and income, which prevent diversion of resources away from production of foodstuffs, and lack of capital to shift to a more extensive and mechanized form of agriculture which might be more productive. Thus the pattern of agricultural output might also be regarded as a result, rather than a cause, of underdevelopment.

And so for each of the other characteristics in Leibenstein's list. Inadequate transport facilities are indeed a barrier to growth, but they are also a product of low levels of income and productivity. Inability to hold sufficient stocks to weather a crisis again reflects low productivity and poverty. High mortality and high fertility rates reflect generally low levels of health and education, which are the result of underdevelopment as well as being a barrier to economic growth. The same is true of low levels of literacy and general education. In underdeveloped countries techniques tend to be relatively inefficient, especially in agriculture, and the low level of technique is a drag on economic growth.

A list of common characteristics is instructive and helps us to understand the nature and magnitude of the problem, but it does not spare us the need to analyze carefully the causes of underdevelopment. Still less does it indicate policies to overcome it. In an earlier publication I coined the outrageously mixed metaphor, "The road to development is paved with vicious circles." [6] Albert Hirschman has recently added, "Yes, but some circles are more vicious than others." [7] The task of economic analysis of the development problem is to discover which of these vicious circles are the basic causes of the others, which can be more readily broken into, and which can be converted into feedback mechanisms bringing sustained growth.

[6] Benjamin Higgins, "Financing Economic Development," *International Conciliation*, 1955.

[7] Albert C. Hirschman, *The Strategy of Economic Development* (New York, 1958).

2 Some Case Studies

In Chapter 1, we saw that underdeveloped countries exhibit some significant common characteristics, but also some important differences. In this chapter we shall consider in more detail the development problems of six countries to illustrate the range of economic situations confronting underdeveloped countries. In three of these, Libya, Indonesia, and the Philippines, the author has been directly engaged in the development planning activities of their respective governments. In India, Italy, and Indonesia, intensive field work has been undertaken by the Economic and Political Development Program of the M.I.T. Center for International Studies (CIS). The sixth, Mexico, is included as a Latin American instance of development problems.

Among them, these countries provide examples of all the major types of underdeveloped country distinguished in the previous chapter. Libya is resource-poor and stagnant. Indonesia is resource-rich and stagnant. The Philippines is relatively well off and currently expanding, but the growth is not diffused and the country faces severe economic and social problems. India is richer than Libya but poorer than Indonesia, both in terms of per capita income and in terms of resource endowment. India is already well into her second Five-Year Plan, but is experiencing great difficulty in achieving a transition from stagnation to sustained growth; the second plan may have to be abandoned. Italy provides the prime example of regional discrepancies in rates of growth. Mexico gives us an example of vigorous, sustained, and apparently healthy growth after generations of stagnation. Moreover, we have in the list three Roman Catholic, two Moslem, and one Hindu country; one country (Mexico) that has been independent for nearly two centuries, one (Italy) that has been independent for 1,500 years but only recently reunited; one country (India) that gained its independence after World War II by an evolutionary process; and one (Indonesia) that fought hard for its freedom. We also have a full geographical spread: Europe, Asia, Africa, and Latin America. We shall treat these countries in ascending order of per capita income, beginning with Libya and ending with Italy.

Libya

Libya's great merit as a case study is as a prototype of poor country. We need not construct *abstract* models of an economy where the bulk of the people live on a subsistence level, where per capita income is well below $50 per year, where there are no sources of power and no mineral resources, where agricultural expansion is severely limited by climatic conditions, where capital formation is zero or less, where there is no skilled labor supply and no indigenous entrepreneurship. When Libya became an independent kingdom under United Nations auspices (December, 1951) it fulfilled all these conditions.[1] Libya is at the bottom of the range in income and resources and so provides a reference point for comparison with all other countries.

Geography: Main Facts

Libya's three provinces (Tripolitania, Cyrenaica, and the Fezzan) represent three distinct economic and geographic units, separated from each other by hundreds of miles of forbidding desert. From a strictly geographic standpoint, it might be more informative to divide the country into areas parallel with the coastline. The coastal strip, varying in width from less than a mile to over ten miles, has relatively high rainfall which permits settled agriculture. Next comes an arid strip, followed by the *Jebel*, or escarpment, which rises sharply from the coastal plain and has another plain on top of it, where extensive agriculture

[1] At time of writing, some petroleum had been discovered in Libya, but the extent of the reserves was still uncertain. In any case the plan to be discussed in Chap. 29 below was prepared before any trace of oil had been found.

(grazing, olive groves, cereals, esparto grass) is possible. The *Jebel* gives way to semidesert and then to complete desert where cultivation is possible only in scattered oases.

Subsoil water is available for irrigation at two or three levels (the two shallow levels may be connected). It is not clear, however, how much the irrigated area can be extended without accelerating the drop in the water table in areas already irrigated.

These grim facts explain why Libya, with an area about equal to that of the United States east of the Mississippi, supports a population of only one and one-quarter million people. The smallness of population, together with the paucity of natural resources and shortage of skilled labor and entrepreneurship, means that Libya faces in unusual degree the problem of scale. Costs of social capital of an indivisible nature (transport and communications facilities, public utilities) are extremely high in per capita terms.

History: Main Facts

The three provinces of Libya never constituted an independent state before 1951; they had been united only as parts of larger empires, from the Roman through the Ottoman to the Italian. None of these imperial powers made any effort to develop the Arab economy. There is, however, a good deal of evidence that in Roman times Libya was more heavily wooded, more fertile, more productive, and more populated than it is today. The classical literature refers to Libya as "the land of the fleeces" and "the grainbowl of Europe." The Delphic oracle spoke of "Libya's pleasant acres." Libya is now a gigantic "dustbowl." Much of the present desert area is the result of overcutting, overgrazing, overirrigation, overtilling, and subsequent abandonment in the past. The development problem is one of arresting decay and launching a new process of progress rather than of initiating economic growth in an area whose development potential had never been realized.

The Economy

The Libyan economy offers discouragingly little with which to work. For decades to come, economic development of Libya must consist largely of raising productivity in agriculture, including animal husbandry. At present, over 80 per cent of the Libyan population is engaged in agriculture and animal husbandry. It is unlikely that this proportion will, or even should, drop significantly during the next few years. Agriculture itself faces extraordinary difficulties. For the population of only 1,200,-000, Libya is a very large country—1,750,000 square kilometers. Unfortunately, however, most of this area is desert. Dr. Lindberg estimates "the potential grazing area at about 12 million hectares."[2] Some 95 per cent of the people are concentrated in the Tripolitanian coastal plain and in the Cyrenaican and Tripolitanian *Jebel*. The rest live mainly in the strings of oases in the Fezzan.

Even in these areas, the soil is not good. The rainfall in Tripolitania and Cyrenaica is both inadequate and unreliable. The Fezzan has virtually no rainfall but has underground water near the surface. Expansion of Libyan agriculture will require extension of the irrigated area, but the degree to which underground water resources will permit such expansion is not clearly known.

If the prospects for rapid expansion of agriculture are not bright, the prospects for industrialization are still more limited. The basis for industrialization is almost completely lacking. Libya has no known mineral deposits big enough or rich enough to justify exploitation, except for such relatively unimportant things as natron, carnallite, and low-grade sulphur. There is no coal and no water power. For the most part, the labor force is unskilled. Even if industries were established, they would be handicapped by the distance of Libyan ports from the major European, or even North African and Middle Eastern centers.

It has become commonplace among observers of Libyan affairs to describe the economy as "deficitary." There are deficits in the budgets of all three provinces, and of most municipalities; the expected budget surplus of the federal government will be exhausted by grants-in-aid to the provinces. There is a deficit in the balance of trade, whether in commodities alone or in goods and services combined, of all three provinces; this deficit is not met by net receipts from foreign investment, as it might be in an advanced country, but by the grants-in-aid, military expenditures, and investments of foreign powers. The wheat-growing experiment at Barce operates at a deficit; the tobacco-growing scheme launched by the Azienda Tabacci Italiani operates at a small deficit; most of the Italian colonization schemes operated, and still operate, at a deficit, perhaps because they were conceived on too grandiose a scale for the nature of the country. Fezzanese agriculture operates at a deficit. The power plant in Tripoli operates at a deficit; the railways operate at a deficit; the harbor and

[2] J. Lindberg, "A General Economic Appraisal of Libya," United Nations Technical Assistance Mission to Libya (A/AC.32/Council/R.143/Rev. 1).

the gas-works at Tripoli have incurred deficits in several years of the last decade, and so on.

These separate deficits reflect the hard fact that the whole Libyan economy operates at a deficit. The country does not produce enough to maintain even its present low standard of living. For four decades, these deficits were made good by foreign governments: by Italy during the thirty years when Libya was an Italian colony; from 1943 to 1952 by the Administering Powers (the United Kingdom in Tripolitania and Cyrenaica, France in the Fezzan); [3] and since then by foreign aid and leases of military bases.

Undeveloped countries are short of capital, almost by definition. Both the existing "real capital" (plant, equipment, and housing) and the flow of monetary savings available for investment purposes, are inadequate in almost any country that could be called underdeveloped. In Libya, however, capital in both these senses is particularly scarce. Outside the Italian sector of the economy the existing plant, equipment, and housing is meager indeed. The capital goods accumulated by the Italians suffered extensive damage during the war, and much of what remains is a drain on the economy. It is expensive to maintain, and much of it is appropriate only to a more advanced economy. Except for the very few wealthy families, the accumulated capital of the Arab population consists mainly of livestock, tools, a little light equipment, and housing that ranges from simple to primitive. Even this capital suffered depletion during the war.

The supply of capital in the monetary sense is restricted by the extreme poverty of the people. No accurate statistics exist, but it is apparent that the share of national income saved is very small indeed. Only a fraction of the population is able to save at all, except in years of very good harvest. Moreover, most Libyans do not save in a form conducive to economic development. In good years, prosperous Libyans may buy land, but this process merely bids up the price of land and is a transfer of assets rather than saving. Alternatively, the population may add to its livestock and to its store of silver ornaments. Neither of these forms of accumulation represents saving in the sense of an offset to increases in private investment and government expenditures. Accumulation of livestock may not even represent a decision to restrict

[3] The Ottoman administration apparently succeeded in collecting more in taxes than it spent within the country, but no reliable information is available concerning the relative levels of production and living standards in that period and today.

consumption; it may be a mere matter of an increased survival rate of livestock in good years. Nor does saving in either of these forms constitute a source of loan capital; it does not increase the lending power of banks, nor provide a market for new issues of securities. The accumulation of livestock or ornaments is "saving" only in the very formal sense that it represents a gap between income (including accruals to capital) and current consumption.

Finally, the bulk of the monetary savings of the Arab population is made available to borrowers only at extremely high rates of interest. The typical Libyan with money to invest likes to keep it by him in a form he can see, and it takes a very high rate of return to tempt him to invest in securities, promissory notes, or the like.

The Problem of Entrepreneurship

With so little to work with, it is not surprising that vigorous entrepreneurship was rare in prewar Libya. The Libyans themselves were almost entirely confined to agriculture of a rather primitive kind, although the Arab garden was in its way an efficient unit. About one-fifth of the population was nomadic and another fifth seminomadic. The only other important occupation of Libyans was textiles and handicrafts. Before the war, a considerable number of Jews was engaged in trading and small enterprises, but the postwar wave of anti-Semitism resulted in the virtual disappearance of this group. By 1951 only 7,000 Jews were left in the country. Large-scale enterprise, whether in agriculture, industry, commerce, or finance, was mostly in the hands of Italians. The Italians were settled in Libya as part of the colonization program and received a variety of aids and subsidies from the Italian government. Some of the large fruit groves, dairies, tobacco farms, wheat farms, etc., are quite impressive technically but none of these ever succeeded in paying its own way. The war brought a substantial exodus of Italians, especially from Cyrenaica, and at the time of transfer of sovereignty there were only 50,000 left, mainly in Tripolitania. The prewar and preindependence Libyan economies were in fact both deficitary; the country simply did not produce as much as it consumed even at the very low income levels prevailing, and the balance was made up by capital imports from the ruling powers.

Islam takes an old-fashioned form in Libya, and lip service is still paid to the ban on usury, which in Libya is often interpreted to mean interest of any kind. The result is that credit transactions are typically disguised as trading operations and the effective interest rates are extremely high—often exceeding 100 per cent per annum.[4] Those Libyans wealthy enough to invest in new enterprises have become accustomed to these extremely high rates of return. In 1951 an issue of securities by the National Esparto Development Corporation failed to attract any significant amount of Libyan capital because it promised a return of only 10 per cent. Certainly the nomadic and seminomadic sector of the Libyan economy offered little opportunity for progressive entrepreneurship, and the tribal organization, which is in some respects inconsistent with private property rights, is a barrier to enterprise of the Western type. Finally, the Arab community has become accustomed to monopoly closely related to social and political privilege. It is normal practice for a Libyan businessman to request a complete monopoly before making an investment in any particular field.

For all these reasons, Libyan capacity to finance its own economic development is extremely limited. Wealthy Libyans must learn to accept lower interest rates, and more Libyans with moderate incomes must learn to put their savings into deposits or securities, before the country can become independent of outside sources of capital.

Population and Manpower

The manpower problem in Libya takes the form of inadequate skill and low productivity, rather than insufficiency of total numbers of workers. Despite the small size of the total Libyan population, there is no evidence that the country is underpopulated relative to its natural resources and existing techniques. Moreover, judging from prewar figures, the ratio of active to total population is higher in Libya than in some other African countries, partly because about one-quarter of the children between ten and fourteen years of age are members of the labor force.

There is, moreover, a large pool of unemployment on which to draw. In the first place, there is a hard core of disguised unemployment, which probably exceeds one-third of the labor force.

[4] In a typical transaction, the merchant may be approached for a loan. The merchant does not wish to leave any record of the loan transaction. He therefore "sells" goods to the borrower on credit for, say, £200, to be paid in three months. He then buys back the goods at once for £150, which he pays immediately to the borrower. Thus in effect, the borrower pays £50 interest on a loan of £150 for three months.

This disguised unemployment is aggravated by seasonal fluctuations and may reach 80 per cent of the labor force in the off seasons. In periods of drought, a substantial volume of visible unemployment also appears in Tripolitania and Cyrenaica. Visible unemployment may exceed half the labor force of some districts when drought is acute. In Benghazi and Tripoli, cyclical unemployment of the kind familiar in advanced countries may also be seen among industrial workers, craftsmen, dock workers, and the like. Finally, there is a substantial amount of "potential" unemployment, in the sense that simple improvements in techniques may release large numbers of workers for absorption into other occupations. Altogether, these various forms of unemployment constitute a substantial reserve of manpower, which could be gradually tapped as economic and social development proceeds. The successive elimination of these various forms of unemployment would be only partially offset by reduced reliance on child labor as education becomes more widespread.

Unfortunately, this over-all labor surplus is of limited value for economic and social development, because of the extremely small range of skills and the low average level of productivity. Nearly 90 per cent of the labor force is engaged in agriculture, for the most part employing only the crudest of agricultural techniques. Industry and crafts together absorb little more than 6 per cent of the labor force, public and private administration about 3 per cent. There are skilled workers among the Italian and Jewish population, but these are employed to a large extent in serving the needs of foreigners, who form a distinct economy within the more primitive Arab one. Outside this small foreign economy, skilled labor is very scarce, and highly skilled or professionally trained people scarcely exist. In the Libyan economy proper, manpower is hardly differentiated as to skill at all, except for workers engaged in handicrafts. Finally, among skilled and unskilled workers alike, the productivity of the Libyan labor force compares unfavorably with those of advanced countries.

Thus the problem of manpower in Libya has three facets: to find means of gradually and progressively eliminating unemployment; to increase the supply of skilled workers through training; and to raise the productivity of the labor force through improvement of tools, equipment, and production methods.

The Libyan birth rate is high—according to Dr. Shanawany, 5.3 per cent per annum.[5] The natural rate of population growth

[5] M. R. el Shanawany, "Report and Recommendations regarding the Organisation of the Vital Statistics Services of Libya," United Nations Technical Assistance Mission to Libya (A/AC.32/Council/R. 167).

is kept down to its present (estimated) 1.1 per cent only by a death rate of 4.2 per cent, which reflects mainly an extremely high infant mortality rate. If the economic and social development plan succeeds, and the population is enabled to share the fruits of success, standards of nutrition will improve and the infant mortality rate will fall, even if medical services are not extended as part of the plan. There is, therefore, a very real danger that the initial gains from economic and social development will soon be swallowed up in accelerated population growth, leaving the average standard of living, and the ability of Libya to finance further development and to achieve true economic independence, no better than before. If the death rate falls to the level of some other underdeveloped countries while birth rates stay where they are, population growth could exceed 3 per cent per year. With an ICOR[6] of 3:1 it would then take net investment of 9 per cent of national income just to keep standards of living from falling. In Libya, of course, they could not fall much without death rates rising again.

The Problem of Scale

The paucity of capital, skilled labor, and natural resources means that Libya is confronted to an unusual degree with the problem of scale. In simple terms, the problem arises because the most efficient scale of operations for many types of undertaking is so large as to require mass production for its effective use. Libya is a very big country in total area but is very small in terms of manpower and natural resources. The problem is aggravated by the scattering of the limited manpower resources over the very large area. Consequently only small capital investment projects can be operated close enough to capacity to be economical. This fact eliminates from consideration for Libya many projects requiring large-scale investment in plant and equipment of an indivisible nature. Such undertakings as the impressive harbor development at Tunis are out of the question for Libya. The fact that the average density of population in Tunisia is forty times that of Libya is a cause, as well as a result, of Tunisia's superior development. In Libya, the scope for electrification, improvement of transport and communications, and similar heavy investment projects is severely limited. Even in the field of agriculture, the problem of scale may arise. Soil fixation for example, is an expensive undertaking; and in a country with a population as small as Libya's, soil fixation is worthwhile only

[6] Incremental Capital-Output Ratio—the ratio of net investment to increases in national income.

for the protection and development of relatively productive areas. This argument applies even more strongly in the less densely populated sections of the country.

The inescapable conclusion is that in Libya any development projects and programs of a kind which cannot be efficiently subdivided into small-scale undertakings must be concentrated in the most productive and most densely populated areas. In the case of soil fixation, for example, it may be that energies must be concentrated on protecting the better agricultural areas, even if this decision involves abandoning some marginal areas to the encroaching desert. Economic development in Libya is no matter of large-scale industrialization; it is not even a matter of greatly extending the total area under cultivation. It is rather a matter of stabilizing the present population in an area which may be little or no larger than the total now cultivated and of increasing productivity per acre and per man-hour in this area. It is worth noting that Tunisia supports a population three times that of Libya, at a higher standard of living, in an area roughly equivalent to the area in Tripolitania between the *Jebel* and the sea.

The Problem of Incentive

Libya also faces a problem of incentive. There is little in Libyan history to convince the people that their welfare can be improved by their own efforts to work and save. There was evidence of material progress in Greek and Roman times, and again under the recent Italian administration; but in both these periods economic development took the form of investment by foreign colonial powers, undertaken at considerable cost, in the interest of their own settlers in Libya. Any benefits the Libyans derived from such development were very indirect. The Turkish regime left the Libyans largely to their own devices, and a few Libyans prospered under it; but at the beginning of this century the Ottoman rulers were no more interested than other imperial powers in Africa in helping the native peoples to improve their techniques, and they did little to alleviate the poverty of the great majority of Libyans. The Italian wars undermined much of what little prosperity there was before 1912, and the three decades of Italian administration did little to bring direct prosperity to the Arabs. World War II brought much destruction, and many Libyans who had made the effort to establish a source of income for themselves saw it swept away in this fresh invasion.

With such a history, it is not surprising that most Libyans have failed to take the long view. To work or save today for benefits to be obtained five, ten, or twenty years hence has even seemed a little foolish in the light of their experience. Certainly that experience has done little to undermine the fatalism of the typical Libyan. Yet the long view is absolutely essential to successful execution of an economic and social development plan.

To what extent can rapid economic and social development take place in Libya without changes in social institutions, attitudes, ideas and customs? Social behavior of a kind inimical to progress has certainly been observed: driving livestock into standing crops, permitting goats to ringbark young trees, selling grain distributed by the government for seed, neglecting good rural housing and equipment, spending for consumption money borrowed for production, breaking up bridges and telephone poles to obtain scrap metal, spending daily income daily, and so forth. However, destructive behavior occurs in the most advanced economies. There is no clear evidence that such behavior is especially widespread in Libya or that it is traceable to basic social institutions and customs, rather than to lack of education, lack of foresight, and centuries of foreign rule. The same observation may be made regarding the widespread tendency to live for today and entrust the future to Providence. Given proper education and greater economic and political stability, planning for the future may become a more normal practice among the Libyan people.

Of course, certain institutions, customs, and attitudes are clearly of major social importance. One of these is the nomadism or seminomadism practiced by some 40 per cent of the Libyan population. Many of the developmental projects and programs recommended in the plan prepared for the Libyan government by the UN mission imply a settled agriculture and stable light industries. Only a few of them can be efficiently carried out by a nomadic people. Yet the economy of the nomads and seminomads is in its way the most successful in the country. It is certainly not a progressive economy, and it provides a standard of living very little above the subsistence level; but it is a means of utilizing otherwise useless resources, it provides its own system of social security, and except in drought years, it is self-sustaining. Moreover, experience with upsetting simple, but stable societies elsewhere, has been none too happy—witness the fate of the Australian aborigines and North American Indians. Before introducing measures for turning nomads into settled farmers, therefore, one must be sure that their lot will really be improved.

Similar considerations apply to the closely related institution of tribes. The tribal organization also has value in the present phase of Libyan development; but there is clearly some inconsistency between tribal organization and national, or even provincial, economic planning. Tribal organization seems to result in lack of respect for any property rights not covered by tribal law; yet the economic development plan assumes, implicitly or explicitly, the institution of private property, with laws to protect it that are respected and enforced. What inducement is there for settled farmers to improve their land, fix soil, plant trees, sow grain, and improve pasturage if the next drought may bring an invasion of thousands of nomads with thousands of animals, to destroy much of their investment of capital and labor within a matter of days?

A social attitude related to the problem of incentives is what the economist calls the "backward-sloping supply curve of effort." The typical Libyan values his current leisure so highly and attaches so little importance to improvement of his material condition, that ordinary income incentives seem to be of limited effectiveness in persuading Libyans to work harder, better, and longer. This problem is certainly not unknown in advanced countries, but the level of the material standard of living at which people prefer more leisure to more income, is apparently very much lower in Libya than in economically developed countries. No doubt, lack of opportunity for earning more by additional effort, the great influence on real income of the vagaries of climate, and also mal-nourishment, help explain this apparent indolence of the Libyan people. But belief that the future is beyond human control, and distaste for unnecessary effort and risk, play their part as well. The same attitudes give rise to the lack of monetary savings referred to above. Can a society where income incentives do not operate, and where no other incentive has yet been provided, develop economically?

Finally, there is the institution of monopoly. This institution is also no stranger to advanced countries, but in countries where rapid economic progress has taken place, monopoly positions have usually been obtained by exercise of superior foresight or introduction of superior techniques, and the monopolist has been constantly threatened by other farsighted entrepreneurs and by the advance of technical knowledge. Temporary monopolies, as a reward for superior foresight or for introducing better techniques, may be conducive to economic progress. Entrenched monopolies based on privilege are almost certainly inimical to economic progress. In most advanced countries, monopoly has been deplored and legal sanctions against it have been provided.

In Libya, monopoly is regarded as normal and is closely related to social and political privilege. Can rapid economic development take place without the spirit and fact of competition?

Conclusions

Some readers may think that Libya has received more attention than a country of one and a quarter million people deserves in a chapter of this sort. But Libya is important in one respect: it has become a pilot plant for a large-scale program of technical and capital assistance in which the UN, the United States, the United Kingdom, France, and Italy are all participating. As a UN baby —and a country with 1,200 miles of coastline opposite "the soft underbelly of Europe"—Libya has been able to obtain preferred treatment. The experiment is worth watching. For Libya combines within the borders of one country virtually all the obstacles to development that can be found anywhere: geographic, economic, political, sociological, technological. If Libya can be brought to a stage of sustained growth, there is hope for every country in the world.

India

No such explanation is needed for the inclusion of India in our survey of countries attempting economic development. India is clearly one of the two most important nations in Asia, which automatically makes it one of the most important in the world. In terms of population it stands second only to its neighbor, China, also an underdeveloped country seeking higher living standards, although by a different route. Comparisons between these two Asian giants are inevitable.

India takes on added interest for us because it was one of the first countries to embark on a formal development plan. Indeed in 1958 India was already halfway through its second Five-Year Plan. Since India has chosen the democratic system and China, the Communist one, these two countries are engaged in a race which the whole world watches with keenest interest. Professor Wilfred Malenbaum, Director of the India Project, M.I.T. Center for International Studies (CIS), has described the situation as follows: [7]

> The contemporary Indian scene is exciting. Of immediate relevance to the present article are two basic aspects of the evolving situation

[7] Wilfred Malenbaum, "Some Political Aspects of Economic Development in India," *World Politics*, April, 1958, pp. 378–79.

in India. First is the fact that there is in process, for anyone to see, a deliberate effort to raise living standards. The government of independent India articulated a framework for economic expansion almost a decade ago, at about the time that President Truman dramatically injected the problems of economic development in the arena of international affairs. Since then India has been proceeding with development activity more or less within this framework.

Elsewhere in the free world—or, better, in the areas uncommitted to the Communist bloc—there has been much talk of development needs and some planning, but relatively little action. Indeed, for any contemporary parallel to the Indian performance one must turn from these areas to Communist China. There one finds *the* other conscious, comprehensive program for inducing growth in what is a classic example of a static economy. These current performances in a Communist and a non-Communist country take on additional interest and significance from the striking similarity in the economic problems of the two neighboring lands. In both, the enormous population, the concentration of employment in agriculture, the unfavorable people/resource ratio, the very low level of per capita income, the long history of hesitant industrialization while the new economies of the Western world marched ahead—all these pose problems of initiating growth that are unequaled in recorded history.

The first important fact, then, is that India has embarked upon a development effort. Second is the fact that this effort is being pursued within a formal system of democratic group relationships. Top leadership in India seems determined to respect the democratic prerogatives of the individual, even in a society where the vast bulk of people is illiterate, where feudal patterns still persist in interpersonal and intergroup conduct and where physical communication and transport are still limited.

The Indian leaders who framed the first Five-Year Plan were well aware of the immensity of the task they had undertaken. In setting forth the objectives of the Plan, they wrote: [8]

The central objective of planning in India at the present stage is to initiate a process of development which will raise living standards and open out to the people new opportunities for a richer and more varied life. . . . An underdeveloped economy is characterized by the co-existence, in greater or less degree, of unutilized or underutilized manpower on the one hand and of unexploited natural resources on the other. . . . In spite of considerable advance in public thinking on the subject, the acceptance of such an approach to the problems of economic development and social change represents a relatively

[8] Government of India Planning Commission, *The First Five-Year Plan* (New Delhi, December, 1952), Vol. I, pp. 1–6.

new phase in policy-making and in administration. . . . The urge to economic and social change under present conditions comes from the fact of poverty and of inequalities in income, wealth and opportunity. The elimination of poverty cannot, obviously, be achieved merely by redistributing existing wealth. Nor can a programme aiming only at raising production remove existing inequalities. . . . A process of all-round and orderly development, such as is indicated above, must inevitably take time to come into full fruition. Large-scale changes in modes of production, in commercial and industrial organization and in the institutional framework of corporate life cannot be seen through within a brief period of four or five years. In the initial stages of development, divergence in the economic and social interests of different sections of the community may create special problems. . . . The rapid advances in science and technology over the last few decades have opened out new possibilities in the direction of abolition of want and the restoration of man to a new sense of dignity, but they also carry potentialities of harm and danger. . . . We should like in this context to stress the essential political and administrative conditions essential to successful planning. Briefly these are:

(a) a large measure of agreement in the community as to the ends of policy;
(b) effective power, based on the active co-operation of citizens, in the hands of the State; and, earnest and determined exercise of that power in furtherance of these ends; and
(c) an efficient administrative set-up, with personnel of requisite capacity and quality.

. . . The task of organizing a democracy for rapid and co-ordinated advance along several lines is one of special difficulty. The party in power has not only to carry public opinion with it; it has to get the active cooperation of all sections . . . Democratic processes are complex, and they make large demands on the government as well as the governed. It cannot be assumed that the apparatus of democratic forms or procedures necessarily ensures the preservation of the basic values which a democratic way of life connotes. . . . But, it must be emphasized that for democratic planning to succeed, it will have to energize the entire community and to place before it a goal of endeavour which will call forth all its latent creative urges. . . . Under the Constitution, India is organized as a federation, in which the Central Government and the Governments of States have their assigned spheres of action. . . . The Centre has certain emergency powers, but, normally, coordination of policies has to be effected through mutual consultation. This system of consultation and of formulation of policies on the basis of over-all national requirements will have to be strengthened in the interests of planning. . . . A planned economy aiming at the realization of larger social objectives entails a vast increase in governmental functions. For these to be discharged efficiently, appropriate local, regional and functional organizations have to be built up and strengthened.

A country with so much vitality and determination among its leaders—in both the public and private sectors of the economy—is inaccurately described as "stagnant." Yet if one looked only at the main economic aggregates one would be inclined to put India into the "poor and stagnant" category. Per capita income is only $60 per year and has risen very slowly in recent years. Only two of the countries listed in Table 1-8 show a slower rate of growth. The proportion of national income derived from agriculture (at constant factor cost) remained within a fraction of 49 per cent between 1950 and 1954 and was just under 48 per cent in 1955–56. The proportion derived from manufacturing, mining, and public utilities remained just under 17 per cent, despite considerable industrial investment.

Actually India has been static in terms of structure for some decades. Industrialization is not new to India. A modern textile industry was established a century ago and a modern steel industry over fifty years ago. Both of these industries were efficient, low-cost organizations which enjoyed healthy expansion, but their establishment did nothing to transform the Indian economy. Similarly, India benefited from early completion of transcontinental railways; and it has a banking system and capital market that other underdeveloped countries might well envy. Yet, says Malenbaum, "modern industry was not more significant as a source of income in 1951 than it was in 1921, and perhaps even earlier."[9]

These are the facts which have impelled the distinguished Indian economist, V. K. R. V. Rao, to refer to his country as "a static economy in progress." A lot of things are happening in India; net investment is taking place, yet there are no signs that the country is safely on its way to sustained economic growth. A Western economist who has specialized on development problems, and who recently visited India, describes the 1958 situation in these pessimistic terms: [10]

[9] In the first chapter of his forthcoming book on Indian economic development.

[10] Berthold F. Hoselitz, "The Prospects for Indian Economic Growth," University of Texas Conference on Economic Development, April, 1958, p. 1.

Rao introduced the expression "static economy in progress" in an article, "Changes in India's National Income," *Capital*, December 6, 1954, Supplement, pp. 15–17. See also chap. V, "A Static Economy in Progress," in Wilfred Malenbaum's forthcoming book referred to in note 9.

[India] has varied and rich natural resources, it has able and well-trained leaders and it has a skillful adaptable population. Yet with all these assets it has remained a poor country, and up to the present its efforts at economic development have not produced very impressive results. Although the total national income of India has hovered around 100 billion rupees, or more than 20 billion dollars, its per capita national income has been one of the lowest in Asia and has shown very little increase in the last decade. Per capita net real output has increased between 1948 and 1956 only by 10.2 per cent, and this increment occurred for all practical purposes in two spurts in the period 1951 to 1954. Since 1954 per capita real output has grown only by 1.4 per cent and the recent discussions on the economic crisis in India, although centering around the lack of foreign exchange and the consequent difficulty in fully implementing the Second Five Year Plan, have, in truth, a much more fundamental aspect—the general poor prospects of economic growth in India.

This stagnation in per capita production and in the structure of the economy is made all the more serious by two other facts: there is danger of an acceleration of population growth, and India's prospects appear to be much more favorable in industry than in agriculture. According to the 1951 census India had a population of 357 million (without Jammu and Kashmir). By 1958 the population was presumably over 400 million. The current rate of population growth is not particularly high, as may be seen from Table 1-6. But even a growth rate of 1.3 per cent on a base of 400 million presents appalling problems in a country like India, and with improvements in public health, death rates are likely to drop. Reductions in fertility rates are a good deal less certain. Demographic data for India are none too reliable, and estimates of the population in 1976 range from 500 to 700 million. Even with the lower figure, India will need substantial expansion of employment and output; with the higher figure, India's growth of productivity must be accelerated considerably just to prevent a declining standard of living.

The handicaps in Indian agriculture are indicated by the spread between the share of income and the share of employment in agriculture, a spread that is even bigger than in other underdeveloped countries. Over 80 per cent of the population is rural, yet only 48 per cent of the national income is produced in the rural sector. Much of India is arid, much of the soil is poor; increasing acreage and raising yields per hectare both require substantial investment. Hoselitz describes the problem as follows: [11]

[11] Hoselitz, *op. cit.*, pp. 3–4. For further demographic material, see Ansley Coale and Edgar Hoover, *Population Growth and Economic Development*

. . . The difficulties of progress in the field of agriculture are exhibited if we look at the achievements of the First Five Year Plan during which special efforts were undertaken to improve India's agricultural output. It may suffice if we cite just two figures, those relating to cropped area, in general, and those to irrigated land. From 1950/51 to 1955/56 the total net area sown in India increased from 293.4 million acres to 319.8 million acres, and the net irrigated area from 51.5 million acres to 56.3 million acres. In each case the increase was about 9 per cent. The total increase in farm production in this period was 13 per cent, a figure which shows that much of the added production was achieved by increase in cropped area rather than by increase in yield per acre.

Additions to the cropped area are becoming more and more difficult to make. To be sure, there exist still some excellent opportunities for irrigation projects, but these are also becoming increasingly more expensive. And any intensification of agricultural production in India depends to a large extent on the availability of water, for, in spite of the impressive quantities of annual rainfall in many parts of the country, the high seasonal concentration of rain during the monsoon is often a menace rather than a blessing to greater productivity in agriculture.

The present writer has expressed a similar view in an earlier publication: [12]

In most of the underdeveloped countries there is just no hope of achieving high living standards through agricultural improvement alone. Sheer arithmetic forbids any such possibility in many of them. In India, for example, where soil and climate are not suitable for a highly productive agriculture, it is likely that an output in excess of $200 per capita (not per worker) in peasant agriculture is a technical impossibility so long as the present size of peasant holdings continues, no matter how much is done in the way of introducing fertilizers, seed selection, improved irrigation, and the like. And if 80 per cent of the labor force remains in agriculture, the achievement of a per capita national income of $400 per year then becomes extremely difficult, and is clearly impossible without developing an extremely efficient industrial sector employing the other 20 per cent of the labor force. . . . Strict application of the comparative advantage principle might well lead to exactly the opposite policy. Soil and climate are not transferable, and populations are hard to move in large numbers. Techniques, however, are easily moved, and become increasingly transferable with technological progress. Thus, while India may never have a highly efficient agriculture, some observers

in Low Income Areas (Princeton, N.J., 1958); and Kingsley Davis, *The Population of India and Pakistan* (Princeton, N.J., 1951).

[12] Benjamin Higgins, "Prospects for an International Economy," *World Politics*, April, 1957, pp. 464–65.

maintain that it already has the most efficient iron and steel industry in the world. On the basis of comparative advantage, India should probably be an importer of foodstuffs and an exporter of products of heavy industry.

Nor are poverty and stagnation the only economic problems in India. Once again we turn to Malenbaum for a summary of the Indian situation in 1958: [13]

(1) Despite an over-all expansion of national output of some 15 per cent—18 per cent in the period from 1951 through 1955—India was not able to absorb current output at a sufficiently rapid rate to counter deflationary pressures.
(2) Most responsible for the expanded produce was the increase in agricultural output which was in turn due principally to unusually favorable weather conditions in two years, 1953 and 1954. For the period as a whole, 1951 to date, India has not been able to achieve its target of a systematic increase in agricultural output, despite a major attention to this sector in the program.
(3) Domestic savings ratios reached high levels (in excess of 10 per cent of national product) during the plan but the expansion seems to have come to an end.
(4) Government has encountered major difficulties in mobilizing any important parts of the increase in national savings. Programs in the public sector have relied more than anticipated upon net imports and government credit creation.
(5) Government has consistently moved back with respect to the Plan's scale of effort. While investment achievement in this area of direct action may be some 20 per cent less than the Plan, government policy has not been encouraging for compensatory action in the private sector.
(6) Pressures on prices, and upon foreign exchange reserves were excessive, given the over-all levels of output on the one hand, and of consumption and investment on the other.
(7) Unemployment, and particularly urban unemployment among the better educated, has been mounting more rapidly than anticipated, without any change in near prospect.
(8) Expanded capital facilities have provided disappointing increases in product. New plant is sometimes underutilized; expanded output is sometimes moving into inventories because of demand shortages in some lines.

Unemployment, open and disguised, is a common feature of underdeveloped countries, as we have seen. In India, however, it takes a particularly acute form, because it is at least as serious in cities as it is in the countryside. The period since World War

[13] Wilfred Malenbaum, *op. cit.*

II has seen rapid growth of Indian cities, particularly the great metropolises of Delhi, Calcutta, and Bombay. This rural-urban migration does not, unfortunately, reflect the "pull" of job opportunities in the cities, but rather the "push" of abysmal poverty and lack of opportunities in the villages. The situation is indicated by the following figures:

TABLE 2-1.

Level of Urban Unemployment, 1956
(millions of persons)

	Small cities	Large cities	Four largest	Total
Population	34.8	24.1	12.6	71.5
Labor force	11.2	8.7	5.1	25.0
Gainfully occupied	10.26	8.05	4.21	22.5
Severely underemployed	.96	.79	1.06	2.8
Unemployed	.94	.65	.89	2.5
Unemployed/labor force (ratio)	8.4%	7.5%	18.4%	10.0%
Underemployed/labor force (ratio)	8.6%	9.1%	20.1%	11.2%
Un- and underemployed/labor force (ratio)	17.0%	16.6%	38.5%	21.2%

SOURCE: Wilfred Malenbaum, "Urban Unemployment in India," M.I.T., CIS, January, 1957.

Particularly distressing is the fact that the *rate* of unemployment is higher among educated than among uneducated people. The distribution of unemployment by educational status was as follows:

Educational Status: Employed and Unemployed
(Per cent)

	Large cities		*Four largest cities*	
Status	Employed	Unemployed	Employed	Unemployed
Illiterate	48.2	21.6	24.9	9.6
Literate below matric	43.1	60.2	53.6	62.5
Matric	5.7	13.1	11.2	18.1
Intermediate	1.5	3.2	4.5	5.8
Graduate and above	1.5	1.9	5.8	4.0
	100.0	100.0	100.0	100.0

Technical Qualification: Employed and Unemployed

Qualification	*Large cities*		*Four largest cities*	
	Employed *	Unemployed	Employed	Unemployed
Nil		61.3	71.4	67.4
Practical, no training .		34.4	20.1	22.4
Certificate or diploma (typing, midwifery, pharmacy, etc.) . . .		2.9	2.3	4.4
Degree or equivalent (engineering, etc.) .		1.4	6.2	5.8
		100.0	100.0	100.0

* Not available.
SOURCE: Malenbaum, *op. cit.*

More surprising is the continued presence of excess capacity. There is excess capacity in social overhead capital—transport, power, and services—although as Malenbaum points out, its existence is more certain "if the term underutilization is also allowed to encompass cases where some modification—relatively small as measured by the outlay involved—is needed in capital." He gives as an example the installation of signaling devices and improved traffic control, which would permit more intensive use of existing railway tracks and rolling stock.

Professors Vakil and Brahmanand give the following figures of industrial excess capacity:

TABLE 2-2.

Industries Classified according to Utilization of Capacity *

Per cent of capacity utilized	*Number of industries*							
	1946	1947	1948	1949	1950	1951	1952	1953
Less than 25	6	4	4	13	8	8	14	[illegible]
	(18)	(10)	(7)	(20)	(10)	(10)	(18)	[illegible]
25–50	9	16	18	20	25	23	25	[illegible]
	(27)	(39)	(32)	(31)	(32)	(30)	(31)	[illegible]
50–75	9	9	19	18	27	18	22	[illegible]
	(27)	(22)	(34)	(28)	(34)	(23)	(27	[illegible]
75 and above	10	12	16	14	19	29	[illegible]	[illegible]
	(30)	(30)	(28)	(22)	(24)	(37)	[illegible]	[illegible]
Total	34	41	57	65	79	78	[illegible]	[illegible]
	(100)	(100)	(100)	(100)	(100)	(100)	[illegible]	[illegible]

* Figures in parentheses give percentage. Figures [illegible] not add up.
SOURCE: Vakil and Brahmanand, *Planning for* [illegible] (Bombay, 1956), p. 23.

The disappointing record of agriculture after the unusually good monsoon years in the mid-1950's is a stiff blow to Indian hopes and expectations. For although the long-run prospects of Indian agriculture are less bright than the outlook for industry, so long as three-fourths of the active population are engaged in agriculture, increases in agricultural output must be obtained, to sustain increases in population and permit some labor to be shifted to industry. India may eventually be able to finance food imports with industrial exports, but that day is not yet. Meanwhile, as Professor Hoselitz puts it: [14]

> Indian agriculture still operates within such a narrow margin in comparison with minimum food requirements for health and survival of its population, that inclement weather, an unfavorable monsoon, or some major disaster, like an inundation, leads to wide-spread famine in large parts of the country. In these situations scarce foreign exchange must be used for food imports, and this affects adversely imports of capital vitally needed for industrial development. The recent crisis of the Indian economy is to a large extent also a food crisis, and a glance at recent changes in the price level of food and other consumers' goods sheds ample light on this.

Professors Vakil and Brahmanand make the point in even stronger terms. In underdeveloped countries like India, they argue, the concept of capital as a stock of wage goods available to support labor in investment activities is still valid: [15]

> We have maintained that unemployment in underdeveloped countries is due solely to the prevalence of the wage-goods gap. It is the inability of the economy to provide in the short-period the required surplus of wage-goods necessary in order that the disguised unemployment can be employed in investment, that inhibits expansion in employment and in investment. Countries like India have an abundance of population, but such an abundance does not necessarily connote a proportionate availability in employable units. If the economy can make good the wage-goods gap through a quick expansion in the output of wage-goods, it is possible to raise the employment potential and thus to initiate an upward cumulative process.

Professor Raj has cast the problem in terms of a "cobweb theory." [16] In India, the Classical theory of profit and investment (discussed at some length in the next chapter) is still valid. The labor cost of food determines the real wage rate, and the spread be-

[14] Hoselitz, *op. cit.*, pp. 15–16.
[15] Vakil and Brahmanand, *loc. cit.*
[16] At a seminar, M.I.T., CIS.

tween real wages and prices determines the real profit. For investors in the industrial sector, profits are also affected by raw material prices. When agricultural yields are good, wages and raw material prices tend to be low and profit to be high. Under these conditions investments (and imports of raw materials and equipment not produced at home) tend to go up. After some lag, manufacturing output increases accordingly. Once the increased supplies of manufactured goods reach the market, their prices tend to go down. If this drop in price of manufactures coincides with a bad harvest, so that wages and raw material costs are rising at the same time, investment may be cut off to a trickle. We shall have more to say concerning this cobweb theory in Chapter 24. At this point, we want only to note that the theory is a realistic one for India, and that the failure to maintain steady growth of agricultural output makes it extremely difficult to obtain steady growth of industrial output, in an economy where the private sector still predominates.

Although commerce, industry, and trade are held in higher regard in India than in some other underdeveloped countries, and although India is blessed with a considerable number of capable and vigorous managers and entrepreneurs, management and entrepreneurship still constitute a bottleneck. As a consequence, Malenbaum points out:[17]

In India, as in other underdeveloped countries, government must not only provide this heavy dose of economic and social overhead investment but must also undertake many specific operations which in the United States, for example, belong distinctly within the scope of the private businessman. The reasons for this needn't be dwelt upon at any length here. They stem from the thinness of the supply of entrepreneurship—even in India, which is more blessed in this regard than are other poor countries. There is also a difficulty in raising enough funds privately for really big industrial investments like steel mills. Of major importance here, moreover, is the fact that there have been decades of relative inaction by the private business sector, after what looked like hopeful beginnings a century or so ago. This interruption of growth has resulted in more than a delay in getting started. In our own economic expansion, we point to the new railroad or the new banking facility or the new research discovery as inducers of further investment. But this is a chicken and egg problem: the railroad, the discovery, the new facilities were results as well as causes in this process. A bundle of things was happening more or less simultaneously. Indian bundles are composed of the old and the new. The big businessman there *has* the new road; he *has* the

[17] Malenbaum, *op. cit.*, pp. 9–10.

capital market; he is aware of the new invention—and along with all these, he is aware of poverty and backwardness, the obvious manifestations of the need for development. But this is no longer a position of disequilibrium to him—one which sets in motion pressures toward balance and at a higher level. Rather he has become psychologically adjusted to the imbalance; he is less sensitive to the new as a spur for improving the old. Be this as it may, government will need to fill a broad big-business leadership role in India.

Professor Walter C. Neale, formerly of the M.I.T. India Project and now of the University of Texas, is somewhat more optimistic with respect to entrepreneurship, especially where small industry is concerned: [18]

Small—very small—industrial establishments have been springing up in the Punjab for a decade, and many of these in small cities and small towns. . . . What do they make? Underwear, sandals, suitcases, utensils, metal boxes, bicycles, typewriters, power saws, jigs and drills, pump parts. Let me describe some operations. Bicycle wheel rims, hubs, and spokes are turned out mechanically, but the wheel is assembled with hands and feet. The worker holds the rim and spokes with his toes and bends the spokes into the hub with his hands, and assembles wheels with remarkable speed. In a box factory a worker sits with metal sheets, hinges, rivets, handles, hasps, and a hammer. In less than five minutes he produces a suitcase, a trunk, or a strong box.

The products are by no means crude. My Hercul*as* bicycle did not differ in looks from its Hercul*es* model, although the steel was soft. Only close inspection showed that the label on a sewing machine did *not* say Singer.

Professor Neale sees another problem here. This kind of entrepreneurship is not easily incorporated into a centralized system of development planning: [19]

It is very difficult to visualize a meeting of minds between one of India's small businessmen, untutored if not illiterate, skillful but not suave, intelligent but not sophisticated, and one of her State Bank executives. America knows no differences so great. The businessman probably distrusts the banker. The banker certainly distrusts, and also lacks respect for, the businessman. What the borrower wants is venture capital while the banker follows the British tradition of lending only for self-liquidating working capital. And of course the borrower cannot produce enough assets as security or enough wealthy friends to stand surety. If he could, he and his friends would already have borrowed elsewhere and set up business.

[18] Walter C. Neale, "Comments on Professor Hoselitz's Paper," University of Texas Conference on Economic Development, April, 1958, pp. 1–2.
[19] *Ibid.*, pp. 3–4.

Finally India shares with other underdeveloped countries a chronic balance of payments problem.[20] Ambitions with regard to economic development are thwarted by simple lack of foreign exchange to get started. Here is another of the many "vicious circles with which the road to higher income is paved." To earn foreign exchange India must build up its industries; but to build up its industries it needs foreign exchange. Let us resort to Malenbaum's special knowledge one final time: [21]

It became clear, within the first year of the Plan period, that important adjustments were in order for India's development effort. In particular, the drain on India's foreign exchange reserves was so much greater than was anticipated (and than India seemed able to maintain) that the need for adjustment acquired the utmost urgency. In the Plan's first year, for example, India utilized $600 million of these reserves (including drawings from the IMF which might need to be repaid before 1961). This is about 50 per cent more than was contemplated for the entire five-year period. While the expected imports for 1956/57 as between government and private sector are not known precisely, it appears that the major contributor to this drain was the very high level of capital imports on account of the private sector. . . . The stringent import policy adopted early in 1957 had significant bearing upon imports by the private sector by the end of the year. Thus, the private sector imported about $85 million less in October to December, 1957, than in the same quarter a year back. Practically all this decline, which really began to take effect in July, 1957, is attributable to reduced imports of raw materials and capital goods. . . . The government now anticipates that India will need net imports from abroad in amount at least 50 per cent above what the Plan visualized. But these are needs for a significantly lower level of total achievement, as will be clear below; for the Plan targets, net imports at least three times those originally planned would be in order.

Conclusions

The Indian case takes on special interest because India has chosen the path of democracy, while her great neighbor China has taken the Communist route. Thus these two Asian giants are engaged in a development race, the outcome of which will influence the course of events throughout the Asian-African bloc. Also, India is now in the middle of her second Five-Year Plan,

[20] Total imports fell by only $11 million owing to the expansion of imports on government account. See Reserve Bank of India, *Bulletin*, May, 1958, pp. 547–50.

[21] Wilfred Malenbaum, *East and West in India's Economic Development* (Washington, D.C., 1958).

and so has accumulated more experience with planned development than most underdeveloped countries.

Unfortunately, so far there seems to have been more planning than development. Whether in terms of the growth of per capita output or in terms of the structure of the economy, India conforms better to the label "static economy in progress" than to the label "developing economy." Unemployment is high and growing and is more of a threat socially and politically for being so much concentrated in the burgeoning cities and among the educated classes. There is also some excess plant capacity. Despite the concentration of attention on agriculture in the first Plan, agricultural output has expanded rather little. The lag in agriculture has acted as a drag on industrial expansion as well. Although better off than many underdeveloped countries for entrepreneurs and managers, India is not spared the presence of a bottleneck in these essential factors of production. Finally, India faces a chronic balance of payments problem that severely inhibits current economic growth.

Indonesia

As we continue our round-the-world tour of typical underdeveloped countries and arrive in Indonesia, we might hope for some alleviation of the gloom surrounding our visits to Libya and India. For here is a country that has been regarded since 1500 as one "rich in natural resources." The foreigner's interest in the country has ranged through time all the way from pepper to petroleum, with sugar, tea, coffee, copra, rubber, tin, and bauxite in between. At every stage of the expansion of Asian trade with Europe and America, Indonesia has been an important exporter of something; one might hope that a country so blessed by nature would afford opportunities for easy and rapid improvements in living standards. If we land in Djakarta in this frame of mind, we are foredoomed to disappointment.

Geography

Indonesia's, like Libya's land area is about equal to that of the United States east of the Mississippi. In terms of transport problems or unification, stating the size of Indonesia this way is misleading, for Indonesia is comprised of a string of islands stretching from a point opposite the northern tip of Malaya almost to the northern tip of Australia—a distance considerably greater than the width of the United States at any point. The equator is the string on which these islands are strung; it cuts three of the major islands, and the whole country is within 10 degrees of it, north or south. The climate is hot and varies little from one season to another. There is more variation according to altitude, and wealthier members of the community find relief from the monotony of the coastal climate by going into the mountains which form the "spine" of most of the major islands.

The total population is about 85 million. Relative to the area of the country, the population is not so great as in some other Asian countries.

The figure of total population, however, is rather meaningless, since over three-fifths of the population are crowded into the one small island of Java. Java is consequently the most densely populated large area in the world, with nearly eleven hundred people per square mile. This extreme population density is made possible by Java's rich volcanic soil and its assured rainfall, which together permit two or three crops a year throughout much of the island.

In the other islands, the soil is for the most part less fertile than in Java, and in some of them the rainfall is less certain, but Indonesia as a whole can be regarded as a fertile land. To this day, Indonesia's soil remains its most important natural resource; it admits not only near self-sufficiency in foodstuffs (of which the most important are rice, cassava, and maize) but also the great plantation industries: rubber, copra, coffee, tea, sisal, tobacco, pepper, teak, and others.

The country also has abundant hydroelectric potential in some areas and a wide variety of mineral resources. Of the latter, petroleum has become most important since the war. Tin and bauxite are also found in significant quantities. There are deposits of gold and silver, iron, coal, manganese, nickel, diamonds, copper, sulfate, lead, and zinc.

No doubt this wide range of natural resources evokes the frequent reference to Indonesia as a country "rich in natural wealth." Closer examination, however, reveals that the quantity and quality of some of these resources is not impressive in relation to the size of the population; the quantity and quality of some others are not thoroughly known. Moreover, the most promising source of hydroelectric power (the Asahan Valley) is not well located relative to population and sources of raw materials, and other regions, with dense populations and larger supplies of raw materials, are power-poor.

Output and Income

The resource pattern is reflected in the structure of production and the level of income. Over two-thirds of the population are still engaged in farming, fishing, and forestry, and about 56 per cent of national income originates in the primary production sector of the economy. Most of the people engaged in this sector are *tanis* (peasants or small farmers) growing rice, maize, cassava, sweet potatoes, and other basic foodstuffs, of which rice is much the most important. This *tani* agriculture sector is not quite able to meet the nation's needs; small amounts of rice and other foodstuffs must be imported, although self-sufficiency in rice is now in sight. However, a good many *tanis* also share smallholdings of plantation products, such as rubber, copra, sugar, kapok, tea, and coffee. This kind of agriculture is particularly important on the island of Java.

Although plantations on Java produce rubber, tea, teak, and oil palm, the large plantations are mainly in Sumatra. This large island is truly the "West" of Indonesia in the "frontier" sense in which the term "West" is understood by Americans. Here are the really great rubber, copra, coffee, sisal, tea, and tobacco plantations. Unfortunately, much of the "great open spaces" of Sumatra, unlike those of the American, Canadian, or Australian West of the nineteenth century, consists of cutover areas, by-product of the wasteful *ladang* system of shifting agriculture. Much of this area is now covered by tough and useless *alang-alang* (cogan) grass which moves in wherever cleared land is abandoned.

The major proved reserves of all four oil companies are in south and central Sumatra.[22] In Sumatra, too, is the city of Palembang, the second port in the country, and site of the Standard Vacuum and the main Shell-Indonesia refineries. Mineral resources also abound in Sumatra—coal, iron, silver, gold, copper. Tin, a major export, is found on the offshore islands of Singkep and Bangka, and bauxite in the nearby Riauw Archipelago. The extent and quality of some of these deposits, however, are not accurately known.

Kalimantan (Borneo) is relatively undeveloped. It is the biggest of the islands, but its population is probably under four million. Much of the coastal area is swamp, much of the center is moun-

[22] The Standard-Vacuum Company, Shell Indonesia, the California-Texas Company (Caltex), and NIAM, a joint Shell-Indonesian government operation.

tain, and in between is dense virgin jungle or cutover land under *alang-alang* grass. Even the swamps, however, grow rice and smallholders' rubber.

The smaller islands play no great role in the Indonesian economy. *Bali*, perhaps best known of Indonesian islands among Westerners, is small both in size and population. Its natural resources are neither rich nor varied, but it is unexcelled as a tourist attraction. The other islands are of even less importance for national output and income.

Thus Indonesia shows a highly regionalized economy devoted mainly to production of food and raw materials. Dutch policy was designed to encourage this kind of limited economic development. Since the transfer of sovereignty, public policy has placed more emphasis on industrialization, but the government's efforts to expand small industries have not as yet met with striking success.[23] There has, however, been some expansion of small industrial enterprises, mainly outside the government program. This expansion is indicated in the available statistics on production, imports of raw materials, licensed capacity, and the like, and includes such industries as clothing and cloth goods, other textiles, printing, household utensils, furniture, building, leather goods, beer and soft drinks, rubber remilling, etc.

With respect to large-scale industrial enterprises there has probably been some net expansion of capacity as a result of the investments of the foreign oil companies. Altogether the three foreign oil companies have invested some 400 million dollars in Indonesia since the war, and they plan to invest still more. Apart from investment in the petroleum industry, however, it is quite possible that there has been net capital consumption (undermaintenance). Some plantations have been abandoned; some have failed to replant. Although other plantations have expanded their capacity, the over-all picture is likely to be one of net reduction in capacity unless conditions favorable to replanting are created in the very near future. There is also some evidence of undermaintenance of roads, railroads, harbors, and the like.

Indonesian exports have always been highly concentrated, and today are more so than ever. The composition of exports has changed since 1938—or 1928—but Indonesian development has not reduced the degree of concentration in the export industries. Of the total value of exports in 1928, rubber accounted for 24.8

[23] For a brief survey of the industrialization program, see Benjamin Higgins, *Economic Stabilization and Development in Indonesia* (New York, 1957), chap. II.

per cent; the two next most important products (sugar and petroleum) accounted for 23.1 per cent and 9.1 per cent respectively. Thus these three products together were responsible for slightly less than half the total value of exports. In 1955, rubber alone accounted for over 45 per cent of the total value of exports. Petroleum and petroleum products accounted for 23 per cent, and tin for 6 per cent, of the total. Thus three products account for three-quarters of the total value of exports. If seven other leading plantation products are included, the total value reaches nearly 95 per cent of total exports.

On the import side, textiles remain the major item. In 1955, textiles and textile raw materials accounted for over one-quarter of the total value of imports. Other major imports were rice (3.6 per cent), paints and dyes, fertilizer, paper and cardboard, iron and steel, automobiles and trucks, bicycles, and industrial machinery.

Economic Problems

Indonesia's basic economic problems are closely related to this structure of output, income, and foreign trade. These problems are poverty, instability, and technological dualism.

Indonesia's fundamental problem is to raise total production faster than the population grows. National income figures for Indonesia are none too abundant and none too accurate; but for what they are worth, they show two facts of particular importance. Today Indonesia is relatively well off among countries of Asia, with a *per capita* income of about $100 per year; but this *per capita* income is apparently lower than it was in 1939, is probably lower than it was in 1929, and perhaps even lower than it was in, say, 1889. Nor is there clear evidence that it is currently rising; there are symptoms of prosperity, but it is prosperity of the speculative, inflationary boom type that benefits a few and injures many. Thus far, the inflation is of the "creeping" variety, but there are indications that "galloping inflation" is just around the corner, unless ways are found of raising *per capita* output while balancing the budget. The Indonesian budget has been in chronic deficit since 1952. Bringing the budget into balance to check inflation must be a major aim of Indonesian policy.

With trade, money income, and employment outside the rural sector so heavily dependent on a narrow range of raw materials and foodstuffs, the Indonesian economy is highly unstable. Few economies in the world suffered a more violent collapse during the Great Depression of the early thirties than the monetary sector of the Netherlands East Indies. Similarly, with the boom in strategic materials during the Korean War, Indonesia enjoyed a species of prosperity, with a highly favorable balance of payments and a budget surplus. From mid-1954, however, Indonesia was losing reserves of gold and foreign exchange more rapidly than any country covered in International Monetary Fund reports, and it suffered serious budget deficits. The country has faced foreign exchange difficulties ever since.

In Indonesia as in many other underdeveloped countries, it is possible to discern two rather distinct sectors, one using advanced, capital-intensive techniques and achieving high man-hour productivity, the other using traditional labor-intensive techniques

TABLE 2-3.

National Income, Net National Product, and Consumption

National income (million rupiahs)	1938	1951	1952	1955
Net national income:				
at current prices	2,700	63,600	78,800	100,000 †
at 1952 prices	81,221	78,000	78,800	96,400
Income per head (rupiahs)				
at 1952 prices	1,230 *	1,000	1,005	1,175

Net national product by sources of origin (in per cent)	1951	1952
Agriculture, fishing, and forestry	55.7	56.5
Mining	2.2	2.3
Industry (including cottage industry)	8.7	8.2
Transport and communications	2.8	3.0
Trade, banking and insurance	15.2	13.4
Government	5.6	6.4
Other	9.8	10.2
Total	100.0	100.0

Consumption of goods and services available in Indonesia (in per cent)	1951	1952
Private consumption	84.4	79.7
Government current expenditure ...	10.8	15.3
Gross domestic capital formation:		
Private	2.6	3.0
Government ..	2.2	2.0
Total	100.0	100.0

* Estimate.
† Preliminary minimum estimate.
SOURCE: *Ekonomi dan Keuangan Indonesia.*

TABLE 2-4.
Indonesia: Regional Imports and Exports
(million rupiahs)

Region	*1955*		*Jan.–Nov., 1956*	
	Imports	Exports	Imports	Exports
Java and Madura	5,123	1,873	6,519	1,500
Sumatra	1,482	7,079	1,887	6,268
Borneo	109	1,267	170	892
East Indonesia	174	399	192	248

SOURCE: *London Economist* Intelligence Unit, "Economic Review of Indonesia," March, 1957.

with low man-hour productivity. The plantation sector, together with the newer mining and industrial sector, is capital-intensive; the capital-job ratio is high. Engineering techniques are largely Western, resulting in a tendency to use highly mechanized production processes rather than labor-intensive ones. In the peasant agriculture and small cottage industry sector, on the other hand, labor-intensive techniques are used. Labor is abundant in this sector, and partial or disguised unemployment is starting to appear. Man-hour productivity in this sector is extremely low.

This problem is relatively new to Indonesia. In the early nineteenth century the entire country was given over to smallholders' and peasant agriculture, with no marked difference in technique from one sector or region to another. The population of Indonesia was less than one-quarter of its present level, and land was abundant. There was no serious population pressure anywhere in the country, and although standards of living were not high there was little real hardship.

The impact of late nineteenth-century industrialization (including plantations as industries) brought an initial increase in *per capita* incomes of Indonesians. Instead of leading to permanent improvement in Indonesian living standards, however, this initial increase in incomes was dissipated through accelerated population growth. The total population increased more than fourfold in some three generations. The sector of the economy in which new investments were being made was totally incapable of absorbing the increase in population which it generated. For as already pointed out, the plantation, oil, and mining sector was land-and-capital-intensive; technical coefficients either were, or were assumed to be, relatively fixed. There was no choice, therefore, but for the increase in population to return mainly to the peasant agriculture and small industries sector, where technical coefficients were relatively variable. With abundant labor and scarce capital—and in Java, scarce land as well—production methods in this sector became highly labor-intensive. Eventually labor became redundant in this sector (marginal productivity fell to zero), and the growing population merely swelled the ranks of the disguised unemployed (static or dynamic). *Per capita* incomes in this sector returned to the subsistence level.

Both the economic and the political aspects of this problem are made more difficult of solution by the fact that the two sectors conform roughly to two regions: Java and the Outer Islands. The main development of plantations, mines, and oil fields occurred on the Outer Islands, especially Sumatra, Kalimantan, and Sulawesi. The big growth of population, however, occurred in Java, where the soil was most fertile and best suited for growing foodstuffs, and where most of the people already were. Employment in cottage and small industry is also highest in Java. Thus two-thirds of Indonesia's population are crowded on one small island, engaged mainly in the production of foodstuffs or simple handicrafts and small-scale manufacturing for home consumption and dependent on imports for textiles and other important items of consumption; the other third of the population is scattered through an enormous area in which there are some highly efficient large-scale industries producing mainly for export. With such a discrepancy in economic conditions, it is small wonder that there are stresses and strains between Java and the Outer Islands. Some increase in output can still be obtained on Java through fertilizer and seed selection, but these will give a "breathing spell" of only a few years. Then the Javanese rural economy will be simply unable to absorb further Javanese population growth without falling standards of living. Once the "breathing spell" is over, increases in man-hour productivity in Javanese agriculture will be obtainable only through a shift to more extensive and more mechanized agriculture. In short, solution of the Javanese problem requires that *somewhat more* than the 300,000 families added each year to Javanese population be absorbed *elsewhere* in the economy—into industries in Java or the Outer Islands, or into agriculture in the Outer Islands. Such a program will be expensive. Providing, say, 400,000 jobs a year in any of these ways would cost at least half a billion dollars per year. Exploiting opportunities in the relatively capital-intensive industries in the Outer Islands will require still more in the way of new investment. The obvious lines of development are the creation of middle-sized import-replacing industries on Java (where the market is) and carrying further the processing of export products of the Outer Islands (aluminum, tin smelting, pulp and paper, petroleum refining, etc.).

Conclusions

Although the richness of Indonesia's known resources has been exaggerated by Indonesian and foreigner alike, Indonesia does have more with which to work, relative to the size of her total population, than many underdeveloped countries. Certainly she is better off than either Libya or India in this respect, and perhaps even better off than the Philippines, where per capita incomes are 60 per cent higher. But Indonesia must take the steps necessary to stabilize her economy before she can hope to develop it. Then she must formulate and execute with enthusiasm a development plan designed to absorb some 400,000 Javanese every year into productive employment outside Javanese peasant agriculture and to make the most of the industrial potential of the Outer Islands. To do that Indonesia must be a good deal more united politically than she has been in recent years.

Since Indonesia is still essentially stagnant, the basic economic problem there is to generate a take-off into sustained economic growth. Stabilization will be easier, and the balance of payments problems more tractable, when a change in structure and higher productivity have been achieved. Meanwhile capital, entrepreneurship, skills, and foreign exchange are all bottlenecks that must be broken—as in most underdeveloped countries. In addition, Indonesia has a peculiar problem arising out of the regional structure of the economy, technological dualism, and the product mix.

The Philippines

Of all the countries discussed in this chapter, Indonesia and the Philippines present the most tempting invitation to direct comparison. They are enough alike to give some hope of isolating cause and effect relationships among the differences between them. They are neighboring archipelagoes, perhaps even once part of the same land mass. Both are mountainous island economies. Although the Philippines lie generally northward and eastward of Indonesia, their climates are much the same. Both countries have a variety of racial groups and languages, but in both the

Malay stock and linguistic roots predominate. Over-all density of population is much the same; Indonesia has some 82 million people and 576,000 square miles, the Philippines has about 22 million people and 116,000 square miles. Thus Indonesia has roughly five times the area and four times the population of the Philippines. After World War II, both countries achieved independence, following more than three centuries of colonial rule. Both were essentially "trading posts" for the metropoles until the late nineteenth century, and both began their life as sovereign nations with a heritage of wartime disruption and devastation.

Economic Problems and Development Plans

Their economic problems and their plans for dealing with them also have common features. In both countries, the central problems are poverty, dependence on a few exports, with consequent pressure on foreign exchange reserves, and unemployment. Solution of these problems in both countries is complicated by "technological dualism." For the Philippines, as well as the Indonesian, economy is divided into two distinct sectors: an industrial and plantation sector that is capital-intensive, fixed-technical-coefficient, technologically advanced, and highly productive, and a peasant agriculture and cottage industry sector which has variable technical coefficients, is highly labor-intensive, technologically retarded, and low in productivity and income.

Major Differences

Let us try to distinguish those major differences between the two countries which are *causal* factors in the development process from those which are *effects*. On the political side, the first *causal* difference is that both Hinduism and Islam preceded European colonization in Indonesia, whereas no advanced culture preceded colonization in the Philippines. The Javanese and Sumatran civilizations of the sixteenth century were highly developed in both a cultural and economic (trading) sense. Vestiges of this civilization remain to this day, and they have their effects on attitudes and actions.[24] Islam has become a powerful political force. Both Hinduism and Islam constitute sources of resistance to certain kinds of change in Indonesia. In the Philippines, on the other hand, the Spanish seem to have encountered a cultural and eco-

[24] See, for example, Clifford Geertz, "Religious Beliefs and Economic Behavior in a Central Javanese Town," *Economic Development and Cultural Change*, January, 1956.

nomic vacuum.[25] There was little resistance to the spread of Roman Catholicism among the people or to adoption of Spanish culture among the elite. Nor was there much resistance to the adoption of American ideologies, techniques, and accents after 1896. When living in the country one has the feeling that neither the Spanish nor the American culture is so firmly entrenched as to provide firm resistance to any powerful new ideology that might appear.

Secondly, there are the various differences between colonization by Spain and the United States on the one hand and by The Netherlands on the other. Particularly significant was the Dutch system of "indirect rule" which prevented the establishment of a strong central government and the training of a modern indigenous civil service. Also important was the tendency of the Dutch to discourage indigenous entrepreneurship while leaving the religion and the culture largely untouched. In the Philippines, on the contrary, administration was highly centralized and the American or Spanish culture was quickly spread. Closely related to these differences is the third major political factor; viz., that the Philippines gained its freedom by evolution and Indonesia by revolution.

On the economic side, an important difference is that, although exports of both countries are highly concentrated on a few commodities, in Indonesia two mineral products, petroleum and tin, rank second and third after rubber, followed by coconut products and tobacco; in the Philippines, all major exports are plantation products: coconut products, sugar, forest products, fruit, and tobacco. Second, the Philippines faces a somewhat higher rate of population growth. The estimated annual growth is from 1.5 to 2 per cent for Indonesia and over 2 per cent for the Philippines. Capital requirements for a given rate of increase in *per capita* incomes, therefore, tend to be higher in the Philippines than in Indonesia. Third, the Philippines has nothing quite like Java, with its incredibly fertile volcanic soil and assured rainfall, which permit two or three crops a year and the sustenance of two-thirds of Indonesia's population on this one small island.

Turning to differences which might be regarded as "effects," of earlier development and which are important for future development planning, perhaps most important is the much more adequate supply of indigenous entrepreneurship in the Philip-

[25] The writer is aware that statements like this make anthropologists shudder or point with scorn. By "cultural vacuum," of course, I mean that the culture was simple and primitive.

pines. Not only does the Philippines have a sizable group of able and ambitious entrepreneurs, but they have essentially American attitudes toward technical change. They also have a nineteenth-century American attitude toward free private enterprise and toward the position of the industrialist, financier, and trader in society. The Philippine elite show none of the reluctance that some Indonesian leaders still have "to sully their hands in trade." The relative prestige of private entrepreneurs and of government officials is just the reverse of what it is in Indonesia. A by-product of this attitude is that in sharp contrast to Indonesia, where the bulk of investment is still in foreign hands, in the Philippines over half the stock of capital is owned by Filipinos. In the government service, too, the Philippines is much better provided with well-trained people.

The relatively liberal policy of the United States in the Philippines, the encouragement of domestic enterprise, and the evolutionary achievement of independence has yielded other results as well. Indonesia is neutralist, but the Philippines is one of three Asian members of SEATO. In the Philippines, too, there is much less concern over the use of foreign aid and foreign investment from the West in the achievement of development aims. Indonesia is paralyzed by a conflict between a "history-minded" group, mindful of Indonesia's recent past and fearful of Western influence in any form, and an "economics-minded" group, attaching top priority to economic development and willing to accept Western guidance and assistance in achieving development somewhat along Western lines.[26] No such conflict exists in the Philippines. Even the Filipino leaders who are keenly aware of their history have little resentment against American behavior toward them in the past; current anti-Americanism arises rather out of the behavior of the United States at the present time, but even the anti-Americanism does not take the form of resisting development along Western lines or with Western assistance.

One offsetting feature of the heritage from Spanish and American colonialism, unfortunately, is the attitude toward corruption in the Philippines. (Presumably learned from the Spanish rather than the Americans?) Corruption among government officials exists in both countries, but the quality is different. In Indonesia, large-scale corruption in high places began only in 1954 and was in the first instance a by-product of party politics. Moreover,

[26] Cf. Benjamin Higgins, *Economic Stabilization and Development in Indonesia* (New York, 1957); and "Indonesia's Development Plans and Problems," *Pacific Affairs*, June, 1956.

the basic Indonesian attitude is that political corruption is sinful and should be punished. The abortive "civil war" of 1958 was in part a reaction by some government and military leaders to this recent growth of corruption. Quite different is the Filipino attitude toward "anomalies," the well-known synonym for corruption in that country. Corruption in high places is more often for personal than for political purposes, and the ordinary Filipino seems to take it for granted that people in positions of power will use the power to line their own pockets. One feels that in the Philippines the sin is not in diverting public funds to your own bank account but in getting caught. Perhaps more important, Indonesian style corruption is less likely than Philippines style to direct public policy away from general ends toward personal goals.

Turning to more purely economic factors, difference in income might be regarded as an "effect" of historical development. *Per capita* income in the Philippines is 60 per cent higher than in Indonesia, and it has been growing at a rate of at least 3 per cent per year. In Indonesia, as we have seen, it is doubtful whether *per capita* income is growing at all, and it is certainly not growing very fast. The Philippines is also more advanced in terms of the structure of production (40 per cent in agriculture as against Indonesia's 55 per cent) and of literacy.[27]

Obstacles to Development in the Philippines

A casual glance at postwar figures of national income and output in the Philippines might lead one to conclude that economic development is no problem in that country. From 1950 to 1956 national income rose by something more than 5 per cent per year, while the price level showed a gently falling trend. In 1957 and 1958 the expansion of real income continued, with relatively modest increases in prices. Here is a record of "steady growth" that has few rivals in economic history; at first blush one might

[27] Whereas a larger share of output comes from the agricultural sector in Indonesia, a larger share of employment is in agriculture in the Philippines. Although the figures for both countries have a considerable margin of error, and the actual differences between them may be less than these statistics suggest, the general picture suggested is what might be expected. Plantation agriculture in Indonesia is highly productive in terms of value produced per man-year, but productivity in industry and mining is higher in the Philippines. A more meaningful comparison might be peasant agriculture and cottage industry on the one hand and plantations, mines, and manufactures on the other, but figures are not available in this form. Superficial evidence suggests that productivity in peasant agriculture is about the same in both countries.

consider the record of the Philippines as one that other countries might well envy. Behind the attractive façade, however, are economic and social disorders that threaten not only economic stability but social and political stability as well.

The Philippines faces four major economic problems. First, maintaining past rates of growth will become increasingly difficult as time goes by; signs of retardation of growth have already appeared. Second, thus far, the rise in national income has done little to relieve the extreme poverty of the vast majority of Filipinos. Third, the balance of payments continues in fundamental disequilibrium. Fourth, unemployment is high and apparently growing despite the rise in national income.

The Problem of Maintaining Growth

The Philippines has shared with other war-torn countries the experience of obtaining large increases in output with relatively little investment (very low incremental capital-output ratios, or "ICOR's" in economist's jargon) during the reconstruction period. In the Philippines, a large proportion of investment between 1946 and 1952 represented reclamation and replanting of agricultural land, a process bringing substantial increases in output with little or no outlay on capital equipment. Fertilizer provided through the foreign aid program brought quick increases in agricultural productivity. The repair of damaged machines, buildings, transport equipment, and the like, permitted the restoration of whole complexes of productive apparatus for very small expense. Large amounts of war surplus equipment were obtained at prices far below cost. All these conditions facilitated significant additions to output for relatively little capital outlay.

Such opportunities, however, will not arise again in the near future. On the contrary, when the time comes to replace this inexpensive capital, costs are likely to be much higher than they originally were. True, in a plantation economy, expansion of output (particularly of coconut products) can continue for some years after investments were made. Nevertheless, it is to be expected that over the next five years capital-output ratios will be higher than they were during the reconstruction period. The figures of output indicate that the rate of economic growth has already tapered off to some degree, with a transition from "reconstruction" to "normal growth" somewhere around 1952.

Trends in the Philippines economy appear very different if, instead of looking at only postwar figures of output and income, one converts production figures to *per capita* terms and compares present levels with prewar. The picture then obtained of the agricultural sector shows restoration and subsequent maintenance of traditional relationships between the number of hectares under cultivation and total population, with little change in output per hectare. For plantation output, both hectarage under cultivation and output is lower in *per capita* terms than it was before the war. The picture for minerals is mixed, but in any case these still play a small role in exports and income.

POVERTY

In 1950, the United States Economic Survey Mission (Bell Mission) noted the large and increasing inequalities in income in the Philippines. There is little evidence that income distribution has since improved. Between 1946 and 1954, entrepreneurial and company incomes rose somewhat more than wage and salary incomes. In the latter year, the proportion of national income going to entrepreneurs and property owners was much higher than in economically advanced countries—56 per cent, as compared to 44 per cent for wages and salaries. In 1950 there were only 6,000 shareholders in the entire country. Wages of skilled industrial workers in Manila actually fell somewhat between 1950 and 1955; wages of unskilled industrial workers in Manila showed only slight improvement. The increase in daily wages of agricultural workers was not sufficient to raise rural wage rates much above prewar or to bring significant changes in their severely curtailed way of life. Nor does this inequity bring high levels of private savings and investment; in the period 1950–56, these ran at only 4 to 5 per cent of national income.

The fiscal process does little to mobilize potential savings or to redress the maldistribution of income. The Filipinos blithely refer to themselves as "the world's worst taxpayers," and the label seems to stick. Total tax revenues in recent years have run at only 8 or 9 per cent of national income, as compared to 10 per cent in Indonesia (with *per capita* income three-fifths as high), 25 per cent in Burma, 16 per cent in Japan, 21 per cent in Ceylon, 22 per cent in the United States and Canada, etc. Tax evasion is widespread among the upper- and upper-middle–income groups. Corporation and personal income taxes together accounted for less than 20 per cent of central government tax revenues in 1955, and only a small fraction of these was paid by Filipinos in the higher-income brackets. More than half the total revenues from income tax is represented by taxes on corporations, a substantial share of which is paid by foreign concerns. Of personal income taxes actually paid, less than half is paid by Filipinos, and these represent mainly deductions from wages in the form of a withholding tax. The tax structure as a whole is highly regressive; the great bulk of revenues comes from commodity taxes of one kind or another which are shifted to the final consumer.

Underlying the unequal distribution of income is the concentration of land ownership, a social problem which has caused much concern among the American advisers to the Philippines government. Legislation of 1954 has improved the tenant's share of agricultural income, but the land reform law of 1955 does not seem to have had much effect on the distribution of land ownership.

By and large, it seems safe to say that the standard of living of the masses of the Philippines people has improved but little over prewar levels, despite the continuous rise in national income. Postwar increases in income, even more than wealth, have been concentrated in the hands of the upper-income groups.

BALANCE OF PAYMENTS

The Philippines has had a chronic import surplus ever since the war, and only large-scale foreign aid, American expenditures on military bases and veterans' pensions, and the like, have prevented more serious losses of foreign exchange than have actually taken place. Even with these extraordinary sources of foreign exchange, it has been necessary to make exchange controls increasingly rigorous to prevent foreign exchange reserves from falling to dangerously low levels.

The favorable balance of Philippines commodity trade before the war depended upon a narrow range of traditional exports, most of which were products of plantation agriculture: copra and other coconut products, sugar, forest products, fruit, and tobacco. These commodities still provide the bulk of Philippines exports. Coconut products alone still account for about 40 per cent of the value of exports and the first four groups for over 80 per cent.

These plantation industries now face serious problems. As in Indonesia, the total area under plantation crops is still below the prewar level. The problems confronting the plantation industries of the Philippines are largely the same as in Indonesia: loss of productive land through destruction, squatters, blight, disease, and inadequate maintenance, combined with increasing competition from synthetics and other rival products. Whereas market prospects for natural rubber are reasonably bright for some years to come, however, and the market for petroleum products is rapidly expanding, the outlook for the major exports of the Philippines is much more dim. The principal use of coconut products is the manufacture of soaps. In the American market, which absorbs 40 to 50 per cent of Philippines exports of coconut products, soap is being increasingly displaced by detergents. Sugar remains the second most important Philippines export, but here the major factor is the American quota of 952,000 short tons. The present agreement with the United States government ends in 1974; if then the arrangements are not renewed, the prospects for Philippines sugar exports would be poor indeed. Among all major Philippines exports, abacá (Manila hemp) has suffered the most severe setback from prewar days. The U.S. Department of Commerce Survey of the Philippines says, "So serious are the problems of the Philippines abacá industry that there is some question of its ability to survive." Meanwhile, no new exports have appeared which seem capable of replacing the traditional ones in the short run.

UNEMPLOYMENT

The National Economic Council estimates the current (1956) level of unemployment, including persons employed less than half time, at 1.9 million people, or 19 per cent of the labor force. When disguised unemployment is included, the figure could, of course, be much higher. At time of writing no reliable estimates of the trend in unemployment were available. The only published figure was in the Central Bank's annual report for 1954–55 which, in conjunction with the National Economic Council's new estimate of increase in the labor force of 275,000 per year, would give an increase in unemployment of more than 100,000 persons per year. However, it seems likely that the Bank's figure underestimated increases in rural employment; a better assumption might be that open unemployment is growing at 50,000 to 70,000 per year and disguised unemployment by 70,000 to 80,000 per year.

From the social and political point of view, the increase in unemployment is made more serious by the tendency for disguised unemployment to move into the cities and become open. The postwar growth of Manila in particular has failed to produce a proportionate increase in the number of productive full-time jobs. A serious aspect of the employment picture, in the Philippines as in India, is growing unemployment among educated people. With nearly 200,000 students in Philippines universities and some

600,000 students in high schools, it would appear that graduates of these institutions are being turned out faster than technical, professional, and administrative positions can absorb them. Indeed, the total number of high school and college graduates each year exceeds the estimated total increase in employment. Moreover, the curricula of Philippines universities are not adapted to a developing economy. Law and humanities still account for a large proportion of university degrees, and relatively few Filipinos receive vocational or technical training. Obviously university and even high school graduates will be less content than the uneducated to return to the *barrios* (villages) if they do not find employment in the cities.

Conclusion

Achieving economic development in the Philippines, then, presents four major problems:

1. Past rates of economic growth must be maintained in the face of increasing difficulties. This will require substantial increases in net investment. Although the general situation was mildly deflationary from 1950 to 1956, the required increase in developmental investment could not be undertaken without inflation unless it is financed by increased voluntary savings or taxes.
2. A larger share of investment must be directed toward providing for the needs of the lower-income groups, and the tax system and its administration must be reformed so as to permit the lower-income groups to share more heavily in the increases in national income.
3. The structure of production, and particularly the structure of exports, must be changed so as to provide new sources of foreign exchange. At the same time, import-replacing industries must be developed. In general, a much more rapid growth of the relative share of manufacturing in national income must be encouraged.
4. Means must be found of increasing the rate of job creation. This can be done in part by increasing the total level of development investment, and in part by giving higher priorities in the development program to enterprises (public and private) with relatively low capital-job ratios.

Mexico

The economic history of Mexico since World War I reads like a success story. The revolution of 1917 released national energies which, in sharp contrast to the Indonesian case to date, have been successfully directed toward economic development. Dr. Alfredo Navarrete, Director of the Department of Economic Studies of the *Nacional Financiere*, puts it this way: [28]

The present Constitution of Mexico establishes a democratic regime to regulate the life of the Nation's 32 million inhabitants who live in an area of 764,000 square miles, approximately one-fourth as large as the continental United States. Drafted in 1917, it sets forth the legitimate aspirations of its people, arising from the profound social, political and economic movement known as the Mexican Revolution—the first of similar 20th-century movements in many parts of the world—initiated in 1910 against the Dictatorship which ruled the country during thirty years. For Mexico, as a result, democracy means more than a legal structure and a political regime. It means essentially a system of life based on the constant economic, social and cultural betterment of its people. Today, forty years after proclaiming its present Constitution, the Mexican people are broadly united about the objectives of its economic system: (1) to attain a rate of economic growth which exceeds its rate of population growth; (2) to attain such economic development with reasonable price and financial stability and (3) to raise the standard of living of the great working majorities by increasing the social justice with which national income is distributed among the factors of production.

Before the revolution Mexico was just another example of a poor and stagnant country.

Mexico [says Dr. Navarrete] lay in the apparently closed circle of poverty resulting from the narrowness of the local market, lack of big social capital, lack of savings, monopolistic advantages possessed by foreign enterprises exploiting local natural resources and from many other hindrances to economic growth. [After the revolution,] having been dormant for many decades, living on the basis of a settled peasant agriculture, the basic concern of Mexicans was to set the national economy into a self-sustaining growth process.

The "pillars" of the Mexican development program were agrarian reform, public investment in social overhead capital, expropriation of foreign-owned railroads and oil properties, labor legislation, education in technical training, and the development of a domestic system of banking and credit institutions. The agrarian reform abolished the feudal system of land ownership, with its "self-contained isolated units and absentee holdings," and redistributed the land in a manner permitting modernization of

[28] Alfredo Navarrete, "Mexico's Growth: Prospects and Problems," University of Texas Conference on Economic Development, April, 1958.

techniques. Improved farming methods, irrigation, extension work, and better farm implements helped to raise agricultural productivity.

The expropriation of foreign-owned petroleum and railroad investments in 1937–38 led to an international boycott of Mexico in protest. Contrary to expectations, and indeed contrary to the objectives of the boycott, it served as a further impetus to Mexican development. For the boycott compelled the Mexicans to make a redoubled effort to manage their productive assets themselves. "A hard-working type of new local managers for the railroads and oil industries," says Dr. Navarrete, "as well as national entrepreneurs interested in agricultural and industrial investments in the home market, started to develop." Once the Mexican economy began to move and new opportunities for profitable investment appeared, foreign capital flowed back into the country, accelerating the rate of economic expansion.

The educational effort included a literacy campaign, agricultural extension work, reorganization of the University of Mexico so as to provide training more suited to the needs of developing countries, and establishment of a National Polytechnical Institute to provide technicians. A National School of Economics was also established, and courses provided in business administration to swell the supply of managers for new enterprises.

Measures in the field of credit and finance included the establishment of the Central Bank in 1925, a national bank for agricultural credit in 1926, and the establishment of the *Nacional Financiere* in 1934 to serve as an industrial bank, development corporation, and investment company. In the early stages of development, the government was responsible for a large share of development finance. Public investment in the "infrastructure" included railroads, highways, power, and housing.

The result has been a rapid rate of increase in national income and an equally rapid transformation of the structure of the economy. Between 1939 and 1945, output of the Mexican economy increased by about 8 per cent per year. In the following decade, the rate of increase declined somewhat, to 5 or 6 per cent per year. Whereas 70 per cent of the labor force was engaged in agriculture in 1930, and 65 per cent in 1940, by 1956 the proportion had dropped to 54 per cent. Thus Mexico seems to be a country well on its way to sustained economic growth.

The change in structure has been accompanied by urbanization. The four largest cities have grown at an average rate in excess of 5 per cent per year since 1940. Mexico City, with four and a half million inhabitants, has become the fourth largest city in the Western Hemisphere and the second largest in Latin America.

The expansion of output reflects partly an increase in employment and partly rising productivity. Between 1946 and 1956, when the index of national production rose by 64.8 per cent, the volume of employment (in man-hours) increased by 46.2 per cent. Thus productivity per man-hour rose by 12.7 per cent.

Since 1939, agricultural output increased two and a half times; the increase can be broken down as follows: 40 per cent was the result of bringing new land under cultivation; 35 per cent resulted from a shift to more productive crops; and 25 per cent was owing to improved yields. Between 1949 and 1955, gross investment in agriculture increased by 148 per cent, three-fourths of this amount representing private investment. Increased use of fertilizers and mechanization contributed to the rise in agricultural output.

Particularly dramatic has been the expansion of cotton output, which in 1955 was six times the 1939 figure, making Mexico the world's second biggest exporter. Coffee output has nearly doubled, and coffee is now Mexico's second most important export. At the same time Mexico has achieved near self-sufficiency in foodstuffs.

The expansion of industry has been even more spectacular. The fish catch increased at an average annual rate of 13 per cent between 1940 and 1949, while the shrimp catch increased more than threefold in that same period.[29] The volume of manufactures has grown by three and a half times since 1939; output of electricity and petroleum products has trebled. The nationalized petroleum industry more than doubled its output of crude oil between 1938 and 1956, trebled its refining capacity, and nearly quadrupled its proved reserves. Manufacturing has been greatly diversified. Iron and steel, sugar, cement, chemicals, tires, "and all the hundreds of establishments that have produced from steel pipe to refrigerators to washing machines, and that indicate existence of modern industrial complexes," Dr. Navarrete points out.[30] Mining as a whole has lagged behind the rest of the economy, but sulphur production has expanded rapidly in recent years. Mexico is now the world's second biggest producer of this mineral. The industrial expansion has been facilitated by a five-

[29] International Bank for Reconstruction and Development Combined Mexican Working Party, *The Economic Development of Mexico* (Baltimore, 1953), p. 36.

[30] Navarrete, *op. cit.*, p. 10.

fold increase in national highway mileage and by extension of air and rail services.

With this spectacular economic growth, what problems remain for Mexico? In the first place, as in the Philippines, the benefits of economic growth have not been equally spread, either among income groups or among regions. As Dr. Navarrete puts it, "Mexicans are aware that their principal task is to reduce wide-spread poverty through relatively high rates of economic growth over a sustained period." [31] A national average income of $220, although higher than in most Asian countries, is still low as compared even to the more advanced European countries, let alone the United States or Canada. Moreover, this average figure "conceals great differences in personal income between upper and lower classes." It also conceals regional differences. As the Combined Mexican Working Party puts it:

> agricultural development between 1939 and 1950 was confined chiefly to the northern states of Mexico and to some tropical and semi-tropical regions where there was scope for irrigation and expansion of cultivation. In the south central plain, traditionally most important agricultural part of the country, development has been slow. In this region where all the arable land is used and where only limited possibility exists for irrigation, increased production could be achieved only by improving farming methods.

Secondly, Mexico—again like the Philippines—will find it more difficult in future than it has been in the past to achieve rates of increase in national income in excess of 5 per cent per year. The rate of growth has already shown signs of retardation during 1956 and 1958. Maintaining even a 5 per cent growth rate in future will require a higher ratio of investment to national income than has been achieved in the past. For as in Indonesia and the Philippines, the "bargain-counter" projects have been largely exhausted. The war gave Mexico an unusual opportunity for industrialization, by increasing demand for its manufactures and industrial metal. It also provided opportunities, both during the war and after, for more intensive use of existing capital equipment. The Combined Mexican Working Party states: [32]

> The Increases in industrial output and in transportation and commercial and other services in 1940–45 were achieved with relatively small capital outlay. . . . In the post-war period there still remained some scope for increasing output without much capital expenditure.

[31] *Ibid.*, p. 14.

[32] International Bank for Reconstruction and Development, *op. cit.*, pp. 4–5.

Between 1945 and 1950, for example, railroad freight traffic was able to increase by 18% in spite of the fact that railroad investment did not even cover maintenance and replacement of worn-out equipment. . . . In the petroleum industry it was possible to increase output substantially in spite of low capital outlay for exploratory drilling because of the existence of plentiful and easily developed reserve in the Poza Rica field; and in agriculture, private investment in land clearing, small scale irrigation and farm machinery up to 1947 yielded large return.

There was considerable excess capacity in industry at the beginning of the war, which permitted substantial increases in output without much new industrial investment. For example, output of textiles increased by an average of 6.6 per cent per year during the war, with almost negligible new investment. Industrial production as a whole grew by 9.4 per cent per year on the average, with relatively little new investment. In general, investment during the period 1939–50 was concentrated in high-yield projects. "Investment could be concentrated in 1939–50 on projects yielding high returns quickly because large numbers of public facilities already existed which were not being used to capacity. The railroads, ports, communication systems, power plants, and community works have all taken on additional loads particularly in the first half of the period." [33] Nearly half the total investment in this period was in agriculture, petroleum, mining, industry, and motor vehicles, and "within each of these fields, projects were available which required only small expenditure to yield the exceptional results." Moreover, only a small part of the investment in this period went into maintenance or replacement. For example, less than 2 per cent of the investment in public irrigation went into maintenance and only 14 per cent of the investment in highways went into repair and maintenance. "Newness of much of the Mexican capital stock kept repair and replacement cost low, but under-maintenance was also partly responsible." Thus investments for maintenance and replacement and repairs are likely to be much higher in future.

The problem of sustaining the rate of increase in *per capita* income is even greater than that of sustaining the growth of national income as a whole. Mexico has a very high rate of population growth, about 3.2 per cent per annum, and it is more likely to increase than to decline in the next few years. As is so often the case with underdeveloped countries, this "population explo-

[33] *Ibid.*, p. 17.

sion" reflects continued high birth rates combined with a sharp drop in death rates brought by improvements in public health. The birth rate increased from 28.2 per thousand in 1893 to 46.2 in 1956, while the death rate has dropped from 39.9 to 13.3 and shows signs of diminishing still further. The expansion of acreage sounds less impressive when it is realized that it is almost exactly equal to the rate of population growth—a fact which provides one more analogy with the situation in the Philippines.

Finally, Mexico has a problem of stabilization. It suffers chronic pressure on its foreign exchange reserves. The marginal propensity both to consume and to import is high. For example, despite the rapid increase in petroleum output, the industrialization of the country and general improvement of living standards have resulted in so great an expansion of domestic demand that petroleum can no longer be counted upon to provide growing amounts of foreign exchange. The Combined Mexican Working Party saw every reason for the rate of growth of imports to continue, in the absence of controls, but thought it unlikely that the rate of increase in exports achieved during the immediate postwar years could be maintained. Some indication of the pressure on the Mexican peso may be obtained from the fact that the peso has been devalued three times since the beginning of war, in 1939, in 1949, and again in 1954. The peso did withstand the American recession of 1957–58, which Dr. Navarrete regards as "sign of the soundness of the Mexican economy." [34]

Moreover, Mexican foreign exchange earnings are uncomfortably dependent on the United States. In 1950, over 84 per cent of Mexico's currency and capital receipt came from the United States. Since the war there has been some expansion of exports to Europe and to Canada, while trade with other Latin American countries has declined. Nevertheless, the dependence on the United States is still a source of potential instability in the economy.

Conclusions

Thus the Mexican and Philippine pictures show striking similarities. Both present handsome façades of rapid current economic growth behind which hide great social and regional inequalities, the specter of population pressure combined with a tapering-off of growth, and a chronic balance of payments problem. Both countries have a Spanish heritage combined with current dom-

[34] Navarrete, *op. cit.*, p. 16.

inance of the United States in their economic and political international relations. Could that be the basic reason for the similarity of their present positions?

Italy

People are sometimes surprised to find Italy, a European power which has made so distinguished a contribution to Western civilization during the last 2,500 years, in a list of underdeveloped countries. There is no doubt, however, that Italy is underdeveloped as we defined the term in Chapter 1. Per capita income in 1952–54 was just over $300, and Italy was receiving technical and capital assistance for economic development from both the UN and the United States. Our reason for including Italy here, however, is that it provides the classic example of regional discrepancies in rates of development. For the average of $300 hides a spread from nearly $500 in northern and central Italy to about $200 in the south (*Mezzogiorno*). Thus incomes in the Italian south are lower than the Mexican average. There are, of course, other underdeveloped countries which show these regional discrepancies, especially those with large oil reserves. Venezuela springs to mind, or Kuwait, whose oil wealth is so great that per capita income there is actually higher than in the United States, although the vast majority of people live in poverty. The Italian case is more puzzling and more interesting than these, however, for since 1880 the Italian north has had a vigorous and varied industrialization. Indeed the north provides a good example of rapid take-off into sustained growth. Why did the development of the north fail to carry the south along with it?

Italy as a whole got off to a late start in its industrialization. As Professor Gerschenkron puts it: [35]

> It is obvious that in the decades following its political unification Italy's economy remained very backward in relation not only to that of England, but also to the economies of industrially advancing countries on the continent of Europe. Whatever gauge one may choose for the purposes of comparison, be it qualitative descriptions of technological equipment, organizational efficiency, and labor skills in individual enterprises; or scattered quantitative data on relative productivity in certain branches of industry, or the numbers of persons employed in industry; or the density of the country's railroad net-

[35] Alexander Gerschenkron, "Notes on the Rate of Industrial Growth in Italy, 1881–1913," *The Journal of Economic History*, December, 1955, p. 360.

work; or the standards of literacy of its population, the same conclusion will result. It is true that there were very large differences in this respect among the individual regions of the Peninsula; but according to Pantaleoni's computations, which—subject to a considerable margin of error as they are—probably give a correct idea of the order of magnitudes involved, the private per capita wealth of the richest and most advanced areas in North Italy in the second half of the eighties was still very much below one half of the contemporaneous figure for France as a whole.

After 1880, however, Italy had a rapid increase in industrial production. It came in two waves, one from 1881 to 1888, and the second from 1896 to 1908.

TABLE 2-5.

Annual Average Rates of Growth of Italian Industrial Output for 1881–1913 and Subperiods *

Period	*Percentage change*
1881–1888	4.6 (Moderate growth)
1888–1896	.3 (Stagnation)
1896–1908	6.7 (Very rapid growth)
1908–1913	2.4 (Reduced rate of growth)
1881–1913	3.8

* Computed on the assumption of a geometric rate of growth between the first and the last years of the specified periods. From Gerschenkron, *op. cit.*, p. 364.

Professor Gerschenkron says of these data: [36]

One point seems to emerge with sufficient clarity from the data contained in the preceding tabulations: Italy did have its period of a big industrial push. While there may be some question concerning the exact choice of the initial and terminal years for the individual subperiods, it seems appropriate to locate the period of the great push between the years 1896 and 1908. Before 1896 lay the years of a laborious return from the low of 1892 to the level of 1888. After 1908, the rates of growth of all the index industries but one were greatly reduced.

Industrialization in northern Italy was resumed after World War I, until interrupted by the Great Depression. Some expansion took place in the late thirties, but the war brought retrogression. A new upsurge began about 1952.

The *Mezzogiorno*, however, has not shared in this expansion. One may dispute the propriety of regarding Italy as an under-

[36] Gerschenkron, *op. cit.*, p. 364.

developed *country*, but there can be no doubt that the *Mezzogiorno* is an underdeveloped *area*. For the Italian south displays nearly all the characteristics of underdeveloped countries outlined in Chapter 1. The dramatic discrepancy between the economic development of the south and the rest of Italy after unification in 1860 has been stated in trenchant terms by Svimez (the Association for the Industrial Development of Southern Italy): [37]

> Between 1861 and 1936 (first and last census years) the population of Southern Italy, if we consider the 1861 frontiers, rose from 9.8 to 15.4 millions showing an increase of 5.6 millions. During the same period the natural increase in the population (births minus deaths) was 9.4 millions. There was consequently a real exodus of 3.8 million persons (to Northern Italy or abroad), equal to more than 40 per cent of the natural increase. In the rest of Italy 3.1 million persons emigrated, equal to 22 per cent of the natural increase.
>
> Of the 5.6 million inhabitants that remained in Southern Italy, only 200,000 were able to find employment there in 75 years; the economically active population (of over ten years of age) rose in fact from 5.6 millions in 1861 to 5.8 in 1936.
>
> Of the remaining 5.4 millions, 4.1 millions increased the size of the inactive (unproductive) population, while the other 1.3 millions represent the increase in the population under ten years of age. This alarming expansion of the inactive population was due partly to social progress (increase in the number of children over ten receiving compulsory schooling, in the number of civil pensioners, etc.), but mainly to the fact that the economic activities of the South were not sufficient to give employment to an appreciable part of the growing population during three-quarters of a century. More or less the same number of economically active persons had to provide a livelihood for 4.2 million inactive persons in 1861 and for 9.6 millions in 1936. On an average, therefore, every occupied person had to provide for 0.75 inactive persons in 1861 and for 1.66 in 1936.
>
> Despite the low income available, Southern Italy brought up and gave a livelihood till the attainment of working age to 40 per cent of the natural increase in the population (3.8 millions), which then emigrated abroad or to the North.

At some point in the period between 1861 and 1936, the south seems to have actually retrogressed. During that period the number of industrial units decreased by 250,000. "Industrial progress in Southern Italy," says the Svimez report, "seems to have limited itself to converting the home worker and craftsman of 1886

[37] Southern Italy, or the south (*Mezzogiorno*), includes Abruzzi, Molise, Campania, Apulia, Basilicata, and Calabria on the mainland and the islands of Sicily and Sardinia.

into a factory worker, reducing thereby the total amount of occupation." With the decline in the capacity of productive apparatus to provide new jobs, emigration to the north and to foreign countries increased.

The lack of development in the *Mezzogiorno* showed up as a greater volume of disguised unemployment in the south, rather than as a greater share of the *population* engaged in agriculture there. In 1936, the proportion of the total population in agriculture in the Italian south was only slightly higher than in the north, and was slightly lower than in central Italy. However, the proportion of the *economically active* population engaged in agriculture in southern Italy was 57 per cent, as against 42 per cent in northern Italy. As may be seen from Table 2-6, the relative backwardness of the occupational structure in the south was even more apparent in 1952. Furthermore, these averages mask discrepancies among major regions within the *Mezzogiorno*. Thus in 1936, the proportion of active population engaged in agriculture in Abruzzi and Molise was 74.5 per cent, and in Basilicata 75.4 per cent.

TABLE 2-6.
Composition of the Working Population in 1861, 1936, and 1952
(percentage)

Occupation	1861			1936			1952			Workers (millions)
	North	South	Italy	North	South	Italy	North	South	Italy	
Agriculture	57.3	57.2	57.2	44.0	56.9	48.1	36.6	52.3	41.6	7.97
Industry, transport, and communication	25.8	30.4	27.6	36.8	27.6	33.9	40.2	28.3	36.4	6.971
Other activities ...	16.9	12.4	15.2	19.2	15.5	18.0	23.2	19.4	22.0	4.241
Total ..	100.0	100.0	100.0	100.0	100.0	100.0	100.0	100.0	100.0	19.182

SOURCE: I. M. D. Little and P. N. Rosenstein-Rodan, *Nuclear Power and Italy's Energy Position* (Washington, D.C., 1957), p. 15.

The relative backwardness of the *Mezzogiorno* is also shown in demographic figures. Before the war the birth rate in the south was 28.8 per cent, as compared to 20.5 per cent in the rest of Italy. The death rate was 15.8 per cent compared to 12.9 per cent, giving a natural rate of population growth of 13 per cent in the south and 7.6 per cent in the rest of the country. Since the war, the death rate in the south has fallen to a figure very close to that of the rest of the country, while the birth rate remains nearly as high as before the war. As a consequence, the *natural* rate of population growth in the south has increased, whereas in the rest of the country it has declined.

The average level of education is also lower in the south than in the rest of the country:[38]

The most serious and decisive shortcoming in Southern Italy, inasmuch as it affects all later development, is the fact that in the elementary schools only 30 per cent of the children (as against 53 per cent in the rest of Italy) take the modest elementary degree, while only 10 per cent (18 per cent in the rest of Italy) finish the secondary schools. In reality, with the extension of compulsory schooling to the age of 14, this should be the limit reached by all who are subject to this compulsion and should therefore be attained by two-thirds of each school generation (after allowance for children who die, fall ill or prove refractory to schooling), instead of by 10 per cent as is actually the case.

Thus it goes; almost any measure that might be applied shows the relative poverty and lack of development of the south. The south lags behind in social overhead capital: with 39.7 per cent of the country's area and 36.5 per cent of its population in 1945, the *Mezzogiorno* had only 11.4 per cent of Italy's communal roads; in 1931, 56.1 per cent of the southern population lived in overcrowded houses (more than two people per room) as compared to 21.8 per cent in the north; the south accounted for only 10.4 per cent of the total electricity production in 1935–38, and only 8.1 per cent in 1948.

Productivity as well as production is lower in the south than in the north. Yields per hectare of wheat, maize, and potatoes were less than half of what they were in northern Italy during 1948. The south had less than half the number of livestock in the north. Only 21 per cent of the industrial establishments, and only 12.1 per cent of the establishments with motor power, were in the south in the years 1937–39. Moreover, the southern establishments were smaller, with an average of only 2.4 persons per establishment, as compared to 5.2 per cent in the north.

A picture of the relative degree of industrialization of south and north is provided by Table 2-7 below. In this table, we show the ratio between the percentage of industrial workers and the percentages of total population in the south, as compared to the whole of Italy. Thus the ratio will be 1 when the workers in

[38] Svimez, *Survey of Southern Italian Economy* (Rome, 1950), p. 17.

the various industrial branches are divided between north and south in the same way as the total population. Only in mining (which must be done where the minerals are) has southern development kept pace with that of the north.

When did this disparate movement between the economies of the Italian north and south begin? There was no such marked difference between north and south at the time of unification, as Table 2-6 suggests. There have been suggestions that unification itself was responsible for the growing gaps in output and income. More recent studies, however, indicate that the seeds of disproportionate growth had already been planted before the unification of Italy. True, the structure of employment in 1861 seems to have been much the same in north and south (Table 2-6); but

TABLE 2-7.

Index Number of the Development of the Various Branches of Industry in Southern Italy, 1937–39

Mining	1.01	Printing	0.28
Food processing	0.81	Metallurgical	0.24
Water, gas, light	0.56	Mechanical engineering	0.21
Miscellaneous	0.41	Leather	0.21
Timber	0.36	Clothing	0.17
Non-metallic minerals	0.32	Textiles	0.09
Chemical	0.32	Paper	0.07
Building	0.30		
General average index number			0.33

a closer look shows that significant differences already existed. For example, at the time of unification, the north was better endowed with social overhead capital, especially transport facilities. As Eckaus puts it, "railways, outside North and Center were a *curioso*."[39] The difference in number of livestock per capita noted above was already apparent in the years 1855 to 1860. And the production of silk—the most important industry at that time—was almost totally a northern enterprise; nearly 80 per cent of the total production occurred in the northern provinces. True, sulphur, the most important Italian mineral product at the time, came almost entirely from Sicily; but "its export earning ability should not be overestimated." Two-thirds of the iron ores were mined on the island of Elba in the north, and employment in

[39] Richard S. Eckaus, "The Development of Regional Economic Differentials in Italy North and South at the Time of Unification," M.I.T., CIS, April, 1958 (D/58-4).

metal-using industries was much lower in the south than in the north.

When the discrepancy in the economic development of north and south began is less important, however, than the fact that it exists now. Dr. Rosenstein-Rodan, director of the M.I.T. Italy Project, emphasizes the fact that "the problem of the South is not just the regional one—it is a problem for Italy as a whole." [40] The Italian ten-year plan is naturally directed mainly toward increasing employment and productivity in the south, primary stress is laid on the creation of employment opportunities:

A survey of Italian economic developments over the past few years and especially since 1950, when real income per head had approximately regained the pre-war level, reveals one particularly striking feature. Despite the very considerable progress made in the direction of increased production and higher national income, the Ministry of Labour figure of registered unemployment has remained undiminished at about 2 million.

During the four years 1951–54 national income in real terms showed an average annual rate of growth of just over 5 per cent, rising (in terms of constant prices) from 8,570 billion Lire in 1950 to 10,450 billion Lire in 1954.

This rate was achieved under conditions of monetary stability and is amongst the highest on record in Italian economic history.

A measure of the effort made by Italy in order to realise this high rate of expansion is given by the investment figures for the same period. The average annual rate of growth in gross investment between 1950 and 1954 was 6.6 per cent, the absolute figure rising from 1,808 billion Lire in 1950 to 2,350 billion Lire (at constant prices) in 1954; and the annual average rate of growth of net investment was over 7 per cent, the absolute figure rising from 1,135 billion Lire to 1,500 billion Lire. Over the four-year period 1951–54 gross investment absorbed about 21 per cent of gross national income, and net investment more than 14 per cent of net national income. These proportions are very high, especially in view of the low level of Italy's national income. A still better measure of the effort made since 1950 is given by the "marginal" saving ratios: over 26 per cent of the increment in gross national income, and about 20 per cent of the increment in net income was devoted to investment purposes.

The other problem emphasized in the ten-year plan is the chronic balance of payments deficit:

A second factor to keep in mind is the large volume of foreign funds that were made available to the Italian economy. During the

[40] P. N. Rosenstein-Rodan, "Programming and Theory in Italian Practice," in *Investment Criteria and Economic Growth* (Cambridge, Mass., 1955).

period 1951–54 the average deficit in the balance of payments on current account was of the order of 200 billion Lire a year. The foreign financial assistance, mostly consisting of outright grants, by which this deficit was covered, was unquestionably a very important factor helping toward the expansion of economic activity during those years.

Conclusion

Thus the development problem in Italy might be defined as raising productivity and employment in the south, while at the same time, sustaining growth in the rest of the country and solving balance of payments problems.

Summary and Conclusions

From our review of the development problem confronting six countries, we can see that not all underdeveloped countries display all the "characteristics" in Leibenstein's list. To some degree at least, each underdeveloped country is a case unto itself. At the same time, it is apparent that all our six countries share certain key problems that must be solved if they are to reach the promised land of sustained growth.

Comparisons among our six cases suggest that the resource base is certainly an important factor in determining the level and rate of increase in per capita income, but that it is by no means the crucial factor. If it were, Indonesian income ought to be higher than the Philippines', instead of the other way around, and Mexico would not have an income and a rate of growth more than three times that of India. We did find that one resource constitutes a strategic bottleneck in all six countries: entrepreneurship and management. Since planned development requires a good deal of economic decision making by government officials, and also efficient administration of ordinary government services, the entrepreneurial and managerial bottleneck applies to public, as well as to business, administration. Capital supply, of course, is another bottleneck in all six countries, although less so in Libya than in the others because of the extraordinary amount of foreign aid received.

All six countries face unemployment problems, although the severity and form of the problem varies somewhat from one country to another. Fluctuations in employment are perhaps most severe in Libya, but the inherent social and political instability is probably more acute in India and the Philippines, because of the degree to which unemployment exists among the urban educated elite. The unemployment, unfortunately, does not assure an unlimited supply of labor for industrial development—not, at least, without extensive manpower training programs—because so many unemployed workers are unskilled.

The "scale" problem varies enormously as between Libya and India, which are at opposite poles in this respect. So long as Indian incomes remain so low, however, the size of the population is of dubious merit as a stimulus to growth; "size of market," for example, depends not on the number of consumers, but on the number with money to spend.

All these countries face in some degree the problem of incentive —the need to find ways of converting the generalized wish for higher standards of living among workers, peasants, and businessmen into decisions to work harder and better, save more, and make risky investments in productive enterprise. All of them, too, are characterized by "technological dualism." Levels of technique and productivity are much higher in the industrial sector than in the rural sector. This problem has been aggravated since World War II by migration into the larger cities.

Finally, all of them have difficulties with their budgets and balances of payments. Execution of bold development programs results in inflation, a drain on foreign exchange reserves, or some combination of the two.

The most stouthearted defender of the new faith in development planning might quail at this array of obstacles to growth. Yet other countries have developed in the past, some recently underdeveloped countries show promise of success, and the popular pressure in poor countries for measures to raise living standards is too strong to be gainsaid. The obstacles must be tackled. What has the combined wisdom of economists to offer by way of an explanation of underdevelopment and means of overcoming it? To this question we now turn.

PART 2 Principles: General Theories of Development

3 The Classical Theory of Capitalist Development: Growth and Stagnation

The economists of the late eighteenth and early nineteenth centuries were very much concerned with the conditions for economic progress. This was the period of the "Industrial Revolution" in Europe. The Classical economists and Karl Marx lived through the period of take-off into sustained growth; Marx and Mill saw peak rates of growth attained in Europe. The observations of these economists regarding the nature and causes of economic progress are, therefore, of considerable interest.

Europe in 1750 differed from Asia and Africa in 1950, as we shall explain in some detail below. Nevertheless, the most dramatic examples of take-off into sustained and cumulative growth are to be found in eighteenth- and nineteenth-century Europe. Economic development of the New World was of course equally spectacular, but it was in part a transplanting of the development of Europe, and it was relatively easy because of the unusually favorable resource-population pattern. What happened in those countries in that period is what we want to happen in Asia, Africa, and Latin America now. Consequently, it is important to find out what the best thinkers of that period regarded as responsible for the current economic growth and what they considered was required to keep it going. The "best thinkers" of the Classical and Marxist schools brought to bear some of the most powerful minds ever to be directed toward questions of economics. Without examining their development theories, we can have no assurance that subsequent work in this field is any more penetrating than theirs, particularly since the field was almost totally neglected between 1870 and 1935. At the very least, any points of agreement in eighteenth- and nineteenth-century theories of growth are well worth our attention.

Since we are interested in basic ideas which may be still relevant today, and in isolating points of agreement and disagreement, we shall treat the literature somewhat differently from the usual history of economic thought. In the first place, we shall be generous in interpreting ideas, translating them into basic functional relationships, and closing up any open ends in the analytical systems. Moreover, we shall translate these ideas into a common contemporary terminology. Not only does this approach help us to evaluate what they had to say, it also makes it easier to see the real points of difference and agreement.

For the most part—despite the controversies that took place within it—we will treat the Classical school as a unit. We shall refer to some differences among members of the school only at the end of this chapter, especially differences between Malthus and the others. Finally, since we want to present the best of the ideas of the Classical school, we shall concentrate on the writings of Adam Smith, Malthus, and Mill rather than those of Ricardo, Senior, and others. To be sure, Ricardo's system was in many respects tighter logically than those of his contemporaries, but his greater rigor was the result of a higher degree of abstraction. More important for us, he was much less interested in economic development than he was in the theory of value and distribution. Schumpeter has gone so far as to state that Ricardo "all but identifies economics with the theory of distribution, implying that he had little or nothing to say about—to use his language—'the laws which regulate total output'." [1] For this reason Schumpeter considered Ricardian analysis as "a detour." [2] This evaluation may be too harsh when considering Ricardo's position in the history of economic thought as a whole, but it is true where the theory of growth is concerned.

A strong case can be made for including Marx in the Classical school. As Schumpeter says, the Marxist system is "part and parcel of that period's general economics." [3] The basic theories of production and value are much the same in Classical and Marxist

[1] Joseph A. Schumpeter, *History of Economic Analysis* (New York, 1954), pp. 568–69.

[2] *Ibid.*, p. 474.

[3] *Ibid.*, pp. 383–85.

models, as is the explanation of the process of economic growth. Even the theory of distribution is not really so very different. Nevertheless, there are good grounds for treating the Classical and Marxist models separately. First, the Marxist prognosis regarding capitalism is quite different from that of the Classical school. Second, Marx paid more explicit attention to interrelations among sectors in the economy, and the sectors he distinguished were different from those emphasized by the Classicists. Third, Marx had a stronger sense of history and of cultural variations than most of his contemporaries. Fourth, there is a more clear-cut suggestion that we cannot rely on "psychological individualism" (generalizing from the behavior of individual workers, capitalists, and landlords), but must conduct our analysis of economic development in terms of groups (classes). Accordingly, we shall confine this chapter to the essential features of the Classical theory of growth, and devote the next chapter to the Marxist model.

The Classical Model

For the Classical economists, the development of capitalist economies was a race between technological progress and population growth, a race in which technological progress would be in the lead for some time but which would end in a dead heat, or stagnation. Technological progress, in turn, depended on capital accumulation, which would permit increasing mechanization and greater division of labor. And the rate of capital accumulation depended on the level and trend of profits.

In order to give form to our presentation and to facilitate comparison with other models, let us translate the basic propositions of the Classical theory of growth into a series of mutually consistent and interacting propositions—or, in mathematical terms, into a set of simultaneous equations, with equal numbers of equations and unknowns, so that the system is soluble or "determinant."

Proposition 1: The Production Function

Smith, Malthus, and Mill all had it quite clearly in mind that total output, O, depended on the size of the labor force, L, the stock of capital, Q, the amount of land available—which we shall denote by K, to mean supply of known resources—and the level of technique, T. Using the common symbol f to mean "function of" or "depends upon," we can then write,

$$O = f(L, K, Q, T) \qquad (1)$$

Repeating this proposition in words for those who find equations a hindrance rather than a help, total output depends on the size of the labor force, the supply of land (or known and economically useful resources), the stock of capital, the proportions in which these factors of production are combined, and the level of technology.

We are perhaps being overgenerous to the Classicists in translating "land" into "supply of known and economically useful resources." Clearly, it is not the area of the country alone, or even the amount of arable land and its fertility that determines output but the total supply of natural resources. In this context "supply" includes only resources currently known to exist and to be economically useful; it does not include resources yet to be discovered or useful only after some future change in technology. Perhaps no member of the Classical school would have denied that only in this sense can "land" be treated as a distinct factor of production along with capital and labor, but much of their discussion was couched in terms of the total area of agricultural land as such. Later on we shall want to use "land" to mean "supply of known and economically useful resources," and we shall denote it by the symbol K—we cannot use L for more than one variable in our system. So let us be generous and introduce it in this sense into the Classical model. Perhaps, after all, they included resource discoveries as part of technological progress, so that at any point of time the supply of land could be treated as fixed.

On the other hand, we may be a little unfair to the Classicists in not including entrepreneurship explicitly in our system. By "entrepreneurship" is meant the function of seeing investment and production opportunities; organizing an enterprise to undertake a new production process; raising capital, hiring labor, arranging for a supply of raw materials, finding a site, and combining these factors of production into a going concern; introducing new techniques and commodities, discovering new sources of natural resources; and selecting top managers for day-to-day operations. As we shall see in Chapter 5, the entrepreneur in this sense plays the vital role in Schumpeter's theory of growth. Of course the Classical economists were aware of the importance of the entrepreneurial function, but they did not make it a strategic part of their system, and they did not make the crucial distinction between entrepreneurship and management.[4] So we omit the entrepreneur until we come to Schumpeter's model.

[4] *Ibid.*, pp. 554–56.

Most Classicists probably thought of the production function as "linear and homogeneous"; that is, they would have expected that if the quantities used of all factors of production were doubled at once, output would double. Adam Smith might have made the case for increasing returns to scale; doubling all factors would increase the opportunities for division of labor. But they would have regarded such propositions as rather uninteresting, because in their view, it would have been nonsense to talk about doubling the supply of land. Any country has so much land, and that is that. It would not be nonsense, however, to talk of doubling the supply of known and economically useful resources over some period—which is the important difference between "land" as we shall use the term and "land" as the Classicists seemed to use it. It is a little inelegant to include all resource discoveries as a form of technological progress, as we must do with the Classical definitions; in any case, they did not seem to regard resource discoveries as an important source of progress. Perhaps for nineteenth-century England they were right, but for a *general* theory we would not want to treat the supply of natural resources—or even arable land—as fixed.

For the Classicists, then, the key cross section of the production function was the one showing what happens to output when land is fixed and the labor supply is increased. This cross section is shown by the solid line in Figure 3-1, which shows the usual four phases: increasing marginal returns, decreasing marginal returns, decreasing average returns, and decreasing total returns. It is also

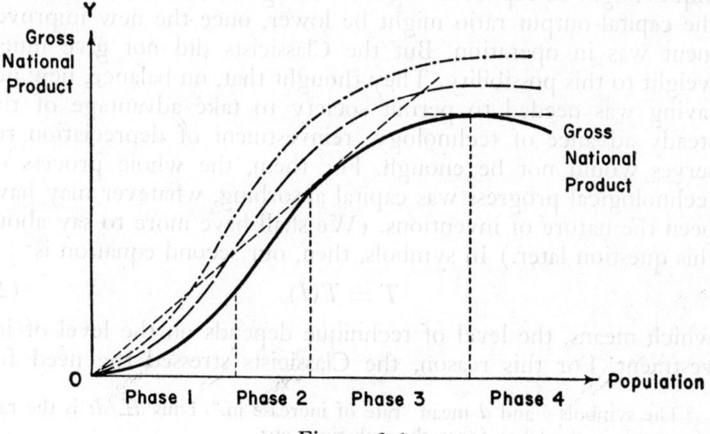

Figure 3-1

clear that the Classicists thought Europe was in the third phase, in which an increase in the amount of labor employed on the land would bring some increase in output, but would reduce output *per capita*, and so well beyond the second phase, where each additional unit of labor would add less to total output than the last one, although still increasing *per capita* output. In symbols, we can write

$$\frac{\delta f}{\delta L} \cdot \frac{dL}{dt} > 0 \qquad \frac{\delta^2 f}{\delta L^2} \cdot \frac{d^2 L}{dt^2} < 0 \quad \text{and} \quad \frac{d}{dL}\left(\frac{O}{L}\right) < 0 \qquad (1a)$$

which says just what we have said in the last sentence.[5]

Now, the solid curve in Figure 3-1 shows what happens if the amount of labor is increased while the land utilized is fixed and nothing else happens either. If additional capital is accumulated, the curve will have the same general shape but will be higher, as indicated by the dotted curves in Figure 3-1. Each successive curve shows the effect of using a larger stock of capital together with the fixed amount of land and varying amounts of labor.

Proposition 2: Capital Accumulation Permits Technological Progress

This consideration brings us to the second basic proposition. The Classical economists seemed to think that there was always a plentiful supply of better techniques and new commodities to be introduced, but they considered that the rate at which these opportunities could be exploited was limited by the flow of capital for new investment. It would be too much to say that their analysis precluded altogether the possibility that new techniques might be capital saving after being introduced; conceivably the capital-output ratio might be lower, once the new improvement was in operation. But the Classicists did not give much weight to this possibility. They thought that, on balance, new net saving was needed to permit society to take advantage of the steady advance of technology; reinvestment of depreciation reserves would not be enough. For them, the whole process of technological progress was capital absorbing, whatever may have been the nature of inventions. (We shall have more to say about this question later.) In symbols, then, our second equation is

$$T = T(I) \qquad (2)$$

which means, the level of technique depends on the level of investment. For this reason, the Classicists stressed the need for

[5] The symbols δ and d mean "rate of increase in." Thus dL/dt is the rate of growth in the labor force through time, etc.

capital accumulation and saving, rather than technological progress as an independent factor.

Proposition 3: Investment Depends on Profits

In common with virtually every economist before or since, the Classicists took it for granted that capitalists make investments because they expect to earn profits on them, and that what they expect with regard to profits in the future depends a good deal on what profits are now.[6] Investment means here net investment, that is, a net addition to the stock of capital. So we can write

$$I = dQ = I(R) \tag{3}$$

where R is return on fixed factors of production (land and capital), or profits. (By definition, net investment, I, equals the increase in stock of capital, dQ.)

Proposition 4: Profits Depend on Labor Supply and the Level of Technique

Of course, the whole nexus of economic events has an effect on profits, and any simple proposition regarding determination of profits is bound to be an abstraction from reality. Since some things are a good deal more important than others in determining the level of profits, one is justified in concentrating on those things, at least to begin with.

For the Classical school, profits were the outcome of the same race mentioned at the beginning of this section. As population grew, diminishing returns would be encountered in agriculture, raising labor costs (man-hour costs of food) and reducing profits. But offsetting this tendency was historically *increasing* returns, especially in industry, through improvements in technique. Which force is more powerful is a question of fact, not of pure theory, and varies from country to country and from time to time in the same country. Most of the Classicists felt that technological progress was winning for the time being, in their own country (England), but that it could not win for very much longer. Our fourth equation, then, is

$$R = R(T, L) \tag{4}$$

That is, the level of profits depends on the level of technique and the size of the labor force.

The labor force and the population were generally conceived

[6] Malthus, however, attached considerable importance to the whole "climate" for investment, as well as actual profits.

to vary together. Of course the Classical economists could ignore neither the existence of unemployment nor variations in the amount of unemployment, especially in the decades following the Napoleonic Wars. But on the whole they regarded unemployment as an aberration, at least in a growing economy, and felt that population growth and employment must move together. Thus population growth always brought a decline in per capita output, *unless* offset by technological progress.

We already have some indication of the circularity of their argument. The level of technique depends on the level of investment, investment depends on profits, and profits depend partly on the level of technique. This circularity is no accident or oversight; it is precisely what the Classicists—and most later economists—have wished to stress; in economic development nothing succeeds like success, and nothing fails like failure. We can express this circularity by substituting Equations (3) and (4) in Equation (2), which gives us

$$T = T(I) = T[I(R)] = T\{I[R(T, L)]\} \qquad (4a)$$

Thus a rapid rate of technological advance will tend to call forth a level of investment that will permit the rapid technological advance to continue, but the reverse is also true. Do we already have a clue to the difference in performance of advanced and underdeveloped countries? Perhaps; but let us go on with the Classical system.

Proposition 5: The Size of the Labor Force Depends on the Size of the Wages Bill

Few of the basic propositions of the Classical school have been so vehemently attacked as the "iron law of wages." The general idea is that the rate of population growth depends on how much money (working capital) is available to pay wages. If the total wages fund is increased and real average rates rise above the subsistence level, larger numbers of working-class children can survive to become members of the labor force. There are no checks on the size of working-class families except the amount of wages available to them and the number of children that can subsist on those wages. Thus there is a constant tendency for real wage rates to return to the subsistence level. An increase in wages paid may bring a temporary improvement in living standards, but this improvement will soon be swamped in an increased rate of population growth.

Sometimes the Classicists seemed to be thinking of subsistence wages as a true physiological minimum, below which children literally could not survive; sometimes they seemed to think rather of an "accustomed normal" living standard, not far above the physical subsistence level, which working-class families would not endanger by having more children. In terms of a systematic model, it does not matter much which explanation is given. In either case, a temporary increase in real wage rates would be squeezed out by accelerated population growth.

This argument often seems far-fetched to people living in advanced countries today, but it probably gave a fairly accurate description of what happened in Europe in the late eighteenth and early nineteenth centuries. It also seems to be true of peasant societies in Asian, African, and some Latin American countries today. Of course we do not know a great deal about the complex psychological, sociological, biological, and technical factors which enter into family size. We can, however, say a few things about it. First, improved standards of public health and nutrition permit a more rapid rate of population growth. Second, every society, from primitive African or Australian tribes through ancient Egypt, Greece, and Rome to modern societies, has practiced population control in some form and to some degree. Third, the technical efficiency of the methods used has varied enormously, even within the same society. Fourth, limitation of family size is practiced only if there seems to be some good reason for it—some vision of a better life if the number of children is restricted. As Professor Myrdal has put it, these facts mean that if people have a very strong desire to keep family size down, they will do so, even if they must resort to infanticide, abortion, complicated and prolonged initiation rites to delay marriage, or similarly crude or brutal devices. If people want larger families, and if the means are available to support them and health standards are high, population growth will attain high levels. And if most people are rather indifferent about family size, because they cannot see that their way of life will be very different with four children or eight, population growth is still likely to reach fairly high levels, so long as health and nutritional standards permit it.

In Europe in the eighteenth century, and in Asia, Africa, and Latin America in recent decades, health and nutrition were improving, while most people could not visualize a significantly higher standard of living to be achieved by acceptable and available means of limiting family size. Thus they were probably rather indifferent about family planning. When wage rates rose, more children could be brought to maturity without impinging on the customary living standards of the working class, and consequently population growth could increase. There was no strong incentive for limiting family size, and no cheap and convenient ways of family planning were available. Under these conditions, the Classical theory of population makes good sense.

We shall have more to say about population growth later; meanwhile we can write the equation for this proposition as

$$L = L(W) \qquad (5)$$

Proposition 6: The Wages Bill Depends on the Level of Investment

The Classical school thought of capital—or at least part of it—as consisting of a "wages fund," an amount of money available for hiring labor. This wages fund was built up by saving and put into effective use through investment. Except for Malthus, who showed a high degree of sophistication in this respect, the Classicists tended to think that savings found their way into investment more or less automatically. Thus the wages bill could be increased only by net (savings and) investment, and our sixth equation is

$$W = W(I) \qquad (6)$$

Closing the System

We now have all the "operational" equations of the Classical system, that is, all propositions expressing fundamental causal relationships. But so far we have listed seven variables and have only six equations; the system is indeterminate. We can close the system by adding an identity, *total output equals profits plus wages*, or

$$O = R + W \qquad (7)$$

We can interpret this equation in either of two ways. If we define profits as we have done above, to include returns on fixed factors of production, including land as well as capital, the equation expresses an identity by definition. The total national income is equal to the total cost or value of all goods or services produced, and this amount is divided between workers and others.

If we want to be more purely Classical, we can think of it in another way, taking account of the somewhat fancy Classical theory of rent. According to the Classical school, value is equal to labor cost of production on "marginal" or no-rent land. Included in this labor cost is the cost of "embodied labor" tied up in capital; so value includes a return to capital as well as to labor. Price is value in money terms. Thus if we think of O as equal to pq, price times quantity of all goods and services, it will be equivalent to the total wages bill plus the total return to capital. If landlords succeed in getting rent, it is because workers or capitalists get less than their actual contribution to the value of output—which is exactly what the Classical economists wanted to imply. As a matter of social ethics they may have had a case; but as a matter of general theory this treatment of rent is a bit of a nuisance. So let us stick to the first interpretation.

We now have a determinate system with seven equations and seven unknowns. If we like, we can add an eighth variable, w, to mean the minimum wage rate, which is a constant, and then add an eighth equation expressing a long-run equilibrium condition,

$$W = wL \tag{8}$$

Summary

Let us now put together our interpretation of the Classical system and have a look at it:

$$\begin{aligned} O &= f(L, K, Q, T) && (1)\\ T &= T(I) && (2)\\ I &= dQ = I(R) && (3)\\ R &= R(T, L) && (4)\\ L &= L(W) && (5)\\ W &= W(I) && (6)\\ O &= R + W && (7) \end{aligned}$$

And in long-run equilibrium, we have also

$$W = wL \tag{8}$$

The circularity that we noticed above is even more apparent when we have the whole system before us. We can break into the circular flow anywhere and show how the system will evolve under various conditions, but let us start with profits as the prime mover of the capitalist system. We could write schematically, $dR \to dI \to dQ \to dT$, $dW \to dL \to dR$. That is, an increase in profits brings an increase in investment, and so an addition to the stock of capital, which permits capitalists to take advantage of the steady flow of improved techniques and also raises the wages fund; that brings an accelerated population growth, which causes decreasing returns to labor on the land, raising labor costs and reducing profits. We could, of course, go on: reduced profits mean reduced investment, retarded technological progress, a diminished wages fund, and slowing down of population growth.

If we want to be a bit more sophisticated, we could make investment a function of the change in profits rather than the level of profits; thus capital accumulation would take place only if profits increase, and capital decumulation occurs when profits fall.

Figure 3-2 presents a diagrammatic summary of the Classical theory of growth. We cannot, of course, present seven or eight variables in one diagram; since we have at best three dimensions, we must pick the variables that tell us most. Moreover, the whole process of growth takes place in time; time is the variable with respect to which all the variables in our equations must be differentiated to get a picture of the growth process. So we are left with two other variables to be shown directly in the diagram. We have chosen to treat population and total production as the key variables; after all, what we are ultimately interested in is the trend of per capita output. The other variables must be treated implicitly, in terms of the circular flow outlined in the equations above. For example, we treat technological progress as depending only on the rate of capital accumulation, and we show variations in both, implicitly, by the change in total output with a given population as time goes by.

We begin at $t = O$, with a stock of capital and a technology which gives us the relationship between labor force and output shown in the curve O_0. Let us suppose that actual population is P_0 and output is at the point GNP_0, in the phase of diminishing average returns on this curve. Profits are earned and some investment takes place, permitting technological progress and increased wage payments. Thus as time goes by we move onto a new curve, O_1, with a higher output than before for any *given* labor force on the fixed amount of land. Meanwhile, of course, the population has also grown, so that at time $t = 1$ our actual position is GNP_1. And so on.

This movement through time has a clearly defined shape. According to the Classical school, when population is relatively small, returns on land will be high, perhaps even increasing; but as population grows we encounter more and more rapidly diminishing returns. Technological progress takes place at a *steady* rate, provided enough capital is forthcoming to exploit opportunities for improvement to the full. Thus in an advanced or "mature" economy, diminishing returns to land, and the consequent rise in labor costs, will outrun effective technological progress. Profits will fall. Then investment drops, technological progress is retarded, the wages fund ceases to grow, and so popu-

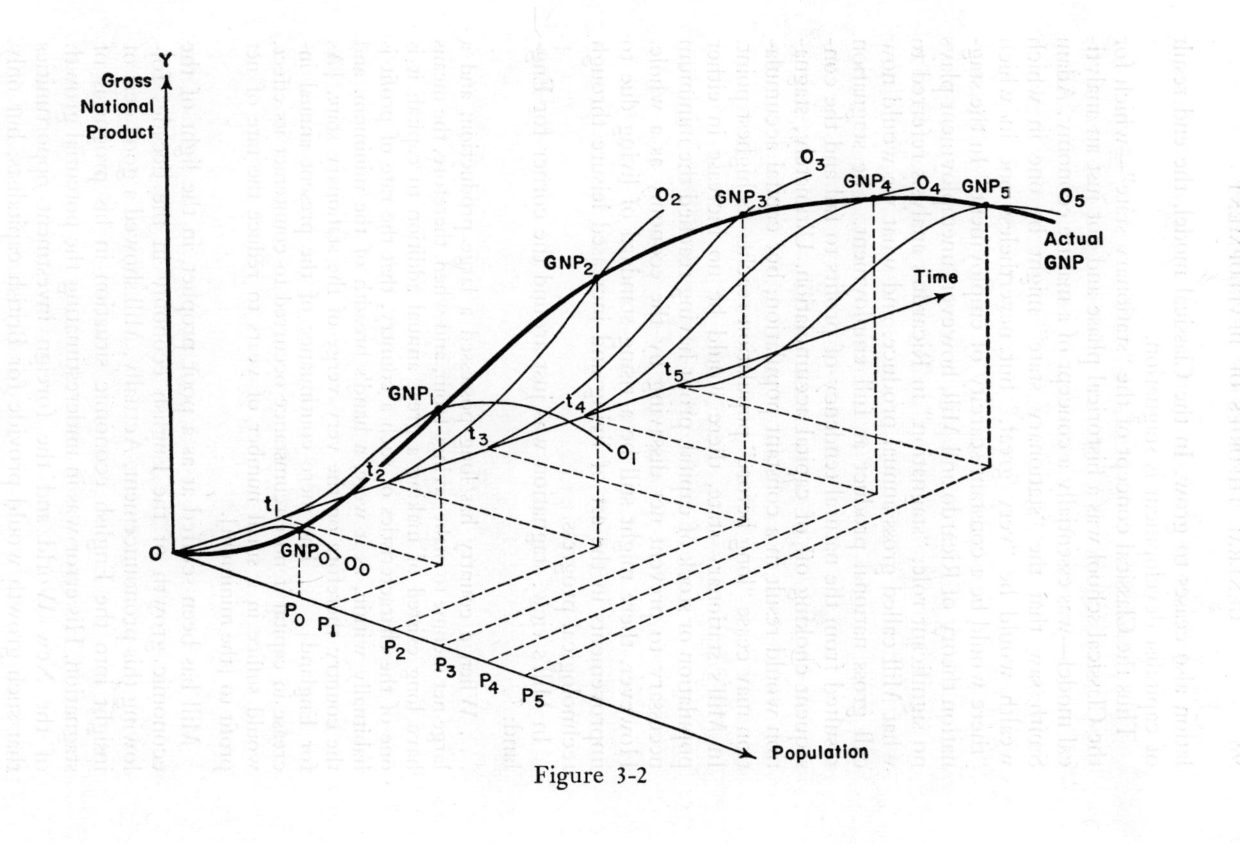

Y
Gross
National
Product
O
GNP_0
O_0
t_1
t_2
GNP_1
t_3
O_1
t_4
t_5
GNP_2
O_2
GNP_3
O_3
GNP_4
O_4
GNP_5
O_5
Actual
GNP
Time
P_0
P_1
P_2
P_3
P_4
P_5
Population

Figure 3-2

lation also ceases to grow. In the Classical model, the end result of capitalist development is stagnation.

Thus the Classical concept of the "stationary state"—which for the Classical school was a historical phase and not just an analytical model—was essentially a concept of a mature economy. Adam Smith saw that the "stationary state" might be one in which wealth would be "very great," but nevertheless one in which "there would be a constant scarcity of employment." In the stagnation theory of Ricardo and Mill, however, unemployment plays no significant role; "stagnation" in Ricardo's analysis referred to what Mill called gross annual produce, and what we would now call gross national product at full employment. The stagnation resulted from the natural tendency of profits to fall and the consequent choking off of capital accumulation. Ultimately, stagnation would result in a constant population; but capital accumulation may cease "long before" population reaches its highest point. In Mill's stationary state, there would be no increase in either population or stock of capital, profit having reached the minimum necessary to prevent net dissaving by the economy as a whole. However, there might still be a rising standard of living due to improvements in the art of living and increased leisure through technological progress.

In Mill's view, stagnation was just around the corner for England: [7]

> . . . When a country has long possessed a large production, and a large net income to make savings from, and when, therefore, the means have long existed of making a great annual addition to capital; it is one of the characteristics of such a country, that the rate of profit is habitually within, as it were, a hand's breadth of the minimum, and the country therefore on the very verge of the stationary state. [As for England] . . . The mere continuance of the present annual increase in capital if no circumstance occurred to counteract its effect, would suffice in a small number of years to reduce the rate of net profit to [the minimum].

Mill has been scoffed at as a poor prophet, in the light of the economic growth of the English economy in the decades following this pronouncement. Actually, Mill showed a good deal of insight into the English economic situation in his prognosis of stagnation. His error was in underestimating the potential growth of the New World and the foreign investment opportunities that such growth would provide for British capitalists; but only

[7] J. S. Mill, *Principles of Political Economy*, Book IV, chap. IV (3d ed.; London, 1852).

this growth of the world economy prevented "stagnation" from appearing in the late nineteenth century instead of after World War I. When Mill wrote his third edition, England was losing out as an industrialist and financier to Germany, France, the United States, and even Japan. Her balance of payments on goods and services account had become chronically unfavorable, never again to become chronically favorable; England had become a *rentier* nation living on returns from its investments abroad. The extent of the trouble with the English economy did not become apparent, however, until World War I reduced this *rentier* income from abroad.

The Malthus Version

We cannot leave our discussion of the Classical theory of development without drawing attention to its refinements in the Malthus version. For although the general theory of Malthus is described by the model presented above, certain features of his theory make it particularly enlightening both for an understanding of the requirements for steady growth in advanced countries and for the launching of development in underdeveloped countries.

To begin with, Malthus showed more appreciation than most of his contemporaries of the importance of a distinct and systematic theory of growth. Book I of his *Principles of Political Economy* [8] was concerned with value and distribution, Book II with "The Progress of Wealth." This book opens with the following statement: [9]

> There is scarcely any inquiry more curious, or, from its importance, more worthy of our attention, than that which traces the causes which practically check the progress of wealth in different countries, and stop it, or make it proceed very slowly, while the power of production remains comparatively undiminished, or at least would furnish the means of a great and abundant increase of produce and population.

He defines the *problem* of development as explaining any difference between potential gross national product ("power of producing riches") and actual gross national product ("actual riches").

There is nothing automatic about economic growth, Malthus

[8] The first edition of Malthus' *Principles* appeared in 1820, the second in 1836. (Page references are to the Augustus Kelly reprint of the second edition; New York, 1951.)

[9] *Ibid.*, p. 309.

warns. To say that population growth by itself is enough to bring economic advance is absurd. In the first place, population growth—despite the strength of the psychological and physiological forces tending to bring it about—is an *end product* of the whole economic process; "an increase of population cannot take place without a proportionate or nearly proportionate increase of wealth." As evidence that the natural tendency toward population growth is no guarantee that either population or income will grow, he cites such "underdeveloped" countries as Spain, Portugal, Hungary, Turkey, "together with nearly the whole of Asia and Africa, and the greatest part of America."[10]

Secondly, mere increases in numbers do not provide a stimulus to economic expansion; population growth encourages development only if it brings an increase in effective demand. "A man whose only possession is his labor has, or has not, an effective demand for produce according as his labor is, or is not, in demand by those who have the disposal of produce."[11] And the demand for labor, in turn, depends on the rate of capital accumulation.

In elaborating his theory of effective demand and its relation to savings and investment, Malthus anticipated some of the basic ideas of such modern writers as Keynes and Kalecki. He flatly repudiated "Say's law," which said in effect that supply creates its own demand and that savings are just a demand for capital goods. Saving, in the sense of planned or *ex ante* saving, or abstinence, means not consuming; and not consuming in itself brings a decline in effective demand, profits, and investment.

Malthus drew attention to a circularity of a kind quite different from the one spelled out by the other Classicists, which has been restated more systematically by Kalecki and others in our own day. Going back to Equation (7) above, we have national income (or output) equal to profits plus wages. Let us rewrite the equation,

$$R = O - W \tag{7a}$$

Now workers, as a class, are too poor to save. They spend all their income on consumption. Let us denote workers' consumption as C_w. Capitalists, however, do save; these savings create income in so far as they are invested. So we may write, substituting in Equation (7a)

$$R = (I + C_c + C_w) - C_w = I + C_c \tag{7b}$$

[10] *Ibid.*, p. 314.
[11] *Ibid.*, pp. 311–12.

That is, national income or output is generated by investment, capitalists' consumption, and workers' consumption. Profits are national income less wages; wages equal workers' consumption—and so profits are equal to investment plus capitalists' consumption. Thus abstinence on the part of capitalists, far from accelerating economic growth, will, in itself, retard it.[12]

Malthus does not, of course, deny the need for saving and investment for economic growth. But he suggests a concept of "optimum propensity to save." Up to a certain point saving is needed to finance (without inflation) the investment for which profitable opportunities exist. Beyond that point, however, saving will reduce consumer spending to such an extent that investment too will be discouraged.[13] High rates of growth do not occur with high levels of *ex ante* savings (abstinence) on the part of the upper-income groups, but with high levels of *ex post* (realized) savings and investment, which are in large degree the result of growth, and do not require reductions in consumer spending:[14]

> . . . The fortune of a country, though necessarily made more slow, is made in the same way as the fortunes of individuals in trade are generally made—by savings, certainly; but by savings which are furnished by increased gains, and by no means involve a diminished expenditure on objects of luxury and enjoyment. . . . The amount of capital in this country is immense, and it certainly received very great additions during the last forty years but on looking back, few traces are to be found of a diminishing expenditure in the shape of revenue.

Thus Malthus had the picture of an advanced economy enjoying steady growth, with consumption, investment, and *ex post* (realized) savings expanding together.

Malthus also demonstrated a number of random insights into the factors which may retard a take-off into sustained economic growth. He attached considerable importance to backward-sloping supply curves of effort—both for workers and managers—in the explanation of the underdeveloped condition of such countries as Mexico and Ireland. He denied that the indolence characterizing underdeveloped countries could be explained by the tropical climate; the scene in the Cordilleras, where the climates "seem to be the finest in the world," is "not essentially different" from that of the "lower regions of New Spain."[15] The

[12] This argument is made in effect in *ibid.*, pp. 311, 361.
[13] *Ibid.*, pp. 326–29.
[14] *Ibid.*, p. 367.
[15] *Ibid.*, p. 338.

problem, as he saw it, was rather a matter of absence of incentives. He suggested that broadening international trade could help a good deal to straighten out these supply curves, by providing incentives for additional expenditure of effort, until an economy could get "over the hump" to the point where its own production was sufficiently varied to provide all the incentive needed for further growth.[16]

> . . . The peasant, who might be induced to labor an additional number of hours for tea or tobacco, might prefer indolence to a new coat. . . . And the trader or merchant, who would continue his business in order to be able to drink and give his guests claret and champagne, might think an addition of homely commodities by no means worth the trouble of so much constant attention.

Meanwhile anything that can be done to widen the market and permit more division of labor by internal measures is well worthwhile; and improved transport is one such measure.[17]

> . . . It has never, I believe, occurred, that the better distribution of the commodities of a country occasioned by improved facilities of communication has failed to increase the value as well as the quantity of the whole produce.

Malthus also noted the phenomenon which Colin Clark has stressed in our own day; economic development entails structural change of a sort which diminishes the relative importance of agriculture in the economy.[18] He argued that technological progress tends to increase employment [19] and that tapering-off of the growth of income and output causes unemployment.[20] He suggested land reform as one means of expanding output.[21]

More important for us than any of these insights, however, was Malthus' anticipation of the theory of "dualism" as applied to underdeveloped countries. We shall see below that our understanding of the problem of underdevelopment can be greatly increased by breaking up the economy into sectors and studying interactions among them; even a two-sector model is a great advance over a single-sector model. A charitable interpretation of the Classical theory of growth can convert it into such a two-

[16] *Ibid.*, p. 354.
[17] *Ibid.*, p. 362.
[18] *Ibid.*, p. 334.
[19] *Ibid.*, p. 352.
[20] *Ibid.*, p. 312.
[21] *Ibid.*, p. 373.

sector model, but the intersectoral analysis emerges more clearly in Malthus' writings than in those of other members of the Classical school.

Malthus envisaged the economy as consisting of two major sectors: one industrial, one agricultural. Technological progress he regarded as a phenomenon confined to the industrial sector—in advanced countries, at any rate. "Increasing returns" was a property of this sector, and unmitigated diminishing returns was the primary characteristic of the agricultural sector. If we think of nineteenth-century England, this picture was probably a good approximation to reality. The first wave of agricultural progress, undertaken by the "improving landlords," had helped to set the stage for the Industrial Revolution, but it was pretty well over when Malthus was writing; and the "industrial revolution" in agriculture itself (mechanization) did not set in until later. The good land was already occupied and no major resource discoveries were taking place. Meanwhile, striking progress was evident in power, manufacturing, and transport.

The Malthusian picture of economic development seems to have been one in which capital was invested in agriculture until all the arable land was brought into cultivation, stocked, and improved; after that there were no more opportunities for profitable investment in that sector, and investment opportunities existed only in the industrial sector. Diminishing returns to increased employment on the land could be avoided only if technological progress in the industrial sector was rapid enough, and if enough investment took place, to absorb most of the population growth in the industrial sector and to reduce the cost of living of workers on the land, permitting reductions in their corn (goods) wage rates.[22]

For those who like equations, we might express this relationship as follows. Let us assume once again that the rate of technological progress in the industrial sector depends only on the amount of capital available for utilizing the steady flow of improvements. Malthus explicitly recognized the possibility of unemployment arising from inadequate investment, so the level of industrial employment can also be treated as a function of investment. Thus we can regard industrial output as depending solely on the amount of capital invested in the industrial sector:

$$O_i = a \cdot Q_i \tag{9}$$

[22] See especially *ibid.*, pp. 278, 284.

where O_i is the output of the industrial sector, Q_i is the amount of capital in the industrial sector, and $1/a$ is the capital-output ratio for the sector. Differentiating with respect to time,

$$\frac{dO_i}{dt} = a \cdot \frac{dQ_i}{dt} + Q_i \cdot \frac{da}{dt} \tag{9a}$$

If technological progress is "neutral" so that the capital-output ratio can be considered a constant, the second term drops out and the trend of industrial output through time depends only on the rate of capital accumulation (investment) in the industrial sector. The rate of investment in turn depends on the level of profits, as we already know; and in this model, the rate of profits will depend on the wage rate (which in turn depends on the cost of producing wage goods, especially foodstuffs) and effective demand, which depends on capitalists' consumption and investment.

In the agricultural sector the situation is different. There are no investment opportunities in the agricultural sector of a "mature" economy, and in underdeveloped countries capital is needed only to increase the effective supply of improved land. So we may write,

$$O_a = f(L_a, K) \tag{10}$$

That is, agricultural output depends only on the supply of labor to the agricultural sector and the stock of improved land. Through time the change in agricultural output is

$$\frac{dO_a}{dt} = \frac{\delta f}{\delta L_a} \cdot \frac{dL_a}{dt} + \frac{\delta f}{\delta K} \cdot \frac{dK}{dt} \tag{10a}$$

In a mature economy, K is constant, so the second term drops out. We are then left only with the first term to explain the trend in agricultural output. Now the first half of that term, $\delta f/\delta L_a$, is the marginal productivity of agricultural labor, which will be positive but diminishing. The second part, dL_a/dt, is the rate of growth of the agricultural labor force. It will increase until net investment in agriculture disappears, because agricultural profits have dropped too low, as a result of falling output per man-year as agricultural employment increases.

The kind of interaction between these two sectors which leads to the stationary state (stagnation) in mature economies has been outlined above. Malthus also, however, makes some suggestions about sectoral interaction in underdeveloped areas, which help to explain why they remain underdeveloped. First, he points out that each sector constitutes the market for the output of the other sector (in the absence of international trade). Thus failure of either sector to expand acts as a drag on the growth of the other; "balanced growth" is necessary if we are to have growth at all. The development of the industrial sector of underdeveloped countries is limited by the poverty of the agricultural sector. Speaking of Latin American countries, Malthus writes:

> Except in the neighborhood of the mines and near the great towns, the effective demand for produce is not such as to induce the great proprietors to bring their immense tracts of land properly into cultivation: and the population, which, as we have seen, presses hard at times against the limits of subsistence, evidently exceeds in general the demand for labor, or the number of persons which the country can employ with regularity and constancy in the actual state of its agriculture and manufactures.

The continuing poverty of the peasant agriculture sector does not arise from scarcity of fertile land; poverty persists because large landowners have no incentive for more intensive cultivation with the present limitations of the market, whereas the peasants lack the capital that would be needed for efficient cultivation, which alone would permit them to pay enough to induce landlords to rent some of their land: [23]

> In the midst of an abundance of fertile land, it appears that the natives are often very scantily supplied with it. They would gladly cultivate portions of the extensive districts held by the great proprietors, and could not fail of thus deriving an ample subsistence for themselves and their families; but in the actual state of the demand for produce in many parts of the country, and in the actual state of the ignorance and indolence of the natives, such tenants might not be able to pay a rent equal to what the land would yield in its uncultivated state, and in this case they would seldom be allowed to intrude upon domains; and thus lands which might be made capable of supporting thousands of people, may be left to support a few hundreds of cattle.

Thus the industrial sector (including large-scale agriculture) remains limited in total size. Because of its land-and-capital-intensive nature it provides employment for relatively few people. The bulk of the population, meanwhile, lives in poverty by means of labor-intensive peasant agriculture which provides no effective demand for further growth.

In other words, there is an "indivisibility" with respect to de-

[23] *Ibid.*, p. 341.

mand; a certain minimum level of effective demand is necessary before cumulative growth can set in.[24]

> Without sufficient foreign commerce to give value to the raw produce of the land; and before the general introduction of manufactures had opened channels for domestic industry, the demands of the great proprietors for labor would be very soon supplied; and beyond this, the laboring classes would have nothing to give them for the use of their lands.

With no alluring use of increased income to tempt them to greater efforts, the landlord-capitalists find themselves on the backward-sloping portions of their supply curves. The concentration of land ownership deprives the peasants of any incentives they might have for raising output through greater efforts.[25]

> And under these circumstances, if a comparative deficiency of commerce and manufactures, which great inequality of property tends rather to perpetuate rather than to correct, prevents the growth of that demand for labor and produce, which can alone remedy the discouragement to population occasioned by this inequality, it is obvious that Spanish America may remain for ages thinly peopled and poor, compared with her natural resources. And so, in fact, she has remained.

And so she remains today, over a century later. As Malthus said then, so now, although "the increase of population and wealth has been considerable, particularly of late years, yet altogether it has been far short of what it would have been, even under a Spanish government," if appropriate development policies had been pursued.

[24] *Ibid.*, p. 342.
[25] *Ibid.*, p. 343.

4 The Marxist Model: Growth and Collapse

Karl Marx is one of those influential thinkers about whom much more has been written than he himself ever wrote. As the prophet of doom for capitalism and chief saint in the Communist hierarchy he is revered by hundreds of millions of people and reviled by other hundreds of millions. Because of the continuing importance of his ideas in shaping policies in Russia, China, and other Communist countries, and in determining the programs of Communist parties the world over, some knowledge of Marxist thought is essential if we wish to understand what is going on in the world.

Here, however, our purpose is quite different. We shall make no attempt to evaluate the Marxist system as a whole, but will do for that just what we have done for the Classical school: isolate the key propositions of its pure theory of economic development. Of course, Marx's theory of development was the core of his system, and because so few people can be detached about this system, our highly condensed presentation of his theory of development is unlikely to please. We cannot deal thoroughly with the Marxist literature. Yet no book on economic development with any pretensions to generality can ignore the Marxist theory. For, as Schumpeter says: [1]

[1] Joseph Schumpeter, *History of Economic Analysis,* p. 573. See also his *Capitalism, Socialism, and Democracy* (3d ed.; New York, 1950), p. 21, for a eulogy of Marx as "a very learned man."

Based upon a diagnosis of the social situation of the 1840's and 1850's that was ideologically vitiated at its roots, hopelessly wrong in its prophecy of ever-increasing mass misery, inadequately substantiated both factually and analytically, Marx's performance is yet the most powerful of all. In his general schema of thought, development was not what it was with all the other economists of that period, an appendix to economic statics, but the central theme. And he concentrated his analytic powers on the task of showing how the economic progress, changing by itself by virtue of its own inherent logic, incessantly changes the social framework—the whole society in fact.

Marx never underestimated the capacity of the capitalist system for economic expansion. Indeed, in this respect he was perhaps more optimistic in his prognosis for capitalist development than Malthus or Mill. True, he expected capitalism to break down, but for sociological reasons, not because of stagnation, and only after a very high degree of development had been attained. To quote Schumpeter once more: [2]

. . . nobody—not even the most ardent of optimists with whom Marx had this point in common—had then a fuller conception of the size and power of the capitalist engine of the future. With a quaint touch of teleology Marx said repeatedly that it is the "historical task" or "privilege" of capitalist society to create a productive apparatus that will be adequate for the requirements of a higher form of human civilization.

We are interested, then, in the basic elements of the Marxist theory of capitalist development and breakdown. We shall proceed as in the previous chapter, by stating the basic propositions and translating them into a set of simultaneous equations. Some of the propositions and equations are the same as those of the Classical school, from which Marx derived them in the first place; these propositions need not be elaborated again. Also, we hope that by now even those readers who have little previous experience with the use of symbols will have acquired the basic idea, so that we need not delay quite so often to translate symbols back into words.

Proposition 1: The Production Function

The Marxist ideas about the production function were the same as those of the Classical school, so we can use the same basic equation:

$$O = f(L, K, Q, T) \qquad (1)$$

[2] *Ibid.*, p. 573.

Marx laid a good deal more stress on technological progress as the "motor" of capitalist growth, and by the same token, assigned a more important role to the entrepreneur. He saw more clearly than his predecessors—and most of his contemporaries—that there is a two-way relationship between investment and technological progress. Certainly investment is needed to take advantage of technological progress, but technological progress also provides the opportunities for profitable investment.

A second difference is that we must now mean by L the labor force actually employed. Marx incorporated the analysis of unemployment into his system, and population and employment cannot be treated as varying together in the Marxist system.

Marx also had a clearer picture of the interactions between development overseas and development in Europe; he thought of England and her colonies, or France and hers, as two sectors of a single economy, administered from the metropolitan country in the interests of the capitalists of that country. Like the Classicists, he regarded the supply of land (natural resources) in Europe as essentially fixed, and he considered Europe to be in the stage of decreasing average returns to labor on the land. But he saw more distinctly than they that foreign trade and investment offered a means of escaping these diminishing returns. His followers built on this insight in developing the Marxist theory of "imperialism" and "colonial wars."[3]

Proposition 2: Technological Progress Depends on Investment

As we have already noted, in the Marxist system this proposition could be stated either way around; but in order to stress points of agreement, we shall write Equation (2) of the Marxist system in the same form as Equation (2) of the Classical system:

$$T = T(I) \qquad (2)$$

Proposition 3: Investment Depends on the Rate of Profits

Although the Marxist theory of investment resembled that of the Classical school, it was a bit more refined. The Classicists tended to think of profits as a category of income, accruing to capitalists, and providing funds for savings and investment. Marx thought of investment as depending, not merely on the size of capitalists' income, but on the rate of return on capital. Using R' to mean this rate of return,

$$I = I(R') \qquad (3)$$

[3] *Ibid.*, p. 49.

Marx himself used the term "surplus value," but surplus value was really what we have previously called profits, or the difference between total national income and the wages bill. He thought of capital as being divided into two parts. The first part is "variable capital," or working capital, which really boils down to payrolls, and which we will accordingly denote by W.[4] The second part is "constant capital," the stock of capital goods including inventories, which we shall continue to denote by Q.

Proposition 4: The Rate of Profits Is the Ratio of Profits to Payrolls Plus Capital Costs.

Instead of the fourth proposition of the Classical school, we can now substitute an identity or definition to which Marx attached great importance:

$$R' = \frac{O - W}{W + Q'} = \frac{R}{W + Q'} \qquad (4)$$

Q' means capital goods and inventories currently used up in producing O. Here Q' can be regarded as having a fixed relation to both Q and O. Thus the rate of return, R', is really a rate of return on turnover; and it is profits in this sense that Marx considered to determine investment.

Now Marx had definite ideas about the historical relationships of these variables in a capitalist economy. Like the Classicists, he regarded technological progress as being labor saving and capital absorbing—as it seemed to be in nineteenth-century Europe. Consequently there was, according to Marx, a tendency for the ratio of "constant capital to variable capital" to rise; or as we would say now, a tendency for capital costs to rise relative to labor costs, or for capital per worker to rise. He seemed to regard the capital-output ratio, as well as the capital-labor ratio, as rising through time. The advantage in new techniques came only from saving labor. The great implications of these tendencies are apparent from a glance at Equation (4); unless they are accompanied by an increased spread between national product

[4] In translating the Marxist concepts into contemporary terms, we are following Joan Robinson, *Essay on Marxian Economics* (London, 1942). It is perhaps worth emphasizing in passing that the Marxist concept of surplus value was not the difference between (the wages bill) and (the marginal productivity of labor) times (number of units of labor employed). It was simply the difference between national product and the wages bill. Throughout most of his analysis, Marx assumed pure competition; prices were equal to marginal labor cost and workers were paid according to their marginal productivity.

or income and the wages bill (increased "exploitation of the working class"), the increase in capital per worker must result in a fall in the rate of profit. By this process, rather than through diminishing returns to labor on the land, Marx explained the tendency of profits to fall.

Proposition 5: Wages Depend on the Level of Investment

The fifth equation takes the same form as in the Classical system, although now it has a somewhat different meaning. For in the Marxist system, the wages bill will depend on the level of employment as well as on the wage rate.

$$W = W(I) \qquad (5)$$

Proposition 6: Employment Depends on the Level of Investment

Employment as well as wages depends on the level of investment. For Marx, however, innovation was essentially a labor-saving device (although he apparently did not think enough labor could be displaced by innovation to prevent the rate of profit from falling). Accordingly he put a good deal of emphasis on technological unemployment. An investment boom would tend to increase employment while it lasted, but each addition to the stock of capital would tend to swell the "reserve army" of technologically displaced workers. Employment rises only if investment goes up relative to the existing stock of capital. Thus we may write:

$$L = L(I/Q) \qquad (6)$$

Proposition 7: Consumption Depends on the Wages Bill

We have seen that Malthus had already pointed out the danger that underconsumption might slow down economic growth; he had recognized that in a closed economy one productive sector constitutes the market for the other. Marx also stressed intersectoral relationships, but he conducted his analysis in terms of capital goods and consumers' goods sectors, rather than of industrial and agricultural sectors. These two kinds of sectoral breakdown are, of course, closely related but are not identical. Whereas Malthus emphasized capitalists' consumption and investment as providing the market for the industrial sector, Marx argued that investment cannot be profitable unless consumption increases enough to absorb the increased output of final products, and that however luxuriously capitalists may live, it is the workers who provide most of the market for consumers' goods. We may therefore write as our seventh equation,

$$C = C(W) \tag{7}$$

Proposition 8: Profits Depend on the Level of Technology and the Level of Consumer Spending

Equation (4) is really an identity, and does not express a functional (causal) relationship. What determines the level of profits —the spread between gross national product or income and the amount paid out in wages? As in the Classical system, the level of technique is a major factor; technological progress is tantamount to the introduction of labor-saving devices, and so permits a given output to be produced with less labor. With wages steady at the subsistence level, an increase in man-year productivity permits an increase in profits. Unfortunately for the capitalists, there is a "contradiction" here—according to Marx. For workers do most of the consuming, and reducing labor costs of production will not raise profits if it lowers worker spending; the output must be sold if profits are to be made. So the profits-determining equation in the Marxist system takes the form,

$$R = R(T, C) \tag{8}$$

It should be remembered, however, that Marx stressed the *rate* of profit (rate of return on capital) rather than the aggregate amount of profit as the factor determining capitalist behavior. It is the rate of profit, not the amount of profits, that must fall in the Marxist system. Thus what happens to R is important primarily for its effect on R' in Equation (4).

Closing the System: Three Identities

We shall have to exercise a bit more ingenuity to close the Marxist system than was necessary for the Classical one. We have, of course, the same identity as in the Classical model,

$$O = R + W \tag{9}$$

and since Marx makes more of the division of the economy into capital goods and consumers' goods sectors, we can add

$$O = C + I \tag{10}$$

Finally, we can treat current capital costs as bearing a fixed relation to the stock of capital, which we shall denote by u to mean "user cost," the added cost of using capital to produce goods and services rather than just holding it. We shall assume that u is given. Then with Equation (11),

$$Q' = u \cdot Q \tag{11}$$

we have eleven equations and eleven unknowns.

Summary

Let us now bring the system together:

$$O = f(L, K, Q, T) \tag{1}$$
$$T = T(I) \tag{2}$$
$$I = I(R') \tag{3}$$
$$R' = \frac{R}{W + Q'} = \frac{O - W}{W + Q'} \tag{4}$$
$$W = W(I) \tag{5}$$
$$L = L(I/Q) \tag{6}$$
$$C = C(W) \tag{7}$$
$$R = R(T, C) \tag{8}$$

and the three identities:

$$O = R + W \tag{9}$$
$$O = C + I \tag{10}$$
$$Q' = u \cdot Q \tag{11}$$

If we put this system side by side with the Classical model, we see both similarities and differences. Equations (1), (2), and (5) are the same in both systems. Equation (6) looks the same, but in the Classical system the L refers to the total labor force, which is thought to vary directly with the total population, whereas in the Marxist system it means labor actually employed. The consumption function, Equation (7), is crucial to the Marxist system, but plays no important role in the Classical system, except for Malthus, who would have written it differently. In Equation (3) of the Marxist system, investment depends on the *rate* of profit rather than on the level of profits, thus bringing into the system the "drag" imposed on new investment by the stock of capital already accumulated. Equation (10) of the Marxist system is really implicit in the Classical system as well, but it plays no great role in the latter, because the division of the economy into capital goods and consumers' goods sectors is less important in the Classical analysis. As we shall see more clearly below, Equation (4) of the Marxist system contains the kernel of his theory of breakdown.

The difference in the form of the profits-determining equation is of particular interest. Both Marx and the Classicists recognized improvements in technique as the one factor that could stave off for any length of time the natural tendency for profits to fall; but where the Classicists regarded population pressure as the cause of diminishing returns, rising labor costs, and falling profits, Marx stressed the "contradiction" that maintaining profits requires reducing the wages bill relative to gross national product, whereas success in doing so reduces workers' purchasing power, so that part of the output goes unsold, reducing profits after all. Marx did not believe that the working class tended naturally to reproduce on such a scale as forever to bring wages back down to the subsistence level; he regarded this Malthusian doctrine as "a libel on the human race." Even today, orthodox Marxists deny that population pressure can occur in a communist country; until recently the Chinese government leaders, well-trained Marxists that they are, have been extremely reluctant to admit that China, with its 650 million people, was, or could become, overpopulated. In the Marxist view, mass poverty is to be explained only by capitalist exploitation. It cannot continue in a communist society, whatever the level and rate of growth of the population.

The System in Operation

It is clear that the Marxist system has all the circularities of the Classical one, and a few of its own besides. With the Marxist, as with the Classical system, we could break into the circular flow anywhere and deduce from our set of relationships how the system will operate. Since Marx had his own very strong views as to how the system must evolve historically, we may follow him a bit further.

As already noted, Marx considered technological change the prime mover of the whole system. The technology of each era in a country's development determines not only the economic situation, but also the "style" of the whole society. As Engels put it in his Preface to *The Communist Manifesto*,

> In every historical epoch the prevailing mode of economic production and exchange, and the social organization necessarily following from it, form the basis upon which is built up, and from which alone can be explained, the political and intellectual history of that epoch.

For Marx, capitalism is merely one of a series of stages in the evolution of society toward the socialist state, which is the inevitable final form of economic, social, and political organization. Each stage of social evolution, with its characteristic technology and "style," breeds its particular kind of class struggle which leads to its breakdown and the emergence of the next, higher form of social organization. Thus feudalism arose out of primitive communism, but feudalism led to a struggle between serfs and feudal lords, out of which arose a class of emancipated serfs who became merchants and launched the first phase of capitalism. Capitalism brings a very high stage of technological advance. But capitalism leads eventually to a bitter class struggle between workers and capitalists, from which the workers will emerge victorious and establish the "dictatorship of the proletariat." This transitional phase will lead gradually to the full-fledged socialist (communist) society. Poverty will disappear. The state will "wither away," as a superfluous institution in a society without conflict. Each will contribute to national income according to his abilities and receive from it according to his needs.

In order to see how this prognosis for capitalism arises from the Marxist analytical framework, let us break into the system at Equation (4), which is the crucial one for the Marxist theory. It will help us to see the full significance of this equation, if we break up the wages bill into employment, L, and the wage rate, w, and if we break up total output into employment and output per man, o. We then have, substituting in Equation (4),

$$R' = \frac{L \cdot o - L \cdot w}{W + Q'} \qquad \text{or} \qquad R' = \frac{L(o - w)}{W + Q'} \tag{4a}$$

Now we can see the pincers in which the capitalists are caught. In order to survive the competitive race, they must be continually introducing improved techniques, which means accumulating capital, using more capital-intensive and less labor-intensive techniques. But the result is that Q, and so Q', increases relative to output. Under the circumstances, the only way to maintain R' is to increase the spread between o and w.

This end may be achieved in several ways. First, the wage rate can be cut to the subsistence level $\bar{w}$ and kept there—it cannot go lower. Second, more labor-saving devices can be introduced, raising o, while wages are held at or near $\bar{w}$. The trouble with this device, of course, is that (according to Marx) it can only be done by further increases in Q and Q'. Technological progress is a treadmill for capitalists—they must run ever faster just to stand still, for technological progress must always keep one step ahead of the rate of capital accumulation. However, labor-saving innovations help in another way; they displace workers, adding to the "industrial reserve army" of unemployed. Chronic technological unemployment weakens the bargaining power of workers, who are always competing for jobs against their unemployed brethren, thus making it easier for the capitalists to keep wages down to the subsistence level. Third, through the "stretch-out," hours can be increased and work speeded up without raising wages, thus again raising o without increasing w. Fourth, monopoly positions can be strengthened, to raise prices without raising wages.

All these devices for maintaining profits prove self-defeating. In the short run, they give rise to economic fluctuations. In the long run, they lead to revolution and the disappearance of the capitalist system.

The Theory of Economic Fluctuations

The Marxian theory of business cycles is scattered throughout his writings, and it takes a somewhat charitable interpretation of his *obiter dicta* on this subject to make them into a tight and systematic theory. Nevertheless, to Marx must go the credit for an early attempt at an explanation of the recurring cycles of prosperity and depression that mark the development of capitalist societies. Moreover, he anticipated some basic ideas of contemporary theories of fluctuations.

Marx really had three different business cycle theories. The simplest stressed the disproportionalities in rates of expansion of different industries in an "unplanned" economy, where investment decisions are made by hosts of independent entrepreneurs. In the course of a boom, some industries turn out to be overextended because the output of complementary goods has not kept pace with them. Put in such terms, this theory of Marx is very similar to the later theory of Spiethoff. But if we lay primary emphasis on unbalanced expansion of the capital goods sector on the one hand and the consumers' goods sector on the other, as Marx seemed to do at points, we approach some of the more modern theories that are built around the savings-investment relationship, such as the "over-investment theory" of Professor F. A. von Hayek.

The second theory is closer to Keynes or Kalecki than to

Hayek and explains the collapse of the boom in terms of the "shift to profits" and consequent underconsumption. The boom starts with innovation, which brings a temporary increase in profits which Marx called "superprofits" to indicate their transitory character and to distinguish them from true "surplus value," which is a more enduring spread between wages and output. The appearance of these superprofits, however, encourages an increase in investment. But this very gain of the capitalists at the expense of the workers proves the undoing of the boom; for capitalists tend to save a large proportion of increases in their incomes, in contrast to workers who spend any increase in income on consumption and who, by the same token, must reduce their consumption to the extent of any drop in their incomes. Monopolization fails for the same reason; capitalists tend to "price themselves out of the market." Thus investment in the boom fails to generate the purchasing power needed to absorb the increase in output of final products. Goods go unsold and profits drop again. Investment falls and depression ensues.

The third theory is less clearly stated than the other two, and at first blush, seems inconsistent with the second theory. For in this variant, the crisis emerges because the investment undertaken in the boom temporarily creates full employment and brings a temporary increase in wages. In such an inflationary boom, the innovations are not enough to maintain an increased spread between o and w; and since capital is being accumulated, the rate of profit must fall, leading to reduced investment and depression. In this model the shift to profits does not occur, and there is no clear reason why consumer spending should not be high enough to clear the market.

The apparent inconsistency between the second and third theories persists in the literature of today; underconsumption, the squeeze on profits through wage increases, and the drag on new investment through the increase in the stock of capital, all have their place in contemporary theories. One way of reconciling these two views is to say that either sequence may occur. "Weak booms" end, before full employment is reached and significant wage increases appear, through the shift to profits and underconsumption. "Strong booms" may survive the initial underconsumption and create inflationary conditions in which wage increases occur; these booms expire because of the squeeze on profits and the accumulation of capital.

Thus in the Marxist system economic fluctuations consist mainly of occasional booms, launched by investment undertaken to introduce new labor-saving techniques, which temporarily carry the economy above the trend line. But sooner or later, and usually sooner, the economy sinks back to its long-run trend, with its inevitable tendency for the rate of profits to fall. This trend toward a growing gap between potential and actual output shows up as deeper and deeper depressions, shorter and weaker booms.

Now everything the capitalists do to maintain profits in the face of this trend increases "the misery of the working class." The increasing tendency toward monopoly has another effect that helps to pave the way for revolution; it leads to the disappearance of the middle class. In the late stages of "high capitalism," capitalists become desperate indeed. Encountering increasing resistence at home, they turn to colonies for more ready exploitation of labor. Colonies also provide sources of cheap raw materials, new outlets for investment, and new markets in which monopoly positions can be established for the sale of final products. So valuable are these colonies in staving off the collapse of capitalism that the advanced capitalist countries fight imperialist wars for their possession.

All in vain. At best, these desperate measures of desperate men can bring only temporary respite. The rate of profits continues to decline, and capitalists cannot resist turning the screws on workers a bit more in the effort to save their way of life. Eventually the workers can stand it no longer; by sheer strength of numbers, they overthrow the system through revolution.

Conclusions: An Appraisal

As indicated above, any appraisal of Marx is likely to displease more people than it pleases; it will have too little vilification for some and too little veneration for others. But let us try, nonetheless, remembering that we are reviewing the earlier literature for the light it may throw on the development problems of today.

Obviously, Marx was a bad prophet. He was right, of course, in predicting the spread of communism, but both the establishment of communist societies and their subsequent evolution have taken forms very different from those envisaged by Marx. In particular, the countries that have gone Communist have not been those in which capitalist development has been most advanced but those in which it has lagged. For in the advanced capitalist countries workers have become increasingly prosperous rather than more miserable, and the middle class, far from disappearing, has grown until it dominates society. And in the

Communist countries, poverty has been slow in disappearing and there are no signs of the state's "withering away."

We cannot attempt here to explain all the reasons for Marx's failure as a prophet; we are concerned only with his analytical framework as a means of explaining economic growth. One obvious mistake was in not foreseeing the rise of powerful trade unions; but it may be questioned whether trade unions would have become so strong if the competitive position of unorganized labor had not become increasingly favorable in the first place. Let us note only two fundamental analytical errors. First, Marx did not see that innovations can be capital saving as well as labor saving. If capital-output ratios fall through improved techniques, as they frequently do, the rate of profit can rise even though wages rise too. Second, Marx was trapped by the labor theory of value which he took over from the Classical school. By measuring everything in terms of man-hours, he attached a quite wrong significance to a fall in the rate of profits in terms of man-hours. He did not see that a rise in man-hour productivity and in real wage rates can be accompanied by a rise in money profits (and real profits), even though profits in terms of man-hours may fall as man-hours become more valuable. And what really counts for capitalists is their actual income, not the number of man-hours' worth of labor a given amount of profit will buy. In other words, Marx did not foresee a process of economic development in which technological progress brings such increases in productivity and total output that both wages and profits can rise together.

On the other hand, Marx introduced certain ideas into the theory of economic development that have been there ever since. Virtually every writer on the subject since Marx has incorporated into his system the basic idea that technological progress is the mainspring of economic growth, and that innovation is the main function of the entrepreneur. By the same token investment decisions and capital accumulation are the core of most modern theories of growth, and in all theories these decisions are related somehow to the rate of return on capital. Another fundamental idea is that economic development under capitalism tends to take the form of fluctuations; economic growth is a destabilizing phenomenon. In particular, as Marx showed, stable growth requires maintenance of the proper balance between investment and consumption, and thus between savings and investment. Marx also pointed to the relationship between the savings-investment relationship on the one hand and the distribution of income on the other, a relationship that has remained a fundamental feature of growth theories ever since. He indicated the slenderness of the tightrope which an economy must walk for steady growth—wages either too high or too low relative to ouput can choke off investment and cause depression. This "damned if you do and damned if you don't" character of the boom has also remained a recognized feature of any complete analysis of cycles and trends. Marx also made employment and unemployment a major variable in the system.

These are sizable bricks for the construction of a theory of growth, even if Marx's own structure collapsed because some of its pillars were faulty. So far as the problem of steady growth in advanced capitalist countries is concerned, Marx's main contribution, apart from these bricks, was in putting capitalism in its historical setting, which helps a good deal in evaluating its past and its future.

So far as its pure economics is concerned, Marx's system is less directly applicable to problems of underdeveloped countries than that of Malthus. Marx did not really think of underdevelopment as an enduring state; underdeveloped countries were simply pre-capitalist ones, which, unfortunately, would have to go through the capitalist phase before they could attain the Elysian Fields of communism. His exclusion of the possibility of population pressure is a severe handicap in trying to apply his system to most underdeveloped countries. Perhaps just because he did not believe population pressure possible he also missed the fundamental feature of "dualism"; he did not see that technological progress might be confined to one sector of an economy while leaving the rest of the economy virtually untouched.

The Marxist sociological and political theory, however, provides some clues to the economic history of underdeveloped countries. It suggests to us that we look at power relations among social classes and see whether these relations are of a sort that imposes barriers to spontaneous growth. It suggests that we should look for an explanation of colonial policies in the economic conditions of the home countries, rather than economic conditions in the colonies themselves. It suggests, too, that part of the explanation of underdevelopment in the former colonies might be traced to these policies. As we shall see in more detail below—for reasons not fully explained by Marx himself—in some underdeveloped countries conditions occurred rather like those Marx predicted for advanced ones: labor was indeed exploited; wages were indeed kept close to subsistence levels; a "reserve army" of chronic unemployment did in fact exist; the class structure was sharply defined and a middle class virtually non-existent; in some cases there is even evidence of "increasing misery." That such conditions could result in revolution of one sort or another few people would deny.

We must be wary of the pitfalls in the Marxist system, but for all its errors, the Marxist theory of economic development has much to contribute to an understanding of development or the lack of it.

5 Unstable Growth: Schumpeter

With the work of Joseph Schumpeter we move into the twentieth century. The basic ideas of his theory of economic growth were presented in his *Theory of Economic Development*, first published in German in 1911. He continued to elaborate his analysis of capitalist development throughout his brilliant career.[1] The most complete statement of it, however, was contained in his *Business Cycles*, published in 1939. It is on this version that we shall draw most heavily in presenting the skeleton of his system.

Apart from his genius and prodigious capacity for work, Schumpeter had a breadth of experience which was unusual for economists of his generation, and which gives particular interest to his pronouncements on the factors involved in economic development. Here is a man who in the course of his career was Finance Minister of a Socialist government in Austria, professor of economics in Bonn and Tokyo, and from 1927 until his untimely

[1] Richard V. Clemence and Francis S. Doody, *The Schumpeterian System* (Cambridge, Mass., 1950), p. 1. "The Schumpeterian System occupies a remarkable place in the history of economic thought. Almost from the beginning of his work on the theories of interest and of business cycles Professor Schumpeter saw a vision of a distinctly capitalist process taking place in historic time. His youthful vision, first reduced to a comprehensive model in 1911, has since been elaborated and refined, but it has been altered in no essential respect to the present day. Such extraordinary consistency is almost unique in our science, and it is by no means a proof of virtue. What it rather suggests is that tests be made of the hypothesis that the model withstands critical attack. That is what we propose to do in this book."

death in 1950, professor of economics at Harvard University. Thus Schumpeter studied the economic scene closely over a period of four decades, during which he lived in four countries and three continents.

Few economists of his generation had so wholehearted an admiration for the capitalist system as Schumpeter. He was not one of those who believed that the capitalist machine produces high rates of economic growth which offset the attendant social evils; Schumpeter heartily enjoyed and endorsed the society and civilization produced by "pure" capitalism as well. He preferred the relatively uninhibited and undemocratic capitalism, accompanied by a high level of cultural attainment, which prevailed in Europe before World War I, to the modified capitalism that has developed since. Even the semifeudal capitalism of prewar Japan struck a responsive chord in Schumpeter.

What his real political position was few people really knew. A few years before his death, in a speech to an organization of French Canadian employers in Montreal, he said bluntly that the way to stem the tide of socialism was to organize the corporative state under the guidance of the Roman Catholic Church.[2] It

[2] "L'Avenir du Capitalisme," in *Comment Sauvegarder l'Entreprise Privée* (Montreal, 1946).

In his address to the American Economic Association in 1949, Schumpeter made the following statement: "Familiar facts of our own trade-union practice suggest that a development toward some form of guild socialism is not entirely off the cards. And other familiar facts suggest that observable tendencies or some of them may be compatible with forms of social reorganization that are not socialist at all, at least not in the sense which has been adopted for this paper. For instance, a reorganization of society on the lines of the encyclical *Quadragesimo anno*, though presumably possible only in Catholic societies or in societies where the position of the Catholic Church is sufficiently strong, no doubt provides an alternative to socialism that would avoid the "omnipotent State."

In the same address he said: "It would spell complete misunderstanding of my argument if you thought that I 'disapprove' or wish to criticize any of these [New Deal] policies. Nor am I one of those who label all or some of them 'socialist.' Some have been espoused, even in the eighteenth century, by conservative or even autocratic rulers; others have been on the programs of conservative parties and have been carried by them long before New Deal days. All I wish to emphasize is the fact that we have traveled far indeed from the principles of laissez-faire capitalism and the further fact that it is possible so to develop and regulate capitalistic institutions as to condition the working of private enterprise in a manner that differs but little from genuinely socialist planning. . . . Having discovered this possibility of a *laborist capitalism* they go on to conclude that *this* capitalism may survive indefinitely, at least under certain favorable conditions. This may be so but it does not amount to a denial of my thesis. Capitalism does not merely mean

would be quite wrong to conclude from these random remarks that he had fascist leanings. At the same time, no one can doubt that he considered the existence of a sharply defined class structure a small price to pay for the continued economic and social progress which he believed unbridled capitalism brings.

We are not concerned here with the personal or political views of this brilliant, vigorous, charming, fascinating, and enigmatic personality. As with the economists already discussed, we are concerned only with his analytical framework and its usefulness for attacking the growth problems of underdeveloped and advanced countries today. These comments on Schumpeter's tastes and views are made for but one reason: Schumpeter's intellectual debt to Marx was greater than his debt to any other figure in the history of economic thought, and it is important to understand that a man may levy upon the Marxist system and still hate communism. Schumpeter's dislike of collectivism extended to a profound distaste even for capitalism in harness or the welfare state.

Much as he admired the capitalist system, however, Schumpeter shared the gloomy prognosis of the Classical school and of Marx. He believed that capitalism will eventually stagnate and break down. This prospect was for him saddening indeed, especially since, in his view, the breakdown would come only from the lack of appreciation of what capitalism can do and the conditions which it needs in order to prosper. According to Schumpeter, not the failures of capitalism, but its very success, would lead eventually to the slaughter of the goose that lays the golden eggs. But we anticipate; let us review his system in the same manner as we have reviewed the Classical and Marxist systems, and see how he reaches this pessimistic conclusion.[3]

that the housewife may influence production by her choice between peas and beans; nor that the youngster may choose whether he wants to work in a factory or on a farm; nor that plant managers have some voice in deciding what and how to produce. It means a scheme of values, an attitude toward life, a civilization—the civilization of inequality and of the family fortune. This civilization is rapidly passing away, however. Let us rejoice or else lament the fact as much as everyone of us likes; but do not let us shut our eyes to it." Joseph Schumpeter, "The March into Socialism," *American Economic Review Papers and Proceedings,* XL (1950), pp. 447, 449–50.

[3] Although Schumpeter's prognosis was certainly pessimistic for someone admiring capitalism and disliking socialism as much as Schumpeter did, he vehemently denied that his attitude was "defeatist." "The report that a given ship is sinking is not defeatist," he insisted. "Only the spirit in which this report is received can be defeatist: the crew can sit down and drink. But it can also rush to the pumps. . . . What normal man will refuse to defend his life merely because he is quite convinced that sooner or later he will have

Proposition 1: The Production Function

Schumpeter had the same general concept of the production function as did Marx and the Classical school. We can therefore use the same Equation (1) once again:

$$O = f(L, K, Q, T) \tag{1}$$

Proposition 2: Savings Depend on Wages, Profits, and the Interest Rate

Schumpeter defines saving as "saving up" for future consumption or for investment. With this definition, workers as well as capitalists are able to save, and both will save more as their incomes rise. However, Schumpeter retained in his system the neoclassical proposition that savings tend to increase with the interest rate. The *proportion* of a given wage or profit income that will be saved will increase as the interest rate goes up. Thus we may write for our second equation

$$S = S(W, R, r) \tag{2}$$

Proposition 3: Total Investment May Be Subdivided into Induced Investment and Autonomous Investment

One of Schumpeter's important contributions was a distinction between two kinds of investment: investment which is stimulated by recent increases in output, income, sales, or profits which we shall call "induced investment," I_i; and investment which is brought forth by such long-run considerations as technological change, which we shall call "autonomous investment," I_A. So far as our third equation is concerned, then, we have an identity,

$$I = I_i + I_A \tag{3}$$

Proposition 4: Induced Investment Depends on the Level of Profits and the Interest Rate

The factors determining induced investment might be expressed in various ways, but Schumpeter laid particular stress on the relationship between profits, R, and the interest rate, r. In this respect, too, he followed the neoclassical tradition. Induced investment tends to rise as current profits rise and to fall as the

---

to die anyhow." *Capitalism, Socialism, and Democracy* (3d ed.; New York, 1950), p. xi. Similarly, he wrote, "If a doctor predicts that his patient will die presently, this does not mean that he desires it. One may hate socialism or at least look upon it with cool criticism and yet foresee its advent. Many conservatives did and do" (*ibid.*, p. 61).

interest rate goes up; the gap between profits and the interest rate is of primary importance in determining induced investment. However, the more capital has already been accumulated, the bigger must be the excess of profits over interest to induce more investment. We may therefore write

$$I_i = I(R, r, Q) \tag{4}$$

$$\frac{\delta I_i}{\delta R} > 0 \qquad \frac{\delta I_i}{r} < 0 \qquad \frac{\delta I_i}{\delta Q} < 0$$

Proposition 5: Autonomous Investment Depends on Resource Discovery and Technological Progress

In his insistence that the most important part of private investment is determined by long-run factors, not directly related to recent changes in income, output, sales, and profits, Schumpeter made his major contribution to the theory of investment. He laid particular stress on what he called "innovation" as the mainspring of autonomous investment. What he meant by "innovation," however, might be regarded either as technological progress or resource discovery (or both), defining these terms broadly. He thought of innovation in general as any change in the production function which would bring an increase in output. "Any doing things differently," he said, which increases the productivity of the bundle of factors of production available (including resources given in the economy but not yet discovered) is an innovation. He listed five major forms of innovation: [4]

Development in our sense is then defined by the carrying out of new combinations.

This concept covers the following five cases: (1) the introduction of a new good—that is, one with which consumers are not yet familiar —or of a new quality of a good. (2) The introduction of a new method of production, that is, one not yet tested by experience in the branch of manufacture concerned, which need by no means be founded upon a discovery scientifically new, and can also exist in a new way of handling a commodity commercially. (3) The opening of a new market, that is, a market into which the particular branch of manufacture of the country in question has not previously entered, whether or not this market has existed before. (4) The conquest of a new source of supply of raw materials, or half-manufactured goods, again irrespective of whether this source already exists or whether it has first to be created. (5) The carrying out of the new organization of any industry, like the creation of a monopoly position (for example through trustification) or the breaking up of a monopoly position.

[4] Schumpeter, *The Theory of Economic Development*, p. 66.

We shall use the term $\dot{K}$ to mean the rate of resource discovery through time, dK/dT, and $\dot{T}$ to mean the rate of technological progress through time, dT/dt. We then have the following relationship: [5]

$$I_A = I_a(\dot{K}, \dot{T}) \tag{5}$$

Readers already familiar with the Keynes-Hansen theory of development, in which population growth plays a prominent role as a stimulant to autonomous investment, may wonder why population growth is not included in Equation (5) of our model of the Schumpeter system. It seems more faithful to Schumpeter's own views on the subject to omit population growth. Schumpeter did not deny that population growth, under some circumstances, may bring forth long-run investment, or that a tapering-off of population growth might result in a drop in investment if not offset by other factors.[6] But he clearly did not attach much weight to population growth as an economic force; he chose to regard it as an "external factor" rather than as an integral part of his system.[7]

[5] Autonomous investment, as well as induced investment, may be retarded by capital accumulation, although the relationship is presumably somewhat less powerful. Also, even autonomous investment may depend somewhat on the level of output. Thus we could write, instead of Equation (5),

$$I_A = \lambda(O) + \phi(\dot{K}, \dot{T}) - \psi(Q)$$

But since in the long run O and Q move closely together and have opposite effects on investment, we can safely drop the first and third terms.

[6] See especially his *Business Cycles*, pp. 1035–1036.

[7] Two quotations will serve to illustrate his attitude toward the population growth factor: "Changes in numbers and age distributions due to other causes than migration sometimes are in fact external factors or consequences of external factors, such as wars. Sometimes they are not, as we may see from the cyclical component in marriage rates. But as it is impossible to accept a minimum-of-existence theory of wages—which it would be necessary to do in order to make the relation between the rate of change of population and economic situations stringent—and as nativity and mortality display substantive independence of economic fluctuations—however much their historic changes have to do with the ulterior cultural effects of the working of the capitalist machine—it has seemed best to class them with external factors. . . .

"Our reason for listing variations in population among external factors was that there is no unique relation between them and variations in the flow of commodities. Hence, it seemed convenient for our purpose, although it would be inadequate for others, to look upon an increase in population as an environmental change conditioning certain phenomena. Moreover, it could be demonstrated by familiar cases (India and China) that mere increase in population does not *bring about* any of those phenomena which presuppose either a certain density or a certain rate of increase in population except a fall in real income per head. Finally, it occurs so continuously as to

He readily admitted that population growth, like saving, can lead to *growth* of the economy, but he made a distinction between growth and development. True *development* requires qualitative change: [8]

> By "development," therefore, we shall understand only such changes in economic life as are not forced upon it from without but arise by its own initiative from within. . . . Nor will the mere growth of the economy, as shown by the growth of population and wealth, be designated here as a process of development. For it calls forth no qualitatively new phenomena, but only processes of adaptation of the same kind as the changes in the natural data. Since we wish to direct our attention to other phenomena, we shall regard such increases as changes in data.

Propositions 6 and 7: Technological Progress and the Rate of Resource Discovery (Innovations) Depend on the Supply of Entrepreneurs

The stress on the leading role of the entrepreneur in economic development under capitalism is the main feature of the Schumpeter system. As we saw in the previous chapter, Marx also considered the entrepreneurial function important, but he did not isolate it for special emphasis in the same degree as Schumpeter did.

The entrepreneur is the man who sees the opportunity for introducing a new technique or a new commodity, an improved organization, or for the development of newly discovered resources. He raises the money to launch a new enterprise, assembles the factors of production, chooses top managers, and sets the organization going. He need not be a "capitalist"—he may not provide any funds of his own. He may not be a day-to-day

---

be capable of current absorption. Short-time variations in marriage rates are obviously the reflex of business fluctuations and do not cause them." (*Business Cycles*, pp. 10, 74.)

[8] *The Theory of Economic Development*, p. 63.

Clemence and Doody paraphrase Schumpeter on this point as follows: "Growth is defined as changes in population, and in total savings and accumulations of households and firms respectively, corrected for variations in the purchasing power of the monetary unit. Growth has so far been excluded from the system on the ground that changes in population and in saving can be currently absorbed without giving rise to cyclical fluctuations. Cycles can be understood without Growth, but not vice versa, and the quantitative importance of Growth, especially of saving, is due to the process of capitalist development. Such saving, of course, may be used to finance innovation, although not without effects on economic contours, such as those of price levels" (*op. cit.*, p. 15).

manager. Nor is he usually an inventor or explorer. Inventions or discoveries by themselves have little economic effect, Schumpeter argues. He instances the Montgolfier balloon, which caused considerable wonderment when invented, but had little effect on economic life. The Patent Registry is filled with files of patent applications for inventions that never see the light of day. For inventions or resource discoveries to be significant, someone with the special talent for seeing their economic potential and bringing them into use must come along. That man is the entrepreneur.

We may therefore write, using $\dot{E}$ to mean the rate of increase in the supply of entrepreneurs, dE/dT,

$$\dot{T} = T(\dot{E}) \tag{6}$$

and

$$\dot{K} = K(\dot{E}) \tag{7}$$

Admittedly, the supply of entrepreneurship is not an easy thing to measure; but in Schumpeter's system the supply of entrepreneurship is the ultimate determining factor of the rate of economic growth, so we must give it a place of honor in our system of equations.

Proposition 8: The Supply of Entrepreneurs Depends on the Rate of Profits and the Social Climate

Like Marx, Schumpeter lay considerable stress on sociological factors, and some of these are not easily reduced to simple mathematical expressions. This stricture applies to Schumpeter's concept of the "social climate," a complex phenomenon reflecting the whole social, political, and socio-psychological atmosphere within which entrepreneurs must operate. It would include the social values of a particular country at a particular time, the class structure, the educational system, and the like. It would certainly include the attitude of society toward business success, and the nature and extent of the prestige and other social rewards, apart from profits, which accompany business success in the society. A particularly important factor in "climate" is the entrepreneur's understanding of the "rules of the game," the conditions under which he must operate. Sudden changes in the rules of the game are particularly deleterious to an increasing flow of enterprise.

With apologies for its inadequacy, we shall use the symbol χ to stand for the whole matter of "climate." We then have, as the determinant of a society's entrepreneurial resources,

$$E = E(R, \chi) \tag{8}$$

Proposition 9: Gross National Product Depends on the Relationship between Savings and Investment and the Supermultiplier

These words are probably not those which Schumpeter would have chosen to state this proposition; but they express the fundamental relationship which was recognized by Schumpeter, as well as by Marx before him and by most of Schumpeter's contemporaries and juniors. An excess of investment over voluntary savings, financed by credit creation, will raise gross national product (in money terms) by an amount which will be some multiple of the original gap between investment and saving. Conversely, an excess of voluntary savings over investment will reduce gross national product, in value terms, by some multiple of the original gap. We can therefore write[9]

$$O = k(I - S) \tag{9}$$

Proposition 10: The Wages Bill Depends on the Level of Investment

Schumpeter carried over into his system the proposition, common both to the Classical school and to Marx, that wage incomes tend to increase with investment, and vice versa. We may therefore write once more,

$$W = W(I) \tag{10}$$

Proposition 11: The "Social Climate" Is Reflected by the Distribution of Income

In order to close the system, we have to stretch a bit. We have already noted that Schumpeter's concept of "climate" is a very complex and subtle affair. However, it is clear from some of his later writings that he considered income distribution to be a good "thermometer" of the general climate. Any development tending to squeeze profits, such as growing strength of trade unions, progressive income taxes, social welfare programs, or any other government intervention designed to limit profits or to redis-

[9] It is useful to differentiate this particular equation with respect to time. We can then write

$$\frac{dO}{dt} = K\left(\frac{dt}{dl} - \frac{dS}{dt}\right)$$

That is, the rate of change in gross national product through time will be some multiple of the gap between the rate of growth in investment and the rate of growth to time in voluntary savings.

tribute income, is tantamount to deterioration of the climate. Thus Schumpeter explained the depth and duration of the Great Depression of the 1930's in terms of the labor legislation, social security, public works spending, progressive tax structure, public utilities regulation, and other "New Deal" policies introduced in the middle and late 1930's. These constituted a change in the "rules of the game" so drastic as to discourage enterprise and thus retard investment. All these forms of government intervention have a direct short-run impact on the relationship between wages and profits (after taxes). The ratio of profits to wages is a mere shorthand expression for all the factors influencing "climate," but it is a convenient shorthand, so we will write

$$\chi = \chi(R/W) \tag{11}$$

Proposition 12: An Identity: Gross National Product Equals Profits Plus Wages

To close the system we can resort once more to the now familiar identity and write

$$O \equiv R + W \tag{12}$$

We now have twelve equations and twelve unknowns and can turn to an analysis of the operation of this system as Schumpeter viewed it.

Scope of the System

The Schumpeter analysis may be regarded as wide or narrow in scope, depending on what one expects from a theory of economic development. Schumpeter himself had this to say of his theory: [10]

> Economic development is so far simply the object of economic history, which in turn is merely a part of universal history, only separated from the rest for purposes of exposition. Because of this fundamental dependence of the economic aspect of things on everything else, it is not possible to explain *economic* change by previous *economic* conditions alone. For the economic state of a people does not emerge simply from the preceding economic conditions, but only from the preceding total situation.

This statement certainly makes Schumpeter's aim sound ambitious enough. On the other hand, as Clemence and Doody point out in their appraisal: [11]

[10] Schumpeter, *The Theory of Economic Development*, p. 58.
[11] Clemence and Doody, *op. cit.*, p. 2.

In comparison with the systems of such scholars as Toynbee and Spengler, the Schumpeterian System has very modest dimensions. No effort is made to achieve a synthesis of world history or even of the history of Western civilization. On the contrary, the whole analysis is concerned with the economic aspects of capitalist society, and most of the resources of modern economics are brought to bear on the comparatively narrow problem of the economic process of the capitalist era. Not only economics, but other social sciences as well are drawn upon heavily in the attempt to develop a model of this process. The important question, however, is not what resources are utilized but what results are achieved, and the present study is part of an effort to find out.

In general, the scope of Schumpeter's system is about as broad as that of the Classical school, and a bit less broad than that of Marx. Schumpeter does not try to provide a systematic explanation of changes in non-economic data; but in explaining changes in economic data he draws on a wide range of sociological, psychological, political, and technological factors.

Operation of the System

Schumpeter starts his analysis with an economy in stationary equilibrium, characterized by a "circular flow" which forever repeats itself. This stationary equilibrium is described by Clemence and Doody as follows: [12]

The Pure Model has as its basis an economic system in general equilibrium. All economic activity in the model is essentially repetitive, following the course of familiar routine, and the model may thus be regarded as a circular flow of economic life. Every firm in the system is in perfect competitive equilibrium, with its costs, consisting of wages and rents, exactly equal to its receipts. Prices everywhere are equated to average costs; profits are zero; profit opportunities are nonexistent; interest rates are zero; and there is no involuntary unemployment of resources. Every household, like every firm, is in full long-run equilibrium, with receipts equal to expenditures, and with a budgetary pattern that cannot, under the existing circumstances, be advantageously altered.

The essence of development is a *discontinuous* disturbance of this circular flow: [13]

Development in our sense is a distinct phenomenon, entirely foreign to what may be observed in the circular flow or in the tendency towards equilibrium. It is spontaneous and discontinuous change in the

[12] *Ibid.*, p. 9.
[13] Schumpeter, *Theory of Economic Development*, p. 64.

channels of the flow, disturbance of equilibrium, which forever alters and displaces the equilibrium state previously existing. Our theory of development is nothing but a treatment of this phenomenon and the processes incident to it.

The discontinuous disturbance comes in the form of an innovation. The innovation entails the construction of new plant and equipment. It may do so in any of three different ways. First, it may hasten the replacement of existing plant and equipment by rendering it obsolete. Second, it may create an expectation of high monopoly profits for the first firm in the new field and thus raise the "marginal efficiency" (expected yield, after allowance for risk) of capital in general, leading to an increase in total net investment. Third, it may produce a new product that seems so attractive that people are willing to cut into their savings to have it, thus raising the propensity to consume and making additional plant and equipment profitable and necessary. Schumpeter himself stresses the second of these types of expansionary process. He also argues "as if" the construction of new plant and equipment was undertaken by New Firms, and points out that historically there is no lack of realism in such an argument; most of the major innovations—such as the railways and steamships of the nineteenth century, and the automobiles, chemicals, and electric power of the twentieth—have in fact been developed mainly by new firms.

Schumpeter also argues that the development of the new firms is usually associated with the rise to business leadership of New Men, and here too he points to history to substantiate his argument. This part of Schumpeter's theory is very important, if it is true, for it means that unless business leadership is forthcoming to build up new firms for the exploitation of innovations, capitalist economies may suffer more or less chronic depression. As we have seen, enterprise of the sort basic to economic expansion, according to Schumpeter, is something different from the genius of the inventor, or the efficiency of the executive of a going concern, or the willingness to risk one's own capital in new enterprises. It consists mainly of seeing and seizing the opportunity for development of a New Firm; historically, it has been this kind of special skill that has been most handsomely rewarded in capitalist economies.

Once the innovator has demonstrated the profitability of his venture, followers will enter the field in "clusters." The original innovator will of course try to maintain his monopoly position. In the past, he has seldom had complete success in this regard.

Today, when a growing proportion of inventions comes from the research departments of existing firms, it is easier for monopolies to protect their positions, and to prevent any "cluster" of would-be followers from entering a new field of production. By the same token, the expansionary force of an innovation is diminished.

The development of the new industry is followed by the adaptation of old industries to the changed pattern of demand. The development of railroads entailed the construction of new towns, relocation of old industries, expansion of the iron and steel industry, and so forth. The development of the automobile industry brought with it the move to the suburbs, the construction of highways, the development of new recreation centers, enormous expansion of the petroleum and rubber industries, and so on. A "big" innovation like railroads or automobiles can generate a huge wave of new investment, through its direct and indirect effects on the economy.

Schumpeter, like most other analysts of economic fluctuations, assumes that the wave of new investment is financed largely by new credit created by the banks. In other words, the investment is assumed to be financed by monetary expansion rather than by an increase in current (*ex ante*) savings, so that new investment produces a spread between investment and *ex ante* savings and generates an upswing. This assumption is, of course, perfectly realistic.

When the "gestation" period is over, and the new plants are completed, the rate of investment drops to the level necessary for replacement only; net investment ceases. Obviously, the operation of a railway involves less current investment than its construction. Moreover, once the new plants are in operation there will be a new and increased flow of consumers' goods onto the market; this factor in itself would tend to reduce prices. The tendency for prices to fall is enhanced by contraction of the money supply; as the new firms begin to sell their product, they come into possession of a "stream of receipts," which enables them to reduce their indebtedness to the banks. Reducing debt means simply the cancellation of deposits, and consequently the money supply contracts. With increasing supplies of goods on the market and a decreasing supply of money to buy them, prices naturally tend to fall. Some firms make windfall losses as a result of this unforeseen drop in prices. Commercial failures increase. Aggregate profits decline. Expectations become gloomy, and the impulse for innovation itself dries up. Depression ensues.

It will be noted that the validity of Schumpeter's theory as an explanation of economic fluctuations depends on the "swarming" of innovations in "clusters" in the early stages of the upswing, when the economy is still close to an equilibrium position. Perhaps no feature of Schumpeter's theory has been so frequently subjected to attack as this one. To the present writer, however, this feature of the Schumpeterian system seems acceptable enough. Two similar opinions might be cited in support of this view:[14]

> Why is innovating activity most favored by equilibrium? A comparison of the difficulties and risks of innovation at different stages of the two-phase cycle shows a heavy balance in favor of this situation. The stability of business conditions, as well as the complete absence of profits, is more conducive to innovation than any other stage of the cycle could be. Since the risk of failure is at a minimum, and the pressure to innovate at a maximum, we should expect that innovating activity, under capitalist arrangements, would be extraordinarily great.
>
> The standard criticism which has been raised against Professor Schumpeter's theory of the business cycle is concerned with the "clustering" of innovations at certain periods of time. The explanation sought by the critics was either in terms of the social psychology of innovations, i.e., that one successful innovation encourages others (a point which Professor Schumpeter himself makes, cf. Vol. i, p. 100, which, however, is not of decisive importance for the theory), or in terms of a clustering in time of technological inventions. These explanations being refuted, the theory was easily rejected. But all this is quite irrelevant. Professor Schumpeter's theory does not rest upon either of these points. The clustering is a consequence of the changing risk of failure. Whatever the time shape of the supply of new inventions, new plans of organization, etc., or of entrepreneurial skill, the actual introduction of innovations will be "bunched" at periods of neighborhood of equilibrium when the risk of failure is the smallest; and as an intensification of the rate of innovation disequilibrates the economy and increases the risk of failure, this rate must slacken again. Thus we can dismiss the standard criticism; the clustering is explained quite satisfactorily in Professor Schumpeter's theory.

Although Schumpeter's theory is not in itself a complete theory of business cycles, it contains elements which must be included in any complete theory. In particular, his analysis of innovations is still the best explanation of how an upswing gets started. Certainly he has made an important contribution to the theory of

[14] Clemence and Doody, *op. cit.*, p. 54; Oscar Lange, review of Joseph Schumpeter *Business Cycles*, in *Review of Economic Statistics*, November, 1941, p. 192.

development by his systematic exposition of the thesis suggested by Marx that capitalist development tends to proceed by leaps, bounds, and falls rather than by a smooth and steady progression. But another aspect of Schumpeter's theory of fluctuations is more troublesome from our standpoint.

Whereas in his original presentation he talked of only one kind of cycle, in his *Business Cycles* he talked of three: the "Kitchin" cycle of three to four years duration; the "Juglar" cycle of seven to eleven years; and the "Kondratieff" cycle of fifty to fifty-five years (in each case the name given the cycle is that of the economist who first provided statistical evidence of its existence and attempted an explanation of it). We are not troubled by Schumpeter's using the same theory to explain all three cycles, although that has bothered some of his critics. It is entirely feasible that the impact of such major innovations as steam or electricity should be felt over long periods and the impact of minor innovations like tubeless tires over short ones, although it is not clear why their impact should be spread over precisely the periods designated by Schumpeter. What does bother us is that, whereas the Kitchin and Juglar cycles appear clearly in the data, the very existence of the Kondratieff cycle is debatable. First, there are very few countries for which reliable time series are available for a couple of centuries—and even a two-century-long time series covers only four Kondratieff cycles, which is not a large sample. Secondly, the "long wave" seems to show up in some time series and not in others. It is fairly clear in prices but it does not appear in figures of total output or employment. It is clear enough that during long periods, such as 1825–50 and 1870–90 in the United Kingdom, or 1870–90 and 1929–40 in the United States, a lot of people talked about "depression." The "Great Depression" of the 1930's and the depression of the 1830's and 1840's show some striking similarities; these were depressions in any language. The so-called "great depression" of the 1870's and 1880's, on the other hand, was a period in which total output went merrily on up throughout. Professor Rostow, who has certainly given the matter as careful study as anyone, finds little evidence of such a cycle in his study of nineteenth-century Britain.

The matter is of some importance for development policy. For if cycles exist in which for twenty-five years a prosperity and expansion phase, interrupted only by the shorter cycles, can be followed by an equally long period of general depression and contraction, it becomes necessary to distinguish the true long-run trend from the movements in the Kondratieff cycle, as well as in the short-run cycle, in order to evaluate the results of a development program. And to do that we would have to know a great deal more about the nature and causes of the Kondratieff cycle than we do. It is also important to know whether there are any cures for the "long wave," and if so what. If a country launches its development program in the downswing of a Kondratieff cycle, it will be very hard to generate enthusiasm for the program by saying that although income is not currently rising, it is rising *relative* to what it would have done without the development program, and that in another twenty-five years or so, when the Kondratieff upturn appears, a rapid rate of increase in per capita income can be confidently expected.

Schumpeter's Theory of Trend

Schumpeter's pure theory is a contribution to the analysis of business cycles rather than to the analysis of economic development. It seems likely that Schumpeter himself became aware of this fact in the course of his career. His great two-volume book published in 1939 is a further elaboration of the ideas in his 1911 *Theory of Economic Development;* it is significant that the title of the later work was changed to *Business Cycles: A Theoretical, Historical, and Statistical Analysis of the Capitalist Process.* Schumpeter's main point was precisely that the capitalist process is necessarily cyclical. He did not provide any systematic explanation of trends; indeed, he treated the trend as a statistical concept —a line drawn through the inflection points of a curve showing the pattern of business cycles. But what determines whether that trend is upward, downward, or horizontal? On this question Schumpeter had little to offer but insights and observations, and although these were very helpful in themselves, they do not really constitute a "theory" of economic development.

Let us summarize the system as outlined above:

$$O = f(L, K, Q, T) \quad (1)$$
$$S = S(W, R, r) \quad (2)$$
$$I = I_i + I_A \quad (3)$$
$$I_i = I(R, r, Q) \quad (4)$$
$$I_A = I_a(\dot{K}, \dot{T}) \quad (5)$$
$$\dot{T} = T(\dot{E}) \quad (6)$$
$$\dot{K} = K(\dot{E}) \quad (7)$$
$$E = E(R, \chi) \quad (8)$$

$$O = k(I - S) \quad (9)$$
$$W = W(I) \quad (10)$$
$$\chi = \chi(R/W) \quad (11)$$
$$O = R + W \quad (12)$$

When we compare this set of equations, summarizing the Schumpeter system, with those summarizing the Classical or the Marxist system, we note three major differences.

First is the introduction of the interest rate as a determinant of savings. Not every economist would regard this feature of the system as a great advantage, since the relationship of savings to the level of interest rates is none too clear. Second is the separation of autonomous from induced investment and the isolation of "innovations" as the factor influencing autonomous investment; many economists consider this feature Schumpeter's major contribution to the theory of development. Third is the emphasis on entrepreneurship as the vital force in the whole economy. This feature was and remains the most distinctive aspect of Schumpeter's system, and it is this feature that has found its way most frequently into later theories of growth.

But what are we to say about it? What determines the supply of entrepreneurship? Without answers to this question, we still do not know why an economy grows, stagnates, or collapses; and Schumpeter does not provide very satisfactory answers. It all resolves itself into the vague concept of "climate" for the rise of the New Men who will do the job of establishing New Firms and making the economy grow.

We have only three indications of what Schumpeter regarded as the essence of this all-important matter of "climate": a more or less offhand remark in his earlier book, some statements about the psychological make-up of entrepreneurs, and his explanation of the Great Depression. The remark is[15]

> The more life becomes rationalised, levelled, democratised, and the more transient become the relations of the individual to concrete people (especially in the family circle) and to concrete things (to a concrete factory or to an ancestral home), the more many of the motives enumerated in the second chapter lose their importance and the more the entrepreneur's grip on profit loses its power. To this process the progressive "automatisation" of development runs parallel, and it also tends to weaken the significance of the entrepreneurial function.

[15] Schumpeter, *The Theory of Economic Development*, p. 155.

The entrepreneur is, among other things, a social deviant: [16]

The third point consists in the reaction of the social environment against one who wishes to do something new. This reaction may manifest itself first of all in the existence of legal or political impediments. But neglecting this, any deviating conduct by a member of a social group is condemned, though in greatly varying degrees according as the social group is used to such conduct or not. Even a deviation from social custom in such things as dress or manners arouses opposition, and of course all the more so in the graver cases. This opposition is stronger in primitive stages of culture than in others, but it is never absent. Even mere astonishment at the deviation, even merely noticing it, exercises a pressure on the individual. The manifestation of condemnation may at once bring noticeable consequences in its train. It may even come to social ostracism and finally to physical prevention or to direct attack. Neither the fact that progressive differentiation weakens this opposition—especially as the most important cause of the weakening is the very development which we wish to explain—nor the further fact that the social opposition operates under certain circumstances and upon many individuals as a stimulus, changes anything in principle in the significance of it. Surmounting this opposition is always a special kind of task which does not exist in the customary course of life, a task which also requires a special kind of conduct.

He is also egocentric, untraditional, and ambitious: [17]

The typical entrepreneur is more self-centred than other types, because he relies less than they do on tradition and connection and because his characteristic task—theoretically as well as historically—consists precisely in breaking up old, and creating new, tradition. Although this applied primarily to his economic action, it also extends to the moral, cultural, and social consequences of it. It is, of course, no mere coincidence that the period of the rise of the entrepreneur type also gave birth to Utilitarianism. . . .

First of all, there is the dream and the will to found a private kingdom, usually, though not necessarily, also a dynasty. The modern world really does not know any such positions, but what may be attained by industrial or commercial success is still the nearest approach to medieval lordship possible to modern man. . . .

Then there is the will to conquer; the impulse to fight, to prove oneself superior to others, to succeed for the sake, not of the fruits of success, but of success itself. From this aspect, economic action becomes akin to sport—there are financial races, or rather boxing-matches. . . .

Finally, there is the joy of creating, of getting things done, or simply of exercising one's energy and ingenuity.

[16] *Ibid.*, p. 89.
[17] *Ibid.*, pp. 91–93.

Schumpeter's ideas about the breakdown of capitalism are perhaps most clearly stated in the final chapter of his *Business Cycles*, where he discusses the "stagnation thesis" in relation to the Great Depression of the 1930's. This theory, which is the subject of Chapter 7, states in essence that the length and depth of the Great Depression was to be explained in terms of vanishing investment opportunity, because of declining rates of population growth, disappearance of the frontier, and a tendency for innovations to become capital saving. Schumpeter does not deny the logical validity of the stagnation thesis: [18]

> The validity of that theory is not denied on the grounds that its basic proposition is wrong. . . . Capitalism is essentially a process of (indigenous) economic change. Without that change or, more precisely, that kind of change which we have called evolution, capitalist society cannot exist, because the economic function, and, with the functions the economic bases of its leading strata—of the strata which work the capitalist engine—would crumble if it ceased: without innovations, no entrepreneurs; without entrepreneurial achievement, no capitalist returns and no capitalist propulsion. . . . The atmosphere of industrial revolutions—of "progress"—is the only one in which capitalism can survive. In this sense stabilized capitalism is a contradiction in terms.

He also accepts "the companion proposition that investment opportunity in this sense may, and in fact is quite likely to, vanish sometime in the future." He even adds "an element of his own." The mechanization of progress may "produce effects similar to those which cessation of technological progress would have. Even now the private entrepreneur is not nearly so important a figure as he has been in the past. We have moreover noticed the implications of chemical and other developments which may result in making innovation capital saving or at least less capital absorbing than, say, it has been in the railroad age." He considers the argument regarding population growth to be "inadequately formulated," but agrees that "provision for an indefinite family future is of central importance in the scheme of bourgeois motivation, and much driving power may be eliminated by childlessness."

However, he flatly denies that such a theory is an explanation of the Great Depression. A particularly deep and long depression was to be expected at that time anyhow, he maintains, in terms of his own theory of long waves. Even the "disappointing Juglar" of 1933–37, which ended in a new downswing long before full employment was restored, is in part to be explained in terms of

[18] Schumpeter, *Business Cycles*, p. 1033.

his general theory: "It did not differ in character from the comparable Juglar prosperities of the preceding Kondratieff downgrades, and therefore does not indicate any fundamental change in the working of the capitalist organism." [19] However, he does feel that more was involved in the Great Depression, and particularly in the disappointing Juglar, than the general nature of interacting Kondratieff and Juglar cycles: to wit, the deterioration of the climate for entrepreneurial activity. For "Capitalism produces by its mere working a social atmosphere—a moral code, if the reader prefers—that is hostile to it, and this atmosphere, in turn, produces policies which do not allow it to function." [20] Moreover, there is no "equilibrating apparatus" to guarantee that this atmosphere will not appear before "the capitalist process will have really spent its force or be spending it." In the United States of the 1930's, he suggests, this atmosphere appeared too soon.

As evidence of this hostile climate, he cites first the burden of direct taxation since 1932. He attaches more importance to the income, corporation, and estate taxes than to some of the newer taxes, such as undistributed profits and capital gains taxes, but he agrees that such "changes in the rules" were inimical to entrepreneurial activity. The tax on payrolls for financing the social security program was also of some significance. In addition, "labor policies reduced investment opportunity—besides employment per unit of output—mainly by forcing up wage rates." [21] His general analysis leads him to expect that "developments in the field of public utilities would be a leading factor of the current, as they had been in the preceding Juglar." The failure of this expectation to be fulfilled he explains in terms of the increasing activity of the federal and municipal governments in this field. The reappearance of "the big stick" with respect to monopoly was another discouraging factor. Finally, "the personnel and methods by which and the spirit in which" the New Deal measures were administered were "much more important than anything contained in any enactment."

Thus Schumpeter's theory of economic growth (as distinct from his theory of economic fluctuations) has a large element of tautology in it, making it difficult to test empirically. It is not set up as a "refutable hypothesis." Economic growth occurs when the social climate is conducive to the appearance of a sufficient flow of New Men, but the only real way to test whether the social

[19] *Ibid.*, p. 1037.
[20] *Ibid.*, p. 1038.
[21] *Ibid.*, p. 1042.

climate is appropriate, is to see whether the New Men are in fact appearing; that is, whether there is economic growth. If vigorous economic growth appears, the social climate is appropriate; when there is no vigorous economic growth, the social climate is by definition inimical to it.

In general, the climate is appropriate when entrepreneurial success is amply rewarded, and where there are good—but not too good—chances of success. If entrepreneurs are to be social deviants, the society must oppose them in some degree, accepting them only after they have proved their success. In contrast to Marx, who thought of "capitalists" as a "class" almost in the sense of caste, a group to which workers could not aspire, an essential aspect of Schumpeter's vigorous capitalist development is rapid circulation of the elite. Success in the innovational process must lead also to the top of the social ladder—if not for oneself, then at least for one's son or grandson—as it did in nineteenth-century Europe.[22]

Accepting the Schumpeter theory of growth raises an interesting question: what can be expected from a society in which entrepreneurs are no longer deviants, since collective entrepreneurial activity is regarded as the most acceptable form of endeavor. Can an economy of "organization men," safe and secure in their junior executive or trade-union positions, produce a rate of economic expansion as rapid as was obtained under unbridled capitalism, in which entrepreneurial activity was highly regarded only when spectacularly successful?

Schumpeter certainly thought not. In his address to the American Economic Association in 1949 (published posthumously) he said: [23]

> The very success of the business class in developing the productive powers of his country and the very fact that this success has created a new standard of life for all classes has paradoxically undermined the social and political position of the same business class whose economic function, though not obsolete, tends to become obsolescent and ame-

[22] One factor that Schumpeter seems to have missed is the importance of the frontier in the circulation of the elite. A major difference between the "open society" of the United States, and the more stratified society of Australia, with its accompanying emphasis on the role of government and social welfare, is that in Australia the same opportunities for rising to the top of the economic ladder, and thus to the top of the social ladder, by "going West" did not prevail. We shall have more to say of this matter in the next chapter.

[23] *American Economic Review Papers and Proceedings*, XL (May, 1950), p. 449.

nable to bureaucratization. . . . The concentration of the business class on the tasks of the factory and the office was instrumental in creating a political system and an intellectual class the structure and interests of which developed an attitude of independence from, and eventually of hostility to, the interests of large-scale business. The latter is becoming increasingly incapable of defending itself against raids that are, in the short run, highly profitable to other classes.

Similarly, in his *Capitalism, Socialism, and Democracy* he wrote: [24]

This social function (of entrepreneurship) is already losing importance . . . it is much easier now than it has been in the past to do things that lie outside the familiar routine—innovation itself is being reduced to routine. Technological progress is increasingly becoming the business of teams of trained specialists . . . personality and will power must count for less in environments which have become accustomed to economic change . . . social and technological change undermined and eventually destroyed the function and position of [the warrior knight]. Now a similar social process—in the last analysis the same social process—undermines the role and, along with the role, the social position of the capitalist entrepreneur.

In concluding this chapter, let us say one word about the relationship of the Schumpeter theory to the problems of underdeveloped areas. Tautological though the theory may be, there can be little doubt of its relevance. The lack of adequate entrepreneurship is one of the most frequently cited obstacles to take-off in such countries, as we have seen in Chapters 1 and 2. It also appears true that the relatively small entrepreneurial group in such countries frequently consists of a deviant class: the Chinese in Southeast Asia, the Hindus in East Bengal, the Jews in Libya, the Indians in Africa, and so on. Schumpeter's theory also raises doubts about the possibilities of successful development in countries which *start* with a climate inimical to entrepreneurship, as is the case in many of the underdeveloped countries. The "socialist" intent of many of these countries has been announced. Such "New Deal" legislation as social security programs, high and progressive income tax rates, labor legislation, and the like have been introduced in many underdeveloped countries in the years following World War II, with levels of income and stocks of capital that are only a tiny fraction of those of the United States in the 1930's. It may be possible for the entrepreneurial function to be performed by government agencies instead of by private individuals, but the Schumpeter theory would throw some doubt on this possibility.

[24] Pp. 132–33.

6 Cumulative Movement away from Equilibrium: Harrod

In this chapter and the next, we shall discuss the growth theories of two leading contemporary economists, one British and one American: R. F. Harrod of Oxford, and Alvin Hansen of Harvard.[1] Readers who are already acquainted with the work of these two men may question our right to include their growth theories in this part of the book, which purports to deal with "general" theories. The work of Harrod and Hansen, some readers may protest, is associated with the particular problem of "secular stagnation" in "mature economies," or as economists put it these days, the problem of maintaining steady growth in advanced industrialized societies. Accordingly, they might argue, the Harrod-Hansen analysis should be treated as a special theory for advanced societies, and not among general theories of development.

This argument would have a certain validity; nevertheless, one may contend that the theories of Harrod and Hansen have as strong a claim to generality as the others outlined in this part. In the first place, Hansen and Harrod are in the direct line of succession. Their models represent further developments of the Classical and Marxist models, with considerable borrowing from Schumpeter, plus new ideas and interpretations of their own. Like Marx and the Classical school, they are concerned with ex-

[1] Dr. Hansen is now professor emeritus of Harvard and a visiting professor at the University of Bombay.

plaining the development of capitalist economies and indicating the conditions under which economic growth may cease. Like Schumpeter, they are interested, too, in showing why capitalist development tends to be irregular, and in indicating how and to what degree the process of growth could be smoothed out. But both Harrod and Hansen provide more systematic theories of trend than Schumpeter did; on this score, their theories are more appropriately termed general than is Schumpeter's.

Second, the concentration of their policy discussion on the problem of maintaining steady growth in advanced economies merely reflects the fact that this problem was uppermost in people's minds at the time they were writing. It does not mean that their theory cannot be applied to other problems. The form of their analytical models is perfectly general. In isolating the factors that may cause stagnation in advanced societies, they also, sometimes by implication and sometimes explicitly, explain the rapid growth of Europe and the New World in the nineteenth century. True, their references to underdeveloped countries are relatively few; but as we shall see, their theories nevertheless throw light on the problem of generating a take-off into sustained growth in such countries.

In contrast to much of the recent literature on "dynamics," Harrod's essay *Towards a Dynamic Economics* has the main attributes of a truly dynamic theory. Harrod concentrates upon the explanation of secular *trends;* he insists that it is precisely this explanation of trends that is the distinguishing characteristic of *dynamic* economics. Comparative statics, he argues, are still statics; more than imperfect foresight, or imperfect knowledge, or mere change, or presence of expectations, or lags and frictions, or "dating" of variables is needed to take us into the realm of economic dynamics. Even trade cycle theory is not dynamic if it merely explains fluctuations around a constant trend. Only a theory explaining secular changes in the volume of output may validly claim to be called dynamic. Harrod's theory is directed toward an explanation of the secular causes of unemployment and inflation, and of the factors determining the optimum and the actual rate of capital accumulation. Although clearly distinct from theories of equilibrium or of comparative statics, Harrod's theory is nevertheless related to them, and it uses those concepts and tools of equilibrium theory and comparative statics that are serviceable in analyzing secular trends. Accordingly, his work provides a foundation upon which it should ultimately be possible to build, brick by brick, an imposing structure of dynamic analysis. Harrod considers the building of such a structure the major task facing economists today:[2]

> The idea which underlies these lectures is that sooner or later we shall be faced once more with the problem of stagnation, and that it is to this problem that economists should devote their main attention.

On the basis of his analysis Harrod concludes that advanced countries will soon confront the problem of a chronic deflationary gap (and by inference that underdeveloped countries will continue to be handicapped by a chronic inflationary gap) unless appropriate policies are pursued. True, the United Kingdom will be faced for the remainder of the postwar transition period with a problem of under- rather than oversaving, and if the secular downward drift of the propensity to save continues, it may be a long time before chronic unemployment becomes the major economic problem in that country. "But the United States," Harrod thinks, "is not likely to be exempt from the problem of chronic depression."[3] And what happens in the United States must affect the rest of the world. It is therefore high time, in Harrod's opinion, for economists to turn their attention once again to problems of chronic and increasing underemployment.

Outline of the Model

This chapter will concentrate upon the systematic theoretical analysis in Harrod's essay. The book also contains some useful discussion of contracyclical policy and some fascinating pronouncements on social philosophy. However, these parts of the essay are readily understandable and do not provide a foundation for system-building to the same extent that the central analytical chapters do. Moreover, these central chapters are frightfully difficult—not for the mathematics, or complicated diagrams, or long-winded discussion they contain, but precisely because all such aids are left out. There are whole paragraphs between the lines that the reader must fill in for himself; and in many cases,

[2] R. F. Harrod, *Towards a Dynamic Economics* (London, 1948), p. v. The literature contains frequent references to the "Harrod-Domar theory," since Evsey Domar presented essentially the same theory, having arrived at it quite independently. (See his *Essays in the Theory of Economic Growth*, Oxford and New York, 1957.) However, Harrod did publish his basic ideas earlier than Domar, and Harrod's formulation seems somewhat more fruitful when applied to underdeveloped areas.

[3] *Ibid.*, p. vi.

it is no easy task to write a paragraph elaborating the argument of one line and come out with something that fits Harrod's next line. We shall be primarily concerned, therefore, with exposition of the Harrod theory.

We shall deviate from the pattern of the earlier chapters in one respect. Harrod's presentation is tight and terse, and he uses his own equations. We shall not, therefore, translate his system into a set of simultaneous equations. We shall only translate Harrod's symbols into our own, as we work our way through his book.

Harrod's first chapter defends his definition of "dynamics," and lays down a few fundamental concepts. He contrasts his approach with that of the Classical theory. In the Classical model, as we have seen, economic development is treated as a race between technological progress and capital accumulation on the one hand, and diminishing returns to a growing population applied to a fixed supply of land on the other. Population growth is a dependent variable, mutually determined with profits, investment, income, and so forth. Harrod follows Marx and discards diminishing returns from land as a "primary determinant," and he considers both the rate of population growth and the rate of technological progress as independent variables in advanced countries. The three "fundamental elements" in his system are (1) manpower, (2) output per head, (3) quantity of capital available. The second of these presumably breaks down into (*a*) level of technique, (*b*) supplies of known resources; but Harrod discusses changes in output per head solely in terms of "inventions."

A "neutral" stream of inventions is one that leaves the ratio of required capital to output ("capital coefficient") unchanged. A "capital-saving" stream of inventions would reduce the capital coefficient, a "labor-saving" stream of inventions would increase it. Thus "labor-saving" inventions are defined as capital-absorbing inventions. Surely an invention could reduce the ratio of labor to output, without raising the ratio of capital to output. This definition also raises the question, which occurs periodically in the course of Harrod's analysis, as to whether he really means inventions when he uses the word, or whether he means innovations. An invention may be capital saving once in place, but the innovation based on it may nevertheless be capital absorbing during the gestation period. What is needed for a growing offset to savings is not a stream of *inventions* that is capital absorbing in the *engineering* sense, but a stream of *innovations* that is capital absorbing in the economic sense.[4] Harrod, unfortunately, fails to make this important distinction. He seems to be talking mainly about inventions, which, he says, may very well be more or less neutral in reality,[5] but at times his arguments make sense only if cast in terms of innovations.

"Capital requirements" are the proportion of income that must be saved and invested to maintain a given rate of increase in income, with a given rate and type of technological progress, and a given rate of population growth. A simplifying assumption that underlies the discussion of capital requirements, which Harrod does not make explicit, is that the labor force and the body of consumers grow in the same proportion; that is, that the ratio of labor force to population and of consuming units to population does not change. Only then would it be true, for example, that capital requirements with no technological advance and no change in interest rates would equal "the increase of population in a period regarded as a fraction of the total income multiplied by the capital coefficient." [6]

More generally, his concept of capital requirements, C_r, could be translated as follows. Let I_r be required net savings and investment, Y be national income, and p (for period of investment) be the "capital coefficient." Then [7]

$$I_r = \frac{\Delta Y}{Y} \cdot p \quad \text{and} \quad C_r = \frac{I_r}{\Delta Y}$$

In chapter 2, Harrod proceeds to analyze trends in (net) savings, for the relation of trends in new savings to trends in new capital requirements is obviously of major importance in determining whether or not there will be a steady growth. He distinguishes three major sources of saving: (1) individual saving to satisfy a person's own needs during his own lifetime (which he calls "hump" saving); (2) individual saving for the purpose of

[4] Benjamin Higgins, "Concepts and Criteria of Secular Stagnation," in *Income, Employment, and Public Policy: Essays in Honor of Alvin Hansen* (New York, 1948).

[5] Harrod, *op. cit.*, p. 28.

[6] *Ibid.*, p. 22.

[7] If L is population and T is level of technique, t is time and Q_r is quantity of capital required for a given level of output, then

$$Q_r = R(R, T) \quad \text{where} \quad L = L(t) \quad \text{and} \quad T = T(t)$$

Then, ignoring cross-derivatives, which would in any case be very small,

$$Ir = \frac{dQr}{dt} = \frac{\delta Qr}{\delta L} \cdot \frac{dL}{dt} + \frac{\delta Qr}{\delta T} \cdot \frac{dT}{dt}$$

L is here defined in terms of output per capita.

enlarging an estate to be passed on to heirs (which we may call "inheritance" saving); (3) saving by business firms (which he calls "corporate" saving). Harrod believes that in a stationary state, with neither population growth nor technological progress (nor, although Harrod fails to distinguish this factor, discoveries of new supplies of natural resources), "hump" savings should be zero for the economy as a whole; saving of the young will be just offset by the dissaving of the aged. It is worth noting, however, that "hump" savings would be zero *only* if tastes regarding the time-pattern of enjoyments throughout a lifetime remained unchanged from generation to generation. Harrod feels less certain about "inheritance" savings, but thinks it most likely that they will be positive, although small and diminishing through time. Corporate saving, which is motivated primarily by the desire of entrepreneurs to expand their businesses without forfeiting controlling interest or unduly enlarging fixed charges, would tend toward zero in a stationary society. If "inheritance" saving is positive, since there would be no demand for saving in a stationary economy at a constant rate of interest, there would be a chronic tendency for savings to exceed investment, and "it would be necessary to have a falling rate of interest to give employment to the savings volunteered." [8]

Even then, the falling interest rate would absorb savings only to the extent that it led to more roundabout methods of production; and the falling interest and longer investment period would probably induce firms to save more themselves, leading to a further decline in the interest rate, and so on. It is hard to say what the effect of falling interest would be on "inheritance" saving; but Harrod concludes that "hump" saving is an increasing function of the rate of interest. This conclusion is derived from putting "reasonable" values into his savings equation,

$$C_1 = C_r\left[1 - e\left(1 - \frac{1}{T^r R^r}\right)\right]$$

in which C_1 is consumption in year one, C_r is consumption in a later year, r, e is the average elasticity of the income utility curve over the relevant range, T is the reciprocal of the rate of time preference, and R the number of pounds to which £1 accumulates at the end of the year at the current rate of interest.[9]

[8] *Ibid.*, p. 47.

[9] It is a pity that Harrod could not have provided his readers with his computations, in a footnote or appendix; but there is little reason to suspect his conclusion. Indeed, if one considers savings as demand for future income

In an economy with a growing population and no technological progress, capital requirements will increase proportionately to the population. So also, Harrod argues, will "hump" savings and "corporate" savings. Consequently, if there is "inheritance" saving to begin with, and all capital requirements are to be met, "inheritance" saving must also grow proportionately to income; that is, it must grow in total volume enough to keep the average per capita inheritance constant. Of course, total savings may tend to grow faster than capital requirements, leading to a condition of chronic excess savings and a need for falling interest rates, even in an economy with a growing population; but the need for a falling interest rate is clearly much greater in a stationary state than in one with a growing population.

In an economy with technological progress as well, it is necessary to ask what is the effect on saving of an increase in per capita output. The effect on elasticity of income-utility is, unfortunately, unpredictable. "On the other hand," Harrod writes, in a mature economy "there seems to be a presumption that time preference will fall (that T will increase). As income rises our consumption is less dominated by basic physical need and becomes more amenable to rational planning. . . . A strong time preference is indicative of a low degree of civilization."[10] Perhaps; but how then does Harrod explain the observed secular tendency for the propensity to save to fall? True, the observed trend is a trend of *ex post* savings, which are necessarily equal to investment; and the observed trend may be causally explained better in terms of a declining ratio of *investment* to income than in terms of a declining *ex ante* propensity to save. Also, in the period for which data are available, there has been some tendency for interest rates to fall, and the fall in propensity to save may be a reflection of the drop in interest rates. However, there is a problem here, and it is rather important for a theory of development. Can underdeveloped countries expect the *share* of any *given* income saved

and translates the interest rate into a price of future income in terms of present income, it becomes fairly obvious that savings out of a given income must vary directly with the interest rate. The conditions for a rising demand curve are the same for "future income" as for any other commodity; the commodity must be one on which a large share of income is spent, and it must be highly competitive with, but inferior to, some other commodity. These conditions are simply not fulfilled for most savers. The effective increase in present income through having to pay a lower price for future income must be insignificant for most people; and although future income might be inferior to present income, it can hardly be considered highly competitive with it.

[10] Harrod, *op. cit.*, p. 53.

to rise as development takes place?

Harrod also contends that "hump" savings are likely to grow faster than income when per capita income is rising. Here we run into the same sort of problem. Harrod's contention presumably means that the trend of the *average* propensity to save (ratio of savings to income) for "hump" purposes will be a rising one. Empirically, it is virtually impossible to separate "hump" saving from other kinds of saving, as well as to measure *ex ante* (planned) savings as a whole. What we know is that historically, neither the average nor the marginal propensity to save (share of increase in income saved) shows any significant long-run change; in any one year, however, families with high incomes have considerably higher average propensities to save, and somewhat higher marginal propensities to save, than families with low incomes. From this combination of facts it has been deduced that there is a downward secular drift of the propensity to save *schedule*, which just offsets the secular rise in incomes, leaving the actual ratio of savings to income unchanged.[11]

There is also some evidence that the downward drift of the propensity to save schedule may be the product of cycles of increasing amplitude. Savings seem to follow income up in the upswing, but to shrink in the downswing as families endeavor to maintain their prosperity standards of living in the face of falling incomes. As higher levels of national income are reached, more families will be able to meet depressions by dissaving.[12] Might not this downward drift in the savings function affect "hump" savings too, and so prevent them from rising faster than income in the long run? In any case, one wishes that Harrod had been more careful to distinguish among the volume of savings, the propensity to save function, the average propensity to save, and the marginal propensity to save, in his arguments.

Regarding "inheritance" saving, Harrod considers the evidence inconclusive, but feels that the increasing capacity for looking ahead in advanced societies would apply here too. Since corporate saving is unlikely to increase less rapidly than income, introduction of "neutral" inventions into the argument increases, rather than decreases, the possibility of chronic excess savings. The existence of a large dead-weight national debt, which historically at least is a feature of mature economies, also adds to the possi-

[11] Cf. Paul Samuelson, "Full Employment after the War," in S. E. Harris (ed.), *Postwar Economic Problems* (New York, 1943), p. 33.

[12] Cf. James S. Duesenberry, "Income-Consumption Relations and Their Implications," in *Income, Employment, and Public Policy*.

bility of excess savings, so long as capital accumulation bears some more or less constant relationship to the existing supply of assets.[13]

In the third chapter which is the heart of his book, Harrod presents a revised version of the "fundamental equations" developed in his *Economic Journal* article of March, 1939, and uses them to derive some extremely interesting "dynamic theorems." The basic equation is $GC = s$: where G is the growth during a unit of time, $\Delta Y/Y$; C is net capital accumulation in the period (including goods in process and stocks), divided by the increase in output in the period, $I/\Delta Y$; and s is the average propensity to save,[14] S/Y. Thus the equation is really a restatement of the truism that *ex post* savings equals *ex post* investment; it could be written:

$$\frac{\Delta Y}{Y} \cdot \frac{I}{\Delta Y} = \frac{S}{Y} \quad \text{or} \quad \frac{I}{Y} = \frac{S}{Y} \quad \text{or} \quad I = S$$

Harrod's second fundamental equation, $G_w C_r = s$, expresses the equilibrium conditions for a steady advance. G_w, the "warranted rate of growth," is the value of $\Delta Y/Y$ that barely satisfies entrepreneurs; C_r, the "capital requirements," is the value of $I/\Delta Y$ that is needed to sustain the warranted rate of growth.[15] It will be noted that s is the same in both equations. Thus in dynamic equilibrium (stable value of $\Delta Y/Y$), $G_w C_r = GC$; the actual, or *ex post* value of I/Y, equals the equilibrium value, which is a subjective phenomenon. Moreover, G must equal G_w and C must equal C_r. For if G exceeds G_w, then C will be below C_r; that is, entrepreneurs will consider the amount of capital accumu-

[13] The second chapter concludes with some remarks about the possibility of a continuously falling interest rate, from the viewpoint of the securities market. Harrod points out, quite rightly, that it is the rate of interest implicit in share prices that is most relevant to decisions regarding new investment, and that "ordinary shares issued by good companies" are not dissimilar to undated government stock. How could the market deal with such things if it came to expect a continuously falling rate of interest? For "the value of stock having no redemption date becomes indeterminate unless we put a term to the fall in the rate of interest" (Harrod, *op. cit.*, p. 60); and even a decline expected to end in twenty or thirty years would produce awkward anomalies in the market. "Dynamic theory strives after the concept of a steadily falling rate of interest, but I do not think that market conditions have been envisaged in which this could become a reality." (*Ibid.*, p. 62.)

[14] These symbols are used in the usual sense: Y is national income, I is net investment, and S is net savings. Since Harrod has preempted C for another use in this chapter, we shall denote consumption by C_n.

[15] If inventions are "neutral," C_r will also be the new capital required to sustain the increase in consumption that consumers want, as a result of the increase in their incomes during the period.

lation inadequate to sustain the increase in total output and will increase their orders for capital goods (and conversely). But then G will depart still further from G_w in the next period, and a cumulative movement away from equilibrium will set in. Thus: "Around the line of advance which, if adhered to, would alone give satisfaction, centrifugal forces are at work, causing the system to depart further and further from the required line of advance."[16]

There are two possible interpretations of Harrod's argument that if G exceeds G_w, C must be below C_r, and vice versa. If $G_wC_r = GC = s$ by assumption, then the proposition follows by mere arithmetic. Harrod's presentation, however, suggests that he thinks G_wC_r *must* equal GC for economic and definitional reasons, in much the same way that *ex post* savings *must* equal *ex post* investment. It is hard to see that such is the case. It is clear enough that G and C must vary inversely with a given I/Y or C. But why should the equilibrium ratio of (*ex post*) savings and investment to income (i.e., the ratio that satisfies entrepreneurs, or $G_wC_r =$ equilibrium$\frac{I = S}{Y}$) be continuously equal to the *actual* ratio of savings and investment to income (GC, or *actual*$\frac{I = S}{Y}$)?

Harrod's main argument does not depend upon the equality of GC and G_wC_r anyhow. It depends rather on the acceleration principle (or better, on the "relation"). For if G exceeds G_w, what this really means is that the rate of increase in total spending is greater than is necessary to call forth the current rate of investment, and consequently investment will increase. By definition, if the rate of investment is below the equilibrium level, C_r is below C. Such a situation would be inconsistent with an excess of GC (actual $I/Y = S/Y$) over G_wC_r (equilibrium $I/Y = S/Y$), since investment cannot be simultaneously above and below the equilibrium level; but it would be quite consistent with an excess of G_wC over GC. That is, $C - C_r$ may exceed $G_w - G$; entrepreneurs may consider actual investment low, not only relative to the actual rate of increase in consumer spending, but also relative to the level of income. In this case there would be a double incentive to increase investment in the next period. The movement away from equilibrium when $G > C_w$, and *in addition* $GC < G_wC_r$, will be greater than if $G > G_w$ but $GC = G_wC_r$.

[16] Harrod, *op. cit.*, p. 86.

Harrod anticipates the criticism that his formulation gives too much weight to the acceleration principle, and he suggests that the criticism could be met by rewriting the first equation $GC = s - k$, where k is investment not due to the current increase in orders for output. It is not quite clear how much investment is meant to go into k and how much into C. C would presumably not include primary investment induced by innovations—let us say, building of automobile factories in the early stages of the automobile long wave, or "Kondratieff." But would the petroleum refineries, rubber plantations, and roadside restaurants brought into being by the automobile Kondratieff go into C or into k? Harrod says k will include "capital outlay which no one expects to see justified or not justified in a fairly short period."[17] How long is that? As will appear below, it is not a matter of indifference how investment is distributed between C and k.

Another problem arises in connection with C and C_r. The "relation" usually expresses the extent to which investment increases as a consequence of increases in demand for the final products of plant and equipment of a given type. For the "relation" to operate in the economy as a whole (without any change in the period of investment, which is not closely related to rates of consumption, and which Harrod excludes from this part of his analysis), there must be a change in the rate of consumer spending. The relation might be expressed as $I = r \cdot dC_n$. Harrod argues throughout as though an increase in income necessarily entailed an increase in consumption, and also as though an increase in investment would always bring with it an increase in consumption. Why else would the increase in investment, C_r, resulting from an excess of G over G_w (excess of C_r over C) carry the system *further* from equilibrium?

Harrod's point is, it will be remembered, that the greater investment brought about by $C_r > C$ will raise G still further above G_w. In the context of his argument, this proposition must mean that the increase in investment in the next period will bring with it an increase in the rate of expansion of consumer spending $\Delta C_n/C_n$. Now, if the increased investment is deficit financed, it is quite likely that the increase in rate of expansion of consumption that accompanies an increase in investment, $\frac{d}{dI}\left(\frac{dC_n}{C_n}\right)$, will be positive; for then the multiplier will operate on the increase in I and so raise consumer spending substantially. But in most of

[17] *Ibid.*, p. 79.

Harrod's argument, savings and investment are always equal; if entrepreneurs consider their investment too low, they also consider their saving too low. An increase in investment financed by an equal and simultaneous increase in saving will not raise income at all, and consumption will actually fall. In this event, investment in period 2 will be too high, rather than still too low, and will be reduced rather than raised in period 3, and so on. The initial excess of G over G_n would in this case set up a series of damped fluctuations, and in the absence of a new disturbance, the system would tend toward a new equilibrium with the actual $\frac{I=S}{Y}$ equal to the equilibrium $\frac{I=S}{Y}$, and so with $G = G_w$ and $GC = G_wC_r$.

To take another example, if half the new investment is financed by new saving and the (instantaneous) multiplier is 2, national income will rise by exactly the amount of the increase in income and consumer spending will remain unchanged, and so on. All kinds of models could be constructed, each giving a different result. Harrod's analytical system is not self-contained. At many points in his argument, conclusions depend on unstated assumptions about entrepreneurial behavior and about the value of functional relationships not explicitly set forth.

Harrod seems to feel that he has excluded the possibility of new investment being financed by new savings, by arguing that ds/dt is small relative to G. "Without any great revolution," he says, "G might easily change from 2 to 6 per cent. This clearly could not cause saving to be trebled. The extreme case of saving being as low as 2 per cent of income, and all extra income, due to a rise in G, being saved may be ruled out. If saving is greater than 2 per cent, then for saving as a fraction of income to increase as much as G, consumption would have to be cut as income rose, and this, too, may be ruled out." [18] The only case in which s could vary proportionately with G, he says [19] is where k is almost as great as s; that is, when the bulk of investment has little to do with current demand (hence the importance of the allocation of investment between k and C).

This argument has several dubious aspects. So long as growth depends on investment to meet current requirements, it would take something of a revolution to change the rate of growth in national income, G, from 2 to 6 per cent. It is precisely such a

[18] *Ibid.*, p. 79.
[19] *Ibid.*, p. 86.

"revolution" that underdeveloped countries are trying to encourage, with so much difficulty, in their development plans. Moreover, the execution of a development plan might easily mean that k would be almost as great as s. Since investment *not* based on increasing demand for final products is ruled out of capital requirements, C, a trebling of G really means a trebling of the rate of increase in consumer spending. Nothing we know about the consumption function implies that degree of instability in it, except perhaps when a cumulative inflation is already under way.

Secondly, Harrod's argument about the cumulative nature of a divergence of G_w from G has nothing to do with the *effect* of a change in G on s; to argue that a $G > G_w$ *must* raise investment, and so *must* raise G, because a rise in investment induced by the rise in G could not raise s proportionately and so prevent the rise in G, is completely circular reasoning. The question is, *must* the investment induced by $G > G_w(C_r > C)$ raise G? We have seen that the answer *depends on* the extent to which entrepreneurs finance their investment by new saving and on the size of the multiplier; it also depends, incidentally, on the value of the relation coefficient itself, which was ignored in our illustration.

In the third place, there seems no a priori reason why, in the real world, the bulk of investment should not be independent of current requirements. Of course, Harrod is assuming "neutral" inventions at this stage; and he points out, quite rightly, that in this case a *constant* rate of technological progress would not require net savings, since replacement reserves would allow for obsolescence. But why should there not be an *increasing* rate of technological progress? To be sure, if the stream of *innovations* is neutral, it absorbs no capital by definition. But a swelling stream of neutral *inventions* could absorb any amount of capital whatsoever, provided the stream swelled fast enough.

The manner in which new investment is financed is crucial to Harrod's analysis. Unless he can demonstrate beyond a shadow of doubt that it is *impossible* for enough of an increase in investment to be financed by new savings to make $\frac{d}{dI}\left(\frac{dC_n}{C}\right)$ zero or negative, he can argue that an initial divergence of G and G_w may start a cumulative movement; but he cannot argue that it must start a cumulative movement.

Harrod's third fundamental equation is G_nC_r may or may not be equal to s; here G_n is the "natural rate of growth" or "that steady rate of advance determined by fundamental conditions."[20] What G_n really seems to be is the rate of increase in output at full employment, given the rate of population increase and the rate of technological progress. A better term would have been "potential rate of growth"; there is nothing very natural about full employment. It will be noted that, whereas Harrod seems to feel that G_wC_r *must* equal GC, he stresses the possibility that G_nC_r may not equal GC, by making G_nC_r equal, or not equal, to s.

With the introduction of G_n, Harrod is able to develop a theory of increasing underemployment for advanced economies. If G_w exceeds G_n (as it well may when population growth tapers off, or the rate of improvement in technique or discovery of new resources tapers off), G will also tend to lie below G_w, C will be chronically above C_r, and the economy will be chronically depressed. (After all, G can exceed G_n only in the recovery phase of the cycle.) Conversely, in a rapidly expanding economy (where population growth, or technological progress, or geographic expansion is at a high level) there will be a chronic excess of G_n over G_w, and also of G over G_n, and thus a chronic excess of C_r over C, and a perpetual tendency for inflationary boom to develop. We might call economies of the former type "deflationary gap" economies and of the latter type, "inflationary gap" economies. We shall have something to say later on as to whether or not underdeveloped countries are, by definition, "inflationary gap" countries as well.

Harrod contrives to get a skeletal theory of economic fluctuations, as well as a theory of trend, out of his analysis. In the recovery phase, $G > G_n$. When full employment is reached, $G = G_n$. If $G_w > G_n$, then at full employment $G_w > G$, $C_r < C$, and a slump is inevitable. Moreover, G_w tends to rise in the later phases of recovery, because "companies are likely to save a large fraction of short-period increases of net receipts,"[21] and G_w rises with s. Thus it is quite likely that G_w will rise above G_n when high levels of employment are reached; and since at full employment $G = G_n$, a slump ensues. If immobilities, frictions, and "bottlenecks" reduce G before it equals G_n, the downturn may come before full employment is reached. If G_w is far above G_n, G may never rise far above G_w and depression may begin "long before" full employment is reached.

On similar reasoning, Harrod argues that "saving is a virtue and

[20] Harrod, *op. cit.*, p. 87.
[21] *Ibid.*, p. 89.

beneficial as long as G_w is below G_n" (and therefore below G at full employment) because saving[22] raises G_w. Why? Harrod does not bother to tell us. Of course, since $G_w C_r = s$, an increase in s must either raise G_w or C_r. By definition, it cannot raise C_r unless G_w rises. In other words, an increase in saving does not cause a rise in G_w, it is a rise in G_w, by definition. However, Harrod's general conclusion about the "virtue of saving" should surprise no one; it is a "good thing" in an "inflationary gap" economy, and a "bad thing" in a "deflationary gap" economy.

The causal relation between G_w and s is one of many problems that could have been made clearer by an elaboration of the central concept, G_w. The term "warranted rate of growth" is not a very happy one for what Harrod seems to have in mind. Nor is "the line of entrepreneurial contentment"[23] a very clear-cut definition of G_w. In his *Economic Journal* article, he defines G_w as "that rate of growth which if it occurs, will leave all parties satisfied that they have produced neither more nor less than the right amount"; it is the rate that "will put them in the frame of mind which will cause them to give such orders as will maintain the same rate of growth." Thus G_w is subjective, but not, apparently, *ex ante;* it is the rate of growth that makes entrepreneurs satisfied with what has happened, rather than a plan for the future.[24]

Although reference to the article makes Harrod's concept of G_w a bit clearer, it still does not tell us what Harrod thinks are the determinants of G_w; and what determines G_w is obviously all-important, for C_r depends on G_w; it is, indeed, defined in terms of G_w. G and C cannot be changed except as a result of entrepreneurial decisions, and these decisions depend on G_w. Thus what happens in Harrod's dynamic economy depends ultimately on G_w. Harrod nowhere presents an analysis of the determinants of G_w, but in the course of his discussion he does indicate the following relationships:

G_w varies (1) inversely with C_n (capital requirements); (2) directly with s (the average propensity to save); (3) inversely with the volume of public works; (4) inversely with the volume of investment, that is, independent of the current rate of growth, k; (5) directly with the rate of interest r (since k and C_r vary

[22] *Ibid.*, p. 88.

[23] *Ibid.*, p. 88.

[24] Harrod also explains in his article that he uses "the unprofessional term warranted instead of equilibrium," because the equilibrium is a "highly unstable one." Stable or unstable, the term "equilibrium" conveys more meaning than "warranted."

inversely with r, and s probably varies directly with r).

The first of these relationships is arithmetic. Given s, G_w must vary inversely with C_r, just as G varies inversely with C. There are no clues to entrepreneurial behavior here. The second relationship has already been discussed; it, too, seems to be a matter of definition rather than of business behavior. Relationships (3) and (4) really amount to the same thing. Public works are one kind of investment that need not depend solely on the current rate of growth of income and that may, therefore, be included in k. Since $G_w C_r = s - k$, by definition, any increase in k must, other things being equal, be accompanied by a reduction in G_w. The fifth relationship is a product of several others:

1. s varies directly with r, and since G_w varies directly with s, G_w varies directly with r.
2. k varies inversely with r, G_w varies inversely with k, and therefore, G_w varies directly with r.
3. C_r varies inversely with r, G_w varies inversely with C_r, and therefore, G_w varies directly with r.

The relationship between s and r is a true causal relationship; $s(r)$ is a savings function with psychological meaning: savings depend on the interest rate. The same is true of the $k(r)$ function, which is really the marginal efficiency of capital schedule: investment depends on the rate of interest. The $C_r(r)$ function is the period of investment, which also has meaningful content: as the interest rate falls, the capital-output ratio will be increased. But $G_w(r)$ has no meaning of its own whatsoever; given the other relationships, the dG_w/dr is given by definition. Thus not one of these G_w relationships is a truly causal one, with meaning in terms of entrepreneurial behavior.

Finally, Harrod adds two refinements. If d represents the fraction of income needed for capital involved in lengthening the production process ("deepening"), then $G_w C_r = s - d$. If inventions are capital saving, d is negative, and the equilibrium rate of growth is enhanced. Thus any tendency toward chronic underemployment resulting from $G_w > G_n$ will be aggravated by capital-saving inventions. Harrod thinks falling interest rates might tend to lengthen the period of production and so keep d positive. This is no place to reopen the Hayek-Knight-Shackle controversy, but it is at least doubtful whether any feasible reduction of interest rates would have a significant effect on production techniques, especially if inventions themselves are capital saving.

In his fourth chapter, "The Foreign Balance," Harrod points

out that when we move to an open economy, the appropriate equations are $GC = s - b$ and $G_w C_r = s - b$, where b is the foreign balance. The equation expresses what is already well known: in a country with chronic underemployment, $G_w > G_n$, a favorable balance of trade on goods and services account helps to reduce the deflationary gap—and conversely for countries with a chronic inflationary gap.

Harrod has little new to offer by way of long-run policy to fill a chronic deflationary gap. Wage policy, he thinks, would not be an effective instrument for this purpose. To alter trends, once-over reductions are useless; a year-by-year reduction in wages would not affect G_n directly (presumably it might ultimately affect population growth or trends in labor productivity) and would be more likely to raise than to lower G_w, by raising "the goods value of money." [25] It might be added that very few governments indeed would dare, or wish to, attempt such a policy even if it would work.

Harrod is doubtful about the expediency of income redistribution as a means of reducing the propensity to save. For one thing, if the number of rich people able to save declines, corporate saving may increase. More important in Harrod's view, is "that there are deep laws relating the distribution of power (money is power) to the stability of a political organism." [26] There remains the possibility of a declining interest rate; but "we must face the possibility that neither deepening nor saving will react sufficiently to a falling interest rate." [27] We must also face the possibility, Harrod thinks, that the "euthanasia of the *rentier*" would result in a deterioration of the quality of our civilization. The *rentier* class is an independent class, the class from which much of science and culture and most of our "modes of decent living" have been derived. "We wish a general levelling up, not a levelling down. If . . . we no longer have an established mode of life that is graceful and charming and delightful, then we take the salt out of socialist hopes." [28]

Yet reduction and ultimate abolition of interest is the only real solution for chronic underemployment that Harrod offers. For if government debt contracted to sustain purchasing power is interest-free, then we need no longer be concerned about a cyclical balancing of the budget; we can fill the long-run deflationary

[25] Harrod, *op. cit.*, p. 93.
[26] *Ibid.*, p. 131.
[27] *Ibid.*, p. 144.
[28] *Ibid.*, p. 150.

gap by deficit-financed government spending. Thus Harrod leaves us with a dilemma; the policies needed to maintain a high level of income and employment in a mature economy may prevent us from enjoying to the full the high level of civilization and culture which are the natural fruits of a mature society.

Application to Underdeveloped Areas

Harrod himself did not apply his system to the problems of underdeveloped countries, but that fact should not prevent us from doing so.

Since it is some time since we have referred to his "fundamental equations," let us recall what they are. First, by definition, the actual rate of growth (G in Harrod's symbols, $\Delta Y/Y$ in ours) multiplied by the relevant incremental capital-output ratio (C or $I/\Delta Y$) gives capital requirements for the actual rate of growth. This rate of capital accumulation must be equal to the actual *ex post* ratio of savings to income (s or S/Y). Hence the first equation:

$$GC = s \tag{1}$$

For growth to be steady, however, the actual rate of growth must be equal to the "warranted rate of growth," G_w, which leaves entrepreneurs content with what is going on. By the same token, the actual rate of capital accumulation must just meet the capital requirements for the warranted rate of growth C_r. In that event, of course, the rate of capital accumulation that keeps entrepreneurs happy will also equal the rate of saving, producing dynamic equilibrium or steady growth. Thus under conditions of steady growth,

$$G_w C_r = s \tag{2}$$

and so, of course, $G_w C_r = GC$.

Now nothing in these equations assures us that the line of "steady growth" is the trend of gross national income with full employment and no inflation. Perhaps entrepreneurs will be content with a rate of investment and increase in national income involving chronic or even increasing unemployment, or a steadily rising price level. Intuition may tell us that they will not, but we cannot be sure until we have studied the question carefully. The trend of gross national income or production with full employment and no inflation is what Harrod calls—unfortunately—the natural rate of growth, G_n; what we would prefer to call the potential rate of growth. It will depend on the rate of population growth, the rate of resource discovery, the rate of technological progress, and on the rate of capital accumulation (which in the long run depends a good deal on the other growth factors). So we have the third fundamental equation,

$$G_nC_r =, \neq s \tag{3}$$

That is, the rate of capital accumulation needed to finance the natural rate of growth may or may not be equal to the actual rate of saving—even in dynamic equilibrium.

Let us consider first a truly stagnant underdeveloped economy. High birth rates are offset by equally high death rates, there is no technological progress and no resource discovery, no capital accumulation, and no net savings. Such an economy is not an absurd abstraction from reality; in Africa one can find cases closely approximating these conditions—or could at the end of World War II. Will the economy suffer from chronic inflation? The answer is no; it will not suffer from anything but poverty, and it will not enjoy much either. For in this case the natural rate of growth is zero, and so, whatever the incremental capital-output ratio, capital requirements are also zero. Thus,

$$G_nC_r = s = 0 \quad \text{and since there is no growth} \quad GC = 0$$

We must also have under these conditions $G_wC_r = 0$. For if, for example, G_wC_r were positive—meaning that only a positive rate of growth would keep entrepreneurs content—either s is also positive and growth is actually taking place, or stagnation does not represent an equilibrium position. The actual rate of growth, G, would be less than the warranted rate, G_w, and the actual (zero) rate of capital accumulation would still be too much to suit entrepreneurs. Capital accumulation would fall below zero, the rate of growth would become negative (income would fall) making entrepreneurs still more unhappy, and so on. Thus in our model stagnation represents "steady growth" at a zero rate, or dynamic equilibrium.

Now let us suppose that some *ex post* saving is taking place, with nothing else changed. We now have $GC = s > 0$; if it is to continue G_nC_r is also positive. But G_nC_r is still zero. How can savings and investment take place? The answer is, through chronic inflation. And if the rate of inflation is just sufficient to keep entrepreneurs content, it can go on indefinitely. Of course, a steady rate of inflation is a phenomenon almost unheard of in history; at some point, it tends to become cumulative. When it does, G will exceed G_w and C will be below C_r, so that still more investment will take place and hyperinflation will set in. All we can say is that an economy with no long-run growth factors to encourage savings and investment is unlikely to have them.

Next, let us introduce population growth, but let us still assume that there is no resource discovery and no technological progress. This model would also approximate certain underdeveloped countries of the real world. Now in such countries population growth is not a stimulus to investment, for reasons that will become clearer in Part 3. There is already a superabundance of unskilled labor, and mere population growth does not permit further capital accumulation without diminishing returns to capital. Nor does population growth raise effective demand, since the increased population merely shares the existing income. Under these conditions, the introduction of population growth has no effect on the actual rate of growth, and no very clear effect on the warranted rate of growth. It looks as though we will still have

$$GC = G_w C_r = s = 0$$

But now the natural rate of growth is positive; if the increased population were employed, output would increase. $G_n C_r > 0$. Thus under these conditions we have stagnation in income, output, and prices, with growing unemployment and falling per capita income.

Let us be a little more kind to our suffering economy, and suppose that prices of its exports rise. In the Harrod equations, this will mean an increase in G, and G will now exceed G_w. Consequently, C_r will exceed C, and investment will increase. Investment will raise G further and encourage still more investment. Unless all this investment is financed by savings from the beginning, or unless it puts to work men and resources which were previously unemployed—both rather unlikely events—the result will be cumulative inflation. We have not helped our economy much after all.

Let us try something else. We will launch a development plan, undertaking some public investment projects, encouraging exploration to raise the rate of resource discovery, and arranging for technical assistance to raise the rate of technological progress. In so doing we ought to stimulate some autonomous private investment as well, provided we have a few Schumpeterian entrepreneurs around. Now all this autonomous investment, public and private, is lumped together by Harrod in his innocent-looking little k. We now have, in dynamic equilibrium,

$$GC = G_w C_r = s - k$$

We have presumably raised G_n, if our plan is successful. But we are still not sure about G, at least in the short run. Suppose the entire development program, public and private, is financed by an increase in saving, so that $s - k$ just equals our previous s. In that case G need not rise; the increased investment is just offset by reduced consumption. In this case there is no particular reason why anything should happen until the new investment bears fruit. What happens then does not show directly in Harrod's equations; for the immediate effect will be a fall in prices just offsetting the increased flow of goods with the flow of money income unchanged. What happens to the all-important warranted rate of growth?

It may fall at the outset. Remember that only induced investment is covered in the left-hand side of Harrod's equations. So if Schumpeter is right, and successful innovation leads to a "cluster of followers" quite apart from what happens to current sales, it means that entrepreneurs regard the current rate of growth as enough, under the changed conditions, to warrant increased investment. Of course, the increased investment will raise G still further above G_w; we will have a boom on our hands, probably an inflationary one at that, since it is unlikely that *ex ante* savings will keep pace with investment throughout the expansion process. When the investment projects mature and new goods are thrown on the market, the rate of increase in money income is likely to slow down; G_w will then exceed G, investment will fall, and we shall have a slump. Thus we end up with a Schumpeterian cycle translated into Harrod's terms.

A second possibility is that G_w remains unchanged. In this case we shall have no initial boom—since G is unchanged—but only the slump when the increased output hits the market. It is unlikely, however, that execution of the development plan will have no secondary effects whatever, and we need not take this case too seriously.

A third possibility, also rather unlikely, is that G_w will rise. If the development program consists mainly of public enterprise and involves a great deal of intervention in the conduct of private enterprise, entrepreneurs may feel that only an increase in the rate of growth would warrant continued investment at current rates. In this case—since G does not rise immediately on our assumption that the whole program is financed by savings at the beginning—the slump comes immediately and becomes cumulative.

Now let us relax our rather artificial assumption that the whole development program is financed by savings at the outset, and let us suppose that the government engages in deficit financing and that some of the private investment is financed by credit.

In this case G, the actual rate of growth, will rise. At the same time C, the actual rate of induced investment, will fall; that is, scarce resources will be bid away from the induced investment sector to the autonomous investment sector, denoted by k. On the reasoning of the earlier models, we can expect G_w to fall: the development program should bring forth some "Schumpeterian" investment, not related to current rates of growth of output. Thus G_w will exceed G, C_r will be greater than C—and inflation will set in.

This application of the Harrod analysis to the conditions of underdeveloped countries does not demonstrate the absolute inevitability of "chronic" inflation in such countries. It does *not* show that in the absence of positive policies to prevent it, prices must always have an upward trend. Indeed, we have seen that under some conditions, which could easily arise in underdeveloped countries, there could even be cumulative deflation. More likely is just plain stagnation. But the analysis does suggest that underdeveloped countries are hypersensitive to forces causing inflation. Relatively small absolute changes in the rate of growth or capital accumulation can constitute big percentage changes, for the simple reason that *initial* rates of growth and capital accumulation are low. Divergence between actual and equilibrium rates of change can therefore arise easily, leading to cumulative movements away from equilibrium, at least until parameters change or until "ceilings" and "floors" are hit. In development-minded countries, these divergences are more likely to be on the inflationary than on the deflationary side.

Thus we see that Harrod's analytical framework can be applied to almost any situation that may exist. In a way, this flexibility is its weakness as well as its strength; his analysis is *too* general. What we badly need are facts, so that we could decide which model best fits the conditions of typical underdeveloped countries. Harrod's analysis does not provide many facts; indeed, it does not even provide us with functional (causal) relationships, which would at least tell us the direction in which other things change if, for example, the government undertakes a program of developmental investment or other changes in strategic variables occur.

Of his fundamental equation, $GC = s$, Harrod says, "I should like to think that it might serve as a target for frequent attack, like Fisher's famous truism, $MV = PT$." This is, in a way, a modest enough hope. Fisher's equation of exchange proved rather sterile; it isolated some important quantities for analysis, but told us nothing of the functional relationships among them or of the functional relationships determining their magnitudes. Some economists might even argue that until the significant *causal* relationships of Keynesian and neo-Keynesian economics were discovered, the Fisher equation did more harm than good, leading to overemphasis of the quantity theory of money. It seems likely that Harrod's hope will be fulfilled, and that his fundamental equations will be attacked on much the same grounds. They, too, merely isolate some significant quantities for analysis but fail to set forth the fundamental functional relationships among them and the causal relations that determine their magnitude.

7 Requirements for Steady Growth: Hansen

Few economic theories have aroused such a storm of protest, or have been so thoroughly and so widely misunderstood, as Alvin Hansen's theory of "economic maturity" or "secular stagnation." The reason is not far to seek; because of the time at which this theory was developed, it was subject to all the passions aroused by the Great Depression and the New Deal. To the more staunch advocates of the free private enterprise economy, the stagnation thesis seemed to offer more serious challenge to the efficiency of that system than the business cycles theories of the 1920's and early 1930's, which regarded economic fluctuations as mere "lapses from full employment" and inflationary booms. These theories suggested that fluctuations were largely the result of misbehavior of the banking system and subject to control by monetary policy. The Hansen thesis went further. It maintained that, in the absence of appropriate monetary and fiscal policy, advanced capitalist countries are subject to chronic and increasing underemployment. It called for government intervention of a more continuous nature than did the prevailing concept of business cycles. Thus it raised more serious doubts as to the efficiency of private enterprise under conditions of laissez faire.

Moreover, because the thesis was advanced during the second Roosevelt administration, at a time when Professor Hansen himself was a high-ranking "brain truster," the theory became linked in the minds of the public with "New Deal economics" in general.

The intensity of political feeling aroused by the New Deal was transferred in some measure to the stagnation thesis. When George Terborgh wrote a counterattack in popular vein, it was declared a "must" for businessmen's reading by the National Association of Manufacturers, was summarized in *Fortune*, was enthusiastically reviewed in *The New York Times* and elsewhere, and was hailed in some quarters as an effective debunking of all that is lumped together as "New Deal economics." [1]

Terborgh labeled those who accepted the Hansen thesis "stagnationists" and "professional pessimists." As we shall see, however, the Hansen theory of economic development is actually the most optimistic of those discussed in this book. The Classical school believed that capitalist development would end in stagnation. Marx and Schumpeter thought that it would end in complete breakdown. The import of Harrod's theory is that maintaining full employment without inflation is extremely difficult in a capitalist society, and that cumulative movements away from equilibrium are always around the corner. Hansen, in contrast, presented the bright vision of a stable yet growing capitalist economy and argued only that the achievement of such an economy required appropriate monetary and fiscal policies.

In the light of the Harrod-Domar analysis, perhaps Hansen's picture was *too* optimistic; that is another matter. But when Hansen was writing, the "new era" psychology had not yet been forgotten; there were still people who felt that the "natural" thing was steady growth with full employment, and to these people Hansen's writing seemed a serious challenge. Thus Shields and Woodward, writing as recently as 1945, insisted that "the general condition over the years was one of prosperity interrupted infrequently by brief periods of adjustment." [2]

Now that twenty years have passed and the policies Hansen recommended have been adopted by most countries in the Western world, one should be able to review his theories more dispassionately than was possible when they were first presented. We shall devote this chapter to such a review; and in addition to considering once again the implications of the theory for advanced countries, we shall endeavor to apply it to the problems of underdeveloped countries as well.

[1] George Terborgh, *The Bogey of Economic Maturity* (Chicago, 1945).

[2] Murray Shields and Donald B. Woodward, *Prosperity, We Can Have It If We Want It* (New York, 1945), p. 112.

The Essence of the Theory

The main contributions of the Hansen thesis to a general theory of economic development are as follows:

1. Providing a more complete theory of autonomous (long-run) investment.

2. Recognition that chronic and growing gaps between potential gross national product (with constant prices) and actual gross national product can arise from acceleration or deceleration of the growth rates of basic factors influencing autonomous investment.

3. Putting empirical content into his model by applying it to a particular country at a particular time.

Let us consider these contributions in that order. We shall first present the bare bones of this theory in the form of simple equations and then go on to consider the causal relations implied in those equations.

Let us write $O_a = k \cdot I_a$, where O_a stands for actual output (gross national product or income at constant prices), I_a for total net investment, and k for the Keynesian multiplier. Dividing investment into its major components and spelling out the multiplier formula, we have:

$$O_a = \frac{1}{dS/dO_a + d\tau/dO_a} \cdot \left[I_i(\dot{O}_a) + I_g + I_A(\dot{L}, \dot{K}, \dot{T}) \right] \quad (1)$$

Here S is saving; τ is taxes; $\dot{O}_a$ is dO_a/dt, or the variation in gross national income through time; I_i is induced investment; I_g is government investment; I_A is autonomous investment; $\dot{L}$ is dL/dt, the rate of population growth; $\dot{K}$ is dK/dt, the rate of resource discovery; and $\dot{T}$ is dT/dt, the rate of technological progress.

Using O_p for potential output (gross national product at full employment) we have also

$$O_p = f(L, K, Q, T) \quad (2)$$

This equation expresses the now familiar production function that has appeared in most of the systems outlined above, except that here L, K, Q, and T stand for the supplies of labor, resources, capital equipment, and technology available, rather than the amounts actually used in production.

We want now to express these two sets of relationships in terms of variations through time. To keep the equations simple, let us assume that both the marginal propensity to save and the marginal propensity to pay taxes are constant through time, in the absence of deliberate government actions to change them. Using $\dot{G}$ for the combined "growth effects" on autonomous investment of population growth, resource discovery, and technological progress,

$$\frac{dO_a}{dt} = \frac{1}{dS/dY + d\tau/dY} \cdot \frac{\delta I_i}{\delta O_a} \cdot \frac{d^2O_a}{dt^2} + \frac{dI_g}{dt} = \frac{\delta I_a}{\delta G} \cdot \frac{d^2G}{dt^2} \quad (1a)$$

Thus the trend of actual gross national product through time will depend partly on the marginal propensity to save and the marginal propensity to pay taxes—the higher either of these, the lower the rate of economic growth, other things being equal. It will also depend partly on the level of induced investment, but induced investment varies in turn with the rate of increase in national income. If national income is constant, induced investment will not appear at all; and if the rate of growth of national income is constant, induced investment will remain at a constant level. Thus induced investment comes into the picture only as an aggravating or amplifying force when something else happens. The volume of government investment, of course, is a matter of policy decision. As we have set up the model, the really dynamic factor is autonomous investment, which depends on the rate of population growth, the rate of resource discovery, and the rate of technological progress. If the combined effects of these are constant, autonomous investment will be constant. If then government investment is also constant, gross national product will rise at a constant rate and induced investment will also be constant.

The rate of increase of potential output through time will be,

$$\frac{dO_p}{dt} = \frac{\delta f}{\delta L} \cdot \frac{dL}{dt} + \frac{\delta f}{\delta dK} \cdot \frac{dK}{dt} + \frac{\delta f}{\delta Q} \cdot \frac{dQ}{dt} + \frac{\delta f}{\delta T} \cdot \frac{dT}{dt} \quad (2a)$$

That is, the growth of potential output will depend only on the rates at which the size of the labor force, the supply of known resources, the stock of capital, and the level of technique rise.

Now let us postulate the conditions which Hansen argued characterized the American economy in the 1920's and 1930's: population growth tapered off; the frontier disappeared and the rate of resource discovery slowed down, while the rate of technological progress remained more or less unchanged. Under these conditions, the combined effect of the growth factors, $\dot{G}$, must fall; in Equation (1a), d^2G/dt^2 becomes negative. With government investment, I_g, constant (and even falling after 1929), the actual level of gross national product must fall; and once that happens, induced investment, I_i, becomes negative as well, aggravating the downswing. Meanwhile, however, the labor force, the supply of known resources, the level of technique continued to rise. Even the stock of capital rose, except in the very worst years of the Depression; net investment fell from 1929 to 1933, but was positive in most interwar years. Thus *potential* output continued to rise throughout the whole period. The result was a growing gap between actual and potential gross national product, which appeared in the form of increasing unemployment and excess capacity after 1929.

It should be noted that in Hansen's view only the drop in induced investment was an ordinary cyclical phenomenon. The drop in autonomous investment was a secular affair, a reaction to much longer-run trends. Whether Hansen thought of the interwar years as the trough of a Kondratieff wave, as Schumpeter did, or something longer-run still, is not altogether clear; some of his writing suggests the former, some the latter.[3] The question of the duration of the tendency toward increasing underemployment, of course, rests on the duration of basic causal factors, viz., the declining rate of population growth and the declining rate of resource discovery. We shall return to these questions of fact below.

Meanwhile, let us note that the major policy implications of the Hansen thesis are already apparent from our two simple equations. The government can do three things to offset the tendency for private investment to fall, and thus for national income to drop and unemployment to appear: it can increase public investment; it can reduce taxes, thus raising the multiplier; or it can redistribute income from savers to spenders, thus reducing the marginal propensity to save and raising the multiplier in that way. A complete policy for maintenance of steady growth might involve a judicious admixture of all three of these measures.

Aggravating Factors: Capital-saving Innovations

In our efforts to keep the equations simple, we temporarily ignored some of the components of the Hansen thesis, concen-

[3] His Presidential Address to the American Economic Association (*American Economic Review*, Supplement, March, 1939) and his *Full Recovery or Stagnation* (New York, 1938) suggest the latter thesis; his *Fiscal Policy and Business Cycles* (New York, 1941) the former one. Hansen's stagnation theory is largely an oral tradition, and it is the present writer's view that Hansen was thinking of trends even longer than the long wave.

trating on its essential features. For example, we have treated the parameter I_A as though it were constant through time; that is, we have assumed implicitly that a given rate of population growth, resource discovery, and technological progress would always bring forth the same level of autonomous investment. The response of autonomous investment to the growth factors might itself vary through time, however, and Hansen argued that it does. There is a tendency, he maintained, for innovations to become increasingly capital saving as time goes by. If so, the response of investment to technological progress becomes weaker and weaker; in terms of Equation (1a), $\delta I_A/\delta \dot{T}$ is itself falling through time. This factor in itself would tend to produce a falling level of (money) income, and so unemployment, if everything else, including the savings function, remained unchanged.

Thus far, we have slurred over the distinction between money income and real income. If money income is Y and the price level is P, then $Y = PO_a$ and $P = Y/O_a$. Once we have made this distinction, we must replace the left-hand side O_a with Y in Equation (1), for what the factors in that equation determine is the money income generated. We must also use Y instead of O_a in the multiplier formula. The question then arises as to whether or not we should also replace $\dot{O}_a$ with $\dot{Y}$ as the determinant of induced investment. If entrepreneurs are subject to the "money illusion," and tend to think that things are getting better when their money profits rise even if the purchasing power of their profits does not increase, we probably should. If there is a significant lag of costs behind prices, so that even real profits rise with expansion of money incomes, we certainly must replace $\dot{O}_a$ with $\dot{Y}$. With this change, a tendency toward capital-saving innovation becomes a retarding factor in economic growth in another way; for it means that the capital-output ratio falls through time. A given level of investment, while generating the same amount of money income as before, produces a bigger increase in output than before. Thus there is chronic pressure on the price level (other things being equal) and a constant level of autonomous investment will be associated with ever lower levels of induced investment.

The "Great New Industries" Argument

Hansen also suggested that recent trends in the nature of technological progress weaken the response of investment to a given rate of technological progress. In the nineteenth century, he pointed out, innovations took the form of "great new industries," such as railroads, iron and steel, electricity, and the automobile. These innovations transformed not only economic organization but also daily life, leading to large-scale supplementary investment in related fields: new cities and towns, suburbs, cinemas, rural electrification, roads and highways, etc. In Schumpeter's terms, innovations of this type, especially in energy and transport, bring forth particularly large "clusters of followers." In the twentieth century, on the other hand, innovations have consisted more in improved techniques for producing the same final products, or of new and improved consumer durables such as radio, television, air-conditioning, etc. These innovations do not bring forth the same volume of secondary investment that "great new industries" do and they bring a high rate of obsolescence into the field of capital equipment, making higher prospective rates of return necessary if investment is to take place.

We might note in passing two related trends which might weaken the response of investment to technological progress. Domar has suggested that the growth of monopoly and institutionalization of research has retarded innovation.[4] In other words, with a given rate of scientific progress, or a given flow of inventions, the rate of introduction of new techniques, or innovation, is slowed down by monopolistic control over research and its application. Obsolescence has become a major threat to the profitability of enterprise, and monopolists tend to delay introduction of new techniques in order to earn additional returns on past investment, unless total costs with the new technique are lower than operating costs with the old ones. With pure competition and freedom of entry, new firms would introduce the new techniques if total costs with them were lower than total costs, including overhead, with the old ones. Second, if Schumpeter is right about the deterioration of the social climate for entrepreneurship, a given rate of scientific progress (or of resource discovery) would bring forth a smaller volume of investment as an economy matures.

Aggravating Factors: The Loss of the "Frontier Spirit"

Although not spelled out or put into systematic form, Hansen's writings suggest another and more intriguing idea about the effect of "the closing of the frontier": the disappearance of the frontier

[4] Evsey D. Domar, "Investment, Losses and Monopolies," in *Income, Employment, and Public Policy: Essays in Honor of Alvin Hansen* (New York, 1948).

is not just a matter of the tapering off of the rate of resource discovery; it also weakens the spirit of adventure in the field of business. The possibility of "going West, young man" to areas where the soil was fertile and mineral resources abundant, kept alive a venturesome entrepreneurial spirit throughout the century and a half of this country's most rapid expansion. The many cases of successful enterprises growing up with frontier communities gave rise to the "log cabin to riches" folklore of the United States and encouraged a generally optimistic attitude toward new commercial, industrial, and agricultural ventures. In the twentieth century, such opportunities for watching a new business grow with a frontier community were disappearing, and "young men" became more cautious in their attitude toward risk-taking. In terms of our equations, then, the "disappearance of the frontier" would show up not only as a drop in $\dot{K}$ (the rate of discovery of new resources), but also as a drop in the parameters $dI_a/d\dot{K}$, and $dI_a/d\dot{T}$, and $dI_a/d\dot{L}$—that is, as a weakening of the response to given rates of resource discovery, technological progress, and population growth.

A Rising Propensity to Save?

As we have seen above, it is not necessary for the propensity to save to rise in order for the Hansen thesis to hold. It is only necessary for *ex ante* (planned) savings to continue rising with income, while at some point, investment drops because of the weakening of long-run growth forces. It is equally clear, however, that the tendency toward increasing underemployment will be stronger if *in addition* there is a secular trend toward a higher ratio of savings to income. Hansen has suggested that such a trend does in fact exist because of the increased "institutionalization" of savings. Corporations have relied increasingly on self-finance, rather than distributing profits in dividends and then appealing to the capital market for the funds needed for expansion. At the same time, increasing shares of personal savings have taken the form of such contractual obligations as insurance premiums, contributions to pension funds, and the like. One result is that the share of total income saved tends to rise through time. Another is that savings are less responsive to short-run fluctuations in income than they were when most savings were generated by periodic decisions of individuals not to spend all their current income.

Yet Hansen has also pointed out an "upward drift in the propensity to consume" in the United States national income data for the interwar period. How could the share of income saved rise if the share spent for consumption rose through the same period? The answer is that the two statements refer to quite different concepts. The contention that there is a tendency toward a rising propensity to save refers to the long-run *ex ante* savings function. This function shows how savings and consumption would change if income rose steadily but nothing else changed. In Figure 7-1, the long-run consumption function at time 1 is $C(Y)_t$. Some years later, this function has fallen to $C(Y)_{t+n}$, reflecting the rise in the long-run *ex ante* savings function with the "institutionalization" of saving. The amount of (actual or realized) *ex post* saving and consumption, however, depends not only on *ex ante* saving and consumption plans but also on the actual level of investment (public and private). The two together will determine the *actual* level of national income, and thus the *actual* level of savings and consumption. Moreover, the level of actual current consumption depends not only on current income, but also on the level of income reached in the last cyclical peak. When incomes rise, standards of living are adjusted to a higher level, after a lag; when incomes drop, an effort is made for some time to maintain these new standards of living. Thus when incomes fall, savings are squeezed out; the more incomes that fall, the more savings are squeezed out. The extent to which savings are squeezed out is reduced by the inflexibility introduced on the savings side by "institutionalization," but the *net* effect is still an increase in the ratio of consumption to income when income drops.

Now the period 1919–35, during which the "upward drift in the consumption function" manifested itself, was one of particularly dramatic fluctuations in income. There were sharp drops in income between 1920 and 1922, between 1929 and 1933, and between 1937 and 1938. Thus this period was one in which the "squeezing out of savings" took place with a vengeance. The result is that the *data* of consumption and income—which by definition are *ex post* or realized positions—record the "upward drift," despite the *downward* drift of the long-run *ex ante* consumption function. In terms of Figure 7-1, the short-run consumption functions (dotted lines) shift in such a way that, in conjunction with the actual fluctuations in income, they yield a scatter-diagram of consumption-income points that can be fitted by the straight line $C(Y)_s$, the statistical long-run consumption function. This curve actually lies above the initial long-run consumption function $C(Y)_t$. Thus the "upward drift in the consumption function" is the *result* of the particular depth and duration of the Great Depression, resulting partly from a rising trend in the *ex ante* propensity to save! This part of the Hansen thesis is thus an application to the theory of trend of a proposi-

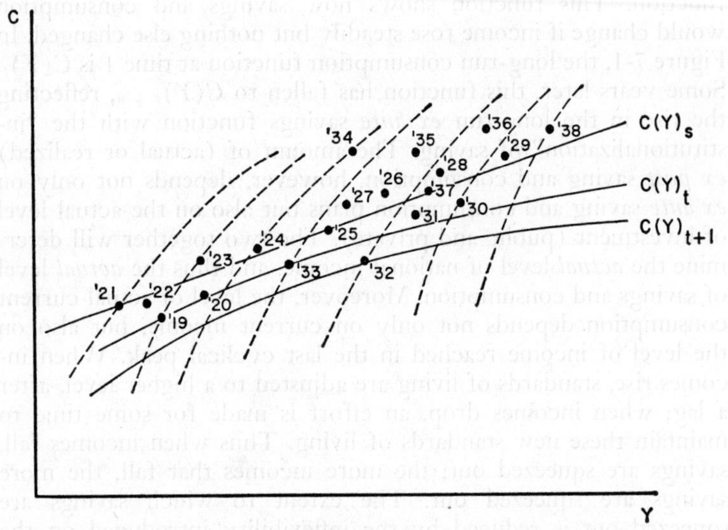

Figure 7-1

tion now generally accepted with respect to economic fluctuations: the *effort* to save more, unless offset by higher investment, will result in the society's *actually* saving less.

Logical Validity of the Hansen Thesis

If the relationships postulated by Hansen exist, and if the variables have behaved as he says they have, there can of course be no question that his thesis of "increasing underemployment" in underdeveloped countries is right. If government policy were "neutral" the pattern of economic development would look like that in Figure 7-2. Once the long-run rate of economic growth generated by autonomous investment begins to taper off, economic fluctuations will take place around a trend of actual gross national product that falls farther and farther below the trend of potential (full employment) gross national product.

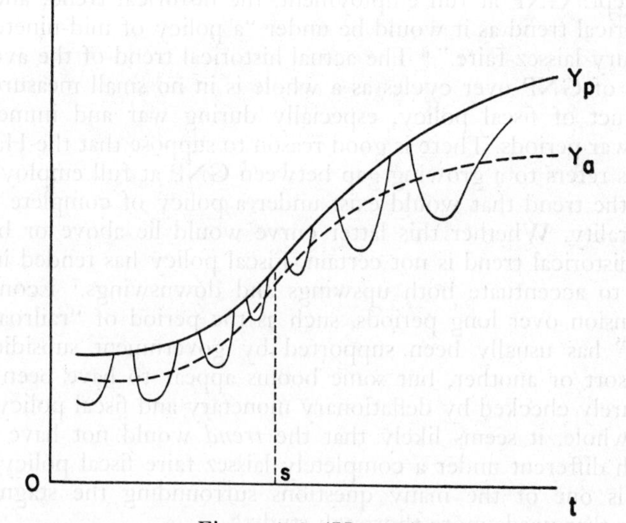

Figure 7-2 (Hansen)

In this diagram the curve Y_p is the trend of "potential income," that is, the trend of national income at full employment and with constant prices. The curve Y_a is the trend of actual gross national income at constant prices, around which economic fluctuations take placc, as indicated by the dotted lines.[5]

[5] As indicated in my note on "The Concept of Secular Stagnation" (*American Economic Review*, March, 1950), "the trend of national income at full employment without inflation" is by no means simple idea: "'Inflation' in this context cannot mean any rise in the general price level; it must mean a rise that takes place (or continues) *after* full employment is reached. Such a definition of 'inflation' is clear enough, but hides certain difficulties. If the points on the Y_p curve represent the levels of gross national income at which full employment is reached in the upswing, the only relevant points on the trend curve are those which lie on cyclical upswings; when national income goes through the trend curve in a downswing, full employment will not prevail. If the Y_p curve is defined as the trend of gross national income at full employment, with prices just high enough to yield full employment, the question arises as to just how high that would be. It is possible—perhaps even likely—that if full employment is reached when prices are rising, only a continually rising price level would maintain full employment. On the other hand, if full employment is reached after a period of fairly stable prices, as in 1929, it is conceivable that full employment could be maintained with a price level falling as techniques improve.

"The first interpretation is, I think, what most economists mean when they speak of 'full employment without inflation' as a goal of economic

Strictly speaking, there are three trend curves in Hansen's concept: GNP at full employment, the historical trend, and the historical trend as it would be under "a policy of mid-nineteenth century laissez-faire." [6] The actual historical trend of the average level of GNP over cycles as a whole is in no small measure the product of fiscal policy, especially during war and immediate postwar periods. There is good reason to suppose that the Hansen thesis refers to a growing gap between GNP at full employment and the trend that would exist under a policy of complete fiscal neutrality. Whether this latter curve would lie above or below the historical trend is not certain. Fiscal policy has tended in the past to accentuate both upswings and downswings.[7] Economic expansion over long periods, such as the period of "railroadization," has usually been supported by government subsidies of one sort or another, but some booms appear to have been prematurely checked by deflationary monetary and fiscal policy. On the whole, it seems likely that the *trend* would not have been much different under a completely laissez faire fiscal policy; but this is one of the many questions surrounding the stagnation thesis that needs more thorough study.[8]

Hansen has little to say about the trend of national income at full employment. His thesis would be quite compatible with an increasing, constant, or declining rate of growth of potential national income, provided the gap was present and growing. No doubt the implication in his discussion is that the rate of growth

---

policy. If the war had ended just when full employment was reached late in 1941, the goal would have been to maintain full employment without a further rise in the general price level. Few economists indeed would oppose a limited price rise during an approach to full employment from a position of unemployment, if the price rise could be checked as soon as full employment was reached. The present situation is more complicated; what does full employment 'without inflation' mean today? It doesn't mean reducing prices to the 1941 level while maintaining full employment, although most economists would probably favour some 'disinflation' if it did not threaten full employment. The main question is, presumably, whether the distortion of the price-cost structure during the *past* inflation can be more easily cured by reducing prices that are too high, or by raising incomes that are too low. "These ambiguities in the concept of 'full employment without inflation' are a strong argument for defining 'potential income' in real terms."

[6] Alvin Hansen, "Some Notes on Terborgh's *The Bogey of Economic Maturity*," *Review of Economic Statistics*, February, 1946, p. 13.

[7] Cf. Benjamin Higgins, *Public Investment and Full Employment* (Montreal, 1946), Part V.

[8] The nature of the underlying trend will affect the amplitude and duration of cycles, thus affecting in turn the statistical trend. See Benjamin Higgins, "Interaction of Cycles and Trends," *The Economic Journal*, December, 1955.

of potential, as well as actual, national income must eventually taper off. Indeed, no other hypothesis is reasonable. Given declining population growth and disappearing frontiers, it would take an ever-increasing rate of technological progress to keep the growth of national income at full employment from slowing down; and population and known supplies of mineral resources cannot be increased at a constant (percentage) rate indefinitely, if only because of purely spatial limitations.[9]

In order to distinguish the Hansen prognosis from those discussed above, we might translate the Classical, Marxist, and Schumpeterian views of capitalist development into a similar form. Although thinkers of the Classical school (particularly Malthus) were not unaware that unemployment might appear in a stagnant society, they were not primarily concerned with the gap between potential and actual income. For them, potential income itself would stagnate when both population growth and capital accumulation were choked off by the drop in profits and investment. Thus the Classical prognosis would look like Figure 7-3, which is simply one cross section of the three-dimensional Figure 3-2.

With Marx, until the downfall of capitalism through the revolution of the working classes, the picture of capitalist growth would be that of Figure 7-4. Here, too, a gap appears between the trend of potential gross national income and the trend of actual gross national income, but this gap is the product solely of increasing amplitude of cycles. Since national income in real terms cannot rise above the full employment level, increasing amplitude of fluctuations in real terms means increasingly severe downswings, which bring the trend of actual income farther and farther below the trend of potential national income.

Figure 7-6 is the Schumpeter version. The curve Y_a represents the trend of actual income at *current* prices, if the behavior of the system conforms to Schumpeter's "two-phase cycle," con-

[9] For a discussion of physical and technological limits to a constant rate of growth of national product, see M. King Hubbert, "Economic Transition and Its Human Consequences," *Advanced Management*, July–September, 1941, pp. 99, 100. He points out that for the percentage rate of increase in production from 1820 to 1910 (when the rate began to fall) to have been maintained, production in 1929 would have had to be 1.5 times its actual level, and in 1941 it would have had to be double its actual level; and he concludes "that any such exponential expansion . . . is a distinctly temporary state of affairs and that this phase must be followed by a long-time period of levelling off or decline." Any exponential expansion approaches infinite absolute growth at some point and is, therefore, an economic impossibility.

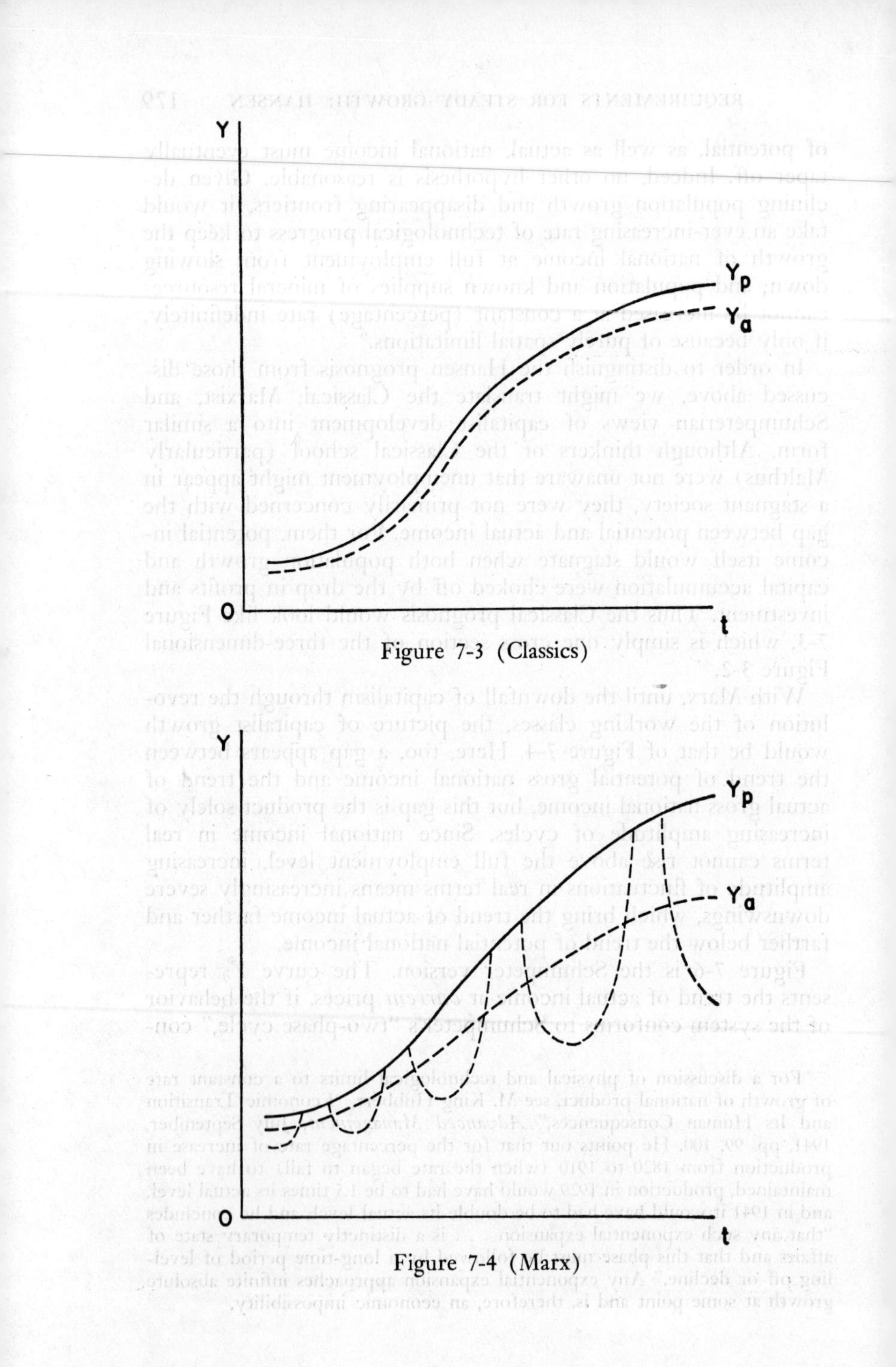

Figure 7-3 (Classics)

Figure 7-4 (Marx)

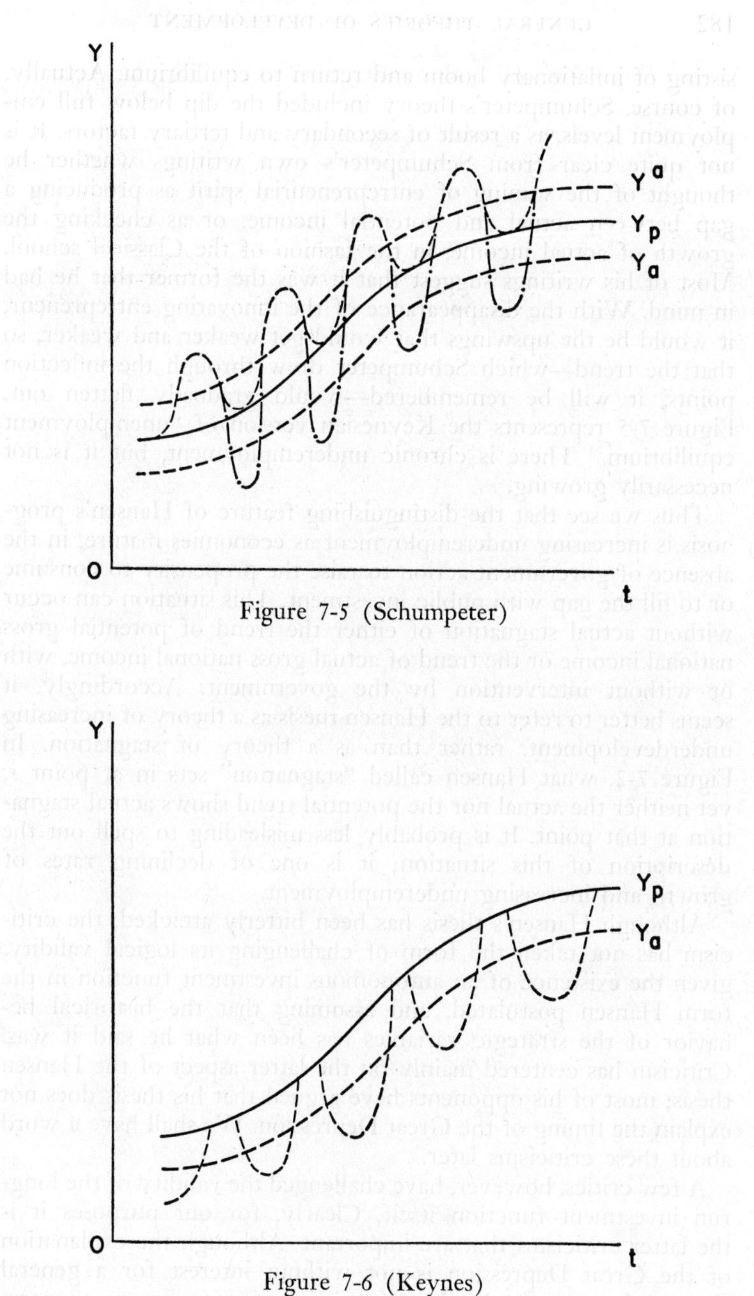

Figure 7-5 (Schumpeter)

Figure 7-6 (Keynes)

sisting of inflationary boom and return to equilibrium. Actually, of course, Schumpeter's theory included the dip below full employment levels, as a result of secondary and tertiary factors. It is not quite clear from Schumpeter's own writings whether he thought of the waning of entrepreneurial spirit as producing a gap between actual and potential income, or as checking the growth of actual income, in the fashion of the Classical school. Most of his writings suggest that it was the former that he had in mind. With the disappearance of the innovating entrepreneur, it would be the upswings that would get weaker and weaker, so that the trend—which Schumpeter drew through the inflection points, it will be remembered—would gradually flatten out. Figure 7-5 represents the Keynesian version of "unemployment equilibrium." There is chronic underemployment, but it is not necessarily growing.

Thus we see that the distinguishing feature of Hansen's prognosis is increasing underemployment as economies mature, in the absence of government action to raise the propensity to consume or to fill the gap with public investment. This situation can occur without actual stagnation of either the trend of potential gross national income or the trend of actual gross national income, with or without intervention by the government. Accordingly, it seems better to refer to the Hansen thesis as a theory of increasing underdevelopment, rather than as a theory of stagnation. In Figure 7-2, what Hansen called "stagnation" sets in at point *s*; yet neither the actual nor the potential trend shows actual stagnation at that point. It is probably less misleading to spell out the description of this situation; it is one of declining rates of growth and increasing underemployment.

Although Hansen's thesis has been bitterly attacked, the criticism has not taken the form of challenging its logical validity, given the existence of an autonomous investment function in the form Hansen postulated, and assuming that the historical behavior of the strategic variables has been what he said it was. Criticism has centered mainly on the latter aspect of the Hansen thesis; most of his opponents have argued that his thesis does not explain the timing of the Great Depression. We shall have a word about these criticisms later.

A few critics, however, have challenged the validity of the long-run investment function itself. Clearly, for our purposes it is the latter criticisms that are important. Although the explanation of the Great Depression is not without interest for a general theory of economic development, it is not our primary concern.

On the other hand, if Hansen's autonomous investment function holds good, it is an important tool of analysis of economic growth in advanced and underdeveloped countries alike. Accordingly, we turn now to an examination of the autonomous investment function.

The Autonomous Investment Function

As has been indicated in the earlier chapters, virtually all writers on economic development, from Adam Smith on, have recognized the importance of resource discovery and technological progress as factors in economic expansion. The Classical school regarded population growth as a drag on expansion, whereas Marx and Schumpeter tended to treat it as an exogenous factor. Thus of the components of Hansen's autonomous investment function, it is the relationship between long-run investment and population growth that is most original. Accordingly, let us begin our discussion of this function with the relationship between population growth and long-run investment.

Population growth affects investment in two main ways. First, a growing population provides a growing labor force. So long as population growth keeps pace with capital accumulation, the marginal productivity of capital will, in the absence of other influences, remain constant; but when population growth falls off, capital accumulation must also fall off, if, apart from other influences, the marginal productivity of capital is not to decline. Second, a growing population provides an increasing demand for goods and services. The correlation between long-run increases of population and of consumption is so high that one can be more or less substituted for the other; and consequently the "acceleration principle" argument, which states that a mere drop in the rate of increase in consumption may cause an absolute decline in investment, can be applied with minor modifications to population.

The early discussion of population growth and investment failed to distinguish adequately between percentage and absolute rates of growth; and although this confusion has now been largely eliminated[10] there is still insufficient clarification as to which is more important and as to which is relevant to what arguments. Speaking generally, the absolute rate of growth is the

[10] *Vide* Hans A. Adler, "Absolute or Relative Rate of Decline in Population Growth?" *Quarterly Journal of Economics,* August, 1945; and Alvin Hansen, "Some Notes on Terborgh . . . ," pp. 13–15.

more important concept, and a falling percentage rate of increase is significant mainly as a harbinger of a later drop in the absolute increase. So far as population as a source of labor is concerned, the percentage rate of increase is important only if it is necessary to maintain a certain percentage increase in quantity of capital in order to offset a given percentage increase in the volume of savings. However, this situation would be the real one to the extent that the volume of business saving in any year tends to equal a certain percentage of existing plant and equipment and, therefore, to rise at a cumulative rate. For the acceleration principle aspect of the argument, the absolute rate of increase is clearly more important.

Hansen's critics have not denied that in a country which starts its expansion with a scarcity of labor, population growth permits a more rapid rate of capital accumulation, without a drop in profits, than would be possible without population growth. The attack has concentrated more on the second part of the argument. Why must an increase in population carry with it an increasing effective demand for final products? What assurance is there that the increased numbers will be provided with additional income? Or conversely, if population growth is slowed down, why should not the rate of increase in per capita spending go up, so that the expansion of final demand remains the same?

Hansen's own argument was cast, not in terms of the effect of population growth on effective demand in general, but in terms of its effect on certain types of demand which seem particularly closely related to population growth:

> It is not difficult to see [he argues] that a country experiencing a rapid increase in population requires a vast capital outlay in order to provide housing, transportation and all the facilities necessary for modern methods of living such as municipal utilities and the like. The enormous capital outlays of the nineteenth century were, of course, in the first instance conditioned by new technological developments, but they were determined also by the vast growth of population.

Hansen estimates that during the nineteenth century, the growth of population accounted for nearly half the outlay of new capital.

The surface plausibility of the argument seems greater if one thinks of a relationship between population growth and housing, transportation facilities, public utilities, and the like, than if one thinks of demand for goods and services in general. Certainly investors in these fields do think a good deal in terms of levels of population and potential rates of population growth. Actually, the same questions arise here as in the case of goods and services in general. What assurance is there that greater numbers of people will have proportionally increased incomes to spend on housing, transport, and the like? Or conversely, if population growth tapers off, why should people not have bigger houses, better transport facilities, and improved public services?

There is, of course, the possibility that people will spend their incomes differently if population is growing rapidly than they will if it is growing slowly, and that the pattern of spending with high rates of population growth is more stimulating to investment than the pattern which accompanies a low rate of population growth. At one point, Hansen does put his argument in those terms: [11]

Now the rate of population growth must necessarily play an important role in determining the character of the output; in other words, the composition of the flow of final goods. Thus a rapidly growing population will demand a much larger per capita volume of new residential building construction than will a stationary population. A stationary population with its larger proportion of old people may perhaps demand more personal services; and the composition of consumer demand will have an important influence on the quantity of capital required. The demand for housing calls for large capital outlays, while the demand for personal services can be met without making large investment expenditures. It is therefore not unlikely that a shift from a rapidly growing population to a stationary or declining one may so alter the composition of the final flow of consumption goods that the ratio of capital to output as a whole will tend to decline.

We would seem to be on more solid ground when the argument is put in these terms, but two questions of fact remain. Is it true that, as family size diminishes and the proportion of older people in the population rises, the demand for housing, transport facilities, and the like goes down while the demand for services goes up? And is it true that the capital-output ratio is lower for services than for housing, public utilities, and the like?

Efforts to test this part of the Hansen thesis empirically have not been very successful. For one thing, the relationship between investment and population growth is hard to isolate. There is, of course, no question that population growth in the United States has been highly correlated with the growth of investment, consumer spending, and national income. If we take the Kuznets data

[11] Alvin H. Hansen, "Progress and Declining Population," *The American Economic Review*, Vol. XXIX, No. 1, Part I (March, 1939), p. 7.

of national income for overlapping decades, and correlate either the level of national income or consumer spending with the level of population, the correlation coefficient for the period 1870–1929 is above .99 in both cases. In the case of investment the correlation with population growth for the period 1870–1919 is again in the neighborhood of .99. Because of the sharp drop in net investment during the 1919–21 depression, and the complete collapse of net investment during the Great Depression of the thirties, the correlation is of course considerably less high if one takes the whole period from 1870–1933.

The difficulty with these figures, as a test of the Hansen argument regarding the relation of investment to population growth, is precisely that population growth does correlate so highly with so many other economic variables. In an economy expanding as rapidly and as steadily as the American one did between 1870 and 1929, high correlations among major aggregate variables are bound to arise. It is very hard to determine causal relationships from such statistical correlations.

The critics of the Hansen thesis have accordingly tried to test the role of population growth in investment in other ways. For example, Fellner [12] endeavors to test the population aspect of the Hansen thesis by examining the relationship of population growth to the consumption function. This approach is unsatisfactory on several counts. First, the Hansen argument regarding population growth is not dependent upon upward shifts of the consumption function—although of course any tendency for the average or marginal propensity to consume to rise with population would strengthen Hansen's argument. Second there is the usual difficulty in historical statistical analysis that the historical relationship between income and consumption is the product of many factors, of which population growth is only one. Third, as we have shown above, the apparent stability of the (marginal) propensity to consume over the long run does not preclude the possibility that the historical relationship is the product of upward shifts in the function. Finally, the "over-all historical consumption function" shows absolute increases in income greater than the absolute increases in consumption over most periods. That is, investment also grew, and the growth of population may have been responsible for the growth of investment, without which the whole historical consumption function would have been different. Indeed, Fellner's figure 16, based on the Kuznets data, actually shows a very close relation between population growth

[12] W. Fellner, *Monetary Policy and Full Employment* (Berkeley, Calif., 1946), Part II.

and capital formation. If the "abnormal" World War I period is left out, the scatter can be well fitted by a very steep curve that is convex downward, suggesting that investment rises more than proportionately to population. The curve is so steep, however, as to suggest that factors other than population growth were dominant in the expansion of investment.

George Terborgh endeavored to test this part of the Hansen theory by comparing rates of population growth and rates of increase in per capita output of various countries in various periods. Since he finds no evidence that countries with high rates of population growth have had a more rapid rise in per capita production than countries with slow population growth, he dismisses the Hansen thesis on these grounds. As any statistician knows, however, the absence of such correlation in historical cases proves nothing in regard to the lack or presence of causal relationships. The countries and periods he compares are so varied that they do not come even close to isolating the effects of population growth on per capita output from all the other factors which were operative. In any case, to test the Hansen thesis Terborgh should have correlated investment with population growth rather than per capita output. Terborgh recognizes this fact but says that we need not worry about what happens to investment so long as production increases. This may be valid, but it is quite irrelevant to the problem of designing empirical tests of the Hansen argument with respect to population growth.

The truth in Hansen's population theory would seem to be something as follows. In Europe during the Industrial Revolution, and in the United States from the very beginnings of European settlement until the present day, population was small relative to resources, and the labor force was limited relative to the demand for labor. Population was chronically below optimum, in the strict sense that per capita output could have been raised by a simple increase in the population and in the labor force. Under these conditions, and with resource discovery and technological progress contributing to the maintenance of high rates of investment, the growth of population was accompanied by higher incomes and higher spending. Moreover, given the "lumpiness" of capital and the need for production at some minimal scale for effective use of some improved techniques, the very growth of the economy with population growth permitted more rapid technological progress. For this reason, entrepreneurs came to associate population growth with an expanding market, particularly for such highly durable consumer goods as housing, transport facilities, and public utilities. Indeed, forecasts of population growth became a major consideration in determining the scale of investment in such fields. For this reason, investment has in fact been highly correlated with population growth in advanced countries, and no doubt will continue to be so for some time to come, unless and until it becomes apparent to entrepreneurs that the relationship between consumer spending in these fields and population growth has broken down.

Resource Discovery and the Frontier

Few people indeed would deny that resource discoveries provide opportunities for investment. Hansen, however, had something more in mind than the rate of resource discovery in a purely quantitative sense. He argued that resource discovery in the *special* form of opening up a geographic frontier has particularly stimulating effects on private investment.[13] If we are to test this thesis, either in terms of the relationship between investment and frontier development, or in terms of the timing of the "disappearance of the frontier," we need a concept of "geographic frontier" more precise than Hansen's "discovery and development of new territory and new resources."[14] Moreover, when is a territory "new"? When it is entirely unpopulated, or when population per square mile is below a certain figure, or when the inhabitants do not practice the most modern techniques, or when its natural resources are not completely known? The mere presence of "unoccupied territory"—that is, land upon which no one is employed[15]—clearly does not constitute a

[13] Adequate investment outlets are necessary to sustain full employment and a satisfactory income level. But investment outlets are more difficult to find in a non-expanding economy. We are living in a period which is, in several important respects, distinctly different from the nineteenth century. It was one thing to find adequate investment outlets in a century quite unique in the world's history—a century with vast, rich areas inviting occupation and large capital outlays on housing, manufacturing, and transportation equipment. In such an expanding economy, investment outlets were easy to find and indeed the main difficulty was a shortage of capital and manpower. Now all this has changed and we are confronted with an economy with no large, rich areas to be occupied anywhere in the entire globe (see Isaiah Bowman, ed., *Limits of Land Settlement*, New York, 1937) and with a practically stationary population in the industrial countries. Cf. Hansen, *op. cit.*

[14] American Co-ordinating Committee for International Studies, "A Report to the Tenth International Studies Conference," Paris, June 18–July 3, 1937.

[15] An alternative definition of "unoccupied" territory would be land for which no legal ownership has been established; but for economic analysis this definition seems less convenient, and Hansen himself has rejected it. "Some Notes on Terborgh . . . ," p. 15.

frontier in the economic sense, if it is worth no one's while to employ someone to do something with it or on it. Yet growth of population in one part of a country may at some stage make it worthwhile to exploit previously unoccupied territory. Similarly, an innovation may make some previously worthless resource highly useful (witness atomic energy and known but untouched uranium deposits) and so make it worthwhile to move people into a region formerly unoccupied. A reduction in transportation costs, or cheaper power, may also result in development of known resources formerly left idle. Development of new territory is clearly one of the incidental effects of population growth and of some kinds of innovation. A shift in demand may also open up new territory.

Many tenable concepts of "geographic frontier" suggest themselves; but it seems most useful to define a *geographic* frontier as an area within which there are increasing returns to both labor and capital with existing technical knowledge, population, and tastes. An area within which increasing returns would appear only with a change in techniques, population, or tastes might be called an *economic* frontier. Thus, "economic frontiers" become "geographic frontiers" as a result of dynamic changes. The frontier might be said to have "disappeared" when the point of diminishing average returns to labor and/or capital has been reached; and might be said to "begin disappearing" when the point of diminishing marginal returns to labor and/or capital has been reached.

As used in the Hansen thesis, however, the concept of "frontier" is a relative one. The existence of a "new" area into which labor and capital are being moved implies the existence of an "old" area from which labor and capital come; and the "opening up of a frontier" involves movement of labor and capital. Increasing returns to labor and capital is a necessary, but not a sufficient, condition for an area to be a geographic frontier; in the nineteenth century, England as well as America would have fulfilled this condition. For a region to constitute a geographic frontier, therefore, one of the following additional conditions must be present as well:

1. It may be an area where the most advanced *known* techniques are not utilized.
2. It may be an area where the marginal productivity of labor and/or capital is less high than in other countries, because the ratio of labor and/or capital to natural resources is lower than in other countries.

3. It may be an area capable of absorbing capital, population, and goods without an equal return flow to other countries, that is, a country able and willing to have an import surplus. (This condition may be a characteristic of all frontier economies, rather than a separate criterion.)

4. A frontier might be said to exist if migration of labor and capital into a "new" area will raise the marginal productivity of labor and capital in the "mature" economy, without raising it above the level in the "new" territory.

A less tangible factor which may nevertheless play some role is "frontier psychology." In economic terms, this factor would consist of a relatively low level of liquidity—and safety—preference, or a relatively high marginal efficiency of capital, for any given set of objective conditions.

These definitions also make it possible to distinguish the development of a frontier from mere migration of industry. If investment of labor and capital in the "new" area is accompanied by a decline in the amount of labor and capital utilized in the "old" area (either in a particular field or in the whole economy of the area), there has been a migration of industry (either in a particular field or in the whole economy). Migration of industry may nevertheless result in temporary increase in *current* investment in the "old" and "new" areas combined, because the fixed plant of the old area cannot be moved to the new one. When the movement into a "new" area results in a rise in the amount of labor and capital utilized in the "old" area, the increment constitutes the development of a frontier. Thus by definition, the opening of a frontier results in an increase in investment in the new and old economies combined.

The importance of the distinction between the geographic and economic frontiers as here defined can hardly be exaggerated. In countries where a geographic frontier exists, there is now, with present knowledge, techniques, and tastes, a supply of fertile agricultural land and mineral resources to be exploited. In terms of the production function, the existence of a geographic frontier has the same effects on the marginal efficiency of capital as population growth; that is, it keeps capital always relatively scarce, and returns on new investment relatively high. Neither industrial nor agricultural investment runs into a bottleneck with respect to natural resources. The existence of a geographic frontier also keeps labor scarce, even in agriculture, a factor of enormous import in the comparison of advanced with underdeveloped economies, as we shall see below. And this was the situation that existed in the United States from the beginning of European settlement until the late nineteenth century, if not later.

Quite different was the case of Europe in the nineteenth century, with the fertile soil already under cultivation, and with the mineral resources that were important with the then *existing* techniques already discovered. The Classical school was right to worry about diminishing returns to increased supplies of labor on the given supply of land; scarcity of foodstuffs and raw materials was truly a barrier to capital accumulation, which was broken only by the development of the New World and the expansion of world trade.

Quite different, too, is the case of countries like Indonesia. Many Indonesians are convinced that there are more natural resources to be discovered, but nobody knows where they are. Moreover, the present distribution of population reflects accurately the relative fertility of the soil. In the Philippines, too, past response to population pressure has been to bring more land under cultivation, so as to maintain customary ratios of labor to land with traditional techniques; but now the point is being reached where this sort of "widening" of capital in agriculture is no longer possible without resorting to inferior land. The "geographic frontier" is disappearing, leaving only a dubious "economic frontier," provided that techniques or tastes change, or something else happens.

In the United States, frontier development, as well as population growth, correlates highly with general economic expansion, whether measured in terms of investment or in terms of consumption or gross national product. In a generally growing economy such correlations are bound to appear. As an approximation to a quantitative measure of frontier development, we might use "westward movement" as shown by the centroid of population. When we plot the degree of west longitude of the centroid of population between 1790 and 1950 on the vertical axis and the year on the horizontal axis, we get an almost perfect growth curve. The inflection point occurs in 1850 at about 81 degrees west; "marginal westward movement," which we take as an approximation to "marginal rate of frontier development," reached its peak at that time. The "average rate of westward movement" or "average rate of frontier development" was at its height toward the end of the nineteenth century, with the centroid of population at about 88 degrees west longitude. Despite variations over time, both private investment and national income follow much the same growth pattern, when the "trend" is separated out from cyclical fluctuations.

In terms of westward movement, investment, and income, one other country would show much the same pattern of development: Canada, the country which has achieved the *second* highest level of *per capita* income. No other country enjoyed the continual presence of a geographic frontier throughout the century and a half of its most rapid growth.

In one respect, however, the American case is absolutely unique. For the westward movement does not tell the whole story of frontier development in the United States; there have been movements north and south from the center as well. Texas and the Pacific Northwest served as geographic frontiers after the westward movement of the centroid of population had virtually ceased. The relative stability of the centroid in this century does not reflect lack of population movement, but rather the diffusion of new resource development north and south, and even east and west, of this centroid. No other country can match the remarkable spread of urban growth throughout its entire area, in wave after successive wave, that has occurred in the United States. In Canada, urban development has been confined to a narrow strip within a few hundred miles of the United States border, and great cities are found only in Ontario and Quebec. Australian frontier development built no cities away from the coast. In Europe, the major cities have grown up side by side over several centuries; there has been no progressive opening up of new frontiers, followed by urban growth, such as has occurred in this country. The story of Chicago, Detroit, Kansas City, St. Louis, Dallas, Houston, and Los Angeles is a purely American story. It is surely not unreasonable to suppose that this continuous opening up of new areas and the concomitant urban growth has been a major factor, both in providing investment opportunities and in keeping alive the "log cabin to riches" folklore and the enterprising spirit that goes with it.[16]

The contrast between American and Australian frontier development is of particular interest. Dr. Carter Goodrich was among the first to recognize that the relative lack of venturesome entrepreneurship in Australia, and the accompanying relative stagna-

[16] For an account of the role of the frontier in American history, see Frederick Jackson Turner, *The Frontier in American History* (New York, 1920) and *The Significance of Sections in American History* (New York, 1932). For an analysis of Turner's and other frontier theories, see F. L. Paxson, *History of the American Frontier 1763–1893* (Boston, 1924). A brief review of these theories and an application to Australia can be found in Fred Alexander, *Moving Frontiers* (Melbourne, 1947).

tion after 1924, can be traced in part to the absence of a "poor man's frontier," of the kind that prevailed in Canada or the United States, and an accompanying absence of westward movement.[17] The acquisition of huge tracts of land by "rich squatters" created employment opportunities in the suburbs of Melbourne and Sydney, but not in the center of the country. Development of the center resulted in population growth on the fringe, not in the center. Clearly, it requires a different sort of attitude to set up a grocery in a suburb of Sydney than to move hundreds of miles to the westward and launch a new enterprise in a strange raw territory. Moreover, the opportunity to start a small business and watch it grow into a large one as the city grew around you was confined to a few coastal centers. The "log cabin to riches" legend had less meaning in Australia than in the United States.

But if a frontier in the Canadian or American sense was lacking in Australia, its absence is still more striking in the case of most underdeveloped areas. For centuries, such economic development as took place brought no obvious movement in the centroid of population. Nothing remotely resembling the westward movements in the United States and Canada, or even the movements from country areas to cities in nineteenth-century England, has taken place in most underdeveloped areas. Consequently, no "frontier spirit" is to be found in these countries.[18] Is it not possible that venturesome entrepreneurship, inculcated by generations of steady movement to new territories, may extend also to the frontiers of technology? May there not be a relationship between the lack of interest in movement to new territories and the lack of interest in the introduction of new techniques?

[17] Carter Goodrich, "The Australian and American Labor Movements," *The Economic Record*, November, 1928. For a generation after 1924 man-year productivity in Australia stagnated relative both to previous trends in Australia and in comparison with other young countries. The role of the "big man's frontier" in producing a mid-nineteenth century Australian society "in terms of a few flockmakers, bankers, and merchants, and a numerous peon class," and the thesis that "Australia owes much of its collectivism to the fact that its frontier was hospitable to the large man," instead of to the small man, as in the United States, are spelled out in Brian Fitzpatrick, *The British Empire in Australia: An Economic History* (Melbourne, 1941).

South African frontier development seems to have been intermediate between the Australian and American cases, but somewhat closer to the Australian than to the American pattern. See S. Daniel Neumark, *Economic Influences on the South African Frontier 1652–1836* (Stanford, Calif., 1957).

[18] North Sumatra and some of the larger Latin American countries may be exceptions to this rule.

Application to Underdeveloped Areas

When Hansen's theory was developed, he, like Harrod, was concerned primarily with problems of advanced countries. Accordingly, he did not attempt an application of his theory to underdeveloped countries. But as with Harrod, so with Hansen we are free to make that application and see what enlightenment can be gained thereby.

In applying the Hansen system, however, we must begin by making changes in the equations to take account of differences in the institutional and sociological framework between advanced and underdeveloped countries; in this sense, because it is specified more completely, Hansen's theory is less "general" than Harrod's.

The Investment Function

The most significant change we must make relates to the role of population growth. There is a sharp contrast in the effects of population growth under conditions in which population is kept continuously below optimum because development starts with a low population base, as it did in the now advanced countries, and its effects where development starts with population far above optimum. As we have seen earlier, where increases in population bring increases in per capita output, merely because labor is a relatively scarce factor, population growth has a favorable effect on investment in a number of ways. The increase in scale of the economy, and the growth of the market, not only provide increasing demand for housing, transport facilities, public utilities, and the like, but permit the use of better and already known techniques. (The selection of better techniques from among those that are already known should be not confused with technological progress, viz., the introduction of superior but hitherto unknown techniques.) It also means that optimal proportions can be maintained between labor and other factors of production, particularly capital, as capital accumulates. Where populations are already above optimum levels, however, where lack of savings rather than lack of effective demand limits investment, and where an addition to the labor supply would lower per capita output and income even if the additional workers were fully employed, population growth is a drag on economic development. It may prevent per capita income from increasing, or even lower per capita income, thus aggravating the difficulty of saving (and investing) enough to generate expansion.

We shall see more clearly below that in the conditions of underdeveloped countries population growth often adds to disguised unemployment rather than to income. Accordingly, entrepreneurs have no reason to associate population growth, particularly in rural areas, with increased demand. Moreover in village communities, housing, irrigation systems, roads, and the like are often provided on a self-help or mutual-aid basis, so that growth of rural population does not lead to any increase in *monetary* investment, but only to a direct "widening" of capital, so long as more land and other natural resources are available.

Hansen was concerned with investment as a generator of money income. Later, when we are concerned with capital-output ratios and the impact of capital accumulation on real income, we shall find it expedient to reintroduce $\dot{L}$ into the investment function. At the moment, however, we shall drop the term $\dot{L}$ from our monetary investment equation and rewrite it in the form:

$$I = I_g + I_i(\dot{Y}) + I_A(\dot{K}, \dot{T}) \tag{1}$$

This alteration is the only one we need make in the actual form of the equation, but there will also be differences in the value of some of the variables. For one thing, for reasons which will become apparent below, we can expect $\delta I_A/\delta\dot{K} \cdot d^2K/dt^2$ (increases in autonomous investment due to acceleration of resource discovery) to be lower in most of the present underdeveloped countries than it was in the advanced countries at the beginning of their industrialization. Considerable resource discovery has already taken place in most underdeveloped countries, and there is little reason to suppose that the *rate* of resource discovery will rise significantly in the future as compared with the last century. True geographic frontiers exist in very few of these countries. As stated above, the distribution of population reflects quite accurately the relative fertility of the soil, and all known mineral deposits have been under development for some time. Few of the underdeveloped countries present the opportunity of moving from the now occupied areas to land *still richer* in agricultural and mineral resources, an opportunity that existed in the New World between, say, 1750 and 1900. And without internal migration the "frontier spirit" will not accompany resource discovery.

On the other hand, there may be some hope that the $\delta I_A/\delta\dot{T} \cdot d^2T/dt^2$ (increases in autonomous investment through acceleration of technological progress) will be higher in underdeveloped countries than it ever was in advanced ones, at least for some time. During the "catching up period," while underdeveloped countries are applying known techniques which have been developed in advanced countries, but for which the necessary capital has not hitherto been available, a very rapid rate of technological progress may be generated. There are limitations even here, as we shall see. The techniques which have been most successful in advanced countries are considerably less suited to conditions in underdeveloped ones. But even with this limitation, a significant rate of technological progress should be obtainable.

It is also possible that the *parameter* I_A (the relationship between autonomous investment and given rates of growth) will increase through time, as the supply of New Men in underdeveloped countries increases, as objective and subjective security is improved, and greater political stability is achieved.

Finally, it is likely that I_i, the parameter relating induced investment to changes in income, will be particularly high and perhaps rising in underdeveloped countries. When inventory accumulation is included in investment, as it should be if we are considering the possibilities of steady growth in underdeveloped countries, we must take account of the readiness of entrepreneurs in underdeveloped countries to speculate on price rises through the accumulation of stock. As entrepreneurs increase in numbers and become more sophisticated, their response to changes in income may be even stronger than it is now.

The Savings Function

In order to take account of all the factors operative in underdeveloped countries, the form of the savings function should also be changed. We could write $S = S(O_a, r, p)$, where r is the interest rate and p is the rate of time preference. In discussing the long-run savings function in advanced countries, we ignored the effects of interest rate and of time preference. There were good reasons for doing so. In the first place, there is considerable evidence that interest rates play a minor role in determining the volume of savings in advanced countries. However that may be, with interest rates as low as they are in advanced countries, the long-run trend toward still lower interest rates cannot have very much effect. Thus the $\delta S/\delta r$ is small, dr/dt is small, and $\delta S/\delta r \cdot dr/dt$ is very small indeed. In underdeveloped countries, however, effective interest rates are sometimes extremely high. Therefore, there is a good possibility that the trend dr/dt may be of quantitative importance. Also, although savings may not alter very much where most savings are institutionalized and interest rates are in any case low, where personal savings play a more important role, and effective interest rates may be in excess of 40 per cent per year, reduction of interest rates may indeed have an effect on savings. Thus $\delta S/\delta r \cdot dr/dt$ (the response of savings to declining interest rates) in underdeveloped countries may be quantitatively significant.

On the other hand, $\delta S/\delta p \cdot dp/dt$ (the response of savings to diminishing time preference) may also be significant, and would tend to move in the opposite direction. There is ample evidence of a high rate of time preference in underdeveloped countries, particularly in the village communities where families will borrow several months' income in order to have an appropriate feast on the occasion of a wedding, funeral, or circumcision. As economies mature and people become more sophisticated, they tend to take more interest in the future—or so Harrod argues—and consequently the rate of time preference drops. On this score one could expect a rising trend in the proportion of income saved. Thus as we move through time, the saving schedule will tend to shift upwards, because of the decline in time preference. Savings will also tend to increase through a movement along the schedule to higher levels of income. There will be one offsetting factor, the drop in interest rates. Taking all these factors together, we can probably expect some increase in the ratio of savings to income, and perhaps also in the ratio of increases in savings to increases in income, in the early phases of economic development. In terms of our equations, this would mean that the multiplier would tend to fall in the first phase of economic growth.

Implications for Steady Growth

Does all this add up to "chronic inflation" in underdeveloped countries, as the other side of the coin of chronic increasing underemployment in advanced countries? Not necessarily; stagnation is another possibility. Looking again at Equation (1), in many underdeveloped countries both $\dot{K}$ and $\dot{T}$ are low and are not increasing rapidly. That is, the rate of technological progress and resource discovery is not particularly high, and is not noticeably rising. Autonomous investment is on a very low level. Public investment is also low, because of limited tax and borrowing capacity of the government. Thus national income is not rising very rapidly either and induced investment will be close to zero. With low levels of income, the average and marginal propensity to save are also low. The multiplier is high, but there is nothing to multiply. The result is an economy which stagnates with levels of per capita income close to the subsistence level.

What is certainly true, however, is that in such a society any event favoring growth immediately creates inflationary pressure. If, for example, public investment for development purposes increases, income will rise; induced investment will come into play, and the high multiplier will begin to operate. Output cannot possibly keep pace with the increase in money income that will be generated, and inflation is the only possible result.

The same sequence will ensue if something happens to raise the rate of resource discovery or technological progress so that autonomous private investment increases suddenly. Since development plans are designed primarily to raise the public investment in development projects and to encourage autonomous investment for development purposes, it is apparent that under the conditions prevailing in underdeveloped countries, the undertaking of a development program will almost inevitably create severe inflationary pressure. The very fact that the rate of resource discovery and technological progress are low in percentage terms, and that both autonomous investment and government investment are small percentages of national income, means that a rather small *absolute* increase in any of these variables can constitute a very large *percentage* increase. Yet the percentage increase in the actual supplies of the resources, labor, and technique, will still be small in the short run. Consequently, the increase in output will also be small in percentage terms, particularly during the gestation period of the new development projects.

Thus although inflation need not be "chronic" if nothing is done to accelerate the rate of economic growth in underdeveloped countries, it is always endemic, and it becomes epidemic whenever vigorous action is taken to increase the rate of economic growth.

8 Summary and Synthesis of General Theories of Development

The years since World War II have seen a return of interest to the problem that attracted most of the attention of economists, and much of the attention of statesmen, in the late eighteenth and early nineteenth centuries: how to assure continually rising standards of living? Currently, this problem is discussed under the heading, "economic development." The term is recent, the basic concept as old as economics. Fundamentally, it means rising per capita incomes. In an effort to make the concept a little more precise, however, we defined it in Chapter 1 as "a discernible rise in total and in per capita income, widely diffused throughout occupational and income groups, continuing for at least two generations, and becoming cumulative."

An underveloped country, then, is one in which this process has not taken place during the last two centuries and where, accordingly, per capita income is still low. "Low" is a relative term and any division between "low" and "high" incomes is necessarily arbitrary. We have chosen the figure of $500 per capita. This choice is designed to include all those countries that are underdeveloped in a policy sense; that is, countries "with announced goals and policies with regard to economic development and which are regarded as candidates for technical and capital assistance under the foreign aid programs of the United States and other advanced Western countries." Such countries have per capita incomes estimated at under $50 to about $500 per year.

There are, of course, significant differences among countries falling into this classification. Obviously, the problem of economic development is more pressing where per capita incomes are below \$100 per year than it is where incomes are between \$300 and \$500. Some underdeveloped countries are resource-poor, some are relatively resource-rich. Some have low but rising incomes; some are both poor and stagnant. But all are alike in considering it important to discover ways to launch and sustain, or to sustain where already launched, a process of continually rising standards of living.

This part of the book has been devoted to a review of general theories of economic development from Adam Smith and Malthus to Harrod and Hansen. In closing, we shall endeavor to pin down major points of agreement in general theories of economic growth and to evaluate this body of knowledge as a basis for policy in underdeveloped countries.

Similarities and Differences

In summarizing the theories outlined in the previous chapters, it may be useful to turn once again to our equations, which permit us to show similarities and differences in schematic form. First of all, there are three equations and two identities which run through all the theories:

the production function . . . $O = f(L, K, Q, T)$ (1)
the technical progress function . . . $T = T(I)$ (2)
the investment function . . . $I = dQ = I(R)$ (3)
and two identities . . . $O = C + I$ (4)
$O = R + W$ (5)

One equation is common to Marx and the Classics:

the wages-bill function . . . $W = W(I)$ (6)

Three equations are important in the Classical system but not in the others:

the population growth function . . . $L = L(W)$ (7)
the profits function . . . $R = R(T, L)$ (8)
the iron law of wages . . . $W = wL$ (9)

Population growth and consequent diminishing returns to labor on the land play a less significant role in the other theories than in the Classical one. These nine equations close the Classical system, since we have specified eight variables, w, the subsistence level of wages, being given.

In their theories of profit, Malthus, Marx, and the "moderns" (Schumpeter, Harrod, and Hansen) differ from the Classics. They recognize the importance of technological progress (and resource discovery) as a creator of profit opportunities, but they also recognize the importance of effective demand and the drag on profit rates and investment of the existing stock of capital. They also stress the relationship between income, effective demand, profits, and investment. Marx considered wages particularly important as a generator of consumer spending. The others are aware that the propensity to consume out of wages may be higher than the propensity to consume out of profits, but would consider both income streams important in determining effective demand. Thus we have instead of the Classical Equation (8),

$$\text{the profits function} \ldots \; R = R(T, C, Q) \qquad (8)$$

$$\text{and the demand function} \ldots \; C = C_1(W) + C_2(R) \qquad (9)$$

The moderns have been more concerned than the nineteenth-century economists with the determination of money income and the whole savings-investment relationship. This concern adds two equations:

$$\text{definition of savings} \ldots \; S = Y - C \qquad (10)$$

$$\text{the multiplier equation} \ldots \; Y = k \cdot I = \frac{1}{dS/dY} \cdot I$$

$$\text{and} \quad \Delta Y = \frac{1}{ds/dY} \, \Delta I \qquad (11)$$

The moderns introduced a distinction between induced and autonomous investment, and for policy purposes, found it useful to separate out government investment as well. They stressed technological progress and resource discoveries as generators of autonomous investment. Hansen and Harrod also emphasized population growth; Schumpeter was more ambivalent about it. Induced investment in turn depends on changes in income (or its major components). This analysis adds three equations:

$$I = I_A + I_i + I_g \qquad (12)$$

$$I_a = I_A(\dot{K}, \dot{T}, \dot{L}) \qquad (13)$$

$$I_i = I_i(\dot{Y}) \qquad (14)$$

These equations close the "modern" system.

Harrod adds an important new factor—or rather, brings it out into the open—in the form of the capital-output ratio. We can express it $Q = r \cdot O$. Later we shall want to use an output-capital ratio which is the reciprocal of this: [1] $O = a \cdot Q$.

Where does all this lead us?

Application to Underdeveloped Areas

First of all, let us note that even the relationships in the "agreed" system tell us some useful things about development policy. Look at the production function, for example. Even so simple a statement as this provides guidance as to the proximate causes of higher standards of living. Without capital accumulation, resource discovery, population growth, or technological progress, increases in output are impossible. When the form of the production function is specified on the basis of empirical knowledge, the equation tells us also that the level of production depends not only on the quantities of factors of production and the degree of technological advance but also on the proportions in which the factors are combined—a very important consideration. In other words, for every "factor endowment," there is an optimal combination of factors of production. One of the purposes of development planning is to find this combination and see to it that it is maintained.

Among the writers discussed, there is, moreover, substantial agreement concerning the relative importance of the factors in the production function and the interrelations among them. In all these theories, pride of place is given to *technological prog-*

[1] We might note in passing that the "moderns" determine the distribution of income between wages and profits through the production function. With an appropriate definition of the factors of production,

$$O = \frac{df}{dL} \cdot L + \frac{df}{dQ} \cdot Q$$

That is, total output is the sum of (marginal productivity of labor times number of units of labor employed) plus (marginal productivity of capital times number of units of capital). Under pure competition,

$$W = \frac{df}{dL} \quad \text{and} \quad \frac{R}{Q} = \frac{df}{dQ}$$

The wage rate equals marginal productivity of labor, the rate of profit the marginal productivity of capital (fixed factors). Thus

$$W = \frac{df}{dL} \cdot L \quad \text{and} \quad R = \frac{df}{dQ} \cdot Q$$

Each factor of production derives from national income what it "contributes" to it. Under monopoly conditions this relationship breaks down and the outcome depends on bargaining power.

ress, the introduction of new techniques which raise the productivity of available resources, especially labor. The Industrial Revolution of the eighteenth and nineteenth centuries was essentially a period of remarkably rapid introduction of new machines, new materials, new sources of power, and new processes. In the advanced countries, this process of "innovation" continues at a high rate, productivity continues to increase, and *per capita* incomes continue to rise. The highly developed countries are also developing most rapidly—one of the many bits of evidence that economic progress is largely a matter of getting started.

The key figure in this process of technological advance is the entrepreneur. He is the man who sees the opportunity for introducing the new commodity, technique, raw material, or machine, and brings together the necessary capital, management, labor, and materials to do it. He may not be, and historically has usually not been, the scientific inventor; his skills are less scientific than organizational. His skills are also different from those of the salaried manager, who takes over an enterprise *after* it has been launched. In any society, the rate of technological progress, and so of economic development, depends greatly on the number and ability of entrepreneurs available to it. But a few entrepreneurs may go a long way in promoting economic expansion. In the now advanced countries, once a leader has shown the way—to steam power, or electricity, or better textile machinery, or automobiles, or airplanes, or whatever—a "cluster of followers" has joined the parade in search of profits, power, or public weal.

The acquisition of new manual, managerial, and professional skills is virtually inseparable from resource discovery and technological change. Economic development can scarcely occur without some improvement of skills, and learning more productive ways of operating rarely takes place without the use of new techniques or the discovery of new resources. Learning to use the *same* tools and the *same* materials more efficiently has seldom brought substantial increases in productivity; it has never been the mainspring of economic growth. It is hard to think of any improvement of skill, in and of itself, that did have revolutionary economic effects. This statement is not meant to belittle acquisition of skills as a factor in economic development; in the present underdeveloped countries, improving skills is exceedingly important. But it is also important to remember that improvement of skills does not take place in a vacuum; for the most part, it means using better tools or better materials. No degree of skill can make a sickle as effective as a well-handled scythe; no amount of training will enable the man with a scythe to cut as much hay as the man with a reaper.

Thus capital accumulation is the very core of economic development. Whether in a predominantly private enterprise system like the American, or in a communistic system like the Russian or the Chinese, economic development cannot take place without capital accumulation: the construction of irrigation systems, use of fertilizers and better seeds or livestock, land reclamation, building dams, bridges, or factories with machines in them, roads, railways, and airports, ships, and harbors—all the "produced means of further production" associated with high levels of productivity. Many underdeveloped countries have a particularly pressing need for "social capital"—equipment used by society at large, rather than by particular enterprises, such as transport facilities, public utilities, schools, and hospitals. But the process of building up the necessary stock of capital equipment has an inescapable financial counterpart—in private enterprise and communist systems alike. Either a part of national income must be saved or paid in taxes to pay for the purchase or production of capital goods, or the necessary funds must be borrowed abroad.

Can capital accumulation take place without technological progress? Society could just go on building more transport facilities, more sources of power, more factories, of the same sort; this process is sometimes called "widening" of capital, in contrast with "deepening," which implies use of more capital-intensive techniques. None of the theories of development outlined above expected progress from "widening" alone. In all of them, capital accumulation and technological progress go hand in hand. Capital accumulation is *possible* without technological improvement, but technological improvement is virtually impossible without prior capital accumulation. For the most part, the most efficient techniques require heavy investment for their introduction, even if they reduce capital costs per unit of output once they are installed and operating. All these theories imply that no nation that is unwilling either to save and pay taxes, or to borrow abroad, will enjoy the fruits of the most advanced techniques.

Equation (2) of the "agreed" system thus becomes a crucial one. Once we recognize that technological improvements of all kinds—including improvements in labor and managerial skills—require investment for their *introduction*, whether or not the innovations prove capital saving when in place, we need not dwell upon whether capital accumulation is as important as technological progress, or whether an underdeveloped country can get out of its rut through technical improvements alone and avoid the harsh necessity of saving more or borrowing abroad. The process of technological progress is inseparably linked with the process of capital accumulation. True, an advanced economy that has already accumulated a large stock of capital, and which generates a continuous flow of capital-saving innovations, may be able to maintain a respectable rate of economic growth without net savings and investment, merely by reinvesting depreciation allowances in ever more efficient equipment and organization. But this possibility offers little comfort to underdeveloped countries, since they cannot take advantage of it until the stock of capital and the level of technique have already been raised far above existing levels.

The third equation of the "agreed" system also tells us something important: if the process of capital accumulation (and thus of improving technology) is to be left to private initiative, it must be profitable—at least as profitable, after appropriate discounting for differences in safety and liquidity of assets, as it is in advanced countries. The point is axiomatic and should also be obvious; but as we shall see in Chapter 25 below, it is a point ignored by the governments of many, if not most, underdeveloped countries. For many underdeveloped countries still rely heavily on private investment in their development planning, while imposing severe limitations on its profitability and introducing measures which reduce the safety and liquidity of assets.

The point is made more strongly in the Schumpeter analysis. In his view neither capital accumulation nor technical progress will reach high levels through private initiative unless the social, political, and economic "climate" is one conducive to the appearance of a large and growing supply of entrepreneurs. Few indeed of the underdeveloped countries have made serious efforts to create such a climate.

Economists of all periods have agreed on three other points arising from analysis of the interactions among the causal relations expressed in the equations. First, all theories of economic development imply a tendency for capitalist economies to stop growing after an advanced stage of development has been reached. Hansen and his followers suggest ways in which this tendency can be offset in a "mixed" economy. Harrod and Schumpeter are less optimistic but would certainly recommend the effort. Second, all are agreed that growth or acceleration of growth tends to bring instability (although the Classical school made little of this point). *Steady* growth is very difficult, perhaps impossible, to attain, although here, too, Hansen and his followers are more optimistic than most economists who have analyzed the problem, contending that the right combination of monetary and fiscal policy can do much to eliminate instability in the economy while sustaining growth. Third, although with varying emphasis, all the economists discussed in this part agree that expansion of international trade and investment provides an "escape valve" from stagnation in advanced countries and helps to bring the transition from stagnation to expansion in underdeveloped ones. The size of the market is treated as a major factor in determining potential growth rates. In Malthus' exposition this concept is stated in terms of "balanced growth": in a closed economy the growth of one sector is limited by the size of the other(s). These limitations can be overcome by expansion of foreign trade, which brings an effective increase in the size of the market for one or more sectors in the economy.

Of these three propositions, only the second is of much use in approaching the problems of underdeveloped countries. The governments or peoples of underdeveloped countries are unlikely to eschew economic development for fear that, having achieved the levels of income of the United States or the United Kingdom, they may need an ingenious set of policy measures to assure further advance. Only if the causes of stagnation in advanced countries were similar to the causes of stagnation in underdeveloped ones would this facet of development theory be of great importance in underdeveloped countries today. At first glance the relationship between the two kinds of stagnation seems rather remote; stagnation in advanced countries results mainly from a tendency for *ex ante* savings to exceed investment at high levels of employment. Stagnation in underdeveloped countries results from low levels of investment *and* of *ex ante* savings at *any* level of employment. Policies designed to cure the first sort of stagnation are unlikely to cure the second, as we shall see more clearly in Part 5. The third proposition seems irrelevant to the present underdeveloped countries. Many of these have experienced substantial inflow of foreign capital and impressive expansion of foreign trade, without any apparent increase in the average incomes of the domestic population. This seeming paradox is the subject of Chapters 14 and 15.

The relationship between growth and instability, however, is one for the governments and peoples of underdeveloped countries to ponder. Our preliminary efforts to apply the modern theories of fluctuations to underdeveloped countries suggest that, once launched, ambitious programs of economic development are almost certain to be inflationary in their original impact; if inflation is checked after it starts, the outcome is likely to be a series of fluctuations. On the other hand, insistence that development must not have any destabilizing effects may hamper economic growth. The problem confronting underdeveloped countries, then, is to determine the maximum rate of growth consistent with stability—or the maximum degree of stability consistent with acceptable rates of growth—and to choose the combination of growth and stability that best meets their aims and wishes. This problem, too, is dealt with in Part 5.

Population Growth

The Classical economists, generalizing from what they saw in Europe at the time, were prepared to treat population growth as a function of workers' incomes. People arrived in the world with both hands and mouths, but because of limitations on the supply of land they tended to eat more during their lifetime than they added to output, barring technological progress to increase their productivity. This analysis suggests a concept of "optimal size of population" which would maximize per capita output at any point of time. The Classicists thought this level of population had already been surpassed in Europe. Marxists have argued that population growth may be a problem for capitalist societies, where capital accumulation depends on profits, but not for a socialist society.

The treatment of population growth by the "moderns" differs in two respects. First, they have been much more reluctant to say just what determines the rate of population growth. By the time they were writing, it was clear that increasing wage incomes did not always bring more rapid increases in population. The importance of death rates as well as birth rates, the obvious fact that people could limit the size of their families if they wished to do so, and the role of migration impressed economists with the complexity of the factors determining rates of population growth in particular societies at particular times. Thus the "moderns" have tended to treat population growth as "exogenous"—outside the system—so far as its causation is concerned. On the other hand, Hansen and others have treated population growth as an endogenous factor—inside the system—in the determination of autonomous investment. It is not just a question of whether hands or mouths prove bigger in economic terms; the rate of capital accumulation itself depends on the rate of increase in the population. This theory suggests a concept of "optimal rate of population growth" in addition to the concept of optimal size of population. Taking account of the impact of population growth on investment, there would be some rate of population growth which would maximize the rate of increase in per capita output. It would be a somewhat complex affair, depending on the rate at which the optimal *size* of population, in terms of the production function, increased with the stock of capital, the precise quantitative effect of population growth on investment, both directly and through pushing people into frontier areas, and on the initial values of all the factors in the production function. There would be *some* rate of population growth, however, at which all the favorable effects on output would be more than offset by the increased numbers of people to share in it.

In both these "modern" aspects, the treatment of population growth is unsatisfactory as a basis for analyzing the problem of underdevelopment. As pointed out in Chapter 6, the relationship between population growth and autonomous investment breaks down when the labor supply is already redundant and there is no assurance that greater numbers will mean an increase in effective demand. In underdeveloped countries there may be nothing for extra hands to do and nothing to put into extra mouths that is not snatched from other mouths. The population may already be above optimum and the optimal rate of growth may even be negative. Nor can we be content to treat the causes of population growth as "exogenous" when we are concerned with raising per capita output and income. If we are to be sure that our policy recommendations will succeed in this respect, we *must* have some idea about what is going to happen to the rate of population growth.

Yet we must agree with the "moderns" that the Classical theory of population growth was too simple. Here is one respect, then, in which a theory of development that is to serve as a guide to policy in underdeveloped countries must differ from those outlined in Part 3.

The distinction between autonomous and induced investment, and the isolation of resource discovery and innovations as the major factors in stimulating autonomous investment in underdeveloped countries are useful additions to our store of knowledge. Once it is recognized that *increasing rates* of resource discovery or technological progress are needed to raise autonomous investment, any easy optimism about prospects of launching growth from this direction should be dispelled.

The reintroduction into the discussion of growth of the capital-output ratio, as a consequence of the contributions of Harrod and Domar and others, is also useful—especially when the relation between capital accumulation, technological progress, resource discovery, and acquisition of skills is recognized. The capital-output ratio—and particularly the incremental capital-output ratio relating investment to increases in output—is a factor that must enter into any serious attempt at development planning. It is a slippery concept when used in plan preparation, as we shall see in Chapter 27. But it is none the less important for that.

Synthesis of General Theories

Let us now attempt a simple synthesis of all the aspects of these general theories that seem to be useful as a guide to policy in underdeveloped countries. Let us write

$$O = a \cdot Q \tag{1}$$

Here a is an output-capital ratio; O is total output, and Q is the stock (quantity) of capital as before. Most of the literature refers to a capital-output ratio, and particularly to an incremental capital-output ratio relating increases in output to additions to the stock of capital. If the value of a is independent of the level of O and Q, it is the reciprocal of the incremental capital-output ratio. Then

$$\Delta O = a \cdot \Delta Q + \Delta a \cdot Q \tag{1a}$$
$$= a \cdot I + \Delta a \cdot Q \tag{1b}$$

(The symbol Δ, remember, means simply "increase in.") This formulation is an improvement over the production function in showing that investment and so investment decisions are the hard core of the development process, while at the same time recognizing that there are ways of using an existing stock of capital more effectively so as to raise output.

To get closer to the decision-making process, we can break up investment into its three major parts: government investment, I_g, determined directly by the plan; induced private investment, I_i, brought forth by recent changes in income, effective demand, profits, etc.; and autonomous private investment, I_A, stimulated by long-run growth factors:

$$I = I_g + I_i + I_A(\dot{L}, \dot{K}, \dot{T}) \tag{2}$$

For our present purposes we can simplify this equation in two ways. First, we can ignore induced investment in an initial approximation. Only if significantly high rates of increase in current income and demand are achieved will induced investment be quantitatively significant; in other words, if short-lived inflationary booms are avoided, induced investment will become significant only if development plans are successful. We must look to the other two kinds of investment for the *generation* of rising incomes. Second, as we have seen, few underdeveloped countries can regard population growth as a stimulus to long-run investment, since in most such countries population is already above optimum. Growth of the total size of the labor force is not needed to permit capital accumulation without a departure from the optimal ratio of labor to capital, nor does it carry with it increased effective demand for housing, transport, public utilities, etc., as it does in advanced countries. Thus we can use a simplified equation:

$$I = I_g + I_A(\dot{K}, \dot{T}) \tag{2a}$$

Substituting in (1b),

$$\Delta O = \Delta a \cdot Q + a_1 \cdot I_g + a_2 \cdot I_A(\dot{K}, \dot{T}) \tag{3}$$

This formulation tells us a good deal about the content and purpose of a development plan. An effective plan must be designed to do the following things:

1. Increase government investment, at least to the point at which opportunities for private investment are maximized. Over a very wide range public investment can provide the impulse to increased private investment. When government investment reaches a level at which it is competing for scarce resources with private enterprise, it may still be worth expanding if the stimulating effects on the rate of resource discovery and technological progress lead to a net increase in private investment nonetheless, or if it raises the output-capital ratio so as to more than offset any net drop in private investment. The methods of financing government investment should be of a sort that will not discourage private investment or result in less effective use of existing capital.

2. Increase the rate of resource discovery and technological progress. In part this objective can be obtained through government expenditures on geological surveys, research, transport facilities, etc. In part it involves providing incentives to private

exploration and development through tax policy, foreign exchange policy, land policy, patents, etc.

3. Raise the parameter I_A; that is, encourage a higher level of private investment with the *existing* rate of resource discovery and technological progress. This might be done by training indigenous managers, entrepreneurs, and technicians; by reducing effective rates of interest and making credit more readily available; by encouraging a "long view" through promotion of confidence, assuring physical security, insurance schemes, etc.; by improved foreign exchange policy; and by improving the climate for foreign investment.

4. To raise the output-capital ratio (reduce the incremental capital-output ratio). This can be done by training managers and workers, inducing improved factor-proportions, improving the product mix, introducing capital-saving innovations, etc.

Equation (3) has the added advantage of indicating that the capital-output ratio is likely to be different for different sectors of the economy, and that the aggregate ratio will, therefore, depend on the sectoral allocation of total investment.

We could go further, introduce different incremental capital-output ratios for each type of investment, and also distinguish between the industrial and agricultural sectors. There would be still further advantages in introducing distributed lags, to take account of differences in gestation periods of investment in various sectors. We would then end up with something like this for each sector:

$$O_t - O_{t-1} = (a_t - a_{t-1}) \cdot Q_{t-1} + a_t^1 I_{i\,t-1} + a_{t-2}^2 I_{t-2}\,(\dot{K}, \dot{T})_{t-3} + a_{t-3}^3\, I_{g\,t-3}\,(\dot{K}, \dot{T})_{t-4} \qquad (4)$$

Here the t subscripts refer to time periods: t is the present income-period (quarter, let's say), $t—1$ is the previous quarter, $t—2$ is the quarter before that, and so on.

These equations might be called "planning equations." By and large, they represent the kind of analysis that underlies the preparation of development plans in a good many underdeveloped countries.

If we are concerned with financing the development program without inflation, we might also make use of "financial equations" derived from the Hansen theory. To make the analysis more realistic, let us take account of the marginal propensity to import, dF/dY, the marginal propensity to pay taxes, dT/dY, and the impact of the development plan on exports, in addition to variables in the simpler version of this equation presented in Chapter 6. We then have:

$$\Delta Y = \frac{1}{\Delta S/\Delta Y + \Delta F/\Delta Y + \Delta T/\Delta Y} \cdot \Delta(I_g + I_A + I_i + X)$$

We know also that $P = Y/O$, P being the general price level, O here standing for physical output. If the price level is to be stable, output must increase enough to offset the increase in money income. We already have

$$\Delta O = a \cdot (I_g + I_A + I_i)$$

So we can readily calculate the increase in output from the data in the plan. Comparing the increase in output with the increase in money income that will be generated by the development program with *existing* tax rates, monetary policies, etc., we can decide how much we must raise taxes and savings to prevent undesirable inflation. We can also calculate the impact on the balance of payments, having both the increase in exports and the increase in imports.

We shall return to these matters in Part 5 and consider them in more detail. Our purpose here is only to indicate what can be done with the sort of theory outlined in this part—which is more or less what *is* done by the planning organizations in underdeveloped countries today. Clearly, theories that enable us to do this sort of planning are very helpful. Just as clearly, however, these theories do *not* tell us how to turn a poor and stagnant economy into an expanding one with hope of becoming truly prosperous. They do not even tell us how underdeveloped countries got that way; and we cannot hope to devise policies to produce growth until we know why some countries have grown and others have not.

It would be pleasant indeed if we had available a theory of economic development general enough to serve as a basis for policy in countries at all stages of economic advance and with all types of economic system. But we do not. Professor Kuznets put the situation this way: [2]

> Can we hope to formulate a theory of economic growth that would indicate the factors in the development of the more industrially advanced nations and thus illuminate the problem of their possible secular stagnation; to frame the factors so that a testable analysis of obstacles

[2] Simon Kuznets, "Toward a Theory of Economic Growth," in Robert Lekachman (ed.), *National Policy for Economic Welfare at Home and Abroad* (New York, 1955), pp. 14–15.

to economic growth of underdeveloped nations and hence a basis for intelligent development policy become possible; to consider the operation of these factors under a system of free enterprise, as well as within the authoritarian system, so that their interplay and potentialities in both become clear; and to distinguish the factors that make for peaceful and for warlike behavior, so that the bearing of each on economic growth can be clearly perceived? To put the question in this way is to predetermine a negative answer—provided that by a theory we mean a statement of testable relations among empirically identifiable factors, such relations and factors having been found relatively invariant under diverse conditions in time and space. Such a theory of economic growth of nations may never be within our reach. But one can safely assert that we do not have it now; and what is more important, are not yet ready for it. The very concern about economic growth is recent; and it is hardly an exaggeration to say that for almost a hundred years, since the mid-nineteenth century, when the economic theories of the long run of the Classical and Marxian schools had already been formulated, there has been no significant theoretical work in this field, excepting the various attempts to revise Marxian theory in the light of subsequent events. Meanwhile with the passage of time our experience in the economic growth of nations has broadened and empirical records have accumulated, but no significant attempt has been made either to utilize these data within a theoretical framework, or even to organize, extend, and test them preparatory to theoretical analysis.

We might do well, then, to abandon the search for a truly "general" theory at this stage, and content ourselves with a quest for a "special" theory of *under*development. Such a theory would be tailor-made for the institutional, technological, sociological, and psychological conditions common to underdeveloped countries. Part 4 is devoted to the quest for such a theory. But before returning to theory, there are two other things we can usefully do. First, we can review ideas concerning the historical causes of growth in the now advanced countries. Secondly, we should look more closely at the underdeveloped countries. What are the significant differences between them and the advanced countries—now, and as they were when the latter began their periods of sustained growth? The next two chapters deal with these questions.

PART 3 Principles: The Lessons of History

9 Historical Theories of the Rise of Capitalism

Economic historians have devoted a good deal of thought and documentary research to the acceleration of economic development in Europe after 1500, which culminated in the Industrial Revolution of the eighteenth and nineteenth centuries. This process of marked acceleration of economic growth has been labeled "the rise of capitalism." Although there is no reason to expect the presently poor countries to follow exactly the same path, it is nonetheless interesting to consider the general theories of the "rise of capitalism" which have come out of these historical studies. They may point to some prerequisites for economic growth which are just as necessary in underdeveloped countries today as they were in the now industrialized countries two or three centuries ago. At their least useful, such theories should indicate some important differences between advanced countries, when their accelerated growth began, and underdeveloped countries today.

The "Rise of Capitalism"

Much historical research has been directed to the question of the date and causes of the beginning of capitalism. When did it arise, and why?

Marx

Karl Marx recognized the existence of a "sporadic" capitalism in the Mediterranean cities of the fourteenth and fifteenth centuries but dated the "era" of capitalism from the sixteenth century. He interpreted the "rise" of capitalism as a successful struggle of the "capitalist class" against the feudal lords and the guild-masters. The basis of its rise was the exploitation of subservient labor. Through enclosures and the breakup of feudalism "a mass of free proletarians was hurled on the labour market." The old nobility was devoured by wars. Cruel legislation failed to stop the movement. This process of forcible expropriation gained new impetus from the Reformation and "hurled" the inmates of the monasteries "into the proletariat." The agricultural people were driven from their homes and then maltreated into a condition and discipline suitable for wage labor. The capitalist class rose out of the class of independent farmers and landlords who exploited labor, and benefited by rising prices. Hand in hand with the breakup of the manor and the expropriation of the peasants went the destruction of domestic industry and the concentration of control of manufacture into the hands of individual capitalists, who gained all the profits. The Middle Ages contributed two kinds of capital: usurers' capital and merchants' capital. Until the breakdown of feudalism, this capital was prevented from being converted into industrial capital. Exploitation of colonies, slave trade, and monopolies also added to the capital accumulation.[1]

Sombart

Sombart considered "capitalism" as an idealized "type" of economic organization, which characterizes a very definite historical period. This "type" of organization developed from 1500 to 1760, was at its height from 1760 until August, 1914, and is now on the decline. The capitalistic "type" of economy has certain characteristics:

1. Technical progress is "typical" of capitalism; in the precapitalistic period technique was stable, bound by custom and tradition.

2. Economic freedom—laissez faire—is also typical of capitalism. Freed from precapitalistic control by guilds, municipal authority, manorial customs and traditions, enterprise was able to

[1] Karl Marx, *Capital: a Critical Analysis of Capital Production,* ed., Friedrich Engels (London, 1887).

make quick use of new improvements, of investment opportunities, etc.

3. Capitalism has its own "spirit," which did not exist previously. It is an unshackled, accumulating, profit-seeking spirit, careless of social consequences and communal relationships.

Sombart was even more emphatic than Marx in his distinction between the Middle Ages and the period following the beginning of the sixteenth century. The medieval organization was not only acapitalistic but was incapable of producing a store of capital. In this essentially localized handicraft economy, it was difficult enough to obtain a bare subsistence, let alone accumulate capital. Capitalism developed mainly out of the operation of the properties of the feudal lords, and from the increased holdings of urban properties.[2]

Later research has shown that many features of capitalism are to be found in medieval economic organization, particularly in commerce, and that commerce was much more important in providing funds for investment than was landholding. Indeed, there is evidence that the commercial capitalists were able to displace the feudal landlords in economic and political control.[3] However, in showing the relation between the rise of the state and of capitalism, Sombart does give a partial explanation. State finance offered one of the best ways for commercial capitalists to increase their wealth, witness the Medici, Fuggers, and other great trading families. Church finance, too, was an important factor in the development of financial institutions, for the heavy taxes imposed by the Popes necessitated the development of both transfer mechanisms and of credit.[4]

The Weber-Tawney Thesis

Max Weber's explanation of the "rise of capitalism" is at once most fascinating and most controversial. The reason for capitalistic development in the sixteenth century is that the Reformation provided the proper philosophical and ethical setting for the "capitalist spirit" to flourish. The impulse to acquisition is common to all times and all places, but Roman Catholicism held in

[2] Werner Sombart, *Der Moderne Kapitalismus* (Leipzig, 1927).

[3] H. Sieveking, "Die Kapitalistische Entwicklung in den italienische Städten des Mittelalters," *Vierteljahrschaft für Sozial und Wirtschaftsgeschichte*, Vol. VII, 1909.

[4] Cf. J. Strieder, "Origin and Evolution of Early European Capitalism," *Journal of Economic and Business History*, November, 1929; F. Scheville, *History of Florence from the Foundation of the City through the Renaissance* (New York, 1936).

check the pursuit of profit and the accumulation of wealth which characterize capitalism. The problem is not the advent of capitalistic activity but the appearance of the sober bourgeois society in which capitalism reached its apex. Even contemporary society gives us a clue to the rise of this middle-class society, Weber argued, for in countries of mixed religion, we find a dominance of Protestants among entrepreneurs, owners of capital, and high-grade labor. It was also true that the more highly developed districts were those which gave most support to the Reformation, finding its creed more suitable to aggressive and progressive ways of life. The spirit of capitalism is typified by Benjamin Franklin's "philosophy of avarice." Acquisition of wealth becomes an end in itself. In the Middle Ages, such ideas were considered as the lowest kind of avarice; after the Reformation, such conduct became highly respectable. At the beginning of modern times, it was not the existing entrepreneurs who represented the capitalistic spirit, for they were bound by traditionalism: fixed profits, limited interest rates, just wages, and just prices. It was in the lower middle class that the spirit was strongest. This spirit, and not new streams of money, stimulated the rise of capitalism. The chief reward for making money was the feeling of having done the job well.

This concept is to be found in Luther's doctrines under the name of the "calling," the idea that each individual is "called" to do a certain job and to do it as well as possible. The highest form of moral conduct is the fulfillment of duty in worldly affairs. The ideal of monastic asceticism was extended to worldly life; one should not indulge in luxury. Yet Luther was opposed to monopoly and to usury, and cannot be regarded as the apostle of capitalism. The real enemy of Catholicism was Calvinism. In order to become one of the "chosen," one must work hard and spend little. One must accept one's lot as part of God's scheme. The intensity of worldly activity alone dispels doubts as to one's being among the "elect." Pietism was a similar doctrine of predestination which influenced the ascetic movement. Methodism was an Anglo-Saxon movement corresponding to Pietism. In practice, the reasoning of the Baptist sects becomes equivalent to Calvinism.

The net result was to justify the pursuit of wealth, provided that happened to be one's "calling." Poverty was not required, but the pursuit of riches must not lead one to reckless enjoyment. Profits are as holy as wages, and interest is not wrong unless wrung from the poor. The cardinal sin is idleness. As for laborers, only when they were poor did they remain obedient to God, but remaining obedient they attained eternal happiness in another world. Thus the Reformation gave to the entrepreneur and to the capitalist a clear conscience to pursue profits to the best of their ability. In condemning expenditure, it provided the basis for capital accumulation. The profits of this era were not absorbed into the life of a new nobility but were reinvested. On the other hand, the new spirit justified a marked class distinction and forbade open dissatisfaction on the part of oppressed labor.[5]

This explanation of the rise of capitalism was introduced to English readers by R. H. Tawney.[6] Although essentially the same as Weber's, his treatment is more general and develops the thesis in relation to its historical setting. Like Weber, Tawney points out that the Catholic Church opposed usury and emphasized the sin of avarice. The outbursts of commercial activity in the fifteenth century made the older teaching an economic anachronism. (It will be noted that Tawney is more inclined than Weber to say that the Reformation stimulated a movement already under way.) Catholic teaching was an effective barrier to capitalistic development despite its neglect in practice. Tawney attributes less positive, and more negative, influence to Luther than does Weber. Luther, he says, was opposed to the accumulation of wealth, usury, monopoly, high prices, speculation, and the luxury trade with the East. But Calvin's teaching was most characteristic and most influential of the new doctrines. He saw economic life with the eyes of a peasant, and recognized frankly the need for capital, credit and banking, and large-scale commerce and finance. Thrift, diligence, sobriety, and frugality are the Christian virtues, and profits and interest are not necessarily evil gains.

Perhaps the most forceful critic of the Weber-Tawney thesis is H. M. Robertson. He regards his *Aspects of the Rise of Economic Individualism* as a "more realistic treatment," historical rather than sociological. The capitalist, he says, is and always has been, a purely secular creature who sees no reason for religion to meddle in his business affairs. Men do not need to be "called" to the pursuit of riches. Weber's philological interpretation of "calling" is unfounded, and there is no essential difference between Catholics and Puritans on this point. The true interpretation of "calling" savors little of capitalism. Secondly, the *Erwerbsprinzip* is not new; society has been acquisitive for thousands of years. There was plenty of capitalism in the Middle Ages. If we look

[5] Max Weber, *The Protestant Ethic and the Spirit of Capitalism* (New York, 1930).

[6] R. H. Tawney, *Religion and the Rise of Capitalism* (New York, 1926).

to Scotland, a stronghold of Calvinism, we find not an advanced but a lagging development of capitalism. As for usury, its approval was no part of the Protestant creed; the literature is full of condemnation of it. In practice, Calvin's own attitude toward interest and that of the Catholic Church were essentially the same. (One could add here that the Catholic Church itself did much to foster capitalism.) As the bases of capitalism, Robertson emphasizes the rise of the nationalist state, the Machiavellian philosophy, and in particular, the "price revolution" following the discoveries.

It is clear that much of Robertson's criticism is justified, but he goes rather too far in his nihilism with respect to the Reformation. It is fairly generally agreed today that the Protestant ethic was one element in the acceleration of capitalistic development.[7] The relationship between predominant religion and per capita income is too close for religion to be dismissed out of hand as a factor in *past* economic history. If we refer back to Table 1-1, we can see that the six countries with the highest *per capita* incomes in 1952–54 were Christian and Protestant. Of the sixteen countries with per capita incomes above $500 per year (the "developed" countries in our definition), all but four are predominantly Protestant, the others are predominantly Roman Catholic. The countries with per capita incomes between $250 and $500 are mainly Roman Catholic; those between $100 and $250 are mainly Roman Catholic and Moslem; those below $100 are mainly Hindu, Buddhist, and pagan. We cannot reach any conclusions about causes and effects on the basis of these facts, but the facts are worth pondering—along with other facts. For in other parts of the world than Europe, quite different religions have produced the spirit of enterprise. Professor Walt Rostow, discussing the role of entrepreneurship in the acceleration of economic growth, writes: [8]

> In this connection it is increasingly conventional for economists to pay their respects to the Protestant ethic.[9] The historian should not

[7] A contemporary critic of Weber is P. C. G. Walker, "Capitalism and the Reformation," *Economic History Review*, November, 1937. He objects to Weber's method of using qualitative rather than quantitative criteria. Moreover, such an investigation cannot take the Reformation as a datum; it must inquire into the causes that lay behind it. He rightly criticizes the emphasis upon the post-sixteenth-century history of capitalism. He follows Robertson in emphasizing the price revolution.

[8] W. W. Rostow, "The Take-off into Self-sustained Growth," *The Economic Journal*, March, 1956.

[9] See, for example, N. Kaldor, "Economic Growth and Cyclical Fluctuations," *Economic Journal*, March, 1954, p. 67.

be ungrateful for this light on the grey horizon of formal growth models. But the known cases of economic growth which theory must seek to explain take us beyond the orbit of Protestantism. In a world where Samurai, Parsees, Jews, North Italians, Turkish, Russian, and Chinese Civil Servants (as well as Huguenots, Scotsmen and British North-countrymen) have played the role of a leading élite in economic growth John Calvin should not be made to bear quite this weight. More fundamentally, allusion to a positive scale of religious or other values conducive to profit-maximising activities is an insufficient sociological basis for this important phenomenon. What appears to be required for the emergence of such élites is not merely an appropriate value system but two further conditions: first, the new élite must feel itself denied the conventional routes to prestige and power by the traditional less acquisitive society of which it is a part; second, the traditional society must be sufficiently flexible (or weak) to permit its members to seek material advance (or political power) as a route upwards alternative to conformity.

In this chapter we are concerned with general theories arising from the study of economic history rather than with economic history proper. To present the history of early modern Europe and the Industrial Revolution that emerged from it would require a book in itself. However, we should note two important points before moving on to other historical explanations of the upsurge of economic development in Europe. First, other things besides the Reformation happened in the sixteenth century. Some of these are discussed below. Others, which may have been equally important—such as the rise of the national state, the new wave of scientific progress during the Renaissance, and the liberal policies of Antwerp as the new financial center of Europe—are not. Second, the Reformation itself had economic effects more direct than those entailed in the change in ideology it introduced. The dissolution of the abbeys and the confiscation and sale of Church properties transferred capital from less enterprising to more enterprising owners. The persecuted Protestants who immigrated into England, West Germany, and Holland brought with them technical skills, scientific knowledge, and managerial talents. Later religious persecution contributed to the development of the New World, and thus indirectly to the development of Europe itself. The impact on ideology may have been an important aspect of the Reformation, but it was certainly not the only one influencing economic history.[10]

[10] See, for example, Herbert Heaton, *Economic History of Europe* (New York, 1948), chaps. XI–XX, and the literature there cited.

The Crusades and Commercial Expansion

Those who associate the "rise of capitalism" with the development of medieval commerce tend to stress the Crusades as a series of events leading to rapid progress. These basically religious movements had as their chief results the colonization of unsettled Continental districts, the opening of new Mediterranean markets and ports, the development of the European luxury trade with the Near East, the introduction of new commodities and new techniques into Europe, improved navigation and ships, better-organized capital and foreign exchange markets, the beginning of the absorption of the old feudal aristocracy by the new commercial capitalists, the economic development of the Italian cities. Indeed, if one wants to risk picking a single cause for the "rise of capitalism," the Crusades would seem to be the choice, for out of the commercial capitalism of the Middle Ages and the capital accumulation that it made possible grew the industrial capitalism of later periods.[11] Of course, one may fall prey to the *post hoc, ergo propter hoc* fallacy in this connection.

Capitalistic Agriculture: Enclosures and the Black Death

In so far as the development of capitalism is synonymous with the decay of feudalism,[12] the causes of the breakup of the manor are likewise causes of the rise of capitalism. Since the enclosures replaced serfdom with a free labor class to some extent, and since the commutation of labor service for money rents replaced serfdom with more or less free enterprise farming for profit, there can be no doubt that the decay of feudalism was a stimulus to capitalistic development.

The growth of the towns was in part a result of the breakup of the manor, but towns were growing up before the enclosures set in and their growth was also a cause of the decline of feudalism. The existence of an artisan and an entrepreneurial class who did not work land to supply their wants for food, clothing, and raw materials directly meant that markets existed for exports from the manors located near the towns. Exporting involved specialization of agricultural output, and specialization is the antithesis of feudalism. The growth of towns stimulated farming for profit rather than farming for consumption.

[11] Since the Crusades are dealt with by almost every author who discusses the development of medieval commerce and finance no specific reference is given.

[12] This is the contention of Marx, as we have seen, and Walker's definition amounts to the same thing.

The growth of towns had another effect through increasing the demand for labor and thus raising wages. This tendency led to the freeing of serfs, and many not freed ran away to take advantage of higher industrial wages.

Another impetus to agricultural specialization was the growth of commerce after the Crusades, and again after the discoveries. These events meant new markets, new commodities, better navigation. The manors could export not only to towns but to other countries. The introduction of new agricultural methods into Europe also made specialization more profitable.

Although there has been some debate on the subject, there can be little doubt that the Black Death accelerated the movement.[13] The immediate effect of the plague and the depopulation resulting from it was an increase in relative supply of and a decrease of demand for commodities, so that prices fell tremendously. Rather than sell livestock and equipment at such prices, landlords sought to acquire more land. This immediate effect was followed by a great reduction in output due to labor scarcity, and prices rose precipitously. This factor made the acquisition of land desirable to expand output and to profit from the high prices. Because of the rise in wage rates, however, it was desirable to replace labor-intensive industries with land-intensive activities such as sheep farming. Here was another reason for enlarging landholdings. The seizure of land was made easier by the frequent arrears in rents due to lack of manpower to obtain the necessary production. The landlords were glad to free villeins because, in face of the high costs and prices, it was too expensive to permit them to go on using the land, at the rents fixed in their leases.

There is little evidence of the "struggle" between feudal lord and commercial capitalist that Marx emphasizes, unless the competition for labor can be called a "struggle." It is not true that all the labor freed was forced off the land by the nobility; in many cases, the villeins were glad to be freed to accept the higher industrial wages. Yet Marx is right in suggesting that feudalism had outlived its usefulness. Indeed, the main reason for its disappearance was its sheer inefficiency and the opportunity for profit in better methods.

Enclosures were accompanied by the concentration of owner-

[13] Cf. Ephraim Lipson, *Economic History of England* (London, 1937–43), Vol. I, pp. 82ff.; H. Robbins, "A Comparison of the Effects of the Black Death on the Economic Organization of France and England," *Journal of Political Economy*, August, 1928.

ship of land into fewer hands. Scattered strips were amalgamated into more workable plots, arable land was converted into pasture, and the commons were appropriated for production. These tendencies were present before the Black Death but are more noticeable afterward. Sheep farming was the most important agricultural industry, and yielded large profits.

Thus in the period from the thirteenth to the sixteenth centuries, and even afterward, we notice a gradual transition from farming for consumption to more specialized and more efficient farming for profit, which is one feature of capitalism.

The Discoveries and the "Price Revolution"

Those, like Henri Sée, who place the period of the "rise of capitalism" at a later date, usually stress the new geographical discoveries, and the consequent inflow of precious metals, as causes. The most important of these discoveries were the Cape route to the Orient (da Gama, 1498), the North American continent (Columbus, 1492), Brazil (Cabral, 1500), and Magellan's circumnavigation of the globe (1522). Hamilton, while admitting the significance of other factors such as the rise of the national state and improvements in agriculture, regards these discoveries as the great cause of capitalistic development.[14] The effects, according to him, were

1. Improved shipping: the effect was similar to the effect upon aviation of the trans-Atlantic flights. Bigger and better ships and new navigation instruments were developed.
2. New techniques: the widening of the market facilitated division of labor and led to technological improvements.
3. The influx of new goods from America and the Orient, including the slave trade.
4. Emigration, which relieved population pressure, provided new raw materials, and markets for finished goods.
5. Guild organization, unable to deal with new problems, crumbled and gave way to the capitalistic employer.
6. The vast influx of gold and silver: this last factor was most important. During the fourteenth and fifteenth centuries, expanding output led to declining prices, which acted as a deterrent to expansion. The gold and silver which came first to Spain and Portugal was distributed throughout Europe through the Ricardian specie-flow mechanism. Prices quadrupled, wages and rents lagged, giving an incentive to speculation, capital building,

[14] E. J. Hamilton, *American Treasure and the Price Revolution in Spain, 1501–1650* (Cambridge, Mass., 1934).

promotion of new industries, etc. Tremendous profits were made from the Oriental trade, and the inflow of gold made possible the importation of Oriental goods without need to sell an equal value of European goods to the Orient. It thus broadened the area of trade, and provided sources for new profits. Without it, the "unfavorable" trade with the Orient could not have been continued. Much of the metal coming from America ended in the Orient.

It should be pointed out that the mere possession of precious metals cannot, in and of itself, provide an incentive to economic development. The countries richest in "treasure" have not always been the most economically advanced. Not the general price level, but the relation between the price of consumers' and of capital goods, determines the amount of new investment. It is profit inflation, due to a lag in costs, that encourages expansion.

In the appendix on mercantilism in his *General Theory*, Keynes provides another rationale for the relation between the "price revolution" and the rise of capitalism. The important aspect of the gold inflow, Keynes argues, was not so much its effect on prices as its effects on liquidity and bank reserves. In a monetary system where the volume of bank credit depends on the size of the nation's reserves of precious metals, the influx of these metals results in low interest rates and "easy money." The volume of private investment and the consequent rate of economic growth is accordingly maintained on a relatively high level.

Did Capitalism "Rise" or Evolve?

Of late some economic historians have become fond of spiking all historical theories about the "rise" of capitalism in one period or another, contending that most of the features attributed to capitalism by Sombart, for example, can be found in the Middle Ages as well. Capitalism, commercial, financial, and industrial, has evolved gradually over several centuries. Some skeptics among historians have contended that one ought not to speak of a "rise of capitalism" at all, or at least not as a phenomenon characteristic of any one period or resulting from any one constellation of events. There has been some degree of capitalism in all civilizations, and the features which constitute the present economic organization have been added gradually and one by one. Nor has the trend been one of continual progress. Features of modern capitalism have existed in one period, have been abandoned in the next, and then reintroduced,—investment banking in Venice, for example. One can speak of a "rise of capitalism" only in the sense that economic development has been somewhat more rapid or more marked in some periods than in others There is, so to speak, a change in the *third* derivative of the function showing the rate of increase in *per capita* output through time.

Commercial Capitalism

In the period following the Crusades, these skeptics point out, a highly organized international trade existed in Europe. The area to develop first was the Mediterranean. Although Italian cities took the lead, Spanish cities, such as Barcelona, and French cities like Marseilles were not far behind. The Mediterranean trade was with North Africa and the Near East and consisted largely of luxury goods. Ships were quite large, capable of handling respectable cargoes. The organization was capitalistic, capital being provided mainly through the *commenda* and *societas* arrangements and often obtained through issuing shares. Ships were sometimes state-owned. Almost contemporaneous with the early development of the Mediterranean trade was the development of the north-to-south trade. This trade took place through the organization of fairs, such as that of Champagne, or of Antwerp, Lyons, Avignon, Bruges, Brussels, as well as those of Genoa, Venice, Barcelona, etc. In the conduct of this trade there was considerable division of labor among wholesalers, retailers, financiers, etc. The purely northern trade between Scandinavia and England, England and The Netherlands, Scandinavia and France, etc., was dominated by the Hanseatic League. The important members of the Hanse, like the great Italian traders, were true capitalists earning large profits; they were often able to become nobles on the proceeds of their financial success. They controlled the peasants and labor and exerted political influence.

The period following the great discoveries at the turn of the fifteenth and sixteenth centuries and up to the eighteenth century is often called the era of "commercial revolution." This term does not give an accurate picture of the period, excluding as it does industrial and agricultural developments and indicating a change more rapid and more violent than actually took place. Yet certain trends can be discerned which begin in the late fifteenth century and continue through the sixteenth and seventeenth centuries. First, there was an enormous expansion in European commerce, both domestic and international. France, England, and Holland began to rival Italy and Spain as trading countries.

The influence of the discoveries on this expansion can be over-emphasized, and the old trade routes were not abandoned. New ones were added, however, bringing new commodities and new markets. There was a relative decline in the importance of the Italian cities and the Hanseatic League in control of international trade. The new routes made the position of the Italian cities less advantageous; the loss of fishing trade and the rise of national states made the Hanseatic League less powerful. Yet the Italian cities continued to dominate the luxury trade until well into the seventeenth century, and many of the Hanse towns continued to be important economic centers. The Commercial Revolution finished the overturn of medieval organization, with its guilds, its manors, and town control of foreign trade. Considerable technical progress occurred in the field of navigation. Ships were built larger and faster, with more decks and more masts and a combination of square-rigged and lateen sails. Knowledge of currents and winds was enlarged. The science of astronomy advanced; the compass and astrolabe made possible more efficient navigation on long voyages. Maps and charts were improved, lighthouses built, and harbors cleared. These developments in the field of commerce constitute a part of the development of "capitalism"—so the skeptics maintain.

Financial Capitalism

Contrary to Sombart, says this group of critics, the development of finance in the Middle Ages had many characteristics that we are inclined to regard as "modern." [15] The most highly developed capital markets were in the Mediterranean cities and in The Netherlands. Commerce was financed to a very large extent by borrowed capital. Capital might be provided under the various *commenda* arrangements, through the *societas*, or even through the *sea loan*. Straightforward loans on personal or commercial security were also made. Often shares were sold to raise capital for ships or cargoes. In Italy and in Spain banks of deposit existed, and payments were made by bank transfers. In certain periods these banks also made loans. Foreign exchange transactions were carried on both as a means of making loans and to transfer capital. The operation of the fairs involved a great deal of sales credit, as did also the transaction of local business. Public finance involved the issue of government securities, state banks, huge interna-

[15] See for example André Sayous, " 'Der Moderne Kapitalismus' de Werner Sombart et Genes aux XII et XIII Siecles," *Revue d'Histoire Economique et Sociale*, XVIII (1930), p. 427.

tional loans, etc. The great financial houses like the Bardi, Peruzzi, Medici, etc., rivaled the Rothschilds and Morgans and Rockefellers of modern times.

The fifteenth and sixteenth centuries, so far as financial capitalism was concerned, were characterized by the spread of these methods of finance to other parts of Europe, notably Germany and England. It might be more accurate to say the development of these financial methods in these countries, since in England, at least, much use was made of credit in the Middle Ages. In the sixteenth century, however, England developed its own class of big capitalists, such as Gresham. In Germany, great houses like the Fuggers became internationally significant in the fifteenth century and were at their height in the early sixteenth century. In England, the development was continued after the sixteenth century, her relative importance increasing. During the sixteenth century, Antwerp was the most important international financial center, overshadowing the Italian cities of Venice and Genoa. The public control of banking made strides in the fifteenth and sixteenth centuries. The legal attitude toward credit operations underwent some revision in this period, particularly in England and the northern part of the Continent. Financial capitalism was perhaps more highly developed in Europe up to 1600 than any other form of capitalism.

In this period there occurred the first modern crisis, based not upon famine nor plague nor invasion but upon overextension of credit. The break came in 1556, and the panic reached its height in 1559. The depression in the financial market continued for several years afterward, and the capitalistic development of Europe was retarded as a result. The basis of the credit inflation was Spanish war finance, with the Fuggers and other large houses making huge loans to the King. Antwerp was glutted with obligations of the Spanish Crown. Gresham noticed signs of disturbance as early as 1553.[16] In France, both King and Cardinal were borrowing constantly. In addition to these public loans, an unestimable amount of private credit was extended by merchants, financiers, and bankers. In 1557, the war between France and Spain broke out. Philip was advised by the Church to repudiate,

[16] "This Bourse of Antwerp is strange. One day there is plenty of money, and the next none, because there are so many good takers and deliveres that if one will not act, another will. Fugger and Jasper Schetz are bare of money and no good can be done with them at present, as the Emperor owes about 300,000 livres." (See William B. Turnbull, *Callendar of State Papers of the Reign of Queen Mary*, 1553–1558, Foreign Series No. 104, London, 1861.)

but he refunded and consolidated for fear of losing his credit altogether. Short-term loans were converted into perpetual *rentes*. Security values fell accordingly. On the date set for payment, only a small part of the interest owed was paid, and the King announced the flotation of a new loan. The market was unable to stand such a strain; both France and Spain became bankrupt and were forced into peace. The "wars of religion" completed the collapse of the international capital market.[17] Thus the financial crisis, which is a characteristic of the capitalistic system, makes its appearance in the sixteenth century. When did "capitalism" arise?

Industrial Capitalism and Urbanism

Some economic historians have maintained that the rise of industrial capitalism coincided with the decay of feudalism and the growth of the towns. If the rise of towns were a mere transplanting of cottage industry from the manor to a town there would be no basis for such a statement. But in fact the growth of towns involved a change in ownership. The cottage workers no longer owned raw materials and products. The raw materials were supplied either by customers or by merchants who bought the raw materials and sold the finished product for a profit. Such merchants were capitalists, and such artisans were dependent workers, hired for piece-rate wages. Such a change is more significant than the growth of factories as such, for factories existed in ancient times with slave labor. Weber mentions various kinds of factory organizations in the Middle Ages: mills, ovens, breweries, iron foundries. With few exceptions, however, such organizations were operated in a communal rather than a capitalistic manner. The independent craftsman, the cottage worker, and the putting-out system were still predominant. Lipson tells us that as late as the sixteenth century the town craftsmen were forbidden to work at their craft during harvest, in order to be available for work on the manors. True there were large workshops, particularly in the textile industry, during the sixteenth century. But one must distinguish between increased use of machinery and division of labor and a mere collection of workers under one roof. Technical specialization was still relatively rare in the sixteenth century. Yet mere size does have some significance; some sixteenth-century manufacturers did rise to considerable prom-

[17] Henri Hauser, "The European Financial Crisis of 1559," *Journal of Economic and Business History*, 1930, pp. 241–55.

inence and contribute to the accumulation of capital. The trend toward the factory system is discernible in the sixteenth century, and even in the fifteenth, as is shown by legislation against large-scale production and the use of machinery. Yet the rise of industrial capitalism is a feature of later centuries.

Technical progress in industry is also not a phenomenon which is limited to the period following 1600, this group of historians insists. One of the earliest and most important advances was the use of water power in place of man or animal power; this opened up many new possibilities in manufacturing. Opposition to the introduction of water power began in the thirteenth century and was largely overcome in the early fifteenth century. The commercial expansion following the discoveries opened up new markets, created new demands, and gave a stimulus to technical progress. Certain new industries grew up: gunpowder mills, cannon foundries, alum and copperas factories, sugar refineries, saltpeter works. Plants were set up involving investments far greater than individual craftsmen or guilds could provide. More important than these new industries were the improvements in old industries. Better methods in mining and production of metals were introduced even before the sixteenth century: drains, pumps, ventilation, etc., in mining and the blast furnace, water-driven hammers, standardization of metal products, machine-drawn wires, etc., in metallurgy. The substitution of coal for wood and charcoal for heating was important in view of the diminishing lumber supply. The sixteenth century saw an acceleration of such technological progress. The advantage of calcining iron ore before smelting it was discovered. William Lee invented the stocking frame. The production of salt from sea water involved large plants. Cranes and pulleys made possible the moving of heavier weights in construction and manufacturing. The finishing of textiles—dyeing, fulling, and calendaring—was much improved and done on a large scale. Thus it is clear that so far as technical improvement is concerned the eighteenth century was more "capitalistic" than the sixteenth only in the sense that the pace was more rapid and the inventions more striking.[18]

Entrepreneurship

Nor can "capitalism" be dated from the seventeenth or eighteenth centuries in terms of appearance of entrepreneurs, say the

[18] Cf. especially J. U Nef, "The Progress of Technology and the Growth of Large-Scale Industry in Great Britain, 1540–1640," *Economic History Review*, October, 1934.

skeptics. Even in the Middle Ages there was a distinct entrepreneurial class in commerce and in finance. During the sixteenth century, if not earlier, the industrial entrepreneur appears. To what extent the development of an entrepreneurial class is dependent upon freedom of enterprise is perhaps debatable. Yet there seems to be some support for the contention that the exhausting struggle between Emperor and Pope in the Middle Ages left the cities free to develop under the domination of merchant capitalists. It is at least worth asking, therefore, whether the rise of the national state and the breakdown of town control contributed substantially to the rise of an entrepreneurial class and the growth of capitalism.

There can be no doubt that town and guild administration involved a complicated and lengthy set of rules for trade and commerce. Severe penalties were imposed for the infraction of rules concerning standards, quality, fraud, adulteration, etc. Particularly important were the laws against forestalling, regrating, and engrossing. An attempt was made to prevent monopolization. The conditions of buying and selling, prices, wages, and hours, were determined by law. It would seem that entrepreneurs hemmed in by such restrictions would be discouraged and pine away into insignificance, but it is doubtful whether the rules were enforced. The impossibility of enforcing the rules against forestalling, etc., led to price fixing. But although prices were fixed, quantity and quality of commodities varied, so that the *de facto* prices actually fluctuated. The large revenue collected from fines imposed for infringement of rules indicated that the rules were not kept and that it paid to break them. It is possible, therefore, that town and guild regulation was not such an impediment to capitalistic development as it may appear at first glance.

When, on the other hand, we turn to the state control and mercantilism that succeeded "town policy," we do not find much relaxation of the administrative regulation of the economy. In practice, mercantilism involved much more than the control of exports, imports, and the foreign exchanges. As always, it was found that intervention in one part of the economy required intervention in others. Control of foreign exchanges necessitated control of the capital market. Regulation of imports and exports meant interference with particular businesses. Bullionist policy was extended to emigration and immigration. There were other types of interference not directly related to mercantilism, such as wage regulation and the legislation against large-scale and machine industry already mentioned.

On the whole, it seems probable that the rise of the national state made commerce and industry somewhat more free within and between towns of a particular country, even if town customs taxes and regulations did not immediately disappear. Also, if one regards monopoly as typical of capitalism, the mercantilist policy aided the development of capitalism, for the creation of monopolies was a feature of this period. The granting of monopolies to creditors of the state was a medieval practice, but the monopolies of the early modern world were more lucrative and contributed more to the accumulation of capital.

Rostow and "the Take-off into Sustained Growth"

The work of economic historians in the last few decades, pushing back the beginning of "the rise of capitalism," is essentially a reaction against the too facile explanation of the Industrial Revolution in terms of a series of inventions in the eighteenth and early nineteenth centuries—the cotton gin, the spinning jenny, steam, the coking process. The difficulty with this sort of research, of course, is that it tends toward agnosticism. If we find evidence of commercial, financial, and even industrial capitalism in the sixteenth century, how do we explain the marked acceleration of economic growth in the eighteenth and nineteenth centuries? To say that there was no fundamental difference between economic organization and activity in the eighteenth century and in the seventeenth or sixteenth is clearly no help.

Recently, an eminent economic historian, who is also well versed in economic theory and a specialist on economic development, has been bold enough to set forth a new synthesis of historical knowledge about the beginnings of economic growth. Walt Rostow opens his discussion of "The Take-off into Self-sustained Growth" with a statement of purpose: [19]

> The purpose of this article is to explore the following hypothesis: that the process of economic growth can usefully be regarded as centering on a relatively brief time interval of two or three decades when the economy and the society of which it is a part transform themselves in such a way that economic growth is, subsequently, more or less automatic. This decisive transformation is here called the take-off.
>
> The take-off is defined as the interval during which the rate of investment increases in such a way that real output per capita rises and this initial increase carries with it radical changes in production techniques and the disposition of income flows which perpetuate the new scale of investment and perpetuate thereby the rising trend in per

[19] Rostow, *op. cit.*, pp. 29–30.

capita output. . . . In short, this article is an effort to clarify the economics of industrial revolution when an industrial revolution is conceived of narrowly with respect to time and broadly with respect to changes in production functions.

Rostow finds it convenient to divide the economic history of any country into three stages: a "long period" of a century or more during which the preconditions for take-off are established; two or three decades into which the take-off itself is compressed; and "the long, fluctuating story of sustained economic progress" when growth becomes normal and "relatively automatic." In terms of this classification, we can see that most of the efforts of economic historians summarized above have actually been directed toward defining and lengthening the period for establishing *preconditions*. Relatively little effort has been directed toward pinning down the timing and causation of the *take-off*. The latter is a more difficult task. It requires a fairly systematic *theory* of development to begin with. "The beginning of take-off," says Rostow "can usually be traced to a particular sharp stimulus." To make such a statement one needs some idea as to what kind of events provide a stimulus to accelerated growth.

The long process of establishing preconditions is summarized by Rostow as follows:

We start with a reasonably stable and traditional society containing an economy mainly agricultural, using more or less unchanging production methods, saving and investing productively little more than is required to meet depreciation. Usually from outside the society, but sometimes out of its own dynamics, comes the idea that economic progress is possible; and this idea spreads within the established élite or, more usually, in some disadvantaged group whose lack of status does not prevent the exercise of some economic initiative. More often than not the economic motives for seeking economic progress converge with some non-economic motive, such as the desire for increased social power and prestige, national pride, political ambition, and so on. Education, for some at least, broadens and changes to suit the needs of modern economic activity. New enterprising men come forward willing to mobilise savings and to take risks in pursuit of profit, notably in commerce. The commercial markets for agricultural products, domestic handicrafts and consumption-goods imports widen. Institutions for mobilising capital appear; or they expand from primitive levels in the scale, surety and time horizon for loans. Basic capital is expanded, notably in transport and communications, often to bring to market raw materials in which other nations have an economic interest, often financed by foreign capital. And, here and there, modern manufacturing enterprise appears, usually in substitution for imports.

Since public-health measures are enormously productive in their early stages of application and, as innovations go, meet relatively low resistance in most cultures, the death rate may fall and the population begin to rise, putting pressure on the food supply and the institutional structure of agriculture, creating thereby an economic depressant or stimulus (or both in turn), depending on the society's response.

The rate of productive investment may rise up to 5 per cent of national income; but this is unlikely to do much more than keep ahead of the population increase. And, in general, all this activity proceeds on a limited basis, within an economy and a society still mainly characterized by traditional low-productivity techniques and by old values and institutions which developed in conjunction with them. The rural proportion of the population is likely to stand at 75 per cent or over.

The take-off is a complex affair; however "a necessary but not sufficient condition" is "the fact that the proportion of net investments to national income rises from (say) 5 per cent to over 10 per cent, definitely outstripping the likely population pressure."[20] He adds two other "necessary" conditions: the appearance of one or more substantial manufacturing sectors with high rates of growth and "the existence or quick emergence of a political, social and institutional framework which exploits the impulses to expansion in the modern sector and the potential external effects of the take-off and gives to growth an on-going character." With these criteria as his major guide, Rostow suggests some "tentative, approximate take-off dates" for twelve countries:

Country	Take-off	Country	Take-off
Great Britain	1783–1802	Russia	1890–1914
France	1830–1860	Canada	1896–1914
Belgium	1833–1860	Argentine ‡	1935–
United States *	1843–1860	Turkey §	1937–
Germany	1850–1873	India ‖	1952–
Sweden	1868–1890	China ‖	1952–
Japan †	1878–1900		

* The American take-off is here viewed as the upshot of two different periods of expansion: the first, that of the 1840's, marked by railway and manufacturing development, mainly confined to the East—this occurred while the West and South digested the extensive agricultural expansion of the previous decade; the second the great railway push into the Middle West during the 1850's marked by a heavy inflow of foreign capital. By the opening of the Civil War, the American economy of North and West, with real momentum in its heavy-industry sector, is judged to have taken off.

† Lacking adequate data, there is some question about the timing of the Japanese take-off. Some part of the post-1868 period was certainly, by the present set of definitions, devoted to firming up the preconditions for take-

In the process, three kinds of sector will appear in the economy: primary growth sectors, with particularly favorable opportunities for innovation and resource discovery; supplementary growth sectors, which expand as a response to, or requirement of, advance in the primary sectors (coal, iron, and engineering in relation to railroads); and derived growth sectors, where advance responds to growth of national income, population, output, "or some other overall, modestly increasing parameter."

All this is very general and far indeed from a tight and systematic theory of economic development. No doubt, historians will raise once again their objections to "stage theories" and insist that the documentary evidence does not permit any precise division of economic history into any such neatly defined periods. Rostow would no doubt agree; but we can also agree with him that his conception of the three stages of growth does correspond roughly to the data and general information about economic development of various countries, however difficult the dating of these stages may be. We can also agree that the lessons of history are more easily assessed if we do make such a distinction among the three stages; for we will not then make the mistake of looking for historical evidence of the causes of take-off during a period when all we can hope to find is evidence on causes of establishing *preconditions*—a mistake to which eco-

[20] Rostow, *op. cit.*, pp. 29, 30. For an earlier statement of Rostow's ideas regarding causes of growth, see his *The Process of Economic Growth* (Oxford, 1953).

---

off. By 1914 the Japanese economy had certainly taken off. The question is whether the period from about 1878 to the Sino-Japanese War in the mid-1890's is to be regarded as the completion of the preconditions or as take-off. On present evidence, I incline to the latter view.

‡ In one sense the Argentine economy began its take-off during the First World War. But by and large, down to the pit of the post-1929 depression, the growth of its modern sector, stimulated during the war, tended to slacken; and, like a good part of the Western World, the Argentine sought during the 1920's to return to a pre-1914 normalcy. It was not until the mid-1930's that a sustained take-off was inaugurated, which by and large can now be judged to have been successful despite the structural vicissitudes of that economy.

§ Against the background of industrialization measures inaugurated in the mid-1930's the Turkish economy has exhibited remarkable momentum in the past five years, founded in the increase in agricultural income and productivity. It still remains to be seen whether these two surges, conducted under quite different national policies, will constitute a transition to self-sustaining growth, and whether Turkey can overcome its current structural problems.

|| As noted in the text, it is still too soon (for quite different reasons) to judge either the Indian or Chinese Communist take-off efforts successful.

nomic historians have been addicted; nor will we make the mistake committed by so many economists of looking for historical evidence on the *take-off* in statistics covering only the period when the process of *self-sustained growth* has already set in.

We can accept all this and still admit to a sense of disappointment at what the economic historian has to offer by way of explanation of how economic development did take place in the now advanced countries.[21] We have added very little to the list of strategic variables included in our synthesis of general theories: the importance of capital formation; the vital role of technological progress and the entrepreneurial function; the widening of the market and expansion of international trade as a means of widening markets; the necessity of structural change, with a relative decline of the agricultural sector at the same time that agricultural productivity rises. All this we knew from our survey of general theory. One hint in the historical analysis, however, is worth recording for future consideration when we turn to the problems of underdeveloped countries today: the Black Death not only gave European countries a respite from population pressure but drastically changed the factor-proportion situation. Labor became scarce even in agriculture, and a shift to more land-and-capital-intensive techniques became profitable to landowners. The expansion of world trade, coming conveniently at the same time, provided growing markets for the product of the new extensive agriculture, and by another strikingly convenient coincidence, the growth of manufactures provided employment for peasants forced off the land by enclosures, or lured to the burgeoning cities by opportunities for self-advancement there.

[21] It seems that economic history must be rewritten with each advance in economic theory. Arthur Lewis has put the situation well: "Every economist goes through a phase where he is dissatisfied with the deductive basis of economic theory, and feels sure that a much better insight into economic processes could be obtained by studying the facts of history. The instinct is sound; yet the enthusiasms of this phase seldom survive any serious attempt to get to grips with the facts of history. This is because there are very few facts in the relevant senses. We mean by this, in the first instance, that it is only for a very few countries and for very recent periods that any adequate quantity of historical records exists; and even when there are plenty of records we cannot always be certain exactly what happened. We mean also, more significantly, that the 'facts' which would interest the theorist are not what happened but why it happened; and while history may record what happened, it is seldom able to record why it happened. . . . Most economic historians explain economic events in terms of the economic theories current at the time of writing . . . and a new crop of economic theories is liable to be followed by a new crop of historical articles rewriting history in terms of the new theory." (*The Theory of Economic Growth*, p. 15.)

10 Economic Development: Past and Present

In the preceding chapter we put this question: "What were the major causes of the rise of capitalism?" Another way to learn from history is to ask: "What are the differences between the present situation of underdeveloped countries and the situation in the now advanced countries at the time of their take-off into sustained economic growth?" Such a comparison may help us to appreciate the dimensions of the task now facing underdeveloped countries as they try to reach higher standards of living. Even a superficial examination of the economic history of the Western world between 1700 and 1950 reveals an extraordinary conjuncture of factors favorable to economic growth. Was this conjuncture a historical accident, an accident that cannot be reproduced by acts of policy?

This chapter is addressed to these questions. For purposes of analysis—and recognizing the arbitrary nature of any such distinction—the various factors are divided among economic, political, sociological, and technological categories.

Economic Factors

In Part 1, we saw that all theories of economic development, from Adam Smith to Hansen, relate increases in per capita income to four major factors: capital accumulation, population growth, discoveries of new resources, and technological progress.

These four factors are interrelated in various ways; indeed, theories of economic development differ mainly with regard to the nature of these interrelationships. Let us examine conditions affecting these four factors in the now advanced countries, during the period of their most rapid growth, and compare those with conditions affecting them in the now underdeveloped countries.

Our review of development theories showed that the effect of capital accumulation on development is ambivalent. Each act of net investment raises national income but retards further net investment. Other things being equal, profits tend to decline as the stock of capital grows. For continued economic expansion to occur, one or more of the other three factors must operate favorably, so as to produce a steady rate of capital accumulation.

In the now advanced countries, net savings and investment during the periods of rapid growth averaged between 10 and 20 per cent of national income. In most, but not all the now underdeveloped countries, net savings and investment run between 2 to 6 per cent of the national income. Here is one of the many vicious circles encountered in any study of the problem of economic development. A high level of national income results in a high level of savings and investment, and consequently, in a rapid rate of economic growth. Underdeveloped countries in general have such low incomes that any substantial volume of savings and investment out of existing income is extremely difficult. To a large degree, the problem of economic growth is a problem of "getting over the hump" to the point where levels of per capita income are high enough to permit sufficient net savings and investment to guarantee continued expansion.

Recently, it has been suggested that significant increases in *per capita* income can be achieved without much capital investment.[1] This suggestion is discussed in Chapter 19 below. In brief, our conclusion is that opportunities for raising *per capita* output in a fashion requiring little *per capita* investment should certainly be seized, but that opportunities for this type of development project are not sufficient in themselves to get the underdeveloped countries "over the hump"—unless a new technology, suited to the factor endowment of these underdeveloped countries, can be discovered. This new technology, which would be labor absorb-

[1] Cf. James Duesenberry, "Some Aspects of the Theory of Economic Development," *Explorations in Entrepreneurial History*, December, 1950; Ragnar Nurkse, *Problems of Capital Formation in Underdeveloped Countries* (New York, 1953); and International Labor Office, *Report of the Director-General* (Geneva, 1953), pp. 37–48.

ing and capital saving, would have to apply over a much wider range of economic activity than the road-building, irrigation, and similar projects proposed for the purpose of absorbing disguised unemployment and raising productivity without much investment.[2]

In this chapter, where we are concerned with a comparison of what did happen in the now advanced countries with what might happen in the now underdeveloped ones, we need make only two observations: first, the "trigger mechanism" of the Industrial Revolution did not consist of such projects as building roads and undertaking irrigation projects, with disguised unemployed labor utilizing known techniques, but rather of technical advance occurring more or less simultaneously over a wide field; second, at least some of the underdeveloped countries have transport facilities and irrigation systems in a relatively advanced state. There seems no way but an increased flow of savings and investment if the less developed countries wish to enjoy high standards of living.

Population Growth

It is useful to distinguish among four types of population situation. First, population may be less than optimum, in the strict technical sense that *per capita* income could be raised merely by increasing the size of the population, with no changes in other strategic variables. Second, *per capita* income may not rise with increasing population alone, but a feasible development program might create a situation in which population growth would have a favorable effect on *per capita* income. Third, the marginal productivity of labor (and thus of population increases) may be positive, although *per capita* income would fall with rising population, despite any measures that could be taken as part of any feasible development program. Fourth, the situation may be one in which the marginal productivity of labor is zero or negative, and will remain so despite the development program.

Some of the now advanced countries, such as Canada, are still in the first category. More important, almost all the advanced countries were in this category *at the beginning* of their periods of most rapid growth. The Industrial Revolution began at a time when European populations were very low. With technological progress, resource discoveries, and expanding world mar-

[2] Problems relating to the choice of technology are discussed further in chap. 27.

kets, the level of the optimum population became steadily higher, so that actual population remained below optimum throughout most of the period of rapid growth.

Some of the Latin American countries appear to be in the second category; a rise in population by itself might not raise per capita income, but appropriate and feasible development plans could create a situation in which population growth would have a favorable effect on *per capita* income. Unfortunately, most of the Middle Eastern and Asian countries (with the possible exceptions of Burma, Indochina, and Malaya) are in the third, or even in the fourth, category.

There is, therefore, a discontinuity in the growth function with respect to population increases. Where population grows in a country with less than optimal population, that growth provides an additional stimulus to expansion, by encouraging investment in housing, transport, public utilities, and the like, and by permitting optimal capital-labor ratios to be maintained as capital accumulates. But where populations are already above optimum levels, further increases act only as a drag on economic development, preventing any rise in per capita income, or even lowering per capita income, and thus aggravating the difficulty of saving and investing enough to generate expansion. Moreover, the population growth of underdeveloped countries takes a very wasteful form. The combination of high birth rates and high death rates means that a large proportion of the population consists of unproductive children, many of whom will not live long enough to repay the community's investment in them.

In short, the now advanced countries had their take-off before their population explosion, whereas many of the now underdeveloped countries have had their population explosion before a take-off. Moreover, as we shall see in Chapter 28 below, European rates of population growth were never so high as they are in some underdeveloped countries today.

Perhaps the most important consequence of this difference in sequence is the contrast in levels of per capita income at the time of actual or attempted take-off. We saw in Chapter 1 that any international comparison of income levels is precarious; it becomes still more precarious when current incomes in some countries are compared with incomes in another country two centuries ago. Nevertheless, the estimates made by Phyllis Deane (Table 10-1) suggest, when allowance is made for subsequent changes in price levels, that incomes in England in the eighteenth century were closer to those of Argentina or Chile today than to those of India or Burma today. Obviously, it is easier to save and invest enough to meet the requirements for take-off out of an average income of $300 than out of an average of $100.

The relatively high incomes in Europe before the Industrial Revolution reflect another factor of great importance—a factor

TABLE 10-1.

Contemporary Estimates of the National Income of the United Kingdom in the Nineteenth Century

Year and derivation of national income estimates	Population, in millions	Average money national income, £	Domestic exports as percentage national income	Estimate of trend in average real incomes 1800 = 100
1800 (Pitt, Beeke, Bell)	15.7	19	13	100
1812 (Colquhoun)	18.4	22	10	94
1822 (Lowe)	21.3	17	10	114
1831 (Pebrer)	24.1	23	7	174
1836 (Mulhall)	25.4	24	8	168
1841 (Spackman)	26.8	21	11	145
1846 (Smee)	28.0	21	10	160
1851 (Levi)	27.4	23	13	193
1860 (Muhall)	28.8	33	14	234
1867 (Levi, Baxter)	30.4	28	21	205
1870 (Mulhall)	31.3	31	22	222
1879–80 (Levi)	34.3	35	18	274
1880 (Mulhall)	34.6	33	19	278
1882–83 (Levi)	35.2	36	21	296
1883 (Giffen)	35.5	36	18	307
1886 (Mulhall)	36.3	34	18	326
1889 (Mulhall)	37.2	35	19	342
1895 (Mulhall)	39.2	36	16	402
1902 (Giffen)	41.9	42	16	405

SOURCE: Phyllis Deane, "The Industrial Revolution and Economic Growth: The Evidence of Early British National Income Estimates," *Economic Development and Cultural Change*, Vol. V, No. 2, January, 1957.

facilitated, and indeed encouraged, by the lack of population pressure. In Europe a long period of agricultural improvement, tending toward more extensive agriculture, preceded the Industrial Revolution. Industrialization in turn permitted a second wave of agricultural improvement in the form of mechanization. As we shall see in more detail in Chapter 14, some underdeveloped countries have had considerable industrialization while agricultural productivity lagged farther and farther behind. This low productivity in agriculture is largely a result of population pressure and consequent division of landholdings into tiny splinters.

No expert can suggest any simple short-run policy to meet this situation. The happy circumstance in which economic expansion took place at a time when populations were below optimum, so that population growth was a favorable factor in the development picture, cannot be reproduced in most of the now underdeveloped countries, except by drastic measures introduced in the social, economic, and technical fields all at once.

Discovery of New Natural Resources

We have seen that the discovery of new natural resources, or the opening up of frontiers, plays a prominent role in recent theories of economic development. Yet all these theories imply, if they do not explicitly state, that resource discovery in itself is not enough to produce economic growth; an *increasing rate* of resource discovery is required.[3] In so far as resource discovery is a factor influencing past and present levels of investment, a constant rate of discovery is needed merely to prevent a *decline* in investment, and thus in employment and output. This consideration is an important one, since most underdeveloped countries have enjoyed substantial rates of resource discovery in the past. In the former colonial areas especially, considerable time, effort, ingenuity, and capital have been devoted to discovery and development of new natural resources. In these areas, producing a rate of resource discovery *more rapid* than that which has taken place in the past will be no easy task.

The problem is complicated by the fact that most underdeveloped areas do not have "frontiers" in the sense that they existed in the New World in the nineteenth century, or even in the sense that they existed in Europe in the eighteenth century. The peoples of the present underdeveloped areas do not have the opportunity of moving to virgin land that is richer than the land now occupied. In most underdeveloped countries, the present distribution of population reflects very accurately the distribution of known resources, including soil fertility. In Libya, for

[3] See, for example: Benjamin Higgins, "The Theory of Increasing Under-Employment," *The Economic Journal*, June, 1950; Evsey Domar, "Capital Expansion, Rate of Growth, and Employment," *The American Economic Review*, March, 1947; and "Investment, Losses, and Monopoly," in *Income, Employment, and Public Policy: Essays in Honor of Alvin Hansen* (New York, 1948); R. F. Harrod, *Towards A Dynamic Economics* (London, 1948); and Burton Keirstead, *The Theory of Economic Change* (Toronto, 1948).

example, moving from the settled areas means moving out into the Sahara. In Indonesia, the areas being considered for transmigration, in order to relieve population pressure in Java and provide opportunities for technically improved agriculture, are far indeed from being easily accessible, virgin, and rich. Some are cut-over areas, once intensively cultivated, later abandoned, and now covered with useless *alang-alang* grass which is both hard and costly to remove. The rest is jungle, virgin perhaps, but extremely difficult and expensive to clear. Moreover, the soil in these areas is less fertile than the rich volcanic soils of Java, from which the settlers are to come. In neither of these countries, therefore—and in few other underdeveloped countries—do people have the opportunity of moving to areas *still richer* in known natural resources than those they formerly occupied.

The outlook with respect to mineral resources is less clear, since surveys are not complete. On the other hand, colonial powers have spent much energy and money in searching for mineral resources. In Libya, these searches have been largely futile, although there is now hope of finding significant reserves of oil. In Indonesia, they have been more rewarding; but at the moment, instead of finding it easy to move to new territories and find new mineral resources, enterprises now operating in the country are worried about exhaustion of present known reserves. A National Planning Bureau Mission was informed that known tin reserves will last six years at present rates of production. Known oil reserves will last for approximately ten years. No clear information is available as to how long the known reserves of high-grade bauxite will last. New exploration and research, new discoveries, and new development are necessary merely to maintain current rates of *production*. In general, in those countries where exploration has been at all successful, past investment in resource development has been high. To discover enough new natural resources to generate *still higher* levels of developmental investment than occurred in the past will be a difficult task.

Apart from the influence on investment through the production function and through presentation of new market opportunities, we have seen that the frontier, as it existed in Canada or the United States, was an important growth factor through the inculcation of a "frontier spirit." The possibility of "moving West" to areas where the land was fertile and mineral resources abundant kept alive a venturesome entrepreneurial spirit throughout a century and a half. We have seen that the absence of such a frontier is one factor in the difference between Australian experience and that of countries of English background in the New World. But if the frontier in the Canadian or American sense was lacking in Australia, its absence is still more striking in the case of most underdeveloped areas. For centuries, such economic development as took place brought no obvious movement in the centroid of population. Nothing remotely resembling the westward movements in the United States and Canada, or even the movements from country areas to cities in nineteenth-century England has taken place in most underdeveloped areas. Consequently, no "frontier spirit" of venturesome entrepreneurship is to be found in these countries.

Technological Progress

The theories of economic development outlined above generally lay primary stress on technological progress. Here too, it is worth remembering that in most of these theories, it is an *increase in the rate* of technological progress, rather than the mere existence of technological advance, which produces economic expansion. Few underdeveloped countries indeed have been without substantial improvements in technique in the past. The problem is not merely one of introducing some degree of improvement in techniques, it is a matter of raising the *rate* of technological progress.

The outlook in this connection is certainly more favorable than in the case of resource discoveries or population growth. The level of techniques is low in the rural sector of underdeveloped areas where the large proportion of the population is occupied. During the "catching-up period," while the level of techniques in these sectors is approaching that of the advanced countries—or of the more advanced industrial sector in the same countries—the rate of technological progress might be very high indeed. Once this catching-up period is over, the problem of *increasing* the rate of technological progress still further will be serious indeed, but this problem need not worry us for some time.

Nevertheless, there are problems with regard to increasing the rate of technological progress in underdeveloped countries. A high rate of technological advance requires both inventions and innovations; that is, it requires that new techniques be not only discovered but also brought into use. Our discussion of Schumpeter's theory emphasized the introduction of inventions into use, or innovation, as the very essence of entrepreneurship. Unfortunately, most underdeveloped countries have little indigenous entrepreneurship. In Europe before the Industrial Revolution, the ideological changes accompanying the Reformation created attitudes favorable to enterprise. The entrepreneurial spirit was enhanced by the opportunities presented by the enclosure movement, the discoveries, and the expansion of world trade. In contrast to this upsurge of enterprise is the feudal attitude toward commerce and industry which still prevails in many underdeveloped countries. In some of these countries today, as in Europe generations ago, the gentleman does not sully his hands in trade. The educated man should be a doctor, a lawyer, a university professor, possibly an engineer, or best of all, a government official. He who becomes a mere businessman is a species of failure. Nor is innovation respected and rewarded in most of these societies.

True, the government may replace private enterprise as innovator. But as Singer has pointed out,[4] government enterprise has disadvantages for development of underdeveloped countries. Most underdeveloped areas are very short of trained people at top levels of government. If these people concentrate on development problems, they may neglect the regular duties of government. The result will be bad administration, which is one of the main barriers to economic development. As Singer indicates, we are confronted here with another of the vicious circles so frequently encountered in this field. It takes good administrators to improve administration. Moreover, Singer argues, it is disadvantageous for economic development policy to be mixed up with nationalism and with local politics.

The Indonesian scene provides illustrations of the effect of nationalism in retarding enterprise. One obstacle to the large inflow of foreign capital so essential to Indonesian development is the continued reluctance of the Indonesian government to return to the Royal Dutch Shell Company the refineries and wells in north Sumatra taken over by the Indonesians during the revolution. Many Indonesian leaders recognize the desirability of returning these properties: the stigma attached to expropriation would be removed; the properties could be fully and efficiently exploited and so contribute as much as possible to Indonesian exports. Against this view is a strong nationalist sentiment, which would oppose the return of ownership and control of Indonesia's "vital natural resources" to a "foreign capitalist-imperialist-monopolistic power." Similar considerations inhibit the govern-

[4] H. W. Singer, "Obstacles to Economic Development," *Social Research*, Spring, 1953.

ment in granting new long-term leases on oil and mineral properties, or accepting other proposals for establishment of new enterprises. The Indonesian government recognizes the importance for Indonesian development of the complex of power and industrial projects constituting the Asahan Valley Program. The launching of this program, however, is blocked by the inability of the Indonesian government to finance and manage such large-scale undertakings itself, and by the reluctance of strong nationalist groups to see natural resources in the hands of foreigners.

The Philippines provides an example of the injurious effects of political control over development activities. There is lip service to the need for a development program, and as we shall see below, the planning techniques are quite sophisticated. But the measures really necessary to solve the country's economic problem—an effective tax system, change in the structure of production, land reform, increased government responsibility—run contrary to the interest of the politically powerful group which has a big stake in maintaining the *status quo*.

There are other economic problems connected with the generation of a high rate of technological progress. Rapid technological progress requires not only entrepreneurship of the Schumpeterian type, but also managerial, technical, and labor skills. Unfortunately, the underdeveloped countries are short of all these. If technological progress consists merely of adapting techniques or introducing commodities already known in the West, there are further disadvantages. Although this process may permit a high rate of technological advance at first, the "leverage effects" may be low. The "geographic multiplier effects" will be felt very largely outside the country, rather than inside it, as was the case where new techniques were developed in the same country as that in which it was applied. If the top management and technicians are brought in from abroad—and it is difficult to imagine how Western techniques could be introduced rapidly otherwise—the process may not become cumulative or self-sustaining, since an indigenous class of top managers and technicians may not develop quickly. Most underdeveloped countries have balance of payments problems, and the importation of capital equipment, in order to take advantage of superior techniques of the Western world, may result in a temporary deterioration of this balance that can be ill-afforded. The advanced countries now have a virtual monopoly of scientific and industrial research, and this research is not directed toward the special problems and the factor endowment of underdeveloped countries. Finally, modern technology brings rapid obsolescence, which only advanced countries with a high ratio of savings and investment to income, can afford.

Despite these limitations, it is a rapid rate of technological progress that offers most hope of economic development of underdeveloped areas.

Importance of Conjuncture of Economic Factors

The extraordinary advance of Europe during the Industrial Revolution, and of the New World in the nineteenth and twentieth centuries, was the result of a favorable *conjuncture* of all these economic forces. Population grew from levels below optimum, so that population growth constituted a further stimulus to expansion. Population growth was accompanied by migration to areas even richer in natural resources than those which were left behind. These two factors were accompanied by a rapid rate of technological progress, which encouraged search for other types of resources and brought new population movements. Population growth also provided additional demand for the new products and for increased output, and it prevented capital accumulation from outrunning the labor supply. Together with resource discoveries, the growing labor force prevented diminishing rates of profit.

Achieving a rapid rate of technological progress in underdeveloped countries is not impossible despite the barriers. What does seem virtually impossible is the achievement of the same *favorable conjuncture of all the economic factors* which was enjoyed by the Western world during its period of most rapid economic progress.

Political Factors

Political as well as economic factors combined to create an atmosphere conducive to economic development of the Western world in the eighteenth and nineteenth centuries. These favorable factors may be divided into two main categories: the politics of the technically superior country during the period and the politics of the relatively underdeveloped areas at the same time.

Politics of Technically Superior Countries

During the eighteenth century, economic development was largely a matter of developing new industries and areas within the geographic area subject to control by the government concerned. The political advantages of this sort of development are too obvious to need stressing here. It will be more fruitful to compare the politics of the technically superior countries during the nineteenth century, when the United States, Canada, Australia, and the New World generally enjoyed rapid growth, with the politics of the technically superior countries today. During the eighteenth and nineteenth centuries, the technically superior countries were the United Kingdom, France, Holland, and Germany. For our purposes, however, we can concentrate our attention on the United Kingdom, as the dominant power in that period. Similarly, the technically superior countries today are the United States and Canada, and possibly Australia, Switzerland, Sweden, Germany, France, and Russia; but we can usefully concentrate on the policies of the United States because of its overwhelming importance in the world economy.

Let us first consider foreign trade policy. During most of the period under consideration, the United Kingdom followed a policy of free trade. There were, of course, good reasons for this policy line. The United Kingdom enjoyed virtually a monopoly position with respect to the sale of its manufactured goods, and a monopsony position in the purchase abroad of agricultural raw materials and foodstuffs. Perhaps because its monopoly-and-monopsony position is somewhat less secure, the United States has followed a high tariff policy rather than a free trade policy. Difficulties in marketing their output of raw materials and foodstuffs, because of the high tariff policy pursued by the United States, operate as a retarding influence on the economic development of the now underdeveloped areas.

The United Kingdom was also a heavy importer. After 1825, its balance of trade in commodities became unfavorable. From 1873 on, its balance of trade in goods and services combined was unfavorable: Great Britain financed its trade deficit from the large amounts of interest and profits earned on its heavy investment abroad.[5] Not only was its balance of trade unfavorable, but the volume of British imports was high relative to national income, probably averaging some 25 per cent. The United States, by contrast, not only has a high tariff but has consistently maintained favorable balances of trade in recent years. Moreover, its imports are a very small fraction of gross national income, averaging less than 5 per cent. Relative to the scale of its own economy and of the present-day world economy, the

[5] Cf. A. E. Kahn, *Great Britain in the World Economy* (New York, 1946), especially chap. VIII.

United States is providing a much less advantageous market for the products of underdeveloped areas, with respect both to the balance and to the volume of trade, and perhaps with respect to the terms of trade as well.

A similar contrast appears with respect to foreign investment. Professor Cairncross has recently estimated that if the United States were to lend abroad on a scale equivalent in terms of *per capita* real income to that of the United Kingdom during the nineteenth century, the United States would have had in 1952 600 billion dollars of foreign investments, on which it would have earned 30 billion dollars a year.[6] In other terms, to match the flow of capital from the United Kingdom in the nineteenth century, relative to its *per capita* real income, the United States would have to carry out the entire Marshall Plan twice every year! The scale of foreign aid and investment would need to be increased tenfold. There was no "chronic shortage of sterling" during the period of rapid growth of the United States, Canada, and Australia, but there is a "chronic shortage of dollars" today.

It has been suggested that the large scale of British foreign investment in the nineteenth century, although dictated largely by private economic interests, was consistent with domestic government policy. The French Revolution instilled a deep-seated fear in Britain's elite, and a feeling that the masses deserved—or might insist upon—more consideration than they had received in the past. There was, therefore, a wish in high places to obtain cheap food. Frontier developments using British capital made cheaper food possible. Thus apart from the immediate economic interest in developing underdeveloped countries through large-scale foreign investment, there was a more subtle political purpose.

Finally, the technically superior countries were able to enforce stability in underdeveloped areas. Originally the "underdeveloped areas" were within their own borders. Later, colonies assumed paramount importance. Later still, the United States and the Dominions became major recipients of foreign investment. Perhaps it was less easy for the United Kingdom to police investments in the Dominions than in its colonies, and less easy in colonies than within its own borders; but the superior military force of the United Kingdom was one factor in promoting confidence among investors. In the underdeveloped countries today, even slight suggestion that Western powers are trying to

[6] A. K. Cairncross, *Home and Foreign Investment, 1870–1913* (Cambridge, 1953), p. 3.

exercise physical control may cause serious trouble for foreign investors. In Indonesia in 1952, the technically superior country (the United States) found itself unable even to obtain a Mutual Security Administration agreement which included military aid—a single example of the difficulty the technically superior country faces in dealing with the underdeveloped areas today.

During the nineteenth century the technically superior countries confronted no major political challenge in underdeveloped areas. The United Kingdom, France, Holland, and Germany, might be rivals but they had a common interest in maintaining political stability in underdeveloped areas. Today, one set of powers has a distinct interest in fomenting unrest in those areas. Efforts of the technically superior country to enforce stability may drive underdeveloped countries into the enemy camp. This fact naturally affects the attitudes of potential investors in the technically superior countries, whether private or governmental, toward investment in the now less developed areas.[7]

Politics of Underdeveloped Areas

In sharp contrast to the current situation in underdeveloped areas, in the New World during the eighteenth and nineteenth centuries nationalism seldom took a form antipathetic to foreign capital. Even in the United States, which won its independence from the British Empire through a revolution, nationalist feeling imposed no serious obstacles to a large and continuous flow of British capital into the country. In colonies, and even in areas which were not legally colonies at all, forced labor and expropriation of property played their roles in economic development, as Bronfenbrenner has pointed out.[8]

How different is the current situation in the underdeveloped countries, most of which are now sovereign nations. Far from being able to force labor or expropriate property, the foreign investor is more apt to find himself at the mercy of powerful trade unions backed by government arbitration boards, and threatened with outright expropriation of his property, or import and immigration restrictions, and foreign exchange controls which are tantamount to expropriation. In many underdeveloped countries today, risks of unpredictable and injurious government action, often based on nationalist sentiment, are added to the normal risks attendant upon investment abroad.

[7] These matters are discussed more fully in Chap. 29 below.

[8] Cf. Martin Bronfenbrenner, "The High Cost of Economic Development," *Land Economics*, May, 1953, pp. 98–99.

Moreover, in the New World of the eighteenth and nineteenth centuries development was undertaken mainly by and with people from the investing countries themselves. As Cairncross has demonstrated, capital and labor flowed together from the Old World to the New.[9] The emigrants who provided the management and the labor force for foreign undertakings spoke the same language and represented the same culture as those providing the capital. This situation naturally led to a higher degree of confidence in foreign investment than can be expected where governments insist on use of nationals of a culture alien to the investor, as they do in many of the present underdeveloped areas. For similar reasons, search for new natural resources by foreign capitalists was more attractive in the New World in the eighteenth and nineteenth centuries than it is in most underdeveloped areas today. Then there were no problems with regard to transfers of profits when earned, or with regard to personal and corporation income taxes, visas for managerial and technical personnel, land leases, and the like. These same conditions facilitated a higher rate of technological progress, since the movement of capital was usually accompanied by a transfer of skills and of technical knowledge.

Another aspect of the internal policies of the underdeveloped areas which is inimical to rapid development is insistence on early introduction of a full-fledged welfare state. In the now advanced countries, the welfare state appeared only after generations of industrialization. In the present underdeveloped areas, the usual policy seems to reverse this process. Most of these countries want the blessings of the welfare state today, complete with old age pensions, unemployment insurance, family allowances, health insurance, forty-hour week, and all the trimmings. Similarly, trade unions became powerful in the now advanced countries only after considerable industrial development had taken place. The statistics are none too good, but it seems likely that the material standard of living of European wage earners *declined* in the first stages of the Industrial Revolution. In terms of actual welfare, industrial slum dwellers in eighteenth-century England were almost certainly worse off than the peasants who were their forebears—and perhaps worse off than the Indonesian *tani* today. Many of the now underdeveloped areas, on the other hand, are encouraging the development of trade unionism in advance of industrialization. In some countries the trade unions, backed by governmental arbitration boards, are demanding higher wages, shorter hours, and "fringe benefits" which do not reflect any

[9] Cairncross, *op. cit.*, especially chaps. III and VIII.

commensurate rise in man-hour productivity. Especially where the employer is a foreigner, trade union members are nationals, and nationalist sentiments run high because of recent release from colonialism, governments are hard put to it to support employers against trade unions, even where economic development is adversely affected by crippling demands. Too few of the trade-union leaders of underdeveloped countries have learned the hard lesson that a higher standard of living for labor as a group requires higher productivity of labor as a group.

Finally, as Hansen has suggested, the fiscal systems of most Western countries in the early stages of industrial development were such as to redistribute income from poor to rich.[10] Taxes consisted almost entirely of customs and excise duties, which fell relatively heavily on the poor, who spent most of their incomes for consumers' goods. Income and inheritance taxes were unknown. Government expenditures, on the other hand, were of a type benefiting mainly the upper-income groups: interest on government bonds, subsidies to private enterprise, transport facilities, and the like. However reprehensible these fiscal systems may have been from the social viewpoint, they added to the flow of savings and investment, and thus accelerated economic development. Most underdeveloped countries today want exactly the opposite kind of fiscal system, with progressive income and inheritance taxes and social security expenditures, designed to improve the distribution of income and wealth. Laudable as these policies are on social grounds, they tend in themselves to reduce the flow of savings and investment and so to retard economic growth.

Sociological Factors

Sociological, as well as economic and political, factors coincided to favor rapid economic growth of the Western world in the eighteenth and nineteenth centuries. There is a whole literature purporting to show how the Reformation raised the propensity to save. The byword of Puritanism was "make what you can, but save what you can." This attitude helped produce a flow of savings sufficient to finance the introduction of new commodities

[10] Alvin Hansen, *Fiscal Policy and Business Cycles* (New York, 1941), chaps. VI and IX. We have seen that in the Philippines a tax structure that is rather regressive in its actual effects has not resulted in a high ratio of private investment to national income. Perhaps Weber was right—the "Protestant ethic" may be needed to convert unequal income distribution into a high propensity to save.

and new techniques brought by the Industrial Revolution. This attitude is lacking in most of the underdeveloped countries today. Not only are these countries poor, so that large volumes of savings entail real sacrifices, but even among the higher-income groups, both the propensity to consume and the propensity to import are high. Especially in urban centers, one sees desire to emulate the Western nations with regard to consumption; hence, unless policy is specifically designed to prevent it, a large share of increases in income tends to be spent on imports. An initial increase in income fails to produce significant increases in savings, and it leads to a deterioration of the balance of payments unless prevented from doing so by policy. Thus, initial increases in income generated by development are likely to be dissipated in higher levels of consumer spending. The people of underdeveloped areas are more eager to consume the goods of the Western world, than they are to duplicate the saving and the quantity and quality of work which have produced the higher standard of living in the West.

A second contrast, which need not be labored for economic historians, is that between present efforts in underdeveloped areas to achieve geographic and occupational shifts on a voluntary basis with the drastic effects of the enclosures in Europe. However painful may have been the social impact of the enclosures, they were a very effective device for moving people out of agriculture into urban industry. The attachment to the village way of life in many of the underdeveloped areas makes it more difficult to achieve the industrialization which is necessary for high standards of living.

Another sociological factor is the difference between incentives in a society organized around the undivided family and those in a society based on the immediate-family unit. The rapid expansion of the European economies in the eighteenth century and of some New World economies in the nineteenth was based on a social system organized around immediate-family units. Whatever the merits or demerits of this system from other points of view, it offered effective economic incentives. The social unit concerned in a choice between income and leisure, between consumption and saving, between more children and a higher living standard, was the social unit that derived the immediate benefit from it. If a man worked overtime for extra pay, his own immediate family benefited from his decision. If he decided to limit his family, he could be reasonably sure that he could provide a better life for the children he did have. If he saved money, it was his own children who benefited from his sacrifice.

In the extended family system prevalent among underdeveloped countries, this consistency between the decision-making social unit and the benefiting social unit does not exist. The man who works harder than others may merely find himself taking care of a larger number of distant relatives, while his own children benefit little from his extra effort. If he limits the number of his own children, he may only be obliged to take care of a larger number of nephews and cousins. His savings may be regarded as at the disposal of the extended family unit as a whole, rather than for his own wife and children alone. Under these conditions, the incentive to work harder or longer, to save, and to practice birth control are obviously much diluted. Either the social organization must change, or the basic choices must be presented in a different fashion, so that the social unit that makes the decision will itself derive any benefit that accrues from it.

A final sociological factor is the "backward-sloping supply curves" of effort and risk-taking in underdeveloped countries. Nearly all observers of individual behavior in these countries point to the difficulty of encouraging additional effort, or additional risk-taking, by the promise of higher money income. One need not agree with Boeke that the people of underdeveloped areas are fundamentally different in their motivation from those of advanced countries to believe that stagnation is self-reinforcing.[11] At whatever level stagnation sets in, it has the effect of converting upward-sloping supply curves of effort and risk-taking into backward-sloping curves. To have an incentive to work harder or better, or to take additional risks with one's capital, one must have a clear picture of the use to which additional income is to be put. A strong "spirit of emulation," or a high "demonstration effect," occurs only where some people actually show that additional effort or risk-taking pays off. "Keeping up with the Joneses" is a dynamic force only when one sees the Joneses move to a higher standard of living. If life in the village has been much the same for generations, and if no one in the village has before him the picture of people moving to ever higher standards of living through their own efforts or their own willingness to risk capital, expending additional effort, or accepting additional risk, will seem rather absurd. Here is still

[11] J. H. Boeke, *Economics and Economic Policy of Dual Societies* (New York, 1953), especially pp. 39–41, 36–52, and 100–112. Boeke's theory is analyzed in Chap. 12 below. See also Wilbert E. Moore, *Industrialization and Labor* (Ithaca, N.Y., 1951).

another of the vicious circles so common in the field of development in underdeveloped areas: a progressive society inculcates attitudes and provides incentives favorable to economic growth; a stagnant one does not.

This analysis only appears inconsistent with the foregoing argument concerning the high marginal propensity to import. If national income rises for some extraneous reason, such as increasing export prices, people will wish to spend a large share of the increased income on imported semiluxuries. But the villagers see no easy way of raising their incomes through their own efforts or initiative, because they do not have before their eyes enough examples of people succeeding in doing so. Thus their wish for imported semiluxuries provides no effective incentive for additional effort or risk-taking. Still another vicious circle: the "spirit of emulation" is necessary to provide incentives to harder and better work and increased enterprise, but if that spirit takes the form of a wish for imported semiluxuries, it aggravates balance of payments problems.

Technological Factors

Finally, technological factors were more favorable to development in the Western world during the eighteenth and nineteenth centuries than they are in the underdeveloped countries today. The simplest of these technological factors is the extent of the resource endowment. If one compares the United States or Canada with Libya or East Pakistan in terms of per capita resource endowment the contrast is apparent. In countries like Indonesia, where there is great diversity of resources, the contrast is less clear; some observers have spoken of Indonesia as a country "rich in natural resources." Closer examination of the Indonesian position in terms of the extent and quality of resources in relation to its population of 85 million people suggests that, although Indonesia is certainly better off than many of the underdeveloped areas, it is far indeed from being as well endowed with natural resources as most of the now advanced countries.

Moreover, in the underdeveloped countries the present factor endowment, in terms of proportions in which land, labor, and capital are available, is a drag on development. The very essence of economic development is a fall in the ratio of agricultural employment to total employment. But the proportions in which factors of production are available in underdeveloped areas favor agriculture against industry: labor is abundant, even redundant, land is relatively limited; capital is very scarce. In agriculture, relatively good results can be obtained by labor-intensive techniques, with much labor and little capital applied to available land. Industrialization with known techniques requires a much higher capital-labor ratio.

Some recent analysis suggests that the techniques which would maximize total value output in underdeveloped countries, even assuming that enough capital was available to introduce them, would not provide full employment. Here is a dilemma: unemployment is a serious social phenomenon; yet maximum value product is needed, not only to raise standards of living at the moment, but in order to permit a ratio of savings and investment to income which would generate continued economic growth.

Unfortunately, technological research has been carried on mainly in countries where labor is a relatively scarce factor. Technological progress is regarded as a synonym for labor-saving devices. Little scientific endeavor has been directed toward raising production in countries where capital is scarce and labor abundant, and where consequently, labor-saving devices make little sense. No advanced technology has yet been discovered which is suited to the factor-proportions of underdeveloped countries. Perhaps such a technology does not exist; but it is important to find out. Meanwhile, the lack of technological advance adapted to their factor-proportions is a serious obstacle to development of underdeveloped areas—an obstacle that scarcely existed in the Western world during its Industrial Revolution.

A related technical problem is the apparent discontinuity in the production function with respect to capital supply. Certain types of production process are inefficient unless carried on at a minimum scale which is itself large in terms of capital requirements. For example, one of the most hopeful projects on the horizon in Indonesia is the complex of power, aluminum, fertilizer, and related industries constituting the Asahan program. A project of this kind runs into hundreds of millions of dollars, yet it is not worth undertaking on a small scale.

Moreover, evidence is accumulating to suggest that raising *per capita* income by a given percentage amount requires a larger percentage addition to the stock of capital in underdeveloped countries than it does in advanced countries. This difference reflects partly the extremely high capital cost involved in providing social capital, such as housing, community facilities, public utilities, and transport, as industrialization takes place. Even in agriculture, however, the incremental capital-output ratio may be very high where land reform is necessary, involving shifts to new types of agriculture, or where expansion requires land reclamation, jungle clearance, and the like. Here is still another vicious circle. Advanced countries can add to their *per capita* income with a smaller (percentage) sacrifice of current income than can underdeveloped countries.

Capital-saving inventions have been suggested as a solution to this problem. However, it is essential to distinguish between capital-saving inventions and capital-saving innovations. Probably most inventions are capital saving, in the sense that they reduce the capital required per unit of output, once the new plant is in place. In this sense, it seems likely that even the steam railroad was a capital-saving invention; capital required per ton-mile of freight carried is probably less on a modern railway than it was with horses and wagons. However, capital-saving inventions of this type do not help very much, if the capital requirements for *introducing* them are beyond the means of underdeveloped countries. In other words, the *installation* of a new technique that may ultimately be capital saving may require very large amounts of capital indeed. Even capital-saving inventions are easier for advanced countries to introduce than for underdeveloped ones. Where a great deal of capital has already been accumulated, capital-saving inventions can be introduced by using existing replacement funds. Where the capital stock is low, however, replacement funds will be insufficient for major innovations, even if they consist in introduction of capital-saving inventions. What underdeveloped countries need is not merely capital-saving inventions in this sense but means of raising productivity without increasing the current rate of total investment, *even temporarily*. Clearly, the technical requirements of this sort of innovation are much more severe than for capital-saving inventions of the usual sort.

There is also a problem of scale, or a discontinuity, on the side of demand. As Rosenstein-Rodan has pointed out, the establishment of a shoe factory may prove unprofitable in an underdeveloped country, since so small a share of the income created by investment in a shoe factory will return to the producer of shoes.[12] Only large-scale expansion, consisting of development of a few industries of very large scale or of a great many small-scale industries, will raise income sufficiently to generate significant increases in demand for all commodities.

[12] P. N. Rosenstein-Rodan, "Problems of Industrialization of Eastern and South-Eastern Europe," *The Economic Journal*, June, 1943.

Moreover, there is reason to suspect that a collection of small industries has lower "leverage effects" than a single large one involving the same initial amount of total investment. The construction of a railway, opening up new territory, facilitating population movements, and making necessary the development of new communities, is likely to have a greater aggregate effect on investment than a collection of shoe factories, textile plants, and the like, even if the initial investment is equally large in both cases. Again we are confronted with a vicious circle. It is difficult to industrialize without the increases in income which would provide the demand for increased output of industrial goods, but such increases in income are difficult to achieve without industrialization.

In those underdeveloped countries which rely heavily on exports of the traditional plantation staples, still another technological problem arises. Most of these industries involve a combination of highly mechanized processing operations with labor-intensive agricultural operations, a combination which puts the plantation industries in an extremely awkward position. The large amount of capital required in the processing plants means that these plants must operate close to capacity if they are to be profitable. But operating *plants* to capacity requires the operation of *plantations* to capacity. Full use of the productive capacity of the plantations would require cultivation of all the land previously conceded to these estates, and the employment of a full labor force working effectively for a full week of at least forty hours. With losses of productive land through destruction, squatters, expropriation, blights, disease, and inadequate maintenance as noted in Chapter 2, the output of many plantations is no longer sufficient to keep the plants operating at capacity. In addition, the effective working week on many plantations is considerably less than what is required. Finally, in direct contrast to the process that took place in other countries during their period of rapid economic advance, growing strength of labor organization and consequent increases in wage rates are preceding, instead of following, increases in labor productivity.

The question is, therefore, whether the productivity of labor can be raised as fast as wage rates, so as to prevent labor costs from rising to a point where the whole operation becomes unprofitable. Certainly, much can be done to improve labor skills, and much more to increase the quantity and quality of effort expended. However, increases in labor productivity from this side will require a long and difficult process of training, not only to improve skills but to increase the sense of social obligation on the part of workers, and to bring an understanding of the relationship of their own efforts to their standard of living. As replanting takes place, higher-yield and disease-resistant strains can be introduced; but this, too, is a slow process, and one that will raise output per hectare considerably more than output per man-hour. The scope for technological progress in the sense of mechanization, or introduction of labor-saving devices, appears to be limited in most plantation industries, although the problem merits further study. The necessity of careful selection in picking and cutting, the importance of skilled tapping, the need to utilize land to the full, and the like, restrict the degree to which labor can be replaced by equipment on the plantations themselves. Meanwhile, no such limitations to technological progress and cost reduction occur in the production of substitute materials through synthetic processes, such as the manufacture of synthetic rubber, nylon fibers, mineral oils, and the like.

An Impossible Task?

In our whole review of strategic factors in economic growth, we have discovered only one with respect to which the now underdeveloped areas have a comparative advantage over the Western world of the eighteenth and nineteenth centuries. All underdeveloped countries have a large sector of their economies, in which the majority of their people are occupied, with levels of technique and skill far below that of the advanced countries or of the more advanced sector of their own economies. There is accordingly an opportunity for a high rate of technological progress, through the application of the most advanced technical knowledge available to the underdeveloped sector.

Even this advantage, however, is doubtful; the equipment and technical skills that have been so effective in raising levels of productivity in the West are largely inappropriate to the factor-proportions of underdeveloped countries. Almost without exception, the technical advances of the Western world have been designed to replace labor with machinery. In countries where capital is scarce and labor redundant, such labor-saving devices cannot add so much to the productivity of the economy as a whole. Even if labor-saving devices can raise the total value of output in underdeveloped countries, they may do so at the cost of adding to the pool of disguised unemployment. In every other respect, the now underdeveloped countries seem to be at a disadvantage as compared to Europe and the New World at the beginning of their periods of rapid economic development.

Must our conclusion be that the task of developing the now underdeveloped areas is an impossible one? My own answer to this question is no: if both the underdeveloped countries and the advanced countries agree on the necessity of economic development of underdeveloped areas; if they understand what is required to obtain this development and recognize the magnitude of the task; and if they accept it nevertheless. The first condition seems to be met. As for the second condition, increasing the understanding of the nature and magnitude of the development problem is the major purpose of this book. Considerable progress has already been made toward a general theory of underdevelopment and we turn now to a consideration of the literature on this subject.

PART 4 Principles: Theories of Underdevelopment

11 General Theories: Geographic Determinism

Nearly all underdeveloped countries are either too hot or too cold. In resource-poor and icy countries like Greenland, the limits to development are fairly clear. But the great majority of underdeveloped countries are wholly or largely within the tropics. Is there a relationship between tropical climate and relative lack of economic growth?

Human Behavior in the Tropics

Before the Second World War it could be said that the tropics were unhealthful. "Most of the diseases of temperate lands," Gourou wrote at that time, "are rife in hot, wet countries, whilst certain terrible endemic and epidemic tropical diseases are unknown in our latitude." [1] This statement is much less clearly true today. The malaria to which Gourou attached so much importance as a killer of men is now being brought under control in a good many tropical countries. The same may be said of yellow fever, bubonic plague, and other tropical diseases.[2]

Professor Gourou also cites some evidence that even before the war bad health was not inevitable in the tropics. "The Europeans in the Panama Canal Zone are in a splendid health and the annual

[1] Pierre Gourou, *The Tropical World: Its Social and Economic Conditions and Its Future Status* (Paris, 1947; English translation, New York, 1953).

[2] Cf. Chap. 28 below.

death rate is only 6.36 per 1,000." Similarly, in northern Queensland "the coastal strip is really hot and rainy; yet on it pure whites cultivate sugar cane with their own hands. The exclusive white population of the sugar belt amounted to 251,000 in 1939, and the people are in perfect health." [3]

The direct impact of climate on human beings seems to be the least important of the various effects of tropical climate on productivity. An Australian Health Department booklet says: [4]

> In tropical Australia . . . there is practically no circumstance which can be laid hold of as representing a definite disability to the white race other than those faulty circumstances of social environment which are inseparable from the opening up of a new country for the purpose of primary production. First-generation, second-generation, and third-generation Queenslanders are performing their life work and following their ordinary avocations as they could in temperate climates, and there is at present no indication that the strain of tropical life is an actual one, or that the outlook for these people is anything but hopeful.

Dr. Douglas H. K. Lee, professor of physiological climatology at the Johns Hopkins University, summarizes his own evidence with regard to the effect of tropical climates on humans in these undramatic terms: [5]

> There is a general tendency to answer questions about possible levels of activity in the tropics in a gloomy fashion and to cite past performances in support. But what has been, is not necessarily what has to be—a Roman soldier stationed in Britain would no doubt have been skeptical about the future productivity of the barbarous inhabitants in so vile a climate; and many a colonial governor has recorded grave disapproval of areas which are now highly successful. Conversely, there have been flourishing empires in areas that are truly tropical (e.g., Southeast Asia) and intense activity can be found in more than one tropical area (e.g., Venezuela).

This conclusion confirms the observations of the present writer. The attitude toward work, leisure, and income in Australia seems much the same from subtropical Darwin, where summer heat is more intense than in most equatorial countries, to chilly Hobart, with its ten-month-long winter and cool summers. Nor is there any significant difference in attitudes or productivity between

[3] Gourou, *op. cit.*, pp. 115–16.

[4] Quoted by Douglas H. K. Lee, *Climate and Economic Development in the Tropics* (New York, 1957), p. 9.

[5] *Ibid.*, p. 100.

Indonesians living at sea level and those living in the invigorating climate 4,000 feet up in the mountains. In the Philippines, the mountain people have remained the most primitive in the country.

These observations are of very considerable importance. In geographic terms, it appears that the comparative advantage of advanced countries is greater in agriculture than it is in industry. Technology can be transported; soil and climate cannot. In very few of the underdeveloped countries is there any hope for achieving levels of man-hour productivity in agriculture comparable to those of the advanced countries. At the same time there seems no reason why many underdeveloped countries should not be just as efficient as the advanced countries in some industries. So long as the majority of its people are engaged in unproductive agriculture, a country is bound to remain poor. We need, then, to explain why the majority of people in the underdeveloped countries have remained in small-scale agriculture instead of moving into occupations where their productivity is higher.

True, people in underdeveloped countries suffer from malnutrition. Indeed, underdeveloped countries might be defined in terms of the difference between the average dietary supply of calories and requirements (see Table 11-1). But this situation reflects the distressing fact that, in terms of output per hectare, agricultural productivity in Asia and Africa is far below that of Europe and America (see Table 11-2).

Reasons for Low Productivity in Tropical Agriculture

Luxuriant vegetation is not necessarily an indication of rich soil. On the contrary, "tropical soils are poorer and more fragile than those of temperate regions." [6] The virgin jungle demands scarcely anything from the soil, because organic matter fallen from the trees provides its own humus. But "clearing causes unpleasant surprises, for, instead of deep humus, sand is found, and the forest may have greatest difficulty in growing up again once man's exploitation has exposed the underlying soil." The relatively poor soil is an important factor in the low yields per acre in Asian and African countries, noted in Chapter 1, and for the same reasons, the shifting, slash-and-burn agriculture common in underdeveloped countries is particularly disastrous. Once cleared, the vegetation does not revert to its original state. Such agriculture is inefficient in terms of productivity per acre, and

[6] Gourou, *op. cit.*, p. 13.

TABLE 11-1.

Average Dietary Supply of Calories as Compared with Requirements

Region and country	Recent level *	Estimated requirements	Percentage difference
Far East:			
Ceylon †	1970	2270	−13.2
India	1700	2250	−24.4
Japan	2100	2330	−9.9
Philippines	1960	2230	−12.1
Middle East:			
Cyprus	2470	2510	−1.6
Egypt	2290	2390	−4.2
Turkey	2480	2440	+1.6
Africa:			
French North Africa	1920	2430	−20.9
Mauritius	2230	2410	−7.5
Union of South Africa	2520	2400	+5.0
Latin America:			
Argentina	3190	2600	+22.7
Brazil	2340	2450	−4.5
Chile	2360	2640	−10.6
Mexico	2050	2490	−17.6
Uruguay	2580	2570	+0.7
Europe:			
Denmark	3160	2750	+14.9
France	2770	2550	+8.6
Greece	2510	2390	+5.0
Italy	2340	2440	−4.1
Norway	3140	2850	+10.2
United Kingdom	3100	2650	+16.9
North America and Oceania:			
Australia	3160	2620	+20.6
United States	3130	2640	+18.5

* Precise dates not given in source.

† Predominantly tropical countries, italics.

SOURCE: Douglas H. K. Lee, *Climate and Economic Development in the Tropics* (New York, 1957).

TABLE 11-2.

Yield of Principal Crops

(100 kilograms per hectare)

Crop	*World*		*Europe*		*N. & C. America*		*S. America*		*Asia*		*Africa*		*Oceania*	
	1948–52	1955	1948–52	1955	1948–52	1955	1948–52	1955	1948–52	1955	1948–52	1955	1948–52	1955
Wheat	10.5	11.7	14.8	16.7	11.6	13.9	10.7	11.8	7.6	8.5	7.2	7.9	10.8	13.1
Rye	13.4	13.9	14.5	15.1	8.0	9.7	7.3	7.4	9.8	9.9	4.1	..	...	...
Barley	11.8	12.6	16.9	18.9	14.3	14.2	11.2	11.1	10.2	10.9	6.7	6.2	12.2	12.4
Oats	13.3	14.1	16.0	17.3	12.7	13.8	10.8	10.6	9.4	10.3	7.0	6.1	7.0	7.5
Maize	15.8	16.7	13.2	16.3	22.1	22.8	12.6	13.2	10.2	11.8	8.4	9.0	18.0	17.1
Millet and sorghum	6.1	6.7	9.8	10.4	12.5	11.7	7.8	10.5	5.8	6.5	...	...	12.8	15.9
Rice paddy	16.0	18.2	43.0	42.3	22.0	27.0	17.2	16.3	15.9	18.2	12.0	14.0	31.1	32.9
Potatoes	123.1	119.7	137.2	131.4	147.6	164.5	52.6	57.2	68.9	72.8	60.8	63.5	98.8	107.7
Sweet potatoes and yams	80.7	90.6	145.0	122.9	45.3	...	77.4	83.8	89.4	103.3	69.2	73.2	...	...
Cotton	2.2	2.4	1.7	2.3	3.2	4.6	1.8	2.1	1.4	1.5	2.2	2.1	...	...

SOURCE: Food and Agriculture Organization, *Yearbook, 1957.*

prevalence of such agriculture is one reason for low density of population.

There are several other reasons why agricultural productivity may be expected to be low in the tropics, where so many of the underdeveloped countries are, in whole or in part. First, the monocultures common to these countries are prone to disease and pests. Second, the use of fertilizer is a good deal more complicated than in the temperate zones. Third, livestock is less productive.

Of the relationship of monoculture to the incidence of diseases and pests, Dr. Lee writes[7]

> It matters little whether the agent be a microbe, an insect, a larger animal, or a plant form; the principle remains the same: pure stands invite disease. [He adds] Under tropical conditions such infestations could easily become widespread epidemics with disastrous results. Blights which have thus affected the cotton, cacao, rubber, and banana industries in the past await the monocultures of the future.

A related factor is the rapid growth of weeds. "Mechanization may speed the clearance of weeds between the rows," Lee points out, "but hand work is necessary to clear them away between plants. In the cultivation of rice the flooding and transplanting of the paddies serves to control weeds, which would soon take over the area if cultivation by United States methods were attempted in the true tropics."

With regard to the use of fertilizers, he concludes: [8]

> The replacement of lost minerals and nitrogenous compounds by the addition of fertilizers is a solution which comes readily to the mind of present-day Western man; but such a program is fraught with difficulties in many tropical regions. In the first place, factory-produced fertilizers are expensive and are often beyond the means of the country concerned, even without the added cost of transportation. Second, the use of fertilizers presupposes a knowledge of what substances are deficient in the soil, the relative acidity of the soil, and the specific requirements of the particular crop. Whereas these facts may be fairly well known for temperate situations, they are very poorly known for tropical areas. Finally, it hardly appears sensible to pour in fertilizer each year, only to have it go out to sea with the next rain. Some control must be introduced over the annual loss by leaching before artificial replenishment can be viewed with equanimity.
>
> The time may come when fertilizers will be economically justified, but in many areas that time is not yet. There is perhaps more point to the utilization of green manure, especially where the manuring

[7] Lee, *op. cit.*, p. 34.
[8] *Ibid.*, pp. 35, 38.

crop fixes atmospheric nitrogen; yet it cannot be blithely assumed that legumes will automatically do this. Both the species and the conditions must be right before the nitrogen-fixing bacteria can operate. Animal wastes may be used, although in many areas the diet of the animal is so poor that the excreta have very little value as manure. In some areas, such as India, it is considered more important to dry the dung for fuel than to apply it to the fields.

Turning to livestock production, Dr. Lee shows that the average output per animal of milk and wool is much lower in underdeveloped than in advanced countries. A part of the explanation for this low productivity is "that tropical grasses and other forage plants, even when abundant, are frequently lacking in nutritive value. In many instances, poor nutrition constitutes a major cause of low animal productivity in the tropics." Accordingly, raising livestock productivity may require importation of feeds, or development of new natural feeds, which may be very difficult in tropical conditions. Heat as such has bad effects on appetite, and "everything man asks of his animals—more meat, more milk, more eggs, more work—involves a greater production of heat." [9] Also, animals as well as plants are more subject to disease and pests in tropical countries.

Professor Gourou also points out that the tropics "are not eminently favourable" to raising livestock. Disease is one factor, difficulty of preserving animal products is another, but most important "is the fact that tropic pasturage of average quality is not good food value." [10] Livestock as well as men are victims of the unhealthiness of the tropics. As yet less progress has been made in raising the levels of health of livestock in the tropics to that of other parts of the world than is the case with human beings.

Here, then, is one of the vicious circles so common in any analysis of underdevelopment; underdevelopment yields low agricultural productivity, yields malnutrition, yields low productivity, yields underdevelopment.

Dr. Lee is much more sanguine with respect to the possibilities of industrial development in tropical climates. He quotes Australia as an example:

> As a youth in Australia, the author frequently heard it said that the country's climate was unsuitable for weaving textiles or manufacturing steel; at a more mature age he learned that it was also supposed to affect the quality of the beer. Some years later he witnessed considerable success attending both the textile and the steel industry and

[9] *Ibid.*, p. 67.
[10] Gourou, *op. cit.*, p. 53.

came to believe that the principal effect of climate upon brewing was through the thirst induced in the inhabitants.

In general, he sees in the field of industry none of the barriers to development in the tropics that he outlines for the agricultural sector.

In previous chapters we have been able to establish very definite and important influences of tropical climate upon crop production, animal husbandry, and the general sweep of human welfare and productivity; and in discussing palliative measures we have had to refer to various nonclimatic factors which may affect the success or practicability of those measures. This was possible without losing sight of the main topic—the role of climate. But when it comes to a discussion of industry, the evidence for direct and important climatic effects is somewhat insubstantial, and a consideration of nonclimatic influences is apt to develop into a full-fledged discussion of the socio-economic forces necessary to the process of industrialization.

He does point out that at present the supply of labor is a serious problem, but here the possibilities of overcoming the difficulty seem relatively good.[11]

The supply of labor may present an equally difficult problem. A superabundance of extremely poor people does not necessarily provide a work force. Undernourishment, disease, lack of education, lack of ambition, or ingrained custom, singly or in combination, may make of the apparent plenitude a veritable mirage. Public health measures and education may, in time, rectify the position, but they must be paid for and presumably treated as an investment in future productivity.

Tropical conditions may impede industrialization indirectly. People living in temperate zones tend to think of the tropics as "fertile" and imagine both luxuriant growth and dense populations. In fact, however, relatively few tropical countries are densely populated. On the eve of World War II the hot and wet regions outside Asia had only 8 per cent of the world's population on 28 per cent of the usable area. The average density was only 2.2 persons per square mile. As Gourou points out, sparsely populated countries do not provide favorable opportunities for industrialization because of the limited size of the domestic market. In his view, it is countries like Indonesia, densely populated yet still at the agricultural stage, which "are obviously by far the most ready for industrialization." Moreover, he says the tropical climate does not impose any special barriers to industrialization.

Gourou does mention another geographic barrier to develop-

[11] Lee, *op. cit.*, pp. 146, 147.

ment in Asia and Africa, which has nothing to do with soil or climate: [12]

> Tropic lands [he points out] suffer from the drawback of being divided into three sections completely separated by broad oceans. Between them, and even between tropical Asia and equatorial Africa, cultural relations have been very difficult and consequently very slight. Agricultural methods are not easily communicated except within the climate in which they originate, nor do they spread, except along parallels of latitude. Hence, isolated from one another by the outline of the continents, the tropical lands in each land-mass have developed independently. These conditions were not very favourable to the progress of civilization. On the other hand, the temperate lands of Europe, Asia, and Africa as a whole offered by their cohesion far greater possibilities of cultural exchange and mutual fertilization of ideas.

Improvements in transport and communications, however, make this factor much less of a handicap today than it was in the past. Gourou concludes that modern civilization opens many other prospects for tropical lands. The endemic diseases can be controlled, and the country made healthful "so long as the work of improving the condition of health is accompanied by complete utilization of the land, for the conquest of disease must keep pace with the control of nature."

Conclusion

Thus the disadvantages of the tropics are steadily disappearing with the growth of scientific knowledge and improvements in techniques with respect to control of disease, seed selection, and use of fertilizer, transport, and industrial production. The relative disadvantages of the tropics are more stubborn in the field of agriculture, however, than in the field of industry.

Finally, we might point out that by no means all the underdeveloped countries are in the tropics. The climate of Korea, for example, is temperate, with long and severe winters; yet levels of per capita income there are not markedly higher than in Asian countries farther south. Similarly, the soil and climate of Japan did not suddenly change in the latter part of the nineteenth century when its transformation to an industrialized country began. Geographic factors have some bearing on per capita income, but we cannot explain development or underdevelopment in purely geographical terms.

[12] *Ibid.*, p. 141.

12 General Theories: Sociological Dualism

The economist who is trying to provide a systematic analysis of stagnation in underdeveloped areas has two choices before him. He may integrate orthodox economic and social theory, as it exists in advanced Western countries, and choose assumptions appropriate to the institutional framework of underdeveloped areas. When we tried this approach in Part 1, we found that the existing general theories leave a good deal still to be explained. The alternative is to try to formulate a new and distinctive general theory. The leading exponent of the latter approach was the late J. H. Boeke, who restated and elaborated his special theory of underdeveloped areas a few years before his death.[1] Boeke's "dualistic theory" is of special interest and importance because of his experience as a Netherlands East Indies civil servant and his subsequent years of reflection as professor of Eastern economics at Leiden University. Although his theory was based largely on Indonesian experience, Boeke thought that it had general application. The reason for his choice of title for his last book, which was

[1] J. H. Boeke, *Economics and Economic Policy of Dual Societies* (New York, 1953), cited as Boeke, *Economics;* "Three Forms of Disintegration in Dual Societies," lecture given in the course on Cooperative Education of the International Labor Office, Asian Cooperative Field Mission, October, 1953, and published in *Indonesië*, Vol. VII, No. 4 (April, 1954), cited as Boeke, "Three Forms"; and "Western Influence on the Growth of Eastern Population," *Economia Internazionale*, Vol. VII, No. 2 (May, 1914), cited as Boeke, "Western Influence."

mainly an amalgamation of two earlier studies of the Indonesian economy was his [2]

. . . conviction that the economic problems of Indonesia are typical for a large and important part of the world, that therefore an analysis of these problems may be illuminating for many similar countries and that the experience gained in several decades of economic colonial policy may serve as a guide to the host of inexperienced planners for the well-being of that part of the world that has not yet conformed to their western ideals.

An analysis based largely on Indonesian experience may prove to have less general application than Boeke believed; but as one of the few prewar attempts at a general theory of underdeveloped areas Boeke's theory enjoyed considerable vogue.[3]

The Theory

Dr. Boeke gives the following formal definition of a dual society: [4]

Social dualism is the clashing of an imported social system with an indigenous social system of another style. Most frequently the imported social system is high capitalism. But it may be socialism or communism just as well, or a blending of them.

This dualism, he says, is a "form of *disintegration*, [which] came into existence with the appearance of capitalism in pre-capitalistic countries." [5] The invading force is capitalism, but it is not colonialism. Colonialism is "a dust-bin term"; both it and "the antithesis native-foreign" are "objectionable," and [6]

. . . it is to be hoped that with the obtaining of national sovereignty the true character of economic dualism will be acknowledged sincerely and logically, for its negation is decidedly not to the interest of the small man.

On the other hand, "dualistic" is for Boeke virtually synonymous with "Eastern." Dualism arises from a clash between East

[2] Boeke, *Economics*, p. vi.

[3] Also to the degree that Boeke reflected attitudes of the Netherlands East Indies government, his ideas are of considerable historical interest. For evidence that the whole structure of government in the Netherlands Indies rested on a theory of "dualism," see Rupert Emerson, *Malaysia* (New York, 1937), especially pp. 420–25.

[4] Boeke, *Economics*, p. 4.

[5] Boeke, "Three Forms," p. 282.

[6] Boeke, *Economics*, p. 20.

and West; Boeke quotes in this context Rudyard Kipling's famous phrase, "East is East and West is West and never the twain shall meet." Boeke contends that "we may use the term 'eastern economics' instead of 'dualistic' economics because both terms cover the same situation, to wit, the situation that is typical for the countries in South and East Asia." [7]

A dualistic economy has several characteristic features. One of these is "limited needs," in sharp contrast with the "unlimited needs" of a Western society. Accordingly,[8]

. . . anyone expecting western reactions will meet with frequent surprises. When the price of coconut is high, the chances are that less of the commodities will be offered for sale; when wages are raised the manager of the estate risks that less work will be done; if three acres are enough to supply the needs of the household a cultivator will not till six; when rubber prices fall the owner of a grove may decide to tap more intensively, whereas high prices may mean that he leaves a larger or smaller portion of his tappable trees untapped.

In other words, the Eastern economy, in contrast to the Western, is characterized by backward-sloping supply curves of effort and risk-taking.

Such needs as there are in Eastern societies are social rather than economic. It is what the community thinks of commodities that gives them their value: [9]

If the Madurese values his bull ten times as much as his cow, this is not because the former is ten times as useful to him in his business as the latter, but because the bull increases his prestige at the bull races.

A closely related feature, in Boeke's view, is the almost complete absence of profit seeking in an Eastern society. Speculative profits are attractive to the Oriental, but "these profits lack every element of that regularity and continuity which characterizes the idea of income." [10] Similarly, there is no professional trading in the Eastern village community. Eastern industry is characterized by "aversion to capital," in the sense of "conscious dislike of investing capital and of the risks attending this," only slight interest in finish and accuracy, lack of business qualities, failure to come up to even the minimum requirements of standard and sample, lack of elasticity of supply, lack of organization and of discipline and corrective local specialization. All this is said to be

[7] *Ibid.*, p. 12.
[8] *Ibid.*, p. 40.
[9] *Ibid.*, pp. 37–38.
[10] *Ibid.*, p. 41.

in sharp contrast to the industry of the Westernized, capitalistic sector of underdeveloped areas. The Oriental is, unfortunately, totally lacking in organizing power where modern Western enterprises are concerned. Where Western industry is dominated by common-sense reason, Eastern society is molded by "fatalism and resignation." [11]

Because of these great differences between Eastern and Western economies, Western economic theory is totally inapplicable to underdeveloped areas. "We shall do well," Boeke sternly admonishes, "not to try to transplant the tender, delicate hothouse plants of western theory to tropical soil, where an early death awaits them." [12] Western economic theory, he says, is based on unlimited wants, a money economy, and many-sided corporative organizations, none of which exists in Eastern societies. Western theory is designed to explain capitalistic society, whereas the Eastern village is precapitalistic. He is particularly critical of any effort to explain the allocation of resources or the distribution of income in terms of marginal productivity theory, mainly because of the great immobility of resources in an Eastern society.

Policy Implications

This picture of the nature of underdeveloped areas led Boeke to pessimistic views on policy. In general, his conclusion is that the kindest thing the Western world can do for underdeveloped areas is to leave them alone; any effort to develop them along Western lines can only hasten their retrogression and decay. Perhaps Boeke's strongest statement of this conclusion was his last one. We cannot reverse the process of social disintegration in dual societies, he said, "because it is not possible to transform the operating forces into the opposite of what they are. The contrast is too all-inclusive, it goes too deep. We shall have to accept dualism as an irretrievable fact." [13] The acceptance of social and economic dualism leads to two policy conclusions: "first that as a rule one policy for the whole country is not possible, and second that what is beneficial for one section of society may be harmful for the other." [14]

Even in agriculture, efforts to bring about improvement in methods are likely to cause retrogression instead, especially if

[11] *Ibid.*, pp. 101–102, 106.
[12] *Ibid.*, p. 143.
[13] Boeke, "Three Forms," p. 289.
[14] *Ibid.*, p. 289.

"mental attitudes" of farmers are not changed in the process. The culture of the village community, Boeke said, is "perfectly adapted to the environment"; and the methods of Eastern agriculture "could hardly be improved upon."[15] The existing agricultural system is a result of adaptation and is not at a low stage of development.

Dr. Boeke doubted the ability of the Javanese cultivator to grow new crops. Nor did he think that Indonesians could[16]

> assume part of the work of the western enterprises, the agricultural part, so as to allow entrepreneurs to devote their energies exclusively to the industrial aspect of the business. This would mean that what is now one united concern, one business, what is being nursed and developed in serried areas, uniformly raised, scientifically guarded and improved, qualified on the basis of the knowledge of market requirements, promoted by means of cheap and plentiful capital, brought into immediate contact with industrial processing, would begin to disintegrate and retrogress at all these points. The present organization of these enterprises is the product of a long history, and handing over cultivation of these products to the petty native peasant would mean a return to an arrangement in the main abandoned as inefficient.

As for industry, "Eastern business will always present a very different appearance from western, even in cases where the two are concerned in the production of the same commodity." Technological progress along Western lines is impossible. "There is no question of the eastern producer adapting himself to the western example technologically, economically or socially." Indeed, if Eastern enterprises endeavor to imitate Western methods, they will merely lose their competitive qualities.[17]

Similarly, Boeke did not believe that there is anything government can do about the unemployment of underdeveloped areas. He distinguishes five kinds of unemployment: seasonal, casual, unemployment of regular laborers, unemployment of urban white-collar workers, and unemployment among Eurasians (he does not specifically mention disguised unemployment). All five kinds of unemployment, Boeke said, "are beyond the reach of government help," because dealing with them "would entail a financial burden far beyond the government's means."[18]

Economic development of any kind is hampered by limited wants. Either an increase in supply of foodstuffs, or industrializa-

[15] Boeke, *Economics*, p. 31.
[16] *Ibid.*, pp. 193–94.
[17] *Ibid.*, p. 103.
[18] *Ibid.*, pp. 318–19.

tion, will lead to a glutting of markets, a fall in prices, and havoc. Even the transmigration program, on which the Indonesian government has placed so much hope for economic development, is worse than useless, according to Boeke. It only transplants Java's population problem to the Outer Islands, while Java itself is worse off than before.[19]

Any effort on the part of the West to improve these harassing conditions by training Indonesian leaders can only hasten decay: [20]

In my opinion, here the western influence tends to divert the attention of the leading classes from their own society to the new and promising western power. The masses, however, unable to follow their leaders on their western way, thus lose the dynamic developing element in their culture. Eastern culture in this way comes to a standstill, and stagnation means decline.

In the field of international relations as well, the outlook for the underdeveloped areas is dismal. For,[21]

after the Second World War disintegrating forces have asserted themselves and binding forces have grown weaker in the international field as well. I am alluding to the formation of new sovereign nations and to the decline of the uniting influence of colonial and imperial powers on all the dual countries.

Boeke had little to suggest by way of positive policy, as a substitute for the "technical- and capital-assistance" approach which he deplores. However, his idea seems to be that any industrialization or agricultural improvement must be "a slow process," small-scale, and adapted to a "dualistic" framework.

The conclusion to which these arguments about industrialization as well as about agricultural reforms lead us can be no other than the one already expressed, to wit, that social-economic dualism, far from being considered as a passing phase the termination of which may be hastened considerably by a western policy of integration, must be accepted as a permanent characteristic of a large number of important countries, permanent at least within a measurable distance of time. [We must have a] dichotomy of social-economic policy, which is fundamentally different according to the social groups at which it is aimed.[22]

What this policy means in concrete terms is not spelled out. "I will expose no plans," said Boeke, except to stress the need for "village restoration." This restoration will not take place through

[19] *Ibid.*, pp. 187, 182–83.
[20] *Ibid.*, p. 39.
[21] Boeke, "Three Forms," p. 294.
[22] *Ibid.*, p. 293.

a revival of the rural gentry, but must "follow more democratic ways." New leaders must spring from "the small folk themselves," and must be accompanied by "a strong feeling of local social responsibility in the people themselves." Just how all this is to be accomplished Boeke did not say; but the sphere of action must be small, the time slow, and the goal won by "faith, charity, and patience, angelic patience."[23]

Appraisal of the Theory

As prologue to any critical appraisal of the Boeke theory, two things should be said. The first is that the late Professor Boeke was one of those devoted and highly trained Netherlands East Indies civil servants who went to Indonesia during the period of the "ethical policy," determined to help raise the standard of welfare of Indonesians. During the period from 1900 to 1930, when the "ethical policy" was pursued, the Dutch had a scientific—even scholarly—approach to their colonial policy. N.E.I. civil servants arrived in Indonesia with a special degree in Oriental studies, speaking the Indonesian language and well-versed in Indonesian history and culture. In that period, a genuine, albeit limited, effort was made to improve the lot of Indonesians. The effort failed. There was even doubt as to whether the Javanese standard of living was not lower in 1930 than it had been two generations earlier. In 1940 the last of a series of Royal Commissions to look into the condition of the Indonesian people was appointed—the so-called Coolie Budget Commission. Boeke himself had cried out in despair,[24]

> But the only popular response to all these nostrums is an increase in numbers, while foreign capitalists and foreign energy take out of native hands a rapidly increasing share of native activities.

Thus Boeke's defeatism must be explained in large measure by the failure of the "ethical policy" in Indonesia. Undoubtedly, there is an element of "hen-and-egg" in the relationship between this failure and sociological dualism. For the dualistic theory did not spring full-blown from the head of Dr. Boeke: similar views can be found in the earlier Dutch literature, some of them lineal descendants of German theories about the "primitive and civilized mind." To some degree the theory of sociological dualism in-

[23] Boeke, "Western Influence," pp. 366–69.

[24] Boeke, "Het Zakelijke en het Persoonlijke Element in de Koloniale Welvaartspolitiek," *Koloniale Studien*, April, 1927.

formed Dutch colonial practices, even under the "ethical policy." The conception of what was appropriate for Indonesians in the way of education, training, and industrialization was very limited; the "ethical policy" was far indeed from the contemporary concept of "the big push," discussed below. In the light of present-day theories of development, one might argue from the strength of hindsight that the "ethical policy" was foredoomed to failure. Be all that as it may, it remains true that the Boeke theory must be explained partly in terms of Indonesian history during Boeke's lifetime.

The second point is that there can be no question about the phenomenon of dualism; it is one of the distinguishing features of underdeveloped countries. Virtually all of them have two clearly differentiated sectors: one confined mainly to peasant agriculture and handicrafts or very small industry, and the trading activities associated with them; the other consisting of plantations, mines, petroleum fields and refineries, large-scale industries, and the transport and trading activities associated with these operations. Levels of technique, productivity, and income are low in the first sector and high in the second. Overcoming this dualism is a major task of economic development policy.

However, it is our view that Boeke looked in the wrong place for his *explanation* of dualism. He thought it had to do with the nature of the society, if not actually of the people themselves. As we will see below, dualism is more readily explained in economic and technological terms; and this explanation withstands scrutiny better than Boeke's sociological explanation. It is well that such is the case; for if Boeke were right, all our efforts to produce a take-off into sustained growth in underdeveloped countries through vigorous development programs supported by technical and capital assistance from the West would be in vain.

The Facts

In examining this gloomy analysis of the prospects for underdeveloped areas, let us first consider Boeke's presentation of the facts regarding Eastern society.

Let us begin with his argument about "limited wants" and backward-sloping supply curves of effort and risk-taking. There is an all-important difference between saying that the people of underdeveloped countries really cannot envisage a standard of living higher than their own, or that they could think of no satisfactory way of spending increases in income, and saying that they see no simple way of raising their standard of living by their own efforts or enterprise. The last of these statements is to some extent true, and the reasons for it receive attention below. The first two are definitely not true, especially in Indonesia. There, both the marginal propensity to consume and the marginal propensity to import are high. Wants of the villagers, far from being limited, are so many and varied that any "windfall," occurring initially through increased exports, is quickly spent on imported semiluxuries unless vigorous import and exchange controls are applied to prevent it. Far up the great rivers of Kalimantan (Borneo), hundreds of miles into the jungle, good rubber prices result in a spate of orders for bicycles, mattresses, watches, fountain pens, and the like. *Sampans* in the remotest canals are loaded with Australian tinned milk and American tinned soup. The same is true of the Outer Islands as well. Indeed, the limitless wants of the Indonesian people confront the authorities concerned with import and foreign exchange controls with their major problem. To turn these wants into a wellspring of economic growth, the people must be shown the connection between satisfaction of their wants and their own willingness to work, save, and take risks—a difficult but not impossible task.[25]

Considering the growing number of enterprises efficiently organized and operated by Orientals, along Western lines, it is difficult to share Boeke's pessimism regarding possibilities of technological progress in Eastern industry. Boeke's characterization of Oriental casual labor as "unorganized, passive, silent, casual" would be acceptable to very few of the employers in Asia who have to deal with contemporary trade unions, especially those where communist influence is strongest.[26] Similarly, it is hard to reconcile Boeke's isolation of "repugnance to alienation from the village community" with the continued growth of the large cities in Asia, noted in Chapter 2. Urban life of the larger cities, with its cinemas, cafés, shops, libraries, and sports events, has proved at-

[25] This point is made, in different terms, by Professor D. H. Burger, "Boeke's Dualisme," *Indonesië*, Vol. VII, No. 3 (January, 1954). See also chap. IX, "Technical Assistance to Underdeveloped Areas," in Lyle W. Shannon, *Underdeveloped Areas* (New York, 1957).

[26] Boeke, *Economics*, pp. 144, 145. At one point, Boeke seems even to deny the possibility of growth of labor organizations. Because of the nature of agricultural enterprises, which are scattered and more likely to support each other in their common interests than to compete, every effort at organization could be nullified, Boeke argues. The fact is, however, that it is precisely in plantation agriculture that the Indonesian trade-union movement is strongest.

tractive to villagers who get a taste of it; the result is congestion, inadequate community facilities, and unemployment in the larger cities. It is also hard to reconcile Boeke's insistence on the inefficiency of native agriculture, as compared with Western agriculture, with the postwar growth of smallholders' exports, in Indonesia, Malaya, Nigeria, and elsewhere.

Again, Boeke's insistence on the difficulty of persuading Javanese people to leave their villages, in order to move to the Outer Islands, is contradicted by the files of the Department of Transmigration in Indonesia which hold two million applications for removal under the transmigration scheme.

At times, Boeke's "facts" seem to conflict with each other. For example, at one point he emphasizes the immobility of labor;[27] at another, he states that wages cannot be raised by industrialization, because[28]

> . . . as soon as, for instance, a new mill is opened or an irrigation work is constructed, from all sides wage laborers, colonists, traders, and partisans rush in, if need be from hundreds of miles away, to seize this opportunity to supplement their scanty means of living.

The latter of these two contrasting pictures conforms more closely to the results of field studies conducted by the M.I.T. Indonesia Project.[29] Plantation owners often complained of the difficulty of maintaining a labor force, in the light of an infinitesimal increase in wage rates on neighboring plantations or in neighboring factories. The drain of trained Chinese workers from the bauxite and tin mines, in response to more attractive wage offers from Red China, has become a major problem. Again, at one point Boeke explained the impossibility of significant expansion of smallholder agriculture.[30] Yet earlier, he complained of the N.E.I. government's difficulty in forcing smallholders to grow less rubber during the 1930's; imposition of what amounted to "penal" export duties resulted instead in an increase in productivity of native smallholders.[31] This experience seems to suggest that expansion of smallholders' agriculture is a matter of finding the right incentive system.

The observations of other economists who have enjoyed the

[27] Boeke, *Economics*, pp. 143–45.

[28] *Ibid.*, p. 177.

[29] C. Geertz, *Modjokuto: Religions in Java*, February, 1958; H. Geertz, *Modjokuto: Town and Village Life in Java*, 1957; A. Dewey, *Modjokuto: The Market*, August, 1957; M.I.T., CIS (mimeographed).

[30] Boeke, *Economics*, pp. 214–16.

[31] *Ibid.*, pp. 124–26.

opportunity for studying economic behavior in underdeveloped countries for themselves confirm the view that economic incentives are at least as powerful there as in advanced countries. Thus Arthur Lewis, speaking of the assumption made by colonizers in Africa that "wants were limited" and that accordingly compulsion would be necessary to obtain an adequate supply of labor, says: [32]

> These compulsions (except slavery) are still to be found in one or the other of the African colonies of all the European powers, but they are not so necessary now as they were formerly thought to be. For imitation has done its work. The Africans have acquired new wants, and are willing to work to satisfy them without compulsion.

Regarding the degree to which people of underdeveloped countries are aware of opportunities for making profits and willing to seize them, he writes: [33]

> It is . . . hard to get the farmers in tropical countries to work as many hours as industrial workers in temperate countries, but this does not prevent them from seizing opportunities to use better seeds, or fertilizers, or to plant more profitable crops. It has not prevented the Gold Coast farmer—who is said, no doubt erroneously, to be one of the laziest farmers in the world—from switching from subsistence production to creating the largest cocoa industry in the world, over a short space of time; or prevented the farmers of Uganda or of Indonesia from taking enthusiastically to cotton and to rubber respectively.

Similarly, Peter Bauer speaks of the "great readiness to migrate, especially to the rubber and tea estates in Malaya and Ceylon," and "their prompt reaction to changes in economic conditions." "There is available a great volume of evidence [which] illustrates prompt and sensitive responses to small differences in prices." Even something so "deeply rooted in tribal custom as bride prices" varies appreciably with economic conditions.[34]

Similarly, Bauer and Yamey deny that the wants of peasants are fixed or static [35] and present many examples of economic responsiveness. "Observation of behavior in many different parts of the underdeveloped world suggest strongly that most producers are aware of current opportunities open to them, and are also anxious to use the information that they seek out or is conveyed to them." In Cyprus "even comparatively small changes

[32] Arthur Lewis, *The Theory of Economic Growth* (London, 1955), p. 39.
[33] *Ibid.*, p. 41.
[34] P. T. Bauer, *Economic Analysis and Policy in Underdeveloped Countries* (Durham, N.C., 1957), pp. 21–24.
[35] P. T. Bauer, and B. S. Yamey, *The Economics of Underdeveloped Countries* (London and Cambridge, 1957), pp. 86–93.

in price ratios bring about large changes in the conversion and disposal of produce." "The ready response of many East African cotton growers to price differences was recognized in an unusual context by an official commission of inquiry into the Uganda cotton growing industry in 1948. . . . It is well known that Africans in various territories are keen and discriminating buyers even though many of them are illiterate. Nor is entrepreneurship lacking in underdeveloped countries." They quote Professor Tax to the effect that "the Indian is perhaps above all else an entrepreneur, a businessman, always looking for new means of turning a penny." Bauer and Yamey are even doubtful as to whether the technological differences are as great as sometimes supposed. The technique which is most efficient in advanced countries is—unfortunately—likely to be most efficient in underdeveloped countries as well, because the more mechanized techniques are not only labor saving but also capital saving.[36]

Is "Dualism" an Eastern Phenomenon?

Some degree of "dualism" certainly exists in underdeveloped areas. Is dualism a special feature of Eastern countries? Merely to raise the question is to answer it. Boeke himself suggests at one point that dualism exists in other underdeveloped areas, including those of Latin America and Africa, as well as those of the Orient. But there is perhaps no country in which "dualism" is more striking than in Italy, with its industrialized and progressive north, and its agricultural and stagnant south. Indeed, one could go further, and argue that some degree of dualism exists in virtually every economy. Even the most advanced countries, such as Canada and the United States, have areas in which techniques lag behind those of the most advanced sectors, and in which standards of economic and social welfare are correspondingly low. Notable examples are the rural sections of the Province of Quebec, rural areas in the Southern hills and northern New England hills, and Mexican communities in Texas, Arizona, and New Mexico. Most economies can be divided into distinct regions, with different degrees of technological advance.

Many of the specific characteristics of the "Eastern" society described by Boeke, seem to the present writer to be attributable to Western societies as well. The preference for speculative profits over long-term investment in productive enterprise appears wherever chronic inflation exists or threatens. Such attitudes pre-

[36] *Ibid.*, pp. 105, 123.

vail in Greece today as they did in Germany, France, Austria, and Italy after World War I. And surely the "conscious dislike of investing capital and of the risk attending this" prevails everywhere. A famous American financier has said, "nothing is so shy as a million dollars"; Western economists have recently developed a whole field of analysis relating to "liquidity-preference" and "safety-preference" to take account of the reluctance of investors the world over to accept risk or illiquidity, and their strong preference for keeping their capital in safe and liquid form. Only the prospect of large and fairly safe profits has called forth the large volume of investment that has resulted in the rapid development of the now advanced countries. Growth breeds growth, stagnation breeds stagnation, in any economy. As for valuing goods according to prestige conferred, rather than direct use-value, what Western society is free from such behavior? Veblen made such behavior a vital aspect of his analysis of American society, and gave it his famous label, "conspicuous consumption."

Similarly, Boeke's distinction between Eastern societies, especially Indonesia, where "export is the great objective," and Western countries, where export "is only the means which makes import possible"—a distinction which Boeke regards of "essential importance"—is hard to understand in view of the popularity of protectionist policies in most countries in recent decades. It is true, of course, that Dutch colonial policy was directed toward expanding exports, and was not much concerned with increasing imports for Indonesians. British policy in India, on the other hand, was very much concerned with expanding imports of British manufactures.

Dr. Boeke also speaks of absenteeism of regular laborers as "undoubtedly in part an expression of the very general pre-capitalistic phenomenon of desiring a large number of holidays." But employers in the United States or Canada in the early part of World War II, or in Australia since the war, would be quick to deny that absenteeism is no problem in the capitalist world. The same is true of the "backward-sloping supply curve of effort," which was all too evident in Australia during the immediate postwar period, and which began to appear at that time in certain industries, such as coal mining, even in the United States. It is the present writer's contention that this "backward-sloping supply curve" is not exclusively a feature of Eastern societies, but appears in any society which stagnates (or slows down) long enough to weaken the "demonstration effect," provided by people moving from one standard of living to another, as a result of their own extra effort, directed specifically toward earning additional income.[37]

Again, Boeke's contrast between colonization in the Western world, where "people on their own initiative and at their own cost leave their country for abroad to better their living conditions"

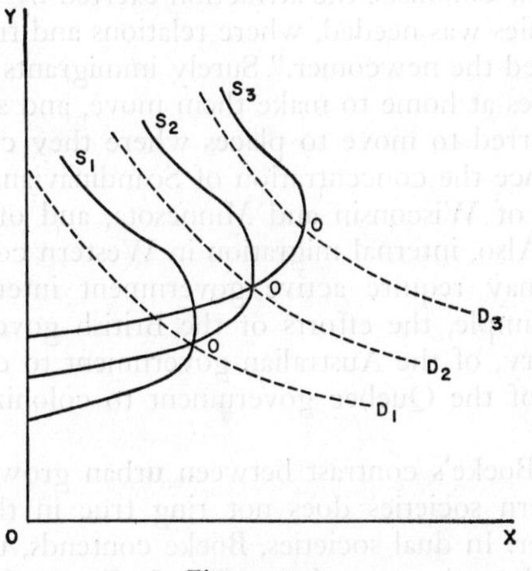

Figure 12-1

[37] The truth may well be that, in a static world, supply curves of effort and risk-taking are normally backward sloping. Where no other changes are taking place, most people would probably like some additional leisure, or some additional safety and liquidity, when rates of pay for effort and risk-taking are increased, so that the extra leisure, safety, and liquidity can be had without a reduction in material standard of living. Can anyone doubt that most academicians would offer fewer man-hours for sale each year if basic university salaries were doubled and nothing else changed? The assumption of more and more outside work by members of university faculties really represents a movement along the backward-sloping portions of their supply curves in response to a cut in real wage rates through inflation. In dynamic societies the *illusion* of upward-sloping supply curves has been created by continuous *shifts* to the right of both demand curves and supply curves, in response to population growth, resource discoveries, and technological progress, as illustrated in Figure 12-1. The increase in demand prices has been *accompanied* by increases in supply; but if the increased demand prices had been offered with all other things remaining unchanged, the result would probably have been a contraction of supply.

For a discussion of response of labor to various incentives in various underdeveloped countries, with special reference to Mexico, see Wilbert E. Moore, *Industrialization and Labor* (Ithaca, N.Y., 1951). In the Mexican villages where intensive field work was carried out, Moore found that there was less resistance to a move from peasant agriculture to factory work in the more purely agricultural and isolated villages than in semisuburban villages with easier access to the city.

and Eastern migration policy which "means propagating migration from overcrowded regions with financial help from the government" seems to overlook the very large role that private and public assistance played in the migration from Europe to the New World. Dr. Boeke also remarked that in Indonesia "when recruiting new colonists, the attraction exerted by the large, well-known colonies was needed, where relations and friends from the village awaited the newcomer." Surely immigrants always needed some pressures at home to make them move, and surely migrants always preferred to move to places where they could join their own kin; hence the concentration of Scandinavians and Germans in the states of Wisconsin and Minnesota, and of Dutchmen in New York. Also, internal migration in Western countries as well as Eastern may require active government intervention. Consider, for example, the efforts of the British government to relocate industry, of the Australian government to decentralize industry, and of the Quebec government to colonize its northern territories.

Similarly, Boeke's contrast between urban growth in Western and in Eastern societies does not ring true in the ears of the present writer. In dual societies, Boeke contends, urban development proceeds at the cost of rural life. In East and West alike, so far as one can judge from available data, urbanization is accompanied by an absolute growth, but relative decline, in the rural population; although in countries where the birth rate has not fallen, the relative fall in rural population and income may not stick. If Boeke means that urbanization has yet to bring true economic progress in Eastern countries, he is, of course, right; but that is because urbanization in the East has not brought the same degree of industrialization, nor the same decline in birth rates. In short, "urban growth" has not been "urban development."

Is Western Social Theory Applicable to Underdeveloped Areas?

If dualism is not primarily the product of a clash of two irreconcilable cultures, its existence is not in itself a barrier to application of Western social theory to underdeveloped areas. Sectoral differences are a challenge to economic theorists, but one that can be met.

The question of usefulness of Western theory is an important one; clearly, the possibility of effective prescriptions for economic and social policy in underdeveloped areas by Western social scientists depends on the degree to which the tools of analysis, in the use of which the Western social scientist is an expert, can be applied in underdeveloped countries.

When Boeke spoke of "the tender, delicate hothouse plants of western theory" he seems to have had in mind the neoclassical theory of a generation ago. All his examples of "inapplicability" of Western theory refer to conflicts between his observations and simple neoclassical theory of value and distribution, with pure competition and "normal" schedules. He referred to no non-Dutch economist more recent that Schumpeter, and even in Schumpeter's case his references were to his theory of economic development, which first appeared before World War I. Most economists would contend that the economic theory of Alfred Marshall was of only limited applicability in the Western world as well; and the inability to derive policy conclusions for underdeveloped areas on the basis of neoclassical theory alone hardly constitutes a proof that contemporary Western economic theory is useless in the East.

In order to demonstrate that Western theory is not so handicapped in explaining phenomena in dualistic economies as Boeke suggested, let us examine two of his examples. Marginal productivity theory, Boeke contended, provides no explanation of differences in rents charged for land leased to Westerners in Indonesia:

> There is no free competition: as land renter the western enterprise has almost always the monopoly; the product undergoes a number of more or less drastic industrial processes before it appears on the market; much capital is involved therein. Under these circumstances, it is impossible to compute what proportion of the value of the product is to be credited to the land. That we are here dealing with a dualistic phenomenon is sure. But this dualism must not be ascribed to a twofold marginal productivity, which varies according to whether land is in the hands of a western enterprise or of a native owner.

Instead, the rent depends on "the scarcity of money in the region concerned." [38]

This case is not unfamiliar in orthodox Western economic analysis. There is not free competition for land in Indonesia and more than one product is involved in estimating the value of marginal product. It is, indeed, a case of monopsony plus joint production, not the simplest model, but one which exists in the Western world and one which can be analyzed with familiar tools.

[38] Boeke, *Economics*, pp. 133–36.

Moreover, there is nothing peculiarly "Eastern" about dependence of rents on "the landowner's need of money." *Supply* price will always depend on "the scarcity of money," as well as on the relative scarcity of the resource in question; it is only the demand schedule that is determined by value of marginal product. If, on the other hand, Boeke argued that rents paid by Western enterprise depend *solely* on the amount of money in the hands of native landowners, as some of his statements suggest, he takes us beyond the limits of credibility. Is the demand for land really infinitely elastic? Is the demand price for land really *totally* unrelated to the income that can be earned from it? At another point [39] he suggests that it is the amount of money in the hands of buyers that determines price of land. Clearly, the demand price for land will depend on how much money buyers have, in the West or in the East; there is no inconsistency with Western theory in that.

To support his theory that rents have nothing to do with marginal productivity, Boeke adduced the following example. In 1920 and 1921, he said, crop failure resulted in a drop in the average rice yield per hectare. The government, accordingly, forced farmers to sell it part of their crop to help it meet the rice shortage. The real income of Javanese farmers fell, through reduced yield, from 67.5 million quintals of paddy in 1919 to 51 million in 1921. Hence, said Boeke, "There was not the least reason for land rent to increase." Yet, there was an increase in the cash income of landowners, because they were selling a larger share of their product for money. As a result, landowners were able to pay off debts at the peoples' credit banks, the number of new loans fell off, and rents of land rose.

This phenomenon is presented by Boeke as evidence of the impossibility of analyzing Eastern economies with tools of economic analysis developed in the West. Yet the simplest explanation would be direct application of marginal productivity theory: the marginal *value* product of land, in money, went up, and so money rents rose. I would agree, however, that this explanation is *too* simple. For an exhaustive analysis, it would be desirable to have further facts. What happened to other crops in the area, and to other prices? However, to the present writer, the sequence of events described by Boeke seems easily explicable in terms of quite ordinary economic analysis. A succession of crop failures does not necessarily bring an expectation of subsequent crop fail-

[39] *Ibid.*, p. 133.

ures. In a country where double-cropping is common,[40] expectations will be short-run, and the discount factor rather small. Under the conditions stipulated, with local supplies of rice reduced and local cash incomes increased, the local price of rice, in barter terms, probably rose.[41] Land was a source of real income in the *near future;* under the conditions described, therefore, it would have been strange if the price of land had not gone up.

In any case, land is an asset, a means of holding wealth, as well as a source of income. It is not uncommon, even in advanced countries, for people to prefer holding land to holding currency. With redundant cash in their hands, why should the Indonesian villagers not have exchanged it for land, raising land values and therefore rents?

Let us next examine Boeke's argument that wage differentials cannot be explained in terms of Western marginal productivity theory. First, Dr. Boeke stated, the profitableness of various forms of culture varies so much that it is impossible to generalize about "the marginal productivity of native agriculture." Moreover, he argued, "marginal productivity presupposes the existence of a real labor market, that is to say mobility of labor. None of these is to be found in native agriculture: the vessels do not communicate, the liquid is thick and slow moving."[42] As we have already indicated, Dr. Boeke himself provided some evidence that *landless* labor is actually highly mobile; all landowners, working their own land, are highly immobile in the Western world as well. In any case, use of the concept of marginal productivity as one aspect of wage analysis is not precluded because of immobility. Even Marshall recognized the existence of "noncompeting groups," among which marginal productivity need not be equalized. Finally, Boeke asks, "How can we make the theory of marginal productivity accord with the phenomenon of wages for the same kind of work varying so greatly at the same time of the year in neighboring localities?" Clearly, the application of marginal productivity theory does not require that wages should be

[40] According to Dr. Metcalf, about 10 per cent of land is double-cropped with rice, and most of the rest bears rice and one other crop each year. John E. Metcalf, *The Agricultural Economy of Indonesia* (Washington, D.C., 1952).

[41] Central market prices of rice rose from 1919 to 1920; they fell slightly from 1920 to 1921, but much less than general price levels. In any case, it would be necessary only for local tenants to *expect* rice prices to rise—a perfectly reasonable expectation. The local *tani* would not be acquainted with *world* economic developments.

[42] Boeke, *Economics*, pp. 142–43.

equalized throughout an economy. Immobility of labor, both geographic and occupational, is a common phenomenon everywhere. Indeed, it may be questioned whether occupational mobility is not greater in underdeveloped areas, where trade unionism is thus far less widespread, than it is in the advanced countries. Moreover, contemporary Western economic theory does not contend that wages must equal marginal productivity of labor. It recognizes a host of market situations, with relative degrees of monopoly and monopsony power, on the part of labor and of employers, and with wages varying from marginal productivity accordingly.[43]

Finally, the present writer has found that one other branch of contemporary Western economic theory, which Boeke did not mention at all—the theory underlying monetary and fiscal policy—is a very useful tool indeed when formulating such policies for underdeveloped areas. The general relationships between flows of money and of goods are the same in underdeveloped countries as they are in advanced ones; it is only a matter of selecting the right institutional assumptions. The same may be said of that part of Western economic theory which provides the basis for policies directed toward the removal of disequilibrium in the balance of payments. Perhaps, since the monetary and fiscal institutions are largely (though not wholly) Western, Boeke would not disagree on this point.

In conclusion, we might quote Bauer and Yamey once again: "There are no special economic theories or methods of analysis fashioned uniquely for the study of the underdeveloped world. But while the tools of analysis are of wide relevance, in a study of underdeveloped countries the situations to which they must be applied vary greatly." Of course, account must be taken of the differences in the institutional framework. "The economist, although equipped with versatile general purpose tools, must proceed with caution both in the way in which he uses them and in the identification of the relevant data in a situation or problem

[43] Cf. John T. Dunlop and Benjamin Higgins, "Bargaining Power and Market Structures," *Journal of Political Economy*, February, 1942. For evidence that Western economists no longer stress "marginal productivity" in the effort to explain the wage structures of the real world, see Lloyd G. Reynolds, *The Structure of Labor Markets* (New York, 1951); and John T. Dunlop, *Wage Determination under Trade Unions* (New York, 1944). Lest some reader fear that such analysis would not apply where there is no *organized* labor market, let me hasten to add that a "market" in this sense exists wherever there is a wage, in money or in kind—even for the self-employed.

to which he is applying them." But the differences between underdeveloped and advanced economies are "of degree rather than of kind." [44]

Thus although it is necessary to take account of differences in institutional framework and of culture patterns, economic behavior is much the same in underdeveloped as in advanced countries. "Those who dispute the relevance of the propositions of economics in the underdeveloped countries," says Bauer, "usually base their arguments on the differences in attitudes and institutions between the underdeveloped world and the Western countries. . . . Usually, however, these views reflect incomplete observation or imperfect understanding of economics. . . . Of course, the institutional framework of the community limits and directs the operations of its economic activities; . . . but all this does not invalidate propositions of economics." [45] Thus encouraged, let us go on.

[44] P. T. Bauer and B. S. Yamey, *op. cit.*, pp. 8–9.
[45] P. T. Bauer, *op. cit.*, pp. 15–16.

13 Partial Theories: Culture Patterns, Achievement Motivation, and Entrepreneurship

One may reject the theory of sociological dualism advanced by Boeke and still consider sociological, cultural, and psychological factors important in economic development. Indeed one may say that *all* economists who have specialized on economic development recognize the importance of the interplay of these factors with economic factors. As Professors Baldwin and Meier put it in their comprehensive textbook: [1]

> The psychological and sociological requirements for development are as important as the economic requirement. They deserve full consideration in their own right. . . . It is obvious that some institutional changes which are not merely economic must accompany successful development efforts. Economic development of sufficient rapidity has not taken place within the present cultural framework. New wants, new motivations, new ways of production, new institutions need to be created if national income is to rise more rapidly. Where there are religious obstacles to modern economic progress, the religion may have to be taken less seriously or its character altered. Fundamentally the backward peoples must recognize that men can master nature; they must be motivated towards economic achievement; they must acquire the means of accomplishing these objectives; and these objectives must become part of the society's value structure.
>
> In general, the economic problems of development are relatively simple compared with the broader and deeper sociological problems

[1] G. M. Meier and R. E. Baldwin, *Economic Development* (New York, 1957), pp. 355–59.

of respecting the general cultural patterns and institutions of the poor countries at the same time that they acquire new wants and the means of attaining them. Not only must economic organization be transformed, but social organization—as represented by such major institutions as caste, the joint family, the rural village, the church, and the schools—must also be modified so that the basic complex of values and motivation may be more favorable for development. Thus, the requirements for development involve both economic change and cultural change. The fundamental problem is likely to be not how much economic change the economy can absorb, but rather how much cultural change the backward peoples can accept and how quickly.

Relatively few economists, however, have had the courage to attempt a systematic theory of development which would incorporate strategic sociological, cultural, and psychological forces. Outstanding among these few is Professor Everett Hagen of the M.I.T. Center for International Studies. Professor Hagen has constructed a theory of entrepreneurial motivation which merits careful attention. Since it depends in large measure on a particular kind of psychological research, in which Professor David McClelland of Harvard University has been prominent, we shall begin with a brief outline of Professor McClelland's theory of "Achievement Motivation." [2]

n-achievement and Entrepreneurship

Professor McClelland begins a recent paper outlining the relationship of his concept of *n*-achievement to economic development, by saying modestly that economists cannot be blamed for their failure to pay more attention to purely psychological factors. "The importance of understanding psychological factors," he says, "has been widely appreciated." The difficulty has been that "psychologists have had very little to offer of a concrete nature to economists and others interested in promoting the development of poor countries." He feels, however, that recent research in the measurement of human motives has improved the capacity of psychologists to provide economists with the "hard facts" which he thinks they should have, if they are to interweave psychological analysis with their economic analysis.

[2] D. C. McClelland, "Community Development and the Nature of Human Motivation: Some Implications of Recent Research" (Paper presented to the Conference on Community Development and National Change, M.I.T., CIS, December, 1957).

The Concept of *n*-achievement

To begin with, says Professor McClelland, we must gain some understanding of what is meant by "Achievement Motivation." Since the concept is technical, we may let McClelland speak for himself:

The "achievement motive" is ordinarily measured by performing a "content analysis" on imaginative thought. The scoring criteria for the "content analysis" were derived by comparing the thought processes of people under the influence of achievement motivation with the thought processes of people not under its influence. "Thought processes" were sampled by asking subjects to write imaginative stories to pictures. It was found that they introduced more ideas of a certain kind into their stories when their motivation to achieve—to do well—was aroused than when it was not aroused. An objective coding definition has been worked out for detecting these "ideas" with high agreement among different observers. Nearly all of the "ideas" can be classified under the heading of "desiring to do well" or "competing with a standard of excellence." This then became the scoring definition for a variable which was named technically *n* Achievement to distinguish it from other common-sense measures of achievement motivation such as one would get from how well a person said he was trying. The *n* Achievement score for an individual is simply a sum of the number of instances of achievement "ideas" or images and their subtypes, and the score for a group of individuals is some measure of central tendency (the average, the mode) of the scores of individuals who make up the group. In this way it can be determined, for example, that the average *n* Achievement of a group of teen-age German boys is slightly but significantly lower than the average *n* Achievement of a carefully matched group of American boys, or that American boys from lower class backgrounds have lower average *n* Achievement than boys from middle class backgrounds.

McClelland goes on to say that by now psychologists know a good deal about the characteristics of people with high *n*-achievement. They work harder at laboratory tasks, learn faster, do better work in high school than others with the same IQ, and "seem to do their best work when it counts for their record and not when other special incentives are introduced such as pressure from the outside to do well, money prizes, or time off from work." They are more resistant to social pressure, choose experts rather than friends as partners in their work activities, and like risky occupations, performing better under longer odds, and choosing moderate risks over either safe or speculative ones. Finally—and perhaps most important in terms of social policy—they come from "families in which there has been stress on early self-reliance and mastery."

McClelland next asks the question which may have occurred to some readers by this time. What has all this got to do with economic development? His answer is "a lot, if we can find evidence to support the two following propositions: (1) that group differences in average level of certain motives such as *n*-achievement, predict differences in rate of economic growth; (2) that certain motive combinations predispose individuals to act like the successful business entrepreneurs, who have played key roles in all previous economic development." [3]

McClelland believes he has evidence to support the first proposition. Table 13-1 presents some of his evidence. It shows that the middle class tends to have a higher average level of *n*-achievement than the lower class. The slightly lower *n*-achievement for upper-class people is a complicated matter, he says, and contents himself by pointing out that "it is probably due in part to traditionalist emphasis in the upper class," in part to the nature of some of the professional occupations in which this group is engaged, and in part simply to "having arrived." In any case, he says, it is the middle class which has traditionally provided the largest number of small business entrepreneurs.

McClelland cites a related study by Havemann and West [4] which shows that among Jews, Protestants, and Catholics with similar college education and similar original economic status, Jews achieve the most economic success, with Protestants next and Catholics third, giving a perfect rank-correlation with the average *n*-achievement figures in Table 13-1. However, McClelland seems to be overburdening his data here. If it is the middle classes who determine the rate of economic development, this table would lead us to expect more rapid progress among Italians, Greeks, and French-Canadians than among Protestant whites. In any case, the categories are not strictly comparable, since these Roman Catholic groups include a larger proportion of people who have had themselves sufficiently strong motivation to immigrate, and who may therefore not be typical of their own original society.

With respect to the correlation between economic success and *n*-achievement in social systems other than the United States, McClelland was able to present only some preliminary results. Since the psychologists were unable to use direct testing in for-

[3] *Ibid.*, p. 6.

[4] E. Havemann and P. S. West, *They Went to College* (New York, 1952).

eign countries, they chose "stories representative of the culture," as an indication of the level of *n*-achievement in that culture. "In other words, it was felt that stories in wide-spread use in a culture might be representative of the way individuals thought in that culture in much the same sense as a sample of actual stories produced for us would be when individuals were tested." Samples were obtained of children's stories in over fifty countries, and the frequency with which various motives and values appeared in these stories were counted, without knowledge of the country from which they came. Some of the results of this study are presented in Table 13-2.

TABLE 13-1.

Average *n*-achievement Scores of Adolescent American Males by Social Class by Ethnicity

Ethnicity	*Social class*			*Average*
	upper	middle	lower	
French-Canadian	10.00	10.92	8.26	8.20
Italian	9.43	12.94	8.75	9.78
Greek	9.17	12.13	9.67	10.81
Jewish	10.06	10.41	11.00	10.53
Negro	11.36	9.00	7.67	8.40
Protestant whites	11.85	11.00	9.03	10.19
Average	10.69	11.34	8.78	

SOURCE: From an unpublished study by B. Rosen.

According to McClelland, "they show a marked relationship between *n*-achievement level in 1925 and rate of economic growth subsequently during the period when the children of 1925 were young adults at the peak of their productivity. In fact, put in their most striking fashion, the *r* results suggest that an *n*-achievement level 2½ times greater in 1925 reached to gain in productivity 7 or 8 times greater in 1938 to 1950." However, McClelland readily admits that there are many shortcomings in these data. No underdeveloped countries are represented, and Holland, with a very low level of *n*-achievement, nevertheless managed to achieve a respectable rate in economic growth.

A third kind of evidence tapped by McClelland and his team is based on analysis of Greek classics from Homer to Aristotle. The average level of *n*-achievement in Greek societies was obtained from analysis of the behavior and motivation in this literature. The level of *n*-achievement was then matched with Greek economic power, as indicated by trading area and other historical measures. The results show, according to McClelland, "that *n*-achievement level was highest long before Greece had developed into much of an economic power, and that in fact, by the time of her golden age, it had dropped significantly, foreshadowing her subsequent decline."

TABLE 13-2.

Relationship between *n*-achievement Level in 1925 and Subsequent Growth Rates in Real National Product per Capita (1938–50)

High n-achievement level in 1925: *		*Average annual gain in real national product per capita, 1938–50 (per cent)* †
Canada	56	4.0
England	44	1.2
Denmark	42	1.2
United States	40	4.2
Average	45	2.7
Low n-achievement level in 1925:		
Germany	29	0.7
Belgium	21	0.3
France	17	0.0
Holland	6	0.6
Average	18	0.4

Rank Correlation = .75 $p < .05$

* *n*-achievement level in 1925 estimated crudely from achievement imagery in children's stories.

† Gains in real national product per capita from G. M. Meier and R. E. Baldwin, *Economic Development* (New York, 1957), p. 248.

McClelland considers analysis of entrepreneurial behavior in terms of *n*-achievement to be a considerable refinement of theories analyzing entrepreneurial behavior in terms of the profit motive alone:

For one thing, as Weber was one of the first to point out, many of the most successful of these business entrepreneurs in England and the United States belonged to fundamentalist religious sects derived from Calvinism and Anabaptism, which were in principle strongly ascetic and successfully prevented their members from sensuous enjoyment of the fruits of their labors. In short, it was the Calvinists, Methodists, Quakers, and other such radical Protestant groups who were most successful in the business sense. But could their chief motive be profit if they were expressly denied the possibility of enjoying material benefits? The phenomenon is by no means limited to the history of the West. In India, for example, it also appears to be the ascetic religious sects like the Jains and the Parsees who have been most successful in business. In neither the East nor the West has it been the secular-minded materialists, primarily interested in money and what it will buy for them personally who have been successful in business.

In McClelland's view, such considerations as money income, the profit margin, or the size of one's business have been important in entrepreneurial motivation "as a means to measuring how well one has done his job," rather than as an end in themselves.

To substantiate his theory that high *n*-achievement results in a flood of Schumpeterian entrepreneurs, one more set of evidence is necessary. "Is there any evidence," McClelland asks "that subjects with high *n*-achievement are attracted to the type of opportunities which business provides?" McClelland thinks there is:

The data are by no means all in but what there are support our expectations. (1) Students with high *n* Achievement prefer risky occupations, particularly of a business nature—e.g., buyer of merchandise, real estate salesman, stock broker—to "safe" occupations of equal prestige—e.g., clergyman, interpreter, statistician— (2) The "highs" also work more efficiently under somewhat "riskier" conditions—when the chances of coming out on top are about 1 in 3—than the "lows" who perform most efficiently under somewhat "safer" conditions—when their chances of winning are about 1 in 2 or fifty-fifty. (3) Even more significantly the "highs," when given a choice of the odds under which they prefer to work, choose a situation in which their objective chances of success are about one in three whereas the "lows" tend to distribute their choices of different types of risk much more evenly so that more often they work under conditions in which they are either *certain* of succeeding or could succeed only if they were extremely lucky.

McClelland summarizes his argument up to this point as follows:

1. Economic development depends on "vigorous activities of a number of individuals who behave in an entrepreneurial fashion."

2. "What appears to make an individual behave in this fashion is a motivational complex not entirely understood as yet but containing a strong need for an achievement as technically measured by economists."

3. There is both direct and inferential evidence that this motivational complex has been in shorter supply in poor countries than in rich countries.

4. If substantial economic development is to occur in poor countries the number of individuals with the entrepreneurial mo-

tivational complex—and particularly with high *n*-achievement—will have to be significantly increased.

Here McClelland parts company with many sociologists and cultural anthropologists. His investigation leads him to conclude that concentration on the *social system* is likely to be ineffective. For if motives are "autonomous forces within individuals," we shall have to "concentrate on changing people." [5] Now the amount of *n*-achievement any particular individual has, McClelland adds, depends on "the pressure for achievement and self-reliance put on him . . . by his parents, particularly by his mother." Such basic motivational characteristics as *n*-achievement are acquired very early in life and are progressively harder to change with age. From this statement McClelland is led to the inevitable conclusion that if we are to promote economic growth, it is necessary first to change the values and motives of individuals. How is this to be done? His answer is "by persuasion or education, by introducing changes in the social system, and by early character training." Of these three approaches, the third "is by all odds the one most likely to succeed. . . ." [6] For in this way, values can be built in from the very beginning. He feels that it is too late to do much toward transforming child training by average parents, "but it certainly is practicable to select carefully a corps of specially qualified nursery and primary school teachers, to bring them to a teacher-training institute, and to make them understand that primary education involves character training fully as much as it does literacy training." Thus McClelland's analysis leads to the conclusion that a take-off into economic development requires a long period of establishing psychological preconditions.

Hagen's Theory of the Transition to Economic Growth

Professor Everett Hagen's theory of economic change leans heavily on the kind of psychological research summarized in the previous section. However, as an economist, he sets forth his theory in the form of a "model." His list of variables is as follows:

R1. The structure of production
- R1.1 Techniques
- R1.2 Rate of technical progress
- R1.3 Composition of output
- R1.4 Rate of saving and investment
- R1.5 Composition of investment

[5] *Ibid.*, pp. 8, 9, 17.
[6] *Ibid.*, p. 37, 42.

R2. The social structure
- R2.1 Geographic scope of
  - R2.1.1 Economic community
  - R2.1.2 Political community
- R2.2 Structure of class relations
  - R2.2.1 Concentration-diffusion of control of production
  - R2.2.2 Social distance between classes
  - R2.2.3 Concentration-diffusion of political power
- R2.3 Pattern of interpersonal relations
  - R2.3.1 Basis for selection of associates: quality-performance
  - R2.3.2 Diffuseness-specificity of rights and obligations

R3. The structure of personality
- R3.1 Scope of knowledge
  - R3.1.1 Knowledge of science and techniques
  - R3.1.2 Knowledge based on external experience
- R3.2 World view
  - R3.2.1 Physical
  - R3.2.2 Social
- R3.3 Needs
  - R3.3.1 Need dependency-need achievement
  - R3.3.2 Need affiliation-need autonomy
  - R3.3.3 Need dominance
- R3.4 Values concerning occupations

These variables, he says, are essentially quantitative in nature, and *could* be set forth in the form of a set of simultaneous equations with appropriate leads and lags. Because of the difficulties of measurement, however, he does not consider it worthwhile translating his "model" into a set of formal equations.

Hagen's essential thesis is apparent from the first sentence of his paper: "Capital formation is frequently regarded as the process immediately responsible for continuing economic growth—growth in per capita output and income in a society. But it is clear that capital formation is important only as it is the carrier or agent of technological progress."[7] The essential task, he says, is to isolate the forces which bring about "the transition from virtually stationary technology to continuing progress." By continuing technological progress he means "technological advances sufficiently frequent and of sufficient effect on production so that output per worker in a society as a whole increases considerably each decade for as many as 3 successive decades."[8] In short, he

[7] Everett E. Hagen, "An Analytical Model of the Transition to Economic Growth," M.I.T., CIS (Document C/57-12), p. 1. An earlier version of this theory was presented in *Economic Development and Cultural Change*, April, 1957, under the title "The Theory of Economic Development."

[8] *Ibid.*, p. 6.

defines continuing technological progress in such a way as to make it identical with our definition of economic development.[9]

To this problem, then, Professor Hagen directs his attention. He believes that "the various social sciences have now progressed to a point at which a first halting general statement of a theory of a transition of a society from virtually stationary technology to continuing technological progress is possible."

The Peasant Society

Hagen begins his analysis by setting up an idealized form of a peasant society, which he then contrasts with an industrialized society in order to isolate the distinguishing characteristics. A peasant society, he says, is first of all a dual society. It consists of a number of agricultural villages with one or more centers, which are trading cities or the king's courts. There is little migration into or out of each village. The occupation of the majority of the people is small-scale agriculture, although there are a few craftsmen and traders. The family form is usually the extended family. Relationships among villages "may be limited to a trickle of trade."[10] The elite live in the center, except for a few officials, teachers, and rent collectors who represent the central government in the villages. The society has little contact with foreign countries, "though a small trickle of trade, and with it a small trickle of ideas across national borders, occurs." When one considers the vigorous international trade in Asia in the sixteenth century and earlier, it is clear that Hagen's "peasant society" is a deliberate abstraction rather than a precise description of underdeveloped countries at any particular phase in their history.

All these characteristics, in Hagen's view, are the exact opposites of "the technologically progressive society." To isolate the differences more systematically, he groups the major variables which determine the nature of a society under five headings, conforming more or less to the variables set forth above. He begins with the structure of production, and the structure of class re-

[9] "By this imprecise but sufficient definition," Hagen excludes the accelerating innovation in ancient Rome, or that of Florence and Venice during the Renaissance, from his category of continuing technological progress. There seems to be a certain circularity in his reasoning here, for he says: "where technological progress has become sufficiently rapid and sufficiently widespread to increase productivity markedly per decade for as much as 3 decades, the advance has continued subsequently, whereas a number of spurts too brief or insufficiently pervasive in the economy to meet this test have proved to be temporary."

[10] Hagen, *op. cit.*, p. 14.

lationships. "In a psychological sense," he states, "the elite and the villagers of the peasant society live literally in different worlds and have extremely few interests in common." In a technologically progressive society, on the other hand, there is a more rapid circulation of the elite, more social mobility through economic success, and a substantial middle class. Again, the peasant society is characterized by crude concepts of the physical world, a rudimentary state of the physical sciences, primitive methods of production, and low literacy. In a technologically progressive society, the physical sciences are well developed and the concepts of the nature and operation of the physical world are refined.

The peasant does not see any connection between his actions and the phenomena of nature, except for such minor matters as irrigation systems to control the flow of water. "Only a rare deviant villager conceives of being anything but a villager." In a technologically progressive society, for a considerable portion of the population "the unconscious frame of reference that determines the scope of their mental activity includes the concept (or fact) that the world can be made to yield increasing fruits by the exercise of their intelligence." They also know that their position in society can be improved by their own efforts. Most important of all, however, is the difference in basic motivation. In contrast to the technologically advanced society with its high *n*-achievement, high need-autonomy (need to be independent of others), and high need-dominance (need to be a leader) the peasant society is characterized by a high need-affiliation (need to please friends and to have their affection, to cooperate with them) and high need-dependency (need to feel inferior to someone; to have ideas and attitudes approved by persons regarded as superiors). With this motivational pattern, the rate of technological progress is likely to be slow. For "the essence of innovation is the solution of problems involving unknown or unique elements—the opposite of rote action—and no one could consistently and effectively apply his energies to the attacking of problems unless he possessed a high need achievement." [11]

The lack of Schumpeterian entrepreneurship in a peasant society is a direct reflection of the value system in such a society. "Villagers and elites alike in a peasant society," Hagen asserts,

[11] *Ibid.*, p. 28. Of course, need-achievement may dominate behavior of business leaders only in some aspects of their life. John Rockefeller, Sr., was "an extremely conventional man in his home and religious life," and "Henry Ford's intense life-long interest in collecting and preserving things of the past suggests a constant fear of venturing too boldly into the new."

"revere the same economic roles, and spurn the same ones." [12] Land ownership, religious position, military position, service to the King—all these are highly respected. In contrast, "both villager and elite spurn trade and business." There is "a feeling of repugnance toward unskilled labor and toward work that soils one's hands." In contrast, in the technologically progressive society, "there is a more diversified attitude toward various economic roles." Life on the land is not so highly regarded, attitudes toward religious life vary, attitudes toward military life change when war is in progress or threatened, attitudes toward art and science are ambivalent, while government service is not highly regarded by most people. "Business has an esteem which contrasts violently with the disesteem in which it is held in peasant society." Technical activities are held in high regard, "and if dirty work is associated with technology the aversion to it disappears."

Finally, Hagen discusses the contrast between peasant and technologically progressive societies in terms of interpersonal relationships, using the Talcott Parsons concept of "pattern variables." In the village, Hagen says, one's attitudes toward other people does not depend on their capability or needs, but upon their status. The peasant does not seek the most efficient worker to help him in his field, he employs members of his family without question. In technologically advanced societies, by contrast, the tendency is to seek the best man for the job.

All these characteristics of peasant society, Hagen concludes, are inimical to rapid technological change. How then can change be brought about?

Hagen suggests five possible forces tending to cause changes in the structure and functioning of peasant society. First, there is "creeping progress of understanding of the physical world and of technology." Second is "social tensions among the elite." It is possible that "high need achievement, aggression and dominance may exist among the elite of a peasant society and the effects of possible tensions among the elite groups merit exploration." The other three causes of change are forces outside the society: pressure which may threaten the structure of social relationships within the society; altered economic opportunities; and imposition of change through physical force, such as colonial rule.

All this analysis leads Hagen to somewhat gloomy prognosis for underdeveloped countries: whatever the initiating force may be, "it will not bring about change from creeping technological

[12] *Ibid.*, p. 30.

progress to continued technological progress without an intervening process of gradual change in the values of all the variables of the model presented above." The individual's view of his relationship with the world must change radically, scientific knowledge and the scope of experience must widen, occupational values must undergo basic alteration, class relationships must alter in their social, economic, and political aspects, and the values of "pattern variables" must change considerably. Moreover, "drastic change in the value of *any* one variable in the peasant society while the others remain at their peasant society level seems unlikely. The entire set of values must probably shift to considerable degree, though of course not equally, before any of them can shift drastically." Hagen considers it extremely difficult, though not impossible, for the entire set of changes to take place within one generation. Nor has he faith in the gradually accelerated effects of mere broadening of contacts.

Historical development does not suggest gradually accelerating technological progress, he says, but "a surge of change."

This line of thought leads Hagen to his theory of entrepreneurship. He agrees with most analysts of economic development that the entrepreneurial function is fundamental in the process of economic change:[13]

> In England, Western Europe, and Latin American countries that are now progressing, as well as in Japan and the Soviet Union, the final surge was carried forward, not by individuals scattered at random among the elite, but by individuals belonging in each case to a selected group or groups. These groups are distinguished in significant ways from the elite as a whole or the population as a whole. In England the group was the Non-conformists, Scotch and other; in Japan, lower-order Samurai, upper-level peasants and a few merchants; in Colombia, the people of Medellia and more generally of Antioquia; in Saõ Paulo selected groups of immigrants and internal migrants, and so on. These facts raise the question whether technological progress would have become rapid when it did, in any of these countries, if circumstances had not caused an important group to channel its energies into economic activities. The facts suggest giving attention to social tensions among the elite as a cause of changes.

The foregoing analysis of the peasant society, Hagen suggests, shows that neither the peasants themselves nor the dominant elite will provide such leadership. What then were the characteristics of these groups which provided the source of Schumpeterian entrepreneurship? First, they must be a "*relatively* elite group."

[13] *Ibid.*, pp. 59–60.

But they must be in "the lower echelons of the elite": The dominant group has no incentive to go into risky financial ventures. The question is, then, "why should the members of a group in the lower echelons of the elite turn vigorously at a certain time in history to economic development?" He reviews the common characteristics of all the groups which have done so in various countries to find the answer.

The *first* part of that answer is that a group does so only if it feels that its social status has been suppressed below its due, or is in danger of suppression. Presumably the feeling arises from an actual reduction of historical status, or from a threat of reduction. In England, the agricultural revolution which preceded the Industrial Revolution was carried out by members of the landed gentry—but they were a country group to whom the urbanite group of gentry manifested a sense of superiority. The Industrial Revolution itself was carried out by *Scots*, who had been conquered by the English, and whose religion was looked down upon by the Church-of-England gentry, and by Non-conformists in England itself. The Intellectuals of Russia; the Antioquians of Colombia who have been looked down upon as "country cousins" by the urbanites of Bogota; and immigrants in many countries, not fully accepted by the local society, provide other examples of the vigor of such lower echelon elite in their reaction to social subordination. The example *par excellence* is provided by Japan.

This principle that "only a group driven by an urge to regain or maintain a rightful social status will carry out the revolutionary actions which complete the transition to continuing technological advance," Hagen calls "*the law of the subordinated group.*" The members of the innovating group, Hagen continues, must have the "combination of world view and motivational structure" which results in a vigorous attack on their problem rather than resignation to their fate. He then states his "law of social blockage."

Some readers may recall that we have already come across these "laws." Schumpeter described his innovating entrepreneurs in much the same terms in his *Economic Development*, written nearly half a century ago. He did not, of course, attempt to provide a complete psycho-sociological theory to support his view of the nature of the entrepreneurial class. Arthur Lewis also explains the rise of an entrepreneurial class in similar terms:

The less the availability of traditional channels of social ascent—either because there are no such channels, class position being traditionally fixed, or because they are blocked to the social group in question—and the greater the apparent possibility of social rise through increase in economic power, the greater will be the tendency to devote energies to economic development.

The resemblance of these laws to Toynbee's challenge and response thesis is also apparent.

All this is, then, readily acceptable and indeed widely accepted. But that being so what are the policy implications? We seem to be confronted here with still another vicious circle: the society which attaches importance to conformity is likely to be stagnant, and a stagnant society is likely to place high value on conformity. Is there any way out of this vicious circle?

Hagen seems to be saying that if people are to have economic growth they must "want it"—in the sense that a sufficient number of the subdominant elite are motivated toward economic activity of a sort bringing technological progress and economic growth, while the motivation of the rest of the society is such as to permit technological progress to spread throughout the society.[14]

His theory might be restated as another kind of psycho-sociological dualism: a dualistic society, with technological progress confined to a small sector of the economy influencing only a small proportion of the population, is unlikely to develop. Cast in such terms, however, the Hagen thesis is almost tautological. What does it tell us in respect to positive action?

On this question Hagen is not very clear. "The conditions suggested above should not be regarded as prerequisites for economic development," he says, "but as forces tending to cause or to prevent change, whose interplay determines the path and speed of movement of the society." External forces may help to break the vicious circle. For example, expansion of the market provides favorable economic opportunities, and increases the intensity of incentives to channel energies into technological progress. However, Hagen maintains that expansion of the export market did *not* play an important role "in the later stages of transition" for the United States, Japan, the Soviet Union, or the newly developing countries of Latin America. Technical knowledge imported from

[14] "If this reaction is to occur," Hagen says, "the society as a whole must have common cultural bonds to be innovated. They must not be so alien, so different from other groups that their activity creates emotional antipathy rather than desire to achieve equal success by doing likewise." *Ibid.*, p. 71.

Migrants also are affected by the influence of having been torn loose from their native culture. They do not fit into the new culture. By observing cultural differences they forcefully learn that social ways are not inevitable, and that man is free to follow new paths. In fact, their old paths are not available and they are forced to tread new ones. These circumstances bring what Toynbee calls the "stimulus of new ground."

abroad may help, but not much: the mere availability of the technical knowledge of other countries does not permit a society "to by-pass that long cumulative growth of scientific and technical knowledge sketched above. While the time period involved can be telescoped considerably, a process of essentially the same nature must be gone through whether the society is developing its own science and the technology or has the knowledge from abroad available."

The reasons for this contention are that science is not simply knowledge, but also an attitude toward the physical world. The people of underdeveloped countries cannot learn science and advanced technology as they might learn a foreign language. "For they will not apply science in their thinking until basic change has occurred in their world view, motivations, and values." In any case, "a complex of production techniques in one society cannot simply be copied in another, as one man might wear another man's clothes." For relationships within a factory or other production organization also depend on the culture of the society. The production process may have to be altered if it is to function efficiently in a society with different patterns of behavior.

Finally, Hagen suggests that an external threat to a nation as a whole may be a powerful force toward development, especially if combined with internal factors in planning the country toward technological change. This kind of combination of internal and external pressures, in Hagen's view, explains the relatively rapid transformation of the Japanese society from a stagnant one into one with sustained technological progress.

Evaluation of the Hagen Theory

What are we to say of Hagen's thesis?

To begin with, is there any reason for attaching more importance to sociological and psychological factors in the theory of economic development than in the theory of equilibrium? Ever since Jevons, Walras, Menger, and J. B. Clark formulated the "psychological theory of value" about 1870, economic theory has been under attack, by economists and other social scientists alike, for its failure to deal satisfactorily with psychological and sociological forces affecting human behavior, or for the naïvete of its underlying psychological and sociological assumptions. The response of economists has been to become less psychological, not more. The history of the theory of value and distribution from 1870 to the present time has been one of progressive "depsychologization." That is, assumptions about basic human behavior have been made so simple and so general as to be virtually axiomatic. Economists felt safer this way than when relying on more specific but unproved theories of motivation—especially when psychologists themselves abandoned for a while their search for a general theory of motivation. The present writer has defended this kind of economics in an earlier publication.[15]

The revolution in economic thought in the late nineteenth century was also accompanied by a new insistence on *Wertfreiheit*, or freedom from value judgments. That is, in making policy prescriptions, economists wanted to be sure that their own value systems or social and political preferences did not enter into their analyses of policy proposals. Recommendations for policy were supposed to be based on "purely scientific analysis," in such a way that economists could state *definitely* that a particular policy would add to social welfare. "Adding to social welfare" was interpreted as giving people what *they* want. The trouble is, of course, that people want different things. Welfare theory has boiled down to a search for policies which would clearly give some people what they want without depriving others of things that they want—or, at least, policies which permit gainers to compensate losers and still be ahead. In this kind of welfare economics the market, or some substitute for it which reflects individual preferences, is the supreme arbiter of what is "good" and "bad" for society. Tastes were taken as *given* by the economic scientist; he expressed no judgment of the relative merit of beer or bibles, but accepted people's preferences for these commodities, as expressed in market choices, as the guide to "welfare."

Why can we not treat economic development in the same way as we treat other aspects of economic policy? Could we not make assumptions about behavior which are essentially axiomatic and still say a great deal about factors which will raise per capita income? Could we not also accept the value systems of a society without passing judgment on them?

Important differences between the theory of value and distribution and a theory of growth warrant answering this question in the negative. For one thing, the professional economist is less justified in maintaining an attitude of scientific indifference where it is not a matter of beer versus bibles but of growth versus equality or growth versus stability. The consumer with only one more dollar to spend knows that he *must* make his choice between

[15] Benjamin Higgins, *What Do Economists Know?* (Melbourne, 1950), pp. 6–8.

another bible or six more beers, and the economist is not especially well qualified to advise him. There is little in the economist's specialized training to make him the right person to explain the ramifications of one choice or the other. But when it comes to economic development on the one hand and equality, stability, and retention of existing sociocultural patterns and attitudes, it is not even clear to the bulk of the people in underdeveloped countries that a choice is involved; most of them want all these things at once, and the economist has a duty to point out that a choice must be made. Even more important, when people say, "Well, if we *must* choose between our social values and higher incomes we prefer to stay as we are," the economist can and should point out that *this* choice is one that many underdeveloped countries cannot make. In countries with high population growth potential, substantial changes in economic and social organization may be necessary merely to prevent a *decline* in living standards. In the worst cases the potential economic deterioration is such that the social fabric could not withstand it anyhow. In such situations the economist cannot simply take tastes as "given" with a clear professional conscience.

Secondly, if we are interested in *prognosis*, the sociological, cultural, psychological, and political factors must be brought in. Here the analogy is market analysis rather than pure theory of price. No market analyst thinks in terms of *Wertfreiheit,* takes tastes as given, or denies himself the use of whatever knowledge the sociologist, psychologist, or anthropologist can provide. In terms of our own foreign policy it may be extremely important to know whether India or China has the best chance for development. For a rational foreign aid policy, it is absolutely essential to be able to forecast with some degree of accuracy the developmental potential of various applicants for assistance. The sociocultural and political frameworks are among the most important elements in "absorptive capacity," which is much the best criterion for allocation of aid funds. A study of economic history suggests that there is an optimal moment for a concentrated effort to produce a take-off, when economic, technical, political, and psycho-cultural factors operate together to create favorable conditions for it. We might call this moment the time of maximum relative absorptive capacity. Ideally, large-scale aid would be poured into each country in turn as this moment is reached; but to discern the moment we cannot be content with axiomatic assumptions about behavior nor can we abjure value judgments about the cultural framework.

Thus the factors discussed by Hagen are important for economic development theory in a way that psychological theories of choice are not important for equilibrium theory. On the other hand, the present writer would stop short of including in his policy recommendations measures designed to operate directly on the sociology, psychology, and culture of any country—even if he knew what measures would be successful. There seems to be no very clear way of *creating* the required attitudes, unless we revert to McClelland's process of gradual change through education, a process which would certainly take a generation or two. Will underdeveloped countries wait that long? And is not the very fact that many of them will *not* wait that long sufficient evidence that the change in motivation has *already* taken place, at least among the elites? Could we not conclude from Hagen's theory that any country which has gone far enough to produce an economic development plan that has become a matter of public discussion has *already* met the psycho-sociological prerequisites for growth? If so, would the economists and technicians who make up most development planning teams not do better to concentrate on the economic and technical problems, rather than to worry about sociological and psychological obstacles?

Certainly, plans which are based on an understanding of existing psycho-cultural patterns are more likely to succeed than those which are not. But there is some evidence that where economic and technical barriers to growth are removed the psychological and sociological barriers melt away rather quickly. Hagen himself refers to one dramatic case of rapid cultural change—the revolutionary development of Manus society as a consequence of occupation of the island by American troops during World War II.[16] This experience suggests that an almost complete transformation of a society can take place within a few years if the external "shock" to the society is powerful enough; Manus society jumped two thousand years in a decade. Hagen says, "I believe the apparent contradictions are not real. If the case of the Manus is an exception to a generalization, it is a limiting case, extremely unlikely to be duplicated elsewhere." Why? Of course, occupation by American troops in numbers many times the total popu-

[16] Cf. Margaret Mead, *New Lives For Old* (New York, 1956). See also Daniel Lerner, *The Passing of Traditional Society: Modernizing the Middle East* (Glencoe, Ill., 1958); and chap. XII, "Experiences in Attempting to Introduce Social Change in Underdeveloped Areas," Lyle W. Shannon, *Underdeveloped Areas* (New York, 1957).

lation is hardly the form of "technical assistance" that is likely to be asked or offered in underdeveloped countries. But where a leadership group is already determined to achieve economic development, an equivalent "shock" effect might be obtained through an integrated economic and social development plan with liberal foreign aid.

14 Partial Theories: Technological Dualism and the Population Explosion

One part of a general theory of underdevelopment is the thesis that in the underdeveloped countries, the initial favorable impact of industrial investment (including investment in plantations as well as in mines, petroleum, etc.) was swamped by population growth, in a way which did not occur in the currently advanced countries. In most countries, an initial increase in population growth seems to have followed the first wave of rapid industrialization. In the advanced countries of the West, however, the rise in *per capita* income was sustained long enough to bring subsequent drops in fertility rates and to permit economic growth to be sustained. The question is why the process in underdeveloped countries was different.

When the colonial powers first came into contact with countries of Asia and Africa, the populations of the latter were apparently not much higher, relative to natural resources, than those of European lands. In the case of Asia, moreover, there is little evidence that the level of technology was markedly below that of Europe in the sixteenth century. India, Indonesia, and China had firearms, navigation instruments, modes of land and water transport, techniques of manufacture and agriculture, and educational systems that compared favorably with Europe's best. We have small evidence that the standard of living of either rich or poor was significantly lower in Asian than in European countries at that time. Like the European countries, the Asian lands were actively engaged in international trade. The sixteenth-century picture would have given little basis for forecasting that in 400 years *per capita* incomes in Europe would be several times as high as in Asia.

During the seventeenth and eighteenth centuries, when the relationship of the colonial powers to Asian and African peoples was mainly a trading one, the countries of Europe seem to have made more progress toward establishing the preconditions for take-off than did those of Asia. In particular, during this period Europe benefited from improvements in agricultural methods and increased transport facilities. Even at the beginning of the nineteenth century, however, populations of many Asian countries were still small relative to resources, and prospects for economic growth would still have been good. By the end of that century, population growth in such countries as Indonesia, India, Japan, and the Philippines was already so high that launching a steady rise in *per capita* incomes had become a difficult problem.

The Population Explosion

The major impact of nineteenth-century industrial investment on rates of population growth probably came through the accompanying reduction in mortality rates. As the colonial powers shifted from trading to settlement, in order to exploit more effectively their new interest in plantations and mines (and later in petroleum), they followed policies which tended to reduce death rates. By maintaining internal law and order the colonial powers hampered the freedom of the native peoples to kill each other. Secondly, when Westerners settled in the country they became more interested in public health. In protecting themselves from malaria, typhoid, plague, and other diseases, they reduced the incidence of these diseases among the native peoples as well. Improved transport lessened the impact of famine. A fourth effect was an initial rise in *per capita* incomes even of native peoples. This improvement in living standards permitted—if it did not cause—a more rapid rise in the size of the population. Educational standards also rose, which may have had an indirect effect on mortality rates.

In some countries industrial investment may have offered incentives for raising larger families. In Indonesia especially, after the shift from trading to the "culture system," which involved compulsory deliveries of plantation products to the colonial authorities, the easiest way for the people to maintain their standards of living and leisure, while meeting the levy of the colonial government, was to have more children, occupy more land, and devote a larger proportion of the land to irrigated rice culture, as distinct from the slash-and-burn shifting agriculture. Something similar may be true of other countries. Harvey Leibenstein, who has devoted much study to demographic aspects of economic growth, is quite ready to generalize on this relationship and to argue that initial rises in *per capita* income will tend on balance to bring initial increases in the "demand for children." [1]

A crucial factor in the course of *per capita* income is the length of the lag between the drop in mortality rates in the early stages of industrialization and the subsequent drop in fertility rates. The population explosions of Asian countries reflect a longer lag between the initial drop in mortality rates and subsequent drop in fertility rates than occurred in European countries or in the New World. No one knows for certain why this longer lag appeared. Some evidence suggests that the drop in fertility rates in Europe and the New World was a concomitant of urbanization. Development in Asia and Africa, centered as it was on plantations, mines, oil fields, and exports of raw materials, brought more *industrialization* than *urbanization;* hence the checks on family size enforced by the urban industrialization of Europe and the New World operated less effectively in the underdeveloped countries. Eventually fertility rates did drop in most Asian countries, but in some that drop came too late to prevent serious population pressure from arising before planned economic development began.

Colonial policy may, at least in part, account for the difference in the demographic patterns in the Asian-African countries and in Europe. Initial investment in Europe and the New World was also directed in large measure toward agricultural improvement, mining, and production of raw materials for export. In advanced countries, this investment gave rise to subsequent marked expansion of the secondary and tertiary sectors of the economy. Colonial policy in most of the Asian countries did not permit development of the secondary and tertiary sectors in the colonies themselves. Where domestic entrepreneurship appeared in the "Western" sector, it was usually discouraged. For example, when the development of the sugar plantations and refineries in the mid-nineteenth century in Java led to a shift from rice cultivation to sugar planting on the part of Javanese landowners, the Netherlands East Indies government sought to nip this local industrializa-

[1] Professor Leibenstein's theories are discussed in Chap. 15.

tion in the bud by imposing a regulation forbidding the sugar refineries to buy cane from native growers. Since the Javanese did not have the capital or the technical skills for large refineries, they had to be content with simple refining methods, producing brown sugar for the local market. Similarly, when smallholders' rubber became an active competitor of plantation rubber, the N.E.I. administration imposed a discriminatory tax on smallholders' rubber (in this case without much success). Thus the secondary and tertiary sectors associated with industrial investment in the colonies developed in the metropolitan countries rather than in the Asian and African countries themselves. The financing, transporting, storing, insuring, and processing of industrial raw materials took place mainly *outside* the colonial country.

Industrialization which is confined to the production of raw materials does not lead to urbanization. Indeed, it can proceed very far without seriously disrupting the pattern of village life led by most of the people. One may conjecture that the disastrously long lag between the initial drop in mortality rates and the subsequent drop in fertility rates is associated with the peculiar form of industrialization in underdeveloped countries, a form which did not bring with it rapid urbanization.

One may doubt whether the reverse process, urbanization without industrialization, such as has taken place in a number of Asian countries since the war, can be expected to have the same effect on fertility rates as the combination of industrialization and urbanization in Europe during the eighteenth and nineteenth centuries. The growth of Calcutta, Bombay, Tokyo, Manila, and Djakarta since World War II reflects the "pull" of employment opportunities in industry less than the "push" of dwindling opportunities for advancement in rural society. There is, of course, no assurance that this kind of urbanization will affect fertility rates in the same way Western urbanization did.

Some sociologists and anthropologists might ask whether there would be any reason for expecting twentieth-century Asian society to behave like eighteenth-century European society even if economic conditions were similar. Two points might be made in reply. First, as a policy prescription no one would recommend urbanization as such; it is industrialization and urbanization together that hold the hope for rising per capita income. Secondly, we have some evidence that even in Asian cities fertility rates tend to fall below those of rural areas in the same country. For one thing, the extended family system tends to break down under urban conditions; indeed, the wish to escape the responsibilities of the extended family system is one of the motives for ambitious young people moving from country to city.

Hagen's "Common Sense of Population"

Everett Hagen takes issue with "Neo-Malthusians" who persist in regarding population pressure as a barrier to economic development, chiding them for excessive gloom. His conception of "The Common Sense of Population" seems at first glance to be in conflict with the concept of the "population multiplier" outlined in the previous section. Closer examination of Hagen's theory, however, indicates that no such conflict exists.

Hagen states his main point as follows: [2]

> The Malthusian thesis suggests that as income rises, the rate of population growth will rise until it reaches the maximum biological growth rate of, say, 3 per cent per year. Only by exceeding this maximum rate of population growth can growth in aggregate output beat population and continue to raise per capita income until it reaches a level high enough to induce new modes of behavior. Indeed, the forecast that population growth if not checked by deliberate action will prevent improvement in human welfare is the heart of the Malthusian message. But while the population of the West has grown, in not a single country has the expected rate of population growth occurred. There is no *single* case of continuing growth in aggregate output of even 1.5 per cent per year, in which population growth has matched it and prevented continuing rise in per capita income. This fact, and not that of growth in world population, may be the fact of recent world history most important for population theory.

This thesis is a projection of the historical record in thirteen countries in Europe and the New World. Hagen's "explanation" of the tapering-off of population growth in these countries is simply that in societies where technological advance becomes habitual, and where significant initial improvements in standards of living are obtained, a "standard of living effect" takes place, bringing a reduction in fertility rates. He outlines this sequence in the following terms:

> Let us now make the further assumption that a standard-of-living effect occurs at any level of income above the subsistence level, if this level of income is sustained for a minimum period (say the period from early infancy to parenthood). There is no reason in logic to

[2] Everett E. Hagen, "The Common Sense of Population" (CENIS Document C/58-14), p. 20.

assume any specific floor of per capita income, below which the standard-of-living effect does not operate. Empirical justification for the contrary assumption made here is presented in Section III.

The tremendously important conclusion follows that technological progress, at any rate above a certain minimum rate, will cause a standard-of-living effect, i.e., will check population growth. First, by raising per capita income, technological progress causes a fall in the death rate, and an accelerated rate of population growth. Then, because continuing technological progress holds per capita income above subsistence, the birth rate falls and with it the rate of population growth. Per capita income therefore rises further; the death rate falls further; and so on, until death and birth rates have reached their minimum levels.

Some Questions of Fact

In appraising this population theory we must first consider the facts on which it is based. Let us note at the outset that by "continuing growth in aggregate output" Hagen has in mind growth sustained for two or three generations.

"The decline in death rate in England," Hagen writes, "probably began some decades before 1800 and elsewhere in Western Europe at latest not many decades after 1800. Throughout Western Europe and Britain the decline in birth rate seemed to have begun only in late 1870s or 1880s. Not until the 1920s has birth rate fallen to a minimum." Thus the interval between the initial fall in death rate and the subsequent fall in birth rate is a matter of fifty to seventy years. He is prepared to admit that during Malthus' own lifetime (1766–1834) there was no clear increase in English per capita output; during the first seventy years or so of industrial revolution, population growth may have prevented the rise in per capita income. The whole ring of the Hagen thesis sounds very different if it is maintained, not that underdeveloped countries need not worry about population pressure, but only that there is reason to hope that *if* they succeed in maintaining expansion of per capita output for fifty or seventy years, there will *then* follow a drop in fertility rate which will permit continuing increase in per capita incomes.

Hagen shows some reluctance to accept figures which do not fit his thesis. Thus he considers the result of studies by Phyllis Deane, showing that between 1770 and the end of the Napoleonic Wars English population grew faster than real income, "difficult to accept."

His tendency to shy away from inconvenient facts is also apparent in his discussion of the Chinese case. The fact that mainland China had in 1953 a population of 582 million, and a rate of population growth of 2 per cent a year, he says, suggests that long-run rapid population growth occurred in China which would contradict his generalizations. But he considers "an estimate of the population growth rate derived from a single census" too flimsy to be evidence "either for or against the thesis presented here." Similarly, he recognizes that "in Ceylon, Malaya, Mexico, Venezuela, Equador, and several Central American countries in the Carribean area . . . the rate of population growth has been about 3 per cent in recent years." He might have added the Philippines and some African countries. These cases he dismisses by saying "we do not know how long this rate of increase may continue." He thinks, wishfully, that because the rate of drop in the *death* rate in these countries has been more rapid than it was in Western Europe and in England, "one may hope that the lag (between the drop in death rate and the subsequent drop in fertility rate) may be correspondingly short." One may indeed *hope* so, but there is little reason to forecast any such relationship. And, as Hagen himself points out, "if in countries already densely populated rapid population growth continues for even one generation results may be tragic."

Some Questions of Causation

From the analytical point of view the main weakness of Hagen's statement of his thesis is his failure to take account of the dualistic character of most underdeveloped economies. A great deal of technological progress can take place in the industrial sector of an underdeveloped country without raising per capita incomes in the rural sector, let alone bringing a built-in habit of technological progress in that sector. If then, as we maintain, technological progress in the industrial sector brings a spurt of population growth, while nothing happens in the rural sector to bring the subsequent drop in fertility rates Hagen postulates, it can indeed happen that the initial spurt of growth in per capita income is subsequently swamped by population growth.

This process is particularly clear in Indonesia, which Hagen chooses to treat as a "limiting case." The process can be traced more easily in Indonesia than in other countries where population growth is now at very high levels, merely because industrialization started earlier there than in other Asian and African countries. The "population explosion" began in Java after 1820, with the introduction of the "culture system" and the first sugar plantations. Why should the Philippines, African countries, and other countries having current rates of population growth near 3 per cent follow the European rather than the Indonesian pattern?

Hagen charges that economists who attach significance to the Indonesian experience have "a misconception" which "arises, not out of empirical research but from the assumption that since men desire to maximize income and examples of improved techniques of West have been available, per capita income should have risen in low income countries, and its failure to rise must be due to some barrier such as population growth." But Hagen himself generalizes from skimpy empirical research. He misses completely the essential point of Indonesian experience. "The official estimates of population in the Netherland Indies," he says, "indicate population increase at a rate above 1.5 per cent per year from 1870 to 1900 and from 1920 to 1930." He suggests that these data may overstate population increase because of progressive improvement in census coverage; or that the population increase was due to introduction of public health measures; "or, more probably, the disruption of the culture by the Dutch created an intense need to strive for emotional security by sexual activity for increase in progeny."

Actually, the Dutch disrupted Indonesian culture very little—certainly far less than any other colonial power disrupted the culture of the native people. It was official policy of N.E.I. administrators *not* to disrupt the local culture any more than they could help. The system of "indirect rule" through local sultans was well designed to carry out this conservative policy. Public health measures and the establishment of law and order, as we have seen above, did indeed bring a drop in death rates. The culture system may have provided the positive incentive for increase in the size of family.

The main point, however, is that the over-all rate of population increase in the Netherlands Indies of 1.8 per cent is almost as meaningless an average as, say, the average rate of population growth in England and India. Under Dutch rule there was probably less contact among the islands constituting the Indonesian archipelago than there had been in the days of the *Madjapahit* empire. The *significant* fact is that the "population explosion" followed the Dutch settlers, beginning in central and east central Java, where Dutch settlement first assumed significant proportions with the development of sugar plantations; proceeding to other parts of Java; and after 1870, as the Dutch began their mining and plantation operations in the Outer Islands, appearing there. The rates of population growth in the areas immediately affected by Dutch settlement and industrialization reached figures very close to Leibenstein's "biological maximum" of 3 per cent.[3] Between 1920 and 1930 the population growth on Java and Madura had dropped from a peak decennial increase of 2.7 per cent to 1.7 per cent, but in Sumatra the rate was 2.7 per cent and in Borneo 2.8 per cent. Much the same pattern can be observed in the Philippines, where industrialization started relatively recently and where the current rate of population growth is between 2.2 and 2.9 per cent, as suggested by a recent sample survey. Far from being a "limiting case," the Indonesian experience, viewed in this light, is a grim warning of what may happen in other underdeveloped countries as industrialization takes place.

With regard to India and China, where populations are large but rates of growth slow, Professor Hagen says that population growth "obviously has not prevented increase in output from raising national income. . . . Per capita income has failed to rise in such countries—because the technological ferment necessary for a rate of growth in output above a minimum rate has not occurred." Maybe. But this is merely a complicated way of saying that where nothing happens, nothing happens. Indian and Chinese experience to date certainly does not entitle us to advise these countries not to worry lest improvements in public health and nutrition bring population pressure that will retard economic growth.

The figures presented by Hagen could be just as well used to support an alternative thesis; viz., that the drop of fertility rates in Europe was an accompaniment of Western style urbanization. Those figures could equally well support the thesis that "population growth occurs when per capita income in excess of $100 is reached, and the subsequent drop in fertility rates comes only when per capita incomes in excess of $200 are reached." This interpretation would leave many underdeveloped countries with the colossal task of surpassing *initial* rates of increase in population growth as they move into the region of per capita incomes above $100 but below $200. As pointed out in Chapter 9, the now underdeveloped countries start their process of economic development from much lower levels of per capita income than the currently advanced countries enjoyed in 1800. Other economic, social, technological, and political differences conjoin to make it less easy for present underdeveloped countries to achieve rates of growth that will assure rising per capita incomes, in face

[3] Harvey Leibenstein, *Theory of Economic-demographic Development* (Princeton, N.J., 1954).

of the possible increases in rates of population growth. Considering his usual caution in forecasting for Asian, African, and Latin American societies responses to given economic situations similar to those we expect in the West, it is surprising that Hagen is so ready to project into these societies Western experience with so complex a matter as population growth.

Although we have reservations about both the facts and theories presented in Hagen's "Common Sense," we can nevertheless accept his final conclusion: [4]

> These considerations do not imply that a densely populated country has no special problem. They are advanced merely to get the superficial argument out of the way in order to get at the sound ones.
>
> One of these is that the country's income elasticity of population growth may be higher than elsewhere. This may be why its population has become large relative to natural resources. If so, it will take a more rapid increase in aggregate output than elsewhere to hold per capita income above subsistence and induce a standard-of-living effect. Moreover, birth mores may be more stubborn, so that it will require a longer period to induce the standard-of-living effect. (Of course, the greater population density may on the other hand merely have resulted from a longer period of human habitation in the country.)
>
> Next, density of population relative to natural resources presumably implies a steep slope of diminishing marginal returns to labor, since the curve of returns is concave downward. If so, it will require a faster rate of technological advance than elsewhere to counter diminishing returns and maintain a given rate of increase in aggregate output. If a faster rate of increase in output than elsewhere is also necessary, the required rate of technological progress may be especially high.
>
> Finally, for any given level of techniques, per capita income will be lower in a densely populated country than in a less densely populated one. (This is true by definition. If it is not true, the country is not appropriately termed densely populated.) *Cet. par.*, the densely populated country will never catch the less densely populated ones in per capita income. Further, because of the difference in factor proportions, its relative progress may be slower, and not only the absolute but the relative gap between it and the less densely populated countries may increase.

Population Pressure as a Stimulant to Growth

In our discussion of the Hansen thesis in Chapter 6 we argued that population growth is less likely to encourage autonomous investment in underdeveloped countries than in advanced ones.

[4] Hagen, *op. cit.*, pp. 35–36.

Where labor is already redundant, growth of the labor force is not needed to permit the optimal combination of labor and capital to be maintained while capital accumulation takes place. Also there is less assurance that increased numbers will be accompanied by increased effective demand for housing, transport facilities, and public utilities. Albert Hirschman, however, suggests that even in underdeveloped countries population pressure may, if it is not so severe as to be demoralizing, provide the stimulus needed to improve production techniques. Once having discovered the ability to raise living standards by their own efforts, people will continue to make such efforts and sustained economic growth will result.[5]

The argument is a little like the more sweeping generalizations of the historian Arnold Toynbee: civilizations progress as a consequence of "response" to some "challenge." Societies where customary ways of life can be maintained without effort and nothing happens to disrupt the traditional economic and social organization are unlikely to progress. Societies confronted with a situation so serious that a universal feeling of hopelessness sets in will not progress either. But where there is both a challenge and a recognized means of dealing with it economic and social advance will ensue.

Hirschman starts from Duesenberry's "fundamental psychological postulate" that people resist any lowering of their living standards and try to prevent it if possible. Duesenberry applied his postulate to savings-consumption patterns during a cyclical downswing in advanced countries: when incomes drop people squeeze their savings in order to maintain their consumption patterns. But if people do that, asks Hirschman, why should they not also resist having their incomes squeezed by population growth? He sets forth two propositions of his own: "that population pressure on living standards will lead to counterpressure, i.e., to activity designed to maintain or restore the traditional standard of living of the community"; and "that the activity undertaken by the community in resisting a decline in its standard of living causes an increase in its ability to control its environment and to organize itself for development."

Of course, Hirschman adds, population growth can provide the stimulus for sustained growth only if there is some slack to be taken up in the economy. Also, a strong reaction is more likely "if the population increase comes as a sudden shock."

[5] Albert O. Hirschman, *The Strategy of Economic Development* (New York, 1958).

"Creeping" population pressure is less likely to result in a successful effort to overcome it than "a dramatic decline in mortality rates" and a consequent population "explosion." Thus Hirschman's argument lends some support to Hagen's suggestion that where drops in mortality rates have been particularly rapid the lag until fertility rates are reduced may be correspondingly short.

Hirschman also believes that action is more likely to be stimulated if population growth is combined with increased urbanization; or if the consequent growth in domestic market and labor force carries the country across "minimum production thresholds in a number of important industries"; or if the original increase affects mainly the upper classes.

Hirschman "certainly does not conclude that underdeveloped countries should institute a generous system of family allowances." For "population pressures are a clumsy and cruel stimulant to development" and "underdeveloped countries are today abundantly supplied with this stimulant." But he does conclude that "if a country is able to offset, be it even partially at first, the effect of the population increase, then we may have confidence that, through the learning acquired in this process, it will be able to do progressively better in marshalling its productive forces for development so that eventually output growth will overtake population growth."

In short, a "population explosion" is one form of "shock" which may move a country off dead center and start it on the path to economic development. There can of course be no denial that it *may* have this effect, and there is good reason to believe that in Europe and the New World in the nineteenth century, and perhaps in Australia since World War II, it *did* have this effect. But it *need not* have this effect, and in a good many underdeveloped countries it *did* not, because of the special conditions that accompanied the population explosions. These special conditions we summarize and analyze under the heading of "technological dualism."

Technological Dualism

If the industrial investment which launched the "population explosions" in Asia, Africa, and Latin America had provided opportunities for productive employment for the whole of the population increase, per capita incomes could still have risen. But industrialization in the form common to underdeveloped countries did not provide a proportionate increase in job opportunities.

Analysis of production functions and factor endowment in an economy with two sectors, two factors of production, and two goods, is enlightening in this regard. Although such a model is necessarily simplified, it approximates reality closely enough to provide significant results. The two sectors are the industrial sector (plantations, mines, oil fields, refineries, etc.) and a rural sector engaged in production of foodstuffs and in handicrafts or very small industries. The first of these sectors is capital-intensive. Moreover, it either is characterized in fact by relatively fixed technical coefficients (fixed proportions in which factors of production must be combined), or is assumed by entrepreneurs to be so. The effect on employment patterns is much the same in either case. The other sector has variable technical coefficients; that is, the products could be produced with a wide range of factor proportions. The two factors of production are labor on the one hand and capital, including improved land, on the other. The two products are industrial raw materials for export and necessities for domestic consumption.

Figure 14-1 represents the production function in the in-

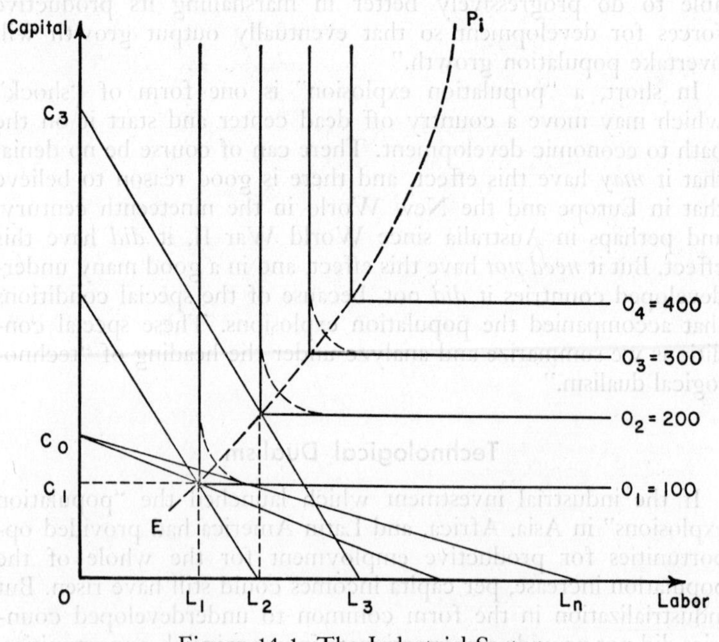

Figure 14-1. The Industrial Sector

dustrial sector. Units of capital are measured on the vertical axis, labor on the horizontal axis. Each curve is an *isoquant* representing combinations of labor and capital producing the same output (sometimes called an "isopod"). As we move away from the origin from curve O_1 to curves O_2, O_3, etc., we move up the "hill" of production to higher and higher levels of output. The diagram is thus a kind of contour map.

The solid curves are drawn to conform to the case of "fixed technical coefficients." In this case labor and capital must be combined in fixed proportions to get any output at all. Output can be increased only by increasing the amounts used of *both* factors so as to maintain these proportions. (Some production processes, such as petroleum refining, actually come very close to having fixed technical coefficients.) The production process in this sector is also capital-intensive; relatively large amounts of capital and relatively small amounts of labor are used. Thus to produce an output of O_1 the industrial sector will use OC_1 units of capital and OL_1 units of labor. If OL_2 units are available, the excess labor supply will have no effect on production techniques, and L_1L_2 units of labor will simply remain unemployed, or must seek employment in the other sector, no matter what the relation of wage rates to capital costs. As more capital becomes available through time, more labor will be employed and output will be expanded. The line EP_i is the expansion path of this industrial sector. However, employment increases relatively little as investment and output in the industrial sector expand along this path.

Perhaps technical coefficients are actually less fixed than entrepreneurs think. If managers and technicians, used to particular methods of production in Western countries which they accept without question as superior, do not look for alternative techniques more suited to the factor endowment, the effect is the same as if coefficients were technologically fixed. The dotted portions of the isopods in Figure 14-1 indicate a situation in which there is actually some flexibility in factor-proportions. It can readily be seen that *small* changes in factor endowments (and in relative prices of factors of production) would not bring marked changes in technique even if entrepreneurs learned that the production function was like the dotted lines rather than the solid ones. But for very large differences in factor endowment (and prices), such as that represented by the line C_oL_n, a more labor-intensive technique would be used if its existence were recognized by the decision makers.

Figure 14-2 represents the production function for the rural sector. Here coefficients are variable: a wide range of techniques and of combinations of labor and capital will give the same output. Accordingly the proportions actually used will be adjusted to the factor endowment (and to the consequent relative prices of labor and capital). In this context capital includes improved land.

Now let us imagine that we begin with production at O_1 in each sector. Then capital begins to flow into the industrial sector, mostly from abroad. The industrial sector expands along EP_i. But we have already seen that this industrialization generates a population explosion. In some countries and some periods, the percentage rate of population increase considerably exceeded the rate at which capital was accumulated in the industrial sector. Because of the actual or accepted fixed technical coefficients in that sector, employment opportunities did not occur at the same rate as that at which the population grew. Far from bringing a shift of population from the rural to the industrial sector, in-

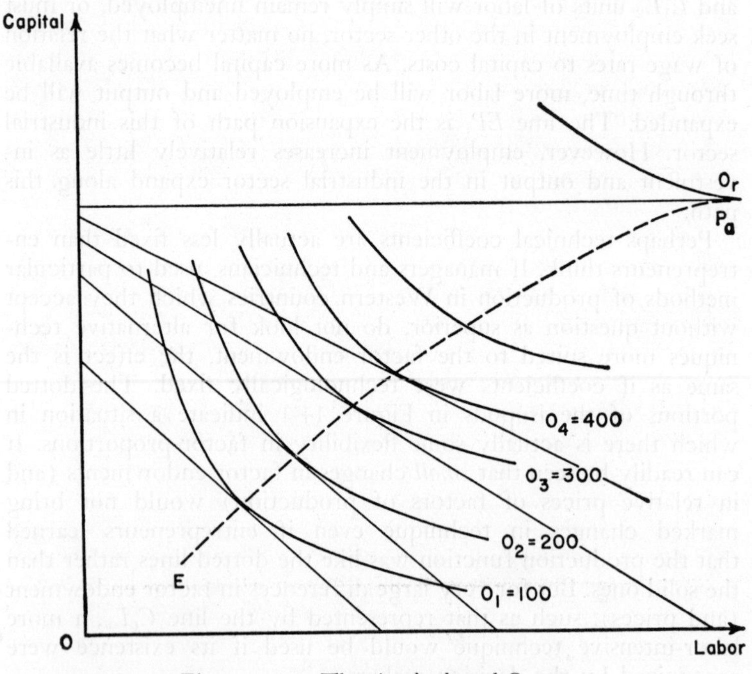

Figure 14-2. The Agricultural Sector

dustrialization, after its first impact, may even have brought a relative *decline* in the proportion of total employment in that sector.

Thus the increased population had to seek a livelihood in the other, variable-coefficient sector. At the beginning of the expansion process, no factor of production was relatively abundant or scarce in this sector. For a while, the response to population growth was to bring additional land under cultivation, so as to keep the ratio of labor to land relatively constant; since other forms of capital were not available in any quantity to this sector, the amount of land that could be effectively worked by one family was in any case limited. Thus for a while the "optimal" combination of labor and capital (mostly improved land) could be maintained, as output rose from O_1 to O_3. Eventually, good land tended to become scarce. The ratio of labor to capital available in that sector rose steadily, and since technical coefficients were variable, techniques in that sector became increasingly labor-intensive. For example, irrigated rice culture was substituted for shifting dry rice culture. Finally the point was reached at output O_n where all available land was already cultivated by highly labor-intensive techniques and the marginal productivity of labor fell below zero even with the most labor-intensive techniques available; with continuing population growth, disguised unemployment began to appear.

Under these conditions there was *no incentive* for groups of individual farmers or small enterprises to make marginal and unrelated investments of capital in the labor-intensive sector, even if they had capital to invest. Nor had they any reason to introduce labor-saving innovations, even if they knew about them and could finance them. And as yet there is no technology designed to raise output per man-hour without also raising the ratio of capital to labor. Labor *as a group* had no incentive to increase its efforts, since the labor supply was already redundant. Thus methods remained labor-intensive and levels of technique, man-hour productivity, and economic and social welfare remained low.

This tendency toward disguised unemployment in the rural sector is enhanced if technological progress takes a form favoring the capital-intensive sector. There can be little doubt that this process is what in fact occurred. Indeed, during the last two centuries little or no technological progress has occurred in peasant agriculture and handicrafts, while technological progress in the plantations, mining, and petroleum sector has been rapid. The tendency toward disguised unemployment in the rural sector will also be aggravated if wage rates are kept artificially high by trade-union activities or by government policy. Industrial wage rates which are high relative to productivity provide an incentive for the introduction of labor-saving devices and consequently diminish still further the capacity of the industrialized sector to absorb the population growth.[6]

Conflict of Output and Employment

Richard Eckaus, as well as providing a more elegant proof of the propositions made in the previous section, also shows that there can be a conflict between full employment and maximization of output in an underdeveloped economy if the pattern of demand does not fit the factor endowment.[7] Dr. Eckaus' diagrammatics are a bit complicated for reproduction here, and his analysis is too tight for convenient summary. However, we can follow him part of the way. He begins with a simple and abstract case:

> In the first case to be considered suppose that only one good is produced in the economy, national product, which requires two factors capital and labor. Assume also for this first problem that only one process can be used to produce national product, i.e., that the factors must be used in fixed proportions. [He introduces here a figure similar to our Figure 14-1.] Quite irrespective of relative factor prices, points *a*, *b*, *c*, etc. represent the combinations of factors which will be used to produce output and the slope of the line joining these points is equal to the constant, capital-labor ratio.
>
> Only when the factors of production are actually available in proportions equal to the fixed capital-labor ratio is there the possibility that both can simultaneously be fully utilized. That is, for full utilization, the factor endowment must lie someplace on the line through points *o*, *a*, *b*, *c*. If the actual factor endowment possessed by the country is at point *E*, there must inevitably be some unemployment of labor which is not amenable to any fiscal or monetary policy for its alleviation. Only by increasing the capital stock available can the unemployment be eliminated. Conventional compensatory fiscal policy would, in this case, only result in inflationary pressures.

[6] With the emergence of national states in former colonial countries after World War II both trade-union activity, supported by government, and direct government intervention in the labor market have tended to create artificially high industrial wage rates in a number of countries. These policies have little or no effect on real wage rates in the rural sector. Accordingly, they aggravate the tendency toward technological dualism.

[7] R. S. Eckaus, "The Factor Proportions Problem in Underdeveloped Areas," *American Economic Review*, September, 1955.

Eckaus next introduces a second, relatively more labor-intensive process for production of the same "good" (national product). He shows that structural unemployment of the relatively abundant factor will still occur, unless the factor endowment (proportions in which the factors of production are available) falls within a certain limited range; with labor-capital ratios as high as they are in many underdeveloped countries, structural unemployment of labor would be extremely likely under the technical conditions assumed.

Next, the effects of adding still more processes are considered, with this conclusion: [8]

> If more than two processes are available to the economy, full employment of all factors will be *possible* so long as the proportions in which factors are endowed fall on or within the limits set by the processes with the most extreme factor-use ratios. This suggests an observation which is, by now, almost trite: reduction of underemployment in over-populated areas depends on the addition of scarce factors.

At this stage, he also demonstrates that adjustment of factor prices will not assure full employment of all factors, although price rigidities can aggravate unemployment.

The next step is to break down national product into two "goods," say, output of Western enterprises which are relatively capital-intensive, and output of local enterprises which are relatively labor-intensive. Once again, he proves that a very high labor-capital ratio will result in structural unemployment of labor, which cannot be eliminated by price adjustments or by creation of increased effective demand.

A special case is also considered, in which the more labor-intensive process would require more of *both* labor and capital to reach a given output—so far as anyone knows at this stage, a perfectly possible situation in underdeveloped countries. In this case, maximizing production conflicts with maintaining full employment, unless "work-spreading" devices are used. Under these conditions, the discarded "lump-of-labor" theory makes perfectly good sense. May not "backward-sloping supply curves" be an intuitive reaction to such a situation, a way of assuring a reasonable degree of work- and income-spreading, and so preventing concentration of employment and income among the relatively few workers who might be willing to provide additional effort for additional income, at the expense of others?

[8] Eckaus, *op. cit.*, p. 6.

An important extension of the analysis of this case proves that the general conclusions are unchanged if variable coefficients replace the fixed coefficients in the more labor-intensive field of employment.

Eckaus next moves several steps nearer reality, and the diagrammatic analysis becomes more complex, involving the introduction of an adapted "Edgeworth-Bowley" box, with isopods for one good measured from one origin and isopods for a second good measured from the other, giving a "transformation curve." With this technique, he analyzes the more complex case in which there are two "goods," two factors of production, and one sector with fixed technical coefficients and one with variable technical coefficients. Finally, he introduces a limited degree of flexibility of technique into the relatively fixed-coefficient, relatively capital-intensive, sector. Thus he deals here with the same "model" as the one presented in the previous section, but with a more refined diagrammatic technique.

Throughout these successive approximations to reality, the conclusion remains fundamentally the same: with a very high labor-capital ratio, structural unemployment of labor in the labor-intensive, variable-coefficient sector is almost certain to appear.

This model is, of course, still a bit simple as compared to the real world. But as Eckaus points out, it has "most of the characteristics of the many-good many-factor case." First attempts at complicating the model still further suggest that the conclusions are not altered by making the model still more realistic.

Eckaus also demonstrates that structural unemployment will be aggravated under any of the following conditions:

1. If wages are kept artificially high by trade-union activity, or by government policy.
2. If technological progress takes a form favoring the capital-intensive sector.
3. If the rate of population growth exceeds the rate of capital accumulation in the labor-intensive sector.

Do we not have here an explanation of "dualism" more fruitful than Boeke's "Orientals are different" approach? Under the conditions postulated in this analysis, unless the indifference maps for the two "commodities" (industrial and rural output) are such that a relatively large share of income is spent on the commodity produced by labor-intensive methods, the allocation of resources that would provide an optimal output may imply unemployment whenever labor supply is large relative to the supply of capital. When we put the underdeveloped countries into their world setting, it is clear that the actual pattern of demand has been such as to bring increasing conflict between the objectives of optimal output and full employment. For the output of underdeveloped countries is sent into a world market for export goods and a domestic market for the produce of its rural sector. Whatever the pattern of demand when expansion began, it is apparent that, in the course of time, demand for exports grew at a much higher percentage rate than demand for domestic products. Indeed, under the conditions described above, the demand for output of the rural sector grew only at the rate at which the total population increased, if not more slowly. The demand for exports, geared to the much more rapidly expanding European economy, increased at a much faster rate.

Moreover, the demand from the *world* market prevailed in the political as well as the economic sense; achieving the optimal allocation of resources from the standpoint of the *European* entrepreneurs and administrators meant an increasing conflict of that goal with the maintenance of full employment in the rural sector of underdeveloped countries. No such conflict arose in the advanced countries. Thus the market forces were such as to bring increasing discrepancies between the standards of living of the rapidly industrializing European countries and those of the underdeveloped countries.

One paragraph in Dr. Eckaus' paper summarizes very well the conditions that actually prevailed in underdeveloped countries: [9]

> Suppose that the respective demands for output are such that a large part of the available capital is drawn into the capital-intensive and fixed-coefficient sector. The amount of labor which can be absorbed in these sectors is dependent on the amount of capital available. Since capital is a scarce factor, labor employment opportunities in this sector are limited by its availability rather than by demand for output. The relatively plentiful labor supply is then pushed into the variable-coefficient sector and absorbed there as long as the marginal value productivity of labor is higher than the wages it receives.

One final point made in the Eckaus analysis is that the disguised unemployment appearing under these conditions cannot be removed by wage-price adjustments alone.

The Solow Model of Economic Growth

The primary aim of Dr. Solow's growth model was to show the limitations on the Harrod-Domar formulation of requirements

[9] *Ibid.*, pp. 559–60.

for steady growth in advanced economies. He demonstrates in his article that "this fundamental opposition of warranted and natural rates turns out in the end to flow from the crucial assumption that production takes place under conditions of fixed proportions."[10] His model, however, can also be used to analyze underdevelopment. If we select from his various cases the ones which seem to conform most closely to the actual conditions of underdeveloped countries, we can show that our thesis regarding technological dualism need not rely on the assumption of fixed technical coefficients in the capital-intensive sector.

Solow demonstrates that with variable technical coefficients there will be a tendency for the capital-labor ratio to adjust itself through time in the direction of an equilibrium ratio. If the initial ratio of capital to labor is above the equilibrium value, capital and output will grow more slowly than the labor force. Applying this analysis to the rural sector of underdeveloped countries, we begin again with a small population and a substantial amount of "capital," which here includes improved land. The ratio of capital to labor is actually *above the equilibrium ratio*. Consequently, after the initial increase in the labor force, there would be a move toward more labor-intensive techniques; man-year output will tend to fall. Once the ratio of capital (including improved land) to labor has fallen to the equilibrium rate, it will be held constant until land begins to give out. From there on maintenance of the equilibrium ratio would require the allocation of more capital, either in the form of land or in some other form, to the rural sector, but under the conditions of technological dualism this will not happen. Instead, once the land gives out, the marginal productivity of labor will fall below minimal real wage rates and unemployment, disguised or overt, will begin to grow.

Solow's figure 2 [11] indicates the possibility of multiple equilibrium, with one unstable equilibrium between rate of growth and ratio of capital to labor, and with two stable equilibrium points, one with a high ratio of capital to labor and one with a low ratio of capital to labor. If the expansion process begins with a

[10] The Philippines today seems to be in this stage of balanced growth in the rural sector, with little capital and land combined with much labor. However, with current rates of population growth, even the Philippines is approaching the point where it will no longer be possible to maintain present ratios of land and other capital to labor. Marginal productivity of labor will then begin to fall below the minimal subsistence real wage rates. In Java, this point has already been reached.

[11] Robert Solow, "A Contribution to the Theory of Economic Growth," *Quarterly Journal of Economics*, February, 1956, p. 91.

relatively high ratio of capital to labor, the system will tend toward a high rate of growth with capital-intensive techniques. If on the other hand, the expansion begins with a low ratio of capital to labor, it will move toward an equilibrium rate of growth with labor-intensive techniques. Applying this analysis to our two sectors, we see the strong likelihood that the industrial sector, which starts with a relatively high ratio of capital to labor, would move toward an equilibrium expansion path with a high ratio of capital to labor, even if technical coefficients were not fixed. In the rural sector, on the other hand, beginning as it did with a high ratio of labor to capital, the tendency will be toward an expansion path which will retain a still lower ratio of capital to labor.

Professor Solow felt that "it would take us too far afield to go wholly classical with a theory of population growth and a fixed supply of land," [12]—an unfortunate decision, since this classical model is the one which would conform most closely to the rural sector of underdeveloped countries. Solow does indicate that in such a model, where savings can fall to zero with income still positive, net investment might cease and the capital stock become stationary while the labor force still grows. He shies away from this case; but it is clear that in such circumstances disguised unemployment must appear as soon as marginal productivity of labor falls below minimal real wage rates. Obviously, too, with fixed techniques, a fixed supply of land, and continuing population growth, per capita income in the rural sector must eventually decline.

Professor Solow's figure 9 [Figure 14-3] is also interesting in this context. Here he treats population growth as a function of per capita income (and so of the capital-labor ratio) instead of treating it as an autonomous variable. On the base axis is measured r, the ratio of capital to labor. On the vertical axis is measured $\dot{r}$, the rate of change in this ratio through time. Population growth is n, shown as a function of capital per head, r. The other curve, $sF(r, 1)$ is a capital accumulation function; it makes the rate of increase in capital per head depend on the relation of output per worker to capital per worker. The pattern of population growth implied in this diagram is that "for very low levels of income per head or real wage population tends to decrease; for higher levels of income it begins to increase, and that for still higher levels of income the rate of population growth levels off and starts to decline." [13] The result is something close to Leibenstein's

[12] Solow, *op. cit.*, pp. 87–88.
[13] *Ibid.*, p. 91.

"minimum effort thesis," to be discussed more fully below. At any initial ratio of capital to labor below r_2, the system will revert to equilibrium at the low ratio of capital to labor, r_1, with the correspondingly low rate of increase of output. If we start with a capital-labor ratio anywhere below r_2, the only way to assure cumulative growth is to make a sudden jump to a ratio of capital to labor above r_2. Combining this analysis with our discussion of population, we can readily see that because of the tendency for increases in investment confined to the industrial sector to accelerate population growth, a *gradual* approach to r_2 is unlikely to be effective.

Finally, Professor Solow introduces rigid wage rates, and concludes that if the ratio of wage rates to price corresponds to a capital-labor ratio that would normally tend to decrease (or drop to less than zero), unemployment develops and vice versa. Once again, these are the conditions in the rural sector of underdeveloped countries; once the first wave of population growth takes place and land becomes relatively scarce, the "fixed" real wage rate, which is a customary subsistence level, tends to be above the marginal productivity of labor. With a low initial ratio of capital to labor and rapid population growth, this relationship is precisely what emerges. Thus the Solow analysis, while starting from a quite different point, tends to corroborate

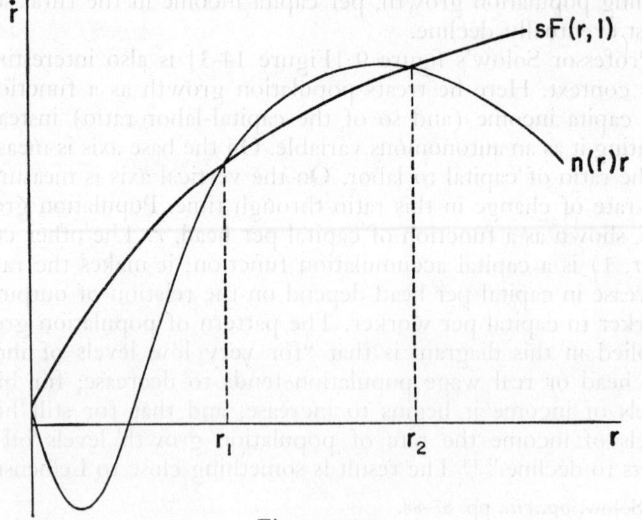

Figure 14-3

the conclusions derived by applying the Eckaus analysis of factor proportions.

The Myint Model

Professor Hla Myint presents his own version of the dualistic theory of underdevelopment.[14] He proposes the following model:

1. The country starts its period of expansion, resulting from its being opened up to economic relations with the outside world, "with a fairly sparse population in relation to its potential natural resources."

2. Its natural resources are then developed in the direction of a few specialized lines of primary production for export. This development is generally carried out by foreign private enterprise, assisted by government policy, and limited by the expansion of the world market for the export goods.

3. The native inhabitants of the country enjoy legal equality with other people in their economic relations, including the right to own any type of property and to enter into any type of occupation. (In some colonial countries this assumption did not hold; but it is all the more interesting that the Myint model does not *need* discrimination against native people to show the tendency toward technological dualism.) In such a model, Professor Myint points out, "The disequalizing factors must be considered as operating not only between the backward and the advanced countries as aggregate units, but also between the backward and advanced groups of peoples within the same backward country itself." The usual "country A and B" approach "is seriously inadequate for our purpose." Disaggregation, at least to the extent of recognizing the two major sectors, is necessary if we are to obtain useful results.

Myint suggests that before the underdeveloped countries were "opened up," they were "primitive or medieval stationary states governed by habits and customs. Their people might have lived near the 'minimum subsistence level,' but that standard, according to their own lights, did not appear too wretched or inadequate. Thus in spite of low productivity and lack of economic progress, there was no problem of economic discontent and frustration: wants and activities are on the whole adapted to each other and the people were in equilibrium with their environment."

He then moves on to the second stage. "Particularly in the second half of the nineteenth century," when "these stationary

[14] Hla Myint, "An Interpretation of Economic Backwardness," *Oxford Economic Papers*, Vol. VI, No. 2 (June, 1954), p. 146.

backward societies were opened up to the outside economic forces. . . . Measures for economic development then consisted mainly in attempts to persuade or force the backward people into the new ways of life represented by the money economy—for example, by stimulating their demand for imports and by taxing them so that they were obliged to turn to cash crops or work in the newly opened mines and plantations."[15] The yardstick of development of such countries was their export and taxable capacity. However, the "opening up" process drew increasing numbers of the native peoples into a new elite, in which the values of Western society were increasingly accepted. This gave rise to "a sense of economic discontent and maladjustment." It was in this third stage that the political problems associated with underdeveloped countries appeared.

The form of development in such dualistic economies was not such as to require a high degree of specialization among the native peoples:[16]

> In spite of the striking specialization of the inanimate productive equipment and of the individuals from the economically advanced groups of people who manage and control them, there is really very little specialization beyond a natural adaptability to the tropical climate, among the backward peoples in their roles as unskilled labourers or peasant producers. . . . Thus all the specialization required for the export market seems to have been done by the other co-operating factors, the whole production structure being built around the supply of cheap undifferentiated labour. . . . Even where a new cash crop is introduced, the essence of its success as a *peasant* crop depends on the fact that it does not represent a radical departure from the existing techniques of production (e.g., yams and cocoa in West Africa).

Indeed, Professor Myint goes so far as to suggest that the process of specialization of a backward economy for the export market is most rapid and successful when it leaves the backward peoples in their unspecialized roles as unskilled laborers and peasant producers using traditional methods of production.

Dual or Plural?

Myint also draws attention to another characteristic of the dualistic—or more properly in this context, plural—economy which has been noted by other observers as well; viz., very often even the middlemen between the big European concerns and the indigenous population are foreigners. He mentions the Indians

[15] *Ibid.*, pp. 149, 150.
[16] *Ibid.*, p. 153.

and Chinese in Southeast Asia, Indians in East Africa, Syrians and "Coast Africans" in West Africa, and so on. He might also have mentioned the Indians in his own country of Burma. These middlemen collect produce from peasant farmers, distribute imported articles to the local consumers, and act as moneylenders.[17] They operate as a buffer between the indigenous population and the advanced Western society, thus depriving the former of "the educating and stimulating effect of a direct contact." Even skilled labor was brought in from abroad. Professor Knowles has said that in the British Empire of the nineteenth century there were three "mother countries": the United Kingdom, India, and China. Immigrant labor from India and China was deliberately introduced into Southeast Asia, Fiji, the West Indies, and part of East and South Africa.

True, some opportunities for acquiring skills occurred on the plantations and mines, but these were diluted by the high labor turnover. Backward peoples are not used to the discipline of the mines and plantations. They keep one foot in their traditional tribal and village economies and look upon the wage labor "not as a continuous permanent employment but as a temporary or periodical expedient to earn a certain sum of money." Thus, "even after many decades of rapid economic development following the opening-up process, the peoples of many backward countries still remain almost as ignorant and unused to the ways of modern economic life as they were before."

The middleman of the Asian type, selling consumers' goods, advancing seed and simple tools on a sharecropping basis, and lending money, was by no means unknown to the West. In the American South or the Canadian prairies, such middlemen were also buffers between the small farmers and the advancing technology of the big cities. The difference is that at a certain point it paid Western middlemen as a class to take over the land altogether, to foreclose on their tardy debtors, and to amalgamate small holdings into units large enough to permit large-scale, extensive, mechanized, and commercial agriculture. From there on the advance of technology spread to agriculture as well as to industry.

[17] It is said in the Philippines, for example, that the growth of a particular village depended entirely on the resources of the local Chinese, for it was his resources that determined the size of the cash crops of which they could dispose. Moreover, there is a continuous draining-off process. The Chinese who becomes successful in the village does not stay there but moves on to a city, installing in his village store a relative whose talents are less striking than his own.

The question is, then, why this process did not occur in underdeveloped countries. Why have the middlemen in Asia and Africa continued to squeeze the peasant rather than maneuver him into a position where they could foreclose on peasant land?

To find an answer to this question, the Myint point must be added to the analysis presented above. In Europe and the New World, a time came when manpower was obviously scarce in the agricultural sector, making it profitable for individual farmers to increase the size of their holdings and to use more capital-intensive methods. The barrier to agricultural improvement in the underdeveloped countries has been that labor never became scarce in the rural sector. The "population explosion," brought by industrial investment in the capital-intensive sector, meant that there was an adequate supply, and later a superabundance, of labor in the peasant agriculture sector.[18] Thus in Asia and Africa the middleman has continued to play his traditional role, directing his efforts to maximizing his share of the output obtainable through labor-intensive methods, rather than endeavoring to get the peasant off the land, so as to cultivate it himself by more land-and-capital-intensive methods.

[18] In my paper for the Conference on Economic Development of the University of Texas (April, 1958), I spoke of a "population multiplier" rather than a "population explosion" and graced the "multiplier" with a mathematical expression. In its simplest form the expression is $\Delta L = k \cdot \Delta L_i$; the increase in total population is a constant multiple of the increase in industrial population. I was led to this formulation by a statement of Dr. Boeke in which he maintained that industrialization of countries like Indonesia is fruitless, since it does not raise the ratio of industrial population to agricultural population. Boeke implied that the reason for this experience in Indonesia is that Indonesians are not suited to industrial occupations; the "population multiplier" was formulated in the first instance as an alternative explanation of the Indonesian experience. The above equation rests on the following assumptions: the ratio of gainfully occupied persons to size of family is constant in both the industrial and agricultural sectors; rate of family formation in the industrial sector depends only on the amount of employment offered in the industrial sector; the capital-job ratio in the industrial sector is constant; increases in industrial employment bring an increase in the birth rate. All these assumptions seem plausible enough, and given the above equation, the ratio of industrial to agricultural employment will, of course, remain unchanged no matter how much industrial investment takes place. On the other hand, the restrictive assumptions needed for such a constant relationship are not necessary to my main argument. For this reason I decided to replace the "population multiplier" with the "population explosion."

Summary and Conclusions

Putting together the theory of the population explosion with the theory of technological dualism we obtain a deeper understanding of some of the "characteristics" of underdeveloped countries outlined in Chapter 1. We saw there that the proportion of the total labor force in agriculture is virtually a measure of the degree of underdevelopment; the more people in agriculture, the more underdeveloped the country. Yet we also saw that it is precisely in agriculture that the spread in man-year productivity is greatest as between advanced and underdeveloped countries. In the industrial sector, techniques are often advanced and productivity is high; in agriculture, techniques are labor-intensive and simple and productivity is abysmally low. Why does labor not shift from the rural to the industrial sector, from low-yield to high-yield occupations, in accordance with orthodox theory?

The same sort of question arises with respect to capital. According to orthodox theory, the marginal productivity of capital ought to be higher in the rural sector, where the ratio of labor to capital is high, than in the industrial sector, where it is low. There is evidence that returns to capital actually are higher in the rural sector than in the industrial sector. George Rosen, on the basis of his extensive knowledge of the Indian economy, concludes that an important factor delaying the development of indigenous industry has been the high returns on investment in agricultural credit.[19] Interest rates on loans in the rural sector range from 16 to 100 per cent; in addition, the rural capitalist, who usually makes loans on a sharecropping basis, is frequently in a position to earn a handsome profit on speculative investment in stocks of food crops. It is easy to see why the rural capitalist is not attracted to industrial investment. But why does not industrial capital flow into agriculture, if returns there are really so much higher than on the plantations and in the mines and oil fields?

Here is the most vicious of all the vicious circles encountered in a theory of underdevelopment. Labor does not flow into the industrial sector because the supply of capital to that sector is limited—each investment project in an underdeveloped country

[19] George Rosen, "Capital Markets and Underdeveloped Economies: A Theoretical Frame-Hypothesis for Empirical Research," M.I.T., CENIS, May, 1958.

competes against projects the world over in the international capital market—and technical coefficients are fixed, or thought to be so. The supply of domestic capital to the rural sector is also limited. It is not directed toward improving techniques, because although the elasticity of substitution of labor for capital may be high, the elasticity of substitution of capital for *land* is low. Relatively small amounts of investment in tools, simple irrigation,

TABLE 14-1.
Arable Land: Acres per Capita of Total and of Agricultural Population

Continent and country	*Per capita* Total	*Per capita* Agricultural
World	1.28	2.20
North America	3.40	18.0
Middle America	1.02	} 2.47
South America	1.47	
Europe	0.96	2.87
USSR	3.26	5.73
Asia	0.64	0.94
Africa	2.22	2.99
Oceania	3.71	11.12
United States	3.1	16.5
Canada	5.3	28.5
United Kingdom	0.4	12.0
France	1.2	5.5
Belgium	0.3	3.5
Netherlands	0.3	3.4
Denmark	1.7	6.5
Sweden	1.4	5.4
Norway	0.7	4.1
Germany	0.7	5.1

Country	*Per capita* Total	*Per capita* Agricultural
Poland	1.5	2.7
Czechoslovakia	1.1	3.8
Switzerland	0.3	5.9
Austria	0.6	5.3
Hungary	1.5	4.0
Portugal	.....	3.1
Spain	1.7	4.6
Italy	0.8	2.7
Yugoslavia	1.2	3.2
Romania	1.7	3.3
Bulgaria		2.5
Greece	1.1	2.9
China	0.29	0.7
Japan	0.20	0.8
Iran	2.47	....
Pakistan	0.69	....
India	0.89	....
Australia	4.06	....

SOURCE: W. S. Woytinsky and E. S. Woytinsky, *World Population and Production* (New York, 1953).

seed selection, and fertilizer could bring the *marginal* productivity of capital down to zero, given the present ratio of labor to land. It may well be that in some underdeveloped countries the marginal productivity of both labor and capital is close to zero in the rural sector.

Dr. Eckaus is, of course, right in saying that the only way to overcome the redundancy of labor in the rural sector is to increase the supply of the scarce factor. But the *immediately* scarce factor is land. The only way to raise the marginal productivity of capital is to increase the ratio of land to labor a great deal. The production function is highly discontinuous in this respect. Increasing the size of the typical family farm from 2 acres to 3 will not raise the marginal productivity of capital very much. The size must be raised to 20 or 200 acres so that mechanization becomes profitable. With high population densities such increases in size of holding can be attained only by luring people out of peasant agriculture into the industrial sector. For *this* kind of program, however, capital becomes the scarce factor once again. It requires heavy investment in *both* the industrial and agricultural sectors. Neither agricultural improvements on the present holdings nor industrialization will, by itself, break through this particular vicious circle.

Industrialization without an agricultural revolution brought the underdeveloped countries where they are. The dangers in neglect of the agricultural sector are even more dramatically illustrated by the postwar development of East Germany. There the limited capital supply has been concentrated in a few relatively capital-intensive industries providing relatively few jobs. The rest of the population has been forced back to the land without the capital for mechanized agriculture. The result is an increase in agricultural population but a *decline* in cultivated area, and a drop in yields both per worker and per hectare, in comparison with prewar conditions. This sort of change is the reverse of development.

The failure of foreign capital to flow into peasant agriculture must be explained in somewhat different terms. The industrial and rural sectors are not part of the same "economy" in the ordinary sense. Geographically, the plantations, mines, and oil fields are in the same country, but economically they may be more closely tied to the metropolitan country providing the capital, technical knowledge, and managerial skill than to the underdeveloped country in which the operation is located. The men who launch, organize, finance, and manage these enterprises —even when they are urbanites of the country itself—know little of peasant agriculture and village life. The rural capitalist relies for his success on his personal and firsthand knowledge of the villagers with whom he deals; he lends to them, sells to them, and buys from them. This is knowledge of a sort the foreign or urban capitalist does not have and does not wish to acquire. As for a wholesale shift to mechanized commercial agriculture, it is not an operation to be carried out on a piecemeal private enterprise basis.

Indeed here is one of the major reasons for government intervention in the development process. Once countries are in the situation analyzed in this chapter, only a unified and large-scale program involving more rapid industrialization and bold schemes for agricultural improvement can launch cumulative growth.

15 Partial Theories: Colonialism and the "Backwash" Effects of International Trade

Malthus and Mill both regarded expansion of international trade as an escape valve, postponing economic stagnation. For nineteenth-century Europe they were probably right. For the underdeveloped countries, however, expansion of foreign trade does not seem to have helped very much in raising domestic standards of living. Recently, some economists have gone so far as to argue that international trade, far from encouraging growth of underdeveloped countries, has actually retarded it by accentuating the dualistic nature of the economy. In these countries, conditions are such that "backwash" (unfavorable) effects outweigh "spread" (stimulating) effects. Secondly, it is maintained that there is a long-run tendency for the terms of trade to turn against countries exporting raw materials and foodstuffs.

Backwash versus Spread Effects

Professor Hla Myint, whose contribution to the theory of technological dualism was outlined in the previous chapter, has also attempted to explain why the growth of foreign trade failed to bring over-all economic growth in Asian and African countries. For these countries did experience some development. During the nineteenth and twentieth centuries, their export sectors expanded very rapidly, as Table 15-1 clearly shows. The value of Indonesian exports grew over tenfold between 1880 and

1920; Malayan exports increased nearly fourteenfold between 1906 and 1950. Other countries show similarly dramatic growth of exports; in Burma, exports grew by 5 per cent per year between 1870 and 1900, and Thailand enjoyed a comparable rate of expansion. Moreover, as Myint points out, capital was not especially scarce in the export sector of underdeveloped countries: "The foreign firms in the export sectors were normally able to borrow capital on equal terms with firms of comparable credit worthiness in the advanced countries."[1] Why did the growth in value of

TABLE 15-1.

Value of Total Exports, Indonesia and Malaya

Indonesia		*Malaya*	
Year	Total value, billion florins	Year	Total value, billion Straits dollars
1870	....	1906	0.293
1880	0.175	1912	.357
1890	.175	1920	.879
1900	.258	1925	1.282
1913	.671	1929	.925
1920	2.228	1932	.323
1925	1.801	1937	.897
1929	1.443	1947	1.295
1930	1.140	1950	3.961
1932	.541	1951	5.991
1937	.990	1952	3.795
1940	0.939	1953	2.897

SOURCE: G. C. Allen and Audrey G. Donnithorne, *Western Enterprise in Indonesia and Malaya* (New York, 1957), pp. 291, 293.

exports have no multiplier effects on per capita incomes in the rest of the economy?

Myint lists these factors operating against spread effects: the high turnover of labor, workers' willingness to accept very low wages, the conviction among employers that the supply curve of labor was backward sloping, and the general lack of industrial skills, which made entrepreneurs feel that it was difficult to recruit an adequate labor force. Wages were not considered low relative to estimates of efficiency. "The attempt to switch over from the cheap labor policy to a policy of higher wages and

[1] H. Myint, "The Gains from International Trade and the Backward Countries," *Review of Economic Studies*, Vol. XXII, No. 2.

more intensive use of labor usually involved taking decisions about 'lumpy investments' both in the form of plant and machinery and in the form of camps and villages where it was necessary to change over from a casual to a permanent labor force."

Professor Myint stresses the reluctance of European entrepreneurs to make heavy investments of a kind which would require a large supply of skilled workers, and their preference for simple labor-intensive techniques which left labor productivity low and afforded few training facilities. As we have seen in the previous chapter, the factors cited by Myint also provided an incentive for a shift to wholly capital-intensive techniques, requiring relatively few workers of any level of skill, where such methods were technically possible. Consequently, we find on the same plantation labor-and-land-intensive methods, of a sort that give little generalized training, in the agricultural side of the operation, combined with capital-intensive techniques in the processing part of the operation. The intermediate kind of technique, requiring fairly large numbers of workers in skilled occupations was shunned by entrepreneurs in underdeveloped countries; and, as Professor Myint suggests, it is these intermediate techniques that provide the best means of training large numbers of workers.

Finally, Professor Myint explains the lack of spread effects from development of the export sector by an appeal to the concept of "non-competing groups": [2]

> Thus it may be possible to find an analogue of non-competing groups in the foreign and domestic sectors of the backward countries which contributes to a lack of secondary rounds of activities. This leads us to the second argument, that the dynamic gains from specialization in industry are likely to be greater because it has a greater "educative" effect on the people of the country than agriculture. Here it must be admitted that in contrast to the tremendous stimulus to further economic development enjoyed by the advanced countries, international trade seems to have had very little educative effect on the people of backward countries except in the development of new wants. Apart from the introduction of modern transport, it is difficult to observe any revolutionary changes in their methods of production and efficiency both in the peasant and in the non-peasant sectors. The peasants specialize for international trade simply by going on producing traditional crops by traditional methods or new crops which can be readily produced by traditional methods.

In a more recent article, Myint shows that, although the "comparative cost" doctrine of the classical theory of international

[2] *Ibid.*, p. 140.

trade is largely inapplicable in underdeveloped countries, the relatively neglected "vent for surplus" aspect of this theory is very useful.[3] The "vent for surplus" was J. S. Mill's term for the idea—at least as old as Adam Smith—that expansion of foreign trade, by widening the market and permitting more division of labor, accelerates economic growth. The comparative cost doctrine assumes full employment of labor and resources before the country enters into international trade. The vent for surplus theory assumes more realistically that "a previously isolated country about to enter into international trade possesses a surplus productive capacity." Exports can be raised without reducing domestic production. Similarly, whereas comparative cost theory assumes a high degree of internal mobility of factors of production and a high elasticity of demand for commodities, the vent for surplus theory assumes—again more realistically—inelastic domestic demand for the exportable commodity "and/or a considerable degree of internal immobility and specificness of resources."

The contribution of Western enterprise to colonial development, Myint maintains, was mainly improvements in transport and communications and discoveries of new mineral resources. Investment of this kind adds to total resources but does not necessarily make existing resources more productive. The contribution of Western enterprise to the domestic (peasant) export sector was to act as middlemen between the peasant and the world market and to stimulate the peasants' demand for imports, thus unbending some backward-sloping supply curves.

The expansion of the export sector was possible without a decline in domestic production because of the labor surplus: [4]

> This surplus labour existed, not because of a shortage of co-operating factors, but because in the subsistence economies, with poor transport and little specialization in production, each self-sufficient economic unit could not find any market outlet to dispose of its potential surplus output, and had therefore no incentive to produce more than its own requirements. Here, then, we have the archetypal form of Smith's "unproductive" labour locked up in a semi-idle state in the underdeveloped economy of a country isolated from outside economic contacts. In most peasant economies this surplus labour was mobilised, however, not by the spread of the money-wage system of employment, but by peasant economic units with their complement of "family" labour moving *en bloc* into the money economy and export production.

[3] Hla Myint, "The 'Classical theory' of International Trade and the Underdeveloped Countries," *The Economic Journal*, June, 1958, pp. 321, 322.

[4] *Ibid.*, pp. 328, 331, 332.

The existence of a labor surplus, unfortunately, did not lead to the use of labor-intensive methods in the export sector. Instead population pressure led to highly labor-intensive and unproductive employment in the rural sector. "Indeed," says Professor Myint, "we may say that these countries remain underdeveloped precisely because they have not succeeded in building up a labour-intensive export trade to cope with their growing population."

Thus population pressure "inflicts a double loss: first, through simple diminishing returns, and secondly, by diverting resources from more to less productive use." Instead of growing rubber or sugar, where his comparative advantage is greater, and importing rice, the Javanese peasant still grows rice. Nor will mere removal of restrictions solve the problem. Given "the combination of population pressure, large pockets of subsistence economy and traditional methods of production which can no longer be made more labour-intensive," only "a more vigorous policy of state interference" is likely to be successful. In the Javanese case, this vigorous policy would include "removal of her surplus population either to thinly populated Outer Islands or to industries within Java and a vigorous export-drive policy supplemented by bulk purchase and subsidies on the imported rice."

Myint closes this article with a highly pertinent word of caution to policy makers in underdeveloped countries. The "export-bias" doctrine outlined above, distorted by "the strong feelings of economic nationalism and anti-colonialism in the underdeveloped countries" can become "very mischievous," supporting the view that to go on producing raw materials for export is tantamount to preserving a "colonial" pattern of trade. Correctly interpreted the doctrine means only that the export sector was artificially expanded relative to the domestic sector; it does not mean that the export sector is absolutely too large. Thus nationalistic governments fail to give enough support to peasant exports and concentrate too much on industrial development. Three home truths remain important: foreign aid is unlikely to relieve underdeveloped countries of the necessity of earning most of the foreign exchange needed for development; the only way to earn more foreign exchange in the short run is by expanding traditional exports; therefore, "export-drive policies" are very important.

Professor Myrdal and the "Backwash Effect"

Gunnar Myrdal carries the argument further than Myint. Because of "circular causation" and backwash effects, Myrdal contends, trade between underdeveloped and advanced countries, far from tending toward equality of marginal productivity and incomes, results in a tendency away from equilibrium, a vicious spiral bringing increasing discrepancies between productivity of advanced and underdeveloped countries.[5] The basic idea rather resembles Harrod's theory of cumulative movements away from equilibrium, but Myrdal's concept is broader, including social as well as economic aspects of equilibrium.

> The idea I want to expound in this book [Professor Myrdal writes] is that . . . in the normal case there is no such tendency towards automatic self-stabilization in the social system. The system is not by itself moving towards any sort of balance between forces, but is constantly on the move away from such a situation. In the normal case a change does not call forth countervailing changes but, instead, supporting changes, which move the system in the same direction as the first change but much further. Because of such circular causation a social process tends to become cumulative and often to gather speed at an accelerating rate.

Myrdal begins his analysis with the tendency toward regional inequalities in a single country. The growing communities will exert a strong agglomerative pull, accelerating their rate of growth and bringing increasing stagnation or decline in other parts of the country. No offsetting forces arise to prevent the acceleration of this shift of economic activity from decadent to progressive regions. Any accident or shock giving a momentary advantage to one region can start this chain of disparate growth movements. Among such shifts in the relative advantages of regions of a country, Professor Myrdal singles out "a change in the terms of trade of a community or a region" as one factor which has historically played this role.

Demographic factors will rank among the aggravating forces, he says, since the poorer regions will have relatively high fertility. This factor, together with net immigration from the decadent regions, makes the age distribution in these regions unfavorable. The poverty in rural regions of Europe during the long period of net immigration to industrial centers and to the

[5] Gunnar Myrdal, *Economic Theory and Under-Developed Regions* (London, 1957), pp. 13, 28, 29.

United States, "has a main explanation in the unfavorable age distribution there, caused by migration and in part also by higher fertility rates."

The expansion of trade only aggravates the process. "The freeing and widening of the markets will often confer such competitive advantages on the industries in already established centres of expansion, which usually work under conditions of increasing returns, that even the handicrafts and industries existing earlier in the other regions are thwarted." As a dramatic example of the growth of regional disparities following liberation of trade, Myrdal cites the expansion of the north and retrogression of the south of Italy following political unification in 1860. For one thing, regions "not touched by the expansionary momentum could not afford to keep up a good road system and all their other public utilities would be inferior." [6]

True, expansion in one region also has spread effects as well as backwash effects; the growth of industrial cities, for example, should create a demand both for agricultural raw materials and for consumers' goods. There is, however, no reason for equilibrium between backwash and spread effects. The preceding analysis offers some reason to assume that the backwash effects will be predominant. The spread effects could outweigh the backwash effects only if income and employment in the leading sectors grew relative to that of the laggard sector, as they did in the now advanced countries. In underdeveloped countries, however, the historical pattern of growth has been such that spread effects were weak. The rural sector (as defined above) did not produce the raw materials for the expanding industrial sector, nor did the expanding industrial sector rely heavily on the rural sector for foodstuffs. (Rice was not the major item in the food budgets of the British, Dutch, or Spanish in their colonies.) Thus the growth of the industrial sector did not much expand the market for cash crops of the rural sector.

Myrdal reports two striking correlations which were discovered in the studies of the Economic Commission for Europe: first, regional disparities are greater in poor countries than in rich ones; and second, the disparities are increasing in poor countries and decreasing in rich ones. "A large part of the explanation for these two broad correlations," he says, "may be found in the important fact that the higher the level of economic development that a country has already attained, the stronger the spread effects will usually be."

[6] *Ibid.*, p. 29.

National policy strengthened these inherent tendencies toward integration in advanced countries and leading and lagging sectors in underdeveloped ones. The poorer countries, and especially those which were colonies, had no effective policies for national integration, of the sort that were introduced in the more highly developed countries.

> Generally speaking, on a low level of economic development with relatively weak spread effects, the competitive forces in the markets will, by circular causation, constantly be tending towards regional inequalities, while the inequalities themselves will be holding back economic development, and at the same time weakening the power basis for egalitarian policies. A higher level of development will strengthen the spread effects and tend to hamper the drift towards regional inequalities; this will sustain economic development, and at the same time create more favourable conditions for policies directed at decreasing regional inequalities still further.

Thus, it is entirely possible for international trade to have "strong backwash effects on the underdeveloped countries."[7] The present pattern of production in underdeveloped countries reflects these backwash effects rather than true comparative advantage. Instead of increasing production of primary goods for export, the true advantage of these countries may lie in improving the productivity of the rural sector and in developing manufactures. Capital cannot be expected to flow to underdeveloped countries simply because capital is relatively scarce there. On the contrary, in the absence of exchange controls capital would flow out of the underdeveloped countries to those more advanced (and more rapidly advancing). Furthermore international adjustment through migration is no longer possible.

The present pattern of production in underdeveloped countries also reflects the past policies of the colonial powers, which often "took special measures to hamper the growth of indigenous industry." Since "cumulative social processes holding it down in stagnation or regression" remain, the colonial heritage cannot be dispelled merely by political independence. For "colonialism meant primarily not only a strengthening of all the forces in markets which anyhow were working towards internal and international inequalities. It built itself into, and gave an extra impetus and a peculiar character to, the circular causation of the cumulative process."[8]

The evidence seems to support Myrdal in this contention. In

[7] *Ibid.*, pp. 34, 41, 51.
[8] *Ibid.*, p. 60.

some measure, the failure of investment in the export sector to have "multiplier effects" on domestic incomes in Asian-African countries and in Europe does reflect colonial policy. In advanced countries investment directed toward production of raw materials for export stimulated expansion of the secondary and tertiary sectors of the economy. In most Asian and African countries colonial policy was directed toward promoting the expansion of those sectors in the metropolis, not in the colony. Most financing, transporting, storing, insuring, and processing of industrial raw materials occurred *outside* the colonial country. Here again, we see the importance of differentiating between a *country*, as a geographic entity, and an *economy* as a nexus of interrelated prices and decisions.

In his final pages, Myrdal calls for a new theory of international trade as applied to underdeveloped countries; he deplores the tendency of the International Monetary Fund and GATT to apply outmoded theory because they "tend continuously to be permeated by the ideological elements which I have referred to as the predilections of economic theory, and which have had a particularly strong influence on the theory of international trade." [9]

Unlimited Supplies of Labor?

Similar conclusions are reached in more systematic fashion by W. Arthur Lewis in his well-known article on "Economic Development with Unlimited Supplies of Labour." [10] He begins by asserting that many underdeveloped countries conform to the Classical model, in which the supply of labor is perfectly elastic at current wage rates. The "widow's cruse" of workers consists of farmers, casual workers, petty traders, domestic retainers, and population growth. Since his conclusions rest on this basic observation, let us begin by examining the premise itself.

Some observers, including the present writer, have pointed out that the optimism concerning development by absorption of disguised unemployment from agriculture was unfounded. It is not possible to transfer large numbers of workers permanently and full time from peasant agriculture to industry without a drop in agricultural output. For, during planting and harvesting seasons, which together amount to several weeks per year, the entire

[9] *Ibid.*, p. 155.

[10] W. Arthur Lewis, "Economic Development with Unlimited Supplies of Labour," *The Manchester School of Economic and Social Studies*, May, 1954.

labor force is occupied. It may even be necessary to bring back members of the village who have gone off to take casual jobs in the industrial sector. Reorganization of agriculture and a shift to relatively extensive and mechanized techniques could release large numbers of workers from agriculture, to be sure, but that requires a certain amount of investment in the agricultural sector itself. Some observers have suggested that disguised unemployment has moved from country to city, and cite as evidence the host of petty retailers. But even the urban peddler, with three empty bottles in one basket and two right shoes in the other, may be performing a real service, and so may be truly employed, if there are customers with left shoes and who want empty bottles. Thus in the static sense, it may be questioned whether supply curves of labor to the industrial sector are perfectly elastic.

If one puts the whole growth process in time, however, as one must to get meaningful results, the Lewis model accords with reality in many underdeveloped countries, so far as *unskilled* labor is concerned. The Lewis argument does not require disguised unemployment. It requires three conditions: that the wage rate in the industrial sector be above the marginal productivity of labor in the rural sector by a small but fixed amount; that investment in the industrial sector be not absolutely large relative to population growth; and that costs of training the necessary numbers of skilled workers be constant through time. The first condition seems to be met in many countries. If the "population multiplier" operates, the second condition is automatically guaranteed. But even if industrial investment does not actually accelerate population growth, the second condition can be met if employment in the industrial sector is a small proportion of the total and population growth is fairly high. Suppose, for example, that the labor force is twenty million, that four million are employed in the industrial sector, that the capital-job ratio in that sector is $2,000 per man, and that the total labor force grows at the rate of 2 per cent per year. To employ the total increase in the labor force in the industrial sector would require net investment of $800 million next year, or 10 per cent of the total stock of capital. Net investment on this scale would double the stock of capital in about eight years, a rate of growth beyond the wildest dreams of most underdeveloped countries. Thus for all practical purposes the supply of unskilled labor to the industrial sector can be treated as perfectly elastic, whereas in the rural sector it is already redundant, in the sense that marginal productivity there is below the subsistence standard of living.

Of course, the industrial employers are interested in skilled labor too. Lewis argues that labor skills are only a "quasi-bottleneck"; if you have unskilled workers, you can convert them into skilled ones.

In the short run, the need to train or import skilled workers may not alter the argument very much; if the cost of training or importing is constant, the elasticity of supply of skilled labor can still be infinite. As we have seen above, it is possible that the cost of training or importing technicians may be high enough to induce entrepreneurs to use capital-intensive techniques in those parts of their operation where skill is necessary, but this fact does not change the argument either, unless these costs are rising. The Lewis thesis is of dubious validity even for unskilled workers if we think in purely static terms, however; and if we think in terms of long-run supply through time, the relevant question about the supply of skills is whether the cost of training or importing is rising through time. The answer will depend on the nature of technological progress; if it is of a sort which reduces both the capital-labor ratio and the capital-output ratio simultaneously, the Lewis thesis may hold for skilled labor as well as for unskilled.

Now if we accept the thesis the process of growth will look like Figure 15-1. Here $\bar{w}$ is the productivity per man-hour in

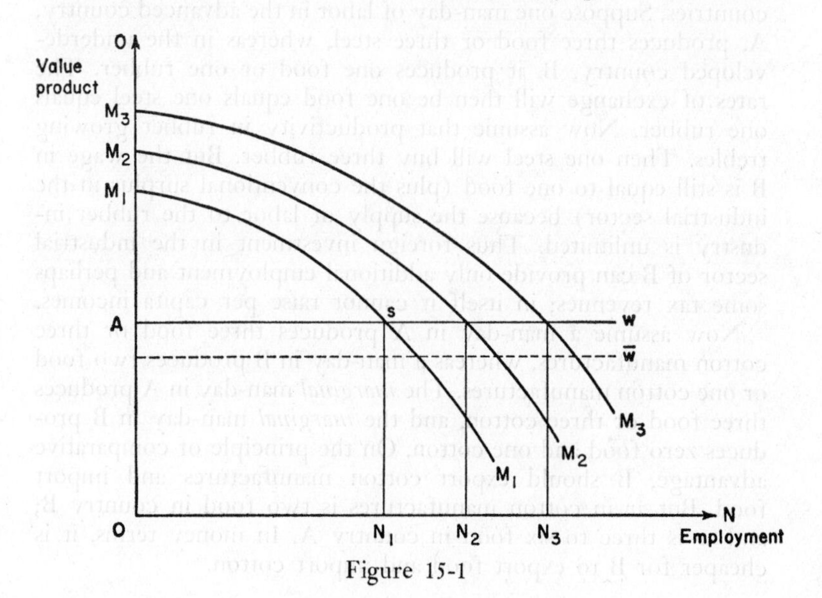

Figure 15-1

peasant agriculture, and w is the conventional wage in the industrial sector. The marginal productivity of labor in industry is MM_1, which permits the capitalist to earn a surplus, AMS. When he invests this surplus—perhaps improving techniques at the same time—the curve of marginal productivity shifts to MM_2, and so on. The per capita income of workers and peasants remains unchanged, and the entire benefits of development accrue to capitalists. Lewis suggests three ways in which the process might be halted: if the expansion of the industrial sector is rapid enough to reduce the absolute population in the rural sector, raising the man-hour productivity in that sector, and so raising $\bar{w}$ and w (this will not happen if the population multiplier is operating); if technological progress in the rural sector raises productivity there, and so raises $\bar{w}$ and w; or if the terms of trade turn against the industrial sector with rising prices of food and raw materials, and so bring a rise in $\bar{w}$ and w (this is the Classical model). The achievement of balanced growth and generally higher living standards requires that the process *must* be halted by either method 1 or method 2, while, at the same time, measures are taken to continue investment in the industrial sector.

Lewis applies his analysis to the impact of international trade. First, he shows that technological progress in the export sector of underdeveloped countries helps only the workers of advanced countries. Suppose one man-day of labor in the advanced country, A, produces three food or three steel, whereas in the underdeveloped country, B, it produces one food or one rubber. The rates of exchange will then be one food equals one steel equals one rubber. Now assume that productivity in rubber growing trebles. Then one steel will buy three rubber. But the wage in B is still equal to one food (plus the conventional surplus in the industrial sector) because the supply of labor to the rubber industry is unlimited. Thus foreign investment in the industrial sector of B can provide only additional employment and perhaps some tax revenues; in itself it cannot raise per capita incomes.

Now assume a man-day in A produces three food or three cotton manufactures, whereas a man-day in B produces two food or one cotton manufactures. The *marginal* man-day in A produces three food or three cotton, and the *marginal* man-day in B produces zero food and one cotton. On the principle of comparative advantage, B should export cotton manufactures and import food. But w in cotton manufactures is two food in country B; and w is three to six food in country A. In money terms, it is cheaper for B to export food and import cotton.

Lewis seems to be correct in his conclusion that countries with inadequate agricultural resources relative to their population (India, Japan, Egypt, the United Kingdom) should export manufactures and import agricultural products. It is impossible to imagine India as a truly efficient agricultural country, but it is easy to see India as an efficient producer of steel and textiles. This kind of misallocation of resources occurs in many underdeveloped countries. The implication is that planning must be based on "shadow prices" as they would prevail *after* a drastic structural change has been achieved.

Finally, Lewis indicates a way out of the vicious circle. Suppose a man-day in A produces five food or five cotton textiles, and a man-day in B produces one food or three cotton. Wages in B are one food, and B will export textiles. Wages in A are five food; A gets all the benefit from trade. Now suppose productivity is raised in B's cotton manufacturing industry. The wage in B is unchanged, and the entire benefit goes to A, as before. But if productivity is raised in B's food production, B's wage will rise. Then cotton prices will also rise, to the benefit of B and the disadvantage of A. Thus economic development requires raising productivity per man-day—not per acre—in the peasant agriculture sector. Given the rates of population growth in that sector, raising productivity per man-day almost certainly requires—sooner or later—a shift to more extensive and more mechanized agriculture.

One final point may be noted. The current nationalist policies, with their emphasis on training and upgrading domestic labor and their limitations on immigration of skilled workers, managers, and technicians, may mean that skilled workers will be a more serious bottleneck to future expansion than they have been in the past. It is a question whether techniques of training, as well as of production, can be improved sufficiently to keep training costs per unit of *output*, at least, from rising as industry expands.

The Terms of Trade

Recently, certain economists have argued that one of the difficulties faced by underdeveloped countries is a long-run tendency for the terms of trade to turn against them. In discussing this thesis, it is important to make two distinctions. First, we must distinguish between a tendency for the prices and volume of exports from underdeveloped countries to fluctuate severely in the course of the world business cycle, and a secular tendency for the prices of their exports to decline relative to the prices of their imports. The first tendency relates to the problem of economic stabilization in underdeveloped countries, and will be dealt with in Chapter 24. Here, we shall be concerned not with the impediments to growth arising from instability of export prices, but with the long-run trend in terms of trade.

Secondly, we must distinguish between trends in the terms of trade of the country as a whole, and trends in the terms of trade between the rural sector of underdeveloped countries and the rest of the world, including the industrial sectors of those countries. As we shall see, the argument is a good deal clearer when cast in terms of trading relations of the rural sectors of underdeveloped countries with the rest of the world. Indeed, there has been relatively little controversy with respect to this question. There has, however, been keen debate with respect to the thesis relating to terms of trade of the underdeveloped countries as a whole. We shall see that this argument is as yet not completely resolved, but that the weight of the evidence favors those who believe that underdeveloped countries do face a problem of deteriorating terms of trade.

The distinction between the problem of instability in prices of exports and of long-run trends in terms of trade has been well stated by Dr. M. K. Atallah: [11]

> The reliance of the underdeveloped countries on their exports of agricultural products to derive a large share of their income is one major cause of their weak economies, because it makes them sensitive to the slightest price fluctuations and imposes additional hardships on their populations. It is the more so, since the prices of primary commodities are known to be subject to wild fluctuations which, although in the upswings bring unusual prosperity, can in the downswings assume the proportions of catastrophes. In the 1930's farm incomes in the whole world were cut to one-half or one-third of their previous levels; and apart from the general depressions, particular price slumps have been experienced frequently for individual commodities, such as coffee, rubber, cocoa and many others.
>
> Since the Second World War, when most of the underdeveloped countries have discovered the differences between their economic conditions and the standard of living prevailing in the developed countries, and decided to decrease this gap by the development of their economies, a further aspect has been added to this problem; because all programs of economic development require large amounts of capital goods obtainable in the advanced countries and must be exchanged

[11] M. K. Atallah, *The Long-term Movement of the Terms of Trade between Agricultural and Industrial Products* (Rotterdam, 1958), p. 1.

—as far as no capital imports take place—for exports of primary products. The ability of the underdeveloped countries to acquire these goods depends, therefore, on the relation between the prices of their exports of primary products and the prices of their imports of capital goods.

Terms of Trade of the Country as a Whole

The recent debate on terms of trade of underdeveloped countries really began with the report of the First Session of the Subcommission on Economic Development of the UN Economic and Employment Commission. This stated that the purpose of borrowing abroad to finance economic development would be defeated unless the lending countries took measures to make capital goods available for export at reasonable prices. The report observed that the recent rise in prices of capital goods had made the task of economic development more difficult, and requested "a careful study of the prices of capital goods and of the relative trends of such prices and of prices of primary products." In response to this request, a study of "Relative Prices of Exports and Imports of Underdeveloped Countries" was published in December, 1949.[12]

The major factual findings of this report are presented in Table 15-2. The index of the ratio of prices of primary products to those of manufactured commodities shows a declining trend, from 147 for the period 1876 to 1880 to 100 in 1938. The report also gives figures for the United Kingdom which show a fall in the relative prices of British imports (mostly raw materials and foodstuffs) to the prices of British exports (mostly manufactured goods). The ratio of American imports of primary goods to American imports of finished manufactures between 1913 and 1948 shows a similar tendency, declining from an index of 141 in 1913 to 108 in 1948.

The report provides figures for price movements of particular exports of underdeveloped countries and evidence of the concentration of exports on a narrow range of commodities in many underdeveloped countries. This latter evidence is set forth in Table 24-1. The report also presents a table listing countries whose terms of trade have improved, worsened, or remained unchanged between 1938 and 1946 or 1947. This table is reproduced here as Table 15-3. From it, no general conclusions can be drawn. The terms of trade

[12] UN Department of Economic Affairs, "Relative Prices of Exports and Imports of Under-developed Countries," New York, December, 1949.

TABLE 15-2.

Selected Unit Value Ratios, 1876–1948
(1938 = 100)

Period	*Ratio*		
	Primary to manufactured commodities in world trade * (1)	United Kingdom imports to exports	
		Current year weights † (2)	Board of Trade index (3)
1876–1880	147	163	....
1881–1885	145	167	....
1886–1890	137	157	....
1891–1895	133	147	....
1896–1900	135	142	....
1901–1905	132	138	....
1906–1910	133	140	....
1911–1913	137	140	....
1913	137	137	143
1921	94	93	101
1922	103	102	109
1923	114	107	111
1924	121	122	117
1925	123	125	120
1926	121	119	117
1927	125	122	117
1928	121	123	120
1929	118	122	120
1930	105	112	109
1931	93	102	99
1932	89	102	99
1933	89	98	96
1934	96	101	99
1935	98	103	100
1936	102	107	103
1937	108	107	109
1938	100	100	100
1946			108
1947			116
1948			117

* Based on League of Nations, *Industrialization and Foreign Trade* (Geneva, 1945). Represents major trading countries and others.

† Based on W. Schlote, "Entwicklung und Strukturwandlungen des eng-

of some countries were better in 1946 and 1947 than before the war, some were worse, some were unchanged. Of course, the short period covered in this table does not tell very much about long-term trends. At best, the figures suggest that the trend indicated in Table 15-2, may have been reversed since World War II.

The report states the general principle that "a favorable change in terms of trade," allows a given quantity of exports to buy more imports and so releases resources for development. But in conclusion, the report warns that the terms of trade constitute "only one factor—and not generally the most important single factor—in determining national income and funds available for economic development." To illustrate this point the authors cite cocoa prices:

> A good illustration of this is provided by the post-war rise in the price of cocoa. As has been indicated in some of the preceding tables, cocoa prices showed a marked increase; hence under-developed countries which concentrated on cocoa in their exports tended to have favourable changes in their terms of trade. This "favourable" change, however, is partly due to a virus disease, the "swollen shoot disease," affecting the Gold Coast, at present the major producing area. The disease reduced supplies and thus tended to raise prices. It is evident that this is not a favourable change for Gold Coast. It merely means that the rise in the price of supplies due to the virus disease, tended to offset to some degree—perhaps only to a slight degree—the unfavourable development by which it was caused.

Thus the facts are not clear. A somewhat longer series covering the terms of trade[13] of the United Kingdom has been prepared by A. H. Imlah, and reproduced by Dr. Atallah.[14] This index does not take account of such "invisibles" as shipping, commercial services, capital movements, and income from foreign investments. It is constructed simply by dividing the index numbers of export prices by the index numbers of import prices. Thus rising numbers indicate an improvement in the British terms of trade and falling numbers a deterioration. The table shows

[13] For a discussion of the main definitions of the terms of trade, see J. Viner, *Studies in the Theory of International Trade* (London, 1937), pp. 555–65. For a detailed survey, see W. W. Rostow, "The Terms of Trade in Theory and Practice," *The Economic History Review*, Second Series, Vol. III, No. 1.

[14] *Ibid.*, pp. 121–22.

---

lischen Aussenhandels von 1700 bis zur Gegenwart," *Probleme der Weltwirtschaft*, No. 62 (Jena, 1938).

SOURCE: UN Department of Economic Affairs, "Relative Prices of Exports and Imports of Under-developed Countries," December, 1949.

that British terms of trade deteriorated between 1800 and the mid-1850's, remained more or less unchanged for a generation, and distinctly improved after 1890. Unfortunately, this series is of limited use for predicting the movements in terms of trade of underdeveloped countries today. The most that can be said is that the terms of trade seemed to turn against the United Kingdom during its period of rapid industrialization and to turn in her favor during her period as an advanced industrialized nation.

As Atallah pointed out, not all economists are satisfied with the simple "commodity terms of trade" as a measure of the influence of foreign trade on the economic position of a particular country:

TABLE 15-3.

Changes in Postwar Terms of Trade of Certain Underdeveloped Countries, compared with Prewar

Region and Country	*Terms of trade of underdeveloped area*		
	Improved	No change *	Worsened
Central America, including Mexico and Caribbean area (17)	8	2	7
Bahamas	X		
Barbados			X
British Honduras			X
Costa Rica	X		
Cuba	X		
United Kingdom	X		
United States	X		
Dominican Republic	X		
Grenada	X		
Guadeloupe		X	
Guatemala	X		
Haiti	X		
United States	X		
Jamaica			X
Martinique		X	
Mexico	X		
Nicaragua			X
Puerto Rico			X
St. Vincent			X
Trinidad and Tobago			X
South America (11)	4	2	5
Argentina	X		

Region and Country	Terms of trade of underdeveloped area		
	Improved	No change *	Worsened
Bolivia			X
Brazil	X		
United Kingdom	X		
United States	X		
British Guiana			X
Chile			X
Colombia	X		
Ecuador	X		
French Guiana			X
Peru		X	
Surinam			X
Venezuela		X	
United States	X		
Europe † (1)	1		
Eastern Europe	X		
Africa (8)	3	1	4
Belgian Congo	X		
French Equatorial Africa			X
French West Africa	X		
Gold Coast			X
Kenya and Uganda			X
Madagascar			X
Sierra Leone ‡			X
Tanganyika		X	
Asia (7)	3	1	3
Burma			
United Kingdom	X		
China			
United States			X
Lebanon and Syria		X	
India and Pakistan ‡ §			X
Iran ‖			X
Turkey			
United States	X		
Total (44)	19	6	19

* Or inconclusive data.

† Eastern Europe–Western Europe.

‡ Prewar composition of trade considered representative.

§ Favorable change in trade with United States; unfavorable change in trade with United Kingdom.

‖ Result obtained on broad commodity classification considered representative.

SOURCE: UN Department of Economic Affairs, "Relative Prices of Exports and Imports of Under-developed Countries," December, 1949.

In their simplest meaning the terms of trade of given country refer to the relation between its imports and exports prices. According to this definition a movement of the terms of trade in favour of a country means an increase in the volume of its imports received in exchange for each unit of its exports. The concept so defined is called "Commodity Terms of Trade." But although straightforward and clear, this definition has often been met with criticism from the economists, mainly because it ignores one or another of the factors which determine the influence of the terms of trade on the balance of payments, the gains from trade, or the income of a country. Consequently, several other definitions have been suggested which take account of one or more of the factors ignored. "The Single Factoral Terms of Trade," for example, correct the "Commodity Terms of Trade" for changes in productivity in producing exports; the "Double Factoral Terms of Trade" correct them for changes in productivity in producing imports and exports; the "Index of Total Gains from Trade" takes account of the volume of trade.

For the sake of completeness, we include estimates of the United Kingdom barter terms of trade made by Colin Clark, Table 15-4(A), a series constructed by Dr. Atallah himself, Table 15-4(B), and another on industrial European merchandise terms of trade constructed by Professor C. P. Kindleberger, Table 15-4(C). The Clark series shows more or less the same movements as the Imlah series. The Atallah series shows improvement in the United Kingdom terms of trade between 1876–80 and 1921, deterioration until 1925, followed by improvement again.

TABLE 15-4(A).

United Kingdom Barter Terms of Trade
(1913 = 100)

Period	Terms	Period	Terms
1801–15	141.7	1886–93	88.8
1816–28	123.6	1894–1903	97.6
1829–42	100.2	1904–10	97.7
1843–50	92.4	1911–13	98.5
1851–59	82.6	1914–18	93.6
1860–69	86.0	1919–23	130.1
1870–76	92.0	1924–32	124.1
1877–85	82.4	1933–37	138.0

SOURCE: Colin Clark, *The Conditions of Economic Progress* (1st ed.), quoted in A. E. Kahn, *Great Britain in the World Economy* (New York, 1956), p. 144.

TABLE 15-4(B).

United Kingdom Import-export Ratio, Based upon Current Year Weights (1938 = 100)

Period	I/E	Period	I/E	Period	I/E
1876–1880	163	1921	93	1931	102
1881–1885	167	1922	102	1932	102
1886–1890	157	1923	107	1933	98
1891–1895	147	1924	122	1934	101
		1925	125	1935	103
1896–1900	142				
1901–1905	138	1926	119	1936	107
1906–1910	140	1927	122	1937	107
1911–1913	140	1928	123	1938	100
		1929	122		
		1930	112		

SOURCE: UN Department of Economic Affairs, "Relative Prices of Exports and Imports of Under-developed Countries," December, 1949, p. 22, Table 5; based on W. Schlote, "Entwicklung und Strukturwandlungen des englischen Aussenhandels von 1700 bis zur Gegenwart," *Probleme der Weltwirtschaft*, No. 62 (Jena, 1938).

TABLE 15-4(C).

Industrial European Merchandise Terms of Trade (1913 = 100)

Year	Terms	Year	Terms	Year	Terms
1900	113	1920	96	1934	137
1901	113	1921	108	1935	135
1902	109	1922	110	1936	130
1903	109	1923	114	1937	124
1904	108	1924	113	1938	134
1905	107	1925	108		
1906	107	1926	109	1947	125
1907	106	1927	109	1948	118
1908	108	1928	108	1949	118
1909	103	1929	109	1950	106
1910	100	1930	119	1951	102
1911	101	1931	129	1952	109
1912	100	1932	136		
1913	100	1933	138		

SOURCE: C. P. Kindleberger, *The Terms of Trade: A European Case Study* (London, 1956), p. 12, Table 2-1.

Kindleberger's series of the industrial European merchandise terms of trade shows declining terms of trade between 1900 and 1920, followed by improvement until 1923, slight decline during the rest of the 1920's, followed by improvement again in the 1930's and deterioration in the postwar period.

The Thesis for Latin America

It is apparent that the available data are rather unsatisfactory as a basis for theoretical speculation about the impact of trends in terms of trade of underdeveloped countries, let alone for prediction as to what will happen in the future. Nevertheless, some economists have been willing to generalize from these figures. Perhaps boldest in this respect is Professor Raoul Prebisch, who has laid great emphasis on deteriorating terms of trade as a factor inhibiting the development of Latin American countries.

The Prebisch Argument

The "schema" of the international division of labor, says Dr. Prebisch, achieved great importance in the nineteenth century and survived as a theoretical concept well into the twentieth century. Under this nineteenth-century schema the specific task assigned to Latin America, "as part of the periphery of the world economic system," was to produce food and raw materials for the great industrial centers. The schema made no provision for industrialization of the newer countries; but "two world wars in a single generation and a great economic crisis between them have shown the Latin American countries their opportunities, clearly pointing the way to industrial activity." [15]

In economics, Professor Prebisch argues, "ideologies usually tend either to lag behind the events or to outlive them." According to the accepted doctrine, countries producing raw materials share in the benefit of technological progress through international exchange. They have no need to industrialize themselves; indeed, if they do so "their lesser efficiency would result in their losing the conventional advantages of (international) exchange." In fact, Prebisch insists, "the industrialization of Latin America is not incompatible with the efficient development of primary pro-

[15] UN Economic Commission for Asia and the Far East, *The Economic Development of Latin America and Some of Its Problems* (New York, 1949), pp. 1–3; see also Raoul Prebisch, "The Role of Commercial Policies in Underdeveloped Countries," *American Economic Review Papers and Proceedings*, May, 1959.

duction." However, for industrialization and mechanization of agriculture, capital equipment must be imported. For that purpose dollars must be made available, directly or indirectly through European countries. But "the import coefficient of the United States has, after a persistent decline, arrived at a very low level (not over three per cent)." Accordingly, the dollar resources made available to Latin American countries are insufficient for the imports needed for development.

Using the UN figures presented in Table 15-2 to support his argument, Prebisch then states that "technical progress seems to have been greater in industry than in the primary production of peripheral countries." Had prices behaved according to the textbook models of pure competition, the prices of industrial products would consequently have fallen relative to those of primary products. "Had this happened, the countries of the periphery would have benefited from the fall in price of finished industrial products to the same extent as the countries of the center, [and] the benefit of technical progress would thus have been distributed alike throughout the world." In reality, the reverse price movement has taken place, and in the 1930's "an average of 58.6 per cent more primary products were needed to buy the same amount of finished manufactures" as in the 1860's. Prebisch considers the price movement between 1938 and 1946–47 a purely cyclical result of the war and postwar boom, and he implies that resumption of the trend against primary products is to be expected.

According to Prebisch, the explanation of these price movements is that "in the center the incomes of entrepreneurs and of productive factors increase relatively more than productivity, whereas in the periphery the increase in income is less than that in productivity. . .[16] In other words, while the centers kept the whole benefit of the technical development of their industries the peripheral countries cannot spare to them a share of the fruits of their own technical progress." He provides no analysis of how this disparate movement in relation of incomes to productivity may have taken place, relying mainly on the figures themselves. The closest Prebisch comes to an explanation of his facts is to point to a difference in the strength of trade-unions. In industrialized countries, prices are pushed up by union action in prosperity and kept up by union resistance to wage cuts in the downswing. In the peripheral countries, "the characteristic lack of organization among the workers employed in primary pro-

[16] ECAFE, *op. cit.*, pp. 8–9.

duction prevents them from obtaining wage increases comparable to those of the industrial countries and from maintaining the increases to the same extent."

Thus the Prebisch argument boils down to the "cost-push" theory of inflation. He really contends that advanced countries have more chronic inflationary pressure than underdeveloped ones, and that this chronic inflationary pressure can be traced to the "cost-push" emanating from trade-union pressure on wages and the unwillingness of entrepreneurs in their turn to accept a squeeze on profits. The question as to whether or not a cost-push alone can generate rising prices is dealt with in Chapter 23. All we need say here is that the Prebisch argument clearly takes us deep into questions of business cycle theory which he himself does not attempt to answer.

Prebisch also argues that technical progress has a "demonstration effect" which creates new wants in Latin America which cannot be satisfied by local production without further industrialization and imports of capital equipment. Technological progress has been greater in the United States than anywhere else; consequently the demand for capital goods needed for industrialization "is preferentially made upon that country."

Five years later Dr. Prebisch restated his argument in briefer and more trenchant form.[17] Here he reverts to the "chronic shortage of dollars" as the factor inhibiting industrialization of underdeveloped countries. "For every one per cent of per-capita increase of income in the USA," he points out "imports of primary goods tend to increase 0.6 per cent." Thus "there is an impressive disparity in the income elasticity of demand. There is no other way of correcting the effects of this disparity than the promotion of industrial production in underdeveloped countries. . . . In other words, protection is economically justified when the possible loss caused by fall of export prices (by expansion of traditional exports) is greater than the higher cost of internal production in relation to imports." Thus protection "does not mean restriction of imports, but rather a change in their composition."

The Singer Version

A very similar argument was made at about the same time by Dr. Hans Singer of the UN Department of Economic Affairs.

[17] Robert Lekachman (ed.), *National Policy for Economic Welfare at Home and Abroad* (New York, 1955), pp. 277–80.

Singer begins his analysis by dispelling any illusions that may remain regarding the importance of foreign trade in underdeveloped areas: [18]

International trade is of very considerable importance to underdeveloped countries, and the benefits which they derive from trade and any variations in their trade affect their national incomes very deeply. The opposite view, which is frequent among economists, namely, that trade is less important to the underdeveloped countries than it is to industrialized countries, may be said to derive from a logical confusion—very easy to slip into—between the absolute amount of foreign trade which is known to be an increasing function of national income, and the ratio of foreign trade to national income. Foreign trade tends to be proportionately most important when incomes are lowest. Secondly, fluctuations in the volume and value of foreign trade tend to be proportionately more violent in that of underdeveloped countries and therefore *a fortiori* also more important in relation to national income. Thirdly, and *a fortissimo*, fluctuations in foreign trade tend to be immensely more important for underdeveloped countries in relation to that small margin of income over subsistence needs which forms the source of capital formation, for which they often depend on export surpluses over consumption goods required from abroad. . . .

. . . Thus the economy of the underdeveloped countries often presents the spectacle of a dualistic economic structure: a high productivity sector producing for export coexisting with a low productivity sector producing for the domestic market.

Singer goes on to distinguish between underdeveloped *countries* and underdeveloped *economies:*

Can it be possible that we economists have become slaves to the geographers? Could it not be that in many cases the productive facilities for export from underdeveloped countries, which were so largely a result of foreign investment, never became a part of the internal economic structure of those underdeveloped countries themselves, except in the purely geographical and physical sense? Economically speaking, they were really an outpost of the economies of the more developed investing countries. The main secondary multiplier effects, which the textbooks tell us to expect from investment, took place not where the investment was physically or geographically located but (to the extent that the results of these investments returned directly home) they took place where the investment came from. I would suggest that if the proper economic test of investment is the multiplier effect in the form of cumulative additions to income, em-

[18] Hans Singer, "The Distribution of Gains Between Investing and Borrowing Countries," *American Economic Review Papers and Proceedings*, May, 1950, p. 473.

ployment, capital, technical knowledge, and growth of external economies, then a good deal of the investment in underdeveloped countries which we used to consider as "foreign" should in fact be considered as domestic investment on the part of the industrialized countries.

Not only was foreign investment of the kind that took place in underdeveloped countries of little benefit to the people of those countries, in terms of the broader aspects of economic development it may have been "positively harmful":[19]

> The tea plantations of Ceylon, the oil wells of Iran, the copper mines of Chile, and the cocoa industry of the Gold Coast may all be more productive than domestic agriculture in these countries; but they may well be less productive than domestic industries in those countries which might have developed if those countries had not become specialized to the degree in which they now are to the export of food and raw materials, thus providing the means of producing manufactured goods elsewhere with superior efficiency.
>
> . . . In the economic life of a country and in its economic history, a most important element is the mechanism by which "one thing leads to another," and the most important contribution of an industry is not its immediate product (as is perforce assumed by economists and statisticians) and not even its effects on other industries and immediate social benefits (thus far economists have been led by Marshall and Pigou to go) but perhaps even further its effect on the general level of education, skill, way of life, investiveness, habits, store of technology, creation of new demand, etc. And this is perhaps precisely the reason why manufacturing industries are so universally desired by underdeveloped countries; namely, that they provide the growing points for increased technical knowledge, urban education, the dynamism and resilience that goes with urban civilization, as well as the direct Marshallian external economies.

Perhaps an even more serious drag on economic development than these backwash effects of foreign investment, however, has been the deterioration of the terms of trade of underdeveloped countries. In making this argument, Singer relies on the same UN data as are presented in Table 15-2. His explanation of these data is essentially the same as that of Prebisch: the gains of technological progress in industrialized countries were distributed to producers as higher incomes, whereas in countries producing primary products the gains from such technical improvement as occurred were distributed to consumers in the form of lower prices. In a closed economy, it does not matter much which form the

[19] *Ibid.*, pp. 473, 474, 476.

rise in real incomes takes; but when producers are at home and consumers are abroad, it makes a good deal of difference: [20]

> The industrialized countries have had the best of both worlds, both as consumers of primary commodities and as producers of manufactured articles, whereas the underdeveloped countries had the worst of both worlds, as consumers of manufactures and as producers of raw materials.

The perverse effects of economic fluctuations on the position of underdeveloped countries also retard economic development by delaying the needed structural change. Good prices for raw materials and foodstuffs provide the means for financing the import of capital goods for industrialization but dilute the incentive to do so. When these prices fall, the incentive to industrialize is stronger but the means are not available.

Dr. Singer concludes: [21]

> The purposes of foreign investment and foreign trade ought perhaps to be redefined as producing gradual changes in the structure of comparative advantages and of the comparative endowment of the different countries rather than to develop a world trading system based on existing comparative advantages and existing distribution of endowments. This perhaps is the real significance of the present movement towards giving technical assistance to underdeveloped countries not necessarily linked with actual trade or investment. The emphasis on technical assistance may be interpreted as a recognition that the present structure of comparative advantages and endowments is not such that it should be considered as a permanent basis for a future international division of labor.

Criticism of the Prebisch-Singer Thesis

The argument with respect to deterioration of the terms of trade of underdeveloped countries has been attacked on both empirical and theoretical grounds. Colin Clark and Arthur Lewis reach quite different results from their efforts to put empirical content into the relationships determining the terms of trade between agricultural and industrial products. Writing in 1944, Colin Clark endeavored to predict the demand for and supply of agricultural and industrial products in 1960.[22] Clark's calcula-

[20] *Ibid.*, p. 479.

[21] *Ibid.*, p. 484.

[22] *The Economics of 1960* (London, 1944). See also "The Future of the Terms of Trade, the Problems of Long-term International Balance," *Proceedings of the International Economic Association*, September, 1950, and "Half-way to 1960," *Loyds Bank Review*, April, 1952.

tions indicated that the terms of trade of agricultural products would improve by 90 per cent between the 1925–34 average and 1960. Arthur Lewis worked out a statistical relationship between the price of raw materials and the volume of manufacturing production, and another for price of food as a function of manufacturing production and the volume of food production. He then calculated that if manufacturing output grows at 3.9 per cent while food production grows at 2 per cent per year, the price of food will fall by 8 per cent; but if manufacturing output grows at 5 per cent while food production grows at 1.3 per cent annually, the price of food will rise by 10 per cent. He estimated that raw material prices will be the same in 1960 as in 1950 if the lower rate of growth in manufacturing production takes place, but will be 10 per cent higher if the higher rate of growth of manufactures takes place. Putting food and raw material prices together, the terms of trade for primary products will move between a lower limit of a fall of 3 per cent and an upper limit of a rise of 10 per cent between 1950 and 1960.[23]

H. G. Aubrey, assuming that any gap between American supplies of major raw materials and demand for them would be filled by imports, projecting domestic production of these commodities, estimating their prices on the basis of prospective domestic supply and total demands, and making similar projections for American export prices, reached the conclusion that the ratio of prices of American imports to American exports would move substantially in favor of imports between 1948 and 1975.[24] A. E. Kahn, appraising the British data, reached the conclusion that terms of trade move in long waves rather than following a continuous trend.

Atallah summarizes the different views about the facts as follows: [25]

a) To some of the authors the movement of the terms of trade has been for a long time a decreasing trend to the detriment of the agricultural products. (Prebisch, Singer). For others long cyclical movements are discernible. (Clark, Kahn, Aubrey).

b) Those who see that the prices of the agricultural products have been and are still falling in relation to the prices of the industrial

[23] W. A. Lewis, "World Production, Prices and Trade, 1870–1960," *The Manchester School of Economic and Social Studies*, Vol. XX, 1952.

[24] H. G. Aubrey, "The Long-term Future of the United States Imports and its Implications for Primary Producing Countries," in *Papers and Proceedings of the American Economic Association*, May, 1955.

[25] M. K. Atallah, *op. cit.*, p. 20.

products explain this by the failure of the prices to adjust themselves to the productivities in agriculture and industry (Prebisch), by the relative decrease in demand for agricultural products and the relative increase in the demand for the industrial products, as well as by the downward rigidity of the agricultural supply (Singer).
c) The long cyclical movement in prices is explained by investment cycles which alternate between the agricultural and the industrial countries. One landmark in this cyclical movement is the Industrial Revolution which resulted in a heavy deterioration of the prices of industrial products. At present, a similar revolution on a world scale is taking place, and will result in an increase of agricultural prices of 90 per cent around 1960 (Clark).
d) According to one view, the Revolution will not be on such a big scale (Lewis). And according to another, the possible effects of the Revolution will be mitigated by the decrease in the demand for agricultural products which will be brought about by the technical improvements and the higher incomes (Kahn).
e) The factors thought to be most important in the long-run determination of the terms of trade, are the supply and the demand for agricultural and industrial products, and the different conclusions about their future movement depend on the different estimates of these magnitudes.

Among the more vehement critics of the underlying theories regarding deterioration of terms of trade is Professor Gottfried Haberler of Harvard University:[26]

The theory has become popular [Haberler says] that the terms of trade have shown a secular tendency to deteriorate for the underdeveloped countries, the so-called "peripheral" world; more precisely for the raw material producing or rather exporting countries.[27] This alleged historical trend is supposed to be the consequence of deep-seated factors and hence capable of confident extrapolation into the future. To my mind the alleged historical facts lack proof, their explanation is faulty, the extrapolation reckless and the policy conclusions irresponsible to put it mildly. . . . Can anyone seriously maintain that the long-run change in the terms of trade is the same for (a) agricultural exporters (Argentina, Uruguay), (b) mining countries (Bolivia), (c) coffee exporters (Brazil), (d) petroleum exporters (Venezuela).

Even if the evidence clearly showed that terms of trade of underdeveloped countries have deteriorated in the last century,

[26] Gottfried Haberler, "Critical Observations on some Current Notions in the Theory of Economic Development," *L'industria*, No. 2 (1957), p. 8.
[27] It should not be forgotten that there are some highly developed and industrialized countries whose exports consist largely of raw materials and foodstuffs. Australia and Denmark, for example, belong to this group.

Haberler continues, it would not be possible to reach policy conclusions from these facts, unless it is certain that the deterioration was likely to continue. Before one could make such a projection, one would need some kind of theory as to why the deterioration took place. Haberler denies the validity of the Prebisch-Singer theory that the prices of finished manufactured goods are kept high by monopolistic behavior of trade unions and cartels.[28]

This argument, as it is usually presented, rests on a confusion of absolute and relative prices. It is true that industrial progress in the developed countries rarely takes the form of constant money wages and money incomes associated with falling prices, but rather the form of constant (or even rising) prices associated with rising money wages. This may be bad from the point of view of stability and is undoubtedly unjust for fixed income receivers, but there is no evidence that it has changed relative prices as between industry and agriculture or between finished goods and raw materials.

Nor will Haberler accept an explanation in terms of "Engel's law," which states that as incomes rise the demand for foodstuffs rises more slowly than the demand for finished industrial products. Haberler admits that Engel's law is "one of the best established empirical generalizations in economics," but he contends that "it cannot bear the heavy burden which is placed on it by the theory under review." For although it applies to food in general, it does not apply to every kind of food, and it is by no means clear that rising income leads in every case to a relative decline in demand for industrial raw materials.

In conclusion, Haberler maintains that "enough has been said . . . to demonstrate that the theory of the secular deterioration of the terms of trade for the underdeveloped countries is completely unfounded and the policy recommendations based on it are devoid of any solid basis." But what Haberler has demonstrated is that the Prebisch-Singer thesis "ain't necessarily so." He has not proved definitively that the thesis could never be right. As is so often the case in economics, the discussion up to this point leads to the conclusion, "it depends."

The Atallah Analysis

But depends on what? This is the question Atallah tackled in his study, which is the most systematic yet attempted. He first sets up three alternative "models" based on reasonable assump-

[28] Haberler, *op. cit.*, p. 9.

tions about the operation of the underdeveloped economy. He next puts into these models the most satisfactory data that he can find. He then calculates what seems likely to happen to terms of trade. His results, although not completely destroying Haberler's conclusion that "it ain't *necessarily* so," show that it is *very likely* so.

Atallah's general model is a two-sector, two-commodities model. It divides the world economy between an agricultural sector producing raw materials and foodstuffs and an industrial sector producing finished manufactured goods. "Since the products which enter international trade are mainly raw materials and foodstuffs from the underdeveloped countries, and mainly manufactured finished goods from the industrialized countries," Atallah says, "the model might be a good approximation of the relations between these two types of countries also." [29] It should be noted, however, that since the model makes no place for minerals and petroleum, it is inapplicable to a good many underdeveloped countries.

Atallah presents three variants of this model. We shall consider only two of them, the ones that seem more realistic for underdeveloped countries. Atallah's Model II seems to fit those underdeveloped countries, such as the Philippines in recent decades or Indonesia in the nineteenth century, where population growth was accompanied by the occupation of additional land, so as to maintain traditional agricultural techniques and per capita output. If population growth is at a constant rate, the result will be a constant rate of increase in total agricultural production, and in this model, Atallah's agricultural production function "says simply that the agriculture production increases by a constant annual rate."

In his Model III, on the other hand, the quantity of land under cultivation is assumed to be fixed, whereas labor and capital are completely complementary to each other. Labor is assumed to be already redundant, and consequently total agricultural output depends solely on the supply of capital. This case would seem to fit "mature" underdeveloped countries, such as Indonesia (or more accurately, the island of Java) today. All the good agricultural land is already occupied; agriculture is carried on with traditional techniques, using small amounts of capital which are nevertheless essential to produce any output at all: seed, some fertilizer, simple irrigation systems, and simple tools. Under such conditions, the *marginal* productivity of *both* labor and capital

[29] Atallah, *op. cit.*, p. 22.

may be zero. Only a discontinuous jump to a completely different technique, and with much higher ratios of land and capital to labor, could bring any significant increase in output.

The equations in Atallah's Model II are as follows:[30]

1. The structural coefficients

   $\psi_0 =$ constant determined by the initial values

   $\psi_1 =$ income elasticity of demand for agricultural products

   $\psi_2 =$ price elasticity of demand for agricultural products

2. The relations

   Technical equations

$$P_1 = \alpha_0 e^{a_1 t} \tag{1}$$

$$P_2 = \beta_0 L_0 \beta_{2e} (\beta_1 + \lambda\beta_2) \, I_2^{1-\beta_2} \tag{2}$$

   Balance equation

$$S_1 + S_2 = \dot{C}_2 \tag{3}$$

   Behavioristic equations

$$S_1 = \sigma_1 p P_1 \tag{4}$$

$$S_2 = \sigma_2 P_2 \tag{5}$$

$$\frac{P_1}{P_2} = \psi_0 (pP_1 + P_2)^{\psi_1} P^{\psi_2} \tag{6}$$

Atallah's variables:

Endogenous:

$P_1 =$ volume of agricultural production

$P_2 =$ volume of industrial production

$S_1 =$ savings in the agricultural sector

$S_2 =$ savings in the industrial sector

$C_2 =$ capital stock in the industrial sector

$\dot{C}_2 =$ the change in capital stock, or investment

$P =$ the ratio of the price of agricultural products to the price of industrial products

Exogenous:

$L_0 =$ labor force in the industrial sector at the initial period

$t =$ time

Data (or structural coefficients):

$\alpha_1 =$ annual rate of technical progress in the agricultural sector

$\beta_2 =$ labor exponent in the industrial sector

[30] *Ibid.*, p. 28.

$\beta_1 =$ annual rate of technical progress in the industrial sector

$\lambda =$ annual rate of growth of the labor force in the industrial sector

$\sigma_1 =$ rate of savings in the agricultural sector

$\sigma_2 =$ rate of savings in the industrial sector

$\delta_1 =$ marginal propensity to consume agricultural products in both the agricultural and the industrial sectors

$\left.\begin{matrix} a_0 \\ \beta_0 \\ \delta_0 \end{matrix}\right\}$ Constants determined by the initial values

Equation (1) is the agricultural production function, which simply states that agricultural output grows at a constant rate. Equation (2) is the industrial production function. It is a "special Douglas production function," implying that an increase in average labor productivity is possible only through mechanization, which requires an increase in the ratio of capital to labor. However, to take account of the possibility of technological progress of a kind which would increase productivity of both labor and capital, Atallah introduces the factor $e^{\beta_1 t}$ to represent such technological progress. The labor force in the industrial sector is assumed to be proportional to the total population in this sector. Equation (3) states that net investment (capital accumulation) is the sum of savings in both industrial and agricultural sectors; in this model it is assumed that no capital accumulation is taking place in agriculture. Equation (4) makes savings depend on the money income of the agricultural sector, which is (agricultural output) times (price). Equation (5), similarly, makes savings in the industrial sector a different proportion of money income in that sector. The price of industrial production is assigned an index of 1; thus P_2 stands for both value and physical volume of output, the money income of the industrial sector. Equation (6) makes the ratio of demand for agricultural products to demand for industrial product depend on the incomes in both sectors and on the price structure.

Model III is as follows:

1. The new variables

Endogenous:

$C_1 =$ capital stock in the agricultural sector

$\dot{C}_1 =$ the change in the capital stock, or investment

The new data (or structural coefficients):

$a_2 =$ capital exponent in the agricultural sector

2. The relations

Technical equations

$$P_1 = \alpha_O e^{\alpha_1 t} C^{\alpha_2} \tag{1}$$
$$P_2 = \beta_O L_O{}^{\beta_{2_e}} (\beta_1 + \lambda\beta_2) t_{c_2}{}^{1 - \beta_2} \tag{2}$$

Balance equations

$$S_1 = \dot{C}_1 \tag{3}$$
$$S_2 = \dot{C}_2 \tag{4}$$

Behavioristic equations

$$S_1 = \sigma_1 p P_1 \tag{5}$$
$$S_2 = \sigma_2 P_2 \tag{6}$$
$$\frac{P_1}{P_2} = \psi_O (pP_1 + P_2)^{\psi_1} p^{\psi_2} \tag{7}$$

As already stated, Equation (1) here sets forth a different agricultural production function, in which labor and capital are assumed to be completely complementary. The industrial production function is unchanged. Net investment in agriculture is here assumed to depend on savings in the agricultural sector, whereas capital accumulation in the industrial sector depends on savings in the industrial sector. Thus this model comes closer to our "dualistic" model of the previous chapter than does Model II. Equations (5), (6), and (7) in Model III are identical with Equations (4), (5), and (6) in Model II.

The next step is to put empirical content into these equations, using the most satisfactory data which can be found—which admittedly are none too satisfactory. As an approximation to agricultural and industrial output, Atallah used Derksen's figures of national income in agricultural and industrial countries.[31] Capital coefficients are derived from figures presented by Tinbergen, Colin Clark, and Kuznets. The industrial labor force is obtained from the UN *Statistical Yearbook*. On the basis of figures presented by Tinbergen and Clark, Atallah chooses an annual rate of increase in efficiency of production of 1 per cent for both the industrial and agricultural sectors.

Atallah had some difficulty in choosing the labor and capital exponents (that is, the proportion of total output attributable to labor on the one hand and capital on the other). The most frequently cited figures are those of P. H. Douglas. These suggest

[31] J. B. D. Derksen, *Statistische en Econometrische Ondersoekingen* (3d ed.; 1956), p. 125.

a labor coefficient of 0.70 and capital coefficient of 0.30, implying that 70 per cent of total output can be attributed to labor and 30 per cent to capital. A recent study of the United States economy by Valavanis, however, which is broader than the Douglas study was, virtually reverses these figures, giving a labor coefficient of 0.20 and a capital coefficient of 0.70. "Although in most of our calculations I used Douglas' results" Atallah concludes "we shall make some alternatives with Valavanis' figures too, in order to inspect the effect of the reversed influences of labor and capital imports on the movement of our variables." [32]

Data provided by Kuznets are used to determine the rate of growth of the industrial labor force, and the UN material yields estimates of the rate of savings in the agricultural sectors. For the rate of savings in the industrial sector Atallah reverts once

TABLE 15-5.

The Terms of Trade, Calculated by Model II

	t	P_1	P_2	P
$\beta_2 = 0.70$	0	125	477	1
	10	138	612	1.03
$a_1 = 0.01$	20	152	785	1.06
	30	169	1005	1.05
$\beta_2 = 0.70$	0	125	477	1
	10	169	612	0.64
$a_1 = 0.03$	20	228	784	0.40
	30	308	1001	0.24
$\beta_2 = 0.30$	1	125	477	1
	10	138	655	1.10
$a_1 = 0.01$	20	152	906	1.22
	30	169	1260	1.32

again to Kuznets' data. Several studies are utilized in determining the income and price elasticity of demand for agricultural products. Some work of Gerhard Tintner is used to obtain the capital exponents in the agricultural production function.

Table 15-5 shows the results of calculations with Model II. Different assumptions are made regarding the rate of technological progress in the agricultural sector (a_1) and regarding the labor coefficient (β_2). With the Douglas labor coefficient and a relatively low rate of improvement in agricultural output (Box

[32] Atallah, *op. cit.*, p. 47.

1) the terms of trade of the agricultural sectors show some improvement over two decades followed by a slight decline in the third decade. In the second box, where a more rapid rate of progress in agriculture is assumed, the terms of trade of agriculture show a steady and drastic decline. Finally, in the third box, the Valavanis estimates of labor coefficient are used. Once again an improvement in terms of trade is obtained.

In giving solutions for Model III Atallah considered the influence of different capital coefficients in both sectors and of different rates of savings in the industrial sector (0.11 or 0.20). These variants give a number of possible solutions; but the interesting fact is that *all of them* show deteriorating terms of trade for the agricultural sector. Table 15-6 presents only those solutions which Atallah (and the present writer) considers most likely. The average propensity to consume agricultural goods is taken to be 0.5, with the income elasticity of demand for industrial products varying between 3 and 4. The capital-output

TABLE 15-6.

The Terms of Trade, Calculated by Model III with Different Values for a_2

		$a_2 = 0.25$						$a_2 = 0.15$					
		III_g			III_h			III_i			III_j		
	t	$\frac{C_1}{P_1} = 0.5$; $\frac{C_2}{P_2} = 4$			$\frac{C_1}{P_1} = 0.5$; $\frac{C_2}{P_2} = 3$			$\frac{C_1}{P_1} = 0.5$; $\frac{C_2}{P_2} = 4$			$\frac{C_1}{P_1} = 0.5$; $\frac{C_2}{P_2} = 3$		
		P_1	P_2	P	P_1	P_2	P	P_1	P_2	P	P_1	P_2	P
$\beta_2 = 0.70$	0	125	477	1	125	477	1	125	477	1	125	477	1
$\sigma_2 = 0.11$	10	164	595	0.67	164	621	0.71	153	595	0.79	153	621	0.82
	20	199	774	0.55	199	806	0.57	180	774	0.68	180	806	0.72
$\beta_2 = 0.30$	0	125	477	1	125	477	1	125	477	1	125	477	1
$\sigma_2 = 0.11$	10	164	644	0.72	164	676	0.76	153	644	0.85	153	676	0.89
	20	200	877	0.61	201	965	0.63	180	877	0.79	181	965	0.85
$\beta_2 = 0.70$	0	125	477	1	125	477	1	125	477	1	125	477	1
$\sigma_2 = 0.20$	10	164	638	0.71	164	658	0.74	153	638	0.84	153	658	0.86
	20	200	844	0.60	201	891	0.61	180	844	0.73	181	891	0.80

ratio in agriculture is taken at the very low figure of 0.5 to 1; the capital-output ratio in industry is taken at either 3 to 1 or 4 to 1. In cases 3G and 3H the ratio of industrial savings to industrial income is taken at 25 per cent; in the other two cases at 15 per cent. The interesting feature of the table is that in every case the terms of trade of the agriculture sector deteriorate over two decades.

Still more rapid deterioration of terms of trade will result if a higher capital-output ratio for agriculture is assumed, as in cases 3E and 3F, not shown here.

What does all this add up to? Atallah cautions against giving his results too much weight because of the simplifications involved:[33]

> The first simplification is the aggregation of all agricultural products in one group and all industrial products in another group. . . . The other simplification is the sharp division of the countries into two distinct groups very different from each other and very uniform within each of them. Beside the divergence which follows from the difference in the commodities, whether agricultural or industrial, which each country produces, there are likely to be specific differences, natural or institutional, which exist even when one commodity is concerned, and which may influence supply. The assumption of one production function for all agricultural products and countries, and for one production function for all industrial products and countries, which is very handy for the purpose of the analysis, has been at the price of this second heavy simplification.
>
> The uniformity of the expenditure patterns is the third major simplification we have made. The behaviour of the consumers differs within each country, though perhaps not as much as is sometimes believed. Price and income elasticities differ from one group of consumers to the other, apart from their differences from one commodity to the other. We have assumed, however, the same elasticities in both sectors. Moreover, we have assumed these elasticities to remain constant over time. This last assumption might constitute a special limitation on the accuracy of our calculations after the first decade.

Let us rephrase these conclusions in terms of our own interpretation of the two models. In agricultural countries where there is very little technological progress and where output barely keeps pace with population growth, there is *some possibility* that the terms of trade of agriculture will improve through time. Even in such countries, however, there is no assurance that *will* occur. In "mature" underdeveloped countries, with no good agricultural land still unoccupied, it is virtually certain that the

[33] *Ibid.*, p. 73.

terms of trade of the rural sector will deteriorate. These results depend, let us recall, on the assumptions made about the interactions of the variables and on our limited knowledge of the quantitative relationships involved. Let us also remember that the argument does not apply to underdeveloped countries exporting mainly minerals and petroleum products, or importing mainly food and agricultural raw materials.

Terms of Trade of the Rural Sector

Although there is, therefore, still room for doubt as to the logical necessity of the terms of trade of underdeveloped *countries* turning against them, the case for deteriorating terms of trade of the *rural sectors* of such countries seems quite clear. Imagine, for example, a typical underdeveloped country exporting, say, petroleum and plantation products; importing textiles, other consumer durables, and luxury foodstuffs; producing rice, fish, and handicraft products in the rural sector, and trading in these. Favorable developments in the industrialized sector (improved techniques, higher world market prices) will not increase the demand for the output of the rural sector. Indeed, in so far as the rise in income of the industrialized sector is shared by domestic workers, the demand for output of the rural sector may even fall, as these workers substitute "superior" imported consumers' goods for home-produced ones. On the other hand, any favorable development in the rural sector will increase the demand for industrial products imported into that sector (either from outside the country or from the industrial sector of the same country) and *reduce* the demand for output of the rural sector.

It is even possible that "Giffen's paradox" may operate. The favorable income-effect of a fall in rice prices, following upon increased yields, may be so strong that the demand for rice *falls* and demand for more "luxurious" imports (into the sector) increases. A large share of the incomes of everyone in the rural sector (including even the rice growers) is spent on rice. When rice is cheaper, they can afford to substitute other foodstuffs and manufactured goods which they consider superior. Thus improvements in rice culture benefit the rest of the world more than they do the rice-growing rural sector itself.

Moreover, when we confine our argument to the rural sector of underdeveloped countries, the differences in bargaining power between people in such sectors and workers in industrialized countries is more obvious. As Myint puts it: [34]

> The backward peoples have to contend with three types of monopolistic forces: in their role as unskilled labor they have to face the big foreign mining and plantation concerns who are monopolistic buyers of their labour; in their role as peasant producers they have to face a small group of exporting and processing firms who are monopolistic buyers of their crop; and in their role as consumers of imported commodities they have to face the same group of firms who are the monopolistic sellers or distributors of these commodities.

In advanced countries such tendencies toward monopolistic exploitation are offset by the development of "countervailing power," to use Professor Galbraith's term. No such countervailing power emerged in the underdeveloped countries before their achievement of independence. Even now workers and peasants have a long way to go before their organization will give them really effective bargaining power. As Myint says, "The first lesson is that some sources of countervailing power, like the co-operative societies, themselves need a fairly high degree of business-like behaviour and 'economic advance' and can only be fostered very slowly in the backward countries. The second lesson is that it is easier to redistribute existing income than to redistribute and stimulate economic activity by the use of countervailing power." Moreover, he points out, countervailing power is sometimes sought in the preservation of traditional social institutions, which do not provide equivalent bargaining power in an economic sense.

The deterioration of the terms of trade of the rural sector in its relations with the industrial sector of the same country must, of course, be reflected in the terms of trade of the *rural sector* with the rest of the world. Obviously, it is the latter which is important to most of the people in the country, since the great majority derives its income from the rural sector. In advanced countries, the primary sector accounts for a small share of income and employment and agricultural productivity is several times as high as in the rural sector of underdeveloped countries. It seems very likely, then, that there has been—and is still—a trend toward deteriorating terms of trade between the rural sector of underdeveloped countries and the rest of the world.

[34] Hla Myint, "An Interpretation of Economic Backwardness," *Oxford Economic Papers*, Vol. VI, No. 2, June, 1954.

16 Partial Theories: Balanced Growth, Discontinuities, and the "Big Push"

The last few years have brought a concentrated attack on "gradualism" and "incrementalism" as an approach to economic development policy. Any such approach is foredoomed to failure, the argument goes: by its very nature, the development process is a series of discontinuous "jumps." The functional relationships among the causal factors in economic growth are full of "lumps" and "discontinuities"; hence a minimum effort or "big push" is needed to overcome the original inertia of the stagnant economy and start it moving toward higher levels of productivity and income. To explain this basic concept, economists often resort to analogy. Leaning on a stalled car with gradually increasing weight will not get it started, for example; it needs a big push. In a *Submission* to the Special Senate Committee to Study the Foreign Aid Program, the Center of International Studies at M.I.T. used another analogy: [1]

> There is a minimum level of resources that must be devoted to . . . a development program if it is to have any chance of success. Launching a country into self-sustaining growth is a little like getting an airplane off the ground. There is a critical ground speed which must be passed before the craft can become airborne. . . .

Essentially, all the arguments in support of the "big push" are related to the old idea of "external economies": benefits which

[1] *The Objectives of U.S. Economic Assistance Programs* (Washington, D.C., 1957), p. 70.

accrue to the society as a whole, or to some members of it, in a fashion that does not bring a direct return to the investor concerned.[2] The basic concept is thus an old one. What is new is the importance attached to it in theories of development.

Rosenstein-Rodan and the Three Indivisibilities

One of the earliest and most often cited statements of the importance of discontinuities, or external economies, in economic development was Paul N. Rosenstein-Rodan's article published in 1943.[3] In this early statement, Rosenstein-Rodan stressed the limitations imposed by the size of the market. More recently, he has restated his argument in terms of "three indivisibilities."[4] The stress upon external economies, Rosenstein-Rodan argues, is a major mark of the difference between static theory and a theory of growth. In static theory, external economies are relatively unimportant. But in a theory of development,

. . . external economies abound because given the inherent imperfection of the investment market, imperfect knowledge and risks, pecuniary and technological external economies have a similarly disturbing effect on the path towards equilibrium. While the distinction between pecuniary and technological external economies becomes practically

[2] This somewhat loose and general definition of external economies has been chosen deliberately over the more rigorous definitions available in the literature. For economic development the important consideration is that certain investments are clearly "profitable" for the society as a whole, but are unprofitable to the individual private investor because the institutional framework does not permit him to charge a price for the by-product benefits his investment brings. It has not seemed worthwhile to digress here on the history of ideas about external economies or to try to unravel the contemporary discussion of the concept. As Francis Bator has pointed out, Marshall and Pigou used the concept to explain decreasing costs in an industry operating under conditions of purely competitive equilibrium—a concern rather different from our own. Bator also shows that these external economies reduce to technological factors which permit suppliers to the industry to produce and sell more cheaply as their market grows. Bator himself prefers the more general "modern version" which treats external economies as part of "a more general doctrine of direct interaction" relating to "interdependences that are external to the price system, hence unaccounted for by market valuations." This definition is tantamount to our own. See Francis Bator, "The Anatomy of Market Failure" and "On External Economies" (CENIS, 1958); and William Fellner, concluding chapter of *Investment Criteria for Economic Growth* (CENIS, 1956).

[3] P. N. Rosenstein-Rodan, "Industrialization of Eastern and Southeastern Europe," *The Economic Journal*, 1943.

[4] P. N. Rosenstein-Rodan, *Notes on the Theory of the "Big Push,"* M.I.T., CIS, March, 1957.

irrelevant in the theory of growth, three different kinds of indivisibilities and external economies may be distinguished.

1) Indivisibilities in the production function especially the indivisibility of supply of Social Overhead Capital (lumpiness of "capital").
2) "Indivisibility" of Demand (complementarity of demand).
3) "Indivisibility" (kink in the) Supply of Savings."

[Because of these indivisibilities] Proceeding "bit by bit" will not add up in its effects to the sum total of the single bits. A minimum quantum of investment is a necessary (though not sufficient) condition of success. This is in a nutshell the contention of the theory of the big push.

Thus in contradiction to traditional static equilibrium theory, development theory maintains that nature does make jumps (*natura fecit saltus*). Why the difference? Because development theory is more realistic in taking account of indivisibilities and "non-appropriabilities" in the production functions, because a growth theory must examine the *path* to equilibrium and not just the equilibrium conditions, and because in underdeveloped countries, markets—especially investment markets—are more imperfect than in developed countries.

Indivisibilities in the Production Function (Lumpiness of Capital)

Social overhead capital (power, transport, communications, housing, etc.) is the most important instance of indivisibility and external economies on the supply side. Its most important products "are investment opportunities created in other industries." Moreover, they usually require "a great minimum size," so that "excess capacity will be unavoidable over the initial period in underdeveloped countries." Social overhead capital is irreversible in time. It must precede other directly productive investment. Its services cannot be imported. Investments in the "infrastructure"—to use another common term for social overhead capital—have a high minimum durability, a long gestation period, and a minimal "industry mix" of several different kinds of public utilities.

Indivisibility of Demand

The indivisibility of demand was stressed in Rosenstein-Rodan's original article and later given wider publicity by Professor Ragnar Nurkse.[5] The basic idea is that investment decisions are in-

[5] Ragnar Nurkse, *Problems of Capital Formation in Underdeveloped Countries* (Oxford, 1953).

terdependent, and individual investment projects have high risk because of uncertainty as to whether their product will find a market. Rosenstein-Rodan uses an example which has by now become famous:

> Let us restate our old example, at first for a closed economy. If a hundred workers who were in disguised unemployment (i.e., with marginal productivity of their labor equal to zero) in an underdeveloped country were put into a shoe factory, their wages would constitute additional income. If the newly employed workers spent all of their additional income on shoes they produce, the shoe factory would find a market and would succeed. In fact, however, they would not spend all of their additional income on shoes; there is no "easy" solution of creating in this way an additional market. The risk of not finding a market reduces the incentive to invest—the shoe factory investment project will probably be abandoned. Let us vary the example: instead of a hundred (unemployed) workers in one shoe factory, let us put ten thousand workers in say one hundred factories (and farms) who between them will produce the bulk of such (wage) goods on which the newly employed workers will spend their wages. What was not true in the case of one single shoe factory will become true for the complementary system of one hundred factories (and farms). The new producers would be each others' customers and would verify Say's Law by creating an additional market. The complementarity of demand would reduce the risk of not finding a market. Reducing such interdependent risks increases naturally the incentive to invest.

Rosenstein-Rodan also points out that a minimum quantum of investment is needed to produce a "bundle" of wage goods on which additionally employed workers can spend their income. In general, unless there is assurance that the necessary complementary investments will occur, any single investment project may be considered too risky to be undertaken at all. There is, in other words, an indivisibility in the *decision-making* process. The present writer would be inclined to stress this indivisibility, perhaps more than Rosenstein-Rodan does. Allocation of capital on the basis of individual estimates of short-run returns on various marginal investment projects is the very process by which underdeveloped countries got where they are. The basic reason for government action to promote development is that each of a set of individual private investment decisions may seem unattractive in itself, whereas a large-scale investment program undertaken as a unit may yield substantial increases in national income. True, the government may be able to arrange for this lump-sum investment to be made by groups of private entrepreneurs; whether it should be done this way or through public investment is a matter of administrative convenience, not of economics. But the needed investment is unlikely to take place without government intervention in the decision-making process.

Rosenstein-Rodan makes a related point in referring to the "psychological indivisibilities" involved in development. "Isolated and small efforts may not add up to a sufficient impact on growth," he maintains, and "an atmosphere of development effervescence may also arise only with a minimum speed or size of investment."

Finally, Rosenstein-Rodan agrees with the writers discussed in the previous chapter that international trade is not always a means of avoiding the necessity of a "big push." International trade may reduce the range of fields in which the big push is required; some of the needed wage goods, for example, can be imported. But the history of the nineteenth century is evidence enough that trade does not eliminate the need altogether.

The Leibenstein Theory

A more systematic treatment of the "minimum effort" thesis has been provided by Dr. Harvey Leibenstein. In outlining this theory, let us begin with an adaptation of one of his simple diagrams illustrating the relationships among population size, investment, and *per capita* income. Figure 16-1 represents the adaptation to our own purposes of Leibenstein's figure 3-2. *Per capita* income is measured on the vertical axis, population size on the horizontal axis. The straight line $x = z$ represents the level of *per capita* income at which there is neither population growth nor capital accumulation.[6]

We are applying the diagram only to the rural sector of the underdeveloped economy. The curves r_1, r_2, r_3, etc., represent the relationship between average output and income and size of population for varying stocks of resources, including land. We

[6] Leibenstein presents other diagrams in which the zero investment line is above the zero population line; but we consider the assumption that complete absence of population growth is accompanied by absence of capital accumulation is more realistic for a peasant economy. Indeed, there is some evidence that in Asian countries a certain amount of capital accumulation took place, even in the absence of population growth, in the form of simple transportation equipment, roads, housing, irrigation systems, and the like. However, for simplicity we shall assume that prior to the beginning of industrialization there is no population growth and no net capital accumulation. See Harvey Leibenstein, *Economic Backwardness and Economic Growth* (New York, 1957).

begin with population at P_1, and *per capita* income at $O_a = P_1E_1$. We now introduce industrial investment in the capital-intensive sector. This investment will withdraw a small amount of population from the rural sector, and perhaps increase somewhat the resources available to the rural sector, in the form of improved roads and the like. Thus the impact effect of the commencement of industrialization is a movement to the left along the popula-

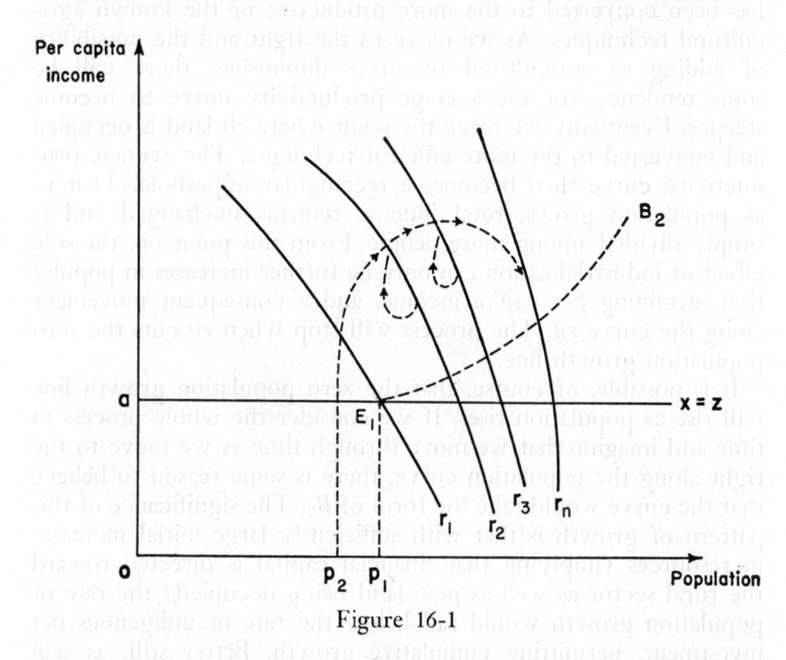

Figure 16-1

tion curve, which in itself tends to raise *per capita* income, and a small shift in the average productivity curve to the right, r_2. On both accounts *per capita* income tends to rise. However, the result (or at least the accompaniment) of rising *per capita* income is an increase in population. Some net investment will now take place, mainly in the form of clearing new land, perhaps accompanied by some shift from "slash and burn" to irrigated agriculture.[7] Thus the average productivity curve shifts farther to the right, to r_3.

As population grows, *per capita* income will tend to move

[7] It is perhaps worth noting that in the tropics improved land meets Professor Hayek's definition of capital; it is a "non-permanent productive resource."

downward along this curve. However, with the next wave of industrial investment, the process is repeated. There is a new shift to the left along the population curve, a new increase in amount of resources immediately available, and a new incentive to occupy new land and improve agricultural techniques.

This process continues so long as the industrial investment takes place, and so long as good new land is available or not all land has been converted to the more productive of the known agricultural techniques. As we move to the right and the possibility of adding to agricultural resources diminishes, there will be some tendency for the average productivity curve to become steeper. Eventually we reach the point where all land is occupied and converted to the more efficient technique. The average productivity curve then becomes a rectangular hyperbola. That is, as population grows, total income remains unchanged and is simply divided among more people. From this point on, the sole effect of industrialization can only be further increases in population, declining *per capita* income, and a consequent movement along the curve *rn*. The process will stop when *rn* cuts the zero population growth line.

It is possible, of course, that the zero population growth line will rise as population rises. If we consider the whole process in time and imagine that we move through time as we move to the right along the population curve, there is some reason to believe that the curve would take the form of B_2. The significance of this pattern of growth is that with sufficiently large initial increases in resources (implying that financial capital is directed toward the rural sector as well as new land being occupied) the rate of population growth would fall below the rate of indigenous net investment, permitting cumulative growth. Better still, as will become more apparent below, would be an initial rate of investment in *both* sectors that would permit a jump to levels of *per capita* income at which steady growth could be maintained from domestic savings and investment.

This point can be illustrated by an adaptation of Leibenstein's figure 3-5. (Figure 16-2.) It is here assumed that as income rises and population grows beyond the present level, the *per capita* income at which population growth falls to zero also falls—a quite reasonable assumption from a demographic point of view. At the same time, the zero investment line is considered to rise with *per capita* income and population. If the "demonstration effect" is operative, this assumption is also reasonable; after a lag, consumption patterns are adjusted to the higher income levels, and when income *falls* again, zero saving is reached at higher levels of income than before. The line *mm* represents the level of *per capita* income at which the rate of population growth falls below the rate of capital accumulation, permitting cumulative growth.

It is apparent that any initial displacement through industrial investment which leaves the system within the area *ezx*, or within the area *exmn*, involves a return to the initial equilibrium position

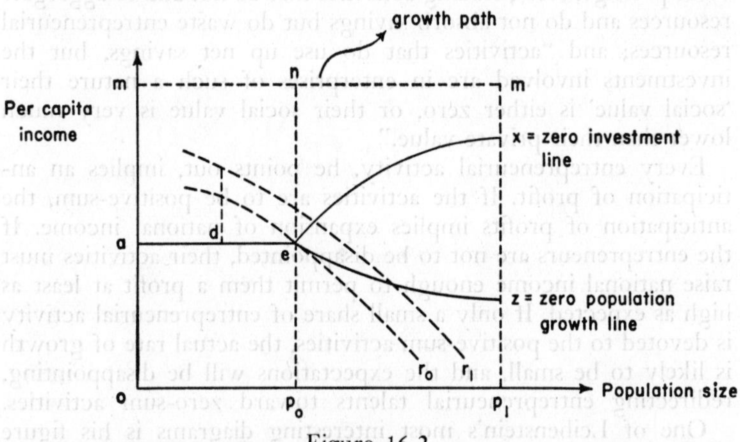

Figure 16-2

e. The former area is one of net disinvestment, which must lead eventually to net decline in population and a return to *e*. The latter area involves net investment, but at a rate slower than population growth, so that *per capita* incomes fall after the initial rise, forcing the system back to *e*.

On the other hand, a simultaneous reduction in the population of the rural sector, such as is involved in the movement from *e* to *d*, combined with an increase in investment in the rural sector which would raise the average productivity curve to r_1, would bring the rural sector into the range of cumulative growth.

Leibenstein also shows that at low levels of income the optimum degree of specialization is rather low. "It is the highly *efficient* special-purpose equipment that, for the most part, is subject to indivisibilities at points where cost per units of capital is quite high. It is the degree of indivisibility per unit of efficiency that matters." This relationship complicates the problem of finding efficient techniques for the degree of specialization called for at the low levels of income in the rural sector.

Leibenstein provides an ingenious explanation of the "vicious circle" with regard to entrepreneurship in underdeveloped countries. The problem, he says, is not that entrepreneurial ability is lacking in these countries. Rather, it is that the conditions of underdeveloped countries incline entrepreneurs toward engaging in "zero-sum" games (those which do not raise national income as a whole) rather than "positive-sum" games. Among the zero-sum games are "non-trading activities in order to secure for their interest a greater monopolistic position, increased political power, more prestige, etc."; trading activities that do not add to aggregate resources and do not absorb savings but do waste entrepreneurial resources; and "activities that do use up net savings, but the investments involved are in enterprises of such a nature their 'social value' is either zero, or their social value is very much lower than their private value."

Every entrepreneurial activity, he points out, implies an anticipation of profit. If the activities are to be positive-sum, the anticipation of profits implies expansion of national income. If the entrepreneurs are not to be disappointed, their activities must raise national income enough to permit them a profit at least as high as expected. If only a small share of entrepreneurial activity is devoted to the positive-sum activities, the actual rate of growth is likely to be small, and the expectations will be disappointing, redirecting entrepreneurial talents toward zero-sum activities.

One of Leibenstein's most interesting diagrams is his figure 15-1. (Figure 16-3 below.) We start with *per capita* income at *oa*. If enough investment is injected into the system to raise *per*

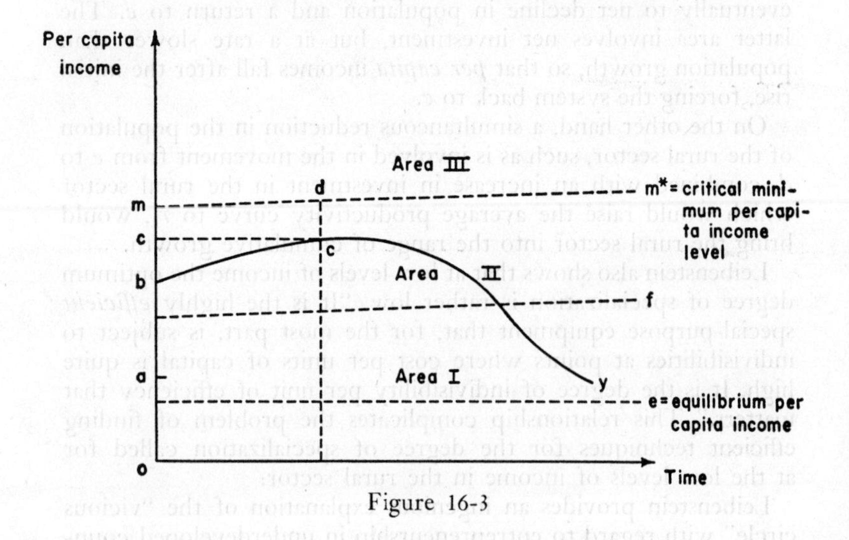

Figure 16-3

capita income immediately to *om*, sustained growth will occur. However, it would be cheaper for the investor (in this context, perhaps a foreign government undertaking a foreign aid program) to make the injection in two stages. The initial injection might be enough to raise income to *ob;* then at time *t*, the second injection could be made to raise *per capita* income by *cd*, to the critical minimum.

Leibenstein readily admits that his theory of the critical minimum effort is an empirical one. In his figure 8-1a (Figure 16-4)

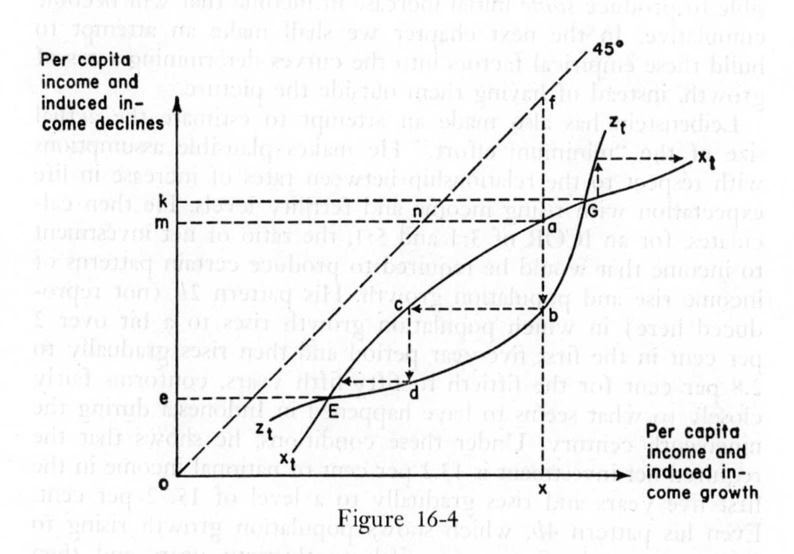

Figure 16-4

the curve X_tX_t represents all income-raising forces, the curve Z_tZ_t all income-depressing forces. Induced increases and decreases are measured from the 45° line. Thus with an income equal to *X*, the income-raising forces are *af* while income-depressing factors are *bf*, income will revert to *E*. Indeed, the relationship of the income-raising and income-depressing forces is such that starting from an equilibrium position, *E*, no investment program which fails to raise *per capita* income to the level, *G*, will produce sustained economic growth. It is of course possible to construct diagrams to show cases in which no growth can occur at all, or in which any initial shock bringing a small increase in *per capita* income would produce steady growth. The reason for assuming that underdeveloped countries in fact face a position where a substantial increase in investment is necessary to yield steady growth relates to the underlying theory of population growth and to actual evidence with respect to internal diseconomies of scale due to indivisibility of the factors of production, other indivisibilities with regard to investment decisions, external diseconomies due to external interdependencies, and the like. Leibenstein has also shown, however, that there is a biological maximum to the (continued) rate of population growth, in the neighborhood of 3 per cent. Consequently, given a sufficiently large volume of technical and capital assistance, it is always possible to produce *some* initial increase in income that will become cumulative. In the next chapter we shall make an attempt to build these empirical factors into the curves determining rates of growth, instead of having them outside the picture.

Leibenstein has also made an attempt to estimate the actual size of the "minimum effort." He makes plausible assumptions with respect to the relationship between rates of increase in life expectation with rising income and fertility levels. He then calculates, for an ICOR of 3:1 and 5:1, the ratio of net investment to income that would be required to produce certain patterns of income rise and population growth. His pattern 2*b* (not reproduced here) in which population growth rises to a bit over 2 per cent in the first five-year period and then rises gradually to 2.8 per cent for the fiftieth to fifty-fifth years, conforms fairly closely to what seems to have happened in Indonesia during the nineteenth century. Under these conditions, he shows that the required net investment is 13.2 per cent of national income in the first five years and rises gradually to a level of 15.72 per cent. Even his pattern 4*b*, which shows population growth rising to 2.42 per cent in the twenty-fifth to thirtieth years and then tapering off, requires investment of 13.2 per cent of national income in the first five years, rising to 14.52 per cent, and then dropping to 13.08 per cent in the fiftieth to fifty-fifth years.

The Low-level Equilibrium Trap

A very similar theory was developed almost simultaneously by Richard Nelson. Since Nelson's version of the theory is presented in an article, it is already highly compressed and hence difficult to summarize. Once again, we suggest that readers who find this summary too sketchy to be persuasive turn to the original article.[8]

Nelson uses an essentially simple model with three equations.

[8] R. R. Nelson, "A Theory of the Low-Level Equilibrium Trap," *American Economic Review*, December, 1956, pp. 894–908.

First, there is an income determination equation. This is fundamentally the same as the "production function" which kept recurring in the various models in Part 1: income depends on the stock of capital, the size of the population, and the level of technique. (The labor force is assumed to bear a constant relationship to the size of the population.) Second, net investment consists of savings-created capital plus additions to the amount of land under cultivation. The savings-created portion is roughly the same as investment in the industrial sector; it represents additions to stock of tools and equipment. No such investment will take place until income rises above the subsistence level, after which it rises with per capita income. The amount of new land brought under cultivation tends to increase with the population, but cultivating fresh areas becomes more difficult as good land becomes scarce. There is a "floor" to disinvestment; "one cannot eat torn-up railroad track no matter how hungry one gets." Finally, there is a population growth equation:

> In areas with low per capita incomes short-run changes in the rate of population growth are caused by changes in the death rate, and changes in the death rate are caused by changes in the level of per capita income. Yet once per capita income reaches a level well above subsistence requirements, further increases in per capita income have a negligible effect on the death rate. The result is a curve of population growth similar in shape to the dP/P curves [in Figure 16-5. The sharp break] is artificial but simplifies exposition . . . A shift in income distribution towards greater equality (or improved medical technique) shifts the function to the left along the Y/P axis.

With these three sets of relationships it is easy to see that an economy may be "trapped" at a low level of income, as illustrated in Figure 16-5. It is necessary only for the rate of increase in population, dP/P, to exceed the rate of increase in income, dY/Y, at a level of national income close to subsistence. For the intersection of the dY/Y and dP/P curves at a level of per capita income, Y/P, equal to S provides a stable equilibrium at that level. Any tendency for income to rise leads to a more rapid increase in population, forcing the economy back to S.

The conditions "conducive to trapping," Nelson points out, are (1) a high correlation between the level of per capita income and the rate of population growth; (2) a low propensity to direct additional per capita income to increasing per capita investment; (3) scarcity of uncultivated arable land; and (4) inefficient production methods. Clearly, in a good many underdeveloped countries, these conditions have been met in the past.

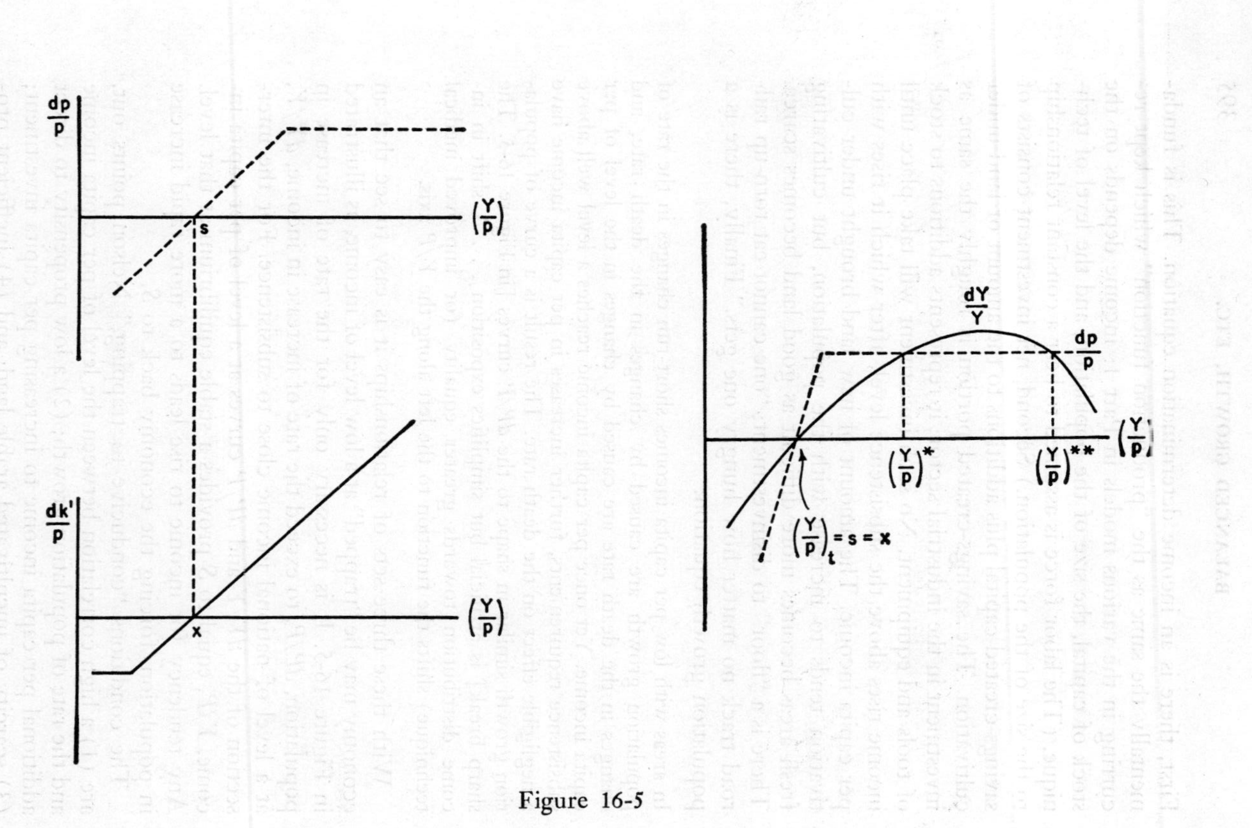

Figure 16-5

Getting out of the trap requires increasing the rate of growth of income to levels higher than the rate of increase in population. The surest way to do this—returning to Leibenstein—is to promote rates of growth of national income in excess of 3 per cent per year. If a jump can be made to the point, Y/P^*, sustained growth will take place, without further government action, until the high level, Y/P^{**}, is reached.

Balanced versus Unbalanced Growth

In presenting his version of the minimum effort thesis, Ragnar Nurkse advocates "a frontal attack . . . a wave of capital investments in a number of different industries," which he calls "balanced growth."[9] Hans Singer and Albert Hirschman have criticized Nurkse's formulation; they insist that what is needed is not balanced growth but a strategy of judiciously unbalanced growth.

The Nurkse Thesis

Nurkse's basic argument resembles Rosenstein-Rodan's; indeed he cites Rodan's famous example of the shoe factory to support his case. Low real income, Nurkse says, "is a reflection of low productivity, which in turn is due largely to lack of capital. The lack of capital is a result of the small capacity to save, and so the circle is complete." The inducement to invest, in turn, is limited by the size of the market—a "modern variant" of Adam Smith's dictum that "the division of labour is limited by the extent of the market." But a crucial determinant of the size of the market is productivity; capacity to buy means capacity to produce. And productivity "depends largely, though by no means entirely, on the degree to which capital is used in production. . . . But, for any individual entrepreneur, the use of capital is inhibited, to start with, by the small size of the market." Another vicious circle.

How to escape? We cannot count on individual investment decisions to do the trick. "Even though in economically backward areas Say's Law may be valid in the sense that there is no deflationary gap, it never is valid in the sense that the output of any single industry, newly set up with capital equipment, can create its own demand." Technical discontinuities call for "jumps" in the rate of output, but "the small and inelastic demand in a

[9] Nurkse, *op. cit.*, chap. I; see also, p. 5.

low-income country tends to make such jumps risky, if not altogether unpromising."

Thus the only way out of the dilemma is "more or less synchronized application of capital to a wide range of different industries. Here is an escape from the deadlock; here the result is an over-all enlargement of the market. . . . Most industries catering for mass consumption are complementary in the sense that they provide a market for, and thus support, each other. . . . The case for 'balanced growth' rests on the need for a 'balanced diet.' "

This is the essence of Nurkse's argument. Two subsidiary points might be noted in passing. First, Nurkse contends (correctly, in the opinion of the present writer) that the choice between public and private enterprise for achieving the required bundle of investment is mainly a matter of administrative expediency. Second, Nurkse joins the growing list of "development economists" who deny that international trade provides an automatic escape from the limitations of the domestic market: "To push exports of primary commodities in the face of an inelastic and more or less stationary demand would not be a promising line of long-run development." He makes a case for building up import-replacing industries behind a tariff wall and points out that the *ultimate* result need not be a reduction in imports—even of goods first receiving protection. He cites Canada for illustration: there "textile manufacturing was one of the first industries to develop, with the aid of tariff protection from 1879 on; yet Canada to-day is one of the world's biggest importers of textile manufactures." [10]

The Singer Critique

Hans Singer has expressed grave doubts about the applicability of this thesis. To understand the problem of balanced growth, Singer asserts, "we have to construct some kind of fundamental structural picture—model if you like—of an underdeveloped country." [11] He defines an underdeveloped country as one with

[10] *Ibid.*, pp. 10, 11, 22. In putting his argument in this unqualified manner, Nurkse opens himself to Haberler's criticisms of the arguments regarding deteriorating terms of trade. Not *all* primary products face an inelastic demand; there is good reason to believe that the demand for natural rubber or petroleum would prove highly elastic in face of significant price reductions. There is still less reason to believe that demand for such products remains "more or less stationary" in an expanding world market.

[11] Hans Singer, "The Concept of Balanced Growth and Economic Development: Theory and Facts," University of Texas Conference on Economic Development, April, 1958, pp. 4, 6.

70 to 90 per cent of the employed population in agriculture, and adds, "Arthur Lewis has defined the process of economic growth as one of transforming a country from a 5 percent saver to a 15 percent saver. We can, with equal justice, define the process as one of transforming a country from an 80 percent farmer to 15 percent farmer." The high proportion of population in farming is another of the vicious circles: it reflects low productivity. "The low level of productivity in farming decrees that the bulk of the people must be in farming in order to feed and clothe themselves, and that they have little to spare over and above their own needs." By writ of Engel's law, a high percentage of low incomes is spent on food and essential clothing, and the demand for other things is "limited to a very small percentage of a very small income." There is thus only a tiny market for these other things and investment in producing them is not attractive. Underdeveloped countries are also, as a rule, net exporters of agricultural goods and net importers of other products.

To make matters worse, productivity in agriculture is significantly lower than productivity in the small industrial sector. "In fact for a surprising number of countries figures come remarkably close to a constant relation of the form, $A = 2/3\ N$, where '*A*' is output per employed person in agriculture and '*N*' is output per employed person in the economy as a whole." From this fact follows an arithmetic law "of considerable political and emotional significance: if an 80 percent farmer economy produces only two thirds of its national per capita average in the agricultural sector, the differential between the agricultural sector and the non-agricultural sector will be much larger than will be the case in a 15 percent farmer economy (i.e., a typical advanced economy) which also produces two thirds of its national average in the agricultural sector. In fact, in the underdeveloped country output per worker outside agriculture compared with agricultural output per worker would be in the ratio of 3:1." Thus a transformation from mainly agriculture to mainly non-agriculture is not only an essential part of the development process, but this structural change also has a "multiplier effect." "As the levels of productivity and of real demand and markets rise, the structural change from an 80 percent farmer economy towards a 15 percent farmer economy, made possible by this rise, will in its turn generate forces which will themselves tend to raise productivity and real incomes." This hen-and-egg riddle, Singer maintains, is "the starting point of the doctrine of balanced growth." The doctrine might be expressed by paraphrasing a metaphor coined in a different context: "100 flowers may grow where a single flower would wither away for lack of nourishment."

Singer agrees that the slogan, "stop thinking piecemeal and start thinking big" is sound advice for underdeveloped countries, but he also feels that there are "several areas of doubt" about the balanced growth theory in its Rodan-Nurkse form. First, if that is interpreted to counsel underdeveloped countries to embark on large and varied packages of *industrial* investment, with no attention to agricultural productivity, it can lead to trouble. Engel's law "certainly does *not* say that the demand for food does not increase at all" when incomes rise, especially when incomes rise from the low levels existing in underdeveloped countries. The big push in industry may have to be accompanied by a big push in agriculture as well, if the country is not to run short of foodstuffs and agricultural raw materials during the transition to an industrialized society that could perhaps obtain these goods in exchange for industrial exports. Once this fact is admitted, the balanced growth doctrine sounds more like the orthodox theory that "structural change must rest on a foundation of raising productivity within the existing structure . . . until real incomes have risen to a level which justifies structural change."

But when we start talking about varied investment packages for industry and "major additional blocks of investment in agriculture" at the same time, we run into serious doubts about the capacity of underdeveloped countries to follow the balanced growth path. Singer quotes Marcus Fleming: "whereas the balanced growth doctrine assumes that the relationship between industries is for the most part complementary, the limitation of factor supply assures that the relationship is for the most part competitive." [12] Singer adds: "the resources required for carrying out the policy of balanced growth . . . are of such an order of magnitude that a country disposing of such resources would in fact not be underdeveloped." The doctrine is premature rather than wrong, Singer concludes; it is applicable to a subsequent stage of sustained growth rather than to the breaking of a deadlock. For *launching* growth "it may well be better development strategy to concentrate available resources on types of investment which help to make the economic system more elastic, more capable of expansion under the stimulus of expanded markets and expanding demand." [13] He instances investment in social overhead capital and

[12] Marcus Fleming, "External Economies and the Doctrine of Balanced Growth," *The Economic Journal*, June, 1958.
[13] Singer, *op. cit.*, p. 10.

removal of specific bottlenecks as examples of such "strategic" investments.

The fundamental trouble with the balanced growth doctrine, Singer concludes, is its failure to come to grips with the true problem of underdeveloped countries, the shortage of resources. "Think Big" is sound advice to underdeveloped countries but "Act Big," is unwise counsel if it spurs them to effort to do more than their resources permit.

One final point of Singer's will serve as a bridge to our next section. The balanced growth doctrine, he says, assumes that an underdeveloped country starts from scratch. In reality, every underdeveloped country starts from a position that reflects previous investment decisions and previous development. Thus at any point of time there are highly desirable investment programs which are not in themselves balanced investment packages, but which represent unbalanced investment to complement existing imbalance. And once such an investment is made, a new imbalance is likely to appear which will require still another "balancing" investment, and so on. Is this not a perfectly good way to develop?

Hirschman's Strategy of Economic Development

Albert Hirschman, at any rate, thinks that it is. He carries Singer's idea further, and contends that *deliberate unbalancing* of the economy, in accordance with a predesigned strategy, is the *best* way to achieve economic growth.[14]

On many points, Hirschman agrees with both Nurkse and Singer. He does not deny the need for a big push. On the contrary, he argues that "ability to invest" is the one serious bottleneck in underdeveloped countries; he readily agrees that ability to invest depends mainly on how much investment has already been made. "The ability to invest," he says, "is acquired and increased primarily by practice; and the amount of practice depends in fact on the size of the modern sector of the economy. In other words, an economy secretes abilities, skills, and attitudes needed for further development roughly in proportion to the size of the sector where these attitudes are being inculcated." He stresses the "complementarity" among investments no less than Nurkse, maintaining that it is of much greater importance in underdeveloped than in advanced countries. He also agrees that analysis based on static assumptions can be very misleading when applied to underdeveloped countries. Thus he says of Aubrey's

[14] Albert Hirschman, *The Strategy of Economic Development* (New York, 1958), p. 36.

argument, that industrialization should take the form of small industries in small towns in order to economize on overhead capital outlays,[15]

> This position is of course entirely valid on the assumption that the supply of capital is fixed. But if we drop this assumption and let ourselves be guided by the rule that during a prolonged phase the essence of development strategy consists in maximizing induced decision-making, then we would favor rather than oppose the establishment of industries in cities precisely because it compels additional or complementary capital formation that otherwise might never have taken place. Obviously, what we are opposing here is not the principle of husbanding capital in general but a policy which in the name of this principle would reduce the stimuli and pressures toward additional capital formation that might emanate from the investments of a given period. Such a policy would . . . "economize" on capital *formation* rather than on capital!

Hirschman also agrees with Singer that application of the balanced growth theory "requires huge amounts of precisely those abilities which we have identified as likely to be very limited in supply in underdeveloped countries." Indeed he quotes an earlier statement of Singer's: "The advantages of multiple development may make interesting reading for economists, but they are gloomy news indeed for the underdeveloped countries." [16] He characterizes the balanced growth doctrine as "the application to underdevelopment of a therapy originally devised for an underemployment situation." In an advanced country during depression, "the industries, machines, managers, and workers, as well as the consumption habits" are all present; in underdeveloped countries "this is obviously not so."

But if we need a big push to get an underdeveloped country off dead center, while at the same time such a country cannot manage simultaneously a balanced "investment package" in industry and the needed investment in agricultural improvements, what are we to do? Hirschman answers: undertake a big push in strategically selected industries or sectors of the economy. After all, he points out, the industrialized countries did not get where they are through "balanced" growth. True, if you compare the economy of the United States in 1950 with the situation in 1850 you will find that many things have grown; but not everything

[15] H. Aubrey, "Small Industry in Economic Development," *Social Research*, September, 1951.

[16] Hans Singer, "Economic Progress in Underdeveloped Countries." Cf. Hirschman, *op. cit.*, chap. III.

grew at the same rate throughout the whole century. Development has proceeded "with growth being communicated from the leading sectors of the economy to the followers, from one industry to another, from one firm to another."[17] Having concluded that the market mechanism will not guarantee growth in the now underdeveloped countries, we need not take "the defeatist view that growth has to be balanced from the start or cannot take place at all."

One of the shortcomings of traditional theory as a basis for development policy is the underlying assumption that the profitability of different investment projects is independent of the order in which they are undertaken. In fact, Hirschman maintains, such need not be the case. He gives the following example: suppose there are two projects, M and N, requiring equal amounts of capital and yielding 10 per cent and 8 per cent respectively. Suppose further that the interest rate stands at 9 per cent. If investment is left to the market, only project M will be undertaken. Once it is in operation the return on project N rises to 10 per cent and so it, too, is launched. But it could perfectly well be, Hirschman argues, that if N had been undertaken first, despite the temporary loss in terms of market considerations, the return on M would rise to 14 per cent. Thus investors as a group—or the society as a whole—would be better off if they reversed the process that would result from independent market decisions. Moreover, the subsequent rate of growth would be faster; for once N was in place M would be rushed to completion, and in the next period other investments would become profitable because M was in operation, and so on. Hirschman admits that this example is artificial, but states that it embodies "a number of concepts that are recurring throughout this essay: the difference between 'permissive' and 'compulsive' sequences, the possible rationality of violating 'first things first' norms and the fact that the difficulty of taking a development decision is not necessarily proportional to the amount of capital it requires."

Hirschman analyzes these concepts in more systematic fashion with respect to the relationship between "directly productive activities," *DPA*, and social overhead capital, *SOC*. For this purpose he makes use of a production function diagram, reproduced here as Figure 16-6. Units of new investment in *SOC* are measured on the vertical axis, and units of new investment in *DPA* on the horizontal axis. The curves are "isopods" showing various quantities of *SOC* and *DPA* which will give the same gross na-

[17] Hirschman, *op. cit.*, pp. 62–63.

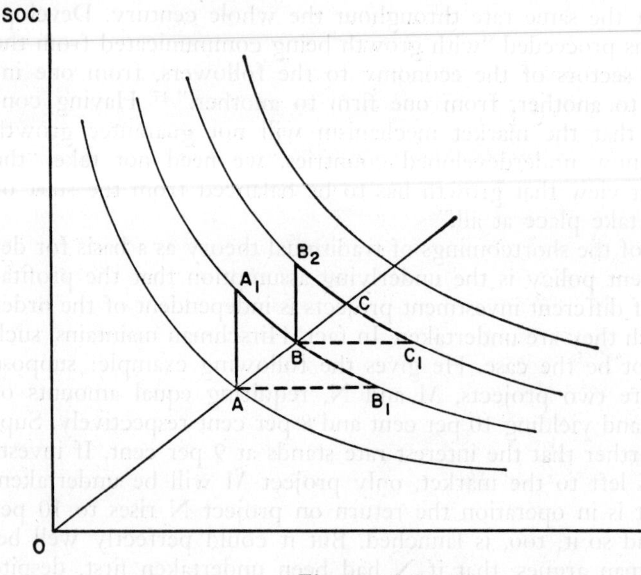

Figure 16-6

tional product at any point of time. Each curve represents a higher gross national product as we move away from the origin. For convenience the curves are drawn so that the 45° line through the origin connects the optimal points on the curves. Thus "this line expresses the ideal of balanced growth of *DPA* and *SOC:* a bit of each at each step no doubt would result in the greatest economy of the country's resources."

The trouble is that "poor countries cannot always afford to be economical." The real scarcity, in Hirschman's view, is not the resources themselves "but the ability to bring them into play." To illustrate this principle, he makes the simplifying assumption that *SOC* and *DPA* cannot be expanded simultaneously, because of this limited ability to utilize resources. Thus the planning problem is to determine the *sequence* of expansion that will maximize *induced* decision making.

We might start either by expanding *SOC* or by expanding *DPA*. If we adopt the first course the economy will follow the heavy line AA_1BB_2C. We begin by increasing *SOC* from A to A_1, which induces increased *DPA* until balance is restored at B, with the whole economy on a higher level of output. We then increase *SOC* further—and can afford to do so because of the higher gross national product already achieved—to B_2; *DPA* follows to point C. Hirschman calls this process "development via excess capacity (of *SOC*)." If we take the other route we follow the dotted line AB_1BC_1C. We begin by increasing *DPA* to B_1; balance requires increasing *SOC* to B. Then *DPA* is expanded further to C_1, and *SOC* has to move to C to catch up. This route is labeled "development via shortage (of *SOC*)."

Either method of unbalanced growth yields an "extra dividend" of "induced, easy-to-take, or compelled decisions resulting in additional investment and output." Balanced growth (of *SOC* and *DPA*) is not only unattainable in most underdeveloped countries, it may not even be desirable. The rate of growth is likely to be faster with chronic imbalance, precisely because of the "incentives and pressures" it sets up.

Having demonstrated the virtues of strategic imbalance, however, we are left with the problem of discovering what kind of imbalance is likely to be most effective. Any particular investment project may have both "forward linkage" (may encourage investment in subsequent stages of production) and "backward linkage" (may encourage investment in earlier stages of production). The task is to find the projects with the greatest *total* linkage. The projects with the greatest linkage will vary from country to country and from time to time, and can be discovered only by empirical studies of the "input-output matrix" variety.

Hirschman thinks that on balance operations which are somewhere in the middle of the production process are likely to have higher total linkage than operations at the beginning or the end of the process; but he does not press the point. He does reproduce a table prepared by Chenery and Watanabe, also reproduced here as Table 16-1. The results must be taken with a grain of salt. The highest backward linkage appears in grain mill products; and "it is highly unrealistic to think of wheat and rice cultivation as being 'induced' by wheat and rice mills." Yet the table is suggestive of the sort of research that may provide useful guides to development planners. And "it is interesting to note," says Hirschman, "that the industry with the highest combined linkage score is Iron and Steel. Perhaps the underdeveloped countries are not so foolish and so exclusively prestige-motivated in attributing prime importance to this industry!" We shall return to considerations of this kind in our discussion of priorities in Chapter 27.

This analysis leads Hirschman to suggest one more way of characterizing underdeveloped countries; they are countries "weak in interdependence and linkage." A ranking of countries in terms of the proportion of intersectoral transactions to total

TABLE 16-1.

Average Degree of Interdependence of Economic Sectors in Italy, Japan, and the United States

Sector	Interdependence through purchases * from other sectors (backward linkage)	Interdependence through sales † to other sectors (forward linkage)
1. "Intermediate manufacture" (backward and forward linkage both high):		
Iron and steel	66	78
Non-ferrous metals	61	81
Paper and products	57	78
Petroleum products	65	68
Coal products	63	67
Chemicals	60	69
Textiles	67	57
Rubber products	51	48
Printing and publishing	49	46
2. "Final manufacture" (backward linkage high, forward linkage low):		
Grain mill products	89	42
Leather and products	66	37
Lumber and wood products	61	38
Apparel	69	12
Transport equipment	60	20
Machinery	51	28
Non-metallic mineral products	47	30
Processed foods	61	15
Shipbuilding	58	14
Miscellaneous industries	43	20
3. "Intermediate primary production" (forward linkage high, backward linkage low):		
Metal mining	21	93
Petroleum and natural gas	15	97
Coal mining	23	87
Agriculture and forestry	31	72
Electric power	27	59
Non-metallic minerals	17	52

Sector	Interdependence through purchases * from other sectors (backward linkage)	Interdependence through sales † to other sectors (forward linkage)
4. "Final primary production" (backward and forward linkage both low):		
Fishing	24	36
Transport	31	26
Services	19	34
Trade	16	17

* Percentage ratio of interindustry purchases to total production.
† Percentage ratio of interindustry sales to total demand.
SOURCE: Albert O. Hirschman, *Strategy of Economic Development* (New York, 1958).

output would probably show a high correlation with both per capita output and proportion of population in manufacturing. Agriculture, especially peasant agriculture, is short on linkage effects. Primary production is low in backward linkage effects by definition; but agriculture and mining are low in forward linkage too. Here is the intuitive source of "the grudge against the 'enclave' type of development," for output of mines, oil wells, and plantations can "slip out of a country without leaving much trace in the rest of the economy." Similarly, "enclave" development in industries providing "finishing touches" may add little to gross national product or to employment, as we saw earlier in discussing the development problem in the Philippines.

However, Hirschman draws a distinction between the long-run effects of enclave export industries and of enclave import industries, a distinction which is of interest in the light of our discussion in the previous chapter of the impact of foreign trade on development. Enclave export industries, he says, have great difficulty in breaking out of the enclave situation and producing "forward linkage" effects within the country. Such need not be the case with enclave import industries; "much of the recent economic history of some rapidly developing underdeveloped countries can be written in terms of industrialization working its way backward from the 'final touches' stage to domestic production of intermediate, and finally to that of basic, industrial materials." He mentions Brazil, Colombia, and Mexico as examples. He might also have included Japan.

He extends this argument to support of the case for protection or subsidization of import-replacing industries, at the right stage of development. Too early encouragement of import-replacers, he points out, may retard economic growth by depriving the country of the "backward" linkage provided by large-scale imports. And backward linkage is more reliable than forward linkage. There is some reason to believe that investment will take place in any industry where demand reaches a certain "threshold." While that threshold is being reached, it is good policy to leave the market to importers. But "it would be absurd to set up any model that would presume to indicate which kind of metal-fabricating industries would come into existence at what point of time in the wake of the establishment of a basic iron and steel industry." Forward linkage should be regarded as "an important and powerful reinforcement to backward linkage" rather than as "an independent inducement mechanism."

Thus Hirschman envisages a kind of "jacking up" process for the economy, using import industries for their backward linkage effects, and then jumping into the production of the import itself when the market reaches a sufficiently large size. When the "threshold" is reached, protection or subsidies to import-replacing industries becomes good policy. The process of starting with final touches has brought a good deal of industrialization to underdeveloped countries, but "much is to be said for biting off as large pieces of value added at a time as the underdeveloped country can possibly digest."

When the whole process is put into an appropriately dynamic context, Hirschman concludes, we are led to a principle that could never be derived from traditional theory: countries tend to develop a comparative advantage in the articles they *import*. "If a country does not produce commodities A and B and if it is importing A in more rapidly increasing volume than B, then it is likely to undertake domestic production of A long before that of B and is acting quite rationally in doing so."

Thus foreign trade policy should go through clearly defined stages with respect to any one industry. In the "prenatal" stage "the opposite of the infant industry treatment is called for." It might even be advisable to restrict *other* imports, to build up an artificial market for the commodity "whose eventual domestic production is to be fostered." [18] Infant industry protection should be given only *after* the threshold is reached and a new industry has been established. Tax concessions are an "apt instrument" for such protection.

[18] *Ibid.*, p. 122.

17 A Synthesis of Theories of Underdevelopment

In this chapter we shall endeavor to weave together the various elements of a theory of underdevelopment presented in the three previous chapters, together with some of the wisdom distilled from the general theories outlined in Part 2. We shall say no more about geographic factors. We have seen in Chapter 11 that resource patterns and climate vary a good deal among underdeveloped countries. Even for tropical countries, geography does not provide a satisfactory explanation of underdevelopment. The soil and climate of the tropics do not produce high agricultural yields, but some valuable agricultural products are hard to grow *outside* the tropics. More important, there is no clear evidence that industrial efficiency is seriously impaired by the tropical climate.

Nor shall we say more in this chapter about the sociological and psychological factors discussed in Chapters 12 and 13. We recognized the value of many of Boeke's observations about the social structure of Asian countries. Nevertheless, we discarded the sociological theory of dualism. Dualism is an important characteristic of most underdeveloped countries, but we found a more acceptable explanation of how dualism arose in these countries in the theory of *technological* dualism. We agreed with Hagen that if economic growth is to occur, a country's culture patterns must be such as to produce "high need-achievement, directed towards economic activity and especially towards innovation" and also to produce "clusters of followers" once innovations are made—just as we agreed with Schumpeter in making essentially the same point. Nor did we doubt that childhood training has much to do with adult motivation. We suggested, however, that the leadership groups of many underdeveloped countries seem to be injected with a liberal dose of need-achievement, and the "revolution of rising expectations" gives reason to hope that the imitators will appear, too. Finally, we saw that Hagen himself opens the door wide to social change by including in his list of "causes" both "outside pressures" and "threats to the existing structure of social relations." For most of the underdeveloped countries *are* subject to external pressures conducive to change, and the very attainment of independence has created threats to the old social order in many of them. We shall have a bit more to say on this subject in the next chapter, when we raise the question as to whether or not economic development is a "good thing." In this chapter, however, we shall assume that the countries with which we are concerned are already on the march from a psycho-sociological point of view—that they "want" development in the relevant sense—and shall concentrate on the economic and technical problems that must be solved to attain it.

Despite the amount of intensive on-the-spot study of underdeveloped countries during the last few years, our chief problem in attempting a synthesis of theories of underdevelopment is still empirical. We do not need elaborate econometric models before we can explain the behavior of underdeveloped economies or prescribe policies. But we do need to know what the strategic functional relations are and we need to know their general shapes. Unfortunately, we are not yet very sure of either of these things. What we have provided in the three previous chapters is a kind of analytical economic history of underdeveloped countries. We have pointed to some strategic relationships which have prevailed in the past. Dare we project them into the future? Let us review briefly the contents of those chapters.

Chapter 12 dealt with the relationship of population growth to industrial development. We showed that in the now underdeveloped countries, investment was made in plantations, mining, petroleum, etc., for the export market, in a way which brought little or no structural change in the economy. It brought rising rates of population growth, but no "built-in habit of technological change," to peasant society.

Concentration of investment in the export sector, combined with population growth, led to increasingly apparent technological dualism. The industrial sector actually was, or was believed to be, capital-intensive and fixed-technical-coefficient in its techniques. It did not provide jobs proportionate to the rate of capital accumulation in that sector. The increased population had to seek employment in the variable-coefficient rural sector. Techniques in that sector therefore became increasingly labor-intensive, and once good land gave out, disguised unemployment began to appear. The shortage of skilled labor, and the effective shortage of unskilled labor where real wages were too low to permit hard and efficient work, aggravated the tendency toward introduction of labor-saving devices in the industrial sector. If population growth is itself a function of the capital-labor ratio (directly or indirectly), Solow's analysis shows the need for a discontinuous jump to a considerably higher ratio of capital to labor if steady growth is to be launched and maintained. Myint points out the barriers to specialization in the rural sector and the vicious circle that develops in this respect. With no specialization, no improvement in skills occurred. Also, the high labor turnover in the industrial sector meant that little effective training was accomplished even there.

In Chapter 14 we outlined some of the reasons why the expansion of foreign trade did not bring generally rising living standards to underdeveloped countries. Myint shows that the rural sector of these countries was confronted by monopolies and monopsonies, without the capacity for developing effective countervailing power of the sort that there is in advanced countries. Wages remained low; techniques were of a kind requiring either little skill or very few workers. Thus industrialization in the export sector had no educative or "spread" effects.

Myrdal goes further, arguing that the world economy is characterized, not by general tendencies toward equilibrium or adjustment to initial changes, but by circular causation, leading to vicious spirals which carry the world economy farther and farther away from an equilibrium position. He demonstrates the tendency both toward regional inequalities in single countries and toward increasing disparities in productivity between advanced and underdeveloped countries. Among the factors which may launch such disparate growth tendencies are shifts in terms of trade; he implies that shifts in the terms of trade in favor of now advanced countries, and against the underdeveloped ones, was one of the factors which resulted in the increasing spread between productivity and standards of living in the two groups of countries.

Far from alleviating these discrepancies, foreign trade tends to aggravate them, especially under conditions of colonial administration in the underdeveloped countries. The colonial heritage is not dispelled by independence alone. Even now, were it not for exchange controls, underdeveloped countries would be exporting rather than importing capital. The marginal productivity of capital is not higher in underdeveloped than in advanced countries, despite the relative scarcity of capital in the former. Only a discontinuous jump to a much higher level of investment, which would have to be made simultaneously in the industrial and agricultural sectors, would create conditions in which the relative scarcity of capital already accumulated could be translated into a higher return on new investment.

Arthur Lewis, on the basis of similar but more systematic analysis, concludes that because the supply of unskilled labor to the industrial sector was virtually unlimited, the "marginal calculus" of individual entrepreneurs became a less and less accurate guide to a socially optimal allocation of resources. Many underdeveloped countries now have a pattern of production just the opposite of what *true* comparative advantage would dictate; they produce agricultural output inefficiently when they could be producing industrial goods efficiently—and exporting them to pay for agricultural imports.

Finally, we saw in Chapter 14 that the terms of trade never moved in favor of the indigenous economy. The statement applies most clearly with respect to internal terms of trade between the rural and the industrial sector of the same country, but it also applies in some measure to terms of trade between underdeveloped countries as a whole and advanced countries as a whole.

We began Chapter 15 with a summary of Rosenstein-Rodan's theory of the need for a "big push," because of indivisibilities in the production function (especially with respect to social overhead capital), demand, and the supply of savings. We next took three major aspects of Harvey Leibenstein's "minimum effort" thesis:

1. If population growth is an increasing function of investment, there is a constant tendency for *per capita* income to revert to a minimum level at which both population growth and capital accumulation are equal to zero. Rising income can continue so long as investment is taking place in the industrial sector and new land is available in the rural sector to absorb the rising population. Once new land gives out, *per capita* income must revert to the minimum level.

2. Only concentration of a large number of entrepreneurs on productive (positive-sum) investments will confirm the profit expectations of individual entrepreneurs. If only a few entrepreneurs are willing to engage in such investments, the rate of growth of the society as a whole is likely to be such that profit expectations will be disappointed, and those few entrepreneurs will revert to unproductive (zero-sum) activities.

3. The configuration of income-raising and income-decreasing factors in underdeveloped countries may be such that only a discontinuous jump to considerably higher levels of capital accumulation will bring the economy into the zone of steady growth.

Leibenstein also quantified the critical minimum effort for various patterns of population growth, and showed that for the conditions prevailing in many Asian countries, investment of 12 to 15 per cent of national income would be necessary to bring these economies into the zone of steady growth. However, there may be advantages in reaching this level in two or more discontinuous jumps rather than in a single jump.

Nelson's "low-level equilibrium trap" is essentially the same idea as Leibenstein's "minimum effort thesis."

Nurkse argues for "balanced growth" to get over the hurdle of indivisibility of demand in a closed economy. Singer points out that few underdeveloped countries can manage a big push in industry and agriculture at once without foreign capital. He urges concentration on investment of a "bottleneck-breaking" sort. Hirschman goes further, favoring deliberate unbalancing of the economy to maximize the "linkage" effects of investment.

Scope and Method

Before attempting a diagrammatic synthesis of these theories, let us note their implications for the scope and method of a theory of underdevelopment. The scope and method of an economics of underdeveloped areas must differ from that of traditional economics for several reasons:

1. Some strategic functions are discontinuous. The discontinuities may take either of two forms. If A is a function of B, instead of a smooth curve relating the two variables, there may be a sudden jump in the value of B at a critical value of A; or the functions may have sharp points. Both the first and second derivatives may have positive signs within one range of A and negative signs in another value of A. These discontinuities are

particularly important in the relationship between capital accumulation and output, in the supply of labor effort, the supply of risk-taking, in decision making, and in production functions.[1]

2. In underdeveloped countries, intersectoral and interregional relations, instead of being a frill to be superimposed on a more or less complete system, are the very core of the analytical framework.[2]

3. Cumulative movements *away from* dynamic equilibrium, or from balanced and steady growth, are typical of underdeveloped countries.[3]

4. In a theory of economic development, population growth and technological progress cannot be treated as exogenous variables, but must be worked into the system. Technological progress, in this context, includes resource discoveries and the spread of managerial, technical, and entrepreneurial skills. The relationship between these factors and economic growth is circular and must be treated as such; that is, population growth and

[1] It is probably true that there are discontinuities in the strategic functions for advanced countries as well; but they are of relatively minor importance. For advanced countries the assumption of continuity gives a reasonably good approximation to reality, and the differential calculus is a useful tool. In underdeveloped countries, on the contrary, the discontinuities are fundamental, and the use of differential calculus can give quite wrong results. Difference equations may help, but a system of mathematics especially designed to take care of discontinuous functions might be more helpful still.

[2] This fact was well understood by the Classical economists, who were always concerned with relations between the agricultural and industrial sectors of the economy. Intersectoral relations played a more explicit role in the Marxist analysis. Specialists like Boeke were groping toward such a framework in their theory of "dualism," but were misled by the feeling that sectoral discrepancies were based on sociological factors, whereas in fact they can be explained in purely economic and technical terms. An important part of the intersectoral relation is the relationship between shifts in location of industry and economic growth, a relationship which has been pointed out by Professor Burton Keirstead in his *Theory of Economic Change* (Toronto, 1948) but which he has not yet worked into a systematic theory of growth.

[3] Cumulative movement away from stable equilibrium is not unknown in advanced countries; but in advanced countries these cumulative movements are important mainly for the theory of fluctuations, where they are limited by a "floor" and a "ceiling," as in the Hicks model of the trade cycle. Where we are concerned with *trends*, however, there are no such limits, at least within very long periods. Trends in the terms and balance of trade, regional discrepancies in productivity, and the like, can continue for decades, even generations. It is this kind of destructive cumulative movement that development policy must endeavor to halt. On this point, see also Albert O. Hirschman, "Investment Policies and Dualism in Underdeveloped Countries," *The American Economic Review*, September, 1957.

technological progress cannot be treated only as factors *influencing* the rate of growth; the system must include the factors which determine them in turn. This is unfortunate, since we know relatively little about the causes of technological progress and population growth, but by leaving them out we produce theories which are not solid foundations for policy recommendations.

5. "Psychological individualism" is of limited use as a method of analysis—not because "people are different" in underdeveloped countries, but because so many of the important decisions are group rather than individual decisions. What may be bad policy for each one of a thousand entrepreneurs may be good policy for the thousand entrepreneurs together; what is unattractive to an individual worker may be very attractive to a trade union or to a village. (This is one aspect of point 1 above.)

6. The analytical framework must be a general equilibrium system, not a partial equilibrium one. It is the *conjuncture* of forces causing economic growth that is important, and no one of them alone will have the same effect as it does in conjunction with others. The system is bound to be rather complicated; it is doubtful whether the method of "successive approximations" will give the right answers. Dealing with the whole system at once enormously increases the intellectual difficulty of handling the problem.

7. The whole process must be put into time; the shape of functions at a point of time is less important than their shape through time.

8. Considering the enormous complexity of the problem and the overweaning importance of the empirical framework, we may be wise to abandon the "purist" approach suggested by the writer on an earlier occasion[4] and to content ourselves with the relatively "sloppy methods of the physicists."[5] That is, instead of insisting on having explanations that are *both necessary and sufficient*, we might adopt explanations that are merely *sufficient*, until they prove inconsistent with other theories or with observations. This method has, after all, worked well for the physicists. At this stage of our efforts to find a general theory of development, any *refutable hypothesis* is well worth stating. Let

[4] Benjamin Higgins, *What Do Economists Know?* (Melbourne, 1951), chap. I, and especially p. 27.

[5] To my knowledge, this expression was first used by Professor Kenneth Boulding in a seminar at McGill University.

us be bold in statement rather than wait until we can set forth *irrefutable* hypotheses (axioms), which are quite likely to be fruitless anyhow. If this approach is adopted, much time and energy must be devoted to empirical testing.

A Diagrammatic Synthesis

Our diagrammatic synthesis of the theories of underdevelopment in this part falls far short of fulfilling all these conditions for a wholly satisfactory theory of underdevelopment. One reason for this failure, of course, is that development is a multidimensional problem, and there is a limit to the number of variables that can be presented in one diagram. However, the writer freely confesses that simple ignorance, not the limitation of diagrammatic techniques, prevents him from presenting a definitive theory of underdevelopment. Our real problem is lack of the necessary factual knowledge about some of the basic relationships involved in the growth process—particularly those relating to population growth, entrepreneurial motivation, political, social, and cultural prerequisites, and the like. Nevertheless, it is the writer's belief that some simple diagrams based on the contents of the previous three chapters, will help us to understand the problem of underdevelopment and to formulate policies for dealing it.[6]

Let us begin by treating the economy as a unit; we shall divide the economy into sectors later. In Figure 17-1 we measure per capita income, Y/N, on the horizontal axis, and various percentages on the vertical axis. The curve n-n' shows percentage rates of population growth (as a function of per capita income). For income below the subsistence level, population declines. Once above this level, it rises rapidly until it hits the "ceiling" of the "biological maximum," which Leibenstein puts at about 3 per cent. (Some countries have growth rates higher than this, but these presumably reflect unusual age distributions that cannot be indefinitely maintained.)

The curve ss' represents aggregate net savings, measured in per cent of national income, as a function of per capita income. It will also be negative for very low levels of income. Experience with low-income societies suggests, however, that some net savings will appear even at levels of income at which population does not grow. Savings will reach a maximum proportion of in-

[6] In the working out of these diagrams, the author has had invaluable assistance from Professor Trevor Swan.

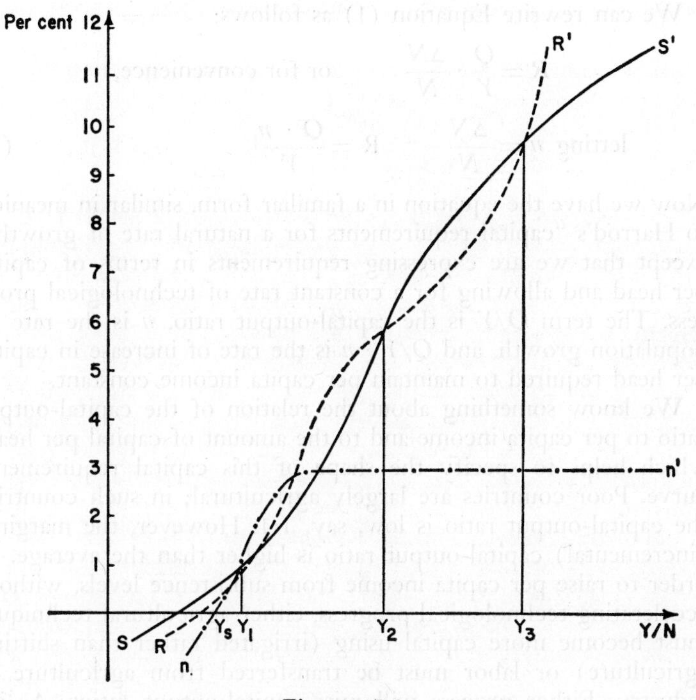

Figure 17-1

come, at some very high level of per capita income, in the neighborhood of 15 per cent.

We are now in a position to derive a "capital requirements" curve, *RR'*, showing the amounts of capital, in per cent of national income, needed to achieve the corresponding level of per capita income. To explain the shape of this curve, we must resort once again to some simple mathematics. We can write:

$$R = \frac{\frac{Q}{N} \cdot \Delta N}{Y} \tag{1}$$

That is, required investment per head, to maintain a constant per capita income with a given amount of population growth, ΔN, is equal to the stock of capital, Q, divided by the population, N, and multiplied by the increase in population. To express this requirement as a percentage of income, Y, we divide through by Y.

We can rewrite Equation (1) as follows:

$$R = \frac{Q}{Y} \cdot \frac{\Delta N}{N} \qquad \text{or for convenience,}$$

$$\text{letting } n = \frac{\Delta N}{N} \qquad \mathrm{R} = \frac{Q \cdot n}{Y} \tag{2}$$

Now we have the equation in a familiar form, similar in meaning to Harrod's "capital requirements for a natural rate of growth," except that we are expressing requirements in terms of capital per head and allowing for a constant rate of technological progress. The term Q/Y is the capital-output ratio, n is the rate of population growth, and $Q/Y \cdot n$ is the rate of increase in capital per head required to maintain per capita income constant.

We know something about the relation of the capital-output ratio to per capita income and to the amount of capital per head, which helps to specify the shape of this capital requirements curve. Poor countries are largely agricultural; in such countries the capital-output ratio is low, say, 1:1. However, the marginal (incremental) capital-output ratio is higher than the average. In order to raise per capita income from subsistence levels, without accelerating technological progress, either agricultural techniques must become more capital using (irrigated rather than shifting agriculture) or labor must be transferred from agriculture to industry. Either process will raise capital-output ratios. As industrialization proceeds and really high levels of income are reached, the capital-output ratio will rise less steeply and will taper off at, say, 3:1. On the other hand the capital-output ratio will rise as the stock of capital per head increases; this is just good old-fashioned diminishing returns to investment. If good land is exhausted, the capital-output ratio may rise sharply as the amount of capital per head is increased.

The shape of the capital requirements curve will depend on these two relationships. For the slope of the curve

$$R = \frac{Q}{Y} \cdot n \qquad \text{or} \qquad \left[\frac{d}{d(\mathrm{Y/N})} \cdot \left(\frac{Q}{Y} \cdot n\right)\right]$$

$$\text{is } \frac{Q}{Y} \cdot n' + n \cdot \frac{Q'}{Y}$$

In order to translate this expression into words, let us coin two new technical terms. Let us call the rate at which the required capital per head rises with per capita income "the marginal capital requirement." This is the expression Q'/Y. Let us call the rate at which population growth rises as per capita income goes up "the marginal propensity to populate." This is the expression n'. Then we have this proposition: capital requirements (for the maintenance of per capita income) are (the capital-output ratio) times (the marginal propensity to populate) plus (the rate of population growth) times (marginal capital requirements).

For very low levels of per capita income, both the rate of population growth and the marginal rate of capital accumulation will be low; n will be very small and the shape of the capital requirements curve will be governed by the marginal propensity to populate and the capital-output ratio, $Q \cdot n'$. Since Q/Y is in the neighborhood of unity the curve will start out with a shape similar to that of the population curve itself. As needs for social overhead capital are met, the capital-output ratio will taper off and the capital requirements curve will do the same.[7]

At some higher level of per capita income, population growth hits the ceiling; n' becomes zero. Thus Q/Yn' is also zero. On the other hand the rate of population growth, n, is high. Thus for higher levels of income the shape of the R curve will be governed by the effect of capital accumulation on the capital-output ratio. Accordingly, capital requirements will tend to rise more steeply again.

Technological progress reduces per capita capital requirements. Exhaustion of good land (decreasing returns) raises them. With very low levels of population growth and high rates of capital accumulation, such as may occur in a "mature economy," labor may become the scarce factor, and returns to investment may diminish on that account. Even in an underdeveloped country, a sufficiently big push could run into bottlenecks other than capital (skilled labor, entrepreneurship), which could raise the capital-output ratio to very high levels.

Where will the R curve cut the horizontal axis? It must do so *at least* as far to the right as Y_8; for with a shrinking population, *both* technological progress *and* increasing returns tend to reduce capital requirements for a given per capita income. In fact, R must cut the s curve at a level of per capita income where technological progress and diminishing returns just offset each other (which might be at zero rates for both, if land is plentiful). This point is likely to occur at a level of per capita income

[7] Professor Trevor Swan has shown, in an unpublished paper presented to an M.I.T. seminar, that so long as the elasticity of substitution of capital for labor is somewhere between 0.5 and 1.0, as it really has to be, the R curve will have an S shape.

somewhat above the zero savings or zero population growth levels.

Thus the *R* curve will have the shape and position of RR'_1 in Figure 17-1.

At a level of per capita income Y_1, the *R* and *S* curves cross. This is a Classical equilibrium position. The rate of capital accumulation is just enough to maintain per capita income slightly above the subsistence level with a modest rate of population growth. This is the "low-level equilibrium trap." The position is stable; any "marginal" move toward higher per capita incomes will be thwarted by capital requirements which exceed savings. On the other hand, to the left of Y_1 savings exceed capital requirements. If "Say's law" holds and inducements to invest are sufficient to make sure that all *ex ante* savings are offset by investment, per capita income will grow to Y_1.

The high-level income Y_3 is also stable, but Y_2 is unstable. In order to assure growth to Y_3, a "minimum effort" is required to provide capital (and everything else) enough to raise income above Y_2.

Figure 17-2 starts with the same situation as in Figure 17-1. We

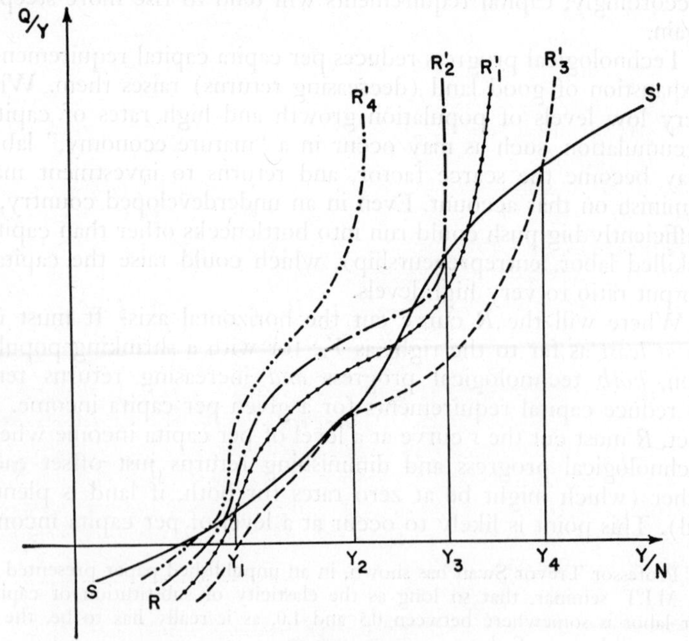

Figure 17-2

have eliminated the population growth curve, since we need it only to derive the curve of capital requirements, and we do not want to clutter the diagram unnecessarily. We are now applying the diagram to the rural sector of the economy. The savings curve is a little flatter, since the range of per capita incomes on the x axis is lower. Let us imagine that investment is taking place in the industrial sector, which does not raise productivity in the agricultural sector, but brings a population explosion in the manner described in Chapter 14. The population explosion will show in the diagram by a shift of the capital requirements curve upward and to the left, to RR_2'. The immediate impact will be a slight decline in per capita income in the rural sector. If the population responds by improving techniques (by shifting from "slash and burn agriculture" to irrigated agriculture, for example), the R curve may shift back to R_1, and income may return to the previous positions.

With the capital requirements curve, RR_2, a stable equilibrium position is established at the rather low per capita income of Y_3. A considerable increase in investment is needed to get even to that level; but truly high levels of income, such as Y_4, are *impossible*, unless technical progress takes place or population growth tapers off again. It is even possible that the population explosion will shift the capital requirements curve to R_4; in this case no escape from the low-level equilibrium trap is possible until techniques improve or population growth tapers off. Otherwise no "effort" is big enough.

Now let us suppose that the "Hirschman effect" sets in; the problems posed by population pressure lead to accelerated technological progress, and a large-scale program of agricultural improvement is launched. A "built-in habit of technical progress" becomes characteristic of the rural sector, the "Hagen effect" takes place and the rate of population growth falls. With luck, we may succeed in shifting the capital requirements curve to the position RR_3. Now the equilibrium position, Y_2, is unstable in an upward direction. Any favorable event bringing an initial increase in per capita income will start the economy on its way to the high-level income, Y_4.

Moreover, the society does not really have the choice between staying in position Y_3 or making the effort to move to still higher levels of income. At this level of income, the rate of technological progress is high enough for the moment to offset the higher rate of population growth generated by the first wave of industrialization. But as good land begins to give out, diminishing returns will operate more and more strongly; accelerated technological progress, or restrictions on the size of families, will be needed just to keep per capita income from falling. Without acceleration of technological progress or reduced population growth, the RR' curve will shift to the left toward RR'_4 and incomes will revert to the subsistence level. With the labor-intensive techniques typical of small-scale peasant agriculture the opportunities for technological improvement are extremely limited. The optimal combination of seed, fertilizer, irrigation, and tools for small family holdings can be reached with relatively little investment of capital, and once attained, the marginal productivity of capital drops to zero. The discontinuous jump to more extensive and more mechanized agriculture can be postponed while this optimal combination is being reached, but it must be made sooner or later. Unless really significant increases in man-year output can still be obtained in other ways, there is a strong case for making the jump sooner rather than later.

It should be noted, however, that although this position is stable in the Classical sense, it may be unstable in the Keynesian sense. That is, savings exceed capital requirements at this level of income. We must make sure that actual investment *exceeds* requirements, so as to offset savings; otherwise, the situation will be deflationary, and private investment will tend to fall off. Investment in excess of requirements for growth is not likely to be forthcoming without an active government policy.

So we see that in the case of the rural sector, the big push cannot be confined to the sort of policy implied in moving *along* the curves. The capital requirements curve must be *shifted*. For some countries such a shift may be possible through seed selection, fertilizer, etc., on present holdings. Sooner or later, however, it will require a transition to mechanized agriculture, while the rate of population growth in the rural sector is reduced by attracting peasants into industrial employment.

Figure 17-3 applies to the industrial sector. Where capital for investment in the industrial sector is provided mainly from abroad, some savings will be provided to this sector even at very low levels of domestic per capita income. The contribution of domestic savings to total capital formation is limited, and the savings curve will therefore be somewhat flatter than in Figure 17-1.[8]

[8] This case would fit Indonesia, Libya, prewar India, and other former colonies. For countries where most of the capital is provided internally, such as Japan or postwar Philippines, the ratio of savings to income would rise somewhat more steeply with income.

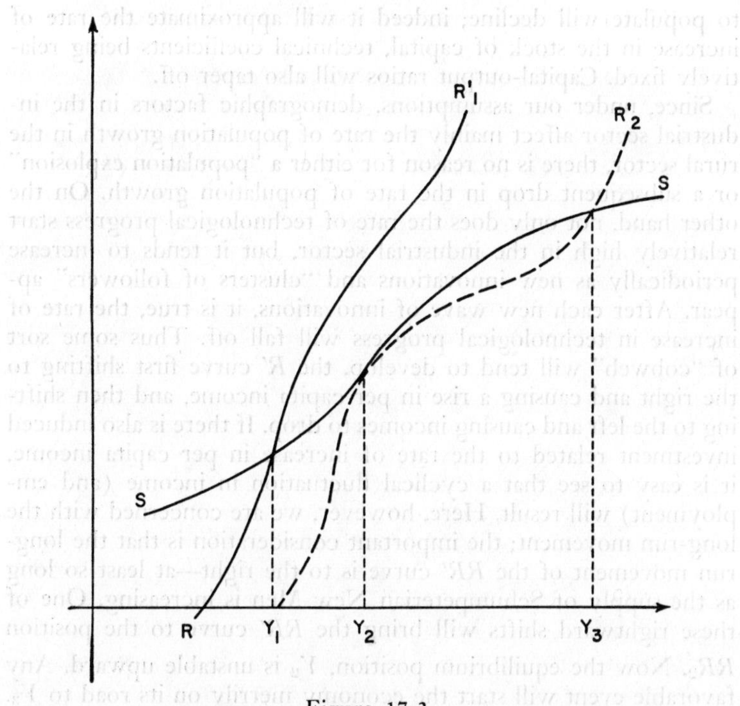

Figure 17-3

Industrial investment is less likely to encounter diminishing returns than agricultural investment, because of the "unlimited supply of labor" to this sector, and because the availability of additional land is somewhat less important to the industrial sector than it is to the rural sector. Finally, population growth within the industrial sector will be closely related to capital accumulation; it is limited by the amount of *employment* provided through investment in these capital-intensive, fixed-technical-coefficient operations. Capital-output ratios will start high, because of the need to provide social overhead capital. As industrial investment proceeds, however, the capital-output ratio in this sector will fall. At levels of investment where bottlenecks appear, it will rise again. Thus at the beginning of industrial expansion both the *marginal* propensity to populate and *marginal* capital requirements will be high. The rate of population growth and the capital-output ratio will also be high. Capital requirements will rise steeply for initial increases in per capita income in this sector. As higher per capita incomes are reached, the marginal propensity to populate will decline; indeed it will approximate the rate of increase in the stock of capital, technical coefficients being relatively fixed. Capital-output ratios will also taper off.

Since, under our assumptions, demographic factors in the industrial sector affect mainly the rate of population growth in the rural sector, there is no reason for either a "population explosion" or a subsequent drop in the rate of population growth. On the other hand, not only does the rate of technological progress start relatively high in the industrial sector, but it tends to increase periodically as new innovations and "clusters of followers" appear. After each new wave of innovations, it is true, the rate of increase in technological progress will fall off. Thus some sort of "cobweb" will tend to develop, the R' curve first shifting to the right and causing a rise in per capita income, and then shifting to the left and causing incomes to drop. If there is also induced investment related to the rate of increase in per capita income, it is easy to see that a cyclical fluctuation in income (and employment) will result. Here, however, we are concerned with the long-run movement; the important consideration is that the long-run movement of the RR' curve is to the right—at least so long as the supply of Schumpeterian New Men is increasing. One of these rightward shifts will bring the RR' curve to the position RR_2'. Now the equilibrium position, Y_2 is unstable upward. Any favorable event will start the economy merrily on its road to Y_3. Thus progress to high levels of per capita income in the industrial sector is virtually assured.

If the development of the rural sector follows the course indicated in Figure 17-2 without a big push in that sector itself, while the industrial sector follows the course of Figure 17-3, it is clear that per capita output and income in the two sectors must diverge, with an ever-widening gap.

Effect of Foreign Trade and Investment

Now let us assume that we have a closed economy with two sectors of production, one agricultural and one industrial. If these sectors are to be considered part of the *same* economy, in the ordinary sense of the term "economy," there must be some transferability of both labor and capital between sectors, and the two sectors must trade with each other. Under these conditions, there is a strong possibility that the barter terms of trade will turn against the industrial sector and in favor of the agricultural sector as development proceeds—as the British terms of trade deteriorated in the integrated world economy of the early nineteenth century. For per capita output and income will be rising considerably faster in the industrial than in the agricultural sector. The rate of technological progress will be much higher in the industrial sector. The size of population will, of course, be much higher in the rural sector, but the rate of population growth within the sectors will be somewhat the same, since both are related to the rate of industrial investment. Thus the supply of industrial products will increase much more rapidly than the supply of agricultural products. Prices of manufactured goods will tend to fall relative to prices of agricultural goods. Capital requirement curves will shift up in industry, down in agriculture. Growth rates will be accelerated in agriculture, decelerated in industry.

There will also be a tendency for capital to move from the industrial sector to the rural sector. For the marginal productivity of capital will tend to be falling (at each point of time) in the industrial sector; it can be prevented from doing so only by accelerated technological progress or cessation of growth. Indeed, if technical coefficients are really fixed, the *marginal* productivity of capital at each point of time will be zero.

In the rural sector, on the other hand, the marginal productivity of capital is high; capital is scarce, labor abundant. So long as there is land to be brought to cultivation or converted to more efficient techniques the rate of return on agricultural investment will be handsome. As we saw in Chapter 14, peasants can pay extremely high interest rates to moneylenders and still survive. In some countries returns in the rural sector may be high enough to attract large lumps of capital for investment in a shift to extensive, mechanized agriculture, thus providing the needed minimum effort in agriculture, as was the case in the Southern United States.

If on the other hand there is no significant amount of trade between the two sectors, and if there is no capital movement between the two sectors, this transition will not take place. Where underdeveloped countries are engaged in foreign trade, this pattern often appears. The industrial sector produces for export, whereas the rural sector sells virtually nothing to the export sector. Under these circumstances there is no reason for the terms of trade to turn in favor of the rural sector. Indeed, if incomes in the rest of the world are rising more rapidly than in the rural sector, the terms of trade may turn *against* the rural sector, as we saw in Chapter 15. Expansion of the industrial export sector may merely attract those villagers with high *n*-achievement, aggravating the tendency toward stagnation in the rural sector. Moreover, foreign capital does not flow into the rural sector because marginal returns are higher there. The high interest rates earned by the moneylenders, we have seen, are based on personal knowledge of and contact with the villagers which foreign capitalists—and even native urbanites—do not have. In any case, this sort of money-making is often distasteful to the foreign or urban entrepreneur. If an economy which already has these two distinct sectors moves from a closed economy to one engaged in foreign trade, the spread between the levels of production and income between the two sectors may be greater than if there were no foreign trade. The *RR′* curves tend to shift continuously to the right in the industrial sector, and continuously to the left in the rural sector. It will take considerable ingenuity in peasant agriculture just to keep incomes from falling, while *average* incomes in the industrial sector tend to rise continuously.

To complete the analysis, we would need a third sector: advanced countries. If it is true that the terms of trade of the industrial sector with the rest of the world tend to deteriorate through time, the rightward shift of the *RR′* curves in that sector would be retarded, and it might even be reversed. In addition, the international flow of capital would be redirected toward the expanding economies of the advanced countries. In that case the influx of capital even to the industrial sector may be insufficient to maintain incomes in that sector. The *SS′* curve in Figure 17-3 may shift downward while the *RR′* curve shifts to the left, until *SS′* is above *RR′* except for one point of tangency. The underdeveloped country is then in a precarious position indeed; any unfavorable shock will send incomes in the industrial sector plunging downward toward Y_1.

Introducing Indivisibilities

Now let us introduce the indivisibilities with respect to supply of capital which were discussed in Chapter 16. These would result in discontinuities in the curve relating the capital-output ratio to per capita income. These discontinuities would be reflected in turn in the capital requirements curve, *RR′*. Capital requirements would rise steeply over a certain range of increases in per capita income, particularly when social overhead capital is being provided, and then would fall abruptly to considerably lower levels. The provision of transport facilities, power, and the like, involves the biggest discontinuities of this kind, but other discontinuities appear at various levels of per capita income. As very high levels of per capita income are reached, however, the discontinuities are less noticeable. In advanced countries, the required "lumps" of new investment are small relative to the existing stock of capital. Thus the capital requirements curve assumes a "saw-toothed" aspect, as in Figure 17-4. The "teeth" become smaller as per capita income rises, and for very high levels of per capita income, a smooth capital requirements curve is a reasonably good approximation to reality.

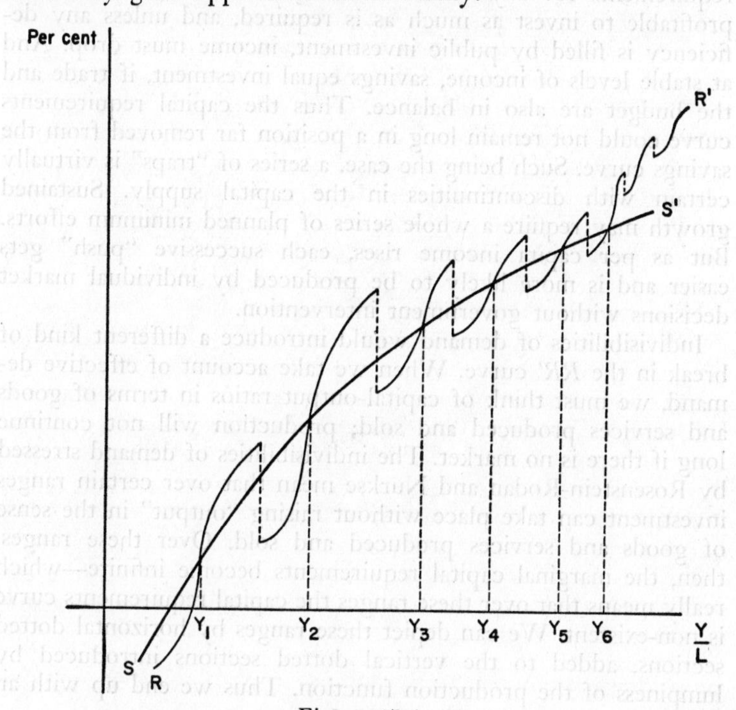

Figure 17-4

The dotted portions of the curve have no economic meaning; equilibrium is possible only on the rising portions of the curve.

It is apparent that with such a saw-toothed capital requirements curve there may be a whole series of income traps at various levels of per capita income. The intersections of the savings curve with the capital requirements curve provide stable equilibrium at the levels of Y_2, Y_3, and Y_4 as well as at Y_1. In the real world, these "traps" would appear as bottlenecks in the supply of capital, or in supply of other factors of production. For example, a shortage of skilled labor may require a shift to a more completely mechanized system of production; lack of trained managers or technicians may lead to inefficient use of capital.

Is there any reason why the *R* curve should remain in the neighborhood of the *S* curve after the initial intersection? Since income equals spending, and actual investment varies with spending, actual investment will not long diverge widely from capital requirements for any established level of income. If it is not profitable to invest as much as is required, and unless any deficiency is filled by public investment, income must drop. And at stable levels of income, savings equal investment, if trade and the budget are also in balance. Thus the capital requirements curve could not remain long in a position far removed from the savings curve. Such being the case, a series of "traps" is virtually certain with discontinuities in the capital supply. Sustained growth may require a whole series of planned minimum efforts. But as per capita income rises, each successive "push" gets easier and is more likely to be produced by individual market decisions without government intervention.

Indivisibilities of demand would introduce a different kind of break in the *RR′* curve. When we take account of effective demand, we must think of capital-output ratios in terms of goods and services produced and sold; production will not continue long if there is no market. The indivisibilities of demand stressed by Rosenstein-Rodan and Nurkse mean that over certain ranges investment can take place without raising "output" in the sense of goods and services produced and sold. Over these ranges, then, the marginal capital requirements become infinite—which really means that over these ranges the capital requirements curve is non-existent. We can depict these ranges by horizontal dotted sections, added to the vertical dotted sections introduced by lumpiness of the production function. Thus we end up with an *RR′* curve like that in Figure 17-5.

Given kinks in the savings function, such as illustrated by the curve *SS′* in Figure 17-5, there could be a whole series of "traps" even with a perfectly smooth capital requirements curve. With discontinuities in both curves, a multiplicity of equilibrium points can occur. Only those levels of income at which solid savings and capital requirements curves intersect have real meaning; only they could be equilibrium points. Only the levels of income that constitute such points are shown in the diagram. We can see at once that the minimum effort for a further rise in per capita income becomes smaller, relative to the existing income and stock

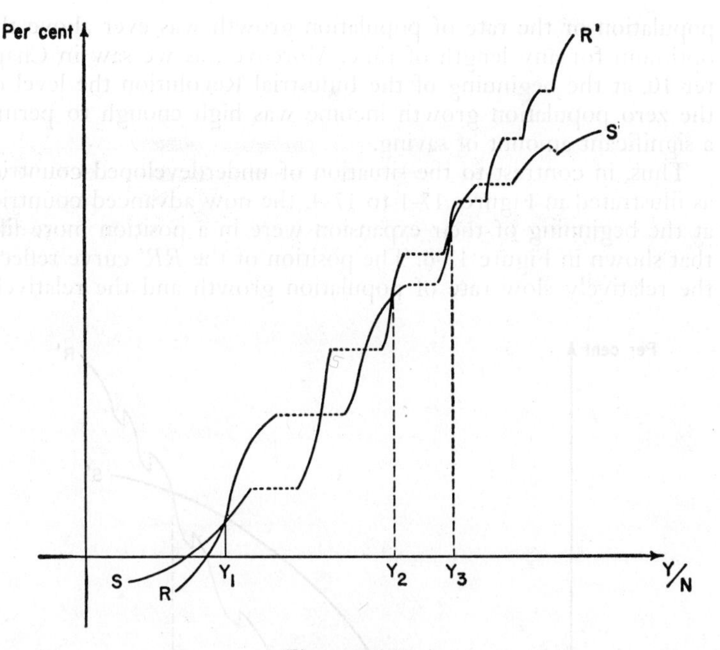

Figure 17-5

of capital, as income rises. At very high levels of income, growth has the appearance of being practically continuous.

Development Past and Present

We can use a diagram of this kind to illustrate some of the differences between the task confronting underdeveloped countries today and the situation of the now advanced countries in the eighteenth and early nineteenth centuries. As we shall show at greater length in Chapter 28, the "population explosion" in Europe and the New World was never quite so explosive as it has been in some Asian, African, and Latin American countries. Moreover, the upsurge of population growth came *after* a marked acceleration of the rate of technological progress in both the agricultural and industrial sectors, and it was owing mainly to economic improvement. With the urbanization that Western industrialization brought with it, fertility rates declined after a lag of two or three generations. Expansion started when the resource-population relationship was relatively favorable, and in most of the advanced countries it is doubtful whether either the level of population or the rate of population growth was ever above the optimum for any length of time. Moreover, as we saw in Chapter 10, at the beginning of the Industrial Revolution the level of the zero population growth income was high enough to permit a significant amount of saving.

Thus, in contrast to the situation of underdeveloped countries as illustrated in Figures 17-1 to 17-4, the now advanced countries at the beginning of their expansion were in a position more like that shown in Figure 17-6. The position of the *RR′* curve reflects the relatively slow rate of population growth and the relatively

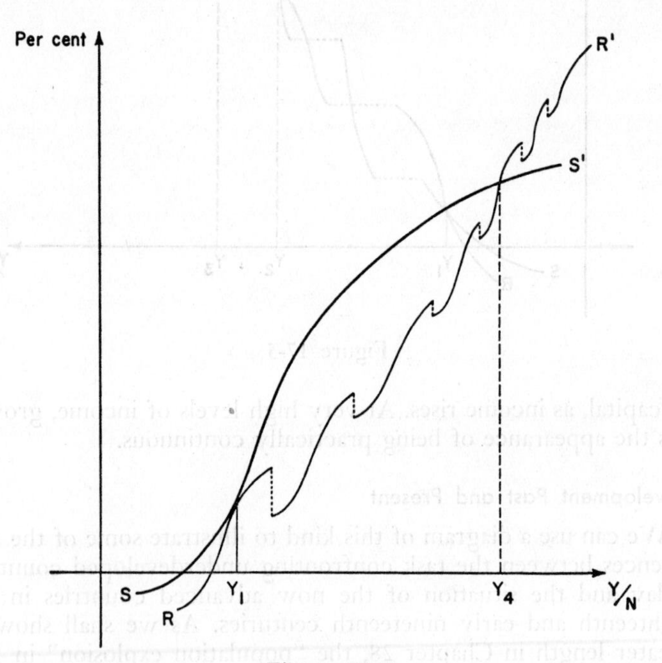

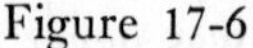
Figure 17-6

high accompanying rate of technological progress. The position of the savings curve reflects the relatively high initial levels of income. Whereas the underdeveloped countries need a big push followed by lesser pushes, no big push is needed for countries in the situation depicted in Figure 17-5. Income can expand steadily (except for minor fluctuations of the sort that characterized nineteenth-century business cycles). Moreover, the *RR′* curve moved steadily to the right, with accelerated technological progress, and particularly after the drop in fertility rates. For these countries, continuous and cumulative growth was fairly easy.

Conclusions

We could go on proposing various models and translating them into terms of these diagrams, but we have now covered the main points made in the preceding three chapters. From the reformulation in this chapter, it should be clear that traditional marginal analysis, however useful it may be as a first approximation to understanding advanced economies, can be very misleading for underdeveloped ones. When such factors as population growth and technological progress are made an integral part of the analysis, instead of being left out altogether as in traditional equilibrium theory, and when the relevant discontinuities are introduced, our analysis can lead us to policy conclusions exactly the reverse of what orthodox equilibrium theory might suggest. Some of the policy conclusions implicit in our analysis have been noted in passing. We have now reached the point where we must turn explicitly to questions of development policy.

PART 5 Policies

18 The Welfare Economics of Growth

The Limits of Theory

We have been using the term economic development to mean a discernible rise in total and per capita income of a country, widely diffused throughout occupational and income groups, and continuing long enough to become cumulative. "Long enough" means a generation or two. Fluctuations may take place around the long-run trend; but a rise in per capita income for a decade or two followed by a relapse—such as seems to have occurred in Indonesia between 1820 and 1840—would not be regarded as economic development as we have defined it.

Thus far, we have merely been trying to answer the question, "What *causes* development or underdevelopment?" We have not asked whether or not development in this sense is a "good thing." Now that we are about to discuss policy, however, we had better face the issues: does economic development always bring an increase in social welfare? How can one tell whether it does or not?

Traditional welfare economics, we have seen, takes preferences as given; it is concerned with using the market, patching it, or replacing it, in such a way as to provide maximum scope for satisfaction of wants through freely expressed individual choices. True, traditional welfare economics has never quite resolved the problem of deciding how income should be distributed. Some economists have thrown in the sponge and admitted the need for a basic value judgment on the ethics of income distribution, although they grace the value judgment with the term "welfare function." Others have tried to rescue *Wertfreiheit* by arguing that an economic change is clearly "good" if it does not cause a "bad" redistribution of income and if the potential losers could not profitably bribe the potential gainers to oppose it. It is also true that such inconvenient possibilities as increasing returns to scale, discontinuities, and kinks, are awkward to handle. Nevertheless, once given a "welfare function" as a basis for income distribution, it is possible to evaluate any current policy proposal in terms of *marginal* rates of substitution between goods and services, and technical possibilities of production as indicated by *marginal* productivities of various factors of production in various uses.[1] The "best" policy is the one that will allocate resources so as to maximize the aggregate satisfaction of the community through the consumption of goods, services, and leisure, with *given* resources, techniques, institutions, and tastes.

We could, of course, state the objective of economic development policy in analogous terms: viz., to maximize the *rate of increase* in this flow of goods, services, and leisure through time. Several writers, indeed, have stated the aim of economic development policy in these terms. Arthur Lewis begins his book by stating his *credo:*[2]

> The subject matter of this book is the growth of output per head of population. . . . The definition of output we leave to the theorists of national income. . . . The definition, however, must relate to goods and services—"economic" output, in the old fashioned meaning of "economic"—and not to some such concept as welfare, satisfaction or happiness. It is possible that a person becomes less happy in the process of acquiring greater command over goods and services. . . . This book is not, however, an essay on whether people ought to have or to want more goods and services; its concern is merely with the processes by which more goods and services become available. The author believes that it is good to have more goods and services, but the analysis of the book does not in any way depend upon this belief.

Having thus set himself free to analyze the factors which will maximize the rate of growth of output, however, Lewis adds an appendix to his book in which he explains why he thinks

[1] For an excellent and relatively readable summary of contemporary welfare economics, see Francis M. Bator, "The Simple Analytics of Welfare Maximization," *The American Economic Review*, March, 1957.

[2] W. Arthur Lewis, *The Theory of Economic Growth* (London, 1955), pp. 9–10.

economic growth is desirable. "The advantage of economic growth," he says there, "is not that wealth increases happiness, but that it increases the range of human choice. It is very hard to correlate wealth and happiness." For "what distinguishes men from pigs is that men have greater control over their environment; not that they are more happy. And on this test, economic growth is greatly to be desired." It gives us the freedom to choose greater leisure. It permits cultivation of the arts and sciences. "Art, music, the study of philosophy itself" can be afforded "only as economic growth permits [a society] to spare increasing numbers from the basic task of growing food." More people hear the work of the best composers, and see the work of the best painters, in the present day than in the times of Mozart or Bach, Rembrandt or El Greco.[3]

Similarly, Bauer and Yamey open their discussion of the role of government in economic development by stating that[4]

> . . . in assessing policies we tend to use as a yardstick their probable effects on the range of alternative courses of action open to individuals, and that we prefer a society in which policy is directed towards widening the effective range of alternatives open to members of that society. . . . We believe that the widening of the range of effective choice is the most valuable single objective of economic development as well as the best single criterion of its attainment.

The present writer shares these beliefs. But to say that we believe in economic development does not really solve the problem; development policy is still left on a very different footing from that of traditional welfare economics. Is it the best we can do?

Observation tells us that practically everyone wants a higher standard of living, in the sense of "command over more goods, services, and leisure." We can also observe that practically everyone is willing to make *some* sacrifice in order to have a higher standard of living. Welfare economics tries to balance the satisfaction of these wants with the sacrifices "at the margin"; each individual is supposed to equalize the marginal rates of substitution among goods and services, between goods and services and leisure, and between income now and income later. But our whole analysis of the development problem, especially in poor and stagnant countries, led us to the conclusion that *current market choices are a very unreliable guide to development policy*.

[3] *Ibid.*, pp. 420–22.

[4] P. T. Bauer and B. S. Yamey, *The Economics of Underdeveloped Countries* (London, 1957).

We have seen that if people are to get over the hump to sustained economic growth they have to "want" it in a way quite different from "wanting" goods and services, in the sense of being willing to pay for them. They may have to work harder and better, save more, and restrict family size even if there is no clear "marginal" increase in their real incomes in the immediate future. They may have to become technology-minded, acquire higher levels of training and skills, shift from agriculture to industry and from country to city, acquire high *n*-achievement, accept changes in institutions and social organization, acquire new tastes—perhaps even a new "way of life"—although many of the people involved in this process of "economic development and cultural change" may not like it at all. For let us be clear on one point; if the pattern of individual preferences was such as to produce economic growth, we would have it now. The present situation in underdeveloped countries is the result of *somebody's* decisions. And no government can launch economic growth where it does not exist without "interfering in the market" in a sense quite different from the intervention involved in the nostrums of welfare economics. We have seen that launching a take-off is *not* merely "patching the market." Even raising the ratio of effective savings and investment to national income to finance a "minimum effort" involves an element of intervention; it would not occur through market forces alone.

We could, of course, treat the development of underdeveloped countries as an item of Western national policy. President Eisenhower, defending his requests for enlarged and liberalized foreign aid, has reiterated the point that development of underdeveloped countries (with *our* assistance) is essential for our security. Similarly, Professors Millikan and Rostow, in their *Proposal* argue that *our* way of life is more secure in a world of "mature democracies" than it is when we are surrounded by poverty-stricken countries with unstable governments.[5]

If economic development is a part of *our* national policy, of course, whether or not people "want" it is a purely technical question. "Absorptive capacity" will be lower in countries that do not want development, and "technical assistance" might have to be directed toward changing the culture and instilling new wants. We might decide, as a matter of efficiency, to concentrate our aid in countries where absorptive capacity is higher and the task easier. In countries peculiarly important to our se-

[5] Max F. Millikan and W. W. Rostow, *A Proposal: Key to an Effective Foreign Policy* (New York, 1957).

curity, however, it may be unwise to frame policy in terms of economic efficiency alone.

If we think only in terms of our own national policy, however, we would be rash to go as far as Gunnar Myrdal and set as our goal "the reduction of the gap between per capita incomes of the United States and Canada and those of underdeveloped countries."[6] Reducing the gap may not prove possible, and if the goal of development policy is to assure our own national security, promising the impossible is not likely to be an effective means to this end. Aiding foreign countries with their development programs will no doubt bring their *per capita* incomes closer to those now enjoyed in advanced countries, but the incomes of advanced countries will meanwhile have risen to new heights. In all likelihood they will rise by bigger amounts than most underdeveloped countries. Even in Latin America, where present incomes and growth rates are relatively high, a level of per capita income *one-third of the United States level* may prove unattainable. The Economic Commission for Latin America has set forth this problem in grimly realistic terms: [7]

In 1953, average per capita income in Latin America stood at 248 dollars (at 1950 prices), or slightly less than one-eighth of that of the United States (2,000 dollars). The targets for a development programme should always be attainable within a reasonable period of time, but it would be expecting too much to suggest that such a high per capita figure could be reached over a short period. In order to discover the first unknown quantity, the figure for the United States may be reduced by two-thirds, or to an average per capita income of 666 dollars, which is two and a half times the average per capita income of 248 dollars in Latin America during 1953. If such income continues to increase at a rate of 2.4 per cent annually, when will the level of 666 dollars be reached? The answer, forty-two years, provides the information for judging whether or not this rate of growth is satisfactory. But the problem does not end here.

Gross income in the United States has not attained a stationary level. The Paley Report based its calculation of the probable income of that country in 1975 upon the assumption that the per capita rate of growth would then be 2.0 per cent annually. If this hypothesis is used as a basis, it is possible to make another illustrative calculation.

[6] Gunnar Myrdal, *op. cit.*

[7] UN Department of Economic and Social Affairs, *Analyses and Projections of Economic Development: A Study Prepared by the Economic Commission for Latin America:* I. "An Introduction to the Technique of Programming" (New York, 1955), p. 11. The Paley Report is William S. Paley (chairman), *Resources for Freedom: A Report to the President by the . . . Materials Policy Commission* (Washington, D.C., June, 1952).

How long would it take Latin America's per capita income to reach one-third of the United States figure, assuming an annual rate of growth of 2.4 per cent in the former and 2.0 per cent in the latter? Given the relatively small difference between the two rates, the period would be extremely long and devoid of all practical significance. In fact, 252 years would be required. Naturally, such an illustration can merely serve to show that a progressive reduction in the very wide margin of per capita income at present existing between the United States and the Latin American countries is impossible, unless the latter make a decisive effort to accelerate their rates of development. In other words, there would be no point in making extrapolations of such long duration since, apart from other factors, a slight change in the rate of population growth would entirely alter the results.

With an investment coefficient of 20 per cent, the average annual rate of expansion in per capita income would rise from 2.4 to 4.0 per cent and, instead of forty-two years, a period of only twenty-five years would be necessary for Latin America to reach one-third of the per capita income in the United States. The shorter time lapse would also narrow the difference between the income levels. Indeed, if Latin America's per capita income could continue to expand after these twenty-five years at the rate of 4.0 per cent annually for a further quarter of a century it would reach 1,830 dollars. This figure would be equivalent to one-third of per capita income in the United States at that date, provided that the annual rate of expansion of 2.0 per cent in that country continued. The target would therefore cease to be unattainable in theory, although it might be rash to draw conclusions about its practical application. A per capita rate of growth of 4.0 per cent is extremely high and in practice would encounter obstacles of another nature.

The present writer has his own "welfare function" in this regard. *Redistribution* of income among *advanced* nations may not be very important, just as redistribution of income among individuals is not very important in advanced countries. What is important and possible in both cases is to *eliminate poverty*. The amount of income redistribution actually achieved by the modern welfare state is relatively small. But where *poverty* has been eliminated by economic and social policy, as in Australia and in lesser degree in the United States or Canada, the presence of a few rich people is not very serious, and redistribution from rich to less rich would not raise incomes of the less rich very much. In the same way, if there were no poor countries, the presence of a few rich ones would not be a menace to world peace and prosperity.

The writer's own "welfare function" is such, however, that he would be sorry to see his profession abandon the attempt to formulate development policies that will give the people of underdeveloped countries what *they* want. Markets may be poor guides, but we still have the polls. Where representative governments have made economic development a major national goal, we can accept it as a policy goal, too. In these cases, the two possible approaches are reconciled in large measure, for absorptive capacity *is* higher where governments are determined to achieve higher living standards for their people. As economists, we can then suggest measures to promote growth; if the governments pursue these measures and the people do not like them, the people can toss the government out. If that happens, the economists may get tossed out, too, unless they can suggest development policies more to people's liking. This approach will give economists plenty to do, for many representative governments are committed to economic development.

The foreign technical assistance "expert" who remains long enough in the field typically goes through three stages. Too often his first reaction is, "Everything here is different from at home; that is terrible, we must change everything." As he lives and travels in these countries, however, he begins to appreciate their culture, civilization, values, and way of life. At this stage the reaction often is, "Why should we force on these happy people the frictions and neuroses of our Western society?" In the third stage, attained after still further experience with underdeveloped countries, the "expert" comes to realize that the question "to develop or not to develop" is not one for the West to answer. Most underdeveloped countries today are determined to achieve higher standards of living, and the events of the last twenty years have injected into their bodies politic the dynamics of economic and social change. Our task is to help these countries to attain their economic goals within a political and social framework that remains democratic.

The present writer would also like to see some of the tenets of traditional welfare theory retained in development policy. Development is for people, and the current wants of people should not be ignored for the sake of raising per capita output in the future. For example, leisure should be respected. Output per capita can be increased, within limits, by the simple device of lengthening the working week; but such an increase in per capita output is not necessarily economic progress. Whether it is or not depends upon how the people concerned value the extra flow of goods and services on the one hand and the loss of leisure on the other. There are problems here; if we are to have growth at all, the choice between a higher material standard of living and more leisure must be made to some degree collectively; it cannot be left to each individual, as it is in traditional welfare economics. There are discontinuities and complementarities in the function relating hours of work to output, and the decisions of various individuals and groups are interrelated. These problems, however, are not peculiar to underdeveloped countries.

Similarly, production can be increased by increasing the proportion of the active labor force to the total population. Part of the increases in output achieved by the belligerent countries during World War II resulted from drawing into employment young people who would otherwise have been in school, older people who had reached the normal retirement age, and housewives who would normally have been fully occupied in their homes. One may doubt whether such increases in output can properly be considered "economic development." At least the people themselves should make their own choice between more goods and services, and more leisure in the form of higher school-leaving ages, lower retirement ages, and freedom of housewives from responsibilities outside their homes.

In sum, the choice between higher material standards of living and more leisure is one that the people themselves should make. The economist's role stops with indicating the nature of the choice to be made. However, the choice cannot be made by each individual separately. Achieving a "minimum effort" requires collective decisions by extended family units, villages, trade unions, employers' associations, or even by the people as a whole through their government.

The choice between a higher level of current consumption and a more rapid rate of economic progress is also one to be made by the people concerned. Here, too, discontinuities appear. Half a railway is useless; power plants, blast furnaces, or refineries below a certain size are too inefficient to be worth constructing; even irrigation projects below a certain scale may not be worthwhile. A certain minimum volume of saving is necessary before significant economic progress can be made. In large measure, the choice between much or little sacrifice of current consumption for a higher standard of living in the future is the choice between a slow or rapid rate of economic progress. This choice, like the choice between material income and leisure, must be made collectively.

As productivity rises it may be translated into a higher level of per capita income or into a larger number of children per member of the labor force. This choice also is for the people themselves to make, and it, too, cannot be left entirely to individuals, since the wishes of some individuals or groups can be thwarted by the decisions of others. A humanitarian society does not permit children to starve; and if some people have more children than they can support, the rest of the community will take care of them through private charity or through the government. In this manner, the income which would otherwise have gone toward swelling the stream of saving and accelerating the rate of economic progress will go instead toward supporting a larger population, in defiance of the wishes of those who prefer smaller families and more rapid progress. Unless income per capita reaches a certain level, the stream of savings cannot rise to the point where an underdeveloped economy is able to finance the whole of its further economic progress from its own resources, without outside assistance in the form of loans or grants. If the population grows so fast that increases in productivity do not bring the country closer to that level of per capita income, the economy will never get "over the hump" to the point where it can finance its own economic development alone and unaided.

Although economic development policy seeks to raise per capita production as quickly as possible, it is not a matter of indifference how this increased output is attained. The limitations imposed by the people's desire for leisure, by their wish to have large families, and their reluctance to sacrifice current consumption for the sake of a higher standard of living in the future, should be considered. Per capita income can be raised if people work harder and longer, if they save larger shares of their income and so release resources for investment projects, and if they restrict the size of their families; but increases in output achieved in these ways are assuredly "progress" only if the gains outweigh the sacrifices in the view of the people concerned.

We shall define the over-all goal of economic development policy, then, as maximizing the rate of expansion of production, while giving due weight to people's wishes regarding the choice between goods and services or leisure, between more income now and more income later, and between a higher per capita income and larger families, as expressed in collective choices made by the smallest group whose decisions can be effective in promoting growth.

Growth through Laissez Faire?

Our conclusion in Chapter 17, based on the analysis of the preceding chapters, was that the problems of underdeveloped countries will *not* be solved by unfettered market forces alone, but will require government intervention in the decision-making process. The various theories of underdevelopment outlined in Part 3 are united in discarding the "marginal calculus" as a guide to policy. However, in accord with our promise in the Preface to make this book "as much of a textbook as is possible," we feel obliged to mention that there are economists—even some with knowledge of underdeveloped countries—who still seem to think that economic development can be achieved by a policy of nineteenth-century laissez faire.

After reading P. T. Bauer, for example, whether he writes alone or in collaboration with B. S. Yamey, one might well conclude that nothing ails the underdeveloped countries but the ineptness of their goverments; if this barrier were removed, they would develop "naturally" without active intervention. The turn of the underdeveloped countries is bound to come, it is just a matter of patience:

> The Creator has not divided the world into two sectors, developed and underdeveloped, the former being more richly blessed with natural resources than the latter. All developed countries began by being underdeveloped by modern standards, which are the opposite ones; indeed they remained in this state until quite recently. The natural resources in their territories, whether rich or poor have only been developed within a comparatively short and recent period of history.

The prosperous nations, Bauer and Yamey insist, are not necessarily those which are particularly blessed with natural resources. They must have *some* resources, of course, "but in most cases advanced countries have largely raised the value of these resources by discovering and developing them through the application of capital, organizing and technical skills and labor."[8] Thus if capital and skills are applied in the now underdeveloped countries, they too will prosper.

Bauer even suggests that there is no particular lack of capital.[9] There are half a dozen different objections, he says, to the argument that

[8] Bauer and Yamey, *op. cit.*, pp. 46–47.

[9] P. T. Bauer, *Economic Analysis and Policy in Underdeveloped Countries* (Durham, N.C., 1957), pp. 63, 73.

the underdeveloped countries are too poor to invest . . . and that they are thereby caught in a vicious circle of poverty. . . . The most obvious objection is that if this argument were valid it is difficult to see how the developed countries could have reached their present position, since all developed countries began by being underdeveloped. The substantial capital formation in agriculture evidenced by the rapid growth of cash crops in underdeveloped countries is a further refutation of the thesis of the vicious circle of underdevelopment.

Capital formation by immigrants "serves as yet another refutation of the idea of the vicious circle of poverty." Thus Bauer entirely overlooks the tremendous differences between the situation of Europe in the eighteenth century, or of the New World in the nineteenth, and of the underdeveloped countries today, outlined in Chapter 10 above.

Bauer seems to believe that the unrelated marginal decisions of individual entrepreneurs are a completely satisfactory means of launching economic growth. "We are impressed that in fact even in underdeveloped countries many individuals and firms are well able to recognize and take advantage of favorable market situations and developments," he says, and instances "the expansion by peasant producers of large acreages of tree crops yielding a delayed income" as "evidence that many are prepared to take the long view."[10] But our whole discussion of theories of underdevelopment shows that each of a set of individual private investment decisions may seem unattractive in itself, whereas, when undertaken as a unit, an investment program may yield substantial increases in national income. Hence, investment on the needed scale will not occur without some government intervention in the decision-making process.

Similarly, Bauer and Yamey deny that backward-sloping supply curves of effort can be a real problem:

With the assumed fixity wants an individual's supply curve of effort to the exchange sector turns back for rates of reward above a certain point; beyond this point the quantity of effort offered varied inversely with the reward per unit. But the slope of the curve and the point at which it turns back will not be the same for all individuals. These differences make it almost certain, even where individual wants are fixed, that, over the range of likely rates of reward or remuneration, the supply curve of effort to the exchange sector from the population as a whole will be of the conventional kind with quantity supply increasing with reward per unit.

But this argument depends on significant differences in wants. In conventional societies, such as those of Asian villages—or even

[10] Bauer, *op. cit.*, pp. 158–59, 85.

that of Australia—where everyone wants to live in an almost identical pattern, a collection of backward-sloping individual supply curves of effort may very well produce a backward-sloping supply curve of effort as a whole. Development can make them unbend, as we saw in Chapter 12—but the development has to be launched somehow.

Bauer and Yamey suggest that those who disagree with them *start* with a predilection for government intervention:

> Advocates of compulsory saving prefer that important decisions be made by the government rather than by dispersed individuals, and that decisions go one way rather than another. Our own preference is for arrangements in which decision-making is dispersed and individual preferences are given full expression.

But this statement misses the real point. It is not that the government is better than private entrepreneurs at judging the outcome of particular investment projects, but that it is better able to judge the outcomes of various constellations, or gestalts, of investment programs. It is also better able to assume the risks associated with them, since many of the rewards accrue, not to the particular projects in which the initial investment is made, but in the form of external economies. No doubt such a constellation of investments could be made attractive to a group of private entrepreneurs; here again, whether a government chooses to do so, or to undertake the investment itself, and how it divides the total task between public and private investment, is a matter of administrative expediency that must be decided separately in each country at each point of time.

How the administrative problem is solved, however, is *not* a matter of preference for government decisions or dispersed individual decisions; it is a matter of finding the most efficient way of making decisions in terms of—let us say—aggregate national income between year ten and year thirty, for each of several gestalts of investment. Such decisions are harder to make than decisions in terms of differences between next year's profits on $100,000 invested this way or that. "Consumer's sovereignty" prevails in either case, but the policy framework which is chosen to influence private investment decisions, and to determine the composition of the public investment program, must be different.

When a Western economist first turns his attention to the problems of Asian, African, and Latin American countries, his first reaction is often one of bewilderment at the sharp differences in social and cultural framework. At this stage he often questions the usefulness of Western economic analysis in tackling the problem of underdevelopment. As his acquaintance with the peoples of underdeveloped countries grows, however—unless his preconceptions are so strong as to blind him to the facts—he discovers to his delight that the basic patterns of economic behavior are really not very different from those of people in the West. He learns that institutional, sociological, and cultural disparities are not insuperable barriers to growth if they are recognized and understood.

This discovery is comforting, but it can also be misleading. The fact that one does not need brand-new psychological assumptions, and that sociological, cultural, and institutional differences do not result in totally different patterns of behavior in similar circumstances, does not mean that one can get the right answers to policy questions by applying traditional textbook theories of value, distribution, and employment. On the contrary, as we have shown at length in Part 4, and especially in Chapter 17, it is precisely the *economics* of underdeveloped countries that is different from that of advanced countries.

The "Keynesian revolution" was not based on totally new assumptions regarding economic behavior or culture patterns; it simply selected a new system of strategic variables, and indicated relations between them quite different from what had been previously accepted. *This* kind of revolution in economic thought is required as a basis for policies to develop underdeveloped countries. We hope that this book will help to establish the "preconditions" for such a revolution.

Foreign Enterprise and Colonialism

Some writers (mostly British) have suggested that economic development can take place through the special kind of laissez faire involved in giving a free hand to foreign enterprise, or through the special kind of "gradualism" involved in colonial administration. In their book on Western enterprise in Indonesia and Malaya,[11] Allen and Donnithorne seem to accept as a foregone conclusion the tenet that Western enterprise *must* have raised per capita incomes of the native peoples. By 1940, in Indonesia, "The standard of life of the native population was still

[11] G. C. Allen and Audrey G. Donnithorne, *Western Enterprise in Indonesia and Malaya* (London, 1957). See also, G. C. Allen and Audrey G. Donnithorne, *Western Enterprise in Far Eastern Economic Development: China and Japan* (London, 1954), pp. 264–65. For a more detailed discussion of the first-named, see Benjamin Higgins, "Western Enterprise and Economic Development of Southeast Asia," *Pacific Affairs,* March, 1958.

low; but the vastly increased numbers certainly enjoyed a higher consumption per head than the tiny population of the early nineteenth century. . . . In Malaya the transformation had been equally striking. A savage and empty land had been peopled. . . . In the early 1950's the population of Malaya enjoyed a higher level of income per head than any other country in East Asia. For these accomplishments Westerners can take most of the credit. . . ."

This judgment on the contribution of Western enterprise to economic development leads the authors to an implicit policy conclusion: for further development, what such countries need is more Western enterprise. They leave the impression that "the outlook is bleak"—especially for Indonesia—because the climate is no longer favorable for Western enterprise. They suggest that what Indonesia and Malaya need for their further development is "more of the same." But the fact is that Western enterprise did not develop those countries, in the sense in which their governments now use the term "develop." Development of Indonesia and Malaya conformed to the pattern outlined in Chapters 14 to 16 above. Western enterprise was limited to land-and-capital-intensive ventures providing incomes and employment for only a small fraction of the population. Western enterprise generated a "population explosion" for which there was no offsetting growth of employment opportunities in the technologically advanced, high-productivity sector. There was not enough capital for high productivity in the peasant agriculture sector where most of the rapidly growing population had to seek a livelihood. In that sector, incomes remained close to subsistence levels.

As a result of the efforts and ingenuity of Western enterprise, in 1937 Malaya had some $455 million, and Indonesia some $2.24 billion, invested in plantations, mines, oil fields and refineries, commerce and finance. Western enterprises had made substantial profits, and as Allen and Donnithorne demonstrate, had shown admirable flexibility in adapting themselves to changing conditions so as to produce a respectable profits record. The Malayan population had grown from a few hundred thousand at the beginning of the nineteenth century to some six million in 1940, the Indonesian population from some five million to seventy million. For the period 1952–54 (no comparisons can be made for earlier years) per capita net national product was about $310 in Malaya and about $90 in Indonesia. Malaya was more highly developed than Indonesia in terms of the structure of the economy, with less than half the national income originating in agriculture as compared to nearly two-thirds in Indonesia.

These differences in results demand explanation. Even more important than the differences, however, is the fundamental similarity in outcome: all this investment and enterprise left most of the people poor in both countries. Satisfactory figures are not available, but it would appear that peasant per capita income in both countries is in the $35–$55 (annually) range prevalent throughout Asia, with Malaya (which has a somewhat smaller proportion of peasants in the total population) somewhat closer to the upper end of this range than Indonesia.[12] No Asian government could contemplate another century of development that produced such meager results as the last one. For it is not at all "certain" that per capita consumption of the *native* population rose during the period under review. Obviously, taking national income and dividing it by total population tells little about living standards of the masses of the people, even where reliable figures are available. Perhaps per capita consumption did rise in Malaya. In Indonesia there seems to have been an initial rise followed by a fall. The Dutch have on the whole taken pride in their performance in Indonesia, but few Dutch writers or politicians have claimed that Indonesian living standards "certainly" rose under their rule. On the contrary, Dutch scholars and administrators have periodically voiced their misgivings and have frequently expressed concern over the declining living standards of the Indonesians, especially on the island of Java.

By the middle of the nineteenth century, the "culture system" was under attack by those Dutchmen who wished a more liberal policy toward private enterprise in the colonies; of their arguments, Furnivall said cautiously, "It is doubtful whether the people were worse off in 1850 than in 1830." [13] Fifty years later, the liberal system was in turn under fire—this time, apparently, with more justice. Queen Wilhelmina herself spoke of the declining welfare (*mindere welvaart*) of the Indonesian people, and a series of Commissions was appointed to investigate its causes. The result was the shift to the "ethical policy" in which improved standards of living for the people was at last a stated aim, but this policy seems to have failed, as we saw in Chapter 12

[12] There seems to be some kind of "iron law" of peasant income. Yields seem to vary inversely with size of holding, so as to keep income per family much the same in all Asian peasant societies.

[13] J. S. Furnivall, *Netherlands India: A Study of Plural Economy* (New York, 1944), p. 138.

above. De Wilde wrote in 1934: "The welfare of the native population has not been noticeably raised, for higher production is counterbalanced by increase of population." In 1939, as we have seen, the so-called Coolie Budget Commission was appointed to look into "Living Conditions of Plantation Workers and Peasants on Java."

The theories of underdevelopment presented in Part 4 explain why foreign investment in plantations, mines, oil fields, and commerce did not bring rising living standards to the peoples of underdeveloped countries. These theories certainly do not show that further foreign investment in these countries is undesirable. On the contrary, there can be little doubt that foreign enterprise still has a substantial role to play in the development of underdeveloped areas. Countries like Indonesia and Malaya lack the capital and the technical and managerial skills for further development. Providing these resources through foreign aid programs is difficult and seldom completely satisfactory. But foreign enterprise must adapt itself to the needs of national economic development; it cannot be just "more of the same." Industrial investment of a capital-intensive nature will not do the job alone; the problem of low productivity in agriculture must be attacked directly, and some capital must be directed into the peasant agriculture sector to permit more mechanized and larger-scale farming. In short, foreign investment must be encouraged, but within a framework of national development planning, not laissez faire. We shall have more to say on this point in Chapter 25.

The Case for Gradualism

It takes courage to say a good word for colonization these days, and Professor Frankel is to be admired for his courage. True, he defines colonization in very broad terms—broad enough, it seems, to include the TVA: [14]

> I submit that if we look below the surface of immediate circumstance we find that colonization is nothing more or less than the process of macrocosmic and microcosmic social and economic growth itself; that the forces which produce or arrest change in any society or social structure, old or new, spring from a common genus, and give rise to problems which are met with in varying degree in all cases of economic and social development.
>
> Colonization is the process by which such new structures are

[14] S. Herbert Frankel, *The Economic Impact on Under-developed Societies* (Oxford, 1953), pp. 9–10.

evolved. It implies the withdrawal of individuals from established structural patterns to found a new colony of endeavour within, and in relation to, the changing natural or human surround. The later structural forms react on the former, and may lead eventually to their complete dissolution. But, let me emphasize again, the process, like all growth, takes time.

The great modern movements of agricultural and consumers' co-operation and communal settlement, the new agencies for the reclamation of the land, for the collective prevention of illness and disease, for the rehabilitation of the injured, and for vaster projects like the re-colonization of neglected regions, on the model of the great experiments in decentralization of the Tennessee Valley Authority—to mention only a few—fall into the same category, and illustrate man's structural inventiveness.

However, colonization also includes in Frankel's concept what is ordinarily understood by colonial development. Indeed, he stresses its international aspects and argues that the process of economic growth "cannot be thought of in terms of any one single nation or state action as a whole." The African miner achieves higher standards of income than his "brother in the bush" because "he happens to have been drawn into a new colony of human activities." But the "focal point of that colony of modern effort lies neither in Northern Rhodesia nor in Africa. It may at one time be found in Europe, or North America." [15]

Frankel seems to regard colonization primarily as a device for achieving a gradual transition from one kind of economic and social organization to another. He would certainly be opposed to the big push recommended above.[16]

It is the attempt to simplify that process, to avoid the gradualness of change in order to pluck the quick fruits of endeavour in one direction—at the expense of inactivity in others—which accounts for social maladjustments. In a society in which all changes were to take place at rates so well adjusted to each other as not to disturb the basic harmony and integration of its constituent parts, there would be no social consequences of change but only harmonious change itself. When, however, rates of change are very discontinuous it may well happen that one sector of the society cannot be meaningfully integrated into the social life of the community at all—so that, as far as that sector is concerned, society as a whole no longer exists.

Change "which is not in harmony with the social resources and needs of a community may well prove to be not a blessing but a curse."

[15] *Ibid.*, p. 13.
[16] *Ibid.*, p. 24.

Not that Professor Frankel is an unquestioning admirer of what colonial administrations have actually achieved. Indeed, he is considerably less sure of the blessings of foreign enterprise than Allen and Donnithorne. The foreign investor, he says, "was not concerned with whether the loan would have good or bad effects on the welfare, health, and social structure of the borrower." The expectation that "the problem of development of the peripheral areas would be solved within the common framework" through international private investment "was an oversimplification of the basic economic and social difficulties of development in them."[17] However, his criticism is that foreign investment tried to bring too rapid change, rather than that it failed to change things enough. "The development of modern methods of economic organization has been accompanied by increasingly rapid disintegration of the indigenous economic and social structure." And this indigenous society had a value that often escaped Western eyes; for it provided the individuals in it "with that sense of psychological and economic security without which life loses its meaning."

Frankel fears that the outcome of efforts to solve the problems of economic development on the basis of "collective criteria directed by national governments" may be even worse; on the whole, he doubts that the task is alleviated by political and economic philosophies "which would make it appear that economic growth is not a decentralized process resting on the enterprise of the many, but one solely dependent upon the exercise of wisdom, foresight and power by the few."

In fact, Frankel doubts that there is any "solution" to the problems of underdeveloped countries. "The very idea of finding final solutions to social problems is the peculiar result of applying to the life of societies and individuals a category of thought which does not fit." Societies cannot solve problems "which constitute the very essence of their being," and analogies with mathematics and mechanics are false.[18]

Obviously Professor Frankel's views are in such complete conflict with ours that our only way to counter his "gradualism" would be to repeat the analysis already presented. But one question might be raised. When Professor Frankel speaks of "change not in harmony with the social resources and needs of a community," whom has he in mind? He seems to think in terms of change forced from outside on a "community" that is a single

[17] *Ibid.*, pp. 71, 73.
[18] *Ibid.*, 134, 74, 155.

integrated whole. We are not talking about such communities, however; we are talking about countries in which the national leadership has determined to pursue a policy of raising the incomes of the masses of the people, in response to a "revolution of rising expectations." True, the economic change may carry with it cultural change, and some people may suffer in the process. But if the majority of the people in these countries support their governments in their aims for economic development, is it for us to say them nay?

Marginalism, the Economic Calculus, and the Phase of Development

The economist's task in advising on development policy is simplest in countries that are already industrially advanced. Here the aim is "steady growth," and the maintenance of full employment without inflation is itself an almost sure guarantee of such growth. The economist may also discern possibilities for improving the allocation of resources; but no "lumpy," discontinuous, or rapid structural changes are required. The usual kind of economic calculus can be applied, comparing marginal (social) costs with marginal (social) benefits. The economist is on familiar ground, dealing with monetary, fiscal, foreign trade, and antimonopoly policy. The planning process is essentially a matter of "patching the market," leaving the broader policy issues to be decided at the polls.

Planning in Underdeveloped but Developing Countries

In Part 1, we saw that although low per capita income places certain countries in the "underdeveloped" category, industrialization and agricultural improvement are proceeding there at a rate high enough to raise per capita incomes. These countries already have enough domestic savings and taxes, plus assured foreign capital assistance, to finance the capital formation needed to raise incomes. At the same time all these countries face bottlenecks—capital supply, skilled labor, managerial and technical skills—and laggard sectors of the economy, which limit the rate of growth and make planning necessary.

In these countries, development planning must be more than "patching the market." The market and the polls do not provide sufficient guidance to the structural adjustments needed for growth, especially in the laggard sectors. Nor are the required adjustments strictly marginal. In such countries growth itself must be "managed," and "sectoral planning" is necessary. The relative rates at which heavy industry, light industry, agricultural improvement, transport and communications, housing, and the like, are to be pushed become a matter of conscious policy.

Planning of this kind still involves a calculus, involving cost-benefit comparisons, but it is no longer a purely marginal calculus, at least not for the more rapidly developing sectors of the economy.[19] Questions arise such as "should we concentrate on accelerating industrialization in the North, building power plants, roads, etc., there, and transfer population from the South, or should we concentrate on agricultural improvements and small industry in the South, with irrigation and drainage schemes, etc.?" Here the usual type of economic calculus is insufficient. The choice involves questions of discontinuous change; and one wants to know not only the direct cost-benefit ratios of the two alternative programs, but also the relative "demonstration effects," impact on attitudes toward enterprise and technical change, attitudes toward work and leisure, and the like.

This kind of calculus requires knowledge of a sort different from that needed for a marginal cost-benefit calculation, but it is not so different as to make traditional economics totally inapplicable. In this phase of development the discontinuities are limited in size and scope; it may be possible to pose the policy questions in terms of decisions on the rates of *acceleration* of trends already under way. Such planning means only looking at second derivatives instead of first derivatives, and market data can still provide a useful guide to development policy.

Underdeveloped and Stagnant (Declining) Countries

The real problems arise in countries where per capita income is stationary or falling, or rising so slowly, and from so low a level, that there is no hope of growth becoming cumulative without a transformation of the economy. Here the task is not merely to sustain or direct growth already under way, but to *launch* a process of growth that can become cumulative at some level of per capita income. Structural change is the most important aspect of development; and if output is to outrun population growth long enough to bring fundamental changes in behavior patterns and thus to get the economy "over the hump" where cumulative growth becomes possible, the required changes are of too discon-

[19] "The decision to develop the South of Italy by a ten-year $1.6 billion public investment program initiated a structural change which no market decision would ever have reached." Rosenstein-Rodan, *op. cit.*, p. 12.

tinuous a nature to be treated as acceleration of existing movements.

For planning of the sort needed in these countries, the domestic market no longer provides any guidance whatsoever. It is not a matter of estimating the cost-benefit ratios of a 10 per cent or even 50 per cent expansion of an existing industry, during a period when per capita incomes rise by, say, 20 per cent. It is a matter of estimating cost-benefit ratios of sudden increases in output ranging from several hundred per cent to infinity, with no previous experience, while national incomes double or treble. The very nature of the problem forbids a step-by-step, trial-and-error approach. It is a question of developing that river valley, with its integrated complex of power, aluminum, fertilizer, and irrigation projects, or not; the cost of one such complex of projects may absorb a country's entire capital budget for several years. Both the scope and the scale of investment must be planned.

Not only are the crucial decisions non-marginal, but they also involve an admixture of economics and other social sciences. The required changes in economic structure are so great that they may be unattainable without changes in social structure as well. Many of the most crucial decisions present themselves in forms which do not lend themselves to traditional economic analysis at all. Should a direct attack be made on the "undivided family," which so seriously dilutes incentives to work harder or better, to save, to risk capital, or to limit the size of individual families, or will industrialization and urbanization automatically break down the undivided family? In resettling people in new areas, should young, childless couples be selected, so as to use the resettlement program as an attack on the undivided family, or must the whole undivided family, or even the whole village, be moved as a unit? Can industrialization take place within the village structure, so as to avoid the high cost in social capital and the social disruption involved in urbanization? Can technological improvements be found that will raise output per man-hour without raising the ratio of capital to labor? How can the willingness to save, pay taxes, or attract foreign capital be increased? Will university training in business administration or industrial management break down the reluctance of the elite to become entrepreneurs? If so, will emphasis on a combination of engineering and economics training be most effective in producing the requisite type of manager, or is it better to stress accounting, which exerts its own discipline on the student and compels him to manage his business in terms of a rational calculus?

Faced with questions such as these, the Western economist who finds himself assisting the government of an underdeveloped country with its development planning finds little in his specialized training to help him; hence, he is apt to flounder. The market provides little or no guidance. The direction that might be obtained from periodic elections is too little and too late. It is doubtful whether any "trigger projects," or even "trigger sectors," can be isolated. What to do?

One field of recent experience may provide some guidance: the planning of "total war." For a short time, the present writer was engaged in wartime planning, and he has been struck since by the similarity between the *nature* of the problem confronting economic planners during the war and in underdeveloped countries now. Rapid expansion of the defense sector of the economy from 5 per cent to 50 per cent involved considerable structural change, as well as rapid absorption of unemployment. The process required breaking a succession of critical bottlenecks. Market criteria were thrown to the winds in determining the size of the defense sector, in allocating resources within the defense sector, and to some extent even in allocating resources within the civilian sector. In short, planning "total war," like planning development of poor and stagnant economies, involves marked and discontinuous structural changes, and resource allocation without reference to the market.

Moreover, we are already a good deal better off for guides to policy than we were ten years ago. We have learned something about the operation of underdeveloped economies, and the theory presented in Part 4 reflects what we have learned. The theory does not, of course, tell any particular country *exactly* what it must do to achieve a take-off into sustained growth. Every country is to some degree a special case, with its own pattern of natural and manpower resources, savings and investment potential, level of n-achievement, and the like. The theory does suggest the broad framework of development policy, and some of the conclusions to which it leads are highly significant:

1. The present allocation of resources in underdeveloped countries may not reflect comparative advantage, either domestically or internationally; it could well be just the reverse of what is required.

2. By the same token, further expansion of international trade without a drastic change in its pattern is no guarantee of a take-off and could even delay a take-off.

3. The "calculus" involved in economic development is one of comparing the effects of one gestalt of investment with another over a period beginning at least ten years hence and extending well into the future. The market provides very limited guidance in allocating resources so as to maximize the degree of development. For this reason development planning is necessary. The need for a plan has nothing to do with the relative importance of the public and private sectors; intervention to alter the decisions of private entrepreneurs is still a plan.

4. The plan must be a long-run one, extending for at least three or four five-year plans. What goes into the current five-year plan must be determined in large measure by the pattern of production established as a goal for the end of the third and fourth five-year plans.

5. In drawing up such a long-run plan, careful studies must be made of the natural resources, manpower resources (including management and technical skills), and capital resources, as they are and as they might be over the plan period. An effort must then be made to estimate the best allocation of these resources *after* a take-off has been accomplished and substantial structural change has been achieved.

6. A gradualist approach is almost certain to be self-defeating. In our foreign aid policy, we should be urging the governments of underdeveloped countries to be more ambitious, not less ambitious, in their planning. The targets for investment and increase in income must be high enough to outrun population growth and bring the needed structural change.

7. If the structural change brought by the development program does not in itself bring a drop in fertility rates to offset the probable drop in death rates, it may be necessary to attack the population problem directly as a part of development policy.

8. It is essential to break through the vicious circle of "technological dualism." Doing so means planning for increased productivity in the rural sector. In the phase when preconditions for take-off are being established, it may make good sense to seize remaining opportunities for raising productivity through fertilizers, seed selection, etc. But sustained growth requires a shift to more extensive and more mechanized agriculture, which means getting people out of the rural sector and getting capital into it.

9. The theory also shows why rising per capita income has been accompanied historically by a relative decline in the share of agriculture in the economy. With a large proportion of the population engaged in labor-intensive agriculture on very small

holdings, the rural sector acts as an anchor sunk deep in the sands of time, so that the ship of state can never move far from its present becalmed position with low levels of productivity and of income. There is no automatic tendency to adjust, either internally or internationally, to the glaring discrepancies in productivity between the rural and the industrial sector, or between average productivity of the economy as a whole and that of advanced countries. Only a rapid change to extensive, mechanized agriculture, with enough industrialization to absorb the population displaced from the rural sector, will assure a take-off into steady growth.

10. A consideration of true comparative advantage suggests that, in a good many underdeveloped countries, leaving large numbers of people in peasant agriculture means continuing to engage in activities for which the economy is not well suited.

11. There is no assurance that fertility will drop significantly in peasant societies unless there are further reductions in per capita income. If small-scale developmental efforts raise productivity faster than they reduce mortality, fertility may rise again in such societies.

In short, economic development is tantamount to getting people out of peasant agriculture. Cumulative growth comes spontaneously only when labor becomes scarce in agriculture, so that a shift to more land-and-capital-intensive techniques becomes profitable from the standpoint of individual farmers. In brief, what is needed is a planned (and less harsh) substitute for the constellation of plague, enclosures, reformation, discoveries, and industrial revolution which launched the process of cumulative growth in Europe.

Industrialization alone is unlikely to produce the desired results. Concentration of a limited capital budget in the capital-intensive sector will merely continue the process which prevailed for two centuries under colonial administrations. So far as industry versus agriculture is concerned, it is not a question of balanced growth or unbalanced growth, but one of balanced growth or no growth at all. At the same time, the most effective development policies will make good use of deliberately created imbalances designed to maximize "linkage."

There is no reason why democratic governments should not carry out policies of this kind. Nor is there any reason why such policies should not be pursued in countries where private enterprise predominates, if that is the preference of the people concerned. Development planning of this kind does not mean that the market is totally replaced by bureaucratic decisions. On the contrary, the more the market can be used the better. The basic decisions regarding the framework of private decision making and the scale and nature of public investment cannot be left to the market, any more than the maintenance of full employment without inflation can be left to the market alone. But once the framework is established, "consumer sovereignty" can reign with respect to all *other* decisions. And the higher the level of incomes, the more decisions can be left to the market, if "workable competition" prevails. Indeed, in development as in stabilization, a "mixed economy" is most likely to succeed. Laissez faire will not do the job, and totalitarian physical planning is unlikely to do the job well. It is the essence of good development planning that the government should take those decisions which it alone can make effectively, leaving to the market the decisions that can be made more effectively there.

The "Affluent Society"

We cannot bring ourselves to leave this discussion without one reference to Professor Kenneth Galbraith's recent essay on "the affluent society." [20] At the beginning of this section we suggested that the market is a better guide to policy in advanced than in poor and stagnant societies. But Galbraith argues that in countries as rich as the United States, the market is no longer an efficient guide to the allocation of resources. For everyone has all the really basic wants: food, clothing, leisure, recreation, security. Most people no longer consider the *marginal* dollar of any great importance, and how it is spent may reflect the relative strength of various "hidden persuaders" and the relative efficiency of different Madison Avenue advertising firms rather than any true relative satisfaction. We need to get back to a basic social philosophy as a guide to spending our money and if we do that we will spend more on public goods and services through our governments and less directly in the market. If Galbraith is right about all this, traditional welfare economics is of little use in affluent societies either. Perhaps future historians of economic thought will conclude that the economics of the marginal calculus was relevant only in Europe and the New World during the late nineteenth century—when and where this kind of economics was developed.

[20] J. K. Galbraith, *The Affluent Society* (New York, 1958).

19 The Primrose Paths

In countries which are both poor and nationalistic neither sacrifices from current consumption nor heavy reliance on foreign aid and investment is popular with the electorate. Hence, governments might be expected to cast about for nostrums that will raise standards of living without following either of these painful paths to development. Four kinds of primrose path for financing development have been seriously discussed: up by the bootstraps, controlled inflation, pump-priming, and expropriation of foreign investments.

Up by the Bootstraps?

Some recent writings suggest that economic development of underdeveloped areas may be possible, without substantial sacrifice of current consumption and without foreign capital, by effective use of the disguised unemployment that exists in most such countries. The argument is twofold. First, it should be possible to devise means of increasing productivity per man-hour which do not require heavy investment of the kind prevalent in advanced countries. Mere transfer of the techniques employed in advanced countries, where labor is more scarce than capital, is inappropriate in countries where capital is more scarce than labor. Secondly, the disguised unemployment in agriculture could be attracted into industrial projects, permitting an increase in industrial output with no offsetting decline in agricultural production. Some kinds of increases in output, it is contended, require much labor and very little capital. Such projects include the construction of irrigation channels and dams, road building, harbor repairs, and the like. Even cement plants, it has been argued, require technically relatively little capital.

Moreover, the argument continues, governments should not be misled by the "financial illusion"; such projects may cost money, but they entail no real social cost, since no alternative production is sacrificed by using on these projects labor that would otherwise be effectively unemployed. Food supply will not be diminished, and farmers who previously provided food to the former disguised unemployed can sell their surplus to the same people, now employed as wage earners. The farmers will therefore be able to pay higher taxes, and these taxes can be used to finance the development project. The completion of the projects will result in increases in agricultural production. In the case of irrigation, the increases in output arise directly from the projects themselves; in the case of improved transport, increased output arises from the greater specialization that becomes possible. The increased income of farmers in turn can then be recaptured in higher taxes, leaving farmers little better off than before, it is true, but permitting the increased output of agricultural goods to be exported, in order to pay for capital imports for further development. The taxing away of the increased yields may also be necessary, to prevent any increased productivity from being dissipated in increased leisure or in higher rates of population growth. Thus, a process of economic development is generated without foreign capital and with only modest and temporary sacrifices of present consumption.

Development of something like this kind has taken place at least once, and possibly twice. England, as the first country to industrialize, was not in a position to finance much of its early economic development by borrowing from abroad. However, it is worth remembering the conditions under which English economic development took place. For one thing, English workers shared very little in the fruits of economic development during its first decades. Men, women, and even children worked ten to fourteen hours per day for extremely low wages. The condition of the English urban worker in the eighteenth century was probably worse than that of the English peasant, or even of the peasant in some underdeveloped areas today. Former peasants, *forced* off the land into the factories through the enclosure movement, lived in the cities under conditions of appalling poverty, misery, and squalor. Moreover, up to the mid-nineteenth century the fiscal structure was highly regressive. With revenues derived mainly from commodity taxes and much of the government expenditures going to servicing the national debt, subsidies to new enterprises, and the like, the fiscal system redistributed income from poor to rich, making possible high levels of saving. Meanwhile, the Reformation had created a puritanical attitude toward consumption and saving, so that the rich reinvested their earnings rather than engaging in conspicuous consumption. Trade-unions were illegal up to 1825 and even then were very weak. There was no "social security" for workers during this period. Public assistance was limited to the dole and the poorhouse. It might also be said that England at the beginning of its period of rapid industrial expansion had a very small population (about four million) and still had undiscovered resources.

Finally, the industrialization of England was neither rapid nor spontaneous. A series of external events spread over centuries contributed to the Industrial Revolution in England: the expansion of European trade following the Crusades; the new trading possibilities opened up by the geographic discoveries of the late fifteenth and sixteenth centuries; the "price revolution" of the sixteenth century, through which a flow of gold and silver from the New World through Spain to Northern Europe provided the base for "easy money" policies; the development of the Dutch and German trading and financial empires. Even in Britain industrialization was not entirely a bootstrap operation.

The second case, although superficially very different, shows fundamental similarities. Under a strong totalitarian government, Russia has been able to industrialize rapidly during the past thirty-five years. However, this industrialization was achieved, at least in its early stages, largely at the expense of the kulaks and peasants. The former were liquidated and the latter seem at times to have been literally starved, to provide a surplus of foodstuffs for the support of workers in the factories and on development projects.

In other words, the "up by the bootstraps" approach has succeeded only where severe sacrifices have been forced on the masses of the people, to provide a basis for capital accumulation. As proposed for underdeveloped areas today, the up by the bootstraps method does not necessarily require reductions in the standard of living to start the development process, but it does mean that the initial increases in output must be denied to the people, in order to provide an export surplus to finance further expansion. An integral part of the scheme is heavier taxation of farmers, first to compel them to produce as much as before although they have fewer mouths to feed, and secondly, to drain off the increase in output and income as the development projects have their effect. This rise in taxation, and consequent prevention of initial improvements in living standards, is necessary, not only to provide an export surplus, but also to prevent the increased productivity from being converted into increased leisure or a more rapid rate of population growth rather than into increased output. The proposed up by the bootstraps route to higher living standards will prove, at best, only somewhat less uncomfortable than the one actually followed in England and in Russia.

Moreover, it is misleading to suggest that this sort of project will produce sustained development with *no* capital. Even road construction or irrigation requires some simple tools. Moreover, better roads are of little use without additional transport equipment, if only ox carts; and improved harbors are of little use without additional ships. Thus some increased saving will be necessary at the beginning, even though the volume required may be less than for a development program consisting mainly of capital-intensive projects.

There is also a serious question as to how much this sort of project alone can raise productivity. Some improvement can certainly be achieved in this manner, but it is doubtful whether the rate of expansion would be sufficient to overcome the inertia of an economy that has been stagnant for centuries and to launch a process of cumulative economic growth. "Capital-cheap" innovations would of course be highly desirable, but thus far they are not available; engineering genius has yet to be directed toward this particular problem in an organized, large-scale fashion. There is no assurance that much in the way of "capital-cheap" innovations can be expected during the next few years. A question also arises as to the degree to which the so-called leisure of the disguised unemployed is actually devoted to productive pursuits, which would have to be paid for by the villagers, if the disguised unemployed are drawn off into development projects.

Finally, the amount of disguised unemployment in agriculture can easily be exaggerated. We saw in Chapter 15 that as knowledge of agriculture in underdeveloped countries has grown, easy optimism about transferring "disguised unemployed" from agriculture to industry has disappeared; in many underdeveloped countries, *static* disguised unemployment in agriculture is at a very low level. With present techniques the entire labor force in the rural sector is needed at planting and harvesting time. Substantial numbers cannot be released from agriculture for full-time industrial jobs without a drop in agricultural production unless the average size of holdings is increased and some degree of mechanization introduced. Cumulative improvement in agricultural productivity on the basis of private initiative will not take place until this initial jump to a more highly mechanized and larger-scale agriculture has been made through government policy. If we want early improvement in *per capita* output, policy must be designed to make labor relatively scarce in agriculture by simultaneously shifting to a more mechanized and larger-scale agriculture and encouraging a rapid rate of industrialization. Such a process is far indeed from a bootstrap operation requiring little net saving and investment.

How effective the up by the bootstraps approach can be is one of the many questions that must be answered differently for different countries. In Indonesia, the Philippines, and Libya, the scope for projects of this sort appears to be rather small. Transport systems are well developed in the areas where economic activity is now concentrated. There are no rich agricultural or mineral resources requiring only improved transport to make them accessible. Land is not obviously misallocated, and better transport alone may not bring much improvement in patterns of land use. Irrigation is not so important in Indonesia as in countries where rainfall is less abundant and less dependable. Where irrigated land is common (as in Javanese rice culture), the irrigation systems are already highly developed, and the advantages of extending the irrigated areas are doubtful at best. Irrigation in Libya is a matter of sinking wells to deeper levels and in new areas; this requires considerable capital equipment and could result in more rapid fall of water tables in the areas now under irrigation unless it is done with skill and care.

At the other extreme is Ethiopia, where it seems that in order to raise output, exports, and living standards the government need only build more roads into the wild coffee forests and persuade the labor force to move into newly opened areas. In India, Pakistan, and other arid zone countries, irrigation can apparently raise output considerably. But whereas the effectiveness of capital-cheap, labor-intensive projects varies substantially from country to country, for underdeveloped countries as a whole their role is likely to be a limited one, unless and until a new brand of "industrial revolution" takes place, consisting of innovations that raise output per man-hour while *absorbing* labor and requiring little additional capital.

It is essential in this connection to distinguish between capital-saving inventions and capital-saving innovations. Probably most inventions are "capital saving," in the sense that they reduce the capital required per unit of output, once the new plant is in place. In this sense, it seems likely that even the steam railroad was a capital-saving invention; capital required per ton-mile of freight carried is probably less on a modern railway than it was with horses and wagons. However, capital-saving inventions of this type do not help very much if the capital requirements for *introducing* them are beyond the means of underdeveloped countries. In other words, the *installation* of a new technique that may ultimately be capital saving, may require very large amounts of capital indeed. Even capital-saving inventions are easier for advanced than for underdeveloped countries to introduce. Where a great deal of capital has already been accumulated, capital-saving inventions can be introduced by using existing replacement funds. Where the capital stock is low, however, replacement funds will be insufficient for major innovations, even if they consist in introduction of capital-saving inventions. What underdeveloped countries need is not merely capital-saving inventions in this sense, but means of raising productivity without increasing the current rate of total investment, *even temporarily*. Clearly, the technical requirements of this sort of innovation are much more severe than for capital-saving inventions of the usual sort.

The indivisibility of demand, discussed in Chapter 16, also constitutes a hurdle hard to jump without a minimum effort. Moreover, there is reason to suspect that a collection of small industries has lower "leverage effects" than a single large one involving the same initial amount of total investment. The construction of a railway, opening up new territory, facilitating population movements, and making necessary the development of new communities, is likely to have a greater aggregate effect on investment than a collection of shoe factories, textile plants, and the like, even if the initial investment is equally large in both cases. Again we are confronted with a vicious circle. It is difficult to industrialize without the increases in income which would provide the demand for increased output of industrial goods; but such increases in income are difficult to achieve without industrialization.

In sum, although the possibilities of promoting expansion by methods requiring little capital should be exploited to the full, we have small reason to hope that these methods by themselves will promote rapid economic growth in most underdeveloped countries in the near future. If our aim is a rate of economic expansion sufficient to outrun population growth and to bring new patterns of behavior regarding work and leisure, we cannot rely on these techniques alone. Some substantial increase in domestic taxes and savings, or a greater inflow of foreign capital, or a combination of the two, will be necessary.

Finance by Inflation?

Some writers have suggested that the simplest way to finance development for underdeveloped areas is to print money or borrow from the banking system—in short, by inflation. In this fashion, it is maintained, the population will be "forced" to save since the rise in prices will necessitate a reduction in the volume of physical consumption.

Of course, in recommending inflation as a financing device, no one is suggesting that underdeveloped countries should subject themselves to the kind of hyperinflation that took place in advanced countries between the wars. It is universally recognized that such cumulative inflations not only disrupt the economy but pave the way for social and political upheavals as well. As Dr. Bresciani-Turroni says at the outset of his classic study of the German hyperinflation: [1]

> The depreciation of the mark of 1914-23, which is the subject of this work, is one of the outstanding episodes in the history of the twentieth century. It was the most colossal thing of its kind in history: and, next probably to the Great War itself, it must bear responsibility for many of the political and economic difficulties of our generation. It destroyed the wealth of the more solid elements in German society: and it left behind a moral and economic disequilibrium, apt breeding ground for the disasters which have followed. Hitler is the foster-child of the inflation. The financial convulsions of the Great Depression were, in part at least, the product of the distortions of the system of international borrowing and lending to which its ravages had given rise. If we are to understand correctly the present position of Europe,

[1] Constantino Bresciani-Turroni, *The Economics of Inflation* (London, 1937), p. 5.

we must not neglect the study of the great German inflation. If we are to plan for greater stability in the future, we must learn to avoid the mistakes from which it sprang.

In hyperinflation, the value of past savings is destroyed in whole or in part. Insurance policies provide increasingly inadequate protection as prices rise. Annuities and pension funds for the aged become insufficient. Persons and families with relatively fixed incomes—and these include some of the most productive members of society, such as scientists, schoolteachers, artists, civil servants, and police—suffer a continuously declining standard of living. Even where labor is well organized, there is often a tendency for wages to lag behind prices, so that labor's share of national income tends to fall. Rational accounting becomes almost impossible, and rational allocation of resources becomes all the more difficult. Moreover, hyperinflations tend to end in crisis and depression. The destruction of the middle classes, impoverishment of workers, and enrichment of speculators and black marketeers intensify social conflict and permit radical parties of right or left to take power. Underdeveloped countries, already prone to political instability, cannot afford the added burdens of hyperinflation.

Even the "controlled" inflations which are advocated, however, may have grave disadvantages for underdeveloped countries. Most of these suffer from a tendency for investment to be directed toward speculative holding of inventories, rather than to the establishment or expansion of productive enterprises. A constantly rising price level tends to aggravate this tendency by making speculation all the more profitable. Who will prefer a possible small gain over a long period, if assured of a large gain in a short period? Moreover, export industries, whose prices are determined in the world market, are confronted with constantly rising costs. Thus export industries tend to become increasingly unprofitable, and balance of payments difficulties are aggravated. Foreign investors are usually not attracted by a situation in which costs are constantly rising, even if their eye is cast toward the domestic market, where there is more hope of recouping increased costs through increased prices. Foreign investors know that even "chronic" inflations tend to break down at some stage. Plants which have been built in high-cost periods become unprofitable in succeeding low-price periods.

Sometimes the advocates of inflation support their arguments by drawing attention to the large amount of unemployment in underdeveloped areas. A development program which is financed in an inflationary fashion to begin with—say, by borrowing from the central bank—will not lead to a serious rise in prices, because any initial rise will result in absorption of the unemployed and increased output of goods and services. This argument, valid enough in advanced countries, does not hold in underdeveloped ones, because there is little excess capacity in farms or factories to match unemployment. As pointed out in a recent ECAFE document: "It is precisely because there are bottlenecks, such as a shortage of capital or skill, in the productive system that resources are unemployed in an underdeveloped economy." [2] Moreover, as this same document points out, the tax system of many underdeveloped countries is so inelastic, that their governments could not count on the yield of taxes rising substantially with prices, so as to impose an "automatic stabilizer" effect. Indeed, the study points out, because of the rise in prices, and the inflexibility of taxes, "the government's command over raw resources through taxation may actually decline as inflation proceeds apace in spite of a higher aggregate productivity." [3] Moreover, many of the investment projects needed in underdeveloped areas are of a long-term nature which will bring increases in output only after a considerable lag. Nor is it certain that the initial increases in income brought by inflationary investment in a development program will bring substantial increases in the propensity to save; once the "demonstration effect" begins to operate, people may spend an increasing share of their incomes on new consumers' goods.

Professor Bronfenbrenner, in an interesting analysis, suggests in effect a concept of "optimal degree of inflation." [4] There are two ways, in addition to those already suggested, in which inflation may prove beneficial. First, it may permit "the authorities . . . to raise the relative prices of the types of labour and capital goods required for development projects without imposing on other sectors of the economy the reductions in money wages and prices which would otherwise be required." This device (which was deliberately used by the Canadian government in the first two years of World War II) permits reallocation of resources, in a manner conducive to development, in relatively

[2] UN Economic Commission for Asia and the Far East, Committee on Industry and Trade, "Inflation and the Mobilization of Domestic Capital" (E/CN.11/I£T/WP.1/L.6), October 22, 1951, p. 3.

[3] *Ibid.*, p. 6.

[4] Martin Bronfenbrenner, "The High Cost of Economic Development," *Land Economics*, August, 1953, especially p. 210.

painless fashion. Second, and more important for Professor Bronfenbrenner's argument, is the "money illusion": [5]

> A slow inflation, or even a rapid one, in its early stages induces labourers to work more intensively for real incomes which are no higher and which may be lower than their previous level. To a lesser extent, owners of land and capital may be induced to put their property to work more intensively in the same way when money incomes rise.

Thus, judicious inflation may call forth increased output which, if properly allocated, could significantly accelerate development. The accompanying forced saving helps to reallocate demand from consumers' goods to capital goods. Beyond a certain point, however, further inflation will reduce output, partly because investment shifts to speculative hoarding of inventories, and partly because supply curves of various factors of production turn backward as higher incomes are reached (workers prefer more leisure to more income, investors more safety and liquidity to more income).

There can be no quarrel with this analysis. The question is only, "Where is this optimum reached"? The question is one of fact. Our hunch is that the optimal degree of inflation is very low in most underdeveloped countries—one which raises prices less than, say, 5 per cent per year. We suspect that the case regarded by Bronfenbrenner as a *curiosum*—where maximum output is reached under *deflationary* pressure at *less* than full employment, because income distribution is very unequal, supply curves of labor turn backward at low income levels, and a large share of income is consumed by idle rich—is approximated by more underdeveloped countries than he thinks. But the question is complicated, and it should be answered by each government in terms of the situation faced in each country.

Economic stabilization and development are closely intertwined. The conflict between unemployment and economic progress is obvious and direct. The productivity of the unemployed worker is zero, and productivity of the entire labor force obviously cannot be maximized when some members are producing nothing. This statement applies equally to overt and to disguised unemployment. But unemployment conflicts with progress in more subtle and indirect ways. Unemployment in export industries can lead to a drain on foreign exchange, making impossible the importation of the capital equipment and raw materials

[5] *Ibid.*

needed for expansion. At worst, it may even make it impossible to import sufficient consumers' goods to maintain a minimal standard of living. The human suffering that goes with a loss of income, or with uncertainty about maintenance of income in the future, the loss of personal pride and dignity that accompanies reliance on the charity of others for a meager livelihood, make unemployment one of the most serious of social evils; consequently, social and political instability are the frequent outcome of prolonged mass unemployment. Economic progress does not take place rapidly in an atmosphere of sudden and violent change in government policies and social attitudes. Avoiding serious inflation, on the other hand, is necessary both to direct private investment into the most effective channels and to prevent disequilibrium in the balance of payments, which could hamper economic development by making impossible the import of necessary raw materials and equipment. Conversely, economic development itself, by raising levels of per capita income, makes the policies needed for stabilization possible without serious sacrifices on the part of the population.

Inflation versus the "Disequilibrium Economy"

It is important to distinguish between ordinary inflation and what may be called a "war finance" approach—or between cumulative price rises and a deliberate policy of creating inflationary pressure, but then offsetting or controlling it so as to reap the benefits and avoid the harm. Inflationary financing of the regular budget in hope that a rising price level will in itself provide incentives for private investment in development projects is unlikely to be successful. Quite different, however, is a system in which a government undertaking a large-scale development program recognizes that the level of public investment is in itself inflationary, and then mops up increases in income through tax policy, monetary policy, and direct controls. This latter system was used with great success by Australia, Canada, the United Kingdom, and the United States during World War II. All these countries had war expenditures exceeding 50 per cent of national income, and budget deficits in the neighborhood of 50 per cent of expenditures; yet the rise in the cost of living index during six years of war was kept under 30 per cent.[6]

There are obvious analogies between the problems of war

[6] One may argue, of course, as to whether or not the official indices were as good a measure of living costs at the end of the war as they were when it began.

finance and the problem of financing an ambitious economic development program, just as there are analogies between planning development and planning total war. The pace of transformation involved an excess of public and private investment over taxes plus *ex ante* savings, creating inflationary pressure that had to be *offset* by tax increases, loan campaigns, price controls and rationing, direct controls over resource allocation—the whole apparatus of the "disequilibrium economy." Financing total war involved deliberate creation and subsequent mopping up of inflationary pressure.

On the other hand, the analogy should not be pushed too far. The objective of wartime planning was more easily understood and more widely accepted than the objective of development planning. The major belligerent powers began their preparations for war with considerable excess industrial capacity as well as unemployment. The wholly or partially unemployed included skilled workers, technicians, and managers as well as common labor. In terms of broad sectors—heavy industry, small industry, agriculture—the structural change was much less drastic than is required for economic development. Wartime administrations were able to use price and income incentives to lubricate the transition to a war economy, so long as unemployment and excess capacity prevailed. Once the war economy was going full blast, the allocation of resources could be "frozen." Underdeveloped countries will have no such interim in which monetary expansion can be used without fear of inflation, and economic development requires *continuous* reallocation of resources. Wartime economic planning is the closest thing in the recent experience of Western economists to the problem of development planning; it is worth reviewing for what help it may provide, but it will not in itself provide the whole answer.

If the government can be responsible for a large share of the economic development program; if it can proceed with this program efficiently; if it is able to regulate and encourage private investment, preventing misallocation of private capital and stimulating private enterprise to expand in conformity with the development program; if, despite inflationary pressure, it is able to prevent cumulative price rises by higher taxes, loan campaigns, price ceilings, rationing, and the like; if it is able to control the pattern and volume of imports; if, indeed, the government is able to run its development program in somewhat the way in which advanced countries ran their war economies during World

War II and thus manage successfully a "disequilibrium economy" —then, a very strong case can be made for this approach.

Pump-priming

Under the combined pressures of continuing depression and "the New Economics," old-fashioned canons of "sound public finance" gave way in the late 1930's to ideas of "compensatory fiscal policy." To a few economists and to larger numbers of businessmen and politicians, however, the concept of increased government intervention in economic life, even for so worthy a purpose as stabilizing the economy, was abhorrent. Yet these people recognized the danger to democratic society of continued mass unemployment. There was a brief phase when persons of this political faith sought an escape from this dilemma in "pump-priming." The basic idea was that the Depression might be overcome by modest and temporary increases in public spending, designed to "prime the pump" and start the "normal" process of steady economic growth flowing again.

Professor Alvin Hansen, writing in 1940, had this to say of the pump-priming idea:[7]

> The term pump-priming carries with it the implication that a certain volume of public spending, varying under different conditions, will have the effect of setting the economy going on the way toward full utilization of resources on its own power without further aid from governmental spending. It is not true, as it has sometimes been suggested, that the pump-priming concept implies that only a very small amount of public spending will set the economy operating at full capacity. A pump may require much or little priming, depending upon a variety of conditions; and similarly the pump-priming concept carried with it no implication as to the amount of spending necessary, but only the implication that, whatever the amount required, sooner or later the economy can operate on its own motive power.

As understanding of the expansionary process increased, optimism about the efficacy of pump-priming dissolved. It was demonstrated that the nature of the expansion path depended upon interactions and relative magnitudes of the "multiplier" (increases in consumer spending resulting from an initial increase in investment) and the "accelerator" (increases in investment resulting from initial increases in consumer spending). If the ac-

[7] Alvin H. Hansen, *Fiscal Policy and Business Cycles* (New York, 1941), p. 262.

celerator were relatively low, the expansion path would have roughly the same shape as if the multiplier were operating alone: after a short period of increasing income, income would return again to its original level—assuming, of course, that the values of the multiplier and the accelerator coefficients did not change in the process. If the accelerator were somewhat higher, damped fluctuations would set in, tending toward the original level of income. A very high accelerator might launch fluctuations of ever-increasing amplitude; and if the multiplier and accelerator were both very high, an "explosion" might occur, with income rising at an increasing rate through cumulative inflation.

More refined analysis still, undertaken by Professor J. R. Hicks and others, introduced a "ceiling" to expansion of output resulting from full employment, and a "floor" representing the maximum rate of capital consumption that was physically possible. This analysis suggested that the most likely effect of a once-over increase in government spending is to set in train a new series of fluctuations. When the psychological impact of initial changes in income on the coefficients themselves is introduced, still other patterns result.[8]

The general effect of this closer study of pump-priming was to show the extremely small possibility that a short period of increased government spending followed by withdrawal would result in resumption of growth. At best, the government could expect to be confronted with a complicated problem of economic stabilization involving "compensatory fiscal policy"; that is, variations in spending and taxing according to the current level of, and recent changes in, private spending, so as to maintain full employment without inflation.

The forlorn hope of finding in pump-priming an escape from the dilemma of continued depression on the one hand or increased government intervention on the other has its psychological counterpart today. In both developed and in underdeveloped countries, some people today, alarmed by the requirements for sustained economic growth, hope to find a means of producing a take-off without either increased taxes and savings at home or increased foreign aid and investment. Will not a large *initial* effort permit a return to "normal" and sustained economic growth as well?

It is true, of course, that economic growth once launched tends to become cumulative. However, this cumulative growth

[8] Cf. Benjamin Higgins, "Interaction of Cycles and Trends," *Economic Journal*, June, 1955, and literature there cited.

does not mean that the need for increased investment disappears. At best, it may mean that, as higher levels of income are reached, the real sacrifices involved in making the necessary savings and investment are reduced.

From the analysis presented in Chapter 17 it is readily seen that there are only two ways of accelerating economic growth. One is to increase the level of per capita investment, the other is to reduce the incremental capital-output ratio (ICOR). There are ways in which the capital-output ratio can be reduced by policy and planning; we have mentioned some of these in Chapter 7. However, the most likely historical pattern with respect to the ICOR is that, after initial reductions (as a result of improved efficiency of management, manpower training, capital-saving innovations, provision of social overhead capital, etc.), ICOR will rise. Thus although it may be true that a big push is needed to launch economic growth, and although it may also be true that *percentage increases* in investment can be allowed to drop once the process of growth is under way, this does not mean that having once started economic growth it will be possible to reduce total investment, or even to reduce the proportion of national income devoted to investment purposes. Steady growth requires that both the amount of investment and the ratio of investment to income should continue to rise for some decades until a level equal to 15 or 20 per cent of national income is reached. This level must then be sustained if growth is to continue unabated.

Thus the concept of pump-priming as an escape from the hard facts of economic life is no more applicable to problems of development of underdeveloped areas than it was to the problem of steady growth in highly industrialized economies. There is no escape from the need to increase the rate of capital formation.

Confiscation of Foreign Enterprises

Most people in the Western world would probably reject confiscation of foreign enterprises as unworthy serious consideration, but the device has been seriously proposed, by Martin Bronfenbrenner among others.[9] It has also been carried through by some governments of underdeveloped countries—notably Mexico, Iran, Egypt, and (on a very small scale) Indonesia—

[9] Martin Bronfenbrenner, "The Appeal of Confiscation in Economic Development," *Economic Development and Cultural Change*, April, 1955, pp. 201–218.

with varying degrees of success. It seems to have worked well in Mexico. In Indonesia, it seems to have delayed a take-off.

Using arithmetic models based on reasonable assumptions as to quantitative relationships and behavior patterns, Bronfenbrenner shows that economic growth can be significantly accelerated by expropriation "in societies whose income distributions include high property shares which are not ploughed back into economic development."[10] In his examples, property income is set at 15 per cent of national income. The initial flow of savings is set at 5 per cent of national income, but developmental investment is only 2 per cent of national income, yielding a 1.7 per cent annual increase in national income. With "Russian style" confiscation, development investment jumps immediately to 10 per cent of national income and the rate of growth to about 2.5 per cent. With "Chinese style" confiscation, permitting some immediate increase in consumption, development investment rises to 5 per cent and the growth rate to about 1.9 per cent.

Obviously, unilateral action by the government of an underdeveloped area to confiscate foreign properties would undermine that country's relations with the outside world and would probably destroy temporarily any hopes of obtaining new capital assistance. Transfer of foreign enterprises to domestic ownership might be arranged on a multilateral basis, however, and this could be the form that foreign aid takes. The United Nations, or one of its Specialized Agencies, or some other organization engaged in capital assistance to underdeveloped areas, might undertake to compensate foreign investors in underdeveloped areas in their own currencies. Ownership of these enterprises could then be transferred to nationals of those underdeveloped countries without loss to the original investors. The effect would be to enrich those countries, in the form of free foreign exchange, by the amount of profits and depreciation now being transferred to foreign investors. This foreign exchange, and its domestic currency counterpart, could then be used to finance economic development.

This approach has some serious limitations. First, there are relatively few underdeveloped countries where the additional financial resources that could be made available for economic development through confiscation would be sufficient to do the job. There would of course be substantial differences in this respect from one country to another; in countries where foreign enterprises comprise a large share of the economy and plough

[10] *Ibid.*, p. 207.

back little of their earnings within the country this limitation would not apply.

Secondly, the necessary technical and managerial personnel for operating such enterprises is often not available among nationals of underdeveloped countries. Obtaining them on a salary basis may not be easy if combined with confiscation, even when the confiscation takes place through international agreement.

Thirdly, the confiscation approach is essentially "isolationist" in character. From many points of view, an approach involving elements of "partnership" between the underdeveloped countries and the advanced ones is more attractive; it seems better designed to produce an integrated international economy.

Conclusions

Unpalatable though it may be to governments of underdeveloped countries, the main conclusion of this chapter is clear: there *are* no "primrose paths" to economic development. Without a certain amount of national sacrifice, economic development will not occur. The sacrifice may take one or all of the following forms:

1. Working harder and better.
2. Saving voluntarily to finance development investment, public or private.
3. Paying higher taxes to finance development investment.
4. Encouraging foreign investment, with whatever temporary sacrifices of opportunities for national businessmen may be involved.
5. Accepting foreign aid, with whatever commitment is required as a condition for receipt of such aid. It is to be hoped that in future the only conditions imposed by grantor countries will be submission by the beneficiary country of a well-constructed development plan, as a basis for aid; but even a good development plan requires some commitment and some sacrifice.

Working harder and better is not "finance" in the ordinary sense, and it will not raise standards of living much unless accompanied by capital formation. The same is true of improved allocation of resources; some increases in output may be achieved in this fashion, but cumulative economic growth will require capital formation as well. In the rest of this book, therefore, we shall concentrate on the four sources of financing for economic development: voluntary savings, taxes, foreign investment, and foreign aid.

20 Public Finance Versus Financing Development

The discussion in Parts 3 and 4 has already shown that the institutional, sociological, technological, and political framework within which economic policy must be formulated and undertaken in underdeveloped countries is very different from that of advanced countries. Fiscal policy is no exception. The sheer poverty of underdeveloped countries makes the raising of the propensity to save, as well as of the inducement to invest, a necessary part of fiscal policy. The absence of frontier areas makes more difficult financing out of profits of individual enterprise, and the government's right of eminent domain is less valuable as a means of financing its own development projects. The possibility that different fiscal systems might have different effects on rates of population growth must be taken into account. The fiscal structure must devote more attention to providing incentives for risk-taking and innovation. In considering the impact of tax measures, the possibility that supply curves of effort, savings, and risk-taking may be backward sloping must be taken into account. "Customary normal" incomes are established at relatively low levels, beyond which additional leisure, or additional liquidity and safety of assets, is preferred to additional income. A closely related phenomenon is what has been called a "high unit-profit" mentality. Entrepreneurs in underdeveloped areas often prefer a high margin of profit on a small volume to a small margin of profit on a large volume.

A large proportion of income is earned in agriculture, a fact which raises administrative problems with respect to the tax structure and to the organization of savings and credit institutions. Even in advanced countries, the assessment of income is much more difficult in agricultural areas, where records are seldom complete, than it is in urban industrialized areas. The administrative problems associated with a large rural population are aggravated in underdeveloped countries by a low level of general education, widespread illiteracy, and by the relatively small number of people with training and experience in public administration. A related problem is the relatively high proportion of income that is earned in kind, rather than in money, which clearly calls for special monetary and fiscal devices.

Special sociological factors further complicate issues of fiscal policy. Where society is organized into villages, operating on a semicommunal basis, or into extended families, the entire incentive system is different from what it is in countries where the basic social unit is the immediate family. Reactions to particular tax measures, or to particular savings incentives, may be affected by such differences in social organization.

Finally, none of these countries can be divorced from its history, which affects attitudes toward particular institutions or policies. This factor is especially important in those underdeveloped countries which have recently emerged from colonial status, where policies or institutions associated with the former imperialist powers may be unacceptable, whatever their intrinsic merits.

To meet these peculiar administrative, political, and social problems, the monetary and fiscal policies of underdeveloped areas must be "tailor-made." Canons of taxation which have become commonplace in advanced countries may be inapplicable in underdeveloped ones. A conference of experts assembled under the joint auspices of the International Program in Taxation at Harvard University and the Fiscal Division of the United Nations Department of Economic Affairs, came to the following conclusions: [1]

(1) Institutional factors and legal systems of underdeveloped countries are to be considered paramount in the formulation of recommendations for tax changes (e.g., in some countries the jurisdiction over land taxes is vested in a level of government whose revenues are

[1] H. P. Wald and J. N. Froomkin (eds.), *Papers and Proceedings of the Conference on Agricultural Taxation and Economic Development* (Cambridge, Mass., 1954), p. 23.

not a promising or desirable source for development funds).

(2) Recommendations for changes must take into account not only the prevailing balance of political power, but also the whole economic, social, and institutional combination of forces shaping the government (e.g., in a country with powerful landlord interests and pressures of population on land, increases in the land tax may be either politically unacceptable or undesirable because they would be transmitted to tenant cultivators).

(3) Another requirement is that the recommendations should be in line with the administrative capacity of the country, so that the taxes can be enforced comprehensively and justly (e.g., sophisticated recommendations with regard to the taxation of land in reverse ratio to its optimum output may be beyond the ability of the underdeveloped country to administer).

(4) One should differentiate between short-term revenue-raising measures for the financing of urgent development projects and long-term tax reforms which are directly articulated to the steady encouragement of economic development.

Even among advanced countries, however, differences exist both in historical background and in legal, institutional, and social frameworks. Economists have long recognized the difference between public finance in general and the public finance of particular countries; the general principles must be applied in a fashion appropriate to the institutional framework of each country. Cannot the same be said of underdeveloped countries as well? Admitting that the differences in institutional background may be greater as between underdeveloped and advanced countries than as among advanced countries, cannot the voluminous literature of public finance be brought to bear on the problems of underdeveloped countries? In short, what excuse is there for starting a separate literature on financing development?

Public Finance

In its theoretical aspects, the literature of traditional public finance, built up roughly between the "marginal revolution" of 1870 and the latter years of the Great Depression of the 1930's, was primarily concerned with the shifting and incidence of taxes. Different tax systems were analyzed in terms of their effects on the allocation of resources and on the distribution of income. Throughout much of this period, "neutrality" of tax systems was regarded by many economists as the final goal; the best tax system was one which left "equilibrium" undisturbed. As more economists recognized that monopoly was the rule rather than the exception, the "neutrality" goal was modified; the fiscal system became a device for "patching the market." Tax and subsidy schemes, designed to make monopolists behave as though they were not, represented the climax of this development in economic thought.

The methodology of public finance was microeconomic, applying marginal analysis to the usual precepts of welfare economics. It was of course recognized that there were occasional "lapses from equilibrium" in the form of inflation or unemployment. These fluctuations, however, were regarded as a monetary phenomenon, to be cured by monetary policy. Apart from theory of taxation, traditional public finance devoted some attention to tax administration and, more rarely, to budgetary administration.

It cannot be said that any of these concerns is unimportant in underdeveloped countries. Assumptions about market behavior and shapes of functions must be made to fit, but the partial equilibrium analysis of orthodox public finance can still be of considerable use in underdeveloped countries. This kind of analysis might be termed "public finance in underdeveloped countries" as distinct from financing development. It is still useful to know who will bear the ultimate burden of a particular tax and what the effects on economic behavior are likely to be. Improved allocation of resources is a part of the process of economic development. Many of these countries suffer from maldistribution of income; certainly a financial system chosen for development purposes ought not to make income distribution worse. There is no denying that many governments of underdeveloped countries need to devote special attention to tax and budgetary administration. Nevertheless full attention to the shifting and incidence of taxes, with budgets confined to government expenditures of a kind considered "normal" in advanced countries, would not in itself assure a take-off into cumulative growth.

Fiscal Policy

With the great depression and the publication of Keynes' *General Theory* and Hansen's *Fiscal Policy and Business Cycles*, the interest of professional economists shifted from public finance to "fiscal policy." Fiscal policy was the use of the government's taxing, borrowing, and spending powers to maintain full employment without inflation. It introduced into the literature the concept of flexible budgetary policy, with budgets deliberately unbalanced to offset inflationary or deflationary tendencies in the economy. It also directed attention toward the planning of public investment from the viewpoint of economic stabilization. Later, emphasis was placed on "built-in flexibility" of the fiscal system. Others were concerned with the problem of stagnation in mature economies. Eventually the theories of cycle and trend were amalgamated in the analysis of "steady growth."

In contrast to the method of public finance, the method of analysis underlying fiscal policy is highly aggregative. It deals with the level of income, output, employment, investment, consumer spending, taxation, government spending, and the like, for the economy as a whole.

We saw in Chapter 18 that in advanced countries the maintenance of full employment without inflation is by itself an almost sure guarantee of steady growth. The consideration of secular trends does not affect very much the methodology of economic analysis, nor the role of the economic adviser. The policy maker is concerned with improving the allocation of resources and distribution of income as well as with stabilization, but no lumpy, discontinuous, or rapid structural changes are required. He can apply conventional economic calculus, comparing marginal social cost with marginal social benefits, and economic policy still reduces to questions of monetary, fiscal, foreign trade, and antimonopoly policy. The policy maker is primarily a trouble shooter. The policy-making process is still essentially a matter of patching the market, with broader issues decided at the polls.

Underdeveloped countries as well as advanced ones face problems of economic instability. Indeed, in arid zone countries where fluctuations are generated from the supply side, fluctuations in income and employment can be more violent than in industrialized countries. In Libya, we saw, unemployment can reach 80 per cent of the labor force, in the off season of a drought year, and there may be labor scarcity in the peak season of a good rainfall year.

Finance in Underdeveloped but Developing Countries

We have seen that there are some countries whose low per capita income places them in the "underdeveloped" category, although industrialization and agricultural improvement are taking place at a rate high enough to raise per capita incomes. These countries, by definition, have enough financial resources to meet capital requirements, but they must contend with bottlenecks, discontinuities, and laggard sectors of the economy.

We suggested in Chapter 18 that, in these countries, planning can be reduced to decisions on selective *acceleration* of trends already under way. It is clear, however, that determination of the appropriate policy requires analysis quite different from the microeconomic "shifting and incidence" theory and macroeconomic "gap" theory of orthodox economics.

Finance in Underdeveloped and Stagnant (Declining) Countries

In Chapter 18 we also saw that the most troublesome policy questions arise in countries where per capita income is stationary or falling, or rising so slowly and from so low a level that there is no hope of growth becoming cumulative without a transformation of the economy. The task is to bring together the constellation of economic, sociological, political, and technical factors that will launch a take-off.

For this job the market provides little guidance, and traditional public finance and fiscal policy are virtually useless. In Chapter 19 we suggested that experience with financing total war might provide some guidance. For the most part, however, principles of financing development must be constructed from the ground up. Traditional public finance and fiscal policy still provides part of the foundation; a larger part is provided by available theories of underdevelopment, such as have been presented in Parts 3 and 4. It would be pleasant if we could go on to construct financial principles with complete confidence in the solidity of this foundation. As it is, we can proceed only with reasonable assurance that the whole structure will not collapse.

21 Measures to Increase Savings

How far can voluntary domestic savings go toward meeting capital requirements where the rate of net investment must be doubled or trebled as part of the "minimum effort" needed for take-off?

In underdeveloped countries, the rate of voluntary saving is low, and existing institutions are not very successful in mobilizing such savings as there are. Most people have incomes so low that virtually all current income must be spent to maintain a subsistence level of consumption. However, there is considerable disparity in income levels among income recipients. Some groups, at least, receive real incomes high enough for a comfortable, even luxurious, standard of living and substantial savings as well. Prewar studies of income distribution in Indonesia showed significant inequalities.[1] In Japan, unequal distribution of income contributed greatly to financing developmental investment after the initial wave of government investment.[2] In an economy still in the stage of establishing preconditions for development, however, upper-income groups often assign considerable prestige value to conspicuous consumption. This propensity seems to be reinforced by what Ragnar Nurkse calls the

[1] J. J. Polak, *The National Income of the Netherlands Indies, 1921–1939* (New York, n.d.), pp. 64–66.

[2] William W. Lockwood, *The Economic Development of Japan* (Princeton, N.J., 1954), pp. 278–80.

"demonstration effect": people at all levels of income try to emulate standards of consumption in economically advanced societies.[3] Thus in the Philippines, despite great disparities in income and wealth, the rate of saving and investment is very low relative to national income.[4]

Moreover, the saving of the upper-income groups in these countries is seldom channeled into developmental investment. High rates of return on short-term loans to consumers, farmers, and traders, and speculative gains from hoarding goods attract capital into these channels instead. Pawnshops, the landlord who lends to tenants during the growing season on a sharecropping basis, the village moneylender, divert the savings of one group to financing consumer expenditures of others. Since the total supply of savings is low and consumption demands for credit are urgent, rates of return may be as high as 50 to 100 per cent per annum for consumer and trade credit while longer-term investments yield considerably less.

If voluntary savings from upper-income groups are to contribute to financing developmental investment, therefore, they must be mobilized by institutions capable of making them available to investors rather than consumers. Of course, this process means enforcing general reductions in consumption. If real income is growing, it is necessary only to restrict consumption to existing levels. The role of voluntary saving is therefore no different from taxation in effect upon consumption.

The political and social reawakening in many underdeveloped countries since the war inclines them toward the welfare state and a more egalitarian distribution of real income. Fiscal redistribution of income, social legislation, and labor union activities backed by government policy, all tend to reduce inequalities in income distribution. Such redistribution usually does little to raise the real incomes in the lower ranges, even where higher incomes have been significantly reduced. This process tends to reduce net saving.

Arthur Lewis has argued that the ratio of voluntary savings to national income is a function, not just of inequality of income distribution, but of inequality of a particular kind.[5] He maintains that voluntary savings have become a significantly large

[3] Ragnar Nurkse, *Problems of Capital Formation in Underdeveloped Countries* (Oxford, 1953), pp. 57–70.

[4] Cf. Benjamin Higgins, *Final Report to the Government of the Philippines* (New York, 1957).

[5] Arthur Lewis, *The Theory of Economic Growth* (Homewood, Ill., 1955), pp. 225–44.

share of national income only where inequality of income distribution is such that entrepreneurial profits are a relatively large share of national income. If unequal distribution of income exists and the society's upper incomes accrue to landlords or to traders, Lewis believes that there is little chance of providing significant amounts of voluntary savings to finance investment. Profits, interest, and rental incomes as a whole are a much smaller share of national income in some underdeveloped economies than is general in advanced economies.

A study comparing these distributive shares as a percentage of national income in Indonesia (1938) and the United States (1951) seems to confirm this hypothesis. Profits, interest, and rental incomes represented about 24½ per cent of national income in the United States, but only 11 per cent in Indonesia.[6] On the other hand, in the Philippines it is clear that the share of entrepreneurial and property income is extraordinarily high, some 56 per cent, and still savings and investment are low. It should be emphasized, however, that this may not contradict Lewis' hypothesis since not all of these high incomes are true "capitalistic profits." Many of them reflect positions of privilege and power rather than returns to entrepreneurial endeavor.

In sum, the social and political context of some newly independent countries is hostile to the accumulation of capitalistic profits of the kind that played an important role in financing economic growth in the West. Both voluntary savings and private investment are likely to be less important in these countries than they were in the development of the now advanced ones. Nevertheless, savings have an important role to play in restricting consumption during the early stages of economic growth. Taxes are never popular, and there is much to be said for encouraging people in underdeveloped areas to save a larger share of their incomes voluntarily. Mobilization of small savings from the agricultural sector might permit more rapid development, if this sector cannot be reached by taxation. Voluntary savings amounting to only 2 or 3 per cent of national income might well prove to be the critical margin in permitting a takeoff.

The literature on development of underdeveloped areas has several suggestions for increasing the supply of domestic loan funds. These suggestions are of unequal merit; let us review them.

[6] Charles Wolf, Jr., "Economic Development and Reform in South and Southeast Asia," *Far Eastern Quarterly*, XII (1952), pp. 29–30.

Savings versus Credit

In assessing such proposals, it is essential to distinguish between savings and credit; the former is anti-inflationary, the latter is inflationary. Credit may be necessary for expansion in some fields, especially small agriculture and small industry. But the expansion of credit is in itself inflationary. Moreover, few underdeveloped countries lack credit institutions; some of them already have *too many*. Consider Indonesia, for example. First there are the government-owned and operated credit institutions: the Bank Indonesia, the Bank Industri Negara, the Bank Negara, the Bank Umum Nasional, the Bank Rakjat Indonesia, the Housing Development Corporation, the *desa* banks, the post office savings system, the government pawnshops, and the credit activities of various ministries. In addition, there are private banks: the few large foreign commercial banks and the many small Indonesian commercial banks. Carrying out an integrated monetary policy is almost impossible with such a plethora of institutions. And this sort of situation is all too common among underdeveloped countries.

To assure adequate credit control by the central bank, banking legislation should have the following features:

1. All banks should be licensed under national law.

2. All banks should be required to have a reasonably high minimum capital. Small banks complicate the problem of monetary control and weaken the banking system. It is much sounder to have a small number of strong commercial banks (preferably not more than ten) with head offices in one center and branches scattered throughout the country, as in Australia, Canada, and England. In this way the whole country can be served, the risks of bank failure are minimized, funds can be moved easily in response to regional shifts in demand for credit, and at the same time an integrated monetary and fiscal policy becomes feasible and a disciplined banking system can gradually be built up.

3. The banks should be required to hold minimum reserves in the form of notes of or deposits with the central bank, subject to change by regulation.

4. In the absence of rediscounting or a broad open market, the central bank should have authority to control the volume of money in other ways. For example, it might be empowered to set a ceiling on deposits beyond which 100 per cent reserves in special reserve-privilege treasury notes are required. This system

permits individual banks to expand, at the expense of others, by bidding away reserve-privilege notes from the less active banks. It also provides a ready market for government securities and so provides the foundations of open market policy. The interest rates paid on the bills can be low, not above 1 per cent.

5. The central bank should also have authority to impose selective credit controls, e.g., restrictions on consumer credit, loans for speculative purposes, for unessential construction, etc. Selective controls have recently proved quite successful in the United States, the United Kingdom, and Canada, and are an essential part of the tool kit for encouraging development and restraining inflation.

6. As a general rule the banks should be restrained from trading and from providing long-term capital. They should not be permitted to lend more than a certain proportion of their total assets to one client.

7. The banks should, however, be permitted to make term loans (one to five years) to finance purchases of equipment.

8. The number of financial institutions should be kept as small as possible. Special institutions for financing agriculture and small business should be brought within the system, and should be subject to control by the central bank.

It is sometimes argued that new financial institutions are needed to "channel" savings more effectively. Savings should be directed toward lending institutions, it is contended, so that they provide the basis for effective extension of credit, rather than being held as cash hoards or invested in jewels, gold, and the like. This argument in this form rests on a misunderstanding. The act of saving is essentially an act of restraint from current consumption; holding cash or buying jewelry (if it is already in the country) is as much saving as putting money into a bank. If the authorities can be assured that money withdrawn from circulation into cash hoards will remain in hoards, they can extend credit for development projects to an equal amount without inflationary effect; the net result will be exactly the same as if the money had been brought into the bank for deposit in the first place. True, money in hoards may be "hot," in the sense that it may suddenly be spent, requiring credit contraction if inflation is to be avoided. But the same situation would arise from any increase in velocity of circulation of existing deposits and notes in circulation; all money in existence is in a sense "hoarded" whenever it is not actually being spent. At most, the control of the authorities over the money supply is slightly greater if savings are channeled into credit institutions, rather than being held in cash hoards, jewelry, or the like.

There is, of course, some difference in the effects of hoarding, depending on the forms it takes. Hoarding currency, or holding unused bank balances, is clearly deflationary. If hoarding takes the form of buying jewelry or precious metals already in the country, the effect is to raise the price of these commodities while reducing inflationary pressure on other prices, permitting an increase in development spending without any rise in the general price level. Indeed, it is not even certain that the prices of jewelry will rise. In some countries, such as Libya, there are dealers in the silver bracelets commonly used to store wealth, who are essentially bankers performing a species of "counter-speculation" function. They buy and sell, by weight, within narrow margins. They "hoard" when the market is "dishoarding," and vice versa.

If hoarding takes the form of importing jewelry or precious metals, the effect is wholly anti-inflationary, but such hoarding is less anti-inflationary than use of equivalent amounts of foreign exchange for imports of consumers' goods to be sold in local markets. From the standpoint of economic development, it is obvious that a much greater contribution would be made by using the foreign exchange to finance needed raw materials and equipment.

If hoarding takes the form of buying land, with a consequent rise in land values, there may be repercussions on prices of agricultural products. However, since *demand* for final products is *reduced* by the process of bidding up land prices, the net effect is still likely to be deflationary on balance, unless the land is actually withdrawn from use.

Hoarding in the form of holding livestock rather than slaughtering, a practice common in arid zones in good rainfall years, is clearly inflationary. Such practices might be regarded as "investment in inventories," rather than hoarding, but they perform much the same function as accumulation of liquid assets in advanced countries.

Thus it is not apparent that channeling savings into financial institutions adds significantly to the amount of development that can be undertaken without inflation. Perhaps use of savings institutions will develop the savings habit and so raise the ratio of savings to income, but this result is not certain. Nor is it clear that monetization of the economy will increase productivity. There is no obvious and significant difference between the motivation to work and to save between peasants living in a partly non-monetary economy, and that of workers on plantations receiving most of their income in a money wage. It is hard to discern any sharp differences in average or marginal propensities to save between peasants and government employees whose entire income is in money. Monetary economies are usually richer than non-monetary ones; but the causal connection is *from* low production *to* poverty *to* a non-monetary economy, not vice versa. Monetization will follow an increase in productivity, but there is no assurance that an increase in productivity will follow monetization. Indeed a mere increase in money supply might be used to finance increased hoarding of goods. In Indonesia, a temporary reduction of the money supply during 1953, which was felt with particular intensity in rural areas, was very successful in forcing dishoarding of goods.

Sometimes the case is made for new financial institutions in terms of high interest rates that now prevail. Interest rates in some underdeveloped countries, especially for certain categories of agricultural loans, are no doubt extremely high. However, these interest rates do not always reflect insufficient monetization of the rural sector or even a lack of credit facilities. Sometimes high interest rates charged by moneylenders exist side by side with low interest rates from government credit institutions in the same locality. The peasant often prefers to borrow at high rates from a moneylender rather than meet the formal requirements of a government lending agency. The high interest rates may reflect accurately the risk of the loan. Moreover, there is a question whether the lower interest rates which can be provided by the government agency represent a real increase in the supply of investible funds or mere monetary expansion. If it is the latter, the gains through such "monetization" will be small indeed.

Proliferation of savings and credit institutions, then, is no substitute for a genuine increase in savings. This is not to say that new and specialized institutions, such as agricultural banks or housing agencies, may not play a useful role in economic development under certain conditions. Sometimes existing financial organizations do a poor job of allocating credit because of the prejudices and limited experience of their personnel. Managers of large commercial banks may underestimate the productivity of small loans to agriculture or may exaggerate the risk attached. In these circumstances, specialized institutions to finance agriculture, with personnel experienced in and sympathetic to this field of endeavor, may be needed to make sure that small farmers get their proper share of total available capital funds. Such organizations can also do a useful job of training, linking "extension work" to loans.

Finally, in such fields as housing and small business, specialized institutions can often operate more flexibly than the more hidebound existing agencies. For example, a case can sometimes be made for giving loans in kind, that is, for a policy of deliberate demonetization of the rural sector. Arab members of the United Nations Working Party on Fiscal Policy in Libya were quite insistent that agricultural credit should be given in kind; if it were given in money, they contended, the farmers would merely buy themselves additional wives.

Government Borrowing

The effects of government borrowing on the spending stream depend on where and how government loans are raised. When virtually all loan funds come directly or indirectly from the central bank, as in Indonesia or the Philippines, the result is highly inflationary. The process is all the more inflationary if commercial banks hold legal reserves in notes or deposits of the central bank; it then increases the flow of money directly and also permits credit expansion by the banks. Borrowing directly or indirectly from the commercial banks is very little better.

Selling securities to the general public is more likely to have neutralizing effects on expenditure of the funds; if the securities are bought with income that would otherwise be spent, whether on consumers' goods or on capital goods, the government borrowing is thoroughly anti-inflationary. If, on the other hand, the offer by the government of safe, liquid securities yielding an attractive return merely diverts savings from other liquid assets, such as currency or savings accounts, government borrowing has little anti-inflationary effect. Generally speaking, the farther down the income scale the government succeeds in placing securities, the more likely it is that the purchase of securities will displace spending, rather than other forms of saving, and the more anti-inflationary the borrowing is likely to be.

It has been suggested that governments of underdeveloped countries should attach special features to their obligations, designed to make them attractive to potential savers. Maturities and interest rates should be patterned as much as possible to fit current savings habits. Government securities should be easily liquidated, perhaps by providing a ready market in the central bank. Issues might be constantly available "on tap" in the central bank and its branches, and always salable to the bank at pre-announced prices. In order to provide an inducement to keep securities rather than cashing them, interest rates might be made to rise as the obligation approaches maturity. Where legal or religious bans on "usury" are a deterrent to purchase of interest-bearing securities (not a problem in most countries), the securities might bear no stipulated interest but might appreciate in value as they approach maturity. Some countries have found it useful to introduce lottery features in connection with their public obligations.

Government securities may be more attractive if attached to particular projects, such as assisting land ownership for small farmers (important where feudal systems of land ownership are widespread), housing, or development projects. In Indonesia, for example, it has been suggested that it may be useful to provide an open market for the bonds of the National Housing Development Corporation, which is to be set up in the first instance with subscriptions out of blocked (*Rurni*) funds of foreign enterprises. Perhaps "National Development Bonds" could be issued, in conjunction with a campaign to arouse interest in and stress the necessity of an economic development program. In the Philippines it has been suggested that special government bonds, salable only after five years, be issued in payment for land to be subdivided among smallholders.

In some countries, it may be worth considering the establishment of a public development and stabilization authority, along the lines of the one now operating in Libya.[7] The advantage of such an authority is its great flexibility; it could derive funds from government budgetary allocations, from public subscriptions to its obligations, from foundations, from international financial organizations, and perhaps eventually from foreign investors preferring a general government-guaranteed obligation, issued to finance an over-all development program, to a more risky investment in a particular project or enterprise.

All these devices are worth trying. It is doubtful whether any very large flow of savings will be stimulated in the near future by such measures alone, but there is no reason for not doing whatever is possible in this way.

Other tailor-made features of government securities may be more effective. There is still a shortage of *credit* (as distinct

[7] This agency is described in Chap. 25.

from credit facilities) in most rural areas, while at the same time some of the more prosperous traders and farmers have occasional surpluses of cash. Perhaps they could be persuaded to buy securities if they were assured that they would always be accepted as collateral for loans from an agricultural or small business loan bank. Of course, this system would bring a net increase in savings only to the extent that the securities were *not* used as a basis for borrowing. Another feature that might be attractive is tax payment privileges; that is, a guarantee that the securities would always be acceptable at face value for payment of taxes. This guarantee would be a partial assurance against the risk of depreciation of the internal value of the securities through inflation.

Some writers have suggested that tax exemptions be granted to investors in bonds; but this feature is useful only if it encourages the growth of savings habits, so that later on savings will continue even if the tax exemption feature is dropped. Paying taxes is at least as effective as saving in preventing inflation from arising out of development spending—perhaps more so, since as pointed out above, the man who has accumulated savings may feel justified in spending a larger share of current income. Perhaps the feature that would be most attractive of all, especially to foreigners, would be a guarantee that principal and interest would be maintained at face value in gold or dollars. This guarantee would be a safeguard against devaluation of the currency, fear of which is a major deterrent to investment in some government securities.

Marketing Boards

In a number of African countries, government marketing boards have been used as an instrument for compulsory saving by paying growers prices below the world market level. The present writer has no direct experience with such boards.[8] Peter Bauer, who has, is not enthusiastic about them. He does not deny that "the heavy accumulation of surpluses by the boards . . . raises total savings" where "the level of capital is very low."[9] But he maintains that the boards reduce private saving,

[8] The Indonesian *Jajasan Copra* is not a good test case for judging the effectiveness of marketing boards in increasing aggregate savings and investment. Squeezing out profits from copra growing was not a purpose pursued vigorously or continuously, and in recent years, much of the copra export was smuggled directly to Singapore, bypassing the Copra Foundation altogether.

[9] P. T. Bauer, *West African Trade* (Cambridge, 1954), p. 313.

TABLE 21-1.

Selected ECAFE Primary Exporting Countries: Gross Domestic Product, Consumption, Savings, and Capital Formation, 1948–56

Country and currency	Gross domestic product at current prices (in million)	Index of gross domestic product (1953 = 100)	Index of per capita real private consumption * (1953 = 100)	Rate of saving †	Rate of capital formation ‡	Excess of rate of saving over rate of capital formation
Burma (kyat):						
1948	3,557	77	108	10.8	16.9	−6.1
1949	3,234	70	65	16.4	8.1	8.3
1950	3,132	68	74	15.4	10.2	5.2
1951	3,690	80	87	19.1	12.9	6.2
1952	4,084	88	91	23.6	18.2	5.4
1953	4,620	100	100	25.2	19.0	6.2
1954	4,593	99	105	19.8	22.0	−2.2
1955	4,808	104	106	21.7	21.0	0.7
1956	5,025	109	98	21.2	18.5	2.7
Ceylon (rupee):						
1948	2,817	61	76	6.8	6.2	0.6
1949	3,077	66	81	7.3	9.0	−1.7
1950	4,096	88	95	14.4	10.6	3.8
1951	4,735	102	103	15.0	11.7	3.3
1952	4,530	98	105	6.3	13.4	−7.1
1953	4,641	100	100	7.6	12.0	−4.4
1954	5,014	108	95	16.4	10.0	6.4
1955	5,538	119	103	16.8	11.3	5.5
1956	5,226	113	94	13.5	12.3	1.2
China (new Taiwan dollar):						
1951	10,821	51	74	17.3	22.2	−4.9
1952	15,750	74	81	17.1	22.0	−4.9
1953	21,203	100	100	12.2	18.1	−5.9
1954	23,158	109	104	8.8	17.9	−9.1
1955	27,889	132	103	10.6	14.6	−4.0
Indonesia (rupiah):						
1951	82,819	. . .	. . .	6.0	4.7	1.3
1952	93,422	. . .	. . .	10.1	5.2	4.9
Malaya (Malayan dollar):						
1949	3,550	61	97	11.6	10.6	1.0
1950	5,345	92	106	29.5	4.5	25.0
1951	7,520	130	121	27.2	6.1	21.1
1952	6,350	110	107	16.6	11.9	4.7
1953	5,780	100	100	11.1	10.4	0.7
Philippines (peso):						
1948	6,222	77	80	10.0	12.3	−2.3
1949	6,196	76	89	2.45	10.7	−8.3
1950	6,655	82	84	9.7	8.5	1.2
1951	7,415	91	87	6.8	7.5	−0.7
1952	7,576	93	93	7.0	7.7	−0.7
1953	8,111	100	100	8.4	8.3	0.1
1954	8,283	102	101	8.1	8.7	−0.6
1955	8,820	109	108	6.8	8.9	−2.1
1956	9,546	118	110	8.8	8.9	−0.1

* Consumption in the private sector deflated by the cost of living index.

† Gross domestic saving as percentage of gross domestic product. "Gross domestic savings" equal "gross domestic product" less "consumption."

‡ Gross capital formation as percentage of gross domestic product.

SOURCE: UN *Economic Survey of Asia and the Far East, 1957*, p. 148.

and in his view this result entails "disadvantages beyond the obvious and substantial adverse effect on the level of supply and on individual incentive to produce." It retards the growth of the personal saving habit in countries where this habit is just getting established, as shown for example by the "great increase and improvement of building, especially house-building, for Africans" in Nigeria and the Gold Coast.[10] To Bauer it seems "paradoxical" to pay producers less than half the market price and then send around teams to encourage increased production, as the Nigerian Marketing Board has done.

Bauer also believes (as one might guess from our review of his attitude toward government development policies in Chapter 18) that the government is likely to use these savings in less productive fashion than would occur if they were left in private hands. He admits the importance of "basic services and subsidization of research" but feels that, apart from these functions, the individual producers are better able to assess the relative merits of alternative uses of funds than is the government. If compulsory saving is ever desirable at all, it can be achieved in less discriminatory fashion through a budget surplus.

It is a little hard to disentangle Bauer's appraisal of African experience with marketing boards from his general dislike of government intervention and his feeling that economic development is a natural process best left to marginal decisions in the market. Our own analysis in Part 4 does not suggest that individual growers are likely to make decisions about the use of savings more conducive to acceleration of growth than those made by an informed and responsible government. If the political and administrative situation is such that financial resources for development can be obtained through marketing boards and not in any other way, the case for them would seem to be a good deal stronger than Bauer indicates. We can agree with him, however, that the question cannot be answered in terms of general theory but must be appraised in terms of the conditions prevailing in a particular country at a particular time.

Conclusions

In general, our answer to the question asked at the beginning of this chapter seems to be, "Not very much." It is highly unlikely that measures to increase voluntary domestic savings alone —or even measures for voluntary and compulsory savings together—can provide all the financial resources needed for de-

[10] *Ibid.*, p. 314.

velopment of underdeveloped countries. At the same time, there is no reason to eschew measures which hold promise of bringing some increase in the flow of savings. There can be no doubt that the ratio of savings to income varies enormously from one underdeveloped country to another, and the differences reflect variations in policy to some extent at least. Table 21–1 includes public savings (taxes) as well as private savings in the figure of gross saving, but it does indicate the wide range in savings efforts among underdeveloped countries. In terms of per capita incomes, Malaya and the Philippines come at the top of the list of countries in the table; in terms of savings, Burma heads the list, with Indonesia and the Philippines competing for bottom position.

22 Tax Policies

Domestic financing of economic development requires increased total savings (including taxes) and investment (public and private). When total output remains relatively constant over time, an economy can generate a higher level of total saving only by reducing its existing level of consumption. If previously idle factors of production can be brought into use, of course, investment can take place without either a reduction in consumption or inflation. Where such excess capacity is insufficient for a minimum effort, where voluntary savings are inadequate, and where foreign aid is not sought or offered in sufficient quantities, the launching of a take-off may require "collective thrift" through taxation.[1]

Taxes versus Savings

Which is better, taxes or savings? There is no simple or general answer to this question. The main purpose of either, from the standpoint of development finance, is to permit increased public and private investment without inflation. Taxes which are paid at the expenses of savings rather than at the expense of current spending are not anti-inflationary at all. On the other hand, it has been argued that taxes not only make people poorer,

[1] This is Nurkse's apt term for savings forced by government fiscal policy. Cf. Ragnar Nurkse, *Problem of Capital Formation in Underdeveloped Countries*, p. 151.

but make people *feel* poorer, whereas an increase in savings, with the accompanying increase in liquid assets, makes people feel better off; consequently, the reduction in spending is likely to be greater if a certain sum is raised in taxes than if it is raised in savings. Much depends also on what income is most affected by an increase in savings or in tax collections. By and large, the upper-income groups tend to be savers, and the lower-income groups spenders. Thus the anti-inflationary effects of taxes or savings are likely to be greater if obtained from lower-income groups, than if the same volume of taxes or savings is obtained from the higher-income groups. The unpleasant task of limiting the consumption of the middle- and lower-income groups—and thus limiting total consumption—is probably easier *administratively* through taxes than through measures to increase savings.

Taxation: The Question of Tax Capacity

With these considerations in mind, let us consider briefly some of the major questions that arise with regard to tax financing of economic development. The first of these questions is likely to be: "How much can be collected in taxes? What is the 'taxable capacity' of underdeveloped countries? What tax burden can they bear?" There is no simple answer to this question either. Today, among businessmen, trade-union officials, government advisers, and even professional economists, from Canada to Indonesia, one hears the statement that, when tax rates reach a certain limit, further increases in tax rates will be inflationary rather than deflationary. It is the present writer's opinion that this statement is based upon a misunderstanding and that its frequent repetition in high places calls for a restatement of home truths regarding the economic effects of taxation.

The Colin Clark Argument

The statement that excessive taxation is inflationary is sometimes supported by reference to Colin Clark's article on "Public Finance and Changes in the Value of Money." [2] The basic thesis of this article is that the ceiling to tax revenues in peacetime is about 25 per cent of national income. However, Colin Clark's main argument was not economic but political. It ran, in effect: if the tax burden becomes uncomfortably high, one or another politically powerful group will bring pressure successfully and

[2] Colin Clark, "Public Finance and Changes in the Value of Money," *Economic Journal*, December, 1945, pp. 371–89.

so relieve the burden. Clark's somewhat scanty data really show only that before World War I, and again between the wars, several countries collected less than 25 per cent of national income in taxes most of the time. In the "analysis" with which Clark "explains" his facts, he argues that since people do not like paying taxes, in democratic countries the government will find it difficult to impose a heavy tax burden for very long, except when the major power groups in the community are in the mood to make sacrifices, as during a war. By the same token, however, Clark's evidence and explanation, carried into the war and post-war periods, suggests that wherever these powerful groups are prepared to make sacrifices, in order to assist the government in carrying out some program entailing heavy expenditures, the tax burden can be increased. For example, if these groups consider an economic development program to be as important as war, they will accept tax burdens as great as those in wartime.

The share of income that people will be willing to pay out in taxes is by no means independent of the level and structure of government expenditures. If the ratio of government expenditures to national income rises, so that relatively more goods and services are being offered in exchange for taxes and relatively fewer are sold for prices, and if the goods and services provided by government yield satisfactions as high as those formerly bought in the market, there is no reason why people should not accept a higher ratio of taxes to income. Indeed, if no redistribution of income and no reallocation of resources were involved there is no theoretical reason why a strongly supported government should not collect 100 per cent of personal income, and pay it out again in family allowances, pensions, interest on debt, etc., without any economic effects whatsoever.

Much the same sort of argument applies here as in the discussions of the burden of national debt; if no redistribution of real income is entailed, there is no real burden and, therefore, no economic limit. There can be a "burden" for particular income groups if they suffer a net loss of real income through the fiscal process, and this burden may have an unfavorable effect on their incentive to work or to invest. There can also be a "burden" for the community as a whole, if government expenditures provide goods and services of a less satisfactory kind than would be provided by private enterprise were the same amount of income spent in the market. But this latter argument amounts only to saying that there is a limit to the extent to which a democratic government can alter the distribution of resources, in a manner reducing psychic income, without destroying the incentives to work and invest, or losing its political support, or both. This statement is axiomatic, but it provides no rationale for an "iron law" regarding the ratio of taxes to income. How much people will pay in taxes, without shifting their political support, and without working or investing less, depends on the value they place on what they get for their money.

How far short of the theoretical maximum the actual maximum is depends on the effects of the fiscal process on various groups, on the relative political power of these groups, and on the degree of enthusiasm felt by the people for the government's program. If the people of the underdeveloped countries could have the same unity of purpose with respect to development as did the people of advanced countries with respect to the war effort during World War II, the ratio of tax collections to national income, for the purpose of financing the development program, could be high. Where such unity of purpose does not exist, and where the fiscal process of collecting and spending money redistributes income from politically powerful groups to politically weak ones, the limit of taxable capacity is likely to be low.[3]

Taxable capacity also depends on the skill with which the tax system is adapted to the institutional framework. For example, it has been suggested that the experience of mainland China, Taiwan, and Korea indicates that higher levels of agricultural taxation are possible if taxes are collected in grain rather than in money. By collecting taxes in kind, the government performs marketing functions which increase the ability of producers to dispose of their surplus output and so raises their taxable capacity.

The question of taxable capacity is therefore related to the question of incentives. Current income may not be a satisfactory indication of taxable capacity because the imposition of the tax may itself provide an incentive for increasing production and income. This situation is said to prevail in a number of Latin American countries, where potentially fertile land is allowed to go unused by big landlords. Consideration such as these influenced a mission from the International Bank for Reconstruction and Development to recommend to the Government of Colombia that land be taxed in terms of potential rather than actual yield.[4]

[3] For a more complete discussion of this point, see Benjamin Higgins, "A Note on Taxation and Inflation," *Canadian Journal of Economics and Political Science*, August, 1953.

[4] H. P. Wald and J. N. Froomkin (eds.), *Papers and Proceedings of the Conference on Agricultural Taxation and Economic Development* (Cambridge, Mass., 1954), p. 17.

Moreover, in underdeveloped countries there is more difference than in advanced ones between taxes that can be *imposed* and taxes that can be *collected*. It is generally agreed that tax revenues in underdeveloped countries could be substantially increased, without increases in tax rates, by improved tax administration and enforcement. Part of the explanation may be found in the large proportion of income earned in agriculture. The assessment of agricultural income, especially in relatively primitive economies where bookkeeping is virtually unknown within the agricultural sphere, is extraordinarily complex and provides opportunities for both laxity and corruption. Sometimes it is easier for local government officials to collect taxes in full than it is for central government officials, who may be regarded as interlopers in the outlying regions of a country. In general, collections could be improved by encouragement to, or where feasible an insistence upon, proper accounting. The organization of marketing cooperatives may help a government collect taxes in the agricultural sector. Each government of underdeveloped countries must assess these factors for itself.

Taxation and Inflation

We have stated above that the main purpose of collecting more taxes is to permit increased government spending without inflation. Some recent literature, however, has suggested that taxation may aggravate rather than alleviate inflationary pressures. Since this controversy has direct bearing on the problem of financing development in underdeveloped countries, a brief discussion of this question is in order.

Some of the confusion about the effects of tax increases in an inflationary period springs from failure to distinguish the effects of collecting taxes from the effects of collecting and spending them. Those who maintain that increases in taxation have obviously been inflationary, merely because prices have risen even where taxes were high enough to balance budgets, clearly fail to take account of the "Haavelmo proposition." Haavelmo has demonstrated that, even without any redistribution of income from savers to spenders, a balanced budget is in itself inflationary. It adds to monetary income an amount just equal to the amount of government spending, and under conditions of full employment, any addition to money income is in itself inflationary.

Although the Haavelmo proposition is by now widely accepted, the simple corollary that a budget must produce a surplus to be "neutral" has not received enough attention. A much simplified version of the Haavelmo argument would be as follows: let Y be national income, E be government expenditures, T, tax revenues, and c, the marginal propensity to consume. The expansionary effects of government expenditures (on goods and services) will then be

$$\Delta Y = E(1 + c + c^2 + c^3 + \ldots + c^n)$$

Since taxes are not an income generator and influence the level of national income only through their effects on spending in the period following their collection, the deflationary effects of collecting taxes will be

$$-\Delta Y = T(0 + c + c^2 + c^3 + \ldots + c^n)$$

Thus if E equals T, the net effect of the budget, $E - T$, is to raise national income by the amount of E (or T). This argument ignores the effects of taxation on investment, but since it is based on the assumption that no redistribution of income takes place through the fiscal process and since net income is increased, there is no reason why investment should be influenced very much one way or the other. If there is any effect, it will presumably aggravate the inflationary pressure. Of course, if the fiscal process redistributes income from savers to spenders, the effects through the multiplier process will be still more inflationary, but the effects on investment may then be deflationary.

The somewhat startling corollary of the Haavelmo proposition is that, if a budget is to be "neutral," the ratio of government expenditures (on goods and services) to tax revenues cannot exceed the marginal propensity to consume. That is, if the marginal propensity to consume is two-thirds, the ratio of government expenditures to tax revenues cannot exceed two-thirds. Put in another way, "neutrality" in the budget requires a ratio of budget surplus to total revenues of 1, minus the marginal propensity to consume. With a marginal propensity to consume of two-thirds, the budget surplus must be equal to one-third of total tax revenues if the budget is to be neutral. Given a marginal propensity to consume of four-fifths, which may be more realistic for some countries, a neutral budget would be one in which the ratio of government expenditures to tax revenues is four-fifths, and in which the budget surplus is one-fifth of total revenues.[5]

[5] In this discussion "national income" means net national income at market prices, and not personal or disposable income. Consequently, the appropriate marginal propensity to consume to use in making an estimate of the budget

This corollary of the Haavelmo proposition can be easily proved by putting figures into the above equation. Let us suppose, for example, that government expenditures are 10 (billion dollars or rupiahs) and that the marginal propensity to consume is four-fifths, giving a multiplier of five. In order for the budget to be neutral, assuming no redistribution of income and thus no effects on investments through the fiscal process, tax revenues must be 12.5 billion and the budget surplus must be 2.5 billion. Substituting these figures in the above equations, it will be seen that the increase in income generated by government expenditures will be 50 billion, and that the reductions in national income generated by collection of taxes will be 50 billion. Thus, on the assumption made, the whole process of collecting taxes and spending them on goods and services will have no effect on the level of national income. With a marginal propensity to consume out of national income of three-fourths, government spending of 10 billion would require tax revenues of 13.3 billion, or a budget surplus of 3.3 billion. With a marginal propensity to consume of two-thirds, a budget of 10 billion would require tax revenue of 15 billion and a budget surplus of 5 billion if the budget is to be neutral.

The limitations of this analysis must be borne in mind. It ignores the effects on investment of the announcement of a particular tax policy, and it ignores the effects of any redistribution of income through the fiscal process. It also ignores the effects on incentives of a change in the composition of national income as a result of extension of government activity. Limited as it is, however, the Haavelmo proposition, with the corollary outlined above, teaches a valuable lesson. The fact that some countries have succeeded in balancing their budgets, or even in producing small surpluses, is no reason to expect that the fiscal policy of these countries should have succeeded in checking inflation, es-

surplus necessary to prevent inflationary effects from government spending should be the marginal propensity to consume out of national income, and not out of personal income or out of disposable income. For the less developed countries, a marginal propensity to consume out of national income of four-fifths may be fairly realistic. In advanced countries, however, a marginal propensity to consume closer to three-fourths or even two-thirds would probably be more realistic. In that case, a neutral budget would be one in which the budget surplus is equal to one-fourth or one-third of total tax revenues.

For a systematic presentation of the requirements for "neutral" budgetary policy in somewhat more complex cases, see Haskell P. Wald, "Fiscal Policy, Military Preparedness, and Postwar Inflation," in Arthur Smithies and J. Keith Butten (eds.), *Readings in Fiscal Policy* (Homewood, Ill., 1955).

pecially when there was strong expansionary pressure from credit-financed private investment or from increasing exports. Budget surpluses in most countries have been far too small to prevent the net effect of the fiscal process alone from being inflationary. Indeed, it seems unlikely that any country in the world has been courageous enough to follow a "neutral" fiscal policy during the postwar period. True neutrality would have required budget surpluses and taxes far higher than most governments were strong enough to impose.

High taxes combined with equally high government expenditures are certainly inflationary. The inflationary component of a large budget is the expenditure side, however, not the tax side. If, in the simple equations presented above, expenditures remain at the stipulated levels, while no taxes are collected at all, it is obvious that the net inflationary effects of government fiscal policy will be far greater than if budgets are balanced. The collection of taxes, in itself, reduces national income (spending) by a multiple of the amount of taxes collected, a multiple that is one less than the multiplier operating on government expenditures. For clear thinking about tax policy, it is essential to distinguish the effects of collecting taxes from the effects of collecting *and spending* them. In what follows we shall assume that the level of government expenditures is a datum and concentrate our attention on the effects of collecting taxes as such.

Taxes and Wages

It is sometimes argued that collecting taxes is inflationary because increases in taxes borne by wage earners will lead to greater pressure for wage increases. It is also argued, by Colin Clark among others, that taxes falling on increments of profits will reduce the natural resistance of employers to wage increases. In other words, the argument is that higher taxes lead to higher wages and that higher wages in turn lead to higher prices.

Let us analyze this argument in terms of the familiar Fisher equation:

$$P \cdot Gv = (M + M')V \quad \text{or} \quad P = \frac{(M + M')V}{Gv}$$

In this equation, P stands for the general price level, G, for the volume of goods and services sold for money during an income period, v, for the velocity of circulation of goods, M, for the quantity of money, M', for the volume of deposits, and V, for velocity of circulation of money. From this equation, it is immediately apparent that, if higher taxes are to lead to an increase in wages and prices, the higher taxes must lead either to a sufficient contraction of Gv, or to a sufficient increase in $(M + M')V$, to support a higher general price level. It is, of course, possible that employers will be faced with stronger pressure for wage increases if taxes on wages are raised. It is also possible that resistance to wage increases may be lessened if taxes on increments of profits are raised. The question arises, however, whether money income will be increased sufficiently, or the flow of goods reduced sufficiently, to support a higher wage and price level.

If the total money income is not increased as a result of collecting taxes, a higher wage-price level can result only in a reduced flow of goods and services, which must lead sooner or later to reduced employment; the level of employment could not be maintained indefinitely in the face of an increase in wage rates combined with a drop in the physical volume of sales and in net receipts. We could also write

$$R = Y - (W + T_r)$$

where R stands for net receipts of business enterprise, Y, for national income, W, for wages and T_r, for taxes paid by capitalists (i.e., by non-wage earners). If profits are to be maintained in the face of increased taxes on profits and higher wages, it is obvious that Y, national income, must rise by enough to offset both the increase in wages and the increase in taxes paid by capitalists. If this does not happen, and wages and prices are raised at the expense of sales and of net revenues, the effect must be unemployment. Increasing unemployment and rising prices cannot march side by side indefinitely, unless each is confined to one sector of the economy and there is little or no interaction between the two sectors.

It is also possible that the announcement of the tax may foster expectations of higher prices, leading to inventory accumulation and a drop in the velocity of circulation of goods, v. The drop in v would raise prices, but inventory accumulation would not proceed indefinitely despite reduced sales. The result might be a subsequent slump in prices through dumping of inventories. In any case, tax increases might foster expectations of price cuts. Once expectations, leads, and lags are introduced, one can produce almost any results one likes by selecting one's assumptions.[6]

[6] See Benjamin Higgins, "Postwar Tax Policy," Part II, *Canadian Journal of Economics and Political Science*, November, 1943.

There remains the alternative that somehow or other the money flow is increased sufficiently to offset both the increase in wages and the increase in tax payments, so as to support the higher price level. Mechanically, there is a way in which this result could occur. If the impact effect of the tax is an increase in wages and prices, and if employers then increase their borrowing from the banks in order to support their payrolls and inventories at the higher levels, it is conceivable that the total money supply would increase sufficiently to support the higher price level, despite the increase in tax collections. Alternatively, idle cash balances may be activated for the same purpose, leading to a sufficient increase in velocity of circulation to support the higher wage-price structure.

In fact, however, such a development is extremely unlikely. Let us substitute numerical values into the "Fisher equation" above. Let us suppose that the average price level, P, is 1, and that the flow of goods, Gv, is 50; and let us suppose also that the quantity of currency in circulation is 5, the volume of bank deposits 5, and the velocity of circulation 5 times per year. We will then have a national income of 50.[7] Now let us suppose that a tax amounting to 10 per cent of national income is imposed and that prices are raised by 10 per cent as a consequence, in order to pay higher wages without loss. If the velocity of circulation is unchanged it will be necessary for the total money supply, $M + M'$, to increase by 1, in order for the equation to remain an equation.[8] That is, the money supply must increase by 1, in order to support the new and higher wage-price structure. The payment of the taxes will in and of itself reduce the money supply by 5. Thus if the net result is to be an increase in money supply of 1, employers must increase their borrowing from the banks by 6. Creation of deposits through extension of credit must be sufficient to offset both the increase in wages and prices, and the increase in tax collections.

It is extremely unlikely that employers, faced with the need of paying taxes amounting in total to 10 per cent of national income, would borrow enough to offset both the tax payments and the increases in wages and prices. In the numerical example given above, they would have to borrow enough to increase their debt to the banks by more than 100 per cent. Even if employers were willing to increase their indebtedness to banks to such an extent, it is highly improbable that the banks would be

[7] $P{\cdot}Gv = (M + M')V = 1 \times 50 = (5 + 5) \times 5.$
[8] $P{\cdot}Gv = (M + M')V = 1.1 \times 50 = (5 + 6) \times 5.$

willing to expand their loans to this degree, when the money volume of business transacted has risen only by 10 per cent. Nor is it likely that velocity of circulation will rise enough (from 5 to 11 times a year) to offset the reduction in money supply from 10 to 5 through collection of 5 in taxes. Indeed, no combination of credit expansion and velocity increase sufficient to support the higher price level is likely to occur. Thus although it is technically possible for an increase in taxes to lead to an increase in wages and prices, it is extremely unlikely that the expansion of credit and increase in velocity resulting directly from the increase in taxes would be sufficient to support a higher price level, despite the contraction of money supply involved in the payment of taxes.

At most, the argument that taxes may be inflationary by leading to wage increases means only that if an anti-inflationary fiscal policy is to be effective, it must be supported by an anti-inflationary monetary policy as well.

Taxes and the Supply of Effort

Another form of the argument that tax increases become inflationary after a certain point runs in terms of the supply curve of effort. If taxes are raised too high, it is contended, output will fall, or costs increase, as a consequence of a reduced supply of effort. The incentive to work hard or well, the argument runs, is destroyed by the necessity of paying high taxes on increases in income. In this case, a higher price level could result, without unemployment, by a contraction of the supply of effort and a corresponding contraction of the output of goods and services. No increase in total money supply would be needed. If the collection of taxes is to result in an increase in prices, however, the flow of goods and services must fall more, as a result of the reduced supply of effort, than the flow of money is reduced by the collection of taxes.

It is of course conceivable that the supply curve of effort is so highly elastic at the income level prevailing before imposition of additional taxes that the contraction of output will be more than proportionate to the contraction of money flow. However, it is worth considering what this situation would mean. If the supply curve of effort is equally elastic for increases in real income, an increase in wage rates would be deflationary, since it would call forth an increase in output more than proportionate to the increase in money income generated through payment of higher wages. At the very least, it would mean that if employers undertook to offset the increase in taxes on wages by an equal increase in wage rates, the net effect on the wage earners would, in itself, increase output by more than it would increase money spending. Very few indeed of those people who have argued that tax increases are inflationary if they fall on wages and salaries have also argued that wage and salary increases would be deflationary, because they would call forth more increase in output than in money spending.[9]

Unfortunately, the supply curve of effort may be highly elastic for reductions in real income and may also be negative for increases in real income. That is, the supply curve of effort may become backward sloping at the present level of wage rates. As suggested in Chapter 12 there is good reason to believe that, in any society, supply curves of effort tend to turn backward, at whatever level of per capita real income prevails, if the standard of living is static long enough for it to become customary. Faced with such a supply curve of effort, the fiscal authorities are indeed in a dilemma. Increased taxes on wages and salaries will reduce the supply of effort and, therefore, the supply of goods and services, but increases in money wages will have the same effect.

We are faced here with a question of fact which cannot be resolved by theoretical analysis alone. In most cases, it seems likely that an increase in taxes will in itself tend to reduce the supply of effort, but is unlikely to reduce the flow of goods and services nearly as much as it will reduce disposable income. Given a marginal propensity to consume of three-fourths, for example, the collecting of an additional 10 per cent of national income in taxes will, through the multiplier process, reduce money flow by 30 per cent. It does not seem likely that the tax would reduce the flow of goods and services by 30 per cent, at least not without leading ultimately to unemployment, which would eventually turn inflation into deflation. This question can be answered only by empirical analysis. Let us recall, however, that in the present context we are talking about an increase in taxes combined with increased development spending. Wage bills would tend to increase on balance, and there is no reason why total supply of effort should be adversely affected, especially if the development projects are designed to absorb open or disguised unemployment.

[9] Of course, a distinction must be made between taxes collected, and wages paid, per unit of effort expended, and taxes collected or wages paid on increments of effort expended.

Taxes and the Supply of Venture Capital

Much the same sort of consideration applies to the effect of increase in taxes on private investment, and particularly on investment in new and risky enterprises. It is, of course, possible that an increase in taxes on profits will reduce the flow of venture capital. The supply curve of risk-taking, as well as the supply curve of effort, may become backward sloping at existing levels of income. If so, either tax reductions or tax increases will have the effect of reducing the flow of venture capital. This situation may develop in an economy which has been reasonably stable for some length of time. Such a situation is certainly awkward for any government constructing anti-inflationary fiscal policy. It is conceivable that the reduction in investments will ultimately reduce current output more than the taxes will reduce money spending. However, this result is even more unlikely in the case of investment than it is in the case of effort.

An increase in investment does not immediately increase the flow of goods and services. On the contrary, the impact effect may very well be a diversion of labor and other resources from current production to the production of capital goods and a consequent decline in current output of final goods. It seems extremely unlikely that an increase in taxes amounting to 10 per cent of national income would reduce the total flow of final goods and services by (say) 30 per cent through reduction of investment. Even if it did, the effect would more probably be unemployment than inflation. A drop in net investment, sufficient to bring the stock of capital down to a level appropriate for a flow of final goods and services 30 per cent below that prevailing when taxes are increased, could precipitate a major depression. That would be unfortunate, but it would not be inflation.

Taxes and Corporate Savings

A variant of the preceding argument is that an increase in taxes on corporate profits will reduce investments, and therefore output, by reducing corporate savings. This argument has some prima facie plausibility. Policy with respect to distribution of profits is determined by earnings net of taxes, and if the earnings drop, corporate liquidity will be reduced. Econometric studies suggest that liquidity is a significant factor in the investment decisions of corporate enterprise. Dividends usually cannot be cut enough to preserve corporate liquidity in face of an increase in corporation income taxes. Thus, it seems quite possible that an increase in such taxes will have the effect of reducing business saving and investment.

However, the initial effect of a decline in savings and investment, in and of itself, must be deflationary. If in the equations presented above, I, investment, is substituted for E, and S, savings, for T, it is apparent that an increase in investment which is just offset by voluntary savings is in itself inflationary and that a decline in savings and investment is deflationary. An increase in investment financed by current savings will increase national income by the amount of investment or savings. It will not, of course, be as inflationary as investment which is not offset by savings but which is financed by expansion of credit. But savings, like taxes, do not generate income in the period in which they are undertaken. They affect national income only through the effect on spending in the subsequent period. In other words, the savings cancel the multiplier effects of the investment, but not the direct effects on income of the investment itself, just as taxes offset the multiplier effects, but not the direct effects of government spending. Thus, the monetary effects of business savings and investment are in themselves inflationary. If at the same time the investment process transfers labor and resources from the production of current goods and services to the production of capital goods, then investment financed out of profits is doubly inflationary. If the effect of higher taxes on corporation income is to reduce both corporate savings and corporate investment, it is almost certain that the effects will be deflationary rather than inflationary.

Of course, another possibility is that, faced with higher taxes, business will borrow more from the banks. Such a development is not inflationary, but neutral; borrowing from the bank cancels the deflationary effects of taxes. However, this possibility points again to the need to support fiscal policy with an appropriate monetary policy.

Conclusions on Taxation and Inflation

The preceding analysis leads to these major conclusions:

1. A balanced budget is in itself inflationary, but a given volume of government expenditures is the more inflationary, the less it is offset by tax collections. A "neutral" budget, so far as multiplier effects are concerned, and ignoring effects through redistribution of income, is one in which the ratio of the budget surplus to total revenues is equal to 1 minus the marginal propensity to consume.

2. An increase in taxes, in and of itself, could be inflationary if it led to an expansion of the flow of money. This result is conceivable but highly unlikely; the tax collections in themselves reduce money supply, and if prices are to rise (without a contraction in the supply of goods), the increase in borrowing from banks, or in velocity of circulation of money, must be sufficient to more than offset the reduction. Increases in money flow of the required volume are highly improbable. In any case, such increases in money flow can be prevented by appropriate monetary policy.

3. An increase in taxes may be inflationary if it reduces the flow of goods more than the flow of money, without creating enough unemployment to cause a cumulative deflation. This result might conceivably occur through the adverse effects of high taxes on the incentives to work and to take risks. However, tax collections have a multiplier effect (although one less than the multiplier effect of the same volume of expenditures). It is highly improbable that output could fall enough to more than offset this effect on money income without causing unemployment and turning inflationary pressure into deflationary pressure, unless the taxation and unemployment were confined to one sector of the economy while inflation continued in other, unrelated sectors.

4. Taxes which reduce net profits may diminish business saving and investment, but this effect would produce deflation rather than inflation. Investment which is just offset by saving is inflationary, and a reduction in both saving and investment is deflationary, in the monetary sense. Reduced investment might also have deflationary effects in the short run by releasing resources from the production of capital goods to the production of consumers' goods. Resort to bank borrowing in face of increased taxation would neutralize the effects of tax collections, but if credit extended just equaled tax collections, the net result would not be inflationary.

5. In discussing the effect of taxation through its influence on incentives, it is necessary to reintroduce the effect of government spending. The collection of taxes in and of itself certainly tends to reduce incentive to work or to take risks. But the receipt of a government contract to produce aircraft or munitions may have a very stimulating effect on incentives to work or to invest. Even the receipt of family allowances and of interest on the national debt may have a favorable effect on incentives, if there is a link in the mind of the general public be-

tween payment of taxes, the receipt of payments from the government, and individuals' own efforts. Here we are brought back to the political argument of Colin Clark. If the general public values the goods and services received in exchange for taxes as highly as the goods and services the same amount of money could buy in the market, there is no reason why the increase of taxes *and* government spending should destroy incentives.

In general, one may say that increases in taxation are in themselves almost certainly deflationary in their effects, no matter what their level. To make certain of this, anti-inflationary fiscal policy should be reinforced by anti-inflationary monetary policy. This analytic conclusion, that preventing inflation requires synchronization of monetary and fiscal policy, is supported by the postwar experience of a good many countries, including the United States, the United Kingdom, Canada, Australia, and Indonesia.

Other Objectives of Tax Policy

Offsetting the inflationary effects of development spending is not the only matter of concern in collecting taxes or encouraging savings. A government must consider the effect of its monetary and fiscal policies on incentives, on the allocation of resources, and on the distribution of income. Administrative problems must also be taken into account.

The collection of taxes may destroy the incentives which are the very mainsprings of economic growth. Taxes which fall on the wage earner may diminish the incentive to work harder and better; taxes which fall on profits of enterprise or on the higher-income groups may undermine the incentive to save and to make investments in new (and hence risky) enterprises. Taxes on output or income of farmers may reduce the incentive to improve agricultural techniques. Somehow the tax system must be devised so as to provide the necessary offset to the inflationary effects of development spending without destroying these incentives.

An incentive problem may also arise with regard to saving. Providing credit for private ventures associated with the development program—such as use of fertilizers or improved tools and the establishment of new industries—is the exact opposite of saving and is in itself inflationary. Yet the provision of such credit may be one of the most effective incentives to these development projects, and failure to provide adequate credit facilities may be a major barrier to expansion. Reconciling the need to provide incentives and the need to prevent inflation is thus a problem of credit policy as well as of tax policy.

Any pattern of government expenditure and taxes affects the relative attractiveness of various occupations and various uses of capital. It will therefore have an effect on the allocation of resources. Unless careful consideration is given to this effect, it may be haphazard or positively disadvantageous. The method chosen to finance a development program should affect the resource allocation in a manner tending to promote, rather than to retard, economic development. Also, the fiscal system should be carefully scrutinized to see whether it may create or strengthen monopoly positions, thus leading to misallocation of resources, and whether it may discourage desirable enterprises or encourage undesirable ones.

The fiscal pattern will also affect the distribution of the fruits of economic development among various individuals and groups. The determination of an "optimal" distribution of income is a matter for the social philosopher rather than the economic development planner; but one must take into account the generally accepted view that greater equality of income distribution is preferable to greater inequality, other things being equal. Where two fiscal systems are equally effective in promoting economic development, but one leads to greater equality of income distribution and the other to greater inequality, the former system would be considered preferable by most people. Thus consideration of the effect of financing economic development on income distribution is a part of the process of planning economic development.

Taxation: The Question of Structure

In nearly all underdeveloped countries some attention should be given to the problem of tax structure. Sometimes the tax system incorporates a large number of "nuisance taxes" which yield very little revenue, which are administratively expensive, and which are an annoyance to the taxpayer. This is true, for example, of the slaughter tax and the "statistical tax" in Indonesia, which were introduced by the Dutch authorities for reasons long since forgotten. Similar items exist in the tax structure of a good many countries. Removal of such nuisance taxes is one of the relatively easy steps toward tax reform.

Foreign "experts" are often struck by the difference between the over-all structure of taxes in underdeveloped countries and in advanced countries. As a general rule underdeveloped countries rely much more heavily on indirect taxes, such as sales taxes, import duties, and the like, and much less heavily on such direct taxes as income and inheritance taxes, than do advanced countries. At first blush this relatively heavy dependence on indirect taxes strikes the foreign observer as highly "regressive." Here, however, caution must be exercised. It is often quite impossible to increase the share of tax revenues from income tax merely by increasing income tax rates. Indeed some of the underdeveloped countries already have income tax structures which are heavier and more steeply progressive than those of more highly developed areas. Moreover, the governments of underdeveloped countries have learned how to build into their indirect tax systems a high degree of progressivity. Tunisia, for example, has commodity tax rates which vary from nothing on essentials to a high rate on luxuries. Indonesia's import surcharge rate varies from zero on necessary imports to 400 per cent on luxuries. Devices such as these may provide a more effective way of relating tax collections to income than an increase in income tax rates; with the institutional framework and administrative system existing in some underdeveloped countries, income taxes are too easily avoided. Finally, with incomes so low and with supply curves of labor and capital turning backward at such low levels of income, unfavorable "incentive" effects may occur at much lower ratios of income tax to income than in advanced countries.

As a long-run policy, increased reliance on income taxes, as administration and compliance improve, should no doubt be a goal of most underdeveloped countries. Meanwhile, however, astute uses of indirect taxes are to be recommended.

Inheritance taxes, on the other hand, could probably be introduced more quickly, from the purely administrative point of view, than extension of income taxes. The problem here is more apt to be political, since in many underdeveloped countries large property owners, who would be most strongly opposed to inheritance taxes, still wield considerable political power. Similarly, corporation income taxes, if not noticeably higher than in other countries, are a good source of revenue for underdeveloped countries. Many corporations are likely to be foreign, reducing the political problem, and they must keep accurate accounts.

In countries so largely agricultural, some use of land taxes would appear to be inevitable if the anti-inflationary potential of taxation is to be fully realized and if an equitable distribution of the tax burden is to be achieved. From the standpoint of equity, and perhaps also from the standpoint of yield, some gear-ing of land tax assessment to the output of the land taxed is desirable. From an incentive viewpoint, on the other hand, a lump-sum tax, which is not related to current output, is preferable. This point is discussed more fully below under the heading of "Incentive Taxes."

Because of the relative ease of control over goods passing international borders and the relative completeness of records of goods moving in international trade, many underdeveloped countries have found it desirable to rely heavily on import taxes and export duties as sources of revenue. As already suggested, it is not too difficult to introduce into such taxes on foreign trade a degree of progressivity, which removes from them any serious disadvantages from the standpoint of equity. Nor need they constitute a more serious interference with the volume and structure of trade than any other kind of tax system.[10] The major disadvantage of this type of tax is its instability. Since many underdeveloped countries are primary producers, exporting foodstuffs, agricultural raw materials, and industrial raw materials, and importing manufactured goods, the volume, balance, and terms of trade tend to move together. Revenues tend to be buoyant during periods of world prosperity and to collapse in periods of world depression. Export duties are particularly unsatisfactory from this point of view, for in their case, there may be a conflict between measures necessary to improve a budgetary situation and measures necessary to improve the balance of payments. In order to close budgetary gaps in period of falling export prices, export duties should be raised. But an increase in export levies, in conjunction with falling world market prices of exports, could prove so discouraging to exporters as seriously to diminish the volume, adding further to the difficulties of earning foreign exchange. If the level of money income is closely related to exports, however, and the non-monetary sector is too poor to tax, no change in tax structure can divorce revenues from the vagaries of the export market.

Local Government Finance

An important aspect of tax structure is the allocation of tax functions among different levels of government. Few underdeveloped countries are wholly free of problems regarding the

[10] Cf. E. M. Bernstein, "Some Aspects of Multiple Exchange Rates"; and B. H. Higgins, "The Rationale of Import Surcharges," *Economics and Finance in Indonesia* (*Ekonomi dan Keuangan Indonesia*), May, 1953.

financial relationships between central and local governments. The precise nature of the problem, of course, varies from country to country. Financial questions are related to responsibility for planning and executing development projects and so to the general division of powers among central and local governments. On the one hand are countries with federal constitutions, such as India and Libya, where central government officials sometimes feel inhibited in the planning, financing, and execution of development projects by the constitutional powers specifically allocated to the provinces. In unitary countries like Indonesia and the Philippines on the other hand, complaints are sometimes heard in areas remote from the capital that financial powers are too heavily concentrated in the hands of the central government. Moreover, there are differences in tradition regarding local government. Some countries, such as Indonesia and Libya, have a strong tradition of village democracy on which local government can be built. In other countries, such as India and Japan, where the feudal tradition was stronger, developing democratic government at the local level is a more difficult task.

Because of such differences in constitutional position and in historical background, intergovernmental financial arrangements, as well as the general tax system, must be tailor-made. The provision in the Libyan constitution, under which legislative powers with respect to personal income tax are in the hands of the central government, while the administrative powers are ascribed to the provincial government, seems curious at first sight, but it is well adapted to the current situation in the country. This provision assures uniform rates of personal income tax throughout the kingdom, but assessment of individual tax liability and the expenditure of income tax receipts are the prerogative and responsibility of the local authorities. Interprovincial rivalries and animosities are thus kept to a minimum, and tax enforcement can be more rigorous than if central government officials endeavored to assess and collect income taxes for expenditure by the central government.

Thus each underdeveloped country must seek its own optimum mix between central and local contributions. Each has certain advantages which cannot readily be transferred from one level of government to the other. Central fiscal devices, for example, are appropriate to levy taxation upon major components of national income which are generated in a particular geographic area or sector of the economy. The taxation of income arising from foreign trade provides one example. Local fiscal processes, on the other hand, are necessarily decentralized in impact and can best be designed to reach income arising from scattered geographic areas. They appear to have special advantages for the direct mobilization of unemployed or partially unemployed resources in many occupations traditional to the underdeveloped economy.

A few generalizations can be made. First, if the rural people who constitute the bulk of the population in most underdeveloped countries are to understand the process of economic development, some projects must be carried out at the local level, so as to demonstrate the relationship between investment and rising standards of living. Only local projects with clear "demonstration effects" will engender widespread support for the overall program of economic development. If a wholehearted effort is to be made to increase domestic financial resources for economic development, widespread popular support for the plan is essential. As already indicated, taxable capacity itself is not unrelated to the degree of enthusiasm for the program of expenditures. There is much to be said for having a substantial portion of the development program planned, financed, and executed at the local government level.

Second, taxes which are likely to be unpopular, or difficult to administer from a distance, are in general more suitable for local governments. In particular, taxes which require much administrative discretion, such as those involving assessment of land values, surmise income taxes, and the like, are as a rule better administered by local government officials who are known to the taxpayers and who are considered to represent them. Against this clear advantage is the danger that personal favoritism and discrimination may be greater if taxes of this kind are administered by local officials, who are subject to more or less continuous pressures, than if they are administered from the center. On balance, in the early stages of a development program, the advantage would seem to lie with local administration of such taxes.

By the same token, taxes which are collected in a form difficult to measure precisely, such as labor services or taxes in kind, are probably more easily administered at the local level. Experience with "community self-help programs" indicates that a substantial volume of resources for economic development can be obtained in the form of labor, if the development projects are organized and executed by local governments for the immediate benefit of the local citizenry.

Incentive Taxes

The literature on public finance in advanced countries has devoted a good deal of attention to "incentive taxation." However important the incentive aspects of taxation may be in advanced countries, their importance in underdeveloped countries is clearly much greater; it is easier to sustain a process of steady growth than it is to initiate it. The purpose of incentive taxation is to stimulate an increase in the flow of labor or managerial effort, or of savings and investment, or to improve the allocation of capital, land, labor, and entrepreneurship.

The term "incentive taxation" has been used with some ambiguity. Indeed it might refer to any of six kinds of tax measures. The term is sometimes used erroneously to mean reductions in tax rates, which are designed to provide incentives for increased effort or risk-taking. In some circumstances, general tax reductions may indeed provide an incentive to increased productivity, but the circumstances under which a general reduction in tax rates would raise the flow of goods by more than it raises the flow of spending are rare. General tax cuts are usually inflationary, and incentive taxation in this sense must be eschewed by most underdeveloped countries.

Secondly, the term may be applied to selective tax reductions, designed to improve the balance of prospective gains and prospective losses on new investment, without necessarily reducing the total tax burden on taxpayers as a group. An example of this kind of incentive measure is the averaging of profits for tax purposes over a number of years, to improve the prospects of average profits after tax, for investment subject to violent fluctuations in demand for its product. The averaging of profits for tax purposes is especially important in such risky fields as mining, petroleum, rubber plantations, and the like, which have a long production cycle and are subject to substantial fluctuations in prices.

Another example of this kind of incentive taxation is the exemption of new investment from taxes for a certain number of years. Investment in new industries always carries more risk than expansion of old ones, and expansion of old ones is more risky than mere replacement. Moreover, there is some reason to suppose that the "chain reaction" effects on the pace of economic development are greater for new investment than for expansion of existing industries. Agricultural taxes which impose lower rates for increases in output than for "normal" returns, thus reducing the risk attached to improvements in agricultural techniques, might also be included under this heading.

Exempting new investment from taxes is a policy to be handled with care; it should be introduced only where it is quite certain to encourage investment that would not otherwise take place. An example of injudicious application of this policy is to be found in the Philippines, where a very wide range of enterprises have been classified as "new and essential" and accorded tax freedom, with no very clear stimulus to private net investment, which remains about 5 per cent of national income. Complete tax freedom is an enormous concession to make and unnecessary for industries that prove profitable in the early years of their lives. Moreover, the concept of "new and essential" is not clearly defined, and the range of administrative discretion permitted in deciding which industries should enjoy this privilege opens the door wide to undesirable practices. Most important, the system is not selective in its effects. For industries making no profits in early years tax freedom is no incentive and no help. For industries making high profits the incentive is adequate without tax freedom and the system merely reduces the volume of public investment that could be undertaken without inflation. Only relatively few cases fall in between, where actual or estimated profits without tax are sufficient to warrant investment but profits less regular taxes would be insufficient. In short, *the present system retards rather than accelerates economic growth.* It is also discriminatory; the tax freedom privilege is obviously much more valuable to some industries—those able to secure a monopoly position, for example—than to others.

Actually, in the Philippines the tax-exempt industries as a group have *not* been of the risky variety that requires special concessions to make investment attractive. The average rate of return on capital has been 16⅔ per cent. Of major branches of industry, the lowest returns (6.3 per cent) were in textiles, a field in which the market was assured and techniques well known and easily transferred from neighboring countries. In some relatively new fields, such as veneer and plywood, profits have been extraordinarily high, 60.5 per cent. Wood and wood fixtures enterprises in general earned an average of 43.2 per cent. Tobacco curing brought profits of 44 per cent, rubber products 33.5 per cent, non-metallic mineral products 31.2 per cent, lithographed metal products 45.8 per cent. With profits at these levels there is no economic justification for continued tax freedom.

Third, tax rates might be increased or reduced selectively, in such a way as to control either the allocation or the timing of investment. One such system of incentive taxation, which has been used with considerable success in Canada and which is recommended in the Five-Year Economic and Social Development Plan in the Philippines, is "accelerated" and "postponed" depreciation. In general, the principle of accelerated depreciation, introduced by the Canadian government at the end of 1944, permits more rapid write-off of plant and equipment for tax purposes. Initially, the privilege of accelerated depreciation was allowed to industries which were converting from wartime to peacetime uses. With the outbreak of war in Korea, the accelerated depreciation privilege was allowed to defense industries and to industries significant for Canada's basic development. The principle of postponed or deferred depreciation introduced into the 1951 budget meant that except for the defense or developmental industries which the government wished to encourage, the right to charge capital costs against income for tax purposes was postponed, in this case for four years.

Thus the system was used to encourage reconstruction from war to peacetime uses in the first instance and to divert investment into defense and developmental industries, at the time of the Korean War. In addition, however, the use of these instruments was related to the general business cycle situation. Accelerated depreciation was first introduced at a time when the government wished to encourage investment, to prevent the widely expected postwar depression. When postponed depreciation was introduced early in 1951, the Canadian economy was suffering inflationary pressure, and this tax device was a means of increasing the ratio of tax payments to business earnings and so repressing investment, especially of a low-priority type. Toward the end of 1951, when inflationary pressure showed signs of abatement, the range of investment exempted from deferred depreciation was expanded. As may be seen from Table 22–1 this set of measures seems to have had a marked effect on the pattern of investment in Canada.

Alternative methods of controlling the timing of investment have been utilized by the Swedish and Swiss governments. In Sweden, corporations and cooperative associations are permitted to deduct from taxable income amounts allocated to special reserve funds for future investment. The funds may be earmarked for construction, for accumulation of inventories, for purchase of machinery and equipment, or for mining and research. The government reserves the right to determine the time at which, the extent to which, and the purpose for which reserves so deducted may be used. In Switzerland the simpler device of allowing rebates of taxes on profits is utilized.[11]

An alternative system, which would have much the same effect, would be for the government to allow a limited proportion of profits to go untaxed in periods of expansion, provided the untaxed profits were used to purchase special non-negotiable and non-interest-bearing bonds. These securities would be cashable in periods of falling income and employment, as designated by the government, for certain stipulated purposes, such as purchase of capital equipment, inventories or housing, payment of wage bonuses, etc.[12]

Fourth, incentive taxes may be imposed not with the purpose of collecting them, but to persuade people to take certain action to avoid them. In this category would be included taxes on hoarding, whether of goods or of money. In underdeveloped countries, speculative hoarding of goods is likely to be the more serious problem. By imposing a penal tax on inventories held in excess of some stipulated "normal," the prospective profitability of such speculation can be removed and goods forced into the market, diminishing the inflationary pressure from development spending.[13] Occasionally hoarding of money also becomes a problem, especially if it occurs side by side with hoarding of goods, as it apparently does in Indonesia at present. Money is held by the urban community as a means of evading income taxes and as a relatively trustworthy asset. Meanwhile there is a scarcity of money in rural areas. Moreover, the hoarded money is "hot"; at any time it may be thrown into the spending stream or into the black market for foreign exchange. Under these conditions, a monthly tax on the average value of cash balances, combined with a "stamp money" system, under which stamps must be attached to currency each week to give it legal-tender status, would have some theoretical merit. In practice, however, such systems have been found administratively unwieldy; the attempt to introduce dated stamp scrip in the Canadian province of Alberta broke down very quickly. Such a system would be of even more dubious merit for underdeveloped countries.

A stronger case could be made for imposing a tax on all assets, with rates diminishing with the degree of risk and illiquidity

[11] For a critical analysis of these systems, see Higgins, *op. cit.*, pp. 473–75.
[12] This system is analyzed more fully in *ibid.*, pp. 475–76.
[13] The administration of such a system is described in detail in Chap. 23.

assumed. Thus rates on cash balances, inventories, and unused land might be high, rates on government securities might approximate the interest paid on them (thus making the national debt self-liquidating), and rates on productive assets might ap-

TABLE 22-1.

New Investment Affected and Not Affected by Deferred Capital Cost Allowances, Canada *

Investment category	*Millions of current dollars*		*Per cent change 1951–52*	
	1951	1952	Current dollars	Constant dollars
1. Total private and public investment (categories 2 and 3)	4,581	5,003	+9	+3
2. Investment by bodies not under income tax regulations	1,875	2,079	+11	+5
3. Investment subject to income tax regulations (categories 4 and 5)	2,706	2,924	+8	+2
4. Investment not affected by deferred capital cost allowances	1,590	1,721	+8	+2
5. Investment affected by deferred capital cost allowances (categories 6 and 7)	1,116	1,203	+7	+2
6. Investment eligible for capital cost allowances, subject to the issuance of a certificate of eligibility	543	729	+34	+27
7. Investment not eligible for capital cost allowances	573	474	−17	−22

* For a more extensive analysis of deferred and accelerated depreciation in Canada, see Benjamin Higgins, "Government Measures to Regularize Private Investment in Other Countries than the United States," *Regularization of Business Investment* (New York, 1954).

SOURCE: Estimates based on returns from the 1952 survey of investment intentions reported in statement of the Minister of Defense Production and Trade and Commerce, in House of Commons, March 14, 1952, *Hansard*, pp. 436–44.

proach zero. Such a system encourages the diversion of saving from cash balances to productive investment. In itself such a tax is not anti-inflationary; but if it results in a net increase in productive investment, it may accelerate the rate of economic growth.

A tax on "profits in excess of a fair return on utilized capacity" has been proposed to compel the absorption of excess capacity. This tax was first recommended as an anti-monopoly device, but it could be adapted to provide an incentive to absorb excess capacity of land and/or of plant. The basic principle is simple; the capacity of the productive unit and its value at capacity production are estimated (perhaps by the entrepreneur himself), and a "fair" rate of return on the value of this plant at capacity production is determined. Profits in excess of the "fair return" on "utilized" capacity are taxed away in their entirety. "Utilization" is defined in terms of output. If production is, let us say, only 50 per cent of estimated capacity, the "fair return" is allowed on the 50 per cent of the estimated value of the plant, and the 100 per cent tax applied to the balance. On the other hand, if output is expanded to double "capacity," the plant is "utilized" at 200 per cent and the "fair return" will be allowed on double the estimated value. The effect of this system is that profits retainable after tax vary directly with output. It then pays the entrepreneur to expand production approximately to the point where the cost of an additional unit is equal to its price, the point usually regarded as the "social optimum." Thus this system provides an incentive for utilizing capacity to the full, and also for introducing the most efficient methods of production.

Sometimes tax proposals are linked with proposals for subsidies. For example, it would be possible to provide a subsidy for investments of a kind which the government wishes to encourage, and then impose a lump-sum or percentage tax on profits, so as to recoup the subsidy plus any "supernormal" profits remaining when the desired scale of production is reached. The subsidy would encourage production of the desired kind, and a lump-sum or percentage tax on profits cannot be "shifted"; that is, it cannot be avoided by reducing output and raising price. In short, the subsidies serve to expand output in the desired direction, and the recapturing of the subsidy through a lump-sum or percentage tax on profits will not be a deterrent to this expansion. The Italian government has utilized subsidies in somewhat this manner, to encourage land reclamation.[14]

Fifth, there are incentive taxes which compel increases in output by the taxpayer, to enable him to meet the assessment. In

[14] For an analysis of tax and subsidy schemes, and of the tax on "profits in excess of a fair return on utilized capacity," see Benjamin Higgins, "Postwar Tax Policy," in Carl Shoup and Richard Musgrave (eds.), *Readings in Public Finance* (New York, 1959).

this category are the poll tax or head tax and lump-sum taxes on land.

It is a long-standing proposition in the literature of public finance that a head tax or poll tax is desirable from the standpoint of incentive, because it is unrelated to the volume of output or to the level of income earned. The tax is not reduced if productivity is diminished nor is it increased if output is raised. In underdeveloped countries, where a larger number of workers, farmers, or entrepreneurs may be operating slightly above the level at which their supply curves turn backward, the case for the poll tax is even stronger; for by reducing income net of tax, more effort or risk-taking is called forth; output must be increased to meet the tax while maintaining "customary normal" standards of living. Unfortunately, in underdeveloped countries this "customary normal" may be close to the subsistence level, a fact which calls forth opposition to the poll tax for such countries. If the tax is too high, so that incomes net of tax are reduced below levels where satisfactory nutrition is maintained, or where the standard of living is so low as to destroy incentives altogether, the imposition of a poll tax may reduce rather than increase output. It has been contended that the poll tax imposed in certain African countries was too high in this sense, disrupting tribal life, and forcing large numbers of people to migrate to cities.[15]

In this connection, however, a distinction might be made between the use of poll taxes to recapture initial increase in income, resulting from the development program, and taxes which constitute a net reduction of income from current levels. As has already been indicated, it may be necessary in some situations to tax away initial increases in income, in order to prevent initial improvements in productivity from being dissipated in accelerated population growth or in increased leisure. Also, if a development program which concentrates on agricultural improvement in the first phase is to provide self-financing for subsequent phases of development, the initial increases in income must be recaptured, in order to increase exports or reduce imports of consumers' goods and thus obtain the necessary foreign exchange to pay for the raw materials and equipment needed for further development. If the general economic situation makes such an austere fiscal policy necessary, a poll tax has much to recommend it, since it would even provide an incentive for increased production, in the event that the tax reduced income below the "customary normal" without endangering health or efficiency.

[15] Wald and Froomkin, *Papers and Proceedings of the Conference on Agricultural Taxation and Economic Development*, p. 26.

If such a "development tax" is accompanied by a progressive income tax, a progressive sales tax, or a progressive land tax, it is less objectionable from a social welfare viewpoint.

A variety of lump-sum tax, of more importance in agricultural countries than a head tax, is a lump-sum tax on land. Like the poll tax, a lump-sum land tax imposes no penalties on increased production and, if farmers are operating on the backward-sloping portions of their supply curves, may even stimulate increased production. In order to diminish the regressiveness of such a tax, it could be defined as a lump-sum tax *per acre*, so that larger landowners would pay proportionately more in total tax. In addition, the tax rate could vary according to the type of product, so that the more productive land would bear a higher rate of tax. If it is desired to use the tax as an incentive for shifting to more desired types of products (exports, for example), the ratio of tax to potential value output per acre could be made to decline, if production is shifted to high-priority products. The Indonesian system of differential rates of export duty for smallholders and plantation operators, which are designed to encourage expansion of smallholders' production, shows some recognition of this principle, although an export tax at any level provides some disincentive to increased output. Several countries, however, including South Korea, Yugoslavia, and the Soviet Union, fix land taxes on the basis of a standard assessment, related to the "normal" productive capacity of the land, so that increases in output do not bring any increase in tax. Similarly, Australia and New Zealand impose land taxes on *unimproved* land values, to avoid barriers to land improvement. New Zealand grants liberal depreciation allowances under its income tax law for land improvements of a developmental type.

A quite different approach, designed for countries where large areas are withheld from cultivation, or cultivated incompletely or inefficiently, by large-scale landlords, is to gear the lump-sum tax to the *potential* output, rather than to the *actual* output of the land in question. Several Latin American countries, including Panama and Brazil, have taxes of this nature.[16]

Sixth, taxes may be classified as incentive taxes, because they are directly linked to government expenditures which have a popular appeal.

The use of lump-sum taxes of the poll tax type is less likely to encounter resistance, and is more likely to have favorable incentive effects, if it is linked to specific services provided by the

[16] For a more complete discussion of incentive taxation in agriculture, see Wald and Froomkin, *op. cit.*, Part III, chap. III.

government, or to specific development projects. Such a system was suggested to the Libyan government by the United Nations Mission of Technical Assistance to that country:[17]

. . . Theoretically, a case could be made for taxing away increases in productivity, and giving away certain goods, notably consumers' durable goods, until these goods become part of the "customary normal" standard of living and people are willing to work in order to buy them; the taxes could then be dropped and the new goods sold instead. Such a scheme would be difficult to administer in Libya, but certain items in the development budget, such as the school feeding program, might be utilized in this way, some social welfare services, agricultural tools, seed and livestock, etc. That is, these goods and services might be provided free or for a nominal fee in the first phase, while the higher taxes or compulsory savings could be justified in terms of the benefits provided through the development program. In the second phase, when the community has learned to appreciate these goods and services, and have come to regard them as part of their normal standard of living, fees closer to actual cost of the services could be charged and taxes (or compulsory savings) reduced. In this way, an incentive would be provided at each stage of development for continuing to work hard and well, despite increases in productivity. Meanwhile, the extra goods taxed away, or sold by producers to meet taxes or compulsory savings, could be used by the government to reduce the import surplus. Such a scheme would entail complex administrative and political problems, but is worthy of serious study.

Similarly in Indonesia, where labor legislation prevents the discharge of redundant labor on plantations, it has been proposed to the government by a working party of the National Planning Bureau that a "development tax" might be imposed on plantation operators, somewhat below the current wages of plantation workers. The receipts would be used to transfer workers to development projects in the same region, of interest to plantation operators and workers alike. In this way, the workers are assured of continuous employment in their own region, the plantations are afforded some relief at a time when falling export prices and rising costs are squeezing profits, and the net cost of the development projects to the government is small. Similarly, road taxes may be justified, in underdeveloped countries as in advanced ones, in terms of need for road improvements; taxes on railway and air fares might be justified in terms of railroad and airport improvement.

[17] Cf. Benjamin Higgins, "The Economic and Social Development of Libya," United Nations Mission of Technical Assistance to Libya, (A/AC.32/TA.16), July 1, 1952, p. 68.

In countries where there is widespread support for development as such, as in India or Yugoslavia, *any* new tax might be more favorably received, if it were labeled a "development tax" and publicized as a measure needed to facilitate the development program.

Finally, taxes may be designed to provide special incentives for saving. One such tax is a compulsory contribution to a provident fund, which has been successfully utilized in Singapore. Deductions from payrolls are justified in terms of the need to build up reserves to meet old age pensions, unemployment insurance, sickness benefits, and the like. While such a system is reaching "maturity" current contributions will exceed benefits, increasing the total revenues of the government and adding to the effective savings of the economy.

A more general measure to stimulate savings is a "spending tax." In an underdeveloped country, spending rather than income should be taxed; saving should be encouraged, and the part of income that is saved should be left tax-free as much as possible. Various devices might be used to convert the income tax into a tax on spending. For example, as already suggested, the portion of income invested in new plant equipment and housing, held idle in savings deposits, used to pay insurance premiums, or to purchase securities issued to finance industrial expansion, might be wholly or partly deductible from taxable income. The tax legislation of advanced countries offers precedents for all these kinds of deductions.

Under appropriate conditions, a general sales tax is a close approximation to a spending tax. Some progression is possible in a general sales tax; rates on luxury items can be much higher than on necessities, as in Tunisia. Basic foodstuffs might be entirely exempt.

Some countries with wide disparities between the standards of living at the top and bottom of the income scale and with administrative difficulties in preventing income tax evasion have resorted to a "surmise income tax," which is also, in effect, a tax on luxury spending. The estimate of taxable income is revised upward in the light of conspicuous consumption of such items as large houses, many servants, expensive cars, foreign travel, and the like. This system is open to abuse because of the large amount of discretion that must be accorded to the officials estimating income for tax purposes. Nevertheless, it is worthy of serious consideration in countries where estimates of income can seldom be checked by reference to account books and where it is desirable to limit luxury spending.

23 A Self-enforcing Incentive Tax System for Underdeveloped Countries

Few underdeveloped countries are in a position to enforce rigorously tax systems of the kind that have become orthodox in advanced countries. Yet it is essential for underdeveloped countries to increase tax revenues, so as to permit increased investment in development projects without disruptive inflation. If possible, tax increases should be of a kind that does not destroy incentives for private undertakings of a developmental nature. Thus the construction of a tax system which by its very nature cannot be evaded, and which nevertheless gives due weight to incentive features, is of particular importance for underdeveloped countries.

This chapter attempts to formulate such a system. The integrated system and even some of its components are so designed that efforts to evade one tax will automatically involve the taxpayer in other tax liabilities so great that evasion is not worthwhile. In short, the system makes it pay to be honest about taxes. At the same time, it has built-in incentive aspects that should contribute to economic growth.

The system might be easier to administer in advanced countries, but where bookkeeping systems are complete and accurate and tax observance prevails, and where accordingly loss of revenue through tax evasion is a small fraction of tax liability, a self-enforcing system may not pay. It is likely to prove somewhat more expensive to operate than traditional income tax systems, and the added costs might outweigh the added collections. Where evasion is the rule rather than the exception, on the other hand, the improvement in tax collections under the self-enforcing system presented here will far outweigh any added cost of operating it.

Kaldor's "Tax Reform"

Various components of the system were developed by the author in the course of advisory missions in Libya, Indonesia, and the Philippines. The idea of a completely closed system, however, came from reading Nicholas Kaldor's book on *Indian Tax Reform.* In the course of a visit to the University of Bombay and the Indian Planning Commission, Kaldor proposed to the government of India a tax system built around a progressive tax on total consumer outlays. The system has subsequently been elaborated in a book.[1] Its main features are as follows:

1. A personal income tax at rates ranging from zero to 45 per cent. Income is defined for tax purposes so as to include all capital gains.
2. A tax on all assets (wealth) ranging from 0.3 to 1.5 per cent, with an exemption for some small minimum holdings.
3. An expenditures tax ranging from 25 to 300 per cent according to the total amount of consumer spending by a family unit, with an exemption for some small minimum amount of expenditure.
4. A gift tax varying from 15 to 80 per cent according to the total value of gifts made in the tax period.
5. To assist in enforcement, Kaldor suggests compulsory auditing of accounts.
6. To check on total spending, income, and wealth every one of the one million taxpayers would be assigned a code number, which would be entered on all documents arising out of capital transactions.

This system goes a long way in the direction of self-enforcement, but it is not a closed system. As Kaldor himself admits, it will not prevent evasion if both parties to a transaction gain by concealing or understating it. In his system the seller of an asset does gain from reporting the sale, offsetting the gain to the buyer from hiding it or understating it. But in the case of goods, both buyer and seller gain from concealment or understatement; the buyer reduces his expenditures tax thereby and the seller his in-

[1] Nicholas Kaldor, *Indian Tax Reform* (Delhi, Ministry of Finance, 1956).

come tax. Ultimately Kaldor relies for enforcement on his compulsory auditing and the difficulty of hiding assets.

An Integrated Self-enforcing Tax System

Although Kaldor's own system is not completely self-enforcing, it provided the present writer with the "missing link." By adding to Kaldor's expenditure and assets taxes a penal tax on excess inventories and a turnover tax, it is possible to devise a closed system, so that anyone failing to report one taxable transaction will either find himself paying more under another tax, or having the transaction reported by the other party to it, because the other party can reduce his tax liability by honest reporting.

The essential components of this integrated system are as follows:

1. A personal income tax of, say, 20 per cent on incomes above, say, $400
2. A flat-rate corporation income tax of, say, 20 per cent
3. A general sales or turnover tax, say, 2 per cent
4. A tax on all assets:
   a) Cash, say, 4 to 8 per cent according to amount (with exemption for *x* per cent of reported income)
   b) Bonds, say, 3 to 5 per cent according to amount held
   c) Equities, say, 2 to 3 per cent
   d) Productive assets (plant and equipment, land in an "appropriate" use), 1 to 2 per cent
   e) Normal inventories, 2 per cent
5. A tax on excess inventories, say, 40 per cent
6. Expenditures tax, say, 6 to 20 per cent according to amount for individuals subject to income tax

Enforcement

Income for tax purposes is defined as profits (dividends, interest, rents, entrepreneurial gains) plus "capital gains" (increase in value of total assets held, less purchases of new assets) plus wages and salaries. In symbols, $Y_t = R + G + W$.

The expenditure tax will apply for income tax payers to all consumption, C. National income may be defined as $Y = R + W = C + I$. (I is "investment" in the sense of all purchases of assets.) Also, by definition $G = \Delta A - I$, where A is total assets. Thus taxable income is $Y_t = C + I + (\Delta A - I) = C + \Delta A$.

The question is then whether any taxable transaction is *worth* hiding or underreporting by both parties, and whether in that case it *can* be hidden or underreported without leading to an increase in tax on other transactions for at least one of the parties.

Wages and salaries paid out will of course be reported by employers as costs, in order to keep down income taxes. If there is any likelihood that some employers may overreport wages and salaries paid, and split the tax savings with employees, exemptions could be set very low so as to remove any difference in *marginal* tax between employers and employees, or a payroll tax could be added to the system.

Profits are equal to gross sales less costs. Sales will tend to be reported by sellers to avoid excess inventory taxes, which will always be higher than sales taxes plus income taxes on the same volume of goods. Wage and salary earners in the lower brackets whose incomes are fully reported will also have an incentive to report sales to them (expenditures for them) since the tax on *their* expenditures will be lower than the assets tax on cash that will otherwise be ascribed to them. That is, income less reported expenditures will be automatically calculated as an increase in assets held; in the absence of reported purchases of other assets, it will be assumed that the assets are held in cash; and this accumulation of cash will also represent an increase in total net worth, and so a capital gain, since no investment has been reported.

Capital gains, in other words, are a residual:

$$G = \Delta A - I = Y_t - (C + I)$$

Purchases of capital goods, I, will be reported by buyers as costs (depreciation for income tax purposes is geared to purchases of capital goods) to avoid the higher assets tax on cash and a tax on capital gains. They will be reported by the sellers to avoid excess inventory taxes. Sales or expenditures, C, will be reported by sellers to avoid excess inventory taxes and by buyers in the lower brackets to avoid taxes on cash balances and capital gains. Buyers in high-income, low-spending brackets will also find it worthwhile reporting consumer spending, rather than adding to their imputed capital gains, which are part of taxable income, and paying the assets tax on imputed increases in cash as well.

Will not taxpayers eager to hoard goods report fictitious sales to avoid the excess inventory tax? It would hardly pay. The seller would have to pay income and turnover tax on the fictitious sale. The buyer must pay the expenditure tax if the transaction involves consumers' goods and capital gains plus assets taxes if the transaction involves assets. If the fictitious buyer is himself a dealer, he puts himself in the position of being liable to excess inventories tax if he makes many fictitious purchases. Moreover, a dealer who reports purchases but no sales would soon arouse suspicion.

The main point, however, is that revelation of *any* transaction in a chain provides the key to the whole chain. There is always someone along the line who will gain by reporting the transaction, exposing any taxpayers who have sought to conceal transactions.

It is true that it will pay both a buyer and a seller to hide a transaction if both have stocks below normal, so that both the sale and purchase for replenishment of inventories can be concealed without penalty. If sales are concealed but purchases for replenishment are reported by either party, the would-be tax evader would soon find himself in an excess inventory bracket. It would be extremely difficult to hide transactions all down the line; at some stage some buyer or seller will *want* to report the transaction to save himself taxes. In the case of imports the whole process would have to begin with smuggling, and in the case of exports it would have to end with smuggling. For most commodities accumulation of inventories could be discovered by physical checks, thus laying bare a whole series of illegal transactions. For all practical purposes, evasion becomes impossible under such an integrated tax system.

Under this system, then, taxes can be profitably evaded by all parties to a transaction only by:

1. Buying goods or assets without reporting or detection and later selling without reporting or detection
2. Reporting false sales (to avoid inventory tax) and later selling without reporting or detection

Method 1 does not apply to imports, unless smuggled, since the initial purchase is recorded on customs slips and import licenses. In the case of large-scale home producers of goods for export, books are usually orderly, and since failure to report sales would be a violation of income tax laws, the risk of detection would be great. Unreported purchases by wholesalers or final exporters from small producers outside the income tax system can be policed by sample physical checks; most export items are too bulky to be hidden in large quantities. As an additional check, however, godowns might be required to report on goods in storage, say, once a quarter, subject to a heavy fine for false information. Some document is always involved in storing goods; the godowns could be required to send a copy to the statistical authorities. Moreover, sellers would have to compensate low-income buyers for the difference between expenditures tax and tax on cash assets, to persuade them not to report the transaction. They would have to compensate high-income buyers for the imputed income tax on capital gains plus tax on cash assets. Enforcement could be tightened by sample checks on bank statements, to disclose false reporting of increases in bank balances.

A retailer may consider it worthwhile reporting fictitious sales, and paying income and sales tax on them, if he can then hold goods for a price rise without paying inventory tax and later sell without reporting sales when actually made. (It would seldom be considered worthwhile to pay income, sales, and expenditures tax twice on the same sale, on the *chance* that the price rise would more than offset the double taxation.) It might even be considered worthwhile for a wholesaler to make an agreement with retailers to report such fictitious sales and share the profits. However, making unreported sales would involve all the usual problems of income tax evasion, plus the problem of physically hiding goods while held for future (unreported) sale. Moreover, if any firm shows a sharp drop in reported sales from one period to another, a clue is provided for investigation; and it would be very difficult for any firm to expand *actual* sales enough to keep *reported* sales on the same level, while adding *unreported* sales of unreported stocks held over from the previous period.

To assist in the detection of such cases, informers could be offered a portion of the tax take. This device, together with sample checks of physical stocks, information from godowns, and investigation of cases where sales drop sharply from one tax period to the next, should prevent significant proportions of evasion by reporting fictitious sales in one period and making unreported sales later.

Professor Carey Brown of M.I.T. has pointed out to the author that in advanced countries the most common form of income tax evasion is one not adequately cared for in the above system: charging as an expense something that is really consumption. "Expense accounts" of various kinds are the most obvious case of such evasion, but there are others. A grocer's wife takes food from the shelves of the shop for family use, reducing sales but not costs; a farmer consumes his own crop but charges full costs against income, or uses farmhands as domestic servants. In most underdeveloped countries, it will be a long time before tax enforcement is rigorous enough for this kind of evasion to become particularly troublesome. In most of them, the trouble now is that people with high incomes do not pay taxes at all. It is doubtful whether evasion of the sort that bothers Professor Brown would be very significant in underdeveloped countries, under the system outlined above. If the grocer's wife takes too much from the shelves, the grocer will get caught on excess inventory tax. Most peasants are not in the tax-paying brackets anyway. In the case of the smallholders or plantation operators, the problem is the same as it is for Texas ranchers, and watertight enforcement would take some policing, perhaps on a sample basis. In any case, the system proposed here does not make this kind of evasion more serious than under the usual kind of income tax, and it makes it at least somewhat more difficult to do undetected.

Administration

A key feature of the system is that computations of tax liability would be made by the Statistical Office, rather than through the internal revenue service. The tax authorities would be left only the simpler task of collecting the tax after each taxpayer's liability had been clearly established. Each income taxpayer would have a code number, as under the Kaldor proposal; each taxpayer would have a card on which his income, expenditures, and assets would be recorded; and whenever a document arising out of a transaction reached the Statistical Office the appropriate entries would be made by machine on the cards of the taxpayers involved. Needless to say, the system would bring as a by-product a considerable improvement in economic statistics, permitting more ready and more accurate computation of national income, production, sales, inventories, input-output matrices, etc. The computations required are by no means beyond the capacity of modern electronic computers, and the cost involved would be a tiny fraction of the improvement in tax collections.[2]

The Tax on Excess Inventories

The most unfamiliar of the taxes in the system is the tax on excess inventories; let us, therefore, consider its administration in more detail. As originally conceived, this tax was designed

[2] In order to avoid the cost of doing the same bookkeeping twice, the government could make quarterly computations for firms requesting this service, in exchange for a reasonable fee which would reduce the net cost to the government.

for incentive rather than enforcement purposes. During 1952 and 1953 the Indonesian Ministry of Finance was concerned with the hoarding of goods, especially goods entering into foreign trade, which was then believed to be taking place on a large scale. Over a period of several months, discussions took place within the government over the possibility of forcing these hoards into the market through a penal tax on excess inventories. In designing such a tax the author worked in close cooperation with Dr. Nathan Keyfitz of the Canadian Dominion Bureau of Statistics, who was then Expert on General Statistics of the Indonesian National Planning Bureau. As the proposal was studied more carefully, it was recognized that the introduction of an excess inventory tax administered through the Central Office of Statistics, together with the income and turnover taxes, would afford opportunities for improved administration of the whole tax system. It became apparent that conceptually simple extensions of existing statistical operations would permit the government to follow the flow of goods through every stage of the economy, providing the basis for a completely efficient system of income, sales, and excess inventory taxes. These extensions also seemed fairly easy from the technical and administrative point of view, except for two "open ends" in the flow of goods:

1. Original purchases of goods from small-scale producers for sale in the home market or for export
2. Final sales to consumers

Except for rice, purchases of home produce from small producers for resale in the home market were not of great importance, and rice sales were already subject to government control. Under the incomplete system then proposed, purchases from small producers for export and final sales of imports would have required policing; these deficiencies disappear in the integrated system outlined above.

Let us consider the general nature of the fact-gathering task. The following sources of information were already available to the statistical services in Indonesia and would be available in many underdeveloped countries:

1. *Imports:* licenses issued, exchange certificates issued, customs slips issued, income tax returns. These were available for each importer and each class of import. There were also data on bank credits issued to importers.
2. *Exports:* estate production, smallholders' rubber production, copra production
   a) Reports by district governments on production

b) Export licenses, by exporter and by product
c) Income tax returns

3. *Rice production for home market:* district government reports, sundry production figures for various commodities

Essentially, the additional material required was as follows:

1. *Importers*
   a) Estimate of *stocks* at starting date (questionnaire plus physical check)
   b) One copy of each invoice of *sales by importers* to be provided to statistical services
   c) One copy of each invoice of *sales by wholesalers* to retailers
   d) If feasible, sales slips of retailers
2. *Exporters*
   a) Estimate of *stocks* at starting date (questionnaire plus physical check
   b) Invoices of *sales by producers* to wholesalers (or exporters)
   c) Invoice of *sales by wholesalers* to exporters
3. *Producers for home market*
   a) Estimate of *stocks* at starting date
   b) Invoices of *sales by producers* to wholesalers
   c) Invoices of *sales by wholesalers* to retailers
   d) *Sales slips* of *retailers*

With these materials and an appropriate system of coding and cards, it would be technically possible to compute, for any period after the starting date, the average stocks, sales, and incomes of every firm. Each firm would be considered to hold the goods in stock, and to be liable for any excess inventories tax, until their sale was confirmed by the purchaser. At that time, the seller must pay any sales tax for which he is liable, and the invoices would be held in his income tax file. Thus with this information in the hands of the government, it would be impossible for any firm to evade any one of the three taxes.

THE PROBLEM OF MARKUP

There is one major conceptual problem. If excess inventories are to be defined in terms of a ratio of the value of sales to the value of stocks, which is the simplest approach, account must somehow be taken of the markup at each turnover. A simple subtraction of value of sales from value of stocks would not measure the value of stocks still held.

It would of course be impossible to take account of the markup in defining a "normal" turnover. If the "normal" turnover is four times per year, and the markup is 12.5 per cent, then the "normal" ratio of sales to stocks is 4.5. However, in an inflationary situation, an entrepreneur may build up a "normal" ratio of sales to stocks by holding goods for a price rise, which is precisely the kind of action the tax is designed to discourage.

The problem is avoided, of course, by defining normal turnover in physical terms. There is then no conceptual or technical problem; given the statistical material itemized above, physical turnover is measurable for every entrepreneur. However, for firms dealing in a wide range of commodities, separate computations for each item would be very time-consuming, and the simplest "index" of the physical volume of sales is total value.

One possibility would be to determine maximum markup for each category of goods, and to value *sales* at the actual price for income and sales tax purposes, while revaluing them *at the maximum markup level* for inventory tax purposes. In evaluating the stocks of the *purchaser*, moreover, the *actual* purchase price would be used. In this way a price control system can be built into the tax system. The incentive to hold goods for higher prices is reduced, because of the penal tax on excess inventories, whereas the purchaser has an added incentive to resist price increases, since he must dispose of his stock at still higher prices to make a profit, and his chances of building up a sufficient value of sales at *ceiling* prices to offset his purchases at *actual* prices, and so avoid excess inventories tax, diminish as his purchase price increases.

The best compromise might be to use physical volume for exporters, who usually deal in a small range of goods and whose markup is limited by world market conditions, and to declare maximum markups for imports.

ASSESSING THE TAX

As already indicated, the tax will be defined as

$$T = \frac{R}{100} \cdot x$$

where T = tax, R = the rate of tax, and x = excess inventories. We define x as $A - N$, where A is actual average inventories over a period, $P_1 - P_6$, and N is normal inventories. In turn, N is defined as $S_A/N = O_N$, where S_A is actual sales and O_N is normal turnover as laid down for the category of goods involved.

Let $S_A = 1{,}000$ and $O_N = 4$
Then $N = 250$

If $A = 350$, $T = \frac{R}{100} = (350\text{–}250)$

If $R = 100$, the tax will be 100

The period of averaging stocks should be long enough to cover erratic or seasonal fluctuations in demand and supply, but short enough to avoid serious inflationary effects through hoarding of stocks in one part of the period for sale in a later part. The best system would probably be to average each quarter a moving average of stocks for two quarters. Suppose $N = 100$, and actual end-of-quarter stocks are as follows:

Quarter:	III	IV	I	II	III	IV
Stocks	0	0	200	200	0	0
Average	0	0	100	200	100	0
x	0	0	0	100	0	0

The firm then becomes liable for excess inventory tax of 100 as a penalty for hoarding through the second quarter of the second year.

If this system involves too much computation, two averages over nine months might suffice.

Quarter:	I	II	III	IV
Stock	0	200	200	0
A } 3			133.3	133.3
N } quarters			100.0	100.0
x			33.3	33.3

The firm is, therefore, liable to excess inventory tax of 66.6

The actual computation need not be made more than once a year, at the same time that income tax is assessed. Excess inventory taxes can then be assessed, and paid along with income tax.

For defining N, four categories of goods, or six at the most, would suffice. Few goods turn over, on the average, more than six times a year, and few less than once. In the author's opinion all goods could be divided into four classes, with turnovers of once a quarter, once every three quarters, and once a year.

The cost of such computation for Indonesia was estimated by Dr. Keyfitz at 1 or 2 million rupiahs per year, say, $100,000 as a maximum, using a reasonably realistic foreign exchange rate for conversion. The improvement in income and sales tax collection which the system would bring would run into hundreds of millions of rupiahs. Moreover, by forcing goods out of hoards into the home market, the tax will make a significant contribution to price stabilization and so save money for the government; each 1 per cent rise in the price level costs the Indonesian government some 150 million rupiahs. Compared to such saving and the increased revenues it could bring the cost of the proposed tax system is insignificant.

Incentive Features

This system already has built-in incentive features. For any taxpayer, with a given income, the total tax burden on that income will be minimized by maximizing the share of income spent on productive equipment. The next most favorable use of income is purchase of equities, which assists others in financing expansion of plant and equipment. The national debt becomes more or less self-liquidating; the tax on bonds is about equal to the interest paid on them. Speculative investment in inventories becomes unprofitable.

In two respects, the objectives of self-enforcement and provision of tax incentives do conflict with each other. The first relates to the treatment of cash balances. In setting out the self-enforcement system above, we defined capital gains as income less consumer spending plus purchases of assets. With this definition, income held as cash is taxed twice, once as earned income and once as capital gains. The "capital gains" tax is needed to make it pay to report transactions in assets. A penalty tax on cash holdings is needed, since only in this way can it be made profitable to taxpayers to report their consumer expenditures. Holdings of cash balances, and especially holdings of currency, which in most underdeveloped countries exceed bank deposits, are the hardest thing to check in the whole chain of transactions. The simplest way of assuring that taxpayers will not underreport expenditures and hold undisclosed stocks of currency is to treat increases in cash balances as a residual, and include them in income as capital gains. This device more or less forces the honest taxpayer to buy securities—treasury bills, say—rather than hold his liquid reserves in cash, in order to avoid the double taxation on cash balances. Purchase and sales of securities, or physical assets, are relatively easy to check, and must be reported by both parties to the transaction.

From an incentive viewpoint, however, the double taxation of cash balances is somewhat severe. In the generally inflationary situation common to underdeveloped countries, holding cash balances is not a particularly serious economic sin; there is no reason for providing a powerful disincentive to cash holdings. True, there are some advantages in having people hold reserves in the form of government securities rather than cash. A market for government securities is built up, broadening the scope of central bank open market policy. It may also make deficit financing less purely inflationary. As people become used to the idea that government securities provide a safe and liquid means of holding wealth, the propensity to save might actually be raised. Moreover, the government authorities have somewhat more control over sudden liquidation of government securities for spending purposes than they do over sudden activation of idle deposits. Cash balances held for speculative purposes are subject to sudden and sharp increases in velocity of circulation which complicate the problems of monetary policy; sudden liquidation of government securities by the general public is possible only if the monetary authorities provide a sufficient market for them. Thus the authorities have a tighter control over the spending stream where reserves are held in the form of securities rather than cash.

Nevertheless, these advantages scarcely warrant the punitive treatment of cash accumulation implicit in the self-enforcement system. Accordingly, it might be desirable to define capital gains so that only increases in cash above some reasonable percentage of declared income would be included.

The other conflict is more serious. From a self-enforcement standpoint, it is convenient to have the tax rate on consumer spending lower than the tax rate on imputed increases in cash balances, so that it will pay to report consumer spending. From an incentive viewpoint, on the other hand, the tax rate on consumer spending should be higher than the rate on any kind of saving. We want taxpayers to report consumer spending, but we want them to save rather than consume.

There seems to be no way of escaping this dilemma completely. However, what we really want taxpayers to do in underdeveloped countries is not just to save, but to save and invest. By buying assets (other than excess inventories) the taxpayer can reduce his marginal tax rate below what he would pay on consumer outlays. It would of course pay to underreport consumer expenditures and overreport purchases of assets; but the document recording the sale of an asset requires two names, and the seller named in a false transaction would be liable for capital gains tax on the imputed increase in *his* cash balances, unless he also reported false purchases and the tax on them—and also the taxes for which the "seller" in the false transaction would be liable. Thus collusion to disguise consumer spending as an assets-transaction would not pay.

A simple way of adding to the incentive effects is to apply the penalty rate on excess inventories to land held idle or put to relatively unproductive or "inappropriate" uses. Land use can be controlled by defining the "appropriate" uses in various areas according to the development plan. Holding land idle for speculative purposes becomes unprofitable. Truly powerful incentive effects can be introduced, however, by adding a tax on "profits in excess of a fair return on utilized capacity" and a tax-and-transfer system for foreign investors.

The former tax has been outlined in detail in an earlier article, and will not be repeated in detail here.[3] The basic idea is simple; capacity is defined for tax purposes in terms of output, and a "fair return" is allowed on the proportion of capacity actually utilized, which may be above or below 100 per cent. For example, if a plant is worth $1,000,000 and capacity is defined as 100,000 units per year, the enterprise will be allowed a return of, say, 20 per cent of $500,000 if it produces 50,000 units, and 20 per cent of $1,500,000 if it produces 150,000 units. Taxes will be 100 per cent of the profits in excess of these amounts. Thus the amount of profits an enterprise can earn and keep depends solely on production. There is accordingly a powerful incentive to expand output up to approximately the purely competitive equilibrium position, and to introduce innovations reducing the capital-output ratio.

A Tax-and-Transfer System for Foreign Investors

The system of business taxes and regulation of profits transfers presented in this section was originally devised to fit within a general policy framework laid down by the Indonesian gov-

[3] Higgins, "Postwar Tax Policy," Part I, *Canadian Journal of Economics and Political Science*, August, 1943.

ernment. At the time, the government wished to attract foreign capital, but was reluctant to allow unlimited transfers from profits for four main reasons: profits higher than 15 per cent or 20 per cent after tax were considered unjustly high, representing exploitation of Indonesian resources and workers; it was considered desirable to block profits in excess of 15 per cent or 20 per cent in order to provide capital for expansion of Indonesian industry and agriculture; it was feared that in the absence of such limits, the privilege of transferring profits would be used to transfer capital, imposing a serious drain on foreign exchange reserves; and it was feared that without limits on transfers, the transfer of excessively high profits would in itself result in serious losses of foreign exchange reserves.

The original context of the proposed system was therefore specifically Indonesian, but the conditions which informed that system prevail in other underdeveloped areas: difficulty in achieving an appropriately anti-inflationary budget, and a consequent need to make every reasonable use of business taxes as a source of revenue, without unduly hampering private investment for development purposes; an unfavorable balance of payments, and consequent need to conserve foreign exchange reserves and, if possible, to attract foreign capital; inadequate domestic savings and taxes (actual or realistically potential) to finance economic development, providing a still more pressing need for foreign capital; strong nationalist sentiment, expressed as opposition to "exploitation" of domestic labor and resources by foreigners through earning and transferring large profits; and, finally, a shortage of trained and competent personnel to administer the tax and foreign exchange control systems, and a consequent need for simplicity in tax and foreign exchange measures.

Fundamentally, the proposed system consists of evaluating capital by discounting returns at an appropriate rate of interest, taking account of the complexity of the managerial problem, and the degree of risk, involved in the enterprise. According to economic theory, the value of an asset is the discounted sum of anticipated future returns on it, or in other words, the sum of the "present values" of annual earnings over the life of the asset. For purposes of tax administration, for firms with an earnings record extending over several years, valuation might more simply be based upon a moving average of returns over, say, five years. The government could permit each firm itself to state what it considers a "fair rate of return" in its field of enterprise. The regular corporation income tax would be kept fairly low (say 20 per cent) but a supertax would be imposed on companies wishing transfer privileges, varying *inversely* with the rate of return selected as "normal." The formula suggested below is gross earnings minus estimated "normal" net earnings times 20 per cent minus the selected "normal" percentage. If an enterprise overstates past earnings in order to build up a high capital value as a basis for estimating transferable profits, it will become liable to additional corporation income taxes and penalties for tax evasion in the past. If it overstates its "normal" rate of return, in order to avoid the supertaxes, its earnings will be capitalized at a high rate of discount, and transferable profits (and depreciation allowances) will be reduced.

Considering this tax in isolation, there is one way in which an enterprise could escape the pincers: by selecting a very low "normal" rate of return (say 2 per cent) which would give it a high capital value for transfer purposes. If earnings do not increase, they will escape supertax even though the return on actual capital investment may be high. Moreover, all profits net of tax could be transferred.

In the integrated system outlined above, the loophole is closed by the general tax on all assets, which destroys the tax advantage of overvaluation of capital. The firm might be allowed to estimate for itself the number of years over which earnings are to be projected in determining capital value. It would then be required to amortize its plant for tax purposes over the same period. The firm itself might be allowed to determine how amortization would be spread over the lifetime of its plant; but when the period is up, the enterprise would of course be allowed no further deductions of depreciation. If a firm overestimates the life of existing plant in order to build up a high capital value for transfer purposes, it would not be allowed foreign exchange for replacement in excess of depreciation allowances accumulated. The government might reserve the option of buying out any firm which is fully amortized by the firm's own definition, or which requires foreign exchange for replacement in excess of its own estimates for tax purposes, for the amount of its accumulated depreciation allowances. Thus no firm could benefit by giving false information about the probable life of its plant.

If depreciation allowances were used for actual replacement, the value of capital, and so transferable profits, would remain unchanged unless earnings rise. If a firm brings in capital in excess of depreciation allowances, the excess could be added to capital value. Transferable profits, and permissible replacement or withdrawal, would increase accordingly.

Capitalization of *past* earnings would be unfair to firms with poor earnings records which can legitimately expect higher rates of return in the future. Such firms may justly contend that the true value of their plant is greater than the sum of present values of average *past* annual earnings, over the expected life of the plant. Such firms might be permitted to estimate their *future* capacity for production and sales, as well as their "normal" rate of return. In this case, however, they would be allowed to transfer only the stipulated percentage of their "utilized" capacity. For example, capital might be valued at $1,000,000 on the assumption that future output will average 100,000 units per year, and that output can be sold at present prices, and that a normal return for such enterprises is, say, 10 per cent. No allowances should be made for price increases since this would be an invitation to speculation and to exploitation of monopoly power. If output turns out to be only 50,000 units, the firm would be allowed to transfer, not 15 per cent on $1,000,000, but only 15 per cent on the amount of plant "utilized," that is, $500,000. In calculating tax liabilities and permissible withdrawals for replacement, depreciation would likewise be permitted only on "utilized capacity." In this case, too, the supertax would be applied to earnings in excess of a "normal" rate of return on "utilized capacity." Under this system, it would not pay firms to overestimate future sales in order to obtain a high capital valuation for transfer purposes.

Firms might be given the option of capitalizing past earnings and applying the appropriate rates to the resulting capital value when estimating transferable profits and excess profits tax, or of capitalizing estimated future earnings (that is, estimated output times present prices) and having depreciation, transferable profits, and excess profits tax calculated on the basis of "utilized capacity." Indeed, they might be allowed to average over *any* five-year period that includes the current year. Only firms confident of their ability to produce and sell more in the future than in the past would choose to capitalize on the basis of future earnings alone. If firms demonstrate an ability to produce and sell more at current prices, they should be rewarded. The whole system then provides an incentive to improve techniques, lower costs, and expand output, and at the same time it destroys the incentive for monopoly restriction or for hoarding.

To provide protection against internal inflation or devaluation of the currency, foreign firms might be permitted to keep their accounts (including taxes, of course) in terms of foreign currencies invested.

Enterprises such as plantations which may suffer wide fluctuations in earnings over very long periods might be allowed to choose a longer averaging period, provided that the replacement period is at least as long. As indicated above, if a firm chooses an excessively long period for averaging and amortization, its depreciation allowances for tax purposes will be very low, and its taxes accordingly high. It will also be a long time before the firm benefits fully from a shift to a higher level of earnings.

This business tax system has several advantages which in themselves would constitute a major tax reform:

1. Unlike the usual progressive corporation income tax, it does not penalize size as such. The *rate* of tax on large profits is the same as on small profits. Taxing size, as such, has never been good economic policy; a small firm with a tidy little monopoly, or a group of traders who have cornered a market on a minor item, may earn 100 per cent return on their capital, whereas a large firm may earn only 5 per cent. The British plantations in Indonesia apparently earned only 2.5 per cent average over recent decades; the oil companies in turn earned 5 to 10 per cent. If the intent is to encourage *new national* firms, these may be exempt from tax for, say, three years, or allowed accelerated depreciation. If it seems desirable to help struggling small firms, profits up to a certain amount might be totally exempt. But large firms are often efficient firms and should not be penalized merely for being big.

2. Since the tax system does not penalize size, neither does it penalize growth. Doubling earnings does not increase the *rate* of tax. The disincentive to expansion involved in a progressive tax structure is avoided. Indeed, if capital is valued according to output, as suggested above, the tax system encourages expansion. Transfers and tax deductions both rise with output. No penalty attaches to earnings of 30 to 40 per cent, before tax, through efficiency or innovation. Indeed, *higher* rates of return can be earned, and the balance after taxes transferred, provided increased earnings come through increased *output*, and not through monopoly restrictions.

3. At the same time, the system has a built-in tax on very high *rates* of earning. Suppose a firm is actually earning 100 per cent. It will not nominate a rate above 20 per cent, even if permitted to do so; otherwise its taxes will rise (through reduced deprecia-

tion allowances) and transfers will fall. At 20 per cent, its capital value will, of course, be valued above cost. But as profits the firm can transfer only 15 per cent of "capital." The balance of its profits (before depreciation) can be transferred only as repatriation or for actual replacement. If transferred as repatriation, its entire capital will be regarded as withdrawn after five years and no more transfers of any kind would be permitted. If used for replacement, the firm must invest much more than the plant is worth. In other words, it must build up its *actual* capital to the *estimated* capital, if it wishes to go on transferring the *same* amount. It gets no reward for reinvesting. But the alternatives are to repatriate, and so give up a profitable enterprise, or have its profits blocked in the underdeveloped country. As suggested above, any temptation to set normal rates of profit too *low* could be removed by a progressive tax on assets.

4. The proposed system provides an incentive for long-term investment in productive enterprise rather than in trading ventures which have a quick turnover. The supertax,[4]

$$T_x = (E_g - E_R) \cdot (20\% - R\%),$$

is also $T_x = (E_g - VR) \cdot (20\% - R\%)$. If E_g and R are given, then $T_x = t(V)$, with $dTx/dV < 0$. But $V = V(P)$ with $dV/dP > 0$. Thus $dTx/dP = dV/dP \cdot dTx/dV < 0$. That is, the supertax falls as the period of investment increases.

5. The system contains a built-in reward for ploughing back profits. By choosing a high rate of "normal" return, 20 per cent, a firm can reduce its tax burden, at the cost of having some profits blocked. These profits can be invested domestically. Thus the system results in lower taxes for firms choosing to plough back profits in domestic investment. This effect could be en-

[4] The following symbols are used:

E_g = Gross earnings (total receipts less operating costs)
E_n = Net earnings (gross earnings less taxes)
E'_n = Estimated net earnings
E_T = Transferable profits
E_d = Net earnings after depreciation
D = Depreciation
R = Estimated "normal" rate of return
V = Value of capital
E_R = "Normal" earnings (i.e., $E_R = VR$)
T_n = Normal tax, defined as $\frac{40}{100}$ of $(E_g - D)$
T_x = Supertax, defined as $(E_g - E_R) \cdot (20\% - R\%)$
T_T = Total tax
P = Period of replacement

hanced by reducing the normal tax to, say, 35 per cent and raising the supertax rate to $(25 - R)/100$. If loss of revenue were no problem, there would be advantages in these rates, which bring the system close to "a tax on profits in excess of normal returns on utilized capacity."

6. The only "discrimination" in the system is the imposition of a supertax on firms wishing foreign exchange transfer facilities. In a situation which requires conservation of foreign exchange, such "discrimination" is perfectly valid. Indeed, the proposed system provides an incentive for firms, nominally "foreign" but actually domestic, not to register as foreign firms in order to avoid the supertax.

7. If it is considered undesirable to discriminate, domestic firms can be brought within the system. Choosing the 20 per cent rate of "normal" return, to eliminate the supertax, would reduce their capital value, and so their allowable depreciation, for normal tax purposes. If it seems advisable to strengthen this effect, a flat-rate deduction for all firms of x per cent of capital might be allowed and offset by a higher normal tax rate. This modification would also strengthen the built-in incentive to undertake long-period productive investment. Other sanctions on undervaluing capital might be imposed on domestic firms. Foreign exchange allocations for imported raw materials and equipment, or permissible bank indebtedness, might be geared to capital value.

8. Indeed, its flexibility is one of the great attractions of the system. By minor modifications, the government can make the system operate in almost any way that it likes.

9. Another great attraction is that most of the work of administration, and most of the decisions, become the responsibility of the firms themselves. The administrative work of the tax authorities is no more complex than with the present tax system. Only figures of output, sales, and costs need be checked by the tax authorities, and these figures usually require checking to administer existing tax systems. The computation of tax and transfer rights involves only the simplest kind of arithmetic. The tax forms utilized can be just as simple as those commonly in use, perhaps simpler.

Conclusion

It is more than possible that the tax system presented here still has loopholes and presents administrative difficulties which have been overlooked by the author. It is his belief, however, that any loopholes others may find could be plugged and the administrative problems overcome. Discussion must begin somewhere, and it is as a starting point for discussion that the system outlined above is presented. The problem of finance is fundamental to the whole problem of developing underdeveloped areas. The tax system outlined here seems to the author to have enormous advantages; if it could be worked out in practical form, it would go a long way toward overcoming financial barriers to economic development.

24 Stabilization Policies

Of all the branches of traditional economics, those most readily applicable to underdeveloped countries are monetary, fiscal, and foreign exchange policies aimed at stabilizing the economy. Even here, however, certain differences between the causes of economic fluctuation in advanced and in underdeveloped countries call for caution in applying these policies to underdeveloped countries.

Beneath the prescriptions of contemporary monetary and fiscal policy lies a theory of economic fluctuations which assumes that the major cause of fluctuations is the instability of private investment. Private investment is treated as depending in some way on the rate of increase in national income or spending. This relationship is called the "accelerator." Consumer spending, in turn, depends on level of investment and the size of the "multiplier," which is determined by the "marginal propensity to consume." An accelerated rate of increase in spending generates additional investment, and additional investment generates an increase in spending. However, the nature of the relationship between consumer spending and income is such that each round of increase in income caused by an initial increase in investment brings forth a smaller increase in consumer spending. There is a built-in tendency for the expansion of consumer spending to taper off. When it does, investment tends to fall; when investment falls, consumption will fall too. Here is the genesis of the downswing. Interactions of "accelerator" and "multiplier" cause fluctuations in income and employment.[1]

In relatively few underdeveloped countries, however, are fluctuations in private investment in response to changes in domestic spending the major factor in economic fluctuations. The instability of underdeveloped economies can usually be traced to one of two factors: fluctuations in output as a consequence of variations in rainfall, and variations in demand for exports. Instability of these kinds requires policies of a different sort from those needed to offset fluctuations in private investment.

Fluctuations in Arid Zone Countries

There are hundreds of millions of people in the world whose incomes depend primarily on the amount of rainfall in the growing season. Of the countries considered in Chapter 2, all of Libya and much of India would be included as part of the "arid zone" where these people live. In the arid zone the rainfall cycle can be the major factor in fluctuations in output, income, and employment.

The similarity of the configuration of rainfall cycles to that of the "Juglar," seven-to-eleven-year cycle in advanced countries has long since been noted by economists. Jevons drew attention to this correlation in his paper for the British Association in 1875, and elaborated on it in his *Investigations in Currency and Finance* some decades later.[2] A more refined presentation of the rainfall cycle theory of economic fluctuations was presented by H. L. Moore.[3] Economists in advanced countries have discarded these theories as naïve and totally inapplicable to the fluctuations in advanced countries. In view of the violence of economic fluctuations in underdeveloped arid zone countries, however, and of the obvious relationship of these fluctuations to rainfall cycles, it may be time to review these theories in relationship to the stabilization problems of such countries.

Jevons seemed to feel that his theory stood or fell according to the closeness of the correlation between sunspot cycles and

[1] This statement is, of course, highly simplified, but we cannot go into detail here on the theory of business cycles in advanced countries. For a good recent statement, see James Deusenberry, *Business Cycles and Economic Growth* (New York, 1958).

[2] Cf. H. Stanley Jevons, "The Causes of Unemployment," *The Contemporary Review*, LCV, LCVI (1909), pp. 548–65; 67–89; and W. Stanley Jevons, *Investigations in Currency and Finance* (London, 1909).

[3] Henry Ludwell Moore, *Economic Cycles: Their Law and Cause* (New York, 1914), and *Generating Economic Cycles* (New York, 1923).

economic fluctuations. Thus in his *Investigations in Currency and Finance*, he wrote: [4]

While writing my 1875 paper for the British Association I was much embarrassed by the fact that the commercial fluctuations could with difficulty be reconciled with a period of 11.1 years. If, indeed, we start from 1825, and add 11.1 years time after time, we get 1836.1, 1847.2, 1858.3, 1869.4, 1880.5, which show a gradually increasing discrepancy from 1837, 1847, 1857, 1866 (and now 1878), the true dates of the crises. To explain this discrepancy I went so far as to form the rather fanciful hypothesis that the commercial world might be a body so mentally constituted, as Mr. John Mill must hold, as to be capable of vibrating in a period of ten years, so that it would every now and then be thrown into oscillation by physical causes having a period of eleven years. The subsequent publication, however, of Mr. J. A. Broun's inquiries, tending to show that the solar period is 10.45 years, not 11.1 [*Nature*, vol. xvi, p. 63], placed the matter in a very different light, and removed the difficulties. Thus, if we take Mr. John Mill's "Synopsis of Six Commercial Panics in the Present Century," and rejecting 1866 as an instance of a premature panic, count from 1815 to 1857, we find that four credit cycles, occupying forty-two years, give an average duration of 10.5 years, which is a remarkably close approximation to Mr. Broun's solar period.

As economists, we need not be concerned about possible association between rainfall cycles and sunspots. We may take rainfall cycles as given and ask whether and how fluctuations in rainfall generate fluctuations in income and employment. Jevons' own theoretical framework was very simple. Concerned as he was with fluctuations in his own country, he argued that drought in the colonies led to famine there and consequent reduction of imports of British manufactured goods, especially textiles, with repercussions on the economy of the mother country.[5]

Probably, however, we ought not to attribute the decennial fluctuation wholly to Indian trade. It is quite possible that tropical Africa, America, the West Indies, and even the Levant are affected by the same meteorological influences which occasion the famines in India. Thus it is the nations which trade most largely to those parts of the world, *and which give long credits to their customers*, which suffer most from these crises. Holland was most easily affected a century ago; England is most deeply affected now; France usually participates, together with some of the German trading towns. But I am not aware that these decennial crises extend in equal severity to such countries as Austria, Hungary, Switzerland, Italy and Russia, which have com-

[4] W. Stanley Jevons, *op. cit.*, p. 206.
[5] *Ibid.*, pp. 212, 215.

paratively little foreign trade. Even when they are affected, it may be indirectly through sympathy with the great commercial nations. . . .

Here again some may jest at the folly of those who theorise about such incongruous things as the cotton-mills of Manchester and the paddy-fields of Hindostan. But to those who look a little below the surface the connection is obvious. Cheapness of food leaves the poor Hindu ryot a small margin of earnings, which he can spend on new clothes; and a small margin multiplied by the vast population of British India, not to mention China, produces a marked change in the demand for Lancashire goods.

Although Moore's analysis was somewhat more sophisticated, he, too, attached primary importance to statistical correlations; his elaboration of Jevons' theory was mainly on the statistical side. Moore's main argument was that rainfall cycles bring fluctuations in yields of raw materials, which in turn bring fluctuations in their prices. Bad rainfall means high raw materials prices, which in turn squeeze profits of manufacturers and lead to a decline in industrial investment and a general downswing. Bad harvests may also result in an increase in real wages (given great flexibility of money wages) and a consequent drop in profits and investment. Moore was satisfied that, with the introduction of appropriate leads and lags, this explanation of fluctuations fitted the facts.

Much more study should be devoted to the process by which such fluctuations are generated; nevertheless, there can be no doubt of the violence of fluctuations in income and employment in arid zone countries nor of their relation to rainfall cycles. The impact effect is clear and direct: no harvest, no work for the rural population, and perhaps even no seed for them to plant for the next harvest. In the pastoral sector of the Libyan and similar economies, drought means that the animals die, leaving pastoralists with no source of income.

However inadequate a "rainfall theory" of economic fluctuations may be for advanced countries, there can be no doubt of its importance in underdeveloped arid zone countries, especially those without petroleum. In Chapter 2 we noted the importance of the monsoon in India, not only for agricultural output, but for industrial investment. Some indication of the cyclical movements of rainfall in India are shown in Chart 24-1. Similar cycles in rainfall occur in Libya. Most important, of course, is rainfall during the growing season; it was in this form that Moore cast his theory. However, cycles of total annual rainfall are closely related to cycles in rainfall during the growing season, in coun-

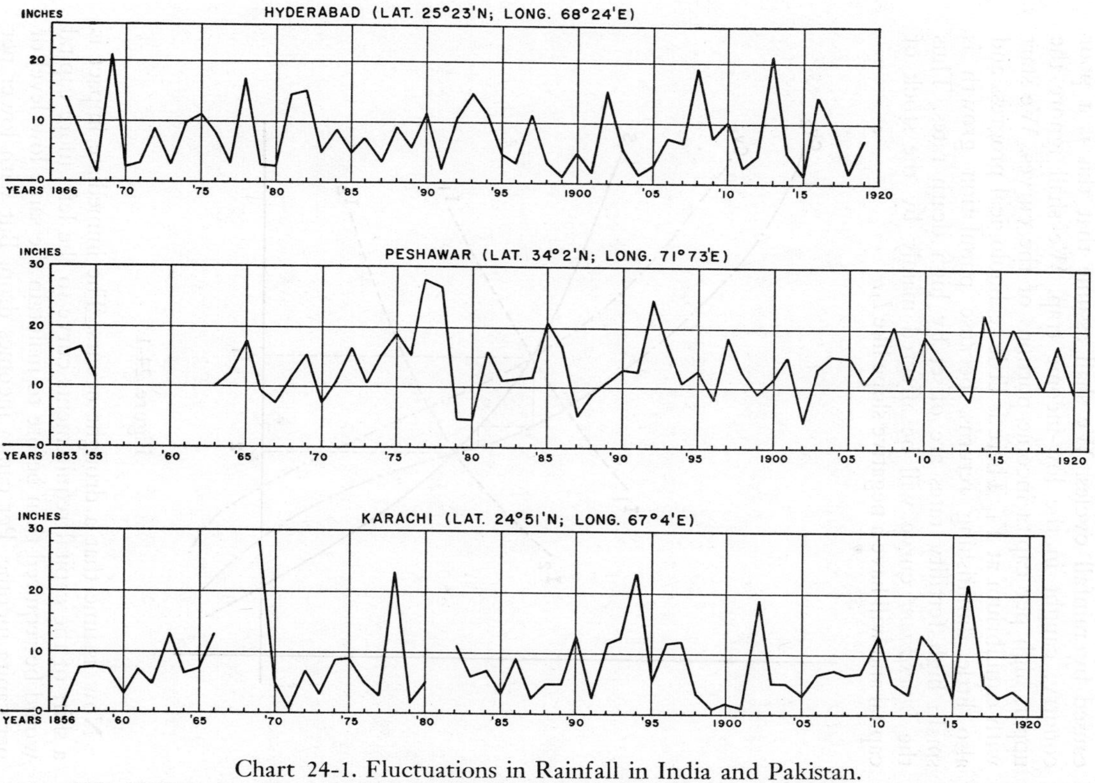

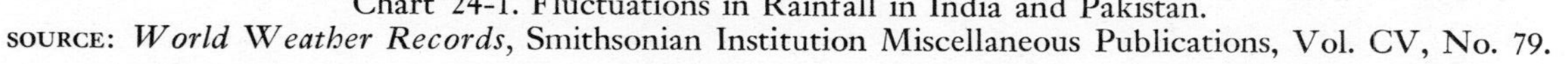
Chart 24-1. Fluctuations in Rainfall in India and Pakistan.
SOURCE: *World Weather Records*, Smithsonian Institution Miscellaneous Publications, Vol. CV, No. 79.

tries that count on more than one crop per year or on grazing.

An adaptation of Figure 17-1 will serve to illustrate fluctuations caused by rainfall cycles. We shall assume that this is a poor country, caught in the low-income trap. We shall ignore the upper, high per capita income portions of the curves. We start with equilibrium at Y_1. There is little technological progress and also little diminishing returns, because population growth is small; high fertility rates are offset by high death rates. Thus the *investment* curve will be affected mainly by the stock of capital and will have a negative slope like I_1.

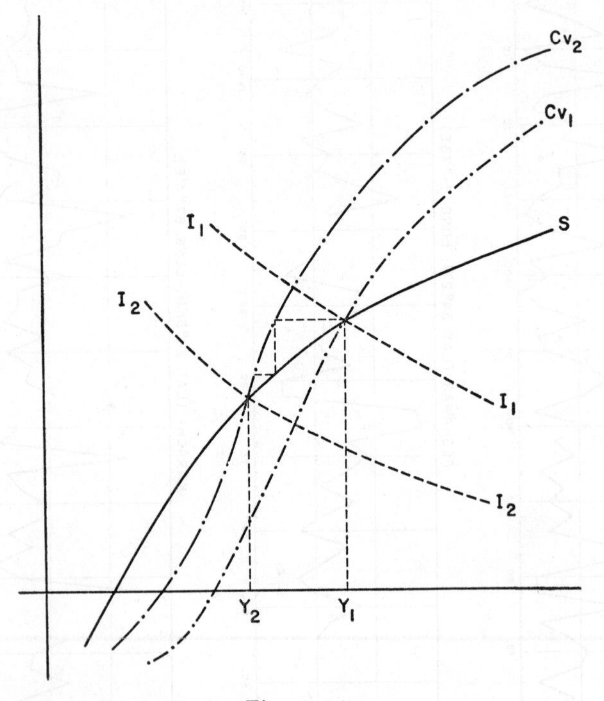

Figure 24-1

Now assume that a drought occurs. The immediate impact is a shift of the capital requirements curve to the left; more capital would be required than before to maintain the same low level of per capita income. Per capita incomes drop. But with lower per capita incomes, savings also fall; the new capital requirements exceed savings at the lower level of income, and income falls farther. Moreover, with a rise in the costs of food and raw materials, industrial investment shifts downward to I_2I_2. The new equilibrium is established at Y_2. If this income is below the subsistence level, income may return to Y_1 through starvation, which reduces the rate of population growth and so reduces capital requirements.

When cycles are generated from the supply side, a different kind of stabilization policy is required from that suggested by orthodox fiscal policy. In these cases, the downswing does not start because of an excess of effective supply over effective demand. Hence, monetary and fiscal measures designed to maintain effective demand are irrelevant; a different kind of stabilization policy is required. Under drought conditions, no amount of internal spending will maintain the output of the private sector of the economy. A major problem in a drought period in such countries is simply to maintain the physical supplies of foodstuffs. For aggregate demand may exceed aggregate supply, and if supplies are not made good by imports or sales from stocks, unemployment and inflation can occur side by side.

In Libya this constellation of problems was met by the establishment of the Libyan Public Development and Stabilization Agency. This Agency has a dual purpose: (1) the stockpiling of barley (the staple food in Libya) and the accumulation of foreign exchange reserves in high rainfall years to permit sales from stocks and imports (if needed) in drought years; and (2) the planning and execution of a development program. The Agency received its funds (directly or indirectly) in the form of grants from foreign governments. Thus the foreign exchange needed to expand development spending while maintaining the legal 100 per cent reserves in foreign exchange against the currency was provided automatically. In drought years, the development program can be speeded up to provide money incomes and employment. Barley can be sold against these money incomes from stocks and, if necessary, from imports as well. Accelerated development spending in itself increases the money supply but the required reserves are automatically provided. As the barley stocks are sold the money supply is reduced again, releasing foreign exchange reserves for further increases in development spending or for imports. Thus food, money income, and jobs are provided simultaneously in a manner consistent with maintenance of stability.

TABLE 24-1.

Share of Prewar * Exports of Principal Primary Commodities in Total Exports from Underdeveloped Countries
(Arranged in order of degree of price increase)

Country	Principal commodities and per cent of total exports	All specified commodities (per cent of total)
Africa:		
Belgian Congo	Seeds and oil, 7; cotton, 12; copper, 26; tin, 6	51
Egypt	Seeds and oils, 6; cotton, 77	83
French Equatorial Africa	Seeds and oils, 11; cotton, 18; lumber, 40	69
French West Africa	Cocoa, 10; seeds and oils, 56; coffee, 7	73
Gold Coast	Cocoa, 29	29
Kenya and Uganda	Sisal, 6; cotton, 42; coffee, 13; tea, 6	66
Madagascar	Corn, 5; coffee, 32; meats, 7; hides and skins, 5	49
Nigeria	Cocoa, 17; seeds and oils, 47; hides and skins, 5; tin, 15	84
Northern Rhodesia	Copper, 90	90
Sierra Leone	Seeds and oils, 21	21
Tanganyika	Sisal, 38; cotton, 10; hides and skins, 5	63
Asia:		
Ceylon	Rice, 45; lumber, 7; petroleum, 25	77
China	Seeds and oils, 6; tea, 65; rubber, 17	88
Burma	Seeds and oils, 6; cotton, 13; raw silk, 5; eggs, 7; tin, 5	36
Federation of Malaya	Tin, 17; petroleum, 10; rubber, 48	75
India	Seeds and oils, 11; cotton, 13; jute, 21; tea, 13	58
Indonesia	Seeds and oils, 6; tobacco, 5; tea, 9; tin, 5; sugar, 7; petroleum, 22; rubber, 20	74
Iran	Petroleum, 73	73
Iraq	Cotton, 6; wheat, 8; barley, 19; cattle, 5; hides and skins, 5; wool, 13	56
Lebanon and Syria	Seeds and oils, 12; wool, 12	24

TABLE 24-1. (*continued*)

Country	Principal commodities and per cent of total exports	All specified commodities (per cent of total)
Philippines	Seeds and oils, 26; sugar, 44	70
Thailand	Rice, 47; lumber, 6; tin, 23; rubber, 14	90
Turkey	Cotton, 7; tobacco, 27; wool, 5	39
Central America, including Mexico and Caribbean area:		
Barbados	Sugar, 50	50
British Honduras	Lumber, 55; bananas, 14	69
Costa Rica	Cocoa, 8; coffee, 49; bananas, 28	85
Cuba	Tobacco, 10; sugar, 70	80
Dominica	Seeds and oils, 21; bananas, 10	31
Dominican Republic	Cocoa, 14; coffee, 8; sugar, 61	83
El Salvador	Coffee, 87	87
Grenada	Cocoa, 47	47
Guadeloupe	Bananas, 29; sugar, 42	71
Guatemala	Coffee, 65; bananas, 27	92
Haiti	Sisal, 9; cotton, 15; coffee, 50; bananas, 6; sugar, 11	91
Honduras	Bananas, 57	57
Jamaica	Bananas, 60; sugar, 17	77
Leeward Islands	Cotton, 15; sugar, 66	81
Martinique	Bananas, 15; sugar, 47	62
Mexico	Cotton, 5; lead, 13; zinc, 10; copper, 5; petroleum, 9	42
Nicaragua	Cotton, 5; coffee, 35; lumber, 6; bananas, 13	59
Panama	Cocoa, 12; bananas, 74	86
Puerto Rico	Tobacco, 11; sugar, 67	78
St. Lucia	Cocoa, 6; seeds and oils, 16; sugar, 48	70
St. Vincent	Cotton, 29	29
Trinidad and Tobago	Cocoa, 8; sugar, 17; petroleum, 66	91
Europe:		
Albania	Cheese, 9; cattle, 8; hides and skins, 14; eggs, 8; petroleum, 22	61
Bulgaria	Tobacco, 43	43

TABLE 24-1. (*continued*)

Share of Prewar * Exports of Principal Primary Commodities in Total Exports from Underdeveloped Countries
(Arranged in order of degree of price increase)

Country	Principal commodities and per cent of total exports	All specified commodities (per cent of total)
Finland	Lumber, 26; butter, 5	31
Greece	Seeds and oils, 6; tobacco, 50	56
Hungary	Wheat, 13; cattle, 12	25
Poland	Lumber, 17; cattle, 4; meats, 13	34
Romania	Wheat, 16; lumber, 11; cattle, 5; petroleum, 43	75
Yugoslavia	Lumber, 16; cattle, 11; meats, 6	33
South America:		
Argentina	Seeds and oils, 13; corn, 13; wheat, 13; meats, 23; hides and skins, 7; wool, 9	78
Bolivia	Tin, 71	71
Brazil	Cocoa, 4; cotton, 18; coffee, 45	67
British Guiana	Sugar, 58	58
Chile	Copper, 48; nitrate of soda, 21	69
Colombia	Coffee, 53; bananas, 5; petroleum, 22	80
Ecuador	Cocoa, 30; coffee, 15; petroleum, 13	58
Falkland Islands	Cattle, 7; hides and skins, 9; wool, 80	96
French Guiana	Lumber, 48	48
Paraguay	Cotton, 37; meats, 9; hides and skins, 9; tea, 6; rubber, 19	80
Peru	Cotton, 18; lead, 5; copper, 17; sugar, 7; petroleum, 34	81
Surinam	Coffee, 7; rice, 6; sugar, 8	21
Uruguay	Seeds and oils, 5; meats, 21; hides and skins, 10; wool, 44	80
Venezuela	Coffee, 5; petroleum, 92	97

* Prewar year is 1938 in the great majority of cases; in a few, figures for the nearest available period were substituted.

Fluctuations in Exports

Underdeveloped countries outside the arid zone are unstable mainly because of their orientation toward exports, often combined with concentration on a very small range of raw materials and foodstuffs (Table 24-1). In recent decades the markets for these exports has been extremely unstable (Table 24–2). This importance and instability of exports is the main factor which, through the action of the "multiplier" and "accelerator," causes fluctuations in income and employment. According to a report of the Economic Commission for Asia and the Far East, "It has . . . been estimated on a global basis that a change of only five per cent in average export prices is approximately equivalent to the entire annual inflow of private and public capital and government grants to under-developed countries." [6] Yet during the nine-year period 1948 to 1956 the actual fluctuation *averaged* 10 to 15 per cent for Thailand rice, for Ceylon tea, for Indonesian and Malayan tin, and Philippines abacá. For Burmese rice, Philippines copra, and Pakistan jute the range was 15 to 20 per cent. Rubber prices showed an average fluctuation of 30 per cent. Volume of exports from these countries showed similar fluctuations in the same directions, adding up to very substantial fluctuations in export earnings.

Some advanced countries, such as Australia and New Zealand, are also export-oriented in this same sense; exports are about as large a fraction of national income as government expenditures and private investment combined, and private investment is closely linked to exports. Variations in income and employment through changes in demand for exports in underdeveloped countries differ in four ways from fluctuations generated in this fashion in more advanced countries. First, a larger proportion of the unemployment resulting from a contraction of exports may be disguised, taking the form of an increase in the number of supernumeraries in agriculture. Second, in some of these countries a large reduction in physical exports cannot be offset by reduced physical imports without causing extreme hardship. Third, the secondary "super-multiplier" effects of a contraction in foreign trade is likely to be less pronounced in underdeveloped than in advanced countries. Underdeveloped economies are less interdependent than advanced ones and the repercussions of

[6] United Nations, *Economic Survey of Asia and the Far East* (New York, 1957), p. 114.

TABLE 24-2.

Average Year-to-Year Fluctuations * in Exports, 1948–53, 1953–56

Commodity and area	*Proceeds* †		*Price* ‡		*Quantity*	
	1948–53	1953–56	1948–53	1953–56	1948–53	1953–56
Rubber:						
Indonesia	40.5	19.7	§	§	14.0	5.2
Federation of Malaya	37.7	18.6	35.8	18.8	3.4	4.0
ECAFE region .	42.6	18.5	§	§	6.0	4.8
Cotton:						
Pakistan	22.7 **	26.5	25.2 **	10.2	15.4 **	28.0
Jute:						
Pakistan	31.5 **	9.3	24.3 **	3.8	23.0 **	10.3
Manila hemp (abacá):						
Philippines	23.3	19.4	11.5	18.6	23.0	11.3
Sugar:						
China (Taiwan)	28.1	19.8	23.7	2.5	46.7	17.8
Philippines	23.8	5.1	5.6	3.4	20.9	6.6
Copra:						
Philippines	30.0	10.3	23.9	10.7	13.2	14.2
Tin:						
Indonesia	21.2	10.9	§	§	5.2	4.0
Federation of Malaya	18.3	6.3	15.2	3.9	14.5	5.4
Petroleum:						
Brunei	20.9	6.0	13.4	1.1	12.3	5.9
Indonesia	15.9	7.3	9.9	5.2	16.5	5.3
Rice:						
Burma	11.7 ‡‡	10.4	13.5 **	17.8	15.9 ‡‡	18.0
Thailand	15.5	13.3 ‖	10.7	11.5	14.2	15.8
Tea:						
Ceylon	8.4	15.0	10.5	12.6	2.9	3.4

* A year-to-year fluctuation is defined as the change from the average for one year to the average for the subsequent year, expressed (for statistical reasons) as a percentage of the higher of the two averages.

† Based on export value in terms of United States dollars.

‡ Except petroleum, for which the price in the United States market is taken, all the rest are market prices at ports of exporting countries or unit values of

changes in income in one sector on employment in another are not as marked. A substantial proportion of the population may be largely outside the market economy, living close to a subsistence, self-sufficiency level, with a large share of trade taking barter form. The accelerator, the chief destabilizer of advanced economies, plays a relatively small role in the less industrialized ones. Cyclical unemployment therefore tends to be more localized and to spread less quickly and less comprehensively than in a complex, interdependent, multistage, industrialized economy.

Finally, if the export industries are in foreign hands and profits are usually transferred, the domestic income is relatively unaffected by fluctuations in exports; the main impact will be on profits transfers, which are not strictly part of the domestic income. Repercussions may be felt through the government budget because of the close tie between revenues and the volume of exports in such economies. As we shall demonstrate more fully below, most of these countries are in a position to offset fluctuations in exports by internal measures. If government expenditures are maintained in the face of a drop in tax revenues, while, despite a drop in exports, imports are maintained from reserves built up during good years, domestic income and employment can be kept quite stable in spite of fluctuations in the world market. Since the export sector is often relatively capital-intensive, it represents a smaller share of *employment* than of national income. This makes stabilization easier in such countries than in advanced ones which are similarly export-oriented; the prevention of widespread unemployment does not require shifting of a large share of the labor force from export industries to others.

An International Commodity Stabilization Authority?

Some underdeveloped countries—in particular those, such as Indonesia, Brazil, Burma, and Thailand, whose national incomes depend a good deal on export markets for raw materials and

---

exports, expressed in terms of United States dollars. Prices or unit values of exports for 1949 are for January–August only.

§ For price fluctuations see figures for the Federation of Malaya, which were approximately the same.

|| 1949–56.

** 1949–53.

‡‡ 1950–53.

SOURCE: UN *Economic Survey of Asia and the Far East, 1957*, p. 118.

Export prices are from International Monetary Fund, *International Financial Statistics;* for export proceeds and quantities see Asian Economic Statistics.

foodstuffs—have recently expressed the view that they would need little in the way of foreign capital assistance if they could get a "fair" and stable price for their major exports. An international agency, perhaps under United Nations auspices, might be set up to perform a "buffer stock" and price stabilization function, holding surpluses in years of excess production and disposing of them in years in which demand exceeds supply at the fixed "fair" price.

In the past, some underdeveloped countries have suffered substantially from violent fluctuations in prices of raw materials and foodstuffs. It is also true that if prices of their exports were maintained at the levels reached, let us say, at the peak of the Korean War boom, they could finance their own development program—if they would. But here is the rub: people in underdeveloped countries, no less than in advanced ones, tend to think of the "fair" price as the highest price in the memory of living man. Yet if prices were maintained at peak levels, the danger is that an international stabilization authority would find itself accumulating continually increasing stockpiles. Moreover, distinguishing cyclical reductions in demand, which will be compensated before long by a cyclical increase, from long-run downward trends, is difficult enough, statistically and analytically, for any group of objective experts. How much more difficult such a distinction will be if deep-seated political considerations are also involved. Suppose, for example, that careful study shows clearly that the cost of production of synthetic rubber has a downward trend, while its range of use is expanding. Will an international stabilization authority have the courage to insist that in the light of this trend the fixed price of natural rubber must be gradually reduced? If it has not, the result will be that countries producing natural rubber will go on producing it for the authority's stockpile, instead of undertaking the structural reorganization of their economies that the situation demands.

The elimination of violent swings in the prices of raw materials and foodstuffs through an international agency could contribute a good deal to the development of underdeveloped areas. It would permit them to prepare and undertake development plans with some assurance that a collapse of the market for their major exports would not prevent their being carried out. The proposal has its dangers, however; if such an agency is established it should not be expected to shore up economies of underdeveloped areas, which have become shaky through failure to adapt to clear-cut and irreversible long-run trends.

Stability and Diversification

Some governments have justified restrictive trade practices on the grounds that diversification of their economies is needed for stabilization purposes.

As a rule, the argument for diversification has been put just the wrong way around. Its function is *not* primarily to stabilize an economy. The argument for diversification as a means of reducing instability arose during a period when the extreme instability of the American economy tended to spread outward to other countries, particularly producers of raw materials and foodstuffs. But let us assume that the United States succeeds in its own brave hopes for steady growth. Let us also imagine that underdeveloped countries diversify to the point of becoming self-sufficient, in investment as well as in production. The main determinant of income and employment in these countries would then be domestic investment. Since some of this investment would be in risky enterprises, domestic investment could be very unstable indeed, and consequently the economy as a whole might be subject to severe fluctuations. If these economies were relatively open, while the American economy was stable, international trade would tend to damp economic fluctuations. Rising national income (inflation) would lead to diminished exports and increased imports, thus checking the boom. Conversely, deflation would lead to rising exports and reduced imports, damping the downswing. This whole question is one which needs reexamination when the assumption that the dominant economy is unstable is replaced by the assumption that it is stable and growing.

The main purpose of diversification is not stabilization but to permit economic growth. If a country wants to increase its output at a faster rate than the world market is expanding, it cannot be content with retaining its share in world markets. Industrialization is then a virtual necessity. Even plantation products, where soil and climate advantages are most clear-cut, face doubtful futures because of increasing competition from synthetics. At best, plantation products can expect a gradual decline in their *share* of the world markets. Such a development is not incompatible with absolute growth of plantation production, but it does imply a falling share of plantation output in national production, if the country is to raise its income at a faster rate than world markets expand. If productivity in plantations keeps pace with productivity in industry—and if it does not, it is likely to lose out even more rapidly to competing synthetics—the share of plantations in national employment will also fall. Industrialization appears to be the only solution.

In short, it is not merely that balanced growth is better than unbalanced growth; rather, these countries must have balanced growth in order to have growth at all. These countries must have an agricultural as well as an industrial revolution. Myrdal quotes Tarlok Singh: "Industrial expansion without agricultural reorganization will leave the bulk of the people in a state of poverty. In other words, we can plan against mass poverty only if we set out to create the conditions of a rapidly expanding and efficient economy both in agriculture and in industry."[7] Myrdal adds, "In most underdeveloped countries improvement of productivity in agriculture is, furthermore, an essential pre-condition for industrialization."

Stability and Commercial Policy

The unbalanced economies of underdeveloped countries do, of course, require special commercial policies. The classical dicta with regard to free trade were based on a kind of marginal analysis which is quite inappropriate where the problem is one of inducing large discontinuous jumps to a completely new structure and level of employment and output. Indeed, given the degree of misallocation of resources already existing in underdeveloped countries, relative to what could be achieved through such a big push, it may well be that any "distortion" of the price-cost structure through government intervention would bring an improvement. Certainly a properly planned intervention will improve rather than worsen the resource allocation of underdeveloped countries.

Myrdal is lukewarm about cooperation among underdeveloped countries with respect to foreign trade. Although he does not deny that such cooperation may be useful, he feels that "the scope for such a cooperation is naturally limited, as almost by definition partnership is more natural between underdeveloped and developed countries than between underdeveloped countries by themselves." This statement seems somewhat inconsistent with Myrdal's insistence that underdeveloped countries be permitted, and indeed urged, to industrialize and shift to a more extensive and mechanized agriculture. It does not follow that there are no limits to the desirable degree of self-sufficiency nor that co-

[7] Gunnar Myrdal, *An International Economy: Problems and Prospects* (New York, 1956), p. 206.

operation among underdeveloped countries is less natural than with advanced ones. Regional planning among countries in Asia and Africa is long overdue. Industrialization is not tantamount to every country's endeavoring to produce everything, and some integration of national plans to avoid costly overlapping is surely desirable. For example, both countries might benefit if Indonesia leaves iron and steel production to the Philippines, while the Philippines stays out of rubber and aluminum, and does not expand its petroleum refining capacity. Such questions require careful study; if ECAFE could be made an effective agency for international planning, this kind of question is one that it might well tackle.

Meanwhile, import-replacers are the most hopeful avenue for industrial development. Both the price elasticity and the income elasticity of demand for agricultural products are very low, whereas agricultural countries have a high marginal propensity to import. Consequently, if underdeveloped countries are not to run into serious drains on their foreign exchange balances through their efforts to develop, they must find either new exports or import-replacers. The latter is clearly easier.

The "precarious balance" in which underdeveloped countries find themselves, with the danger that large-scale development investment will lead to both inflation and a drain on foreign exchange, is an added reason for import controls. Of all kinds of possible import restrictions, multiple exchange rates come closest to being "a free trader's dream." Recent Indonesian experience would seem to support this contention; in 1956, thanks to higher advance payments and import surcharges, it was possible to let the market govern foreign exchange allocations and grant virtually all applications for import licenses.[8]

If economic development plans are successful, import restrictions do not involve a decline in total imports of underdeveloped countries. They imply rather a shift in the composition of imports and limiting the *increase* in imports as national income rises.

Monetary Policy

Since few underdeveloped countries have highly developed systems of commercial credit or capital markets, it is customary to discount monetary policy as a stabilization device in these

[8] This experience is analyzed more fully in Benjamin Higgins, *Economic Stabilization and Development in Indonesia* (New York, 1957).

countries. If we include in "monetary policy" all government measures to increase or decrease the money supply through the banking system, however, there is some evidence that monetary policy can be very effective. Efforts at stabilization in Indonesia are a case in point.[9] One of the most interesting aspects of Indonesia's economic policy between 1950 and 1958 is the success of the measures undertaken to reduce the money supply during the two periods when Dr. Sumitro was Minister of Finance. This experience corroborates the evidence provided by the failure of the "cheap money" policies in the United Kingdom, the United States, Canada, and Australia, during the postwar period. This failure, and the consequent reversal of policy by one after the other of these countries, showed that an anti-inflationary fiscal policy is likely to be ineffective unless it is supported by an anti-inflationary monetary policy. The Indonesian story is even more dramatic. It suggests that, where political and administrative barriers prevent the pursuit of the fiscal policy appropriate in an inflationary situation, powerful anti-inflationary forces may be generated by monetary policy alone.

The methods used by the Indonesian government to check monetary expansion were unorthodox in terms of central bank policy of advanced countries. Quantitative and qualitative controls that have become standard central bank policy in advanced countries were not available to the Indonesian government. The revised statutes of the Java Bank, setting it up as a full-fledged central bank with the new name of the Bank of Indonesia, under the control of a monetary board, and with sweeping general powers for monetary control, did not come into force until July, 1953. Even with these statutes in effect, control through ordinary central bank policy was virtually impossible. The Bank of Indonesia statutes were not supported by general banking legislation governing the activities of the commercial banks until 1957. The largest of these were branches of foreign banks whose reserves were held abroad; hence they could not be controlled by ordinary measures to increase or decrease the quantity of commercial bank reserves. There is as yet no "open market" in Indonesia, and the commercial banks do not follow the practice of rediscounting commercial paper with the central bank. Accordingly, during the period in question it was necessary to resort to a species of monetary "gadgetry" designed to fit the institutional framework.

On the whole the "gadgets" worked well. The most effective

[9] For a more detailed exposition of these measures, see *ibid.*

of them was probably the system of advance payments for foreign exchange. Under this system importers, instead of waiting to take up foreign exchange grants when goods arrived in Indonesian ports, were compelled to make rupiah payments when the foreign exchange license was granted. They also had to pay in advance any "import surcharges" (special duties) to which they would become liable. The 40 per cent advance payments, at their peak at the end of 1952, withdrew nearly 600 million rupiahs from the money supply. The 40 per cent and 75 per cent advance payments combined, at their peak in mid-1953, reduced the money supply by close to a billion rupiahs, or by about 15 per cent. During 1955 the net prepayments of importers rose no less than 2 billion rupiahs, or some 17 per cent of the money supply. To some extent, these reductions in money supply may have been offset by financing of importers by wholesalers, or, in the case of standardized commodities such as bicycles, by consumers. To the degree that this financing by wholesalers or consumers represented use of otherwise idle currency or deposits, it meant an increase in velocity of circulation of money which would offset in some measure the reduction in money supply. On balance, however, there can be no doubt that the system of advance payments was a powerful offset to forces tending to increase the money supply. Perhaps the most convincing evidence of the effectiveness of these policies was the reduction in the black market price of the rupiah, despite the strong pressures tending to raise the price of gold and foreign exchange in the black market. The system of advance payments was admirably supplemented by a "gentleman's agreement" with the banks limiting credit to importers, and by a prohibition of transfers of profits by firms indebted to banks, which compelled liquidation of bank loans by foreign firms.

The Indonesian experience supports some of the recent developments in the pure theory of interest, particularly the writings of G. L. S. Shackle. These studies suggest that variations in interest rates influence two kinds of investment decisions: those pertaining to investment in inventories, and those pertaining to investment in long-run projects of a relatively safe nature. These types of investment predominate in a number of underdeveloped countries. Manufacturing, which is characterized by investment in equipment with rapid but uncertain rates of obsolescence, is relatively unimportant in these countries. Investment in inventories, and investment in such long-range projects as rubber and copra plantations, petroleum, and mines, are the major alternatives. Under present circumstances, the latter type of investment may not be considered particularly "safe" in some underdeveloped countries, including Indonesia. Moreover, interest rates in foreign capital markets may be more important than interest rates in the country where the operation takes place. However, the policy regarding transfers of profits probably persuaded foreign companies to obtain working capital abroad rather than through the Indonesian banking system, which in itself was an anti-inflationary move since it permitted a larger volume of imports with a given balance of payments deficit. Certainly the Indonesian "tight money" policy succeeded in forcing goods out of speculative hoards into the market, which is a particularly desirable kind of anti-inflationary move.

To be sure, the monetary measures in Indonesia were all of a type which has only a once-over effect. The impact on money supply of the system of advance down payments dwindles as the lag between application for foreign exchange and sale of imports in Indonesia disappears. The gentleman's agreement imposes a ceiling on, but does not reduce, credit to importers. Similarly, the limit on transfer of profits by firms indebted to banks loses its effect once those debts have been liquidated. Improving fiscal policy was no easier, and offsetting inadequate fiscal policy by ingenious monetary policy was more difficult, for the succeeding government than it had been for the Wilopo government. In 1957, Indonesia finally introduced reserve requirements for banks, partly in cash and partly in treasury bills. By controlling the supply of treasury bills, the central bank has a more orthodox influence on bank reserves.

In general, we may conclude that underdeveloped countries may need monetary measures of a sort tailor-made for their own institutional framework, but that such measures can be an effective instrument of economic stabilization.

Anticyclical Timing of Public Developmental Investment

In the past, economic development has been a powerful destabilizing factor. The theories presented in Chapters 4, 5, and 6 show some of the reasons why. Proper planning, however, can convert *public* investment for development into a stabilizing device. The chronic structural unemployment of the sort common in underdeveloped countries requires steady expansion of investment, public and private. Where *cyclical* unemployment also exists as a consequence of fluctuations in exports and related private investment, it can be offset by timing the expansion of public investment inversely with these fluctuations.

The process of bringing forward public investment projects in order to offset cyclical unemployment has been called "telescoping." Telescoping does not mean diverting physical or fiscal resources to make-work projects; it means only offsetting the temporarily low level of private investment and exports with worthwhile public projects already included in the development plan because of their high priority ratings. Nor does it mean inflation, since the increased public investment merely replaces private investment. As private investment recovers, the public investment sector can be contracted simply by not starting new projects as earlier ones are completed. The development plan should include a reserve of useful projects at the regional and local levels which can be used to absorb cyclical unemployment if necessary. Experience in other countries indicates that the relatively small and labor-intensive projects typically undertaken by regional and local governments have greater flexibility than the heavier construction projects normally undertaken by the central government. Regional and local projects will meet this requirement. The Philippine approach to development planning, with annual revision and addition of another year's projects to replace the projects already completed, permits adjustment more easily than a fixed-period plan.

The problems of timing public investment to help maintain full employment are not intrinsically different in underdeveloped and advanced countries. The present writer has dealt with these problems at some length in an earlier publication, and so will not repeat the discussion in any detail here.[10] It may be worthwhile to point out, however, that underdeveloped countries with ambitious development programs including a substantial volume of public investment are in a better position to use public investment as a stabilizing device than are most advanced countries. For such countries should always have a reserve of highly useful public works that can be brought forward whenever private spending falls. Moreover, a large proportion of the projects should be of the small-scale, labor-intensive type that permits greatest flexibility.

In both underdeveloped and advanced countries there is a widespread, but essentially erroneous, idea that public investment is a less flexible instrument of employment policy than variable

[10] Benjamin Higgins, *Public Investment and Full Employment* (Montreal, 1946), especially Part III.

taxes or transfer payments (such as unemployment insurance). Yet even American experience illustrates the great flexibility of public works on the expansion side. The Civil Works Administration had men at work ten days after it was created, had 814,000 workers on its payroll on the first payday. By the week following, this figure had been doubled and a month later the agency was providing jobs for nearly four million men.[11] The worst that could be said of this remarkable record is that not all the projects were of high priority, but this deficiency reflects lack of advance planning, not lack of flexibility. On the contraction side, the chief requirement for flexibility is a sufficient sprinkling of small-scale projects that can be finished within a few months. Here again the CWA record is impressive; employment was cut from 4.2 million at the end of January, 1934, to 2 million at the end of March, when the operation was transferred to the FERA.

The flexibility of an employment policy has economic, legal and administrative, and technical aspects. The economic aspects consist of the rate at which income and employment can be varied with a given fiscal cost, in the absence of legal, administrative, or technical barriers. On economic grounds, public expenditures on goods and services ("public investment") are clearly *more* flexible than taxes or transfer payments, for the simple reason that variations in public investment affect income and employment in the same income period as that in which action is taken, whereas variable taxes and variable transfer payments affect income and employment only after a lag.[12] Moreover, the marginal propensity to consume is likely to be higher for public investment than for taxes, since the great bulk of public investment goes into wage incomes, whereas a large share of almost any kind of taxes comes out of non-wage incomes. Transfer payments of the family allowance or unemployment insurance type also go mainly to wage incomes. Moreover, the relevant income period itself will tend to be shorter for variable public investment than for variable taxes, since the average lag between receipt and re-spending of income is much shorter for wage than for non-wage incomes. When all these factors are taken into account, it is apparent that, on purely economic grounds, a policy of varying public investment would be more flexible than a policy of variable transfer payments, and a good deal more flexible than variable taxes. This argument, of course, holds a fortiori when unemployment is concentrated in partic-

[11] Cf. *ibid.*, chap. IX.

[12] This proposition is the basis of the "balanced budget multiplier" theorem.

ular industries or regions.

By the same token, reliance on variable tax rates and transfer payments for the achievement of a flexible employment policy will necessitate more accurate forecasting than a program which also includes variable public investment. To have expansionary (or deflationary) effects starting at the same time as would be produced by increases (or decreases) of public investment, the decision to reduce (or increase) taxes must be made at least one income period sooner. It should be noted also that the sort of built-in flexibility that is achieved with stable tax rates can be obtained in a public investment policy merely by assuring that public investment falls less than other components of national income. Automatic rules for variations in tax rates would be more effective, especially if coupled with automatically varying or even stable transfer payments. (In Canada such a policy exists in part through the family allowance program.) However, automatic rules for variable expenditures are just as easily formulated. No rule could be more simple than one requiring the government to take onto its payroll any worker discharged by private enterprise. The truth in the proposal to achieve flexibility through tax policy alone is simply that if the budget is big enough, a substantial compensatory effect can be achieved by varying taxes while keeping expenditures stable.

The chief legal and administrative requirements for flexibility of any type of employment policy are two: there must be departments at all relevant levels of government with legal powers to take all necessary steps without delay, including powers to collect or spend funds; and these departments must be going concerns with efficient personnel. These requirements can be met for any type of policy, and the achievement of complete flexibility of any policy requires the concession of a wider range of independent decision to the executive branch of government.

More specifically, the requirements for a flexible tax policy are that the executive branch of government must have power to vary taxes; that channels must be established for giving notice of tax changes or issuing forms and instructions, and so forth; and that some inducements must be available to persuade regional and local governments to integrate their tax policies with the central policy. Requirements for a flexible public investment policy are a fully planned reserve of useful projects, power of the executive branch to subsidize acceleration of central, regional, and local public investment programs, advance acquisition of sites or sweeping powers of condemnation, and reliance on government force-account work or advance letting of contracts with an "escalator clause."

The technical barriers to a variable tax policy or a variable transfer payment consist mainly of paper work and are not very important. The technical problems in a public investment program consist mainly of the engineering limitations on the speed with which projects can be started and finished. A program heavily weighted with relatively small-scale projects, which reach peak employment quickly and have an average duration of about six months, would involve no serious technical barriers to flexibility. Within two months of starting the expansion, some projects would mature each month. Within six months, some 15 to 20 per cent of the total program would mature each month. Consequently, the program as a whole could be rapidly contracted merely by failing to replace maturing projects with new ones. If large projects of long duration are launched in a downswing of private investment, they should be of a sort that has social priority so high that prompt completion is desirable even under prosperity conditions.

Thus, on economic grounds, public investment is most flexible, transfer payments are next most flexible, and tax policy is least flexible. On legal and administrative grounds, all types of policy could be made equally flexible. On technical grounds, public investment presents the greatest problems, but these can be overcome.

In underdeveloped countries, however, there may be an incompatibility between stability and growth of a more subtle form. In Chapter 16 we indicated that maximizing the rate of economic growth requires an *optimal sequence* of projects, a point which we shall elaborate in Chapter 27. This optimal sequence may require undertaking projects in a different order from the one that would be most efficient in terms of telescoping. Where such a conflict arises, the society must choose between greater stability and more rapid development.

25 Foreign Investment

In most underdeveloped countries, the scale of development investment to date has been too low to promote vigorous economic growth. It is doubtful whether many of them can raise the additional capital resources they need without some foreign aid or foreign investment. Even if they could, as total outlays for development are increased, foreign exchange requirements will also rise; few underdeveloped countries can hope to produce in the near future all the raw materials and equipment needed for economic development. Heavy equipment, such as turbines, railway locomotives and cars, diesel motors, steam shovels, must be imported. More modest projects also will need some imported materials; it will be some time before all underdeveloped countries can hope to be self-sufficient in fertilizer, cement, and agricultural tools. Even a development program concentrating in its first phase on agricultural improvement will impose some additional burdens on supplies of foreign exchange. A substantial proportion of government capital budget expenditures is made in foreign exchange. Developmental investment by private enterprise also entails allocation of foreign exchange for materials and equipment. Thus even countries fortunate enough to be able to meet total capital requirements from domestic taxes and savings may nevertheless face a foreign exchange problem.

The foreign exchange needed for development must be obtained in one of four ways: by restricting imports of other goods and services; by increasing exports; by obtaining loans or grants from foreigners; or by repudiating foreign obligations and expropriating foreign enterprise. The limitations on the last of these devices have been outlined in Chapter 19.

1. *Reducing imports.* Foreign exchange problems are general in underdeveloped countries. Restrictions on luxury imports are already common. In most underdeveloped countries, finding the foreign exchange for an ambitious development program by cutting other imports would require inroads into the semi-necessity or necessity category, with accompanying sacrifices by the masses of the people. Moreover, reducing imports, in and of itself, is inflationary; it lessens the flow of goods and releases cash for spending in other ways. Many underdeveloped countries must have an austere import policy, but that offers no panacea for financing their development.

2. *Expanding exports.* There can be no argument against a policy to increase exports. However, four observations might be made. First, the volume of exports is not entirely under the control of government policy; it depends very much on world market conditions, on which individual underdeveloped countries may have little influence. Increasing the total value of exports is virtually impossible in a period when world market prices of major exports are falling. Second, measures to increase exports are for the most part likely to operate rather slowly; it is a matter of improving techniques and strains, labor skills and managerial methods, introducing new industries, and the like, so as to increase productivity per hectare and per man-hour and to reduce costs. Increasing exports in this fashion is one of the major *results* to be expected from *carrying out* a development plan; it is another thing altogether to *launch* a development program by an initial increase in exports. Third, an export surplus, no less than a cut in imports, involves sacrifices; an export surplus means sending more abroad than one gets in return—using labor and resources to provide goods and services to foreigners. If the surplus is used to finance imports of capital goods, it will assist development, but it will not alleviate the immediate sacrifice of consumers' goods. Using an export surplus of other items to finance imports of capital goods means reducing current consumption below present levels in order to raise productivity and so have more to consume later; it is another form of saving. Finally, an export surplus is in itself inflationary; it reduces the supply of goods and increases the supply of money. It is not, therefore, a substitute for increased savings or taxes at home.

Foreign Aid or Private Foreign Investment?

Can the additional capital needed by underdeveloped areas be better obtained from foreign private investors, from foreign governments, or from international agencies? This question is not an either-or proposition. There is no reason why underdeveloped countries should not obtain part of their additional requirements in each form. Certain development projects can be more easily organized and more efficiently managed if carried out on a private enterprise basis. Other development projects, important to the country, and perhaps producing "external economies" or other benefits not easily sold in the market, may be better handled through government channels. Sometimes top managerial and technical personnel feel happier if working for a private enterprise, in other cases the reverse is true. The question must be decided on an *ad hoc* basis for each project in each development plan.

One thing, however, is clear: underdeveloped countries will not find it easy to attract large amounts of foreign private capital at this stage of their development. Even if every reasonable effort is made in both lending and borrowing countries to encourage foreign investment in underdeveloped areas, the flow of private capital in itself is not likely to fill the gap between capital requirements and domestic financial resources, current or potential.

Encouragement of Private Foreign Investment

Many people in underdeveloped countries still believe that a huge flood of foreign capital is waiting to inundate those lands if the gates are opened. Nothing could be further from the truth. Currently there is a *world* shortage of capital. Even countries with high standards of living, such as Canada and Australia, still find it necessary to borrow abroad to finance their economic development. The most highly developed country of all, the United States, offers investors earnings above 10 per cent on the highest-grade industrial securities. Far from being a matter of "permitting" foreign capital to enter under restrictive conditions, it is a matter of competing for capital against other countries in both the highly developed and the less developed categories.

In countries recently emerged from colonial status, the general public must learn the difference between "colonialism" and foreign investment. Foreign investment in a sovereign country, with its own corporation, tax, and monetary legislation, foreign exchange control, etc., is a totally different thing from investment in colonies by citizens of a colonial power. Certainly, big business tends to exert an influence on government policy in any country where it exists; but this fact is no less true when the big business is owned by nationals than when it is owned by foreigners, and the foreigners are often easier to handle, just because they are foreigners with less influence on the electorate, than nationals would be.

The United Nations Economic Commission for Asia and the Far East (ECAFE) has summarized very well the requirements of foreign investors regarding investment in less developed countries—the requirements that must be met if any significant volume of foreign capital is to be attracted to these countries: [1]

The question of encouraging private foreign investments in the countries of the (ECAFE) region has recently assumed very great importance. The prospective investor, however, wants to be sure about the climate for foreign investments in the receiving countries. The elements that constitute a favourable climate from his point of view may be briefly indicated as follows:

(1) Political stability and freedom from external aggression.
(2) Security of life and property.
(3) Availability of opportunities for earning profits.
(4) Prompt payment of fair compensation and its remittance to the country of origin in the event of compulsory acquisition of a foreign enterprise.
(5) Facilities for the remittance of profits, dividends, interest, etc.
(6) Facilities for the immigration and employment of foreign technical and administrative personnel.
(7) A system of taxation that does not impose a crushing burden on private enterprise.
(8) Freedom from double taxation.
(9) Absence of vexatious controls.
(10) Non-discriminatory treatment of foreigners in the administration of controls.
(11) Absence of competition of state-owned enterprises with private capital.
(12) A general spirit of friendliness for foreign investors.

Guarantees for Foreign Investors

What measures can be suggested for meeting the twelve requirements listed above, without sacrificing any degree of sov-

[1] United Nations Economic Commission for Asia and the Far East, Committee on Industry and Trade, Second Session, "Foreign Investment Laws and Regulations in the ECAFE Region," (Bangkok, March, 1950), pp. 4–5.

ereignty and without compromising the government's freedom with respect to economic policy?

1 and 2. The question of international security and political stability is of course outside an economist's field of competence. Internal security is also a non-economic question. Insurance provisions might help. The governments might consider setting up their own insurance organizations for the purpose or, lacking experience and personnel for such a task, might enter into discussions with foreign insurance firms. It might pay to give some subsidy in local currency to insurance companies assuming the risks of loss of life and property of foreigners, if such subsidies would help to bring significant amounts of foreign exchange into the country. Of course, foreigners would want only policies with benefits payable in foreign currency, but any insurance company will have local currency expenses, so a local currency subsidy would be acceptable to them. Alternatively, the government of the lending countries might expand the scope of insurance of approved foreign investment.

3. No special policy is necessary to provide opportunities for profitable investment; in some fields, they certainly exist. Governments might provide information to foreign business and industrial organizations regarding investment opportunities, however, and they might undertake to provide the complementary public utilities, public works, and community services needed to permit new enterprises to operate, attract personnel, and market products.

4. With regard to nationalization, there are two possible approaches: First, to guarantee that no nationalization shall take place until initial and supplementary investments have been recouped, and a reasonable aggregate profit on the investment has been earned. The only obvious objection to this approach is need for a government to put up with an inefficient foreign firm indefinitely, just because its rate of earnings is low and accordingly it requires a very long time to accumulate the stipulated aggregate profit. In such cases, the foreign investor would usually be willing to sell out for a reasonable price. Secondly, to promise prior consultation and notice, plus "fair compensation," to be determined in cases of dispute by the International Court of Justice at The Hague. Some combination of these two provisions might be worked out, the first to apply in general, and the second to be resorted to in special and unusual circumstances, which might be itemized.

5. If foreign capital is to be attracted in significant quantities,

freedom of transfer of profits (net of tax) must be accorded, including transfer of depreciation allowances if the foreign investor wishes to withdraw his capital gradually over a period of time. Also, facilities should be provided for the transfer of ownership from one foreigner to another, subject to approval of the authorities. The only restrictions on transfers should be on transfer of proceeds of sales of assets for local currency.

6. Direct investment (which is the only form likely to be attractive to foreigners in the near future) will not take place unless the foreign firms can bring their own managers and technicians.[2] No restrictions, other than those essential to security, should be imposed on immigration of such personnel; on the contrary, every facility should be afforded to assist such immigration. Indeed, except for diplomatic status, skilled personnel of foreign firms should be accorded the same sort of treatment as experts brought in under the UN Technical Assistance program; assistance should be provided in obtaining passage and visas, in finding suitable living accommodations, etc.

Foreign firms should, however, take on some obligations with respect to training local staff. Perhaps amounts spent on training local staff might be made deductible from tax, instead of from taxable income.

7. The tax problem is most complex of all and cannot be analyzed fully here. Some of the problems regarding taxation apply equally to foreign and to domestic firms. However, some major points may be made:

a) The regulations governing foreign investment should promise identical treatment with respect to taxes of foreign and domestic firms and their personnel; there must certainly be no discrimination against foreign firms.

b) The governments might also promise prior consultation of foreign investors when tax legislation clearly injurious to their interests is under discussion.

c) Some tax concessions might be made to encourage investment. A difficulty here is that concessions on personal and company income tax may be of no use, because they would merely mean that foreign firms and their staffs would pay more taxes in their own countries. However, it would be possible and helpful to exempt new firms, or new investments of existing ones, from export and import taxes for a limited period.

[2] Cf. paper by Everett Hagen, "The Problem of Management in an Underdeveloped Economy," M.I.T., CIS, October 18, 1954 (Document Control #C/54–18).

d) Income taxes present a special problem, since the rates are often higher in the underdeveloped country, on salaries which are at customary levels for managerial and technical personnel, than they would be in the lending countries. That is, when translated into local currency at official rates, a normal salary in United States or Canadian dollars for a production manager, say, would put him into a higher tax bracket than he would be in at home, with the same salary. Thus exemption from income tax for a limited period would be significant for many foreign investors. Another possibility would be to permit the employers to pay income tax, in order to attract efficient staff, and allow the firm to deduct such income tax payments on behalf of staff from tax liability, instead of from taxable income. Any such privilege should then be accorded also to new investments of domestic firms, to avoid discrimination. It is unlikely that such a scheme would reduce revenues of the government; by bringing a larger proportion of employees into the range of accurate bookkeeping, it might very well improve personal income tax collections so much that it would more than offset the loss on corporation income tax.

In general, care must be taken not to drive out existing firms by giving new firms competitive advantages. Potential foreign investors will get their impressions of possibilities in underdeveloped countries mainly from the reports of foreign firms already operating in the country. Also, experienced firms are likely to contribute more to development than inexperienced ones.

e) Certain types of "incentive tax schemes," which might be applied to investment in general, would be of special interest to foreign investors. These include:

(1) Averaging profits for tax purposes over a longer period, say, ten years
(2) Liberal provisions for accelerated depreciation on new investments of a type, or made at a time or place, designated by the government
(3) Permitting profits used for new investment of a kind, or made at a time or in a place, approved by the government, to be deducted from taxable income

Certain less developed countries, such as India and Pakistan, have already taken steps of this kind.

8. Double taxation must certainly be avoided, and the governments should sign treaties concerning double taxation with all the countries likely to provide significant amounts of capital.

9. The question of controls is a sore point among foreign

businessmen and investors. Many of the controls which irritate foreign investors are not essential to the achievement of the government's true policy objectives. Existing controls should be thoroughly reviewed to distinguish the essential from the non-essential.

With respect to controls, the ECAFE report comments: [3]

> A large number of economic activities are subject to government control in various countries of the region. The controls may cover trade, industry, banking, insurance, foreign exchange, transport services, real estate, mining, capital issues, sale of securities, payment of dividends, etc. The scope of these controls, however, varies from one country to another. Except in a few cases, they generally do not discriminate against foreigners; but discrimination can be exercised in their actual administration. Countries which want to attract foreign capital would find it to their advantage to ensure non-discriminatory administration of the controls.
>
> Further, controls are generally a drag on free enterprise. When they are first introduced, there are usually very good reasons for so doing. But as time passes and circumstances change, these reasons may lose much of their force. It is, therefore, possible that some of the controls may continue for a longer period than necessary. They should be kept under constant review, so that they may be gradually relaxed or completely abolished when circumstances permit.

10. Foreign investors should be guaranteed treatment regarding controls identical to that accorded to nationals.

11. An outright guarantee that no publicly owned enterprise would compete in the same field would leave the door open to monopolistic exploitation by foreign firms. It should be given, therefore, only in conjunction with some provision for control of monopolistic exploitation.

12. A "general spirit of friendliness" is not something that can be written into regulations but public information could be so phrased as to indicate such a spirit, where it exists.

No government, of course, can undertake not to devalue its currency; a situation might conceivably arise in which devaluation was necessary. The guarantees regarding nationalization might be stated in terms of the currency of the investors' home countries; that is, the Canadian investor would be assured of no nationalization until he had got back his capital plus reasonable cumulative profits, in terms of Canadian dollars. Apart from this assurance, the only other possibility would be some sort of insurance against loss through devaluation. Perhaps the lending

[3] *Op. cit.*, p. 28.

countries could be induced to provide such insurance, along the lines of the Canadian Export Credits Guarantees Corporation or the Mutual Security Administration's guarantee program. Permitting foreign firms to do their accounting in the currencies they initially invest would also help.

Again, no government could guarantee foreign investors against labor difficulties. The governments might, however, improve the arbitration machinery and publicize this improvement abroad. They might also embark on a campaign, similar to that undertaken by the Labor government in the United Kingdom after 1946, to teach organized labor its responsibilities toward the nation, and to teach workers that only through increased output can they gain a higher standard of living for themselves. Publicity abroad could then be given to this campaign as well.

Raising labor productivity through training and improved equipment is of course a long-run approach. Meanwhile, for export industries facing genuine difficulties because of high labor costs and falling prices, some system of wage subsidies might be worked out. Such subsidies should accrue in the first instance to the employer, to permit him to cover the gap between current wage rates and value productivity per man-hour. For social and political reasons, there would have to be an accompanying benefit for workers, but it should not take a form that would permit workers to maintain a customary normal standard of living while working less hard or less well. It might, for example, take the form of a government contribution to an employer-managed old age pension fund, or an employer-managed health scheme, or something of the sort, with the government contributions exceeding the actual cost to the employer.

Handling foreign investment problems so as to offer every possible inducement to foreign investors, while protecting vital national rights, requires a special high-level organization, which might be called the Foreign Investment Board. The Board would need a secretariat, which might be called the Foreign Investment Bureau. This Bureau would be comprised of technicians and experts, who would be responsible for administering policy regarding foreign investment, along the general lines laid down by the government. The logical place for this Bureau would be either in the central bank, or in the development planning agency.

It would be helpful if this "F.I.B." had on its staff one or two foreign experts, provided under one of the technical assistance programs, who could "talk the language" of foreign investors, not merely in the sense of knowing English, French, or German, but in the sense of knowing what attitudes and worries they have, and what various words mean to them. These experts should have experience with capital markets abroad. It would also be desirable for the F.I.B. to have a representative attached to the embassy in each country likely to furnish significant amounts of capital, to provide information to potential investors. The F.I.B. might also prepare prospectuses of particular investment possibilities, for distribution among potential investors abroad.

In order to make it unnecessary for the F.I.B. to deal separately with hundreds of small foreign firms, parallel organization of foreign investors should be encouraged. This organization might retain legal counsel and possibly a small research staff, and contributions to the expenses of the organization might be made deductible from taxable income. The organization could then deal with the F.I.B. on matters of taxation, import regulations, foreign exchange regulations, etc., of interest to all foreign investors. Large-scale foreign investors, such as oil companies, would of course retain their right to deal directly with the Board, or even directly with the government in the case of very large interests.

Factors Limiting Foreign Private Investment

It is unlikely that even highly favorable laws governing foreign investment will encourage sufficient inflow of private capital to meet a large share of the requirements of underdeveloped areas. We deal here only with the two most highly developed countries, the United States and Canada, for which studies of limitations on investment in underdeveloped areas are available. Much the same considerations, however, would apply in other industrialized countries.

The United States

The U.S. Department of Commerce has undertaken two studies which throw light on the problems that must be overcome to encourage a substantial flow of American capital to underdeveloped areas. The first was *Foreign Investment of the United States*, the second, *Factors Limiting U.S. Investment Abroad*, both published in 1953. The latter report incorporates "the findings of several months of investigation undertaken in compliance with Section 516(C) of the Mutual Security Act of 1951, as amended." That subsection directed the Department of Commerce to conduct a study of "the legal and other impediments to private investment abroad and the methods and means whereby these impediments can be removed or decreased."

The figures show clearly that the bulk of American foreign investment is made in advanced countries, or at least, in the relatively advanced sectors of underdeveloped ones. Canada is by far the most important single country for American foreign investment. Canada absorbs 30 per cent of total direct American investment abroad, 37 per cent of the foreign branches of American firms, 50 per cent of all American foreign investment in manufacturing, and 70 per cent of "the interest of United States owners not affiliated with United States reporters." Yet Canada is the second most highly developed country in the world, as well as one which is currently developing at a very rapid rate. Of total foreign direct investments amounting in 1950 to $11.78 billion, $3.58 billion were in Canada (see Table 25-1).

TABLE 25-1.

Direct Investments Abroad, 1950
(In millions of dollars)

Industries	All areas, total	Canada	Latin American republics	Western Europe	Western European dependencies	Other countries
All industries, total	11,788	3,579	4,735	1,720	435	1,318
Agriculture	589	21	520	1	9	39
Mining and smelting	1,129	334	628	21	88	57
Petroleum	3,390	418	1,408	424	296	844
Manufacturing	3,831	1,897	780	933	9	214
Transportation, communication, and public utilities	1,425	284	1,042	27	18	54
Trade	762	239	243	186	13	81
Finance and insurance	425	313	71	37	*	3
Miscellaneous	237	72	45	92	1	27

* Less than $500,000.

SOURCE: U.S. Department of Commerce, *Foreign Investment of the United States* (Washington, D.C., 1953).

It is interesting to note (Table 25-2) that Canada also absorbed nearly twice as much of the *increase* in investment between 1943 and 1950 as its nearest rival, the Persian Gulf. This investment is an important factor in Canada's recent expansion. The Latin American countries combined absorbed a somewhat larger amount

TABLE 25-2.

Investment in Specified Countries, 1943 and 1950
(In millions of dollars)

Country	1950	1943	Increase
Canada	3,564	2,378	1,186
Persian Gulf area *	726	61	665
Venezuela	981	373	608
Brazil	627	233	394
United Kingdom	840	519	321
Panama †	349	110	239
Chile	530	328	202
France	285	167	118
Mexico	399	286	113
Cuba	638	526	112
Union of South Africa	140	50	90
Australia	198	114	84
Colombia	194	117	77
Peru	140	71	69
Liberia †	82	18	64
Philippine Republic	149	95	54
Total for specified countries	9,842	5,446	4,396

* Includes Saudi Arabia, Iraq, Jordan, Lebanon, Syria, Aden, Bahrein, Kuwait, and Qatar.

† Increases represent mainly ships registered under foreign flags and owned mainly by subsidiaries of United States corporations.

SOURCE: U.S. Department of Commerce, *Foreign Investment of the United States* (Washington, D.C., 1953).

of direct American investment, $4.7 billion. However, a large share of this total is represented by petroleum investment in Venezuela. About one-fifth of total American investment in Latin America is in Venezuela, and the bulk of this investment is in the petroleum industry. Moreover, most of the remaining Latin American investment is either in the relatively advanced A B C countries or in Cuba, where most American investment takes the form of producing raw materials and foodstuffs for the American market. Much of the Latin American investment outside the petroleum industry is in the meat-packing industry, where again an American market is assured. Europe accounts for another 20 per cent of American foreign direct investment, whereas "other countries" combined absorb only some 11 per cent of the total.

Manufacturing and the petroleum industry are the two categories of investment which have absorbed the larger share of American foreign investment (see Table 25-1). In the "other" countries, however, the petroleum industry is by far the most significant sector. In this connection, it should be noted that Southeast Asia has shared very little in the increase in American foreign investment in petroleum since 1929 (see Table 25-3).

TABLE 25-3.
American Investment in Foreign Petroleum Industries
(In millions of dollars)

	Total	Canada	Latin America	Western Europe	Other	Persian Gulf
1929	1,117	55	617	231	214	....
1950	3,390	418	1,408	424	1,140	659

SOURCE: U.S. Department of Commerce, *Foreign Investment of the United States* (Washington, D.C., 1953).

The preference of American investors for familiar and relatively developed countries is shown also by the figures of net receipts (Table 25-4). As a ratio to investments in 1950, net receipts amounted to 6.5 per cent in Western Europe, 8 per cent in Canada, 11 per cent in Latin America, and 20.4 per cent in other countries. In other words, to attract even the relatively small amounts invested in "other countries" in 1950, rates of return more than three times as high as in Western Europe, and two and a half times as high in Canada, were required. Even in Latin America, rates of return were nearly double those in Western Europe.

In summarizing these results, the U.S. Department of Commerce writes: [4]

It is apparent that American individuals and others venturing to make investments abroad without acquiring control of a foreign enterprise did so primarily in countries, such as Canada and the United Kingdom, with familiar business practices and enterprises; in com-

[4] U.S. Department of Commerce, *Foreign Investment of the U.S.* (Washington, D.C., 1953), pp. 22.

panies supplying raw materials to the U.S., such as sugar, copper, or tin; and in senior securities of companies owned or controlled in the United States, like shipping enterprises incorporated in Panama or Liberia. . . . The only significant exception is the heavy investment in Canadian mining companies. However, the more important of these securities are traded on the New York stock exchanges.

In the second report, the Department of Commerce lists the following factors as the major impediments to higher investments in Latin American countries: differences in political traditions and legal concepts; the small size and limited population and resources of some of the countries; the large measure of governmental intervention in political, social (including labor-management relations), and economic affairs; the exclusion of foreigners from participation in some activities in some countries; the threat of expropriation or nationalization; foreign exchange controls,

TABLE 25-4.

Net Receipts of Income, 1950, by Area and Industry
(In millions of dollars)

Industries	All areas, total	Canada	Latin American republics	Western Europe	Western European dependencies	Other countries
All industries, total	1,294	294	522	111	98	269
Agriculture	91	1	76	*	4	11
Mining and smelting	112	31	64	1	12	3
Petroleum	555	3	262	9	75	212
Manufacturing . .	357	211	55	69	1	22
Transportation, communication, and public utilities	44	9	33	*	*	1
Trade	72	17	17	21	3	14
Finance and insurance	40	21	9	4	2	5
Miscellaneous . . .	23	8	7	7	*	1

* Less than $500,000.

SOURCE: U.S. Department of Commerce, *Foreign Investment of the United States* (Washington, D.C., 1953).

and particularly "the problems and difficulties inherent in the delays and administrative complexities of exchange controls"; difficulties with customs, in connection with imports of equipment and raw materials; inadequate prior surveys and investigations; and finally, "creeping expropriation." This latter factor, says the report,[5]

. . . has been a more serious problem for large investors than outright nationalization. . . . Some countries have harassed foreign-controlled enterprises with fines and discriminatory tax and labor requirements, or have refused to permit utilities to charge rates high enough to yield adequate returns. . . . Foreign firms may also be subject to discriminatory application of exchange rates.

In summarizing the experience in Latin America, the report states: [6]

Most of the barriers to foreign investment arise out of national policy designed (1) to protect or favor national ownership and employment, or (2) to regulate financial or other activities for specific national or social objectives.

There are obvious analogies between Latin America and other underdeveloped countries with regard to these impediments to foreign investment.

Of particular interest are the statements made in the report with respect to investment in Venezuela, a country which has relied heavily on foreign capital for its economic development: [7]

Venezuela's economic growth has coincided with a huge increase in foreign investment. Direct investment of United States capital alone in Venezuela—representing perhaps two-thirds of foreign direct investment in the country—rose from $232.5 million in 1929 to $993 million at the end of 1950 and as of that date constituted the second largest United States direct investment in any foreign country. The country's rich petroleum reserves have provided the basis for the entry of an amount estimated as high as $2 billion of foreign capital. Petroleum development and the estimated $175 million of other foreign investment could not have taken place without Venezuelan Government cooperation and approval and the maintenance of conditions generally favorable to the conduct of business by foreign enterprises.

The Venezuelan Government recognizes the role that new private foreign capital can play in diversifying the economy, now largely dependent upon petroleum, by continuing a minimum of purely legal

[5] U.S. Department of Commerce, *Factors Limiting United States Investment Abroad* (Washington, D.C., 1953), pp. 4–6.

[6] *Ibid.*, p. 6.

[7] *Ibid.*, pp. 40–41.

barriers to the establishment of foreign enterprise. At present, petroleum provides directly or indirectly, two-thirds of the Government's revenues, and crude petroleum and refined products account for 97 per cent of Venezuela's exports."

The comments with respect to Turkey may also contain some lessons for other countries: [8]

The primary problem with respect to private foreign investments in Turkey is the fact that the Government still plays a dominant role in the economy of the country. Although since 1950 the Government has relaxed its policy of statism and has been looking increasingly to foreign capital for development in some fields, its attitude is still cautious. This caution is due in large part to experiences during the period of the Ottoman Empire when the Turkish economy fell under foreign control through a series of capitulations and concessions. . . . Although Turkey has a wide variety of mineral resources, such as chrome, copper, manganese, and coal, they are largely owned and developed by the Government. While there is some indication that private operation of some mines is contemplated, these fields are not presently open to private foreign investment. Other resources not controlled by the Government are of limited interest to foreign investors. . . . This deficiency of investment capital has been partially remedied by the creation of the Industrial Development Bank in 1950. This bank has the function of providing medium- and long-term credit for private enterprise as well as the task of encouraging Turkish investment in private industry by underwriting issuances of share capital. The Bank's rate of interest, 6 per cent, was set by agreement with the Government. This Bank has loaned over $24 million to 136 industrial enterprises. As mentioned above, the IBRD assisted in establishing the Bank and provided it with foreign exchange through a loan of $9 million. Most of the Bank's equity capital was subscribed by private interests.

In the section devoted specifically to the Far East, the report lists the following factors as major impediments to American investment: the uncertainty created by the present political situation in that area; the policies or practices of most Far Eastern countries with respect to foreign capital investment; the relatively low level of economic development and the lack of trained labor in much of the region; the growing sphere of government activity; and the limited knowledge of the Far East on the part of many American businessmen.

The particular impediments stressed in the case of India are the nature of India's screening policy, which has denied admission

[8] *Ibid.*, pp. 92–94.

to some types of investment and proved slow and costly for others; the import, export, foreign exchange and other controls; a government policy which favors nationalization of some industries and government participation in industry in general; the unfamiliarity of Americans with Indian business ways; the relatively low stage of Indian economic development; and the absence of a double taxation agreement.

The particularly gloomy discussion of opportunities for investment in Japan is also of interest: [9]

Japan has an extremely low ratio of natural resources to population and those relatively meager resources are already highly developed. Per capita income in 1951 has been estimated as equivalent to $150–$160. The country does not have the capacity within its boundaries to produce enough food, clothing, shelter, or fuel to maintain 86 million people at the present standard of living. Furthermore, the population is growing at the rate of more than a million annually and the productive capacity of some resources is declining. Japan must import one-fifth of its food supply and virtually all of its cotton and wool. Its forests cannot meet normal demands for construction, fuel, and the manufacture of paper and artificial fiber. Large quantities of potash and phosphate must be imported if agricultural production is to be maintained at its present level. Sea water is the only domestic source of salt for the chemical industry. Japan is deficient in iron, lead, aluminum, tin, manganese, antimony, tungsten, nickel, petroleum, and coking coal suitable for large blast-furnace use. Although there may be new discoveries, and technical improvements may result in more efficient uses, presently known resources, with the exception of water power, offer little opportunity for further development.

Japan's chief resource, as well as its greatest problem, is its large and growing population, the principal reservoir of skilled labor in the Far East. Owing to the paucity of natural resources, the maintenance of the present economic level is dependent in large part upon earnings from industry and trade. It is these two fields, rather than the primary industries, in which prospective investors are interested. In 1951, 29.5 per cent of the national income was produced by manufacturing and 18.3 per cent by trade, as compared with 15.9 per cent by agriculture, 3.9 by mining, 2.6 by fishing, and 2.5 by forestry.

Obviously, these impediments cannot all be removed quickly and easily by legislation in the underdeveloped countries; it is also obvious that legislation can remove some of them.

A similar picture is presented in the Report of the Canadian Advisory Committee on Overseas Investment—except that on balance Canada is a substantial capital importer.

[9] *Ibid.*, pp. 112–13.

The origin of the Committee is described by the Minister of Finance in the foreword of its Report:

At the Tripartite Discussions held in Washington in September, 1949, the representatives of the United States, the United Kingdom and Canada reached the conclusion that a high level of North American investment in overseas countries, both public and private, could make an important contribution toward reducing the sterling-dollar disequilibrium. The three governments agreed that every aspect of this constructive approach to a problem of common concern should be explored. In line with the recommendation at the September talks, a Canadian Advisory Committee on Overseas Investment was established last April under the chairmanship of Mr. Gordon Ball. The Canadian Committee maintained throughout close liaison with the President's Committee for Financing Foreign Trade (The American Committee) headed by Mr. Winthrop W. Aldrich. The report of the Canadian Committee, which is presented here, was submitted to the Government on September 19th, 1950.

Although the contribution of Canadian foreign investment to the solution of the sterling problem was the major interest of the Committee, it also had in mind the need of underdeveloped areas for foreign capital. Many of the questions in the questionnaire were slanted toward special problems in underdeveloped areas. The countries covered by the questionnaire included most of those in Asia and Southeast Asia, Latin America, Africa, and the Middle East, which are usually classified as underdeveloped.

Major Conclusions

The findings of the Committee lead to a number of conclusions significant for underdeveloped areas.

1. One significant fact is that Canada, the country with the second highest *per capita* income in the world, and the one which is apparently the most rapidly advancing, has been a net importer of capital since the war (Table 25-5). In discussions regarding possibilities of attracting foreign capital, the governments of underdeveloped countries frequently overlook the important fact that the United States is the *only* country in the world which has been a large-scale net exporter of capital since the war, and which can be expected to be so in the next decade. This fact does not mean, of course, that underdeveloped countries must seek foreign capital only in the United States. Capital will be available from other countries, including Canada, for investment in particular enterprises in which the businessmen of

other countries have a particular interest or knowledge. It does mean, however, that meeting the capital requirements of underdeveloped countries as a whole will be possible, without aggravating the dollar shortage in other countries, only if the total flow of United States dollars for investment purposes is increased.

2. Most Canadian foreign investment is made in highly industrialized countries, rather than in underdeveloped countries (Table 25-6). At the end of 1949, Canadians had total investments abroad of $3.5 billion, of which $1.5 billion were in the United Kingdom, and $1.1 billion in the United States. Thus even to the extent that capital is available for investment abroad,

Table 25-5.

Canadian Capital Movements, 1926–49

(In millions of Canadian dollars)

		Canadian investment abroad		
Year	Non-resident investment in Canada	Direct and portfolio investment	Governmental credits	Total *
1926	6,002	890	36	926
1939	6,913	1,390	31	1,421
1947	7,175	1,401	1,816	3,217
1949	7,977	1,531	2,000	3,531

* Excluded from the estimates of Canadian investments abroad are official holdings of gold and foreign exchange, and external assets of Canadian banks and insurance companies which are regarded as offsets to the external liabilities of these concerns.

SOURCE: *Report of the Canadian Advisory Committee on Overseas Investment* (Ottawa, 1950).

the underdeveloped countries will be competing against highly industrialized countries for this scarce capital, and they will have to overcome the established practice of most investors of seeking assets in the United States, Canada, and Europe rather than in less well-known countries.

3. Moreover, the foreign investment of Canadians was almost entirely direct investment, and only to a very minor extent portfolio investment. Of the total foreign assets of Canadians at the end of 1949, only $195 million were in stocks and bonds; the remaining investments outside the United States, about $500 million, were all direct investments. For the most part, these direct investments were made to provide either outlets for

TABLE 25-6.

Geographic Distribution of Canadian Investment, as at December 31, 1949
(In millions of Canadian dollars)

	United States	United Kingdom	Other countries	Total
Investment in Canada	5,890	1,752	335	7,977
Canadian investment abroad:				
Special government credits	......	1,434	566	2,000
Direct, portfolio, and miscellaneous	1,133	100	298	1,531
Total investment abroad *	1,133	1,534	864	3,531
Net investment in Canada	4,757	218	−529	4,446

* Estimates exclude holdings and assets as in Table 25-5.
SOURCE: See Table 25-5.

Canadian products or a source of supply for Canadian companies (Table 25-7). In other words, such capital as underdeveloped countries are able to attract is likely to consist mainly of investment in fields of industry in which the foreign companies are already active, and it is likely to take the form of direct rather than portfolio investment.

4. Government policies toward foreign investment are a relatively unimportant factor in limiting Canadian foreign invest-

TABLE 25-7.

Apparent Motive for Investing

Nature of venture	Number of ventures	Source of supply for Canadian companies	Distribution of Canadian production	Other
Manufacturing	47	3	24	20
Mining	30	16	....	14
Trade	20		17	3
Transportation	6	5	....	1
Other public utilities	7	....	....	7
Other	9	1	3	5
Total	119	25	44	50

SOURCE: See Table 25-5.

TABLE 25-8.

Problems in Overseas Countries *

Nature of problem	Number of problems incorporated in questionnaire	Number of times reported	Incidence per 100 ventures
Retarded economic development	6	103	87
Attitude of government and labor:			
Labor problems	8	154	129
Other factors (political, etc.)	5	64	54
	13	218	183
Problems arising directly from governmental action, etc.:			
Foreign exchange controls	4	136	114
Tariff factors	4	71	60
Tax problems	4	30	25
Government policies toward foreign investment	5	26	22
	17	263	221
All problems	36	584	491

* Distributed according to nature of problem, and showing the relative incidence of problems per 100 ventures; number of ventures used in compiling this table, 119.
SOURCE: See Table 25-5.

ment. Of much greater importance than the actual government policies regarding foreign investment are labor problems, foreign exchange controls, and retarded economic development (Table 25-8). In the "special arrangement countries," labor problems and foreign exchange controls are by far the most serious problems in the view of actual or potential Canadian investors. In Asia and Oceania, however, retarded economic development is considered just as serious a barrier to investment as labor problems and foreign exchange controls; here too, government policies toward foreign investment are of minor significance (Table 25-9).

For mining, retarded economic development ranks highest among the problems listed in the questionnaire. Labor problems are second; foreign exchange controls third. In the field of manufacturing, on the other hand, foreign exchange controls rank first, labor problems second, and retarded economic development third.

TABLE 25-9.

Problems in Overseas Countries: Incidence of Problems per 100 Ventures by Principal Geographical Areas

Nature of problem	Incidence per 100 Ventures: South and Central America, West Indies, and Bermuda (35) *	Africa (12) *	Europe, including United Kingdom (51) *	Asia and Oceania (21) *	All areas (119) *
Retarded economic development	149	133	14	133	87
Attitude of government and labor:					
Labor problems .	203	192	63	133	129
Other factors (political, etc.) .	46	67	53	62	54
	249	259	116	195	183
Problems arising directly from government action, etc.:					
Foreign exchange controls	134	108	94	133	114
Tariff factors	77	58	41	76	60
Tax problems ...	37	8	21	24	25
Government policies toward foreign investment	23	25	16	33	22
	271	199	172	266	221
All problems	669	591	302	594	491

* Number of ventures reported on.
SOURCE: See Table 25-5.

This analysis indicates that underdeveloped countries cannot hope to attract significant quantities of Canadian capital merely by legislating attractive regulations covering foreign investment. More important will be the settlement of labor problems, release from irksome foreign exchange controls, security, political stability, and the like. There can be little doubt that the attitude of

Canadian investors in this regard is typical of foreign investors in general. In such fields of investment as mining, however, the provision of transport facilities, housing, and other community facilities, may provide a significant stimulus to foreign investment.

5. The Committee considered it worthwhile to quote at some length a commentary by one company with an interest in numerous overseas countries, as typical of the attitude of Canadian investors with respect to labor problems: [10]

(a) One of the principal difficulties met by us when considering making investments overseas is getting competent personnel, who know our methods and way of doing business, to go to these foreign countries to watch over such investments or, in the case of a . . . plant, if necessary, to actually operate or assist in its management to ensure that it is successful.

(b) Prior to the war there was not too much difficulty in getting personnel to go abroad. While there were the same physical drawbacks that exist today, the final return to the individual was much higher. In the backward and undeveloped areas where investment is most needed there were few if any taxes. It was possible to make large personal savings. The individual enjoyed a good standard of living at a very low cost.

(c) Since the war all this has changed. Today the Canadian going abroad has to pay as high if not higher income taxes than he would have paid had he stayed at home. He saves little if any money, and because the cost of living has in most places increased to the point where it is higher than in Canada, the great drawback is that it is no longer possible to enjoy the previous high standard of living. In addition, there is the deterrent of foreign exchange control. An employee is dissatisfied if he earns and perhaps saves an amount of sterling and finds on his return to Canada or the United States that it is blocked and frozen in his former place of work. Canadian personnel serving abroad also require foreign exchange to educate their children in Canada and to meet Canadian commitments, such as insurance policies, etc.

(d) We are not anxious to invest money abroad unless we can have them accompanied by the minimum number of staff drawn from our world-wide organization to protect our investment. They may be Canadians, Americans, Swiss or any one of several nationalities. From our point of view the personnel angle is a very important phase in this whole problem of overseas investment.

[10] *Report of the Canadian Advisory Committee on Overseas Investment* (Ottawa, 1950), pp. 36–37.

6. The Committee also quotes another company with respect to the importance of political stability as a prerequisite for a flow of Canadian capital: [11]

The threat of Soviet domination is felt in many parts of the world, and one company sums up the situation as follows:

Political Instability and the "Cold War":

(a) The continuance of political unrest in many areas and the spreading influence of Soviet Communism restrict the overseas areas attractive to investment by Canadian firms.

(b) In many areas, such as Africa, the West Indies, the East Indies and Southeast Asia, there is an understandable but growing ferment in favour of self-government and universal suffrage. Undesirable types of trade unionism are being actively fomented among illiterate workers often by irresponsible labour leaders. The pattern of political institutions and political morality that will eventually emerge is far from clear. This is an additional risk that must be faced in placing investments in such areas.

(c) Other areas of the world, notably Central Europe and the Far East, are now either behind the Iron Curtain or dangerously close to it and are no longer possibilities for foreign investment.

7. In its conclusions, the Committee makes several comments worthy of repetition.

. . . It is perhaps paradoxical but nevertheless true that one of the greatest inducements that can be offered for the attraction of new capital and the voluntary retention of capital already established is the absence or removal of all restrictions on withdrawal. . . . One deterrent feature that arises out of nearly all the problems discussed in this report is the cumulative labour, expense and loss of time involved in complying with regulations and seeking interpretations thereof, and completing complex forms, in obtaining permits and visas, and in calculating and filing complicated tax returns.

However, as a final conclusion the Committee states

. . . Despite the domestic demands for Canadian capital there appears to be a sizeable volume of capital seeking outlets overseas for specialized direct investment purposes, and the impression is gained that any reasonable relaxation of existing obstacles and restrictions would be sufficient to encourage a further outward flow.

Thus although attracting capital from countries such as Canada will not be easy, it is by no means impossible. However, it will probably be easiest to attract capital into fields in which Canadian enterprise is already active (such as mining, pulp and paper,

[11] *Ibid.*, pp. 41, 64, 66.

chemicals, agricultural machinery), and some improvement in labor and security conditions, as well as generous regulations, may prove necessary.

Increasing the flow of private capital to underdeveloped countries will probably require a recasting of economic policies in both underdeveloped and advanced countries. Professor Gunnar Myrdal has suggested that ways should be found of inducing the international capital market itself to play its proper role in channeling capital from countries where it is relatively abundant to those where it is scarce. He points out that financial institutions are no longer permitted to pursue shortsighted and selfish profit-maximizing policies so far as their domestic operations are concerned. On the contrary, they have been compelled to serve the interests of national policy, including improvements in income distribution, maintenance of full employment without inflation, and the like. The problem now, Myrdal argues, is to make these institutions play a similar role internationally, promoting the aims of agreed international policy.

To the present writer two things seem essential to any such policy. First, capital must be provided in bigger lumps than private organizations have hitherto found feasible. As shown earlier, in underdeveloped countries it often happens that each of a series of one hundred $1,000,000 loans would be rejected on banking principles, whereas a single investment of $100 million may be very worthwhile indeed. Some means must be found to persuade private institutions to make loans of this order.

Institutional rearrangements would be necessary on the marketing side as well. The major benefits derived from such large-scale investments are often in the form of "external economies," rather than direct returns through sale of the immediate product. Consequently, if such large units of investment are to be made attractive to private enterprise, methods must be found to permit either the borrower or the lender to cash in on the external economies as well as on the direct returns. These two requirements probably involve collective action by groups of financial institutions, and we may need to recast our thinking about the merits and demerits of "combination" in the field of finance.

The problem of inducing a larger volume of international capital movements, however, is not merely one of increasing the *supply* of international capital; in some of the countries that need it most, it is also a matter of increasing the *demand*. Nationalist revolutions and the recent emergence from colonialism, especially in the neutralist countries that count most in this context, have left an aftermath of suspicion of foreign enterprise. In some of these countries there is a firm resolve not to allow "foreign-monopoly-capitalist-imperialists" to gain access to the country's "rich natural resources." Yet as we have seen above, direct investment in resource development is often the most attractive form of investment to foreigners.

One solution to this dilemma is the "management contract." Where there is a large domestic market for an existing product, a contract can sometimes be arranged to set up a national company, with management hired from a foreign company producing the product. The new national company is granted licenses to import from the foreign "managing" concern in certain amounts and for certain periods. During this time the new company, with technical and managerial advice from the foreign firm, builds a local plant to produce the same commodity. The foreign firm might continue to operate the new plant until the host country can take over. In the case of exports for which there is no significant domestic market, the foreign managing firm must set up a plant immediately, which is not quite such an attractive proposition as a rule. However, the arrangement can involve handsome profits for the foreign concern even if they are disguised as management fees. Some management contracts between Latin American countries and foreign oil companies have actually proved more profitable to the companies than the usual "fifty-fifty" arrangement. At the same time, the arrangement has the great advantage that the *ownership* is national from start to finish. Tax concessions for investment in underdeveloped countries and special insurance arrangements as sketched earlier in this chapter might also help to promote a flow of capital to underdeveloped countries.

26 Foreign Aid

Even with the most liberal policies toward foreign investors in both lending and borrowing countries, the flow of private capital from advanced to underdeveloped countries is not likely by itself to fill the gap between capital requirements and potential domestic investment. Some role—and probably a substantial one—will remain for foreign aid. In order to assess the need for new policies and new institutions in the field of foreign aid, we shall first appraise existing foreign aid programs.

The International Monetary Fund and the International Bank for Reconstruction and Development

In July, 1944, representatives of forty-four nations assembled at Bretton Woods, New Hampshire, and after three weeks of discussion, agreed on the Articles for the International Monetary Fund and the International Bank for Reconstruction and Development. Ten years later, when the delegates of these two organizations met in Washington for their annual conference, the membership had increased to more than fifty countries, including a good many of those considered "underdeveloped." By that time, the Bank had been in actual operation for more than eight years, the Fund for more than seven. At this tenth anniversary meeting, however, the representatives of underdeveloped countries expressed dissatisfaction with the contribution the two institutions had made to solution of their problems. The attitude with respect to the Fund was typified by some remarks of Dr. Sjafruddin, Governor of the Bank Indonesia. Dr. Sjafruddin pointed to the peculiar problems of underdeveloped areas, and argued that they need special treatment: [1]

> The large deficits in our balance of payments resulted *inter alia* in considerable dollar transfers to the Netherlands in settlement of Indonesia's transactions with EPU countries. Indonesia's gold and dollar reserves have continued to fall rapidly.
>
> These facts have led to the introduction in my country of measures which undoubtedly diverge strongly from the measures recommended by the Fund in the sphere of economic and monetary policy. The balance of payments difficulties, for instance, necessitated the maintenance of a rigorous foreign exchange control system, and the introduction of restrictive measures in the realms of both goods and services. Unfortunately, it doesn't look as though appreciable relaxations can be introduced within a short time.
>
> . . . But this conviction must logically lead to a realization that the Fund should establish rules and pursue policies especially aimed at the achievement of the Fund's purposes with regard to the underdeveloped countries. Questions such as those referring to the transitional period, in which a member may free itself from exchange and trade restrictions and assume the responsibilities as laid down in Section 2 of Article VIII, and the availability of the Fund's resources to member countries, should be interpreted in a more liberal manner with regard to underdeveloped countries than would be the case for countries in a more favoured position. The Fund should dare to take risks in extending a helping hand to underdeveloped countries.
>
> The dream of convertibility may, for many developed countries, be realized tomorrow. This may lead to a more stringent policy of the Fund in the observance of its rules and regulations before these rules and regulations have been adapted to the special needs and problems of the underdeveloped countries. For most of them there is still no room for a convertibility dream, in a delightful Washington Indian Summer atmosphere, or, to stay within the picture evoked before us by our Chairman, most of us underdeveloped countries have still no water to swim in, struggling as we are for a mere glass of water.
>
> I hope not to be misunderstood. What I am pleading for on behalf of the underdeveloped countries is not a privilege from the Fund but a fair treatment, which is not always identical with equal treatment. Aid is good for those who can get it. Trade is good for those who are in a strong bargaining position. But the only thing which underdeveloped countries request is a fair treatment, a fair share of the world's

[1] From the statement by the Hon. Sjafruddin Prawiranegara, Governor for Indonesia, at the discussion of the Fund's Annual Report, September 27, 1954. (Press Release No. 41.)

income, based on a good understanding of our needs, not from the viewpoint of bare commercialism, but from that of human idealism. This may not be quite in line with the ideas of our founding fathers, something of which I am not quite sure, but certainly quite in line with the ideas of our Father who created us.

The attitude of delegates from underdeveloped countries toward the Bank was well expressed by Mr. Cuaderno, Governor for the Philippines: [2]

. . . Economic conditions in many countries during the past year have also been encouraging.

But, as was pointed out in the Fund report, there were exceptions to this over-all improvement, and the exceptions occurred in the case of the underdeveloped areas of the world, Asia and Latin America. These regions have suffered by the recession in the export prices of raw materials, and their exports of only a few such raw materials, which are subject to violent fluctuations in the world market; in a word, their basic trouble is that they are underdeveloped.

It was also observed by Mr. Black in his address of September 25th that advances in these countries have been uneven, and harder to observe, which suggests that there are difficulties in their situation.

Distinguished Governors of underdeveloped countries have been unanimous, in their addresses during this meeting, in expressing their concern over the lack of means to speed up the pace of economic development in them. Conditions there are now reaching the point of economic and political crisis and psychological disillusionment. The seriousness of the matter has been recognized in an editorial in a leading periodical in this city, which appeared even while we were holding our deliberations, on "How to Save Asia."

Four years ago, at the Paris meeting in 1950, I took occasion to urge the Bank, since the other areas of the world had already received ample aid from it, to give due consideration to the needs of Asia and the Far East. At that time I warned: "The need of the Far East for such a program is great and merits increased attention from the Bank. . . . Time is of the essence and the time is now."

If, however, there is no disposition on the part of the influential members of the Bank to do this, then I believe that they should give their support to the desire of the underdeveloped countries to establish institutions which would enable them to accelerate their ecenomic development. I refer to the proposed U.N. agencies already alluded to by several of the distinguished Governors here, namely, the Special Fund for Economic Development and the International Finance Corporation. If the need for such agencies was great in 1950, it is critical

[2] Statement at the closing session, ninth annual meeting, International Monetary Fund and International Bank for Reconstruction and Development, Washington, D.C., September 29, 1954. See *Guideposts to Economic Stability and Progress* (Manila, 1955), pp. 57–59.

now, and the free world can ignore it only at the risk of its own survival. I would urge, therefore, the fullest support of all member countries for the formation of these agencies.

The records of the Bank and Fund provide some evidence that the complaints of the delegates from underdeveloped countries were justified. As may be seen from Table 26-1, it is not the underdeveloped countries that have drawn most heavily on the resources of the Fund. Indeed, up to April 30, 1954, a good many of the underdeveloped countries had made net contributions to the resources of the Fund. Brazil, India, and Japan were the only underdeveloped countries which made substantial net withdrawals from the Fund, and the assistance provided to these countries was a small fraction of the total, and small relative to the assistance to such advanced countries as the United Kingdom and France.

The operations of the Bank are summarized in Table 26-2. Of the total loans outstanding on June 30, 1954, only about 12.5 per cent had gone to Asia and the Middle East, and a bit over 10 per cent to Africa. For both areas, electric power and transport constituted the purpose for the bulk of the loans. Latin America accounted for nearly one-quarter of the loans outstanding, but these went mainly to such relatively highly developed Latin American countries as Brazil and Chile.

However, the Bretton Woods organizations were not set up with the primary aim of assisting in the development of underdeveloped areas. The chief purpose of the Fund is "To promote exchange stability, to maintain orderly exchange arrangements among members, and to avoid competitive exchange depreciation." The purpose of the Bank includes assistance in developing less developed countries, but at the time of Bretton Woods, the reconstruction of war-devastated areas was uppermost in the minds of the delegates: [3]

(i) To assist in the reconstruction and development of territories of members by facilitating the investment of capital for productive purposes, including the restoration of economies destroyed or disrupted by war, the reconversion of productive facilities to peacetime needs and the encouragement of the development of productive facilities and resources in less developed countries.

(ii) To promote private foreign investment by means of guarantees or participations in loans and other investments made by pri-

[3] "Articles of Agreement of the International Bank for Reconstruction and Development," in *The International Bank for Reconstruction and Development, 1946–1953* (Baltimore, 1954), p. 237.

TABLE 26-1.

Summary of IMF Transactions, beginning of Operations to April 30, 1956 *

(In millions of dollars)

Countries	Currency purchased by member against own currency (1)	Member's currency sold by Fund to other members for their currency or gold (2)	Member's currency repurchased by member with convertible currency or gold (3)	Withdrawing member's offset (4)	Member's currency used for repurchases by other members (5)	Effect of operations on Fund's currency holdings (columns 2 and 6 minus 3, 4, 5) (6)	Fund's currency holdings on April 30, 1956, expressed as percentage of quota (7)
North America:							
Canada	...	...	...	...	...	...	75
United States	...	1,035.2	...	...	789.5	−245.7	65
Total	...	1,035.2	...	...	789.5	−245.7	...
Latin America:							
Brazil	168.5	...	103.0	...	...	65.5	119
Other	96.4	...	63.5	...	...	32.8	...
Total	264.9	...	166.5	...	...	98.3	...
Europe:							
United Kingdom	300.0	191.7	112.0	...	...	−3.7	82
France	125.0	...	147.9	...	...	−22.9	75
Other	152.7	15.8	193.1	2.4 †	...	−58.6	...
Total	577.7	207.5	453.0	2.4	...	−85.2	...
Asia:							
India	100.0	...	99.9	...	...	0.0	93
Indonesia	15.0	...	...	...	...	15.0	100
Japan	124.0	...	124.0	...	...	0.0	75
Philippines	15.0	...	...	...	...	15.0	175
Other	76.2	...	44.0	...	...	32.2	...
Total	330.2	...	267.9	...	...	62.2	...
Australia	50.0	...	50.0	...	...	0.0	96
Africa (Total)	13.6	...	20.5	...	...	−6.9	...
Grand total	1,236.4	1,242.6 ‡	957.9 §	2.4	789.5	−177.3	...

* Totals may not equal sum of items because of rounding.

† The settlement with Czechoslovakia involved an offset of $2.04 million in respect of Czechoslovakia's drawing of $6 million. The first installment paid by Czechoslovakia under the settlement increased the offset to $2.37 million.

‡ $1,236.4 million sold for currency and $6.2 million for gold.

§ $789.5 million repurchased with convertible currency and $168.4 million with gold.

SOURCE: International Monetary Fund, *Annual Report, 1956* (Washington, D.C., 1956), p.136.

TABLE 26-2.

IBRD Loans Classified by Purposes and Area, June 30, 1954, and June 30, 1956

(In millions of United States dollars, net of cancellations and refundings)

Purpose and type of supplies financed	Total		Area									
			Asia and Middle East		Africa		Australasia		Europe		Western Hemisphere	
	1954	1956	1954	1956	1954	1956	1954	1956	1954	1956	1954	1956
Grand total	1,874	2,667	232	439	199	347	204	259	782	969	457	653
Reconstruction loans: France, The Netherlands, Denmark, Luxembourg	497	497	.....	.....	.....	.....	.....	.....	497	497	.....	.....
Development loans:												
Total	1,377	2,170	232	439	199	347	204	259	285	472	457	653
Electric power	509	789	63	136	88	178	33	33	35	130	290	312
Transport	397	656	86	128	71	125	74	97	63	59	103	247
Communications	26	26	2	.....	.....	2	.....	.....	.....	.....	24	24
Agriculture and forestry	167	228	47	41	.....	.....	71	89	29	51	20	47
Industry	168	331	32	134	.....	2	26	40	90	132	20	23
General development	110	140	2	.....	40	40	.....	.....	68	100	.....	.....

SOURCE: International Bank for Reconstruction and Development, *Ninth Annual Report, 1953–1954* (Washington, D.C., 1954), p. 12; *Eleventh Annual Report, 1955–1956* (Washington, D.C., 1956), p. 58.

vate investors; and when private capital is not available on reasonable terms, to supplement private investment by providing on suitable conditions, finance for productive purposes out of its own capital, funds raised by it and its other resources.

Thus although the Bank and Fund have not done very much to solve the financial problems of underdeveloped countries, it is perhaps a little unfair to criticize them on this score; they were not set up to do so.

To what extent, then, is the claim of underdeveloped countries for special treatment justified? Do the underdeveloped countries really require special policies with respect to foreign trade, foreign exchange, and foreign investment, which differentiate them from the advanced countries? Are new institutions needed to deal with the peculiar needs of underdeveloped countries?

To some degree, the claim of underdeveloped countries for special treatment is indeed warranted. First of all, the link between foreign and domestic policy is, if anything, even stronger in underdeveloped than in advanced countries. Foreign trade is a large share of the economic activity of many of them, and some depend on their exports for the maintenance of their current standards of living, low as those are. Not only is the ratio of exports to national income high, but the secondary and tertiary effects of fluctuations in export income are marked. Moreover, exports are often very narrowly based. World market conditions for rubber in Indonesia, petroleum in Venezuela, coffee in Brazil or Ethiopia are the major determinant of the level of economic activity in the monetary sector of these countries.

Since these major exports are mainly raw materials and foodstuffs, they have been subject to extraordinarily violent fluctuations in both price and volume. Indeed, unlike most advanced countries, in many underdeveloped countries the volume, terms, and balance of trade tend to move together.

In the course of world economic fluctuations, prices of manufactured goods have proved more stable than prices of raw materials and foodstuffs. Accordingly, countries whose exports consist mainly of manufactured goods, and whose imports consist mainly of raw materials and foodstuffs, enjoy a kind of "built-in stabilizer" in their foreign trade. An increase in exports may be accompanied by a decline in the export surplus, since imports continue to rise with rising income levels, and prices of imports go up more than prices of exports. The reverse is true when exports fall off. Even more certain is that the *terms* of trade will vary inversely with its volume. When exports decline, the number of man-hours of work in export industries required to finance a given volume of imports also falls, since import prices drop more than export prices. The improvement in the terms of trade during the Great Depression, for example, was one of the reasons for the relative stability of real income in the United Kingdom during the downswing of 1929 to 1933.

In underdeveloped countries, however, the volume and value of trade, the export surplus, and the terms of trade all move together. When exports collapse, the export surplus also falls (or the import surplus increases), because of the tendency for imports to lag behind exports, and because import prices fall more than export prices. For the same reason, the *terms* of trade also decline when exports fall off. The number of man-hours that must be devoted to producing exports in order to finance imports, increases during a downswing. In some of the underdeveloped countries, the marginal propensity to import (increase in imports accompanying an increase in income) is very high, and an initial rise in income due to improvement in exports may be rapidly dissipated in increased imports.

In arid zone countries, the volume of foreign trade may be quite unrelated to world market conditions. In a year of drought, exports fall off because the export products are simply not available; yet imports must be increased, to maintain food supplies above starvation levels.

Thus foreign trade and foreign exchange policy of underdeveloped countries must also be tailor-made, and the governments of these countries are right to question whether the usual norms can be applied to their foreign trade and foreign exchange policy.

There is some evidence that the Bank has heeded the demands for greater attention to the special problems of the truly underdeveloped countries. Its pattern of new lending during the fiscal year 1956 was quite different from the pattern up to the end of fiscal year 1954. As stated in the Bank's Report for 1955–56: [4]

> There were a number of notable features in the past year's lending operations. One was the increased activity of the Bank in Asia, where lending totaled $166 million (out of total new lending amounting to $396 million). Another was the size of projects assisted: the Kariba power loan of $80 million was the largest yet made for a single project by the Bank and also the largest loan in Africa; the Tata Iron and

[4] International Bank for Reconstruction and Development, *Eleventh Annual Report, 1955–1956*, p. 7.

Steel loan of $75 million was the largest yet made for industry and also the largest for any purpose in Asia.

Thus in fiscal 1956 about 45 per cent of new loans went to Asia (including the Middle East). Nearly 30 per cent more, $115.2 million, went to Africa, and nearly 20 per cent, $75.1 million, to Latin America. Moreover, the Latin American loans in that year went entirely to the smaller and less developed countries of the region.

The shift in pattern of new lending is too recent, of course, to alter very much the distribution of total loans made in the course of the Bank's entire operation since 1947. At the end of fiscal 1956, total loans made amounted to $2.72 billion. Of this amount a total of $440 million, 16 per cent, had gone to Asia; $347 million, 13 per cent, to Africa; $653 million, 24 per cent to Latin America. About two-thirds of the Latin American loans went to Brazil, Colombia, and Mexico. No underdeveloped country has yet received assistance on the same scale as Australia or France.

The International Finance Corporation

The IFC came into existence as a branch of the Bank on July 20, 1956. On that date the required thirty members had joined the organization and subscribed a total of $78,366,000 to the capital of the new agency, somewhat more than the minimum of $75 million laid down in its statutes. Some $50 million of this amount came from the United States and the United Kingdom. Thirteen of the members are Latin American, eight European, seven from Asia and the Middle East.

The purpose of the IFC is "to promote the growth of productive private enterprise, particularly in less developed countries." [5]

The IFC is empowered to sell its own obligations and its portfolio securities in private capital markets to raise additional funds. It is not expected that the IFC will provide equity financing, although it might hold debentures convertible into stock or securities paying interest only if earned.

The Special Fund for Economic Development

Useful as the IFC may be, it is quite clear that it will not fill the gap between capital requirements for development of underdeveloped countries and the amounts that these countries can

[5] *Ibid.*, p. 27.

be expected to provide themselves. Many of these countries have supported a proposal to create a new UN agency, the Special United Nations Fund for Economic Development (SUNFED), to make "soft" loans and grants. As the *London Economist* puts it, "The backward countries' demand for SUNFED will not be silenced by the creation of the IFC." [6] Neither the quantity nor the quality of assistance added to the total by the IFC alone is adequate for meeting the needs.

The proposal for SUNFED is also modest in terms of quantity—$250 million—but it comes closer to meeting the bill in terms of quality. For SUNFED would provide loans of a non-profitable nature, or make outright grants, as the situation demanded. The proposal has a long history, going back to a resolution of the Economic and Employment Commission in 1946. A report submitted in 1947 by the Subcommission on Economic Development reflected the view of underdeveloped countries that they should obtain loans under more flexible conditions than those of the IBRD. A concrete proposal for a new fund came from V. K. R. V. Rao in 1949, as Chairman of the Subcommission on Economic Development. In 1951, the experts' report, *Measures for the Economic Development of Underdeveloped Countries*, recommended the establishment of an International Development Authority, with distribution of grants-in-aid as one of its functions. In December, 1953, upon a recommendation of the Economic and Social Council, the General Assembly passed Resolution 724 A(VIII) stating that the members were prepared to ask their nations to contribute to an international fund for development of underdeveloped areas. In the subsequent discussion of this resolution, the fund became known as the "Special Fund for Economic Development."

A questionnaire submitted to member governments in 1954 regarding their attitude toward SUNFED brought forty replies, none of which expressed disapproval in principle. Different views were expressed on such details as whether the Special Fund should seek a fully paid-up capital fund or annual contributions; whether contributions should be voluntary or assessed; whether any private contributions should be deductible for taxable income; whether contributions should be convertible; whether the proposed initial capital of $250 million was adequate—here views ranged from "inadequate" (an underdeveloped country) to "very high" (an advanced one)—and the like.

These differences of opinion are not serious, except those per-

[6] "Dollars for Development," *The Economist*, November 20, 1954, p. 654.

taining to the size of the Fund, which is quite clearly inadequate for the task proposed for it. More serious is the cool reception given to the proposal by the countries who might be expected to contribute most to it: the United States, Canada, and the United Kingdom, and the lukewarm reception from such other advanced countries as France, Sweden, Switzerland, and New Zealand. None of these countries expresses willingness to contribute until substantial progress has been made with disarmament. It is clear, therefore, that a change of heart on the part of these governments will be necessary before SUNFED can materialize, even on the modest scale proposed for its initial operations. Meanwhile, the UN Special Fund has been established as a compromise solution. Its initial resources are only $26 million, and it has decided to use them for large-scale surveys of a sort that will generate future investment rather than for capital assistance.

Bilateral Capital Assistance

In addition to the international agencies discussed in the previous section, there are several programs of bilateral capital assistance to underdeveloped areas. The United States has provided most of this bilateral assistance through a series of government agencies of which the most recent is the International Cooperation Administration. Australia, Canada, New Zealand, and the United Kingdom have provided useful amounts of capital assistance through the Colombo Plan organization; France, Sweden, and Switzerland have also undertaken modest bilateral programs, mostly in the form of technical assistance. In addition, Belgium, Holland, France, and the United Kingdom have financed development projects in their own colonies. These programs cannot be considered in detail here; we shall confine our discussion to the American aid program, which is the biggest, and to the United Kingdom's Colonial Development Corporation, which is perhaps the major case of a postwar organization set up specifically to finance economic development of dependent territories.

American Loans and Grants

From the end of the war to the end of fiscal 1956, net grants and loans from the United States reached a total of $56.92 billion (see Table 26-3). However, $17.81 billion of this sum was for military grants. To the degree that such grants cover local currency expenditures for military purposes, as well as imports of military equipment, they improve the balance of payments of the recipient country and so may assist economic development. They may also accelerate economic development if they finance from abroad military programs that would have been undertaken in any case. On the other hand, if they induce underdeveloped countries to embark on defense programs more ambitious than they would otherwise have considered, such grants may retard economic development while contributing to

TABLE 26-3.

Distribution of United States Government Foreign Grants and Credits *
(In millions of dollars)

	Postwar period	Before Korean invasion	After Korean invasion	July 1, 1955–June 30, 1956
Total	56,918	26,347	30,571	5,051
Military	17,809	1,438	16,371	3,044
Non-military:	39,108	24,909	14,199	2,077
Europe	26,115	18,996	7,119	441
Japan	2,588	1,973	615	−11 †
Canada	−10 †	1	−11 †	−12 †
Main defense support countries:	6,273	2,657	3,616	897
China (Taiwan)	1,321	819	502	113
Greece	1,362	776	586	66
Indochina	563	....	563	256
Korea	1,483	367	1,116	254
Pakistan	258	....	258	123
Philippines	846	620	226	26
Turkey	440	75	365	59
All other:	4,140	1,281	2,857	669
India	444	12	432	101
Other Near East, Southeast Asia, and Africa	1,137	−3 †	1,140	164
Other Far East	372	184	187	145
American Republics	1,154	356	798	188
International and unspecified	1,033	732	300	71

* Includes sale of agricultural products for local currencies.
† Net repayments.
SOURCE: The American Assembly, *International Stability and Progress* (New York, 1957), p. 62; prepared by staff of Committee for Economic Development, January, 1957.

security. About $1 billion of this total represents contributions to international agencies, leaving some $38 billion as clear-cut bilateral capital assistance for economic reconstruction and development.

Thirty-eight billion dollars is a substantial sum; but most of this amount consists of Marshall Plan aid to Europe. Over $26 billion of this total went to Western Europe, mainly for reconstruction purposes. This region includes some countries, such as Greece, Italy, Turkey, and Yugoslavia, that could properly be considered underdeveloped; but these countries together received less than $5 billion, or less than 5 per cent of the total aid to Western countries, and of this fraction the largest share went to Italy, whose claim to be "underdeveloped" is least strong among countries in this group. The biggest sums went to such advanced countries as the United Kingdom, France, and Western Germany.[7] The Near East and Africa received less than 1.5 per cent of the total, and some three-fifths of this went to Israel, the country with the highest per capita income in the region. Asia and the Pacific were accorded some 13 per cent of the total, but over half of this portion went to Japan and Formosa; apparently defense considerations guided the distribution of funds in this region. Latin America obtained less than 2 per cent of the total, of which half went to Brazil and Mexico—one relatively advanced country and one neighbor. Thus although the United States has spent considerable sums on *foreign aid*, it has spent rather little on *economic development of underdeveloped areas.*

Among agencies making loans for reconstruction and development, the United States Export-Import Bank has operated on much the biggest scale. In the allocation of its loans, however, the Eximbank has followed exactly the "to him who hath shall be given" pattern revealed in American grants and loans as a whole. Much the biggest share of total loans has gone to the relatively advanced countries in Western Europe. Latin America has received a beggar's portion in comparison, and even within Latin America it has been the relatively prosperous countries that have benefited most from Eximbank activities. The Middle and Far East, most in need of capital assistance, have received least of it from the Eximbank (see Table 26-4).

Since the fiscal year 1954, American foreign aid expenditures have shown a more or less continuous shift away from Europe and toward more obviously underdeveloped countries. In fiscal

[7] A small fraction of aid to The Netherlands was used for the Netherlands East Indies.

TABLE 26-4.

Export-Import Bank Operations, by Countries and Areas, June 30, 1954, and June 30, 1956
(In thousands of dollars)

Country	*Net credits authorized* *		*Outstanding loans*	
	1954	1956	1954	1956
Latin America:				
Argentina	101,675	286,282	96,148	76,143
Bolivia	37,583	47,031	33,747	34,678
Brazil	653,839	986,753	426,420	442,615
Chile	124,560	158,329	79,238	65,258
Colombia	72,139	103,743	33,341	24,126
Costa Rica	6,985	23,053	6,039	10,025
Cuba	24,000	116,422	12,000	12,000
Dominican Republic	.....	3,300	.....	.....
Ecuador	34,271	40,390	16,805	25,539
Guatemala	.....	2,620	.....	571
Haiti	19,000	40,350	9,120	26,023
Honduras	.....	2,766	.....	.....
Mexico	230,239	380,945	114,595	119,337
Nicaragua	2,600	6,158	530	420
Panama	4,000	8,530	3,560	1,006
Paraguay	3,000	17,283	1,292	515
Peru	22,894	163,653	15,662	14,815
Salvador	1,476	1,825	303	.....
Uruguay	19,454	49,259	11,349	8,206
Venezuela	14,200	65,820	7,168	7,953
Various	8,575	128,791	532	38
Total Latin America	1,380,490	2,633,303	867,849	869,269
Asia:				
Afghanistan	39,500	39,500	19,900	28,400
China	34,651	221,737	32,537	31,639
India	.....	16,270	.....	.....
Indonesia	100,000	200,000	53,000	70,632
Iran	.....	80,766	.....	359
Iraq	.....	310	.....	.....
Israel	134,998	135,000	122,636	119,807
Japan	139,850	360,058	85,070	59,767
Philippine Islands	25,001	118,615	10,027	20,513
Saudi Arabia	14,768	105	8,768	6,085
Syria	.....	49,000	.....	50
Thailand	1,040	3,607	882	1,219
Turkey	28,170	53,206	6,403	5,361
Total Asia	517,978	1,278,174	339,223	343,832

1956, total expenditures under the ICA program (as it had then become) amounted to $1.63 billion. Of this amount $794 million went to the Far East, 48 per cent of the total. Another $370 million went to South Asia and the Near East, $54 million to Latin America, and $11.3 million to Africa. Only $279 million was spent in Europe, as compared to $830 million in fiscal 1954 and $1.65 billion in fiscal 1952.

However, this picture is not as favorable as it may look at first glance. The *total* amount is only half the estimated absorptive capacity of the underdeveloped countries. Moreover, the great bulk of the aid funds went to defense support, not to straightforward development assistance. In terms of obligations, the total for the fiscal year 1956 was $1.47 billion; of this $1.17 billion was for defense support; only $113 million was for development assistance, whereas $127 million was for technical co-operation.

The concentration on defense support affected the distribution of funds *within* regions. For example, of the $763 million obligated to the Far East, $594 million went to Korea, Vietnam, and Taiwan, the countries in which the United States is providing the heaviest military aid. Less than $40 million was available to the Far East for development assistance and technical co-operation, and most of that was for technical assistance. Similarly, in the Near East, Africa, and South Asia region the biggest allotments went to Turkey, Pakistan, and Iran. These three countries accounted for some two-thirds of total obligations.[8]

The 1957 program showed only slight improvement in any of these respects. Total appropriations were $3.8 billion, but of this amount $2.01 billion was for military assistance to be administered by the Department of Defense. Another $1.16 billion was for defense support, leaving $250 million, 7 per cent of the total, for development assistance, and $152 million, 4 per cent of the total, for technical co-operation. The remaining $100 million represented the President's emergency fund. Total ICA non-military obligations for the fiscal year 1957 reached only $1.66 billion, and of this amount $1.14 billion was for defense support. Another $145.7 million was obligated for technical co-operation, leaving

[8] All figures from International Cooperation Administration, *Operations Report*, as of June 30, 1956, September 30, 1956, and December 31, 1957.

---

* These represent active credits as of June 30, 1954, and June 30, 1956, and were authorized at various times since the Export-Import Bank began operations.

SOURCE: Export-Import Bank, *Annual Reports* for 1954 and 1956 (Washington, D.C., 1954 and 1956).

only $206.4 million for capital assistance to economic development. Most of the capital assistance did, however, go to the Far East, Near East, South Asia, and Africa, with India receiving the biggest single amount. For the fiscal year 1958 (to the end of June, 1958) total non-military obligations were down to $1.47 billion, of which $777.7 million was for defense support and $148 million for technical co-operation. The capital assistance program was transferred to the new Development Loan Fund, which had approved loans of only $228 million. The geographical distribution was much the same as in the previous year.

Of course, some of the aid classified as "defense support" contributes to economic development, just as some military aid has the effect of retarding economic growth. It is not easy to distinguish with precision those loans and grants which encourage economic development from those which discourage it or leave it unaffected. Table 26-3 presents one effort to make such a distinction by separating "main defense support countries" from all other.

The Colonial Development Corporation

Apart from release of blocked sterling balances accumulated during the war by Commonwealth countries (notably India and Pakistan), as a contribution to the Colombo Plan, the United Kingdom has concentrated its postwar assistance to underdeveloped countries in its own colonies, mainly through the Colonial Development Corporation. This agency was established in 1948 and "charged with the duty of securing the investigation, formulation and carrying out of projects for developing resources of colonial territories with a view to expansion of production therein of foodstuffs and raw materials, or for other agricultural, industrial or trade development therein." The initial capital of £100 million ($280 million) might seem small in comparison to the estimates of capital requirements made above, but in practice it has proved that other factors than loan capital were the critical bottlenecks in development of British colonies. As pointed out by one observer,[9] loan funds are of little use unless materials, technicians, and managerial skills are available to combine with them, and rearmament at home reduced the supply of these strategic resources to the colonies. In addition, the armament-induced prosperity at home provided outlets for

[9] The Rt. Hon. L. John Edwards, O.B.E., M.P., "CDC and Economic Development," *Colonial Development*, Summer, 1954.

private investment more attractive than investment in the colonies.

Perhaps even more important, however, were the restrictions imposed on the character of the Corporation's lending activities, restrictions similar to those which have inhibited the International Bank for Reconstruction and Development. The Corporation is limited to operations that are in the aggregate self-liquidating over fairly short periods—not the sort of capital assistance the colonies most urgently need. As L. John Edwards points out, the problems faced by the colonies "require the expenditure of foundation capital which will bring little or no monetary return, many need highly expert technical and administrative personnel who may never yield a profit." [10]

Another more complex and more delicate question arises in connection with operations such as those of the CDC. In certain underdeveloped countries, particularly those which have recently emerged from colonial status, the whole issue of "colonialism" is one which still arouses strong passions. This issue shapes the attitude of these countries toward the political and economic development policies which the remaining imperial powers adopt for their dependent territories. Any suggestions by such advanced countries as the United Kingdom, France, Belgium, and The Netherlands that their ability to contribute to general programs of assistance to underdeveloped areas is limited by their obligations in their own colonies is likely to be received in "neutralist" countries as one more manifestation of "Western imperialism." Progress toward international harmony might be more rapid if the imperial powers contributed to an international development agency, which would consider the claims of dependent territories along with others.

Soviet Bloc Aid

Up to February, 1958, aid from the Sino-Soviet bloc to underdeveloped countries in Asia was on a small scale as compared to total aid from the United States, even when only Asian countries are considered (Table 26-5). However, the allocation of Sino-Soviet assistance was in sharp contrast to that from the United States. Whereas American aid has continued to flow mainly to countries that might be regarded as safely in the Western camp, Sino-Soviet aid has been used to woo the uncommitted neutralist countries. Neighboring Burma has been the chief beneficiary, although the $100 million loan to Indonesia will constitute larger-scale aid as it is put to use.

[10] *Ibid.*

TABLE 26-5.

Sino-Soviet Bloc Economic Aid to Free Countries of the Far East as of February 7, 1958

Recipient	Donor	Year offered	Amount promised, equivalent in millions of dollars	Interest rate (per cent)	Repayment period, years	Use and remarks
Burma	USSR	1956	30 *	None stated	20	Equipment and technical assistance for construction of technological institute, hotel, hospital, cultural-sports complex, permanent agricultural-industrial exhibition, theater, and conference hall. In form of "gifts" to be repaid by "gifts" of rice.
	USSR	1957	4.2–6.3	2.5	12	Credit for construction of two irrigation projects. Repayment in rice.
	USSR	1957	3.1	2.5	5	Credit for construction of agricultural implements factory. Repayment in rice.
	Communist China	1957	4.2	2.5	Unknown	Credit for construction of 40,000-spindle textile mill. Repayment in rice.
Estimated minimum total			41.5			

Cambodia . .	Communist China	1956	22.4	None	None	Grant aid. Shipments of Communist Chinese goods sold to pay local costs of agricultural development and social welfare projects and projected textile, cement, plywood, and paper plants.
Indonesia . . .	East Germany	1955	7.9	4.0	6	Credit for equipment and technical assistance for construction of sugar refinery. Repayment may be in goods.
	Czechoslovakia	1956	1.5	4.0	6	Credit for construction of tire factory. Repayment may be in goods.
	USSR	1956	100.0	2.5	12	Line of credit for surveys for road, inland waterways, and mineral (including petroleum) development; equipment and technical assistance for construction of industrial facilities, possibly including iron and steel plants. Repayment in goods, sterling, or other acceptable currencies. Agreement signed September, 1956, and formally approved by the Indonesian parliament in February, 1958.
Minimum total			109.4			
Estimated minimum grand total			173.3			

* Estimated.

SOURCE: U.S. Department of State, "Intelligence Report No. 7670," Washington, D.C., 1958.

During 1958 Soviet aid to India, not shown in the table, was a major part of the Communist bloc aid program. The projects for which Russian assistance has been promised include the Bhilai steel plant ($115 to $130 million), a steel machinery plant in Bihar ($56 million), a thermal power plant ($32 million), a coal mining machinery plant ($21 million), and development of the Korba coal field ($16 million).[11] It is interesting to note that this assistance is all directed toward accelerating India's industrial development.

The Over-all Picture

Tables 26-6 and 26-7 provide an over-all picture of aid given and received during the years 1954–56. (In these years Sino-Soviet aid was not important.) Three features stand out. First, the United States has been much the most important source of aid, not only in total amount, but for nearly every country listed. On this count as on so many others, Libya is exceptional; most of her aid in this period came from the United Kingdom. Second, for most countries the amount of aid received per capita has been very small. Third, the allocation of aid among countries bears little relationship to absorptive capacity. Israel, a special case, heads the list, and Libya, another special case, is next. Indonesia, with its great resource potential and desperate need for capital, stands at the bottom. India, with its elaborate planning organization, with one Five-Year Plan already behind it, with its excellent civil service, stable government, and vigorous Schumpeterian entrepreneurs, is next to the bottom. Israel gets large-scale aid because many individuals are interested in her success; Libya, because she is a UN baby and has 1,200 miles of coastline facing the "soft underbelly of Europe"; Korea, because of American military interest in the area. Hardly a country so far has received large-scale aid because it needed it and was able to use it effectively in a well-planned economic development program. The IBRD loans to Italy are the one obvious exception, although at time of writing it seemed likely that United States aid to India was about to be considerably increased.

Determinants of Absorptive Capacity

We have been using the term "absorptive capacity" in a common-sense fashion to mean the amount of technical and

[11] Cf. Wilfred Malenbaum, *East and West in India's Development* (Washington, D.C., 1959).

capital assistance that can be effectively used. The previous paragraph suggests some of the factors that influence absorptive capacity. If we are to use absorptive capacity as the major criterion for allocation of foreign aid, however, it would be reassuring to have a more precise definition of it and a clearer idea of what determines its size.

TABLE 26-6.

International Economic Aid to Underdeveloped Countries in Relation to Population and per Capita Gross National Product, 1954–1956

Country and per capita gross national product	*Aid received per capita (dollars)*
Group I, under $100 per capita:	
Burma	0.9
India	0.6
Indonesia	0.5
Pakistan	3.8
Thailand	2.0
Korea	31.4
Group II, $100–$200 per capita:	
Ceylon	2.1
Egypt	2.1
Libya	54.8
Paraguay	3.6
Group III, $200–$300 per capita:	
El Salvador	4.0
Mexico	2.7
Philippines	2.0
Group IV, more than $300 per capita:	
Israel	83.0

SOURCE: United Nations, *Statistical Yearbook*, 1957.

Had we not discovered in Part 4 that marginal analysis is of little use in understanding the process of economic development and prescribing policies to promote it, we could fall back on marginal productivity to define absorptive capacity: the amount of capital that can be absorbed without the marginal productivity of capital falling to zero, and the amount of technical assistance that can be used without the marginal productivity of this kind of skilled labor falling to zero. This definition will not do; the marginal productivity of capital might be zero, in the ordinary sense that additional investment financed by foreign aid results in no early increase in output, and yet the investment might start a

Table 26-7.

International Economic Aid to Underdeveloped Countries, 1954–56
(In millions of dollars)

Contributing country or agency	*Recipient countries*															
	Libya (1.1) *		El Salvador (2.2)		Mexico (29.7)		Brazil (58.5)		Burma (19.4)		Ceylon (8.6)		Nationalist China (8.9)		India (381.7)	
	Grants	Loans	Grants	Loans	Grants	Loans	Grants	Loans	Grants	Loans	Grants	Loans	Grants	Loans	Grants	Loans
Bilateral aid:																
France	2.4	...	...	...	...	...	...	...	...	...	...	...	...	...	...	...
Italy	1.5	...	...	...	...	...	...	...	...	...	...	...	...	...	...	...
Portugal	...	...	...	...	...	...	...	...	...	...	...	...	...	...	...	...
Spain	...	...	...	...	...	...	...	...	...	...	...	...	...	...	...	...
Netherlands	...	...	...	...	...	...	...	...	...	...	...	...	...	...	...	...
Australia	...	...	...	...	...	...	...	...	0.7	...	3.7	...	...	...	2.8	...
Canada	...	...	...	...	...	...	...	...	0.1	...	7.0	...	...	...	32.1	...
India	...	...	...	...	...	...	...	...	9.2	...	0.3	...	...	...	...	...
Japan	...	...	...	...	...	...	...	...	...	...	0.1	...	...	...	0.1	...
New Zealand	...	...	...	...	...	...	...	...	...	...	0.8	...	...	...	1.0	...
Norway	...	...	...	...	...	...	...	...	...	...	...	...	...	...	1.3	...
Sweden	...	...	...	...	...	...	...	...	...	...	...	...	...	...	...	...
United Kingdom	29.3	−1.1	...	...	...	...	...	...	...	...	...	...	...	...	1.2	−8.6
United States	25.8		3.0	−0.5	8.3	19.8	12.6	226.4	4.1	−1.1	0.2	...	201.3	15.1	179.5	20.0
Total	59.0	−1.1	3.0	−0.5	8.3	19.8	12.6	226.4	14.1	−1.1	12.1	...	201.3	15.1	218.0	11.4
Multilateral aid:																
UNTA	2.2	...	0.5	...	0.9	...	1.8	...	2.3	...	1.7	...	1.0	...	4.2	...
UNICEF	0.2	...	0.2	...	2.4	...	0.8	...	1.4	...	0.3	...	0.9	...	4.9	...
IBRD	...	...	...	5.6	...	49.4	...	51.1	...	...	...	3.6	...	...	...	6.7
Total	2.4		0.7	5.6	3.3	49.4	2.6	51.1	3.7		2.0	3.6	1.9		9.1	6.7
Grand total	61.4	−1.1	3.7	5.1	11.6	69.2	15.2	277.5	17.8	−1.1	14.1	3.6	203.2	15.1	227.1	18.1

Contributing country or agency	Recipient countries													
	Indonesia (81.9)		Korea (21.5)		Malaya (7.3)		Pakistan (82.4)		Philippines (21.8)		Thailand (20.3)		Vietnam (26.3)	
	Grants	Loans	Grants	Loans	Grants	Loans	Grants	Loans	Grants	Loans	Grants	Loans	Grants	Loans
Bilateral aid:														
France	...	...	...	...	...	...	...	...	...	...	...	...	10.0	...
Italy	...	...	...	...	...	...	...	...	...	...	...	...	...	...
Portugal	...	...	...	...	...	...	...	...	...	...	...	...	...	...
Spain	...	...	...	...	...	...	...	...	...	...	...	...	...	...
The Netherlands	...	14.7	...	...	...	...	...	...	...	...	...	...	...	...
Australia	2.2	...	...	...	...	...	9.6	...	...	...	...	...	0.7	...
Canada	0.4	...	0.7	...	0.2	...	23.3	...	...	...	...	...	0.1	...
India	0.1	...	...	...	...	...	...	...	...	...	...	...	...	...
Japan	...	...	...	...	...	...	...	...	...	...	...	...	...	...
New Zealand	0.8	...	...	...	...	...	2.7	...	...	...	...	...	...	...
Norway	...	...	1.7	...	...	...	...	...	...	...	...	...	...	...
Sweden	...	...	2.0	...	...	...	0.1	...	...	...	...	...	...	...
United Kingdom	...	...	...	...	11.2	4.7	1.5	11.8	...	...	...	...	...	...
United States	18.6	29.3	595.2		0.7		214.0	7.7	52.7	−11.7	33.1	−1.4	316.3	25.0
Total	22.1	14.6	599.6	...	12.1	4.7	251.2	19.5	52.7	−11.7	33.1	−1.4	327.1	25.0
Multilateral aid:														
UNTA	2.7	...	0.2	...	0.5	...	3.5	...	1.2	...	1.8	...	0.3	...
UNICEF	2.5	...	3.3	...	0.1	...	2.0	...	0.9	...	0.7	...	0.2	...
IBRD	...	...	...	...	...	...	...	33.2	...	...	...	6.4	...	...
Total †	5.2	...	77.8 †	...	0.6	...	5.5	33.2	2.1	...	2.5	6.4	0.5	...
Grand total	27.3	14.6	677.4	...	12.7	4.7	256.7	52.7	54.8	−11.7	35.6	5.0	327.6	25.0

* Figures in parenthesis, population in millions.

† Total of multilateral aid recorded includes $74.3 million given by the UN Korean Reconstruction Agency.

SOURCE: United Nations, *Statistical Yearbook*, 1957.

sequence of events that will result in considerably higher levels and rates of increase in income ten or twenty years hence, and thus be highly desirable. Exactly the same thing may be true of particular kinds of technical assistance. Advice given one year may be put into effect ten years later, when (for example) the young student who understood the advice has become Minister of Agriculture.[12]

A modification of the concept of marginal productivity to meet the needs of a development policy brings us closer to a useful and precise definition of absorptive capacity. We might say, for example, that it is the total amount of capital and technical assistance that a country can use in one year and still add to aggregate income during the period twenty to thirty years from now. (This aggregate, remember, will depend partly on the level of income reached in twenty years and partly on the rate of growth thereafter.) Such a definition presents two analytical and two practical problems. The first analytical problem relates to the choice of period for measuring the contribution to economic growth. We do not really know enough about the process of growth in particular countries to say exactly when the crucial period will be, the period when a country achieves self-sustained growth or fails to do so. No doubt the period will be different for each country. Close study of conditions in each country may help to pin down the crucial period; otherwise, the only solution to this problem is to widen the limits of the period to, say, five to forty years from now. The second theoretical problem is that the significance of a given aggregate will depend somewhat on how it is distributed through the period.

The first practical problem, to be sure, is to make any kind of forecast that far ahead. The second practical problem is that the *amount* of assistance which can be "absorbed" in this sense depends on the *form* in which it is offered. Capital assistance, of course, consists basically of foreign exchange which is in itself uniform. But the amount of capital assistance that can be absorbed may depend on the currency in which it is offered, on whether it is "tied" to the donor country or free for expenditure anywhere, and on the limitations imposed by the donor country on the use of capital. In the case of technical assistance this problem is much more acute. An expert on rodent control is clearly a very different sort of assistance from a financial adviser. Moreover, a

[12] The writer has had the experience of having recommendations put into effect six years after they were made, when the economic and political conditions made the time "ripe" for them in the eyes of the government leaders.

country may have more "capacity to absorb" one financial adviser than another; personality traits can make a great deal of difference in the impact of an adviser on the policies of an underdeveloped country. Even the country from which he comes makes a difference. Generally speaking, the capacity of underdeveloped countries to "absorb" additional technical assistance in the form of high-level advisers is greater if they are provided through the UN, Colombo Plan, or Ford Foundation and from such countries as Australia, Canada, New Zealand, Switzerland, and Sweden than if they are provided through the ICA. The fear of "new-style economic imperialism" from the United States and other Western powers is an important factor in many underdeveloped countries; hence an expert can be more effective if he is not an official of any government and if he comes from a relatively small country that never had and could not hope to have "imperialistic ambitions."

In short, it is not possible to estimate exactly the "absorptive capacity" of a particular country at a particular time. It is possible, however, to make reasonable "guesstimates" and to rank countries in order of their absorptive capacity. Among the things to look for as evidence that a country still has such capacity are the following:

1. Unutilized capacity of some kind to combine with additional capital.
2. Simple and obvious opportunities for improvements in technique.[13]
3. A well-construed development plan, plus the domestic financial resources for a large share of it.
4. Public and business administrators capable of executing projects in the plan expeditiously and efficiently.
5. A strong and united governmental leadership group with the support of the majority of the people.
6. A society that is already undergoing cultural change; hence is fluid and flexible.

[13] When technical assistance programs were first launched it was expected that many such opportunities would appear; the "expert" from the technologically superior country would go to the underdeveloped one, tell people what to do, and productivity would rise. Occasionally such obvious opportunities do appear. The expert on leather production in Libya was able to bring improvements in the methods of cutting and tanning hides in a matter of weeks after his arrival; better ways of cutting, sorting, grading, and scouring wool were introduced by the wool expert in a matter of months. Unfortunately, improvements of this kind do not transform an economy from an underdeveloped into a developing one.

7. A society in which substantial numbers of people already indicate willingness to shift from agricultural to industrial occupations.

8. An economy in which a movement toward more extensive and mechanized agriculture is already under way.[14]

9. A high level of literacy and an effective system of general education.

10. A "technology-minded" and "development-minded" populace.

Obviously, many of these indications of a high degree of absorptive capacity are not easy to express in quantitative terms; even if they were, a complex problem of "weighting" would remain. Nevertheless, on the basis of guides such as these, a team of experts with experience in the field could probably reach agreement on the relative scores of various applicants for foreign aid.

The M.I.T. Proposal

The Millikan-Rostow proposal, parts of which were reiterated in the M.I.T. Submission to the Special Senate Committee on Foreign Aid, prompted a good deal of discussion. Yet this proposal differs from others mainly in the depth and breadth of the research underlying it. Its major aspects—enlarged, liberalized, and long-term foreign aid as a strategic factor in American security—were included in other major presentations to the Senate Committee and in other publications. They have been stated subsequently by leading members of the Administration and by the President himself. The Millikan-Rostow proposal deserves particular attention because it reflects the distilled wisdom of several years of research on problems of developing underdeveloped areas by a

[14] Russia's ability to meet requests for aid in a hurry does not always redound to the benefit of the recipient country, especially when the recipient overestimates its own absorptive capacity. During Khrushchev's tour of India, an Indian official mentioned to him the need for farm machinery. Five weeks later Russian equipment suitable for the operation of a 30,000-acre farm began arriving at Indian ports, but no such farm existed. The Indian government hurriedly set up a farm at Suratgarh but the site has no water and will not be ready until the end of 1959. Some 5,000 acres have been sown, but some of the equipment does not fit the soil and 60 per cent of the machinery still stands idle.

The writer himself has seen tens of thousands of dollars worth of imported earth-moving equipment sinking gently into the mud 300 miles up the Barito River in the interior of Borneo. It could not be moved or it would disappear into the swamp altogether, and it had never been used for the drainage project for which it had been bought months earlier.

sizable team of social scientists, the members of which combine a scientific interest in problems of economic development and of United States foreign policy with experience in advising governments on development policy.

These are the main features of this proposal:

1. The foreign aid program must be substantially larger than anything yet undertaken. Indeed, only the absorptive capacity of the beneficiary country should limit the amount of aid granted.
2. Aid should be given without military or political strings.
3. The sole criterion for the granting of aid should be the presentation by the beneficiary country of a solid plan for economic development.
4. The program should guarantee continuity of aid over several years.
5. The administration of foreign aid should combine international and bilateral aspects. A new international agency, working in cooperation with the World Bank, should have the function of reviewing development plans and declaring them satisfactory or unsatisfactory as a basis for aid. This agency should have a small international secretariat. There should also be a Consultative Committee comprised of representatives of both donor and recipient governments, as under the present Colombo Plan organization. The actual capital assistance, however, can continue to be largely on a bilateral basis, as under the present American and Colombo Plan programs.

In the view of the present writer, technical assistance of an advisory nature should be provided internationally rather than bilaterally, to avoid the danger of a "boomerang" effect. Foreign experts (especially economists) might do three quite different jobs in an underdeveloped country: they might provide economic intelligence for their own governments; they might give economic advice to their chief of mission and to their national headquarters; and they might give advice to the host government. It is important to distinguish sharply between those experts who are doing the third job and those who are doing the other two; linking aid with advice may render both useless or worse from the viewpoint of the grantor countries. If they are closely linked, it is almost inevitable that experts in the field will become administrators of the capital assistance program, rather than true technical assistants to the government of the underdeveloped country. They may succumb to the temptation to use their research primarily as a basis for their own policy decisions and to use capital assistance as a club to persuade the host government to accept these policy decisions. The inevitable result is increased friction between the grantor country and the host country.

Loans or Grants?

Although proposals of the Millikan-Rostow type are gaining favor in the advanced countries, "budget-minded" leaders in those countries, particularly in the United States, tend to prefer loans to grants, feeling that no net loss of revenues over the long run is then involved. Against this view, others cite the unfortunate experience with reparations loans after World War I, when the recipients of the "reconstruction loans," particularly Germany, were more heavily indebted at the time of the Hoover moratorium in 1931 than they were at the time of the peace settlement. Critics of the loan approach also point to the bad record of United States loans to Latin American countries and to the friction and destruction of confidence that accompanies default. They prefer the less complicated approach of outright grants. People in underdeveloped areas who wish to retain a sense of independence, and are concerned with national pride, may prefer loans to gifts. Others, concerned with the burden of servicing loans, point to the extreme poverty of their countries as a barrier to the undertaking of foreign obligations and stress the need for outright grants.

The unhappy experience with reparation loans and with some American loans to Latin American countries, should not be regarded as an indication of the probable fate of loans to the now underdeveloped countries. Between the wars, American lending was unstable, combined as it was with fluctuations both in American national income and in American trade policy. If loans flow in a steady and increasing stream from the advanced to the underdeveloped countries, as United Kingdom lending moved during the nineteenth century, no problems of repayment need arise. In the early stages, the servicing of old debts was financed by new loans. If this process continues until underdeveloped countries have raised their outputs sufficiently to permit *net* repayment, loans need be little more burdensome than grants. If the loans are to be repaid in currencies of the lending countries, however, the advanced countries must follow a liberal policy with respect to imports from underdeveloped ones and must maintain full employment at home. They must avoid a collapse of national income that would greatly reduce imports and so make impossible the servicing of loans.

Some proponents of the loan approach also contend that a requirement to repay will compel the governments of recipient countries to plan more thoroughly and select projects more carefully than would a "giveaway" program. There is an element of truth in this contention, but if the Millikan-Rostow approach were adopted no country would receive either loans or grants unless it had completed a well-designed development plan, and aid would be available only for projects within such a plan. Moreover, the broad category of "underdeveloped countries" includes countries with widely varying degrees of development and with quite different balance of payments positions. The ability to meet ordinary international loan commitments varies accordingly. Restriction of aid to a "hard loan" approach would remove from candidacy for aid some of the countries that need it most.

Soft Loans?

Some politicians have sought a reconciliation of the arguments for and against restriction of aid to loans by making provision for "soft loans," that is, loans repayable in domestic currency. They believe that even a soft loan which must be repaid will encourage more caution in soliciting aid than a straightforward grant, yet it avoids the balance of payments problems inherent in hard currency loans. The latter part of the argument is incontestable; loans are easier to repay in local currency than in dollars. The former part of the argument is open to question. No country in which there is a government-controlled central bank can ever experience difficulty in raising domestic currency for any purpose, including the repayment of foreign loans. The psychological effect of a soft loan may be little different from that of a grant. True, excessive borrowing from the central bank may be inflationary, but whether it is so depends on how the local currency is ultimately used by the lender. If it is used for purposes for which the lending country would otherwise purchase local currency, such as costs of foreign missions, the effect may not be inflationary on balance, but the loan will be little easier to repay than a "hard" loan; repayment will mean a reduction of the influx of foreign exchange. If the result is reduced imports of consumers' goods, repayment may be inflationary as well. If the local currency is used to finance local expenses of additional development projects, in the manner of counterpart funds, the net effect of repayment by borrowing from the central bank will certainly be inflationary. If the borrowing government obtains local currency for repayment through taxation, and then uses it for further development spending, the result is not very inflationary, but neither will the re-lending of the local currency by the lending country add to total developmental investment. The result will be the same as if the loan were canceled altogether and the borrowing government raised the same amount of taxes for its own development program.

The main advantage of provision for repayment in local currency seems to be that the loan can then be administered so as to be virtually a grant, while meeting the objections to a "give-away" program from budget-minded people in the granting countries.

In any case the "hard loans, soft loans, or grants" question is not an either-or proposition. There is no reason why a foreign aid program should not include a judicious mixture of all three.

An International Investment Bank?

A simple way to increase the total resources for capital assistance would be to establish an International Investment Bank, perhaps as a branch of the IBRD. The function of such a bank would be to underwrite approved securities issued in underdeveloped countries, either by governments or by private undertakings. Having studied and appraised any particular issue, the bank would announce its readiness to buy unlimited amounts of it, in hard currencies, at par, at any time. This offer would guarantee stability of the price of the security in the international capital markets; and since the rates of interest offered would presumably run somewhat above the return on government bonds issued in the United States or Canada, the securities of underdeveloped countries would thus be made attractive to private investors the world over. In this fashion substantial amounts of private capital could be channeled into the development of underdeveloped countries.

Surplus Commodity Disposal

During 1956 and 1957 the surplus commodity disposal program became an increasingly important form of aid from the United States; and other countries with surpluses of foodstuffs and raw materials, such as Canada and Australia, were showing increasing interest in such programs. Under the usual form of American surplus disposal (under PL 480) the commodities are sold for local currency which is then made available for the financing of development projects. From the standpoint of most underdeveloped countries, as *recipients* of such aid, there can be little objection to it. As indicated above, a good many of them are, and probably should remain, net importers of foodstuffs; if they can get foodstuffs free, they can devote foreign exchange and real resources to development projects. Objections are more likely to come from other exporters of the same commodities whether in advanced or underdeveloped countries. They sometimes regard the surplus disposal programs as unfair competition creating disorderly markets.

It would seem desirable that surplus commodity disposal be handled by international agreements involving both recipient countries and all major exporters of the surplus items. A specialized agency within the United Nations might act as secretariat; perhaps the Food and Agriculture Organization and the World Bank could establish a joint committee to service the agreements.

A more fundamental question, of course, is whether surplus disposal is good policy for the granting countries. There can be no surplus disposal without surpluses, and the surpluses reflect price maintenance of one kind or another. In pure market terms, the surpluses represent overproduction at current prices. From a very long-run point of view, however, it may make sense to retain the present agricultural capacity of the advanced countries, while the underdeveloped ones are industrializing. As industrialization proceeds, the developing countries, one after the other, will reach the point where they can finance imports of foodstuffs and raw materials from industrial exports. Industrialization of Asia and Africa could provide an expanding market for these items even at current prices.

Should Foreign Aid and Investment Equal the Foreign Exchange Component of Development?

In capital assistance programs in the past there has been some tendency to match foreign aid against the foreign exchange requirements of a development project or program. There is no clear rationale for this approach. Any underdeveloped country needs foreign exchange, not only for its development program, but also for the raw materials and equipment necessary to maintain production in existing enterprises and to provide certain essential consumers' goods. It makes little difference which of these foreign exchange requirements carry the "foreign aid" label and which are covered by foreign trade or foreign investment.

One might contend that the purpose of foreign aid is to provide the *additional* exchange needed to undertake *additional* development projects. The problem is not as simple as all that, however; launching a development program, even if financed by foreign aid, will require local currency expenditures as well. These outlays will tend to raise national income and so to increase the demand for imported consumers' goods. If inflation is to be avoided, the government must either find ways of financing its *local* currency expenditures that will prevent any rise in money income before the development projects begin to bear fruit, or offset the rise in money income with increased imports. But if a maximum effort is already being made with respect to domestic finance, such non-inflationary financing of the local currency counterpart of foreign aid projects will be impossible.

In other words, the problem confronting underdeveloped countries is the gap between their own capacity for financing development and their capital requirements. It is this gap which must be filled by foreign loans or grants; and this gap may be greater or less than the foreign exchange component of the development program.

In this connection, questions arise with respect to counterpart requirements. The traditional approach to capital assistance has required a matching of assistance provided in foreign exchange by advanced countries by a local currency contribution from the governments of underdeveloped areas. There may have been a certain unconscious wisdom in this approach, taking underdeveloped countries as a whole; the available studies suggest that a wholehearted effort on the part of the underdeveloped countries might enable them to raise domestically half the necessary increase in financial resources. However, there are great differences among underdeveloped countries in their capacity to match capital assistance by local currency contributions. A country like Ethiopia, which has recently accumulated reserves because of a favorable export position, is clearly in a different situation from countries like Indonesia and the Philippines, which in some postwar years have lost foreign exchange reserves at a phenomenal rate and have had budgetary difficulties as well. Some counterpart requirement may be desirable as a general provision, in order to give underdeveloped countries a sense of participation. But this requirement should be flexible, determined in the light of the country's over-all economic situation, and in relation to its development program as a whole.

Another question which is sometimes raised with regard to counterpart funds is whether or not the projects for use of such funds should be "additional" to those carried out by the original foreign assistance. This question, too, is really meaningless. If a country has a well-constructed development plan, requiring outlays in foreign exchange and in domestic currency, it matters very little which specific projects are assigned to the initial capital assistance program and which to counterpart. For example, if a development program includes a hospital and a school, each costing $10 million, half in foreign exchange and half in local currency, the country's financial position, and the pace of its economic development, is precisely the same whether foreign aid takes the form of $10 million for the school, without counterpart requirements, and the country raises both the foreign exchange and the local currency for the hospital; or whether the capital assistance provides $5 million each for school and hospital, and the balance is financed out of something called "counterpart." Nor does it matter if regulations prevent the application of counterpart to the same projects as those for which capital assistance is provided; if in the development plan there are other projects costing $10 million in local currencies, these projects can be presented for the counterpart program.

There would be much to be said, therefore, for having no specific counterpart requirement. Instead, countries providing capital assistance to underdeveloped areas might require that the aid be given in support of a well-worked-out development plan, with broad assurance that the country itself is making every effort to raise domestic financial resources. If counterpart requirements are necessary to "sell" foreign aid programs to the legislatures of advanced countries, the requirements as to the amount of counterpart, and as to its use, should be as flexible as possible. An interesting example is the device recently worked out for India. The IBRD, in agreement with American authorities, permitted the use of counterpart funds to purchase the junior securities in a development corporation. The Bank itself provided new capital in foreign exchange and held the "senior securities." Such flexible arrangements for use of counterpart funds are likely to prove most successful.

Conclusion

The main conclusion of Chapters 25 and 26 is that no policies, institutions, or agreements which can significantly increase the flow of capital from advanced to underdeveloped countries should be eschewed, providing they do no offsetting harm to beneficiary or granting countries and do not introduce new friction into international relations. Private international investment should be encouraged in both advanced and underdeveloped countries, and thought should be given to devices for regulating the international capital market so as to induce it to play a larger role in financing economic development. Foreign aid will also be necessary, and grants, soft loans, hard loans, technical assistance, and surplus commodity disposal can all play useful roles. It is unlikely that the total flow engendered by a maximum effort on all fronts will exceed aggregate absorptive capacity if the capital is allocated among countries with absorptive capacity as the major criterion and on the basis of well-worked-out development plans. What is important, however, is that neither private investment nor foreign aid be used—or even appear to be used—for any purpose other than raising total output in the country where the investment is made.

27 Planning Economic Development

We have left the most difficult and delicate questions to the last. In the next chapter, we discuss population policy; here we tackle development planning.

Financing economic development has its problems, as we have seen. We have also seen that the orthodox tools of monetary, fiscal, and foreign exchange policy are useful in underdeveloped countries, provided we give full weight to differences in the institutional framework. When we come to development planning, however, we encounter the very essence of the development problem. To plan effectively, we would have to understand completely the nature of underdevelopment and the process of transition to sustained growth. In the previous chapters, we have contended that this or that measure is the wrong way to promote economic growth. Unfortunately, it is easier to say what not to do than to say what should be done. As we admitted in Chapter 17, we do not yet have a general theory from which could be derived concrete policy proposals for every underdeveloped country. To a great degree the development plan of each country must be tailor-made, in terms of conditions ruling in that country. Nevertheless, the theory outlined above does provide some guidelines that should help to increase the general effectiveness of development planning. Reduced to its essentials, a development plan has the following main components:

1. A capital budget, comprised of public investment projects

of a developmental nature.

2. A budget of government expenditures not usually regarded as capital outlays, but which contribute to economic and social development. These expenditures might be termed a "human investment budget" (education, manpower training, health, etc.).

3. A program of legislation and regulation governing the activities of private individuals, enterprises, and institutions, so as to redirect, guide, and encourage these activities in a manner contributing to economic and social development, including proposals for new institutions, or for reorganization of old ones, so as to facilitate the execution of measures included in the plan.

Each of these three major components of a plan involves decisions affecting the allocation of resources, human and material. To make wise decisions of this kind, the objective of the plan must be clear and cast in concrete terms, if possible, in terms which submit to measurement. A development plan is not static but subject to constant revision as portions are completed and new information becomes available. In revising a plan, it is of the utmost importance to know whether progress is being made toward the ultimate goal; and for this purpose progress should be defined, as much as possible, in measurable terms.

Measuring Economic Development

We have defined the over-all goal of an economic development plan, as maximizing the rate of expansion of production, while giving due weight to people's wishes regarding the choice between goods and services or leisure, between more income now and more income later, and between a higher per capita income and larger families. How can economic development in this sense be measured, as a check on the degree of success of the development program?

A conceptually simple measure would be the trend of gross national income at constant prices. There are, of course, statistical difficulties involved. Measuring national income is itself a complex task in underdeveloped countries, and determining the proper "deflators" to eliminate the effects of price changes is a ticklish operation. The elimination of cyclical fluctuations so as to get a picture of the actual trend is also a statistical operation of some complexity. However, these problems are not insoluble. A more fundamental inadequacy of national income trends, as a measure of economic progress, is that in itself national income tells little about the standard of living of the people. A rising national income might reflect rapid population growth, while the standard of living was actually falling. Income or output *per capita* is accordingly a better measure.

Changes in *per capita* income, however, may result from changes in the length of the working week or in the ratio of labor force to total population. To measure increases in *productivity*, which are the essence of economic development, adjustments must be made for such changes. One way of making these adjustments is to concentrate on the increase in productivity per man-hour. Reducing the increases in output to man-hour terms automatically eliminates the effects on output of increases in total population, in the ratio of the labor force to total population, and in the length of the working week.

Strictly speaking, of course, economic development consists not in raising productivity per man-hour alone, but in raising productivity per unit of factor of production used. Let total output be O; the size of the total labor force (employed or unemployed) be L; the quantity of natural resources used ("land") be K; the amount of plant and equipment used ("capital") be Q. For convenience we can subsume risk-taking under Q and management under L. Then we have the familiar production function of Part 1:

$$O = f(L, K, Q) \tag{1}$$

where f is the production function. The factors of production can always be defined so as to make this function linear and homogeneous; that is, so that doubling the quantities of all factors would double output. In that case, the sum of marginal products of each factor times number of units of that factor just equals total output:

$$O = L \cdot \frac{dO}{dL} + K \cdot \frac{dO}{dK} + Q \cdot \frac{dO}{dQ} \tag{2}$$

Economic development can then be defined as an increase in f, or an improvement in the ratio $L{:}K{:}Q$ at full employment. With optimal proportions and full employment, the rate of economic progress reduces to df/dt, where t is time.[1]

Given the data, the time, and the skill, it would be possible

[1] This definition makes the "rate of economic progress" tantamount to "the rate of innovation" in Schumpeter's sense, plus the rate at which the optimal proportion of factors (with "full employment" of all factors) is reached. With "full employment" and an optimal combination of factors, economic development consists only in Schumpeterian innovation.

to make econometric studies to measure both f and df/dt. In practice, however, especially in underdeveloped countries where data are incomplete and facilities for econometric research limited, so complex a concept and measure of economic development is inconvenient. The rate of increase in productivity per man-hour, $d/dt(O/L)$, is the simplest close approximation to the combined effects of df/dt and improved factor proportions.

To be sure, one might conceive of two sets of conditions under which an increase in productivity per man-hour would not reflect true economic progress. First, productivity per man-hour might be raised by accelerating the depletion of natural resources; what may appear at first sight as an increase in f may really be an increase in K. But this problem is merely an accounting one; it is only necessary to deduct from total output the value of the resources used up, so as to get a "net" figure for output, or to add to L an estimate of the man-hours "embodied" in the resources used up. Moreover, although resource conservation should not be ignored by development planners, the resources used up in any period should probably not be valued much above their market price, which is already deducted from net production, as a cost. Given a rapid rate of technological progress, means of replacing depleted resources are usually forthcoming.

Secondly, under a totalitarian government, man-hour productivity might be made to rise by forcing a rate of domestic capital accumulation far in excess of the wishes of the people. What looks like an increase in f, or improved factor-proportions, may be an excessive increase in Q through forced saving. Although much of what has passed for economic progress in the past has taken precisely this form, it is doubtful whether capital accumulation through enforced sacrifice of current consumption warrants the term "progress." If one wanted to be strictly accurate in one's measurement of productivity, one could (conceptually) discount the value of capital goods produced at an appropriate rate of interest, reflecting the marginal rate of "time preference" of the community as a whole.

Of course, following standard social accounting practice, depreciation, imports, and the service on foreign debt should be deducted from gross output in calculating output per man-hour.

With these adjustments, an increase in productivity per man-hour always reflects either a rise in f, or improved factor-proportions, and can, therefore, be accepted as a measure of economic progress.

Some development planners have argued that plans should be based on maximizing the productivity of the *scarce* factor.[2] This argument is based on a double confusion: between average and marginal productivity, and between selection of the optimal point on an isopod of the production function (optimum combination of factors), and policies to raise the whole function. Certainly, in determining the optimal combination of factors, the relative abundance or scarcity of factors must be considered, and larger proportions of the abundant cheap factor should be used wherever possible. The selection of a maximum *rate of increase* in productivity per man-hour as the objective of economic development, *does not mean* that the appropriate aim of current policy is to maximize the *marginal* productivity of labor *at each point of time*. But economic progress cannot take place without a rise in output per man-hour *at some point* on the cross section of the production function relating total output to man-hours worked. Suppose that the society prefers working 100 hours for 1,000 units to working 120 hours for 1,140 units. Now suppose a new technique is introduced which permits the production of 1,170 units in 120 hours, and that this situation is preferred to the original one. This change will represent economic progress, even though output per man-hour is only 9.75 in the new situation as compared to 10 in the old; productivity per man-hour has risen, and also f, at least for the range of the production function between 100 hours and 120 hours. This possibility (on the whole rather unlikely) means that when hours worked and output rise together (or output and the ratio of gainfully occupied to total population and labor force) but output per man-hour fails to rise, we can never be *absolutely* sure whether or not economic progress has taken place. We would need to know what the product per man-hour would have been before, at the new level of hours, or the new ratio of gainfully occupied to labor force. Such cases will be rare, however; whenever output rises without a rise in output per man-hour as well, we may suspect that no progress has occurred.

The argument against maximizing output per unit of scarce factor can be put another way. Assuming that the optimum com-

[2] Even Dr. Tinbergen comes dangerously close to this argument, in suggesting that where capital is very scarce, the "priority figure" for investment projects will "coincide approximately" with the ratio of net returns per unit of capital. See Jan Tinbergen, "The Relevance of Theoretical Criteria in the Selection of Investment Plans," paper prepared for M.I.T., CIS, SSRC Conference on Economic Growth, October 15–17, 1954, p. 4. (mimeographed)

bination of factors is continuously achieved, it is productivity per unit of the *abundant* factor that must be maximized. Total output can, of course, be expressed as output per unit of any factor, multiplied by the number of units of that factor; that is mere arithmetic. But if we divide total output into one part, O_q which is produced by workers, L_q, in optimal combination with capital, and another part, O_s, which is produced by the remaining labor supply with little or no capital, it is clear that $O_q/L_q + O_s/L$ will always exceed O_q/L_q, so long as capital is scarce relative to labor. Thus maximizing output per unit of capital alone, in the optimal combination, will not maximize total product, but maximizing the output per unit of labor, with as much labor used in optimal combination with capital as the available capital supply permits, will maximize output.

The question may also be considered in terms of the importance in the development plan of increasing the *supply* of the factor. We may write $f = L \cdot O_l$. To maximize f by a variable plan which we may call P (and which may be quantified in terms of investment, say) we must set $Df/dP = O = L \cdot dO_l/dP + O_l \cdot dL/dP$. But dL/dP may be regarded as zero; it is no part of the plan to maximize the size of the labor force as such. The size of the labor force depends on the level of the population and on the ratio of gainfully occupied to population. Changing the proportion of the population in the labor force is not one of the accepted goals of economic development, although reducing it (by raising school-leaving ages or lowering retirement ages) may be a goal of social development. If the "plan" seeks to affect the level of population or of the labor force, it will do so, not for its own sake, but for its effect on productivity. Thus maximizing f reduces to maximizing productivity per man-hour.

In the basic equation, either O_q or O_s may be substituted for O_l and the equation will still hold. But in the maximization equation, the result is different; for the terms $O_k \cdot dK/dP$ or $O_q \cdot dQ/dP$ are not insignificant. Increasing the rate of discovery of new natural resources, or accelerating capital accumulation, may very well be part of the plan. Discovery of resources or capital accumulation may be a prerequisite to the improvements in technique (increase in f) which constitute the core of economic progress. Thus maximizing f cannot be reduced to maximizing the productivity per unit of land or per unit of capital. A still simpler way of putting the argument is to say that where land and capital are scarce relative to the existing labor supply, the "plan" should include increasing the supply of land and capital;

but increasing the supply of *labor*, to raise output per unit of capital or per acre, would be sheer nonsense or reactionary politics.

Unfortunately, measurement of the increase in man-hour productivity carries with it a conceptual and statistical difficulty of its own. An important part of development planning is the absorption of unemployment, disguised or overt; it is the increase in output per man-hour in the *total labor force* that must be maximized. But how does one measure the "total labor force" in an underdeveloped country? How does one determine the volume of disguised unemployment that should be considered part of the "labor force," which a good development plan would bring into full employment? Having determined the labor force in numbers of persons, how should it be converted into man-hours? Where there are statutory regulations governing the length of the working week, paid vacations, and the like, one might accept the statutes as a basis for this conversion. However, labor regulations are themselves a matter of policy, and decisions concerning them might be considered part of the plan.

As a matter of practical procedure, it may therefore be easier in some countries to use per capita income as a measure of economic progress, with suitable adjustments for changes in the working week, ratio of gainfully occupied to labor force, etc., than to use increase in man-hour productivity and calculate the size of the total labor force in man-hours. In any case, there is no reason why planning authorities should not try both; if both methods give roughly the same result, the authorities can be confident that they have a reasonably good picture of the over-all rate of economic progress.

Aspects of Development Planning

This attempt to pin down the over-all objective and measure of economic development provides several clues to the source of economists' present discomfort regarding their role in development planning and of their disagreement as to scope and method both of development planning and of a general theory of economic development. In the development field, one is immediately confronted with problems of choice involving discontinuities rather than marginal changes. We have seen above that the economics of development is distinguished by the overwhelming importance of the choices which must be made by large groups rather than by individuals; which must be made in terms of "lumps," "jumps," or structural changes rather than marginal adjustment; and which may involve fundamental changes in social organization and perhaps even in social philosophy.[3] Faced with problems which cannot be solved with the tools provided in the standard kit, some economists tend to argue that economists should "confine themselves to" one or another aspect of development planning. At the Conference held at the M.I.T. Center for International Studies in the fall of 1954, several such suggestions were made, with widely varying implications: the economist should limit himself to "trouble shooting," pointing out obvious mistakes in policy; he should be content with "project planning," recommending at each stage a few specific projects of obviously high priority; he should confine himself to broad aggregative questions, including questions of structural change, which can be subsumed under the heading of "sectoral planning"; he should concentrate on "target planning," selecting a few broad targets (such as the rate of absorption of disguised unemployment or the rate of increase in the ratio of industrial to agricultural employment) and suggesting means of achieving them.

Each of these aspects of planning has a contribution to make. Efficient planning cannot ignore any of them. But none of them—not even all of them together—does the whole job of development planning.

Trouble Shooting

In many underdeveloped countries, growth is hampered by bad monetary, fiscal, and foreign trade policies, by monopolies which have no offsetting advantages in terms of efficiency of large-scale production, ineffective marketing methods, visibly disproportionate development of various related sectors, and the like. Appropriate policies can sometimes help to remove such barriers to development, and such "trouble shooting" is certainly part of the development planner's function. Not all the "trouble" is economic; engineers, training experts, public health experts, and other technicians have important places on a development planning team, even if the team's activities are confined to "trouble shooting." Furthermore, since one cannot transplant, without modification, policies and institutions designed for industrially advanced countries, no more serious mistake could be made than

[3] Cf. Everett Hagen, "The Allocation of Investment in Underdeveloped Countries: The Case of Burma," in *Investment Criteria for Economic Growth* (Cambridge, Mass., 1955).

to underestimate the ability of people in underdeveloped countries to do their own trouble shooting.

Project Planning

In the context of a particular underdeveloped country at a particular time, the temptation to "confine oneself" to project planning is certainly strong. Usually a few projects are so pressing as to be of very high priority, and the planner feels that at least he will do no harm in recommending that they be carried out and in making suggestions for their financing, timing, and organization.[4] Unfortunately, although the economic development planner may do little harm in limiting himself in this fashion, he also does little good. Ultimately any plan must be reduced to specific projects, but the really difficult problem is to determine the optimal nature and pace of structural change in an economy. The regular government departments can usually discern a few high-priority projects.[5]

Sectoral Planning

The concept of "sectoral planning" seems to vary considerably from one economist to another, with accompanying differences in degree of ambitiousness. For some, it seems to mean essentially a forecast, based on a type of input-output analysis or linear programing, given some assumed "target" rate of growth of the entire economy. For others, it means also making *recommendations* as to the relative rates at which various sectors of the economy should grow, presumably with additional recommendations as to how this growth is to be achieved. Others would suggest a combination of these two things, with *projections* in sectors where the plan calls only for "steady growth," combined with *planned* and *discontinuous* structural change in "development" sectors.[6] This approach to development planning is usually attractive to economists whose interest is in aggregative eco-

[4] Dr. Tinbergen's Conference paper is almost entirely concerned with how to "calculate a 'priority figure' for each of a number of projects of which the execution is under consideration," Jan Tinbergen, in *op. cit.*, p. 1.

[5] Cf. Albert O. Hirschman, "Economics and Investment Planning: Some Reflections Based on Experience in Colombia," in *ibid.*

[6] Rosenstein-Rodan seems to stress "sectoral planning" in this sense. See Paul Rosenstein-Rodan, "Programming in Theory and in Italian Practice," in *ibid.* Dr. Chenery places his emphasis on statistical projections of the structure, given certain targets. Dr. Hirschman would limit the economist to trouble shooting and planning high-priority "sectors" so narrow (electric power) as to be virtually "projects."

nomics, or in the econometrically derived *tableaux économiques* involved in input-output analysis. Certainly, sectoral planning involves some of the most basic problems of economic development, such as the desirable rate and form of industrialization.

Target Planning

The "five-year plans" associated with Soviet bloc countries, and some of the postwar reconstruction plans in Western Europe, are not stated only in terms of public investment projects, technical assistance, manpower training, new regulations and institutions, and the like, but include quantitative production "targets": so many more tons of coal and steel, so many kilowatts of additional power capacity, so many miles of road or railway, so many tons of cereal, so many dollars worth of additional exports, and so on. Although this sort of "multiple target" planning may lose sight of the ultimate goal of raising productivity in the economy as a whole, it may nevertheless provide useful gauges of the success of the development program and focal points for public discussion. A development program may succeed in raising over-all man-hour productivity and yet be inadequate because certain strategic sectors of the program fail to share proportionately in the progress. It is always a bit dangerous to use any single average to measure the effectiveness of economic policy; the average may hide overconcentration in some fields and neglect of other important sectors.

In order to avoid unwarranted satisfaction with an increase in productivity of the economy as a whole, therefore, it may be worthwhile to lay down additional subtargets in quantitative terms.

1. *A target for approach to equilibrium in the over-all budget and balance of payments position*

Many underdeveloped countries face a combination of budget and balance of payments deficits. No country can go on indefinitely living on foreign exchange reserves; and when imports are restricted in an effort to avoid exhaustion of foreign exchange reserves, the budget deficit must be reduced as well, if dangerous inflationary pressure is to be staved off. Economic policy must be designed to bring about such equilibrium sooner or later, if healthy economic growth is to be possible. At the same time, the scale of the development program that is feasible is limited by the steps necessary to reach this equilibrium. This "target," therefore, must be taken into account in framing the development plan.

2. *A target for foodstuffs*

In many development plans, increasing production of foodstuffs is a top-priority project. It is desirable to cast this objective quantitatively, either in terms of expansion of local production or in terms of reduction of imports. (Some countries should plan for *increased* imports of foodstuffs, and for earning the foreign exchange to pay for them.)

3. *A target for industrial production*

It is useful to set forth a "target" in terms of the desired increase in aggregate industrial production over the period covered by the plan, and to break this target down into smaller categories, such as power capacity, transport facilities, manufactured goods, and the like.

4. *A target for capital accumulation*

A closely related "target" would be the over-all rate of capital accumulation, stated in amounts, or as a percentage of national income.

5. *A target for transfer of population from agriculture to industry*

As a rule, economic development requires a net transfer of population from agriculture to industry. It would be helpful to translate this "target" into as precise quantitative terms as possible, the goal being expressed in terms of thousands of persons. In determining this target, account must, of course, be taken of the rate of net population growth. Thus a "target" with respect to net increase in population is implied.

6. *A target for resettlement of population*

In addition to moving people from industry to agriculture, some development programs also call for movements from overpopulated to unsettled areas. Any such transmigration program should be defined in terms of the numbers of people to be moved year by year. It is apparent that this target, too, implies some target with respect to over-all population growth.

7. *A target for manpower training*

Manpower training should be a major part of any development program. This "target" should state the numbers of persons to receive training in each major field of industry and agriculture, the numbers at various levels of training, the length of the training program, etc.

With these separate "targets" as a check on the effectiveness of the development program, in addition to measurements of changes in per capita income and in man-hour productivity as a whole, the planners, the government, and the general public should be well informed of the progress of the economy.

When quantitative targets are established they can be tested for mutual consistency or "complementarity." Certain types of facilities must be provided together and in more or less fixed proportions. For example, as Tinbergen points out, investment in transport has in the past run a fairly constant 20 to 25 per cent of total investment. A refined form of this sort of testing is input-output analysis. Such analysis is highly useful—even if only *x*'s can be put in the boxes, indicating interrelationships among different industrial activities and the need to provide resources for all interrelated production processes. If figures can be obtained indicating the precise quantitative nature of these relationships, so much the better. On the other hand, since the development process involves changes in industrial structure and introduction of new activities, mere projection of past input-output relationships can be highly misleading, and simple transfer of experience from more highly developed countries may also be dangerous.

Aspects of Planning and Phases of Economic Development

All these aspects of development planning have their proper role. They are not rival sets of rules for planners to follow, but aspects of an over-all planning process, of varying significance in successive phases of economic growth.[7]

Development Planning in Advanced Countries

In industrially advanced countries where the aim is "steady growth," development policy is largely a matter of trouble shooting. Economists may also collaborate with engineers, public health experts, architects, town planners, agriculturalists, and the like, in planning specific projects in the public sector, and in devising regulations to direct investment in the private sector. In short, in advanced economies development policy can be confined to trouble shooting and project planning.

Planning in Underdeveloped but Developing Countries

In underdeveloped countries where industrialization and agricultural improvement are taking place at a satisfactory rate but where bottlenecks and laggard sectors of the economy must be overcome, development planning must be more than "patching

[7] This idea was first suggested to the author by Professor Adolph Lowe of the New School for Social Research.

the market." Trouble shooting is still useful and indeed necessary; growth can still be hampered by inappropriate monetary, fiscal, and foreign trade policies. The development planner can still be of assistance in preparing projects in the public sector and in devising regulations to control and direct private investment projects. But trouble shooting plus project planning is no longer enough. In such countries, growth itself must be "managed," and sectoral planning is necessary. The relative rates at which heavy industry, light industry, agricultural improvement, transport and communications, housing, and the like, are to be pushed becomes a matter of conscious policy. It will usually be found helpful to break down over-all objectives into specific "targets." Countries in this category will need all aspects of planning: trouble shooting, project planning, sectoral planning, and target planning.

Underdeveloped and Stagnant (Declining) Countries

In countries where per capita income is stationary or falling, or rising so slowly and from so low a level that there is no hope of growth becoming cumulative without a transformation of the economy, "structural planning" is much the *most* important aspect of development planning. As we saw in Chapter 17, for structural planning of the sort needed in these countries, the very nature of the problem forbids a step-by-step, trial-and-error approach. Rather, one must proceed on a take it or leave it basis even if an affirmative decision requires a country to put its entire capital budget into one complex of projects for several years on end.

The other aspects of planning will still be present, of course, but they will be relatively easy. Once the sector plan is made, translation into specific projects, or recasting in terms of targets, will not be too difficult. Trouble shooting will still be necessary, but will not be different in *kind* from trouble shooting in the two more advanced phases.

Not only are the crucial "sectoral planning" decisions nonmarginal, but they also involve an admixture of economics, engineering, and other social sciences. The required changes in economic structure are so great that they are unattainable without changes in social structure as well. Much depends, too, on what is technically possible. Many of the most crucial decisions present themselves in forms which do not lend themselves to traditional economic analysis at all. Should a direct attack be made on the "undivided family," which so seriously dilutes incentives to work harder or better, to save, to risk capital, or to limit the size of individual families, or will industrialization and urbanization automatically break down the undivided family so that no special consideration need be given to this problem? Questions such as these clearly involve knowledge—and value-judgments—outside the scope of traditional economics.[8]

Estimating Capital Requirements: The Incremental Capital-Output Ratio

The first question in development planning is, "How much total investment is needed to produce target increases in per capita income?" Answering this question requires determining the relationship between investment, I, and the consequent increase in income, Y. This relationship, $I/\Delta Y$ is called the incremental capital-output ratio (ICOR). Some ICOR is always implicit in any development plan, and it is helpful to make assumptions about ICOR explicit so that they can be scrutinized. However, the conceptual and empirical problems surrounding the use of ICOR are such that it should be handled with great care. This section is concerned with an exposition of some of these problems.

Conceptual Problems

As Professor Everett Hagen has pointed out in a pioneering paper on ICOR:

> Measurement of ICOR for any given country involves obtaining conceptually comparable wealth estimates for at least two different dates, income estimates for the same dates, and calculating the ratio between the increment in capital and that in income. The dates must be far enough apart in time so that the probable margin of error in the estimate of capital or income at each date is small relative to the increment between the dates. But long income series are available for

[8] In this respect Dr. Tinbergen's discussion seems to the writer to be exactly the wrong way around. He suggests (*Design of Development*, Baltimore, 1958, pp. 25–26) that "detailed programming" is inappropriate in the early stages of development, and that in more advanced stages of development "more diversified action will be called for, distributed over more sectors and based on a more detailed type of programming." This error, as the writer regards it, springs from Dr. Tinbergen's tendency to think of planning as a statistical or econometric operation which remains in large measure a projection of observed market behavior. Dr. Tinbergen and the writer agree, of course, that the market is a better guide in advanced countries than in underdeveloped ones; but where Tinbergen concludes that more detailed planning is therefore *possible* in advanced countries, the writer concludes that more detailed planning is *needed* in underdeveloped ones.

only a relatively few countries. Measurements of the aggregate capital stock of various countries are even less common, and are imprecise. For these reasons the number of countries is small indeed for which the necessary set of estimates can be made without a feeling that the statistical margin of error present renders the conclusions very doubtful.

Where long series of income and wealth are lacking there is a strong temptation to derive ICOR from national income statistics available over short periods. However, an ICOR derived from a short period in the past is not really what is wanted as a basis for projecting capital requirements. To determine the capital requirements of a given income target, one needs a figure (preferably one for each major sector of the economy) approximating an average relation between additions to the stock of capital and increases in national income over some period in the future. The use of an average over five previous years is justified only if those five years are part of a much longer period, so that there is a solid basis for assuming that the average for the five years is an approximation to a ratio that is stable in the long run, and if the planning period will not be significantly different from the last five years. If, for example, the previous five years represents the completion of a reconstruction period, while the plan explicitly provides for a long-run structural change, a projection of the ICOR in the recent past can be dangerous. Moreover, over short periods, the net investment figures in the national accounts are seldom an accurate measure of actual increases in the stock of productive capital. The net investment is usually derived from gross investment and a depreciation figure that is based on an accounting concept, rather than an estimate of the actual depletion of the stock of productive capital.

ICOR and Priorities

Further problems arise if, as a result of using ICOR for determining total capital requirements, planners slip into the error of using ICOR also as a factor in determining priorities. What should be compared in choosing among investment projects is not their ICOR's, but their contributions to income during a crucial period. As has been pointed out in an earlier paper,[9]

> The goal of development policy is not the maximum output at a point of time but a maximum rate of growth over time. Consider the following example of two potential investments:

[9] U.S. Department of State, "Intelligence Report No. 7013," February 7, 1956, pp. 9–11.

	Investment A	Investment B
Initial investment	100	100
Annual output	40	20
Investment life (years)	4	20
Annual straight-line depreciation	25	5
Total output over investment life	160	400
Capital-output ratio	2.5	5.0

The total output over the life span of Investment B is 400 as against 160 for Investment A. The capital-output ratios, on the other hand, are 5.0 and 2.5 respectively. In each case annual output net of depreciation is 15. Which investment yields the greater increase in national output?

Overlooking any costs other than that of the investment, the output streams may be reduced to comparability by means of discounting. Given a rate of interest, it is possible to assign a present value to the income streams of $40 for 4 years and $20 for 20 years. Assuming an interest rate of 5 per cent, the present values would be $142 and $249, respectively. Thus Investment A is "worth" $142 in output and Investment B is worth $249. The choice would clearly favor Investment B and the fact that the capital-output ratio is less "favorable" is irrelevant. . . .

How is the appropriate rate of interest to be determined? In the more primitive and more socialized economies, the market rate of interest for various reasons is likely to understate the social cost of delayed increases in output. This is an example of divergence between private and social costs, analogous to the subsequently cited divergence between wages and the social cost of labor.

Statistical Problems

The use in any country of ICOR's derived from experience in other countries where statistics are more complete also has its dangers. The work done on ICOR at the M.I.T. Center for International Studies turned up only five countries whose statistics could be considered complete enough to give a reasonable approximation of a long-run ICOR (see Table 27-1). With the possible exception of Japan all these countries are highly developed, and Japan is much more industrialized than other countries in Asia. The range of ICOR among these five countries is itself very wide: from 3 in the United States to 7.4 in The Netherlands. It would be difficult to decide from these figures what would be an appropriate ICOR for any particular underdeveloped country.

Moreover, the averages for individual countries hide wide fluctuations in the figures from one year to another, or even from one decade to another. For the United States, ICOR varies from 4.8 for the decade 1899 to 1919 to 1.9 for the decade 1919 to

1929. For Britain the figure ranges from 8.4 for the decade 1885 to 1895 to 0.4 for the period 1905 to 1909. Much wider fluctuations occur from year to year.

In addition to the long series for the five countries with reasonably reliable data, there are figures over fairly long periods

TABLE 27-1.

ICOR for Various Countries and Periods

	Period	ICOR
Long periods, reasonably reliable data:		
United States	1879–1953	2.3:1 (3.0) *
Japan	1924–1939	4.7:1 *
Denmark	1864–1939	3.5:1
The Netherlands	1900–1952	7.4:1
Sweden	1896–1929	3.5:1
Long periods, unsatisfactory data:		
Canada	1895–1920	4.2:1
	1895–1929 †	2.7:1
United Kingdom	1865–1933	5.9:1
Australia	1913–1938	3.9:1
France	1852–1913	7.4:1
Italy	1861–1895	4.5:1
	1891–1938 †	7.5:1
Underdeveloped countries: short (plan) periods:		
Czechoslovakia	1948–1953	3.3
Poland	1950–1955	2.0
Hungary	1950–1954	3.2
Bulgaria	1949–1953	1.2
Yugoslavia	1947–1951	2.2

* Reproducible capital only.
† Different basis.

for five other countries which are subject to a greater margin of error. These show a range of ICOR from 3.9 to 7.5. For underdeveloped countries figures are available only for short periods. These show a range from 1.8 for Czechoslovakia to 2.5 for Poland.

There is also a very wide range of ICOR from one sector to another of the same economy. For the United States, for which the sectoral figures are by far the most complete, the highest sectoral ICOR's are more than 100 times as high as the lowest one (Table 27-2). For India, the only other country for which sectoral estimates are available at time of writing, the range is from 1 to 5; but these are for broad sectors rather than for individual industries. Even with this range of structural variation, it is apparent that the aggregate ICOR will depend a good deal on the investment structure in the development plan, and that it will change as the structure of investment changes in the course of economic development.

TABLE 27-2.

ICOR's for Various Sectors

Country and Sector	*ICOR*
United States: *	
Trade and services	0.1 or less
Manufacturing	1.3–2.0
Housing and public utilities	10 or more
India: †	
Calculations:	
Cement	3.0–3.5
Pulp and paper	3.5–4.0
Iron and steel	3.5–4.0
Agriculture	1.0
Estimates:	
Small industries	2.0
Factories	3.0
Mining	4.0
Communications and transport	5.0

* U.S. Department of State, "Intelligence Report No. 7670," Washington, D.C., 1958.
† M.I.T., India Project.

The effect on estimates of capital requirements of relatively small errors in ICOR estimates is borne out by an arithmetic example. Assuming an investment coefficient of 0.1 (that is, that net investment is 10 per cent of net national income) one obtains the following results:

ICOR	Rate of Growth (per cent)
3.0	3.3
1.8	5.5
4.2	2.4

As stated in the earlier study already cited,[10]

[10] *Ibid.*

Bearing in mind that the problem of economic development is essentially one of raising the growth rate by one or two percentage points, it is clear that the uncertainty surrounding the value of ICOR renders its application difficult. Assume, for example, that the development target is a 4 per cent growth in output per year and that we wish to determine the investment coefficient required to meet this target. The development equation would then yield the following results for the various ICORs:

ICOR	Required Investment Coefficient (per cent)
3.0	12.0
1.8	7.5
4.2	16.8

If the determination of an ICOR suitable for prediction in the most developed and statistically sophisticated countries is difficult, in the economically and statistically underdeveloped areas it may be sheer guesswork.

Some Tentative Generalizations from ICOR Data

For what they are worth, the available data indicate certain relations between ICOR and other economic variables. First, in the figures for advanced countries, there is some indication that ICOR falls with the achievement of high levels of industrialization (Table 27-3). This tendency is explained by the necessity of making heavy investments in social capital (housing, transport facilities, public utilities, schools, hospitals, etc.) in the early phases of development, together with the very high ICOR for such investments. However, this experience with unplanned development may not be a reliable guide to results of planned de-

TABLE 27-3.

ICOR and Stage of Development

Country	Period I	ICOR	Period II	ICOR
United States	1889–1929	3.0	1929–53	1.8
Japan	1900–1924	6.0	1924–39	4.7
Denmark	1864–1909	4.5	1909–39	2.0
Canada	1895–1920	4.2	1920–29	2.0 *
Mexico	1940–45	1.54	1946–50	2.75
Czechoslovakia	1947–48	1.4	1949–50	1.8
Bulgaria	1947–48	0.9	1949–52	1.9
Hungary	1940–49	0.7	1949–52	2.4

* Rough estimate.

velopment. If, for example, it is planned to concentrate on agricultural improvement in the early phases and gradually to increase the pace of industrialization, it is conceivable that ICOR would rise rather than fall in the course of the country's development.

There is also some slight indication that ICOR's may be particularly low in reconstruction periods, when existing plant and equipment, land, skilled labor, and management are being brought back into productive use. Indeed, the only case of ICOR's as low as 1.7 have occurred in Soviet bloc satellites during their postwar reconstruction phase.

There is also some evidence that ICOR's are lower where population growth is more rapid (Table 27-4). There are two possible explanations for this relationship: rapid population growth prevents waste of capital by assuring markets for almost any investment; and a rapid increase in the labor supply permits capital accumulation without departing from the optimal ratio of labor to capital.

There is also some rough evidence that ICOR will vary inversely with the ratio of population to natural resources. One would expect capital to be more productive when combined with relatively large amounts of natural resources.

These relationships suggest interesting areas for further study. The evidence is too scanty for them to be received as empirical laws until a good deal more data have been collected and analyzed.

An Example: ICOR in the Philippines

The national income data of the Philippines give an average ICOR for 1950–54 of 0.67. The average, however, cloaks fluctuations within that short period between 0.3 and 2.0. The gross ICOR for the same period (ratio of gross investment to the increase in gross national production) is 1.5:1. At one time the Office of National Planning of the National Economic Council contemplated the use of these figures for determining capital requirements. However, it was difficult to accept at face value an ICOR as low as 0.67. As was pointed out by Dr. Ahrensdorf, an ICOR of 0.67 implies an average rate of return on new investment of 150 per cent.[11] Moreover, no other country had quoted an ICOR as low as this—not even the Soviet satellites during their reconstruction period.

[11] J. Ahrensdorf, "Capital Formation and Public Policy," National Economic Council Seminar Paper, 1956.

TABLE 27-4.
Relationships between Incremental Capital-Output Ratio and Other Variables
(eight countries)

	A		B		C	
Country	ICOR	Rank inverted	Income per worker *	Rank	Population per sq. mi.	Rank inverted
United States	3.0	1	1,414	2	41	4
Sweden	3.3	2	666	6	35	3
Australia	3.9	3	1,326	3	2.2	1
Canada	4.2	4	1,676	1	2.8	2
Great Britain	5.9	5	858	5	491	7
Japan	6.1	6	370	8	435	6
The Netherlands	7.4	7.5	1,014	4	610	8
France	7.4	7.5	516	7	201	5

		D		E		F	
Country	ICOR rank	Increase in income, % per yr.	Rank	Increase in working force, % per yr.	Rank	Increase in income per worker, % per yr.	Rank
United States	1	0.0372	2.5 †	0.0223	1	0.0165	2
Sweden	2	.0375	2.5 †	.0141	3	.0132	3
Australia	3	.0233	4	.0160	2	.0071	6.5 †
Canada	4	.0208	5	.0123	4.5 †	.0078	4.5 †
Great Britain	5	.0192	6	.0110	6	.0081	4.5 †
Japan	6	.0625	1	.0096	7	.0524	1
The Netherlands	7	.0169	7	.0119	4.5 †	.0049	8
France	8	0.0108	8	0.0038	8	0.0071	6.5 †

		G		H		I	
Country	ICOR rank	E ÷ D	Rank	F ÷ D	Rank	E ÷ F	Rank
United States	1	0.599	3	0.444	3	1.352	4
Sweden	2	.375	6	.352	6	1.068	6
Australia	3	.687	2	.305	7	2.254	2
Canada	4	.591	4	.375	5	1.685	5
Great Britain	5	.573	5	.422	4	1.358	3
Japan	6	.154	8	.838	1	0.183	8
The Netherlands	7	.704	1	.290	8	2.429	1
France	8	0.352	7	0.657	7	0.535	7

* Average initial and terminal dates.
† Differences of less than 0.0005 ignored in ranking.

It turned out after review that the extraordinarily low ICOR's derived from the national accounts were due partly to statistical factors and partly to the special economic circumstances prevailing in the reconstruction period in the Philippines.

1. *Gross Investment.* Gross investment had been underestimated in the national accounts in several respects. Perhaps most important, the estimate of capital formation included no estimate of the increase in number or growth of coconut trees. In this respect the National Income Unit was following the suggestions made by the Third Regional Conference of Statisticians of ECAFE. However, Dr. Wu, Chief of the Statistics Section of the UN Economic Commission on Asia and the Far East, pointed out that this recommendation was made on the assumption that the increase in stock of trees was difficult to estimate and an unimportant factor in capital formation. In the Philippines, where 40 per cent of exports are derived from coconut products, failure to include this type of capital formation resulted in significant underestimation of gross investment. The underestimation was particularly serious for the postwar period, in view of the replanting and the consequent increase in output.

With respect to equipment, there were four sources of underestimation. First, the value of imported equipment (which constitutes the bulk of this item) was based on customs valuations. Using this source involved a systematic understatement of the true value of this equipment. Secondly, from 1946 through 1953, a constant figure was added each year as an estimate of locally produced equipment; this figure was very low (a million pesos per year) and may well have increased since the census year 1948. Figures for 1954 and 1955 included estimates of durable equipment actually manufactured in the Philippines. Third, the inclusion of imported equipment at C.I.F. values plus a single 50 per cent markup, with final output at market values, distorted the ICOR through failure to take account of the exchange premium.

Similar considerations apply to the estimate of farm improvements. The original estimate of capital formation in farm improvements was based on figures obtained during the Macmillan Survey in 1951. This estimate was extrapolated according to growth in farm income. This method probably underestimated capital formation of this type in recent years. Growth of hectarage is a better basis for extrapolation than increase in farm income. The increase in area planted has been much higher in recent years than it was in 1951. The figures for earlier years are of dubious accuracy.

There may also have been an underestimate from the non-inclusion of items under the heading of "Repair and Maintenance" in government accounts which actually represent a net addition to the stock of capital. The practice was to include only "Major Repairs" as new investment, and it is not clear exactly where was the dividing line between "major" and "minor" repairs.

2. *Net Investment*. The figure for net investment was even more of an underestimate than the figure of gross investment, since the figure for depreciation almost certainly exceeds the actual withdrawals of capital from productive use. Depreciation on equipment was taken at 10 per cent per year of an estimated stock of prewar capital plus net additions (mostly imports) adjusted by a price index. Since much of the equipment added to the stock since the war was new, the actual annual withdrawals from use would be much less than 10 per cent. Similarly, a constant figure for depreciation of buildings was included, although actual withdrawals from use after 1946 were probably negligible. As the National Income Unit of the Bank has pointed out, the depreciation figures provided in the national accounts cannot be used for determining actual net investment. Indeed, it seems possible, in the light of the observations regarding depreciation, together with those already made concerning underestimation of gross investment, that the actual addition to the stock of capital exceeded the figures given for gross investment in the national accounts.

ECONOMIC FACTORS

In addition to these statistical inaccuracies, a number of factors were operating during the postwar period to bring extraordinary increases in output for relatively small levels of investment. A large proportion of the actual addition to productive assets represented the rehabilitation and replanting of agricultural land. Some of this rehabilitation involved no monetary outlay for capital equipment whatsoever, but brought substantial increase in output. The increase in agricultural productivity was enhanced by greatly increased use of fertilizer, much of it provided through foreign aid. Such expansion of hectarage and introduction of fertilizer cannot be repeated on the same scale in future years. Similarly, rehabilitation of buildings and equipment adds more to the effective stock of productive capital than it costs. It may bring back into use whole blocks of capital equipment, with consequent large increase in output, for relatively little capital outlay. For example, the repair of a single bridge might bring back into use 100 kilometers of road; the stock of capital is increased by the whole length of road thus made usable.

Finally, substantial amounts of war surplus equipment were disposed of at prices far below cost. The opportunity for addition to the stock of capital thus provided will not occur again in the near future.

Superficial analysis suggests that the reconstruction period lasted until 1951, after which a tapering off of expansion is apparent. The declining rate of increase in output is especially clear when expressed in per capita terms. This is true despite the lag of five to ten years between increased output and investment in plantations, and despite the fact that much of the war surplus equipment is still in use. In other words, when the time comes to replace these additions to the stock of capital which were inexpensive when made during the reconstruction period, the capital costs may be well above their original cost and the ICOR may rise still higher.

When all these factors were taken into account it appeared that a net ICOR in the neighborhood of 2.0 was a more accurate reflection of relationships likely to prevail in the future than the figure of 0.67 derived from the national accounts. However, it was also clear that the margin of error was so great that no aggregate ICOR could be accorded a strategic role in development planning.

Conclusions

This example illustrates clearly the kind of problems that can arise in estimating ICOR, and the dangers implicit in incautious use of the concept. The ICOR is unquestionably a useful tool for determining the broad order of magnitude of capital requirements for meeting income targets. As Jan Tinbergen has pointed out, the very facts that aggregrate ICOR's for countries are usually between 2 and 4, and that the planning team can usually decide whether it is closer to one limit or the other, are highly significant.[12] However, the use of this tool is beset by pitfalls which must be carefully avoided if serious errors are to be prevented. Relatively small changes in evaluation of ICOR can yield big changes in estimates of capital requirements. In particular, the following points should be borne in mind when making use of this concept:

1. The measurement of ICOR should be attempted only if

[12] Tinbergen, *op. cit.*, p. 13.

data are available for a long period—at least one full cycle, and preferably much more.

2. If the period covered by the data is less than three or four decades, every effort must be made to make sure that the period is in some sense "normal," as contrasted, for example, with periods having special characteristics, such as the years following a major war.

3. It must be remembered that the undertaking of a development plan will in itself change the ICOR. Straightforward projection of past ICOR in the same country is seldom satisfactory. It would be better to use comparable figures from other countries for the phase in their economic development which the planning country is about to enter; but great care must be exercised that the figures from other countries are truly comparable.

4. In estimating net investment, one must be very wary in utilizing national accounts, especially in estimating depreciation.

5. The purpose of calculating ICOR is only to determine total capital requirements; the ICOR should not be used for establishing priorities among investment projects or sectors.

Although this section has stressed the difficulties in utilizing ICOR, it should also be remembered that any investment budget contains an implicit ICOR. Accuracy is not gained by making no effort whatsoever to estimate the appropriate ICOR for a particular country in a particular phase of development. It is always worthwhile to make the most accurate possible estimate of the appropriate ICOR as a check on the total scale of the proposed investment budget.

Investment Criteria and Priorities

The most difficult task of all is to establish priorities for the various investment projects which constitute a development program. The dangers in using ICOR to determine total capital requirements are mainly technical and statistical; the difficulties in establishing priorities spring directly from our continuing ignorance of the nature of the development process—or in other words, our lack of a definitive general theory of economic development.

Several economists, including Hollis Chenery, Benjamin King, and Jan Tinbergen have endeavored to reduce the problem of priorities to a formula.[13] One underdeveloped country, the Philip-

[13] Hollis Chenery, "The Application of Investment Criteria," *Quarterly Journal of Economics*, February, 1951, pp. 38–61.

pines, is actually using a modified version of the Chenery formula as a basis for allocating scarce resources. The nature of the problems involved in determining criteria for investment can be conveniently illustrated by a review of this one attempt at practical application.

The policy objectives which the government wanted to see reflected in the priority formula were the following: [14]

1. To direct resources toward the most productive uses
2. To conserve foreign exchange
3. To reduce unemployment
4. To improve the distribution of real income
5. To promote economic growth

These objectives, in turn, reflected the economic situation in the Philippines as outlined in Chapter 2.

The guiding principles of the system were stated as follows:

(1) Other considerations being equal, preferences will be given to an industrial project that will make per unit of scarce resources expended the highest contribution to the national income. This is represented in the formula by the sum of earnings of the productive factors involved in the industrial project including those of labor, land, capital and entrepreneur.
(2) Other considerations being equal, preference will be given to an industrial project that will give per unit of scarce resource expended the highest measure of improvement in the country's balance of payments position. This is measured by the annual foreign exchange value of the product minus the value of foreign exchange directly or indirectly used in production per unit of investment.
(3) Other considerations being equal, preference will be given to an industrial project that will make the greatest use of domestically produced raw materials and operating supplies.
(4) Other considerations being equal, preference will be given to an industrial project that will make the most use of domestic labor. This is measured by the annual value of such labor per unit of scarce resource expended.
(5) Other considerations being equal, preference will be given to an industrial project that will produce goods that meet the more basic needs of the people and will produce the greater effect on the external economies.

For the purpose of the formula the value of this last factor (the essentiality factor) is applied to the first factor (national income contribution) to reflect the effect produced on the external economies to take

[14] Philippines National Economic Council, *The Five-Year Economic and Social Development Program for Fiscal Years 1957–1961* (Manila, 1957), pp. 253–54.

into account other social benefit considerations such as the relative essentiality of the product for consumption purposes. This in effect will encourage the production of goods consumed by the low-income groups in greater volume, resulting in the improvement of real income distribution.
The application of the essentiality factor to the national income contribution of the enterprise is a substitute for the direct measurement of the impact of the project on the external economies which is extremely difficult to make.

The formula that finally emerged from months of discussion based on these principles was:

$$IP = R_1 + R_2 + R_3 + R_4$$

where[15] IP = Industrial Priority

R_1 = The value added to the national income by the factors of production involved in the project including labor, land, capital, and entrepreneur, as corrected by an essentiality factor to account for the impact of the project on external economies and for other social benefit considerations, the whole per unit of capital resources utilized.

R_2 = Impact of the operations of the firm on the country's balance of payments position.

R_3 = The extent of additional economic values derived from the use of domestic raw materials and supplies.

R_4 = The social value derived from employment of Filipino labor.

Why a Formula?

It should be emphasized that the important decision was not the decision to use a formula, but the decision to intervene in the market to allocate scarce resources. A formula is only precise measurement of the factors which the government wishes to consider in making these allocations. Difficulties of measurement are no reason for abandoning a formula. If the factors in the formula are of major importance for determining allocation of scarce resources, they must be considered anyhow. No precision is gained by refusing to make the attempt to express these factors quantitatively. At the same time, no simple formula can cover all the

[15] The statistical definition of these terms is presented in the Appendix to this chapter.

factors germane to a particular case. The formula must be applied with discretion by well-informed administrators who understand both the usefulness and the limitations of the formula.

What Is to Be Allocated?

To be strictly logical a formula should be designed to allocate all scarce resources in accordance with the aforementioned list of objectives. In the Philippines, however, two types of scarce resources were most clearly in short supply: foreign exchange and capital. Skilled labor, technicians, managers, and entrepreneurship are also scarce; but the Philippines government was not prepared at that time to adopt policies which would involve direct allocation of human resources. In any case the numbers used would correlate fairly closely with the amounts of foreign exchange and the capital required.

In addition to foreign exchange and long- and middle-term credits (scarce capital) the formula might also have been used for determining tax privileges. Although tax privileges are not in themselves a "resource," they may be regarded as a subheading of allocation of capital; tax privileges encourage investment in particular fields.

The purpose of the formula, then, was to compare investment projects according to the ratio of benefits obtained relative to the cost in terms of scarce resources: foreign exchange and capital. The formula as adopted sought to achieve this purpose by relating annual benefits to annual costs in capital and foreign exchange, both reduced to pesos. Benefits in turn were measured by three factors: net contribution to foreign exchange earnings, net contribution to national income, and net contribution to employment.

The Employment Factor (*L*)

The technical committee set up to prepare the formula took the view that the purpose of introducing an employment factor into the formula was to accord higher priority to investment projects that would reduce unemployment (other things being equal). It was thought, therefore, that this factor should include only those categories of labor among which there was some unemployment. The absorption of those kinds of labor which were already in short supply obviously would not reduce unemployment, and giving high priority to projects requiring scarce labor skills could result in serious disturbances in the labor market: bidding-up wages of skilled workers, hijacking skilled workers by those who already have foreign exchange allocations from employers whose applications had not yet been processed, etc. It could also be an open invitation to excessive and wasteful use of skilled workers merely in order to obtain a high priority rating.

Taking an extreme example to illustrate this point, it would have been absurd to accord a high "employment factor" to a project requiring a thousand atomic physicists; not only would such a project make no contribution to solution of the employment problem, the required skilled workers could not possibly be found in the Philippines. It is doubtful whether such a project could even use foreign exchange or credit granted to it. Although less obvious, the same principle might apply to projects requiring large numbers of toolmakers, diemakers, steel rollers, welders, chemists, etc. Not only does use of such skills do nothing to reduce employment, since most of the unemployed are unskilled, but expansion of any industry requiring such skills necessarily brings *contraction of others* requiring the same skills. The net effect could be a *decline* in employment in the economy as a whole.

Although there is no case for including types of labor in short supply in an employment factor, there may nevertheless be a good case for considering the upgrading of labor as a factor promoting economic growth. A nation of unskilled workers can never be highly productive and will find it difficult to compete in world markets. If industries needing skilled workers are never started, a corps of skilled workers can never be built up. There may also be more intangible results on the rate of economic growth through increasing the degree of "technology-mindedness" of the population through introduction of industries needing relatively high technical skills. And, of course, craftsmanship and efficiency should be rewarded.

In order to measure as accurately as possible the contribution to employment without losing sight of these economic growth factors, it may be advisable not to lay down hard and fast rules for measurement of L in the formula, but instead to lay down a set of principles to be followed in assigning a value to L. The efficiency factor is already given full weight in the modified Chenery formula and need not be considered again. Among the principles to be taken into account would be the following:

1. All unemployed workers who would be given jobs through the project should be included.

2. One should not include skilled workers of a kind in short supply, who cannot be obtained in a reasonable length of time

by training unskilled workers, but who must on the contrary be attracted away from other employers.

3. Where the need is for labor skills of a kind not presently available in the market, but which can be provided in a reasonable length of time by upgrading unskilled workers through a training program, such workers might be included in the *L*. It might even be good development policy to give a premium to workers so upgraded—but in that case, the administering authorities should be quite certain that the prospective employer can and will provide the necessary training facilities.

As may be seen from the Appendix to this chapter, the Philippines government sought an approximation to these principles by deducting from the wages bill 50 per cent of salaries of non-Filipinos remitted abroad in calculating value added, and by including in the employment factor only Filipino workers to whom a uniform wage of 2,000 pesos per year is attributed.

Domestic Materials (M_d)

Somewhat similar considerations apply to the use of domestic materials. Some spokesmen for industry felt that domestic raw materials should be treated as costless in calculating the contribution of an investment project to national income. But failure to include *as a cost* domestic materials that are in short supply would be an open invitation to inefficiency and waste. The same is even more true of inclusion of such materials as a *positive* factor in the formula.

Consider the following example: Firm A produces 110 units of final product with 300 units of domestic materials; Firm B produces 100 units of the same final product with 100 units of domestic materials. If M_d were eliminated from the formula, or included as a positive factor, Firm A would (other things being equal) be accorded the higher priority, which would be contrary to good economic policy unless the raw material was so abundant as to become a free good. If it were a scarce material, home-produced steel rods, or exports such as chromite or petroleum, there would be no basis whatsoever for according a higher priority to a firm using large quantities of the material by deliberately wasteful methods. As in the case of scarce labor, use of domestic materials that are in short supply by one project will require *contraction* of other operations using the same scarce raw material. It should also be pointed out that a premium for use of domestic rather than foreign materials is already accorded through the balance of payments factor in the formula.

On the other hand, there may on occasion be cases in which a certain domestic material is temporarily in excess supply although the long-run prospects for producers of this material are good. There may be other cases where temporary assistance may lead to the development of an import-replacing industry processing domestic materials. Under these conditions projects using relatively large amounts of this particular material may deserve a premium. Accordingly the same procedure might be followed as was suggested above for labor: some discretion might be allowed in the evaluation of M_d according to the current market situation and future prospects for the material in question. Among the principles to be considered would be the following:

1. Domestic raw materials of kinds currently in short supply and likely to continue in short supply should be deducted in full from value added, as a social cost, and should not be included as a positive factor.

2. Where domestic materials are temporarily in excess supply, but have good long-run market prospects, the authorities might be empowered to estimate the cost of M_d at a figure lower than actual market value of materials used, or to add a positive factor for their use.

3. Where domestic materials are, and are expected to remain, in excess supply, but where the land, capital, or labor used to produce them cannot possibly be shifted to alternative uses, the authorities might be empowered to value the materials below market price for estimating cost, or to include a positive factor for their use.

4. Use of domestic materials might also receive positive treatment in cases of "infant industries" that can replace imports by processing domestic materials, given temporary protection.

5. Where materials are in excess supply, are expected to continue in excess supply, but the land, labor, and capital producing them can be shifted to alternative outputs for which the long-run prospects are better, the full value of the materials should be deducted from value added, as a social cost.

The formula adopted, in effect, regarded raw materials as a cost by deducting the value of raw materials used from gross sales to determine value added. However, the use of domestic material was reintroduced in another component of the formula, R_3, in a form that makes it a relatively small positive factor in the total priority rating.

External Economies

The main weakness of the formula is its failure to include a direct measure of external economies (contribution to output of the rest of the economy) or of the impact on distribution of income. The first of these omissions is a serious defect. Our whole analysis in Part 3 indicates that an enterprise may serve economic development more by its indirect contribution to the output of the economy as a whole than by its own direct contribution to output.

In the system presented in the five-year program an effort was made to approximate the effect on income distribution through the "essentiality multiplier." Higher ratings were assigned to essential consumers' goods than semiessential consumers' goods; semiessential consumers' goods ranked higher than non-essential consumers' goods. In this context, "essentiality" refers to importance in the budgets of lower-income groups: a consumer good is regarded as "essential" if it plays an important role in worker-peasant budgets. Thus the priority system was designed to improve income distribution by encouraging production of goods consumed by the lower-income groups rather than those consumed mainly by upper-income groups.

The essentiality multiplier also involved an approximation to external economies. A higher rating was given to essential producers' goods in primary industry than to essential producers' goods in secondary industry, or to semiessential producers' goods in primary industry, and so on. The "multiplier" system is shown in the Appendix to this chapter. The assumption is that production of goods with the higher priority ratings will have a bigger impact on total production of the economy as a whole than production of those with lower priority ratings. The question here is one of fact. The assumption may be valid for the Philippines economy: it is true that most of the processing industries recently established there to put finishing touches on imported semifinished goods have done little to stimulate expansion in other sectors of the economy. Hirschman's analysis, however, would suggest modification of the multiplier ratings. Once the market is built up and the labor and managerial skills are available, "backward linkage" may appear; that is, earlier stages of production may be taken over by Filipino enterprises. Also, Hirschman's figures, presented in Table 16-1 suggest that higher "multipliers" should be accorded to enterprises in the *middle* of the chain of production than to those at the beginning.

Since the essentiality multiplier is introduced as an approximation to external economies, it should be applied only to the net national income produced, and not to the sum of *all* the ratios.

It should also be emphasized that the difficulties of measuring external economies cannot be overcome by altering the formula in other respects. For example, in the course of testing various formulas, it was found that inclusion of the foreign exchange cost in the denominator resulted in a drop of a twine mill from third to twelfth place in a list of twenty firms. Since this firm was producing fish-net twine essential to the highly important fishing industry, this low priority rating clearly reflected a defect in the formula. But it does not follow that, because eliminating foreign exchange cost would raise the rating of this project, the inclusion of foreign exchange cost in the denominator is the weakness. If foreign exchange is one of the scarce resources which the government wishes to allocate, logic *requires* its inclusion in the denominator of the formula.

The formula was wrong in that it did not properly measure the external economies of the twine industry; a perfect formula would accord this industry a high rating, despite the fact that its direct contribution to income and employment is small relative to capital and foreign exchange cost, because of its big contribution to the income produced by the fishing industry. The only way to improve the formula is to improve the measurement of external economies.

Nor is it desirable to manipulate multipliers so as to get a ranking of a small number of cases that seems "reasonable." At one stage of discussion it was proposed to use multipliers ranging from 1 to 64. But to apply essentiality multipliers ranging from 1 to 64 is equivalent to throwing out the formula altogether; only the ranking in terms of essentiality will be of any significance between groups and the formula would be operative only *within* groups. If the government wishes the groupings to be of paramount importance, it would be simpler not to introduce an essentiality multiplier at all but to use the formula only to establish ratings within major groups. It might be advisable to begin the priority system in this fashion, and to apply the formula between groups only as the accumulation of knowledge permits more accurate measurement of external economies.

Use of the Formula

The original motivation behind the proposal to draw up an industrial priorities formula seems to have been a wish to assure co-ordinated treatment by various government agencies of requests for foreign exchange, transfer privileges, tax privileges, intermediate and long-term loans, etc. Another motive was to relieve the pressure on those government agencies which were concerned with applications of various sorts emanating from the private industrial sector. By providing a ready device for evaluating such applications, the system was expected to speed decisions and remove them from personal influence by the applicants.

The underlying logic of the formula was such, however, as to make it equally applicable to the public and to the private sector, to the agricultural and to the industrial sector. Whatever the investment project, the most important considerations were its cost in capital and foreign exchange and its yield in contribution to national income, employment, and the balance of payments. To be sure, measuring external economies (positive or negative) may be more difficult for public projects, which produce nothing for the market, than for private projects; it may also be more difficult to measure external economies of agricultural projects (particularly such projects as reafforestation, soil conservation, and flood control) than of industrial projects. But as argued above, the difficulties of measurement are no excuse for not making the effort, since these are the factors relevant to decisions regarding priorities.

On the other hand, there are two kinds of applications which the formula does not fit at all. One of these is the import of final consumers' goods. The import of consumers' goods cannot be said to "produce" anything; here only the "essentiality factor" counts. The other consists of enterprises seeking some permission or commitment from the government but requesting no foreign exchange or capital. An example would be a foreign petroleum company wishing to build a refinery and requesting both permission to do so and a commitment of profits transfer, but providing its own capital and foreign exchange and undertaking to save the country foreign exchange on balance. Since the formula is designed to allocate the country's own capital and foreign exchange, it is not relevant where no such allocation takes place. In such cases, the only questions are: "Will the project save the country foreign exchange? Will it absorb an excessive amount of scarce skilled labor or scarce domestic materials?"

The Market and the Planner

The interesting feature of the Philippines formula is that it combines market with non-market considerations. Value added is a pure market factor; if only this component of the formula were in operation, allocation would be no different from what it would be in a free market operating on the profit principle. The fact that the "essentiality multiplier" is applied only to value added means that *current* market factors remain a major factor in allocation of scarce resources. Since development requires allocation in terms of market considerations in the *future*—perhaps twenty years hence—it may be that the Philippines formula still gives too much weight to *existing* market relationships. Obviously, where *new* industries are being considered, an estimate of *future* value added must be made.

The treatment of R_2, the impact of investment projects on the balance of payments, is also estimated primarily in terms of current market relationships. In the consideration of creating employment and using domestic materials "shadow prices" are used, but they are still *current* shadow prices.[16] Only the "essentiality multiplier" reflects the judgment of planners as to the impact of various investment projects on future economic growth.

In the light of our analysis in Part 3, perhaps the Philippines formula is still too market-oriented; but it is a first attempt at rational allocation of resources, to promote economic development and other policy objectives, by a government committed to democracy and free private enterprise. The experiment will bear watching.

The Tinbergen-King Formula

The priority formula developed by the Netherlands Economics Institute, on the basis of earlier work by Jan Tinbergen and Benjamin B. King, was not aimed at early application in a particular country with a peculiar set of economic and political problems. Accordingly, it is more general and more precise than the Philippines formula. For example, whereas the Philippines formula differentiates between the gestation period and the operations period only for foreign exchange costs, the Tinbergen-King formula does so for every aspect of an investment project. Similarly, where the Philippines formula uses an "essentiality multiplier," which is given empirical content on the basis of an implicit theory of linkages, the Tinbergen-King formula includes direct influences (immediate contributions to production) and indirect influences (all other effects on the economy) in general form. The method consists of comparing real national income for all future periods, appropriately discounted to ac-

[16] For a brief and simple discussion of the use of "shadow" or "accounting" prices, see Tinbergen, *op. cit.*, pp. 39, 76–78.

count for national time preference, and with appropriate accounting prices, with and without the investment project or projects in question. No cost calculations are necessary, because any inputs involved in a project have an immediate effect on national income, if they must be withdrawn from other uses.

The basic equations are quite simple:

$$Y^o = pv^o - p^i i^o - \delta p b^o \quad \text{(M.1)}$$

$$Y^h = pv^h - p^i i^h - \delta p b^h - m^i K^{ih} \quad \text{(M.2)}$$

where the symbols are defined as follows:

Y^o = the contribution to net national product of the rest of the economy

Y^h = the contribution to net national product of project h

v^o = the quantity of the gross product produced in the rest of the economy

v^h = the quantity of gross product for project h

i^o = the required volume of imports for the rest of the economy

i^h = the required volume of imports for project h

b^o = the real value of the capital stock in the rest of the economy

b^h = the real value of the capital stock created by project h

K^{ih} = the amount of foreign debts incurred for the execution of project h

m^i = the interest rate for foreign debts

p = the price level of the national product

p^i = the import price level

In determining the rate of growth of income, with and without project h, the rate of capital accumulation (growth of the capital stock) and the capital-output ratio become strategic variables.

The very fact that this formula gains precision through greater generality makes it more difficult to put into it the necessary data than is the case with the Philippines formula. The general theory behind the two formulas is much the same; both try to measure the impact on future national income and both calculate separately the impact on the balance of payments. The Philippines formula sacrifices theoretical accuracy in order to have something that is operable with the statistics available to the planning authorities.

Although the Tinbergen-King formula is less market-oriented than the Philippines version, making use of accounting prices and measuring the effect on national income as a whole for as far in the future as the project has any effect, it is still essentially "marginal" in concept. With such a formula there would be a temptation to compare the impact of particular *projects*, rather than the impact of constellations and sequences of projects. The formula could still be used for such constellations and sequences, but for this purpose it would be of limited use, since it does not isolate the strategic variables that would determine the outcome; these are lumped together in the "contribution to real national income," which is just the thing that is so difficult to measure.

We have suggested above that the impact of various constellations and sequences of projects be measured in terms of aggregate income during a "crucial period," rather than from the time a project is launched to infinity. For planning practice, there are advantages in this formulation, although the Tinbergen-King formula is formally more correct. On the one hand, it is hardly worthwhile trying to estimate the impact on national income beyond a "crucial period" ending twenty to forty years hence; our forecasting is not that accurate, and if a discount factor is applied, the contribution in later years will be of minor significance anyway. On the other hand, leaving out the impact during the next five to ten years helps planners to make the necessary break from traditional engineering or economic concepts of "cost-benefit ratios" of individual projects, and to think in terms of model sequences over a considerable period, a period which should tell the tale with respect to stagnation or progress.[17]

On much the same sort of grounds we have not thought it advisable to measure the impact on income during the crucial period in terms of a discounted series of annual incomes. It is true that if a discount factor is applied the value of aggregate income during the crucial period will vary with the way in which it is distributed among the individual years during the period. However, there are two arguments against using a discount factor. It is virtually impossible to decide what figure to use. Secondly, use of a figure based on some concept of a "pure interest rate" could be highly misleading. For example, with a discount factor the aggregate income during a period would be higher if income were 200 in the first year and fell during the next ten years to 100 than if it were 100 in the first year and rose steadily to 200; yet clearly the prognosis would be better in the second case than in the first. If the concept of a "crucial period" is to be utilized,

[17] For an example of the "old-fashioned" type of cost-benefit comparison, see *Formulation and Economic Appraisal of Development Projects* (New York, 1951), Part II. The UN agencies themselves have moved a long way from the approach outlined in this document.

a negative discount factor might be more appropriate than a positive one. Once again, the real problem is lack of knowledge about the nature of the growth process. Some sort of weighting of aggregate income during the crucial period is certainly necessary, but it must be based on the best judgment possible of the effect of different patterns of income on future growth.

Priorities, Linkage, and the Sequence of Projects

Since development is a cumulative process in time, a more important question than "Will education or improved transport add more to national income during the next few years?" is, "Will expenditure on education or on transport in the next few years stimulate the most investment in other fields in subsequent years?" As Professor Hirschman puts it: [18]

> The question of priority must be resolved on the basis of a comparative appraisal of the strength with which progress in one of these areas will induce progress in the other(s). In these basic types of development decisions, it is therefore not sufficient to supplement, qualify, and otherwise refine the usual investment criteria. We must evolve entirely new aids to thought and action in this largely uncharted territory of efficient sequences and optimal development strategies.

The relative strength of these backward and forward "linkage" effects is among the all-important factors bundled together in the "essentiality multiplier" of the Philippines formula. And this, of course, is the weakness of the formula. Our most important need is a formula for determining the size of the essentiality multiplier —and that we do not yet have. As experience with planned development accumulates, however, and as more planning authorities begin thinking in such terms, it will become easier to determine the "optimal sequence" for particular countries at particular times.

In determining the sequence of projects, planning authorities should also give attention to the alternation of "pressure-creating" and "pressure-relieving" investments recommended by Hirschman. In countries with vigorously expanding private enterprise sectors, the government's function can be largely limited to "pressure-relieving." As private investment takes place, shortages and shortcomings will appear in transport facilities, public utilities, education, and other activities traditionally assigned (in whole or in part) to public enterprise in such societies. Governments ought not to feel "restless and slighted" when confined to this

[18] Albert O. Hirschman, *Strategy of Economic Development* (New York, 1958), p. 79.

"induced role," Hirschman maintains, because "knowledge on the part of private operators that bottlenecks and shortages will be efficiently taken care of if and when they appear acts as a considerable spur to further development."

Where expansion through private investment is not assured, the government's role must be more active. For example, it might build an iron and steel plant. In Chapter 16, we saw that there is some evidence that iron and steel industries have high total linkage effects. If so, such government action will lead to a spurt of investment in a variety of fields. This investment in turn will reveal deficiencies that government must fill. When filled, further private investment will take place, and so on.

This sort of sequence, says Hirschman, casts doubt on the view that "the government should not get itself involved in making steel ingots when it is not even capable of keeping the roads in passable condition." On this issue, the present writer tends to side with Hirschman. In his view, the team of American engineers invited to advise Indonesia on its industrialization program in 1951 did that country a dubious service in insisting that the government ought not to think of new industries when it could not properly maintain the plant and equipment already in the country. Had a program of industrialization been launched at that time, when the government had both the internal revenues and the foreign exchange to do it, a sequence of developmental investment might have been initiated. Indonesia might now be on her way to higher levels of productivity, instead of being substantially where she was seven years ago.

Hirschman concludes his discussion of the optimal sequence of projects in the following words: [19]

> Thus our division of governmental activities into these two "inducing" and "induced" or "unbalancing" functions seems to be useful in a variety of ways. It is not suggested that governments should appoint a Minister for Initiating Growth and a Minister for Restoring Balance, but to think in terms of these two tasks may perhaps serve to give ministers and governments a clearer conception of their role within the development process. The frequently prevailing lack of clarity in this matter is a distinct handicap not only for the peaceful coexistence and collaboration of the public and private sectors but also for the effectiveness of governmental action.
>
> In this respect, the contemporary fashion of drawing up comprehensive development plans or programs is often quite unhelpful. For the very comprehensiveness of these plans can drown out the sense of

[19] *Ibid.*, pp. 204–205.

direction so important for purposeful policy-making. A plan can be most useful if, through its elaboration, a government works out a strategy for development. While the choice of priority areas must of course proceed from an examination of the economy as a whole, it may be best, once the choice is made to concentrate on detailed concrete programs for these areas, as in the first Monnet Plan for France's postwar reconstruction. The attempt at comprehensive programming usually exacts a high price in terms of articulateness and persuasiveness, qualities that are essential for the plan's ability to come to grips with reality.

The Choice of Technology

The simple argument with respect to choice of techniques in underdeveloped countries is derived from the orthodox theory of production: where labor is abundant and capital is scarce, efficient production calls for labor-intensive techniques. But this theory is essentially "static"; it is relevant to conditions ruling at a point of time and is accordingly not very suitable as a basis for development planning.

Some advocates of this approach, it is true, recognize that the labor-intensive techniques prevalent in the rural sector of underdeveloped countries are so inefficient that output per unit of capital, as well as output per unit of labor, is lower than with more advanced methods. We saw in Chapter 1, for example, that yields per hectare are lower, even with the labor-intensive methods of Asia and Africa, than they are with more mechanized techniques in advanced countries. These advocates proceed to call for a *new* technology, to raise output per man-year without increasing the ratio of capital to labor. The present writer has himself expressed concern, in his report to the Philippines government, over the tendency to use capital-intensive techniques in the industrial sector of that country despite the presence of high and growing unemployment. Other writers, however, have maintained that underdeveloped countries should always use the most advanced techniques. What is the truth of the matter?

Let us begin by stating the obvious. If it is possible to find techniques which will indeed raise productivity per man-hour without increasing capital per man; if this kind of technological progress contributes as much to "technology-mindedness," industrialization, and urbanization, drops in fertility rates, acquisition of skills, "linkage," and subsequent capital formation as does the usual kind of labor-saving innovation; then we should certainly use such techniques wherever labor is abundant and capital scarce. In stating the principle in this way, however, we also indicate the limitations of this approach to the question of choice of technology. When and where are these conditions met?

In peasant agriculture, where the size of farm is likely to be limited for some decades to come in many countries, there is indeed a case for seeking better tools rather than introducing "tractor pools" and other heavy agricultural equipment where it cannot be effectively used. In India, China, Japan, or Java, for example, it is unrealistic to think of average holdings in excess of, say, five hectares for a long time to come. If possible, technological progress should take the form of tools which would permit a family to cultivate efficiently holdings two or three times what they now have. Specialized weeding tools, scythes instead of sickles, Persian wheels instead of *dahlu*'s, these are the kinds of things that come to mind. These innovations *do* raise the ratio of capital to labor, but not very much, and they can bring a substantial increase in total output, thus reducing capital costs as well as labor costs.

Probably, managers of industrial plants have not devoted as much ingenuity as they might to finding ways of using more labor-intensive techniques without loss of efficiency. Engineers in particular tend to think that the *latest* device is the best. Such is not always the case. The team of American engineers referred to above suggested to the Indonesian government that the ancient "Opelettes" (model "A" Fords, jeeps, etc., with tiny bus bodies), which ply the streets and roads of Indonesia, be replaced by modern busses running on fixed schedules. But the engineers overlooked some important points. First, the average age of these machines was over twenty years, and only the mechanical genius of their owner-operators kept them running. Thus they had long ago been written off, and the *capital cost* of operating them was zero. Gasoline was a domestic product and cheap. Maintaining them provided training in automotive mechanics to a lot of people. The busses would have employed far fewer men; they would have been very expensive in terms of capital and foreign exchange, and it was doubtful that fuel costs per man-mile would have been significantly reduced with busses.

Moreover, the busses would have given less satisfactory service. The "Opelettes" ran in steady streams over a great variety of routes. The villager going to market had only to squat by the road beside his village (and in Java there is nearly always a road beside a village) with the assurance that an Opelette would come along soon, and that it would drop him very near the market.

Incredible numbers of small Indonesians could be crowded into these tiny vehicles, making this semi-taxi-service very cheap. Busses running on regular schedules, on the other hand, would be limited to a certain number of stops at certain times of the day. They would have involved a considerable loss of convenience to the user. In short, in the Indonesian setting, the "Opelette" represented a *superior* technique to the modern bus. It constituted a labor-intensive, capital-cheap method of providing services of a kind the local people wanted.

There is also some evidence that labor-capital ratios can be varied a good deal without loss of efficiency in certain kinds of construction work. As the story goes, there is a dam in India half of which was built by foreign contractors using heavy equipment and the other half of which was built by traditional Indian methods, with women carrying baskets of concrete on their heads. The two halves look the same and are equally effective. Some studies made in the United States showed that even there, where contractors are used to highly mechanized techniques, costs on PWA projects executed on private contract with standard techniques were only 13 per cent lower than on WPA projects providing 3.8 times as much direct employment. In countries where labor-intensive techniques are traditional, one might expect construction costs to be lower where such techniques are used.

The Division for Balanced International Growth of the Netherlands Economics Institute has been conducting a series of studies of the flexibility of capital-labor ratios. Some of their results are presented in Table 27-5. These show very wide differences in capital-labor ratios between advanced and underdeveloped countries in certain industries. The biggest spreads occur between the United States and India in the sugar refining, flour, and iron and steel industries. Even among underdeveloped countries there is a marked variation in technique in these industries, with Mexico and Colombia—where the supply of both capital and entrepreneurship is relatively favorable—using considerably more capital-intensive techniques than India. In other industries, such as pulp and paper and printing, the range is rather small. The absolute figures are also of some interest; in the industries shown, even in India where the most labor-intensive techniques are used, capital-job ratios range from $1,800 for cotton textiles to $6,100 for alcoholic beverages. These figures provide some indication of the possibilities for establishing and maintaining full employment in underdeveloped countries with development programs on the scales now planned.[20]

The table shows that in some industries, at least, there is a good deal of flexibility in capital-labor ratios. It does not tell us directly whether the technology chosen is actually the most efficient for the country and industry in question. For that purpose, cost figures would be necessary. Here much more information

TABLE 27-5.

Capital per Person Employed
(In thousands of dollars at 1950 prices)

Industry	U.S.	Mexico	Colombia	India
Flour and gristmill products	39.1	10.4	19.9	5.6
Bread and bakery products	5.0	1.7	1.3	3.5
Sugar refining	26.8	8.2	12.4	2.6
Starch	...	9.4	3.8	3.3
Alcoholic beverages	16.0	6.6	18.0	6.1
Tobacco manufactures	12.4	8.6	2.0	...
Iron and steel industries	32.1	10.8	5.4	5.7
Wood pulp, paper, and paper products	10.2	8.9	4.8	6.6
Printing and publishing industries	5.1	3.5	5.1	..
Cotton yarn and cloth	8.7	2.1	6.2	1.8
Rubber products	7.0	3.4	6.1	...

SOURCE: Netherlands Economics Institute, Division for Balanced International Growth, December, 1955.

is needed than is yet available. Another study of the Netherlands Economics Institute analyzes costs of lathing with three types of machines, representing increasing degrees of mechanization: a center lathe (I), a turret lathe (II), and an automatic lathe (III). Costs are estimated with wages, *W*, at 1.50 florins per hour and an interest rate, *i*, of 4 per cent, and with wages of 0.05 florins and an interest rate of 15 per cent. The first case might be considered typical of an advanced country, the latter typical of an underdeveloped one. What the study shows is that for levels of output up to 150 units a single center lathe is most efficient in either country. In the advanced country a single turret lathe is best for outputs of 150 to 785, whereas in the underdeveloped country this remains the best technique up to an output of 1,000. When output reaches 2,800 in the advanced country, it pays to

[20] Cf. Benjamin Higgins, *Public Investment and Full Employment*, p. 164.

shift to a pair of automatic lathes, but it takes an output of 3,600 to make this technique worthwhile in the underdeveloped country. In a sense, the results of this study are encouraging: it shows that for this kind of process an underdeveloped country can keep costs down by using relatively labor-intensive techniques. In another sense it is discouraging; it means that an underdeveloped country must achieve a *higher* level of output than an advanced one, in order to make it profitable to use the most advanced techniques.

A later study of filing and grinding techniques led to the conclusion that for wages below a certain level the wage level has a good deal of influence on break-even points, whereas for higher wages the actual level has rather little effect on break-even points. Thus over a wide range of output, "a choice between labor- and capital-intensive techniques is relevant only when the wage rate is sufficiently low." [21] The study also showed that higher interest rates did not much affect the choice of technology.

What these studies seem to add up to, as far as they have gone, is that in some industries it pays to use labor-intensive techniques if labor is relatively abundant and cheap, at least over some ranges of output. At the same time, the opportunities for turning a scarcity of capital and an abundance of labor into advantages are strictly limited.[22] There *is* no technology which can be applied to a wide range of productive activities, and which obtains higher yields per unit of capital used by using more labor in conjunction with each unit of capital. Small-scale agriculture and construction seem to be exceptions rather than the rule. The more advanced techniques tend to save both labor and capital; underdeveloped countries can afford to deny themselves their use less than advanced ones, because underdeveloped countries can ill afford to waste capital. By the same token, capital-scarce countries can less afford losses through obsolescence than capital-rich countries; it is particularly important for the underdeveloped country to choose techniques that will *not* become outmoded soon. In any case, only unskilled labor is abundant; skilled workers, technicians, foremen, and managers are scarce—even more scarce than capital. For this reason, one finds Stanvac in-

[21] Netherlands Economics Institute, *Alternative Techniques of Production* (Rotterdam, January, 1957), p. 33.

[22] See also Netherlands Economics Institute, "Subsidies and the Substitution of Labour for Capital" (January, 1956); "The Economics of Mill vs. Handloom-Weaving in India" (a progress report on method, September, 1956); and other reports in this series.

stalling a fully automatic refinery in Bombay, and the municipality of Djakarta choosing a fully automatic French design for its water filtration plant.

More important still, however, are dynamic factors of the kind discussed in the previous section. When one considers the impact on the whole process of economic growth, the case for the more advanced techniques becomes very strong. Hirschman suggests, for example, that there is much to be said for "show-pieces" that are so expensive and so complex that they *have* to be carefully planned in advance, and carefully operated and maintained by properly trained workers once they are installed. A government which builds an iron and steel mill or a hydroelectric plant "places itself under a far stronger compulsion to 'deliver' than if it were to spend the same funds on a large number of small projects." We have already pointed out that a few large-scale projects seem to have a greater total impact on an economy than a lot of small ones costing the same amount. Similarly, Hirschman argues, there is more assurance that workers will acquire the necessary skills if the limits of tolerance are so small that errors are disastrous, as in the case of precision instruments. An untrained labor force, he says, performs better on machine-paced operations than on operator-paced operations. Management, too, tends to become more efficient if subjected to the discipline of machine-paced operations.

Hirschman formalizes his argument with the use of a diagram which is a modification of Figure 14-1 above. All the points made above add up to a situation in which, for the labor-intensive operations common in underdeveloped countries, the loss of a unit of capital requires the addition of *more* labor to maintain output constant than is the case in advanced countries. Thus the isopods of advanced and underdeveloped countries will coincide only for the upper portions of the curves representing capital-intensive techniques; these tend to be the same everywhere. But for more labor-intensive techniques the curves for the underdeveloped countries (shown by the dotted lines) will lie upward and to the right of those for the advanced countries (solid lines). Thus despite the lower ratio of labor costs to capital costs in an underdeveloped country, it should use at least as much capital to produce a given output as in advanced countries. In Figure 27-1 the underdeveloped country uses the same amount of capital and more labor; but one could construct a similar diagram to show it using the same amount of labor and more capital than an advanced country to produce a given output.

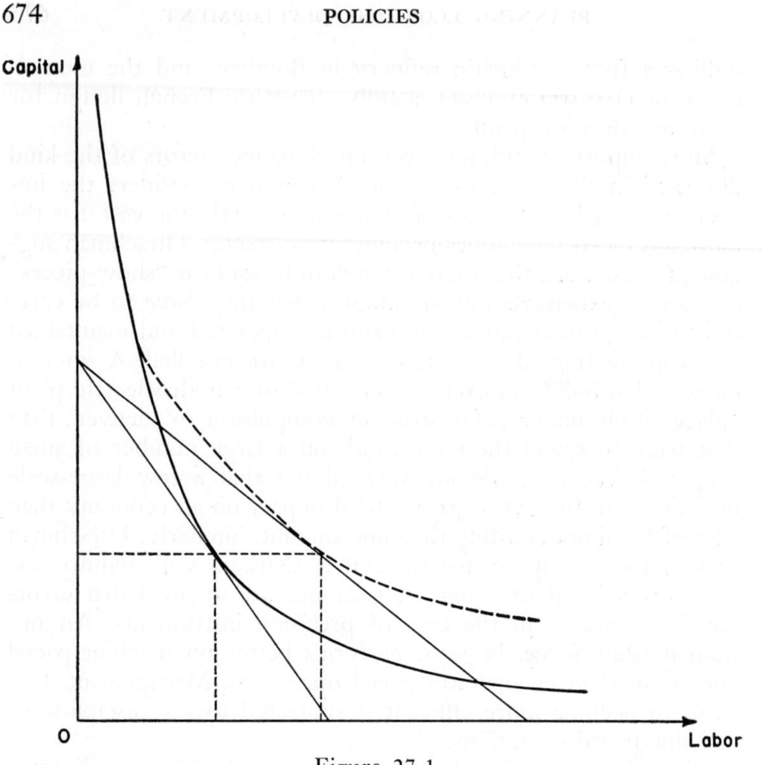

Figure 27-1

Hirschman reaches the following conclusion with respect to choice of technique: [23]

[23] Hirschman, *op. cit.* Hirschman's article also pointed out that Leontief's celebrated findings about the comparatively high labor content of United States exports could be considered corroborative evidence. (See his "Factor Proportions and the Structure of American Trade: Further Theoretical and Empirical Analysis," *Review of Economics and Statistics*, Vol. XXXVIII, November, 1956, pp. 386–407, and literature there cited.) Conversely, our analysis provides an explanation of Leontief's statistics, related to the one he has proposed himself. It has been suggested that underdeveloped countries may find it easier to approach the efficiency standards of the advanced industrial nations in capital-intensive, process-centered, than in labor-intensive, product-centered, industries. Therefore, as world-wide industrialization progresses, the comparative advantage of the advanced industrial countries may come to lie increasingly with certain types of labor-intensive goods and services. This can best be illustrated by a fanciful hypothesis. Let us imagine that certain labor-intensive services such as maintenance of roads, buildings, and machinery, could become objects of international trade at moderate transport costs. I have no doubt that in this eventuality the older industrial nations would specialize in the export of services, quite possibly importing steel and cement in exchange!

Nevertheless, in combination, the criteria developed here do point toward certain highly capital-intensive pursuits as particularly well suited for underdeveloped countries. The list includes thus far: large-scale ventures, activities that must be maintained in top working order, that must maintain high quality standards for their output, machine-paced operations, and process-centered industries. For the time being, these criteria can of course be considered only as hypotheses. Empirical verifications should not be too difficult to undertake. If we are correct, labor productivity differentials between an underdeveloped and an industrial country should be much larger in certain industries (e.g., metal fabricating) than in certain others (e.g., cement) even when essentially similar techniques are used in both countries.

The general principle for choice of techniques is easy enough to state: the country should use the technique that will contribute most, for a given cost as measured with appropriate accounting prices, to the aggregate national income during the "crucial period" some years in the future. But it is not easy to decide what this technique is in a particular case, and it may prove that the total capital supply would not permit enough projects to be carried out with the optimal technique to create and maintain full employment.

Choice of Technology versus Choice of Product Mix

The over-all capital-labor ratio for the country as a whole depends not only on the techniques chosen to produce a particular commodity but also on what the country chooses to produce. Some commodities require a lower ratio of capital to labor, with the most effective technique, than others. A country with much labor and little capital would do well to include in its product mix a large proportion of commodities which can be produced efficiently with relatively labor-intensive methods.

Even here, however, caution is necessary. "Efficiency" in this context has to mean once again contribution to gross national product during the "crucial period," and not merely the immediate increase in output of the product directly concerned. All the interactions, sequences, linkages, and external economies must be taken into account. It is more than likely that the products which can be produced cheaply with labor-intensive techniques are goods which the country has been traditionally producing, and continuing to produce them rather than something new may prove to be a way of retarding take-off. Careful study, sharp foresight, and keen judgment are needed to make the right decisions in each particular case.

Another point that must be borne in mind in choosing a product mix is that the execution of a development program usually requires increasing foreign exchange earnings. The necessity to engage in foreign trade on an expanding scale imposes limits on the choice of products. For as Jan Tinbergen has pointed out, both highly capital-intensive and highly labor-intensive activities seem to turn out "products that do not enter easily into international trade."[24] Tinbergen also points out the importance of distinguishing between the establishment of an industry (building an electricity plant) and operating it (producing electricity); one may be labor-intensive, the other capital-intensive. Finally, it should be noted that a simple way of raising the capital-labor ratio is to increase the number of shifts.

Land-use Planning

Some underdeveloped countries have prepared regional and city plans as well as national economic development plans. At these three levels, plans obviously overlap with respect to land use. A national development plan is usually presented in terms of levels and patterns of investment, income, output, employment, etc., but it *implies* a certain location of industry and a certain distribution of population and thus a certain pattern of land use. Regional development plans are more frequently stated in terms of land use, and the land-use pattern is usually the core of a city plan; but the execution of city and regional plans affects investment, output, employment, and income.

The question therefore arises, "Is planning at national, regional, and city levels integrated with respect to land use—either in theory or in practice?" Not only is the planning at the three levels done by different people under different kinds of authority and different laws, but the planners themselves usually have different kinds of training and use different kinds of analytical tools. It is therefore high time for giving serious thought to integration of national, regional, and city planning, both in terms of principles and in terms of their application, into a national urban policy.[25]

Some progress toward a national urban policy can be made by improvements in administration. City and regional planners

[24] Jan Tinbergen, *The Design of Development* (Baltimore, 1958), pp. 72–73.

[25] Cf. C. Haar, Benjamin Higgins, and L. Rodwin, "Economic and Physical Planning: Coordination in Developing Areas," *Journal of the American Institute of Planners*, October, 1958.

need a two-way street to the planning organization charged with responsibility for a national development plan. The draft plans of city and regional planners should be among the data studied by national development planners in preparing the overall plan. National development plans should be submitted in draft to city and regional planners, for analysis of the impact on their area of execution of the national plan. This analysis of the city and regional planners should in turn be made available to the national planners and utilized in preparation of the final draft of the national plan. Once development plans are in final form, they should be made available to city and regional planners immediately so that they can make their final plans accordingly.

This process of solving a system of simultaneous equations should be continuous. Ideally, no plan, whether at the national or at the city or regional level, would have legal status for more than one year. In this fashion, there would be a continuous process of revision of national development plans for next year in terms of the city and regional plans of this year, as well as the degree of success in carrying out the national development plan this year. Direct contacts among the professional planners, and also of the planning authorities at all levels of government would help a good deal to promote integrated national planning. However, there must also be greater uniformity of approach and methodology than now exists in the fields of physical planning on the one hand and economic planning on the other. The usual economic development plan concentrates on *capital use;* it assumes implicitly that, if an appropriate allocation of *capital* is obtained, the appropriate allocation of management, labor, and land will follow automatically. Thus economic development plans do not as a rule include a plan for land use. Decisions as to land use are left to private investors, local governments, and to central government implementing agencies, within the framework of capital allocation which is provided in the economic development plan.

There are exceptions. Some public investment projects are defined in place terms. The detailed presentation of the plan, listing roads, railroads, airports, harbors, land reclamation, resettlement projects, and the like, will very often provide place tags for these projects. More rarely, the economic development planning process includes an analysis of location factors, and the plan may include suggestions as to location of new private industries as well. In the rare cases where such suggestions are made, they are usually connected with new public investment projects, such as power and transport, which are expected to open up new opportunities for private industrial or agricultural investment.

Indeed, here is one of the major weaknesses of economic development planning as ordinarily undertaken. Virtually no consideration is given to the optimum location of enterprises. Certainly development planners need not be concerned with street patterns, design of public buildings, and the like. But even the crucial questions of rural *versus* urban growth, and the distribution of new enterprises among cities, small towns, and villages, the selection of growing points and leading sectors, which are the very core of economic development, are frequently neglected.

The first requirement for the development of a national urban policy, as a guide to inclusion of land-use aspects of development in the development plans, is an analysis of what is happening now. Most underdeveloped countries show a disturbing tendency toward agglomeration, conurbation, and the like. Why have these trends appeared since World War II? Is it a healthy or an unhealthy development? What objections are there to permitting the pattern of land use to develop "naturally"? These questions deserve much more study than they have yet obtained. Conditions seem to vary from one country to another. For example, the available evidence suggests that in India people move from partial employment in rural areas to total unemployment in the cities. In Indonesia, on the other hand, it seems that unemployment among in-migrants is lower in the capital city of Djakarta than it was in the rural areas whence they came.

The Role of Community Development

This section is concerned with the relationship of community development to general programs for launching a take-off into economic growth in now underdeveloped countries.

By "community development" is meant here the range of activities described in the ICA statement of *Community Development Guidelines:*[26]

A. "Community Development" is the term used to describe the technique many governments have adopted to reach their village people and to make more effective use of local initiative and energy for increased production and better living standards. Community development is a process of social action in which the people of a community organize themselves for planning and action; define their common and individual needs and problems; make group and individual plans to

[26] Community development is also known as village development, rural development, village agricultural and industrial development, community action, and community education.

meet their needs and solve their problems; execute these plans with a maximum of reliance upon community resources; and supplement these resources when necessary with services and material from governmental and nongovernmental agencies outside the community. Governments have learned that when local people have a chance to decide how they can better their own local conditions, better sanitation, greater literacy, and other desirable improvements are more easily introduced and have a more lasting effect.

B. More specifically, community development is technical assistance at the village level in how people work together for better living. Its objectives are to help people find methods to organize self-help programs and to furnish the techniques for cooperative action on plans which the local people develop to improve their own circumstances. It can result in greater literacy, improved health, more productive agriculture. Its immediate concern is not only these results but what happens in the process of achieving them. The heart of community development is village organization and all of the techniques in how people are brought together; how they are democratically organized; how to get the individual villager to take part; how to get discussion and thinking started; how people arrive at the things they think they need; how they judge the priority of the things they want; how committees operate; how people are brought around to the decision that they can do something for themselves; how they proceed to get from a higher level of government the help they need. It helps to bring a whole range of technical knowledge to bear on the programs which the people themselves feel are necessary to their economic and social progress. Community development fosters a unified approach to the problems of the villages. It capitalizes on and puts to work manpower, the greatest resource of underdeveloped countries. It produces its own end result in the form of experience and skill in democratic procedures.

It is apparent that there is a close relationship between community development, as an approach to economic development, and the "up by the bootstraps" approach outlined in Chapter 19. The governments of several underdeveloped countries, discouraged by the magnitudes of the capital requirements suggested by calculations of the sort outlined earlier in this chapter, have seized upon community development as an easier path. It is of some importance, therefore, to consider the potentialities and limitations of community development as an instrument for promoting sustained economic growth.

If the theory outlined in Chapter 17 is correct, any policy designed simply to keep people on the land is antidevelopmental. Any such policy must fall instead into one of two categories: (*a*) it may be a policy designed to establish the preconditions for take-off, or (*b*) it may come under the heading of rural social work.

ESTABLISHING PRECONDITIONS

It is possible that in some underdeveloped countries resources are so limited that they cannot plan realistically for a take-off in the near future. In that event, there may be a case for concentrating on raising agricultural productivity in the short run, so as to produce the surpluses that can be recaptured to finance the next phase of economic growth. If this route to a take-off is the only one open to a particular country, of course, no argument can be made against it. However, it is a route that can easily lead instead to further stagnation. For raising agricultural productivity as part of a program for establishing preconditions for a take-off means preventing the increase in agricultural output from improving rural living standards; otherwise, it may merely freeze the existing structure. With further population growth, no permanent gains may be attained even in rural welfare. Yet recapturing initial gains in agriculture to finance further development is politically very difficult.

As we have seen in Chapter 19, the "up by the bootstraps" approach has succeeded in the past only where severe sacrifices have been forced on the masses of the people, to provide a basis for capital accumulation. The "up by the bootstraps" approach proposed for underdeveloped areas today may not require reductions in the standard of living to start the development process, but it does mean that the initial increases in output must be denied to the people, in order to provide an export surplus to finance further expansion. An integral part of the scheme is increased taxation for farmers, first to compel them to produce as much as before although they have fewer mouths to feed, and secondly to drain off the increase in output and income as the development projects have their effect. This increase in taxation, and consequent prevention of initial improvements in living standards, is necessary, not only to provide an export surplus, but also to prevent the increased productivity from being converted into increased leisure or a more rapid rate of population growth rather than into increased output. Given the tax structures and general political situations of most underdeveloped countries, it is highly questionable whether small increases in *per capita* income, obtainable through improvements in techniques with the present structure of the economy, can be recaptured in their entirety.

RURAL SOCIAL WORK

If it is felt that development is impossible, there may be a case on purely humanitarian grounds for doing everything possible to alleviate the misery of people living in the peasant agriculture and handicrafts sector. A good deal of what has actually been done by community development programs would seem to fall into this category. Moreover, a good deal of the urban community development now being recommended to supplement rural community development would also have to be characterized as urban social work rather than economic development. There is of course nothing wrong with endeavoring to improve levels of social welfare; but we should be perfectly clear when we are engaging in social welfare programs and when we are assisting countries with their economic development.

ROLE OF COMMUNITY DEVELOPMENT

Can the social work aspects of community development be carried out without absorbing scarce resources? The basic idea of community development is to use resources that would otherwise remain idle. If in fact no scarce resources are used, community development programs may not retard development, even if they are exclusively of the social work variety. There is of course some danger that raising levels of social welfare will accelerate population growth once more; nothing in our demographic knowledge suggests that it would not, unless a deliberate effort is made to introduce family planning along with improved public health. If population growth is accelerated, community development may make a later take-off all the more difficult. In that case community development would be directly opposed to economic development.

Unfortunately, however, community development does absorb some scarce resources. In so far as community development programs remain part of the technical assistance provided by Western countries, they absorb budget funds, reducing the amounts available for other foreign aid projects. They utilize technical *expertise* from the Western countries which is scarce even in these countries. The same is true of administrative personnel in aid-giving countries. Community development also uses at least some budget funds and capital goods of underdeveloped countries, no matter how simple the community development projects may be. Most serious, they absorb the extremely scarce administrative and technical capacities of personnel in the underdeveloped country.

There is thus a real danger that expansion of community development programs may actually retard economic development. The extent to which they do so will depend on the extent to which community development takes the social work form, improving levels of rural welfare and making it more attractive for people to stay where they are.

Could community development programs be designed to *accelerate* the removal of people from agriculture? It would be useful to review community development projects in these terms. Which of them could properly be considered projects designed to get people off the land? The improvement of transport facilities, which permit a higher degree of specialization and increased contrast between rural and urban centers, might accelerate the flow of people from the rural to the industrial sector. General education may provide the basis for acquisition of industrial skills. Community development programs might give more weight to the kind of training which will either produce industrial skills directly or permit their more rapid acquisition on the job. Health programs may improve the industrial work capacity of people now living in rural areas. The same is true of increases in agricultural productivity which permit rising levels of nutrition combined with reduction of the numbers of people on the land.

Thus the theory in Chapter 17 does not constitute an argument against community development as such, but only against community development projects of a kind designed to make life more attractive in the villages, as opposed to projects designed to facilitate a flow of people from the rural to the industrial sector. Economic development requires *both* agricultural improvement, of a kind involving a shift to more extensive and mechanized agriculture, and more rapid industrialization. In a word, it means vastly increased levels of investment, which in turn means increased foreign aid.

Appendix: Meaning of Symbols and Definition of Terms

$$R_1 = \frac{e(w + r + i + p)}{K}$$

where $e =$ Essentiality factor determined according to (1) economic importance of the product either as a commodity for export or for domestic use, (2) source of raw materials and supplies used, (3) source of capital equipment, and (4) source and nationality of financing.

$w =$ Compensation of all officials, employees, and laborers, including salaries, wages, bonuses, commissions, and others. From this value is subtracted the 50 per cent of the compensation of officials and employees who are not Philippine nationals which is remitted abroad, or such portion as is estimated to be remitted abroad in the case of prospective firms.

$r =$ Rent for the use of the land, buildings, and other facilities. The following rental rates shall apply for prospective firms: land, 8 per cent of its declared value; buildings, 12 per cent; and machinery and equipment, 16 per cent. For operating firms the imputed rent for facilities owned is already included in the profits, but rent for facilities not belonging to the firm is included. Equipment and process rentals and similar payments remitted abroad shall not be included.

$i =$ Interest paid for borrowed capital. An interest rate of 6 per cent shall be assumed whenever actual interest rate is not known. Interest payments on foreign borrowing shall not be included.

$p =$ Profits or returns (actual or estimated) on paid-up capital, but only to the extent of 15 per cent of such paid-up capital. Any balance between the total fixed assets plus circulating capital based on production and the value of the rented facilities, the paid-up capital, and the borrowed capital is also to earn a return to the extent of 15 per cent thereof. To be subtracted from the above are profits and dividends remitted abroad by the firm and its stockholders.

$k =$ Total investment in the firm which is equal to fixed assets (owned and/or rented) plus circulating capital. For this purpose the peso component of both fixed assets and circulating capital shall be adjusted to 70 per cent thereof. The amount of circulating capital of prospective firms shall be determined according to the nature of the industry but in no case shall it be less than the peso operating costs during three months (excluding depreciation changes) plus the foreign exchange operating costs (in peso equivalent) during six months.

$$R_2 = \frac{F \cdot E \cdot s/e - F \cdot E \cdot c}{K}$$

where $F \cdot E \cdot s/e =$ Foreign exchange earned or saved arising from the operation of the firm. The foreign exchange earned is the peso equivalent of the foreign exchange received by the country for the export product. The foreign exchange saved is the peso equivalent of the foreign exchange value of the "import-substitute" product. Import substitute is defined, as (1) any product that was imported into the Philippines at some time in the past or is an acceptable substitute thereof; (2) any product which, although never imported, will serve a useful purpose or is otherwise necessary for economic development. The foreign exchange value to be credited in the case of consumer goods shall be adjusted to the amount of foreign exchange expenditure which the economy could sustain if the product were to be imported. In the case of producer goods the foreign exchange value of which is indeterminate, the foreign exchange rates shall be taken to be equal to 70 per cent of the wholesale value of the product.

$F \cdot E \cdot c =$ Actual foreign exchange cost ($C + F$ or CIF) incurred in production including that for imported raw materials and supplies, salaries of foreign personnel, profits and resident remittances, interest payments, amortization of value of assets acquired with foreign exchange, royalty payments, technical and consulting services, business trips abroad, and all other foreign exchange outlays.

Where the imported component of a domestically processed intermediate product exceeds valuewise 50 per cent of the cost of that product, the value of the imported component shall also be considered as part of the foreign exchange costs of the firm. If the foreign exchange for the acquisition of assets is supplied by the Central Bank, it shall be amortized over a period of ten

TABLE 27-6.

Check Sheet A for Essentiality Rating (e)

Criterion	Points allowed				
	2.5	2.0	1.5	1.0	0.5
1A. Economic importance of export product	Product to be largely exported in finished form.	Product to be partly exported in semifinished and partly in finished form.	Product to be largely exported in semifinished form.	Product to be partly exported in semiprocessed form and partly in raw form.	Product to be largely exported in raw form.
1B. Economic importance of the domestic product	Product largely for use by other industries.	Products partly for other industries and partly for consumption.	Products largely for basic human needs.	Products partly for basic and partly for less basic human needs.	Products largely luxurious or unessential.
2. Materials and supplies used	Materials largely from domestic sources.	Materials partly imported and partly in domestic raw form or largely imported in raw or semifinished form but their early availability from domestic sources is fairly certain.	Materials partly imported and partly domestic in raw and semifinished form.	Materials largely imported in raw and semifinished form.	Materials largely imported in finished and semifinished form.
3. Capital equipment	Uses capital equipment entirely fabricated locally.	Uses capital equipment largely fabricated locally.	Uses capital equipment partly imported and partly locally fabricated.	Uses capital equipment with very little local fabrication.	Uses capital equipment entirely imported.
4. Source of financing	Financed entirely by nationals, with paid-up capital more than 50% of total investment required.	Financed entirely by nationals, with paid-up capital less than 50% of total investment required.	Financed largely by nationals and partly by foreigners and/or aliens, or with foreign loans.	Financed partly by nationals and largely by foreigners and/or aliens, or with foreign loans.	Financed entirely by foreigners and/or aliens.

SOURCE: Philippines National Economic Council, *The Five-Year Economic and Social Development Program for Fiscal Years, 1957–1961* (Manila, 1957).

years. If not supplied by the Central Bank, the actual amortization shall be used.

$$R_3 = \frac{0.5 \cdot rmd/rmt \cdot rmd}{K}$$

where *rmd* = Value of domestic materials and operating supplies used in production, excluding the value of the imported component of domestically processed intermediate products whenever such imported component exceeds valuewise 50 per cent of the value of that intermediate product.

rmt = Value of the total raw materials and supplies used in production.

The coefficient, $0.5 \cdot rmd/rmt$, represents a measure of the additional economic value generated by the utilization of the domestic materials and supplies.

$$R_4 = \frac{ld \cdot 2{,}000}{K}$$

where *ld* = Number of paid Filipino workers (officials, employees, and laborers employed during at least 300 days a year). A uniform average of 2,000 pesos per annum, corresponding to 300 working days, is to be used in determining the social value arising from the employment of the Filipino workers.

28 Population Policy

In Chapter 17 we saw that getting out of the low-income trap and staying out requires some combination of accelerated technological progress and retardation of population growth. We have already indicated that in the past these two developments have had some tendency to come together; conditions of rapid technical change have also been conducive to declining fertility. The possibility must be faced, however, that in some countries *no* feasible rate of technological progress will guarantee sustained economic progress, unless the rate of population growth drops. In these countries, a positive population policy may prove to be an essential part of over-all planning for economic development.

The cold diagrammatic analysis of Chapter 17 may destroy for the reader any sense of the intense human and social problems involved in the very concept of "population policy." Let us borrow some more picturesque language from a leading anthropologist: [1]

> In summary, every society would like to improve its economic position, and every society is capable of learning to operate the machines and follow the scientific procedures which might lead to such improvement. Let us turn now to the cultural and social factors which may operate to inhibit or retard economic growth.

[1] Ralph Linton, "Cultural and Personality Factors Affecting Economic Growth," in Berthold F. Hoselitz (ed.), *The Progress of Underdeveloped Areas,* Harris Foundation Lectures (Chicago, 1952) pp. 79–80.

The first and perhaps most important of these is unrestricted breeding. This is no more and no less natural than other features of human behavior. It is intimately wrapped up with the society's culture, and birth control is infinitely older and more widely distributed than the use of rubber. Where such relatively humane methods of keeping down population are not in use, the balance between societies and their food supply has, until recently, been maintained by periodic famines and plagues. What happens when modern science and charity step in to prevent these can be seen in the case of the Navaho.

When I first visited the Navaho in 1912, there were supposed to be about twenty thousand of them. Exact figures were lacking, since many of those living in the back districts could not be caught to be counted. Today there are over sixty thousand, with no signs of a letdown in the rate of increase. Since there are already enough Navaho to weave all the blankets and herd all the sheep for which white Americans can provide a market, no solution to the problem is in sight.

Not all underdeveloped countries face population pressure in the same degree. We have seen from Table 1-6 that there is a wide variation in current rates of population growth. Table 28-1 shows similar data grouped by geographic regions. Between 1952 and 1956, East Asia had rates of population growth just equal to the world average. South Central Asia was below the world average, Central America far above it.

Of course, recent rates of population growth do not tell the whole story. The level and density of population are also important. So far as prognosis is concerned, a growth rate of 2 per cent as a consequence of a 4 per cent birth rate and a 2 per cent death rate has quite different implications from one resulting from a 3 per cent birth rate and a 1 per cent death rate. For in the latter case the death rate is already about as low as it can go, and acceleration of population growth through further improvements in public health is just about impossible. In the former case, on the other hand, death rates can be cut in half and the rate of population growth can be raised still higher. In predicting natality, age distribution counts; obviously a population heavily concentrated in the age brackets between fifteen and forty is more likely to have high birth rates in the next few years than one with heavier concentrations in the lower or higher age brackets.

Demographers have developed a concept of "population types," which permits them to classify countries into "low-growth potential," "high-growth potential," and "transitional," on the basis of all the relevant demographic data. Countries tend

TABLE 28-1.

Population, 1956, and Annual Average Birth, Death, and Population Growth Rates,* by Regions, 1952–56

World and regions	Population, midyear 1956, in millions	Birth rates	Death rates	Population growth rates in per cent
World	2,737	34	18	1.6
Africa:				
Northern Africa	72	42	28	1.7
Tropical and southern Africa ..	148	50	33	1.8
America:				
Northern America	186	25 †	9 †	1.7
Middle America	60	42	16	2.7
South America	129	39	17	2.4 ‡
Asia:				
South West Asia	73	42	22	2.5 ‡
South Central Asia	506	40	27	1.4
Southeast Asia	190	44	28	1.8
East Asia	745	35 †	16 †	1.6 ‡
Europe:				
Northern and Western Europe .	138	18 †	11 †	0.6
Central Europe	135	19 †	11 †	0.9
Southern Europe	139	21 †	10 †	0.9 ‡
Oceania:	15.1	25 †	9 †	2.3 ‡
USSR:	200 §	26 †	9 †	..

* Rates are annual averages for 1952–56; birth and death rates are per 1,000 population; population growth is the per cent rate, calculated by compound interest formula.

† Based on recorded statistics.

‡ This rate reflects the combined effect of natural increase and migration.

§ For April 1.

SOURCE: UN *Demographic Yearbook*, 1957.

to go through phases with respect to their demographic patterns. Thus we see from Table 28-2 that rates of growth between 1920 and 1950 were not markedly different in countries classified as low-growth potential from what they were in countries of high-growth potential. But when we look at the differences in birth and death rates, and take account of age distributions as well, it is apparent that the countries in Asia and Africa have much higher growth potential than other countries in the world. There are, of course, differences from country to country not shown here; but most of the underdeveloped countries in the world are still in the high-growth potential group. Latin America as a whole, however, falls into the "transitional" classification. There death rates are already low, and many demographers would expect fertility rates to drop in due course, following the pattern that has been set in the past by Europe and the New World.

Some demographers doubt whether the high-growth potential countries can be expected to follow the same demographic patterns as the advanced countries did. These were still high-growth potential up to the end of the eighteenth century, although natality in Western Europe was never so high as in present-day Asia and Africa, and mortality seems to have been somewhat lower and so had less far to drop. The declines in both death rates and in birth rates came slowly. Professor Spengler summarizes the process as follows: [2]

> In the course of the nineteenth and twentieth centuries, populations situated in the European sphere of civilization which were subjected to the pressures of industrialization and urbanization underwent a number of transformations: (1) Age-specific fertility and mortality, together with crude natality, declined below eighteenth-century levels, often to less than half. (2) The age structure changed (the relative number of younger persons diminishing while that of older persons increased) and this change eventually re-enforced the impact upon natality of the forces making for a decline in age-specific fertility. (3) Intragroup differences in fertility for a time were intensified, since at first fertility declined relatively more in such groups as urban dwellers, professional families and the better educated. Then the factors making for family limitation became sufficiently diffused so that the diverging fertility pattern gave place to a converging one, and a comparatively stable pattern of small differences was again in process of being established. (4) Because the per capita demand for farm produce was comparatively constant (i.e., both price and income inelastic), improvements in agricultural methods caused the rural population to decline relatively and then absolutely. The associated drift of the population

[2] Joseph J. Spengler, "Demographic Patterns," in H. F. Williamson and J. A. Buttrick, *Economic Development: Principles and Patterns* (New York, 1954), pp. 90–91. Spengler adds:

"It is easy to exaggerate the role of migration. Around 1850 the annual number of emigrants from Europe formed about 0.1 per cent of the European population and, at the emigration peak around 1905–15, only 0.3 per cent. In the decades 1880–90 and 1900–10, immigration increased the population of the United States only about 0.9 and 0.7 per cent, respectively."

TABLE 28-2.

World Population, Growth Rates, Birth Rates, and Death Rates

Area	1950 Population, in millions	Annual increase 1920–50, per thousand	*Annual rates, 1946–48, per thousand*			*Annual rates, 1936–38, per thousand*		
			Birth	Death	Natural increase	Birth	Death	Natural increase
World	2,406	9	35–37	22–25	11–14	34–38	24–27	8–13
Low-growth potential (type I):	486	9	.....	.....	10	.....	.....	5
North West Central Europe	215	6	19	12	7	17	13	4
North America	166	13	25	10	15	17	11	6
South Europe	92	9	23	12	11	23	16	7
Oceania	13	14	28	12	16	20	11	9
High-growth potential (type II):	1,387	8	.....	.....	12	.....	.....	7–13
Far East *	670	5	40–45	30–38	7–13	40–45	30–35	7–13
South Central Asia	442	11	40–45	25–30	12–18	40–45	30–35	7–13
Africa	199	13	40–45	25–30	12–18	40–45	30–35	7–13
Near East	75	10	40–45	30–35	7–13	40–45	30–35	7–13
Transitional (type III):	533	11	.....	.....	15	.....	.....	13–17
Soviet Union and Eastern Europe	287	7	28	18	10	30–34	17–21	11–15
Latin America	162	19	40	17	23	40–45	20–25	17–23
Japan	84	14	31	15	16	28	17	11

* Excluding Japan.

SOURCE: United Nations, *Demographic Yearbook*, 1957.

to towns and cities was accentuated by the development of urban and industrial employments, until today the number of potential emigrants in rural situations in most industrially developed countries is very small. (5) Because populations grew at different rates in different countries and because the multiplication of economic opportunities proceeded more rapidly in some countries than in others, the nineteenth and early twentieth century witnessed considerable international migration. This was finally halted by restrictive legislation and a narrowing of differences between prospects at home and prospects abroad, as envisaged by potential migrants.

In other words, in the Western world economic development came first, and the initial declines in death rates reflected mainly improved economic conditions. The impact of medical science on death rates came considerably later. In the now underdevel-

TABLE 28-3.

World Population, Age Compositions, and Density, 1949

Area	Population, in millions	*Age distribution of population, in percentages*			Persons per sq. km.
		Under 15 yrs.	15–59 yrs.	60 yrs. and over	
World	2,378	36	57	7	18
Low-growth potential (type I):					
North West Central Europe	214	24	62	14	78
United States and Canada	163	25	64	11	8
Southern Europe	91	30	59	11	88
Oceania	12	28	62	10	1
High-growth potential (type II):					
Far East *	661	40	55	5	41
South Central Asia	436	40	56	4	100
Africa	198	40	55	5	7
Near East	74	40	54	6	12
Transitional (type III):					
Soviet Union and Eastern Europe	288	34	59	7	12
Latin America	158	40	55	5	8
Japan	83	37	55	8	223

* Excluding Japan.
SOURCE: United Nations, *Demographic Yearbook*, 1957.

oped countries, on the other hand, dramatic declines in death rates are being produced by medical science *before* any substantial economic development has taken place. Thus in Ceylon the death rate dropped by 34 per cent between 1946 and 1947, as a result of residual spraying with DDT and the consequent reduction in the incidence of malaria and related diseases. The Ceylonese case is the most spectacular for so short a period, but the same sort of thing has been happening in many underdeveloped countries, as Tables 28-4 and 28-5 show. Malaria, "the world's most potent single cause of sickness, invalidism and death" is on the run in a good number of these countries, and other diseases are also being brought under control. Dr. Kingsley Davis points out that "the drop in the death rate has tended to go much further without a significant decline in the birth rate than was the case in the West." [3] Consequently, a good many of these countries are now expanding their populations at figures close to 30 per thousand, Leibenstein's "biological maximum."

Thus considerable evidence supports our statement that in some countries economic development may require a positive population policy. What might such a policy be?

To begin with, we may repeat what we have mentioned at several points in this book: economic development itself may bring falling birth rates as well as falling death rates. Industrialization may cut the birth rate through the operation of such factors as urbanization, the breaking up of peasant society, general education, higher school-leaving ages (especially for girls), and a "built-in habit of technological progress." Yet such indirect effects on birth rates may be too little and come too late to prevent a long postponement of take-off in some underdeveloped countries. To quote Professor Spengler again: [4]

> What has been said may be reduced to this: The aspirations of the populations living in underdeveloped countries will be under continuing upward pressure from many sources. These pressures will be reinforced by urbanization as industrialization proceeds. While rural populations are not immune to forces making for rising aspirations, city milieus seem to intensify them. If an expanding labor organization is coupled with governmental intervention, the share of the national net product going to the masses may be increased unless firmly established ruling groups are able to appropriate much of the country's

[3] Kingsley Davis, "The Amazing Decline of Mortality in Underdeveloped Areas," *American Economic Review Papers and Proceedings*, XLVI (May, 1956), p. 314.

[4] Joseph J. Spengler, *op. cit.*, p. 97.

TABLE 28-4.

Average Percentage Decline of Crude Death Rates as between Specified Periods in Eighteen Underdeveloped Countries

	Number of countries *	Average percentage decline from previous period †
Half-decade changes		
1920–24	....	....
1925–29	15	6.0
1930–34	16	4.6
1935–39	18	6.3
1940–44	16	8.5
1945–49	16	15.2
1950–54	18	20.1
Average	....	10.1
Thirty-year change		
1920–24	....	....
1950–54	15	46.9

* Eighteen countries were used, but in some cases data were missing for one or the other of the periods compared.

† The percentage change in average crude death rate was computed for each country. Then the percentages were added and divided by the number of countries involved in each comparison.

SOURCE: Kingsley Davis, "The Amazing Decline of Mortality in Underdeveloped Areas," *American Economic Review Papers and Proceedings,* XLVI (May, 1956), p. 311.

product for capital formation or the development of military strength. It is not likely, in any event, that income growth can keep pace with the growth of aspirations. Instead, aspirations will be apt to press ahead of income, and as a result the disposition to regulate family size will be widely diffused and strengthened.

Increases in the disposition to regulate family size, however, are not likely by themselves to produce a marked decline in natality even though folk methods of birth control are fairly effective. In addition, effective and suitable means for the control of births must be widely distributed. This may well be undertaken by governments in most of the high-growth-potential countries. These countries appear to be largely free of religious influences opposed to birth control, the principal exceptions being parts of Latin America and countries in the presently anti-Malthusian, Communist orbit. Moreover, the heavy expenditures required by social legislation will put those governments under pressure to reduce natality since some expenditures may thus be avoided.

TABLE 28-5.

Natural Increase for Different Periods, Developed and Underdeveloped Countries

Countries	Average natural increase per 1,000 per year					
	1735–99	1800–49	1850–99	1900–49	1940–49	1950–54 ‡
Industrial:						
England and Wales	....	10.2 *	12.7	6.5	....	....
Denmark	2.8	8.5	12.2	10.9	....	....
Norway	6.6	9.3	14.0	9.0	....	....
Sweden	5.6	8.1	11.5	6.9	....	....
Switzerland	....	....	7.9 †	7.0	....	....
Average	5.0	9.0	11.7	8.1	....	....
Underdeveloped:						
Barbados	....	....	....	....	14.7	18.6
Ceylon	....	....	....	....	19.9	27.8
Costa Rica	....	....	....	....	27.6	37.3
Cyprus	....	....	....	....	19.6	20.2
Egypt	....	....	....	....	16.1	26.0
El Salvador	....	....	....	....	25.0	33.2
Fiji	....	....	....	....	27.5	29.6
Jamaica	....	....	....	....	17.4	22.1
Malaya	....	....	....	....	22.6	29.6
Mauritius	....	....	....	....	12.3	33.0
Mexico	....	....	....	....	24.6	28.7
Panama	....	....	....	....	24.9	26.2
Puerto Rico	....	....	....	....	26.0	27.6
Surinam	....	....	....	....	20.6	27.0
Taiwan	....	....	....	....	25.0	35.0
Thailand	....	....	....	....	14.9	18.9
Trinidad and Tobago	....	....	....	....	22.7	26.6
Average	....	....	....	....	21.3	27.5

* For 1841–50 only.
† For 1871–99 only.
‡ For 1954 or the latest year available.

SOURCE: For 1940 to 1954, United Nations, *Demographic Yearbook*, 1953 and 1954. For earlier years, statistical yearbooks of various countries, and H. Gille, "Demographic History of the Northern European Countries in the Eighteenth Century," *Population Studies*, June, 1949.

Dr. Notestein, in another publication, has endeavored to summarize what might constitute an active population policy for countries facing population pressure. We are thankful to be able to quote an eminent demographer on so complex a question: [5]

Something of the scope of changes required to bring as rapid a decline of fertility as possible is suggested by the following outline.

1. Economic—The Substitution Within Feasible Limits of the Rounded for the Colonial Economy.

a. The development of industries to support large urban populations. Such a development takes people out of their former con-

[5] Frank W. Notestein, "Problems of Policy in Relation to Areas of Heavy Population Pressure," in J. J. Spengler and O. D. Duncan (eds.), *Population Theory and Policy* (Glencoe, Ill., 1956), pp. 478–79.

text, breaks the cake of custom, and permits the growth of new individualistic aspirations. Moreover, it is essential to draw a surplus and ineffective agricultural population into effective production. The development of light industries, such as textiles, in which women can be employed away from the home, is especially important as a means of giving women new independence and a milieu for the dissemination of new ideas.

b. The rationalization and extension of agriculture. Such rationalization would include the improvement of techniques, the reform of land tenures and credit systems, the development of new areas, and such diversification of production as the requirements of high productivity permit. It would not include the extension of subsistence farming as a substitute for commercial agriculture.

c. The promotion of international trade. Trade is one of the most important means of diffusing new ideas and attitudes.

2. Educational. The rapid extension of popular education through all available mediums designed, unlike the education in some colonial systems, to create new wants for physical and material well-being, and the skills appropriate to modern techniques in industry and agriculture.

3. Birth Control. It is important that specific and widespread propaganda be directed to developing an interest in the health and welfare of children rather than in large families for their own sake. Such education would also involve propaganda in favor of controlled fertility as an integral part of a public health program. As a matter of economic necessity, the efforts would have to be confined largely to the educational level.

4. Public Health. The matter cannot be rigidly proved, but the writer is profoundly convinced that only a society in which the individual (child or adult) has a reasonable chance for survival in healthy life will develop that interest in the dignity and material well-being of the individual essential to the reduction of fertility. He therefore firmly believes in directly fostering public health *as part of the program required to reduce growth potential.*

5. Political. It is important to develop a native leadership that will acquire new values rapidly and serve as a medium for their diffusion. To this end native political leaders, civil servants, and native middle classes are needed.

6. Social. It is important that caste and other barriers to the advancement of the individual be broken down as rapidly as possible.

7. Migration. If a train of events of the sort suggested above were under way, migration could be of invaluable assistance in facilitating the transition to low fertility. Under such circumstances emigration becomes more than a substitute for reduced fertility. By relieving the pressure of population during the transitional stage of rapid growth, it fosters the rising levels of living essential to the maintenance of that

transition. Much of Europe's migration to the United States has been of this character. If the curtailment of the growth potential is the object, the world's areas available for settlement should be reserved for migrants from regions in which the downward trend of fertility is already established. The empty regions are none too plentiful and should be used to some lasting effect.

Temporary migration, seasonal or other, should in all circumstances be encouraged as part of any program for the reduction of fertility. It is one of the most effective means of spreading new ideas, new skills and new interests in the home population.

At least two countries have taken note of the problem of population pressure in their official policy statements. In the second Five-Year Plan, the Indian government stated its position as follows:[6]

> The problem of regulating India's population from the dual standpoint of size and quality is of the utmost importance to national welfare and national planning. The objectives set out in the first five-year plan were:
>
> (1) to obtain an accurate picture of the factors which contribute to rapid increase of population,
> (2) to gain fuller understanding of human fertility and the means of regulating it,
> (3) to devise speedy ways of education of the public, and
> (4) to make family planning advice and service an integral part of the services in hospitals and health centres. . . .
>
> The family planning programme has now gone far enough to call for its further development on systematic lines, for continuous study of population problems and for a suitable central board for family planning and population problems. Such an organisation should be more or less autonomous in its working. The main constituents in the Central Board's programme will be:
>
> (1) extension of family planning advice and service;
> (2) establishment and maintenance of a sufficient number of centres for the training of personnel;
> (3) development of a broad-based programme of education in family living, which should include within its scope, sex education, marriage counselling and child guidance;
> (4) research into biological and medical aspects of reproduction and of population problems;
> (5) demographic research, including investigations of motivation in regard to family limitation as well as studies of methods of communication;
> (6) inspection and supervision of the work done by different

[6] Government of India Planning Commission, *Second Five Year Plan*, 1956, pp. 553–54. See also, *The New York Times*, Feb. 16, 1959, p. 1.

agencies, governmental and non-governmental, to which grants are made by the Central Board;

(7) evaluation and reporting of progress; and

(8) establishment of a well-equipped central organisation.

It is proposed to establish clinics, one for 50,000 population, in all big cities and major towns. As regards small towns and rural areas, clinics will be opened gradually, in association with primary health units. These clinics are intended to create a general awareness of the problem and to provide advice and service. The establishment of a central training and clinical institute and a rural training unit near Bangalore are under consideration. A contraceptive testing and evaluation centre is being developed at Bombay. It is necessary that training in family planning should be imparted to all medical and nursing students. All hospitals and an increasing number of dispensaries should develop in due course a family planning service. It is also proposed to promote actively medical, biological and demographic research.

So far the Indian family planning program is in too preliminary a stage to judge results.

In Japan, on the other hand, the results are clear. Birth rates have dropped sharply since the war and a stable population is now in sight. A major factor in this rapid change in Japan's population picture has been legalized abortion. However, it is important to remember that Japan has undergone a process of economic, sociological, and cultural change over the past three generations. A part of this change was a decline in the proportion of the population in peasant agriculture and an increase in the proportion living in industrial cities. As Dr. Irene Taueber has put it, "Declining fertility and hence the solution to the problems of growth created by modernization appeared to inhere in urbanization, itself an essential correlate of industrialization. Residential and occupational movement away from the peasant village and its agrarian activities was the overt manifestation of the cultural psychological transformation that signalized the 'Westernization' of the Japanese and their escape from the economic difficulties of increasing numbers." [7] Legalized abortion has no doubt contributed to the drop in Japanese birth rates, but it may be asked whether the Japanese people would have been so receptive to this rather crude form of family planning had the long process of industrialization and urbanization not taken place

[7] Ralph Linton, "Cultural and Personality Factors Affecting Economic Growth," and Irene B. Taueber, "Population Increase and Manpower Utilization in Imperial Japan," in J. J. Spengler and O. D. Duncan (eds.), *Demographic Analysis* (Glencoe, Ill., 1956), p. 723.

first. In her book on the population of Japan, Taueber has this to say: [8]

> The sharp reduction of births in recent years has not been the result of Government policy to "solve" the population problem. It was due, instead, to the decisions of Japanese men and women from the remote fishing villages of Hokkaido and the mining slums of Tokyo and Osaka, that the number of children had to be limited. The Government permitted designated private physicians to perform abortions and sterilizations, but it neither subsidized nor sponsored them.

However, Dr. Taueber points out that today the majority of Japanese live in cities and work in an industrial economy. She also maintains that the influence of the American military occupation on standards of living and on the vision of still higher standards was "favourable to declining fertility in Japan." She mentions also the Institute of Public Health's comprehensive program to spread contraceptive practice although she contends that this program was not "population policy" but an effort to "reduce the harmful effects of excessive childbearing."

Taueber is optimistic about the Japanese example's spreading to other Asian countries. It would be "unsafe indeed," she writes, "to assume that other Asian nations will continue to move toward population catastrophe without a most careful inspection of how and why birth rates declined in Japan." Here we have another of the hen-and-egg problems with which the analysis of economic development abound. Is there any reason to suppose that other Asian or African countries will follow the Japanese example with respect to population *before* they have a similar process of industrialization and urbanization? Many demographers would say no. On the other hand, one must admit that the case is not clear. Village studies in India and Indonesia indicate that even in peasant societies the *women* are interested in family planning; provided with any method that is simple and cheap, they would like to restrict the size of their families.[9]

[8] Irene Taueber, *The Population of Japan* (Princeton, N.J., 1958).

[9] In another article, Irene Taueber appraises the Japanese and Chinese experience as follows:

"It is widely recognized that industrial Japan offers no firm basis for assessing the probable future in agrarian Asia. It should be noted, however, that drastic changes did occur in the fertility of the Japanese including both peasants and urban dwellers, and that these declines were not foreseen by statesmen or by publicists. They were not predicted by demographers, whether in or outside Japan. And, as far as the author knows, no students predicted the legalization of all means of population control by Mainland

What of the religious factor? The present writer dares not tread far into this uncertain ground. We shall confine ourselves to two observations: in Hindu and Islamic societies, what was long regarded as a religious taboo on family planning seems now to be a sociological problem instead; secondly, among the first countries to achieve essentially stable populations by limiting birth rates were the Roman Catholic countries of France, Italy, and Spain.

China and the advances of political and educational activities to spread the practice of birth control in a Marxian state. These are segments of the evidence which suggests that eighteenth- and nineteenth-century Europe and historic Asia may be unsafe guides to the population prospects of Asian countries."

The opening guns in the Chinese campaign against excessive population growth were fired in an article in the *People's Daily* early in March, 1957. The article expressed doubts as to the possibility of an economic development program surpassing the 2.2 per cent annual population growth, recommended the use of contraceptives, and advised postponing marriages until the age of twenty-five. (Cf. *The New York Times*, March 6, 1957.)

29 Some Lessons of Experience

Of the six countries discussed in Chapter 2, all but Mexico have embarked on formal plans for economic development since 1950. India is well into its second Five-Year Plan; Libya has completed its first six-year plan; the other countries are several years along in their first five-year plans. It should be useful, therefore, to appraise the preparation and execution of plans in these countries against the background of the analysis presented in the preceding chapters.

Libya

We saw in Chapter 2 that when Libya became independent at the end of 1951, the country ranked near the bottom of the scale of national income or recent rates of economic growth. Moreover, the resource pattern was one which imposed formidable obstacles to development along orthodox lines. Human as well as natural resources were scarce, and the economy was deficitary in virtually every respect.

So peculiar a country required a peculiar development plan. The six-year plan prepared by the United Nations Mission provided for relatively little in industrialization through private enterprise. For the first six years covered by the plan there were no proposals for completely new industries, for new types of transport facility, for new public utilities, or for gigantic investment projects of any kind. Far from being designed to increase the relative share of industry and the degree of urban concentration, it was designed to make agriculture a more remunerative and attractive occupation. The plan consisted entirely of projects and programs for the improvement, expansion, or restoration of existing plant, skills, and undertakings. As stated in the UN report, "Libya has only one major untapped resource: the latent skills of its people. Raising the productivity of the Libyan economy must consist largely of improving the production methods used by the people in their present occupations. The emphasis in the plan is accordingly on teaching the Libyans to do better what they are already doing." The education program included training in agriculture, light industry, and handicrafts, as well as improvements in general education.

Financing

In one respect, the task of the planning team was simpler in Libya than in many underdeveloped countries; before the plan was finished it had become clear that foreign aid would be available on a scale permitting the execution of a sizable development plan. Two financing institutions were set up. The Libyan Public Development and Stabilization Agency receives grants from the Libyan and foreign governments and makes grants for public development projects. The Libyan Finance Corporation receives subscriptions from the Libyan and foreign governments and makes intermediate and long-term loans for development projects, mainly to private enterprise. In addition, the United Kingdom government undertook to make budgetary subventions to assist the Libyan government in meeting its deficits, and the French government undertook similar grants for the province of the Fezzan. As the net result of the agreements between the Libyan government and the British, American, French, and Italian governments, finance has been the least serious bottleneck in the economic development of the country.

The Approach

The Libyan plan has been successful in the sense that the Libyan government has not found it necessary to depart very far from it as the years have gone by. There is also some evidence of success in raising productivity. Such success as the Libyan plan has had derives mainly from two aspects of the *approach* to the planning in that country: the undertaking of an extensive resource survey as a first step, and the selection of the *planning* team according to the results of the resource survey.

Actually the planning involved three stages. The first step was to send a small team to make a rapid survey of the country's problems and potential, as a basis for selecting a larger team to make a more comprehensive resource survey. The first phase was accomplished in a matter of weeks. The resource survey team required approximately six months for completion of its task; in countries with more complex resource patterns, the job would of course take longer. In addition to studies of agricultural, mineral, and water resources (the latter being of particular importance in arid zone countries like Libya) studies were made of the country's balance of payments, national income, and finances.

On the basis of this survey, the broad outline of a development plan could already be discerned. It became clear which sectors of the economy provided some hope of expansion and called for more intensive study. The *planning* team was composed of experts in each of these areas of potential development. For example, the team, which numbered some fifteen experts in all, included a mineralogist, a hydrologist, a war damage expert, a social welfare expert, a power engineer (all provided by UNTAA), a fishing expert, a tanning expert, an expert on the cleaning, grading, and packaging of wool, and other FAO experts on dates, animal husbandry, olives, and citrus fruits. Also participating were an ILO team on manpower training, a UNESCO team on general education, and a WHO team on public health, with a chief economist to coordinate their work into a comprehensive plan and a public finance expert to help.

To indicate the underlying principle, it may be useful to elaborate a little on the reasons for selecting some of these experts. Libya had suffered from several years of warfare, and a good deal of the transport and public utilities facilities had been severely damaged. Some of these facilities seemed more appropriate to Italy's plans for colonizing the country than to development of a new independent nation. Rehabilitation would be expensive; would it be worthwhile? This was an important question on which expert advice was needed. Similarly, the steam turbine power plant in Tripoli, and the smaller power plants in Bengasi and other small cities, had insufficient capacity to cope with any significant degree of urbanization, industrialization, or rural electrification. But with no domestic coal and no water power, electricity was expensive. Would it pay to expand electricity capacity? Here again special *expertise* was required.

Libya had once been a wool exporter. Significant quantities of wool were still being grown, but because of inefficient clipping and almost total lack of scouring and sorting, high-grade and low-grade wools alike were bringing the lowest prices in the market. Here was an area for potential increase in the value of output, and an expert in this field was included on the team.

These examples should serve to illustrate the basic principle underlying selection of the team: each man was chosen to deal with a particular problem, or with a particular sector of the economy where there was reason to hope for increased productivity.

The Plan

Since the entire development plan was to be financed by the Stabilization and Development Authority and the Finance Corporation, the plan took the form of a budget for these agencies, together with a recommended technical assistance budget for the UN and its Specialized Agencies and the Libyan-American Technical Assistance Service. On the basis of the analyses prepared by the various experts of the possibilities in particular sectors of the economy, the determination of priorities for these budgets was not too difficult.

Top-priority projects were put into an A category; these projects together constituted the budgets of the financing agencies for the first year of the plan. Projects to be started within the second five-year period were put into a B category. Other useful projects for which assured financing was not available in the first six years, were put into a C category as a reserve. In the event of a drought it was expected that the Authority would first canvass the B category, for the projects to bring forward, but that C-category projects with a particularly high degree of flexibility might be updated in the event of severe but temporary unemployment. The plan was presented in great detail both in terms of technical assistance requirements and in terms of physical and financial capital requirements—even to the number of square feet of classroom space.

Although the detailed budget covered only six years, the planning team looked much farther ahead and envisaged three phases of development. In the summary version of the plan these three phases were described as follows: [1]

[1] Benjamin Higgins, *The Economic and Social Development of Libya* (New York, 1953), pp. 13–14.

Timing by Phase of Development: Summary

The recommendations for timing by phase of economic development might be summarized in schematic fashion:

Phase 1: first six-year plan. Emphasis on training and education, agricultural research, experiment, demonstration, and improvement. Agricultural production should be increased by all possible means, including training of farmers, improvement of tools and techniques, and, when and where feasible, by expansion of cultivable acreage of individual farms and of the country as a whole. Large role of repair of war damages, other public works, and public utilities. Net absorption of manpower into public development program. Increased import surplus, large budget deficits, reliance on foreign financial and technical assistance. Capital accumulation of 5 to 10 per cent of national income, half covered by domestic savings. If necessary, tax away increase in productivity to maintain supply of effort and restrict population growth, providing free (or nearly free) public goods and services in exchange.

Phase 2: second and third six-year plans. Increased emphasis on agricultural processing and similar light industries with domestic markets and using domestic raw materials. Possible further decline in proportion of labor force in agriculture through labor-saving innovations. Mechanization of handicrafts begins. Decline in outlays for war damages and, in second half (with completion of new Tripoli power plant), in public works and public utilities as a whole. Net release of manpower from public development program to private industrial sector. Reduced import surplus, reduced budget deficits, reduced reliance on foreign grants, some borrowing abroad. Net reduction in foreign technical assistance. Capital accumulation of 10 to 15 per cent of national income, domestic savings of at least 10 per cent of national income. Reduced taxes and increased sales of consumers' goods.

Phase 3: fourth and subsequent six-year plans. Accelerated development of agricultural processing and similar light industries. Further mechanization of handicrafts. Balanced trade, balanced budgets (apart from cyclical fluctuations), independence of foreign financial and technical assistance. Capital accumulation and domestic savings of at least 15 per cent of national income.

In an effort to ensure public acceptability of the plan and to utilize the special knowledge of members of the community, several working parties were established to assist the planning team. These included Italians, Arabs, and representatives of foreign enterprise. Separate working parties covered agriculture, power, transport, small industry, etc.

In general, because of the severe limitations imposed by the poverty of resources and power, little structural change was contemplated in the plan. Manpower training, agricultural extension work, and general education constituted a large part of the program. However, the plan did provide for carrying further the processing of Libyan natural resources. Pressing olives and refining olive oil, freezing fish, canning fruits and vegetables, as well as weaving factories, a dairy, etc., were included among the recommended projects.

Economic Development: 1952–57

Such development as took place in the first five years covered by the plan was mainly the result of government enterprise, partly because the most important source of capital has been foreign aid granted to and administered by the Libyan government. Interim arrangements were made at the time of transfer of sovereignty with the British, American, French, and Italian governments. Toward the end of 1953, Libya concluded a long-term (twenty-year) agreement with the United Kingdom under which Britain promised £3,750,000 per year for 1952–57; of this, £1,000,000 per year was specifically earmarked for development projects. In July, 1954, the United States agreed to pay $4,000,000 per year for five years and a lower sum in the following years, plus $3,000,000 in the fiscal year 1955 for specific projects. The United States also provided 24,000 tons of wheat for relief and $1,500,000 million in technical assistance. The UN Technical Assistance Program amounted to $850,000. In 1954, France offered £100,000 for development and £163,000 for budgetary subventions. Italy and Turkey each granted £10,000 to the Development Agency. Moreover, since the agreement with the United Kingdom was made retroactive, the Libyan government found itself with a surplus of £1,250,000 at that time. Thus total foreign aid in 1954–55 was running in excess of $26,000,000 per year, or more than half the estimated national income.

In 1956, both the British and the American grants were running at even higher rates: the budgetary subvention from the United Kingdom was raised by £250,000 in the fiscal year 1956 and by £750,000 in the following year; American assistance reached $12,000,000 per year, of which $5,000,000 was specifically earmarked for development. The sums earmarked for development alone exceeded 20 per cent of national income; and since all foreign aid relieves both the budget and the balance of payments, the whole amount might be regarded as adding to the financial resources for development. These grants were large only relative to the very low national income; truly large-scale projects were still not possible in Libya. But the lack of natural resources, technical and managerial skills, and entrepreneurship was a much more serious bottleneck than lack of capital.

Part of the American grants was used by the government to establish a National Bank of Libya, which took over the function of issuing currency from the Currency Commission in March, 1957, and undertook to rediscount good commercial paper at 4½ per cent. The government also set up an Agricultural Credit Bank, but this institution has been slow in getting under way, partly for lack of a co-operative movement through which to operate.

Among the government enterprises that have been established (with technical assistance from the UN and the United States) are a date-packing plant, a central milk pasteurization plant (which has apparently fallen into disuse), and the Tripolitanian Esparto Corporation. The latter organization has endeavored to assist small-scale private enterprise by granting £10,000 to establish a handicrafts committee for promoting the production and sale of handicraft products. This venture does not seem to have been outstandingly successful; a trial order from the UN Gift Shop remained unfilled at time of writing. A potassium deposit has been found but there is no information regarding its exploitation.

For some years, it had been apparent that the Tripoli steam turbine electricity plant would have to be rehabilitated and expanded. SECI, an Italian company, owned the plant; the government did not want to leave it in the hands of the company but lacked the capital needed for modernization. The American grants made it possible to earmark £1,000,000 for this purpose. The Italian company retained a 30 per cent interest in a new mixed company, with directors appointed according to shares. The Italian shareholders received 5 per cent cumulative participatory preference shares.

THE LIBYAN FINANCE CORPORATION

The Libyan Finance Corporation was slow in getting under way and it has never reached the scale recommended in the plan. At the end of 1954, it had total capital of £100,000 and had made fifty-three loans of three to five years amounting to

£98,000. The Italian parastatal corporation participating in the Libyan Finance Corporation then promised an additional £40,000 and the French government another £20,000, to be paid early in 1955. Until the spring of 1954, the Corporation tried in vain to persuade the banks to underwrite its loans and few applications were received. The Libyan Finance Corporation then decided to lend without guarantees and lowered its rates from 6 to 5 per cent. By October of that year, 157 applications totaling £460,000 had been received, but few of the applicants had either credit ratings or assets. The small scale and unimaginative nature of the projects financed by the Libyan Finance Corporation is indicated by the following table (of somewhat earlier date):

Number of Loans	*Purpose*	*Amount*
33	Irrigation equipment	£40,000
6	Tractors	17,000
8	Olive oil refineries	30,600
2	Citrus marketing co-operative	3,000
1	Pest-fighting co-operative	£ 600 of 1,500
50		£90,300 of 91,800

The last two projects in this list were FAO projects; the basic entrepreneurship involved was essentially foreign.

LIBYAN PRIVATE ENTERPRISE

Very little genuinely Libyan private entrepreneurship has appeared. The penchant for monopoly privileges continues to be a barrier. During the early part of 1957 the government was approached for grants of monopoly privileges in match production, date processing, production of industrial alcohol, fisheries, and various agricultural ventures. The government's experience with concessions already granted has not been too happy and these applications were refused.

The few new ventures have usually involved government participation in the innovational process. The citrus fruit co-operative was able to raise exports in 1954 to a level 70 per cent higher in volume and more than 100 per cent higher in value than any figure previously attained; but this expansion was based not only on improved cleaning and grading with the use of a new machine (and FAO technical assistance) but also on an agreement with the Italian government to import and permit through transport of the fruit, an agreement arranged by the UN Resident Representative. Similarly, the tanning industry achieved greater sales at higher prices with FAO assistance. Another successful venture in which the government participated was the sale of new potatoes and other fresh vegetables in the London market; it was found that Libya could beat European countries into this market by a month.

FOREIGN ENTERPRISE

Foreign enterprise remains chiefly Italian. In the spring of 1956, the Libyan government finally reached an agreement with Italy regarding Italian residents and property which included non-discrimination against Italian enterprises by the financial institutions. This agreement may provide the basis for expansion of Italian enterprises, although the Libyan government does not of course intend to continue subsidization of the former "Ente" ventures.

Enactment of the Petroleum Law in June, 1956, has led to active drilling by a number of foreign oil companies, the most important activity of non-Italian foreign enterprise in the country thus far. Some oil has been found, but at time of writing its commercial importance could not be assessed. Early in 1956, the government also approved a set of general principles on treatment of foreign investment in general, but so far this step has had little impact.

LESSONS FROM LIBYAN EXPERIENCE

Four lessons may be gleaned from the experience with development planning in Libya. *First*, it is much easier to prepare a plan of lasting value if the planning team has extensive and intensive information on the natural and manpower resource pattern. *Second*, the assembly of a plan and the determination of priorities is greatly facilitated by having in the planning organization experts with special knowledge of each of the major sectors or industries in the economy. *Third*, if stabilization is considered simultaneously with development, the development program, far from being a destabilizing factor, can be utilized to increase the stability of the economy. *Fourth*, even in a country as poor in natural resources and with such limited markets as Libya, the lack of indigenous entrepreneurship can be a major obstacle to accelerated economic growth. Capital has been available in substantial quantities, and even in Libya there are possibilities for establishment of new enterprises; but there are not enough "Schumpeterian entrepreneurs" who can see and seize the opportunities for joining the available capital with the available resources in new combinations.

India

India entered its first Five-Year Plan period with both advantages and handicaps. Professor Malenbaum describes the Indian position this way: [2]

On the eve of the First Plan in 1951, national income per capita in India was about $55, near the bottom of the range of national observations available. Population density was one of the highest among the poor countries. The percentage of population directly dependent upon the land for a livelihood was a high 70 per cent, and 85 per cent of all the people lived in rural areas. From this resource point of view, therefore, Indian prospects for accelerating growth might not be as favorable as those of other economically underdeveloped lands, even in Asia and Africa, to say naught of Latin America. But unlike most others, India has had a long history of modern industrial development. While modern industry by 1951 had not become a very important contributor to total national product, it did give India significant groups of people skilled in modern business enterprise. Indeed, India's intellectual leadership, including the top ranks of an outstanding civil service, finds few equals in the underdeveloped countries of the world. Such leadership may perhaps explain the Indian head-start among nations newly aspiring to improved economic conditions.

The Planning Commission itself, in its *Review of the First Five-Year Plan*, lists the pressing problems confronting the country in 1951. There were acute shortages of raw materials and foodstuffs; in 1951, 4.7 million tons of food grains had to be imported. Industrial production was below capacity. The transport system was in bad shape. Millions of displaced persons poured over the border from Pakistan. The Korean War and a bad harvest created inflationary pressure. Co-ordination of central and state government operations had yet to be achieved. The balance of payments on current account was unfavorable. In these conditions, the first Plan set itself two main targets: to correct "the disequilibrium in the economy caused by the War and the partition of the country"; and "to initiate simultaneously a process of all-around balanced development which would ensure a rising national income and a steady improvement in living standards over a period." [3]

[2] Wilfred Malenbaum, *East and West in India's Development*, (Washington, D.C., 1959), chap. II.
[3] Government of India Planning Commission, *Review of the First Five-Year Plan* (Delhi, May, 1957), p. 1.

The First Plan

In the opening chapter of the first Five-Year Plan, the Planning Commission raised two basic questions: "What increase in per capita income can we reasonably hope to attain over a given period of years? What rate of capital formation will be required to achieve it?" The Commission stressed the fact that the Indian people were confronted here with a "definite problem of choice—a choice between, on the one hand a small or moderate increase in the standard of living in the near future but with only relatively small additions to capital equipment and hence no marked and sustained upward trend; and, on the other, a substantially higher standard of living for the next generation at the cost of continued austerity and privation to the present generation in the interests of rapid capital formation." The Commission assumed that the "weight will incline towards the second alternative."

The Commission went on to state two basic assumptions: that population growth would continue at the rate of 1.25 per cent annually, and that the Incremental Capital-Output Ratio (ICOR) would start at 3:1 and rise gradually to about 4:1.

TARGETS

On the basis of these assumptions, the Commission chose modest targets for its plans. It hoped to double per capita national income in one generation, but expected to do no more than lay the groundwork for this expansion during the first five-year period. Although recognizing that rapidly expanding economies have invested (net) 12 per cent to 15 per cent of the national income the Commission did not consider it feasible during the first five years to do more than to raise net investment in India from 5 per cent to 6.75 per cent of national income. It was contemplated, however, that this increase in investment would occur at an increasing rate, so that by the end of the first five-year period, 50 per cent of *additional income* could be saved and invested and that "by 1967–68 the annual saving would amount to no less than 20 per cent of the aggregate national income—a rate which it would not be necessary to exceed."

The Commission also stated as objectives of the plan reduction in inequalities of income and wealth, and reducing the rate of population growth to about 1 per cent per year.

PUBLIC AND PRIVATE INVESTMENT

In accomplishing these objectives, the Indian government depended primarily on public investment. With respect to the private sector, the Commission pointed out that the state "cannot determine absolutely the investment of the savings of private individuals and corporations; it can only influence their investment by offering facilities and incentives to encourage their flow into certain channels while discouraging or even prohibiting them from being drawn off into others." For encouraging and directing private investment the Commission recommended credit controls, fiscal policy, licensing, and, if necessary, price controls.[4]

DEFICIT FINANCE

In the light of subsequent developments the Commission's statement with regard to deficit financing is of some interest:

> The dangers of "creating" money are sufficiently well known. Such a course means the depreciation of the existing currency and consequent inflation of prices and, if carried beyond certain limits, may completely undermine public confidence in the currency with catastrophic results. Deficit financing can be countenanced only if there is an assurance of steady supplies of the essential commodities of consumption. The injection of increased purchasing power into the system is apt to lead to increased demand for basic commodities and, if their supply cannot be expanded quickly, their prices rise and push up the cost of living. It will thus be apparent that the scope for deficit financing is intimately bound up with the policy of controls.

RESULTS UNDER THE FIRST PLAN

The budget for the first Plan and the actual outlays under it are compared in Table 29-1. It will be noted that the emphasis in the first Plan was on agriculture (including community development and irrigation) and transport. Power projects received a substantial allocation (especially railways) and social services were not neglected. Very little was allocated for industry and mining. The percentage distribution of actual outlays conformed closely to the Plan, except that investment in large-scale industry and mining was even less than planned, and investment in railways even more. There was, however, an over-all shortfall of about 15 per cent in actual outlays.

This developmental investment brought useful but not dra-

[4] Government of India Planning Commission, *First Five-Year Plan*, pp. 15, 21–22, 32–33.

matic increases in output. As may be seen from Table 29-3, national income at constant prices rose 17.5 per cent and per capita income 10.5 per cent. Despite the emphasis on agriculture, it was mining, manufacturing, and transport that showed the biggest percentage expansion. Favorable monsoons were an im-

TABLE 29-1.

Allocations and Outlay under the First Five-Year Plan by Major Heads of Development

Allocation	*Total plan provision (including adjustments)*		*Outlay, 1951–56*	
	Rs. Crores	Per cent	Rs. Crores	Per cent
Agriculture and community development	354	14.9	299	14.8
Irrigation and power	647	27.2	585	29.1
Industries and mining	188	7.9	100	5.0
Transport and communications	571	24.0	532	26.4
Social services	532	22.4	423	21.0
Miscellaneous	86	3.6	74	3.7
Total	2,378	100.0	2,013	100.0

SOURCE: Government of India Planning Commission, *Review of the First Five-Year Plan* (New Delhi, May, 1957), pp. 2–3.

TABLE 29-2.

Distribution of Plan Outlay by Major Heads of Development

Allocation	*First five-year plan*		*Second five-year plan*	
	Total provision, rs. crores	Per cent	Total provision, rs. crores	Per cent
Agriculture and community development	357	15.1	568	11.8
Irrigation and power	661	28.1	913	19.0
Industries and mining	179	7.6	890	18.5
Transport and communications	557	23.6	1,385	28.9
Social services	533	22.6	945	19.7
Miscellaneous	69	3.0	99	2.1
Total	2,356	100.0	4,800	100.0

SOURCE: Government of India Planning Commission, *Second Five-Year Plan* (New Delhi, 1956), pp. 51–52.

portant factor in the increase in agricultural output.

The feared inflation did not develop. Deficit financing (which in Indian parlance means borrowing from the banking system) accounted for 21 per cent of the government expenditures under the Plan, and market borrowings another 10 per cent; deficits in the ordinary sense were therefore nearly one-third of the total outlays. Taxation, together with surpluses of the state-owned railways, provided only 38 per cent of the needed funds. Yet prices fell and unemployment grew during the Plan period—facts which greatly influenced attitudes toward the scale and financing of the second Plan. The reasons for the coexistence of deficit finance, deflation, and growing unemployment seem to

TABLE 29-3.

Increases in Output under the First Five-Year Plan

Category of output	*Percentage increase*
Agriculture, etc.	14.7
Mining, manufacturing, and small enterprise	18.2
Commerce, transport, and communications	18.6
Net domestic product at factor cost	17.5
Per capita net output	10.5
Population	6.6

SOURCE: Government of India, *Review of the First Five-Year Plan* (New Delhi, 1957), pp. 7–8.

have been the favorable monsoons, foreign aid which permitted an import surplus, and investment of a kind that provided more output than jobs. Some Indian officials, however, apparently translated the experience under the first Plan into a proof of excessive pessimism on the part of others who warned of the dangers of inflation and unduly ambitious plans.

Professor Malenbaum offers this appraisal of the results of the first Plan: [5]

Without playing down an Indian achievement without parallel among free world nations, it is true that circumstances surrounding the Indian effort were unusually favourable. Notable, of course, was the weather—with excellent monsoons, at least after the first two years of the Plan. The international political and economic environment was such that India could obtain assistance from abroad, beyond what she

[5] Wilfred Malenbaum, "Some Political Aspects of Economic Development," *World Politics*, April, 1958.

actually used during the First Plan. The First Plan years did not involve reductions in current consumption levels, or even unpleasant choices about what to do with increased incomes. True, government did want more tax revenues than it collected, but at the same time when people were prepared to lend, especially to government, more than seemed to be demanded. The economy actually suffered somewhat from deflationary pressures.

The Second Five-Year Plan

Early in 1956, the Indian Planning Commission released its second Five-Year Plan. The Commission noted that participation in preparation of the Plan had been much broader than in the case of the first Five-Year Plan. "The enthusiasm and the widespread participation which have gone into the making of the Second Five-Year Plan" says the Commission, "are the best augury for its fulfillment." [6] The assistance of the Indian Statistical Institute, under the direction of Professor Mahalanobis, and of the Commission's panel of economists, is especially mentioned.

THE MAHALANOBIS "FRAMEWORK"

Indeed the final plan follows closely the draft prepared by the Statistical Institute, as approved by its panel of economists, although it is somewhat less ambitious in its income targets and less optimistic with regard to the capital-ouput ratio. In the preface to this Plan framework, public attention is called to the decision of the National Development Council that "the widest possible publicity be given to the draft outline so as to facilitate a discussion on the overall objectives of the plan and the means of obtaining them." The substantial success of the first Five-Year Plan "has laid the foundations for a bolder plan in the second five-year period." Although it is recognized that complete control over the private sector of a mixed economy is impossible, the achievement of balanced growth requires conformity of the activities of the private sector to the program of production "in a general way." [7]

The first Five-Year Plan is regarded as having been unsatisfactory in terms of employment creation; unemployment is still increasing, especially in urban areas. Agricultural prices are declining. Thus despite modest deficit financing for the first plan,

[6] Government of India Planning Commission, *Second Five-Year Plan* (New Delhi, 1956), p. 3.

[7] *Ibid.*, p. 8.

the trend within the economy has remained deflationary. Accordingly, the draft plan called for more vigorous development and a more expansionary approach for the second Five-Year Plan. In particular, "a large increase in employment opportunities must be regarded as the principal objective—the Kingpin—of the second plan."[8] The plan recognized that maximizing employment may conflict with maximizing output, especially where cottage industries are concerned; accordingly, it was felt that development of basic industries should not result in destruction of the small-scale industries that provide opportunities for employment.

OBJECTIVES OF THE SECOND PLAN

For this second phase of planning the Commission itemizes four principal objectives:

(a) a sizeable increase in national income so as to raise the level of living in the country;
(b) rapid industrialization, with particular emphasis on the development of basic and heavy industries;
(c) a large expansion of employment opportunities; and
(d) reduction of inequalities in income and wealth and a more even distribution of economic power.

The Commission added that a low standard of living, underemployment, and maldistribution of income are all symptoms of "the basic underdevelopment which characterizes an economy depending mainly on agriculture." Rapid industrialization is thus the core of the new plan.

Much more attention is directed toward the problem of employment creation in the second plan than in the first. "The question of increasing employment opportunities," states the Commission, "cannot be viewed separately from the programs of investment envisaged in the plan";[9] for there is general agreement that "the Second Five-Year Plan should have a distinct employment bias."[10] Employment creation must be designed to reduce existing unemployment in the urban and rural areas, to absorb an increase in the labor force of about two million persons per year, and to lessen underemployment in rural and household occupations.

[8] *Ibid.*, p. 66.
[9] *Ibid.*, pp. 7, 8.
[10] *Ibid.*, p. 41; see also Table I, p. 43.

COMPARISON WITH THE FIRST PLAN

The increase in plan outlay and the changes in its composition are indicated by Table 29-2. Over-all expenditures under the second Plan are more than doubled. The most striking changes in composition are the increased investment in industry and mining and the reduced investment in irrigation and power (especially irrigation). The actual capital-output ratio under the first Plan was calculated at 1.8:1, somewhat better than anticipated. Making allowance for the favorable monsoons and the shift in structure of investment, the ICOR for the second Plan was set at 2.3:1; it was estimated that in the course of subsequent Plans it would rise to 2.6, 3.4, and 3.7. The long-run expectations with regard to increase in investment were scaled down. The target was an increase from 7 per cent of national income in 1955–56 to 11 per cent in 1960–61. Instead of reaching 20 per cent by 1968–69 as originally hoped, it would rise to 16 per cent by 1970–71.

The Plan document notes the lack of change in occupational structure in the past, stating that, although immigration to cities may have resulted in some decline in agriculture's share of total employment, "the change is unlikely so far to have been of any noteworthy character." The objective must be to keep increases in agricultural employment to a minimum. However, the targets set up for structural change are still very modest: to reduce the proportion of agricultural employment to 60 per cent of the total by 1975–76. At the same time, the Plan undertook to protect cottage industry, while stressing the need to find new products and develop new techniques in this sector of the economy.

As may be seen from Table 29-4, the new Plan relies much more heavily on deficit finance in the public sector than the first did. Of the entire budget, 4,800 crores of rupees, tax revenue will provide only 800, and of this more than half is hopefully assigned to "new taxes." The "other budgetary sources" might be regarded as anti-inflationary sources of finance, but these add only 450 crores of rupees. The bulk of the program is to be covered by what is actually called deficit financing, borrowings from the public that may or may not be inflationary in effect, external resources, and an unspecified "gap."

RESULTS UNDER THE PLAN

The second Plan was hardly more than a few months old when it became apparent that it was heading for trouble. The chief symptom of trouble was the loss of foreign exchange, already noted in Chapter 2; during the first Plan year, India lost $600 million in reserves (including drawings on the International Monetary Fund that may have to be repaid before the end of the Plan period)—50 per cent more than was contemplated for the entire Plan. The deficit on current account in 1956–57 amounted to 332 crores of rupees, more than double the estimate in the Plan. Imports were nearly 200 crores above estimates, exports more than 60 crores below estimates; net income on invisibles was somewhat better than expected. The consequent

TABLE 29-4.

Financing the Public Sector, Second Five-Year Plan

Source of funds	*Amount, crores of rupees*
Surplus from current revenue	800
At existing (1955–56) rates	350
Additional taxation	450
Borrowings from the public	1,200
Other budgetary sources	400
Railways' contribution	150
Provident funds, etc.	250
Resources to be raised externally	800
Deficit financing	1,200
Gap—to be covered by additional measures to raise domestic resources	400
Total	4,800

SOURCE: Government of India, *Second Five-Year Plan* (New Delhi, 1956), pp. 77–78.

foreign exchange crisis has been met in the first instance by drawings on the IMF equal to 50 per cent of the Indian quota and by import restrictions. It was soon recognized, however, that the implications were much more serious. Unless greatly increased foreign aid were forthcoming, the second Plan would have to be abandoned. At best, it might be possible to finish the "hard core" projects.

It should be emphasized that, for the most part, this drain on foreign exchange was not the result of any unhealthy trend in the Indian economy. On the contrary, it reflects unexpectedly vigorous expansion, particularly in the private sector. During 1956–57, private imports of capital goods were nearly 50 per cent higher than in the preceding year and nearly 25 per cent above plan estimates. Capital goods imports on public account were more than double the 1955–56 level, but somewhat below Plan estimates. Raw material imports showed relatively little expansion over the previous year. Food imports were three and a half times the 1955–56 level and more than double the Plan estimate. In part, this increase means failure to maintain expansion of food production, but since much of this increase represents United States commodity surplus disposal, it does not impose an immediate drain on Indian foreign exchange. Another part of the drain was due to unexpectedly large outlays for defense.

For those who wish to see India achieve her aims with respect to economic development, then—and particularly those who would like to see her do so with private enterprise playing an important role—the most unfortunate aspect of these trends is that they cannot continue without outside help. Mr. Jagdish Bhagwati has estimated that if the Plan were carried out in full, and the implications of the trend with regard to balance of payments projected throughout the period, the total deficit would reach 1,700 crores of rupees, broken down as follows: [11]

Excess of Imports over the Plan Period

Category	*Amount*
Defense	200
Food	150
Private capital goods	950
Raw materials	125
Consumer goods	275
Total	1,700

The foreign exchange crisis is not the only fly in the Indian ointment. It is the one on the surface that has caught the public eye, both at home and abroad, but there are others deeper down. Perhaps most serious of all is the failure of the investment undertaken thus far to produce the predicted increase in output; the estimates of the capital-output ratio have proved too optimistic. As Malenbaum says, "an average increase of 5 per cent per annum in national income is a high goal but a goal which may be necessary for a country seeking to shift rapidly from stagnation to progress." [12] Disappointments have occurred even in the

[11] Jagdish Bhagwate, "The Present Imbalance in Indian International Accounts," M.I.T., CIS, November, 1957.

[12] Malenbaum, *op. cit.*, p. 12.

field of community development, where much effort has been concentrated and a special ministry established. Here is an approach to increased agricultural productivity that seems tailor-made for India's traditional village pattern in mobilizing mass effort; yet continuous application of effort, personnel, and funds from the central government seem necessary to achieve continuous improvement.[13]

In appraising results thus far under the second Plan, Malenbaum emphasizes the failure of the Indian government either to plan in accordance with the traditional patterns of savings and investment or to undertake the measures necessary to change them. He considers the target with respect to aggregate saving and investment—an average of 8.5 per cent of national income over the five years—realistic enough. But the plan also calls for diversion of a large share of total savings, including non-monetary private savings, into heavy investment, particularly in the public sector. The present tax system is quite inadequate to achieve this result. Revenues have not kept pace with national income, and evasion is rampant. Some 20 to 25 per cent of total savings and investment is non-monetized, concentrated in peasant agriculture and very hard to shift to anything else. Moreover, much of the monetized saving tends to be invested directly in enterprises that generate it. Under these circumstances the planned doubling of real public investment calls for drastic measures for the reallocation of real savings, and it may be impossible without additional resources from abroad. If so, the attempt to carry out the public investment program can lead only to inflation.

Planning and Performance

To what extent can the imperfections in performance under the Plan be traced to imperfections in the planning process? To answer this question we must first take a look at the manner in which the second Plan was put together. The Introduction to *The Second Five-Year Plan* says,[14]

> The Plan which is now presented to government for submission to parliament is a result of the labours of large numbers of persons in the Central Government, in the States at various levels and leaders of thought and opinion in every part of the country. In its preparation, men and women from all walks of life have given generously of their time and experience.

[13] Cf. Malenbaum, "Some Political Aspects of Economic Development in India," *ibid.*, p. 385.

[14] Government of India Planning Commission, *op. cit.*, p. xiv.

Certainly a sincere effort was made to base the second Plan on "planning from below." As early as April, 1954, the Planning Commission asked the state governments to encourage the preparation of district and even village plans. Discussions took place between the states and the districts and between the states and the Central Government to iron out differences in conception of the Plan. Analysis and co-ordination was the task of the secretariat of the Planning Commission, which had the advice of a panel of economists. Malenbaum doubts "that there is any conceptual device, statistical tool or theoretical argument known to economists anywhere which has not in some way been used, or been mentioned, in the two Five-Year Plans." [15]

However, as Malenbaum also points out, "a flow from the bottom can scarcely exist where more than 80 per cent of the population is illiterate, where an even larger number may be only remotely concerned with the need for a development plan or program—to say nothing of a land where higher authority is traditionally accepted." [16] He gives India credit for "retaining the semblance of this multiple interchange" but says bluntly that at the moment planning is still from top to bottom. The Deputy Chairman of the Planning Commission, the Minister of Planning, the Finance Minister, and the Statistical Adviser all played extremely important roles, but most important was the Chairman of the Planning Commission, the Prime Minister himself. Nehru, Malenbaum points out, "is clearly India's top politician," and "progress on the Plan . . . is an excellent political point of contact with the people," a fact that Nehru clearly understands.

What flaws have appeared in this planning process? Malenbaum stresses the failure of those responsible for framing the Plan to study *India:* [17]

> There is a much narrower gap between the economic theorists and planners of the world's nations than there is between the general economies of different nations. India's planners are less well versed in India than they are in the more developed economic systems. It is therefore understandable that India's plans seem to rest so little upon economic characteristics and relationships known to pertain to India. And this also helps to explain why there is relatively little appreciation of what is actually occurring on the Indian economic scene today.

[15] Malenbaum, "Who Does the Planning?" (Paper presented to the Seminar on Leadership and Political Institutions in India, University of California, August, 1956.)

[16] *Ibid.*, p. 4.

[17] Malenbaum, *East and West in India's Development*, chap. I.

For example, in a Plan which leaves so much to individual and group initiative, it is necessary to know much more about motivation, especially in the rural sector, so as to decide what measures are most likely to bring the actions implicit in the Plan. "The structure and dynamics of Indian economic life . . . are only beginning to become known."[18] The excessive optimism with respect to the capital-output ratio is one example of inadequate study of actual conditions in the country.

A closely related point is the failure of the Plan to make full allowance for and use of the dynamism of Indian private enterprise. The point here is technical, not ideological; if the dynamism can be diverted to the public sector in accordance with Indian social philosophy, well and good; if not, failure to encourage it where it exists means a slower rate of growth than would otherwise be possible. The balance of public and private enterprise underlying the second Plan, together with the lack of measures to change the structure of the economy, has turned out to be quite unrealistic. Malenbaum thinks that the lack of realism is particularly apparent with regard to agriculture and small enterprise. In the first Plan, the balance of public to private investment in agriculture and irrigation was roughly 1:1; in the second Plan it is about 2½:1, 800 crores of rupees, public and 300 crores of rupees, private. How was this shift in balance to be achieved? What reason had the planners to assume that such an increase in public investment would not encourage a proportionate increase in private investment—considering, for example, that the Italian planners made precisely the reverse assumption?

Indeed, another flaw in the planning process is a general failure to think in terms of implementation and control as well as in terms of setting targets. As Malenbaum puts it:[19]

> . . . an economic development program is much more than a total of inter-related projects and of the resources for their implementation. The program must specify the machinery which will make these savings, these borrowings, these imports, these investments, and the like actually take place. Will the people and institutions of the society simply respond to the announcement of the program, both because they are motivated to the objectives of the program and because the particulars of the program were in fact worked out on the basis of specific response patterns of Indian society? Or will new action be needed, primarily by government, to assure the fulfillment of the Plan? Clearly these are the two extremes. To some extent the Plan will

[18] *Ibid.*
[19] *Ibid.*, chap. II.

require direct action by public authorities, including perhaps direct restraints upon popular action; on the other hand, there will also need to be a broad response from the people. Given decades without progress in India, there is ample justification for considerable attention in the Plan to the underlying mechanism which is to assure the implementation of the specific programs.

The truth is that despite the emphasis on planning and the announced socialist philosophy (which really means a social welfare philosophy) India is one of the least regulated economies in the world. Professor Galbraith points out that [20]

> . . . by almost any test, the economy of India is less responsive to public guidance and direction than that of the United States. Indeed it is one of the world's least controlled or "planned" economies. In the United States the several levels of government dispose of about 20 per cent of the total production (or $434 billions in 1957). In India the corresponding figure is not over 10 per cent. By this test—the size of state activity in relation to all activity—more than twice as much of the American economy is managed or planned by government as is the case in India. . . . In the aggregate there can be little doubt that ours is both much the more manageable and the more managed economy. India has, in fact, superimposed a smallish socialized sector atop what, no doubt, is the world's greatest example of functioning anarchy.

Perhaps the basic trouble with the second Plan is that it is an admixture of physical planning and economic planning, of ideology and *ad hocery*, which reflects the basic splits in Indian society as a whole. The Indian government is committed to democracy and to socialism, to preserving traditional values and to getting on with the job of development, to raising productivity and to avoiding technological unemployment,[21] to steadfast independence and refusal of political commitments, and to use of foreign aid in development. India's neutralism, like Indonesia's, reflects the strength of opposing viewpoints within the society rather than complete political unity. The election of a Communist government in the state of Kerala and a Communist mayor in Bombay, the strength of the Communist Party else-

[20] J. K. Galbraith, "Rival Economic Theories in India," *Foreign Affairs*, July, 1958.

[21] "Mr. Nehru can talk about the greater appropriateness of energy from cowdung than from atomic fission at India's present stage of progress; Indian political and governmental leaders can give abundant lip service to Gandhian proclivity for rural and handicraft activities. But the effective force is one for rapid modernization, for a quick transition to the industry and power in the U.S. and the U.S.S.R. prototypes." Malenbaum, *op. cit.*, chap. III.

where in the country, the restiveness within the Congress party itself, the success of Communist China—all mean that left-wing viewpoints cannot be ignored. Yet majority opinion is still anti-communist. The Plan tries to please both sides, incorporating some Russian style physical target planning and some Western style economic planning, with neither being completely carried through. The physical planning was not carried as far as input-output analysis, although the facilities of the excellent Statistical Institute would have permitted that to be done. Had full use been made of these facilities, the foreign exchange crisis and inflationary pressure could have been predicted. The same is true if economic planning had been carried through in terms of the usual sort of multiplier analysis. Indeed, such predictions were made by a number of private economists.[22]

The mixture of incomplete physical planning with incomplete economic analysis reflects the personalities involved in the planning process as well as the political differences in the country as a whole. Both the Statistical Adviser and the then Minister of Finance, as well as the Minister of Planning, were trained originally as natural scientists, and tend toward a physical planning approach. The top staff of the Planning Commission Secretariat, together with the panel of economists, lean toward an economic policy approach to development. Apparently, in the preparation of the second Plan, the influence of the former group outweighed that of the latter, but the Plan reflects the ideas of both groups without completely co-ordinating them.

Was the Second Plan "Too Ambitious"?

The Indian experience illustrates very well the point made in Chapter 16 regarding the necessity of "planning big," in order to assure a take-off into sustained growth, while not planning more than available resources permit, so that the economy runs into serious loss of foreign exchange or inflation or both. In terms of what is needed to provide a "big push," bring the required structural change, produce simultaneous agricultural improvement and industrialization, and to assure increases in productivity that will significantly outrun population growth, the second Plan was certainly too small. In Malenbaum's view, the necessity for the Indian leadership to show results that would not be so obviously at a disadvantage in comparison with China

[22] See for example the articles on the second Plan in the *Quarterly Economic Report* of the Indian Institute of Public Opinion, especially Vol. I, No. 3, 4, 8, 1955.

as to shift public opinion further to the left, plus the fact that over the first Plan national income actually did grow by 17 per cent or 18 per cent, "meant that over-all targets for 1961 could not have been significantly smaller than the 25 per cent increase actually established." Malenbaum also holds that "given the drive and excitement of the process of a transformation from stagnation to growth, the resource potential of India and especially the knowledge and ability of Indian business and governmental leadership, such targets were not unreasonable."[23]

On the other hand, it is clear in retrospect that India planned beyond its actual capacity, given the amount of foreign aid that was forthcoming and the limited measures for mobilizing and directing India's own saving and investment potential. If the second Plan is to be realized, more vigorous efforts will be needed on both these fronts.

If sufficient foreign aid is offered, the government is likely to give private enterprise its head, no matter whether the aid itself is designated for public or for private projects. The "socialist" philosophy may prevent the government from allocating more foreign exchange to private investment projects at the expense of the public sector; but if the public investment program is provided for, the Indian *ad hocery* would incline the government toward granting any extra foreign exchange to private enterprises that could use it for development. A case in point is the World Bank loan to the Tata Company for the construction of an iron and steel plant, which the Indian government approved even though iron and steel had been allocated to the public sector. The most effective way of encouraging expansion of private enterprise in India might be to provide generous capital assistance for public projects.

India versus China

We saw in Chapter 2 that democratic India is engaged in a development race with Communist China, a race watched with great interest by all underdeveloped countries and particularly by those still uncommitted in the Cold War. How is the race going so far?

As of early 1958, China was well in the lead. In India, real income was 28 per cent higher at the end of March, 1958, than it had been eight years before, an average annual increase of 3.5 per cent. In the seven years ending January 1, 1958, China achieved an increase in real income of 85 per cent, indicating a

[23] Malenbaum, *op. cit.*, chap. II.

rate of growth almost three times as high as in India. Over the periods of the two first Plans (April, 1951, to April, 1956, for India; January, 1953, to January, 1958, for China) gross national product grew 20 per cent in India and 50 per cent in China. (See Table 29-5.) The rate of population growth was somewhat higher in China than in India, but even when allowance is made

TABLE 29-5.

India and China, Gross National Product and Gross Investment

(Prices 1952; ratios, 1952 = 100)

India (billions of rupees)

Year *	GNP			GI		
	Amount	Ratio	Ratio † per capita	Amount	Ratio	% GNP
1950	95.9	93.4	95.7	9.05	85.2	9.4
1951	98.7	97.1	97.2	9.99	94.1	10.1
1952	102.9	100.0	100.0	10.62	100.0	10.3
1953	109.1	106.1	105.0	11.18	105.2	10.2
1954	112.5	109.4	106.0	14.02	132.1	12.4
1955	114.8	111.6	107.5	16.30	153.4	14.3
1956	120.3	117.0	111.3	17.90	168.5	14.9
1957	122.5	119.1	112.0	19.40	182.8	15.8

China (billions of yuan)

Year	GNP			GI		
	Amount	Ratio	Ratio per capita	Amount	Ratio	% GNP
1950	54.7	79.2	84.0	5.85	61.2	10.7
1951	63.0	93.0	93.8	7.75	81.0	12.3
1952	67.9	100.0	100.0	9.57	100.0	14.1
1953	77.7	114.5	112.2	12.65	132.1	16.3
1954	82.1	121.0	116.1	14.25	149.0	17.3
1955	84.9	125.0	118.2	14.60	152.5	17.2
1956	96.2	141.7	131.0	16.90	176.8	17.6
1957 ‡	101.9	150.1	135.2	22.35	233.5	22.0

* For India, years begin April 1; for China, January 1.

† Based on census data. Indian growth rate about 1.35 per cent; Chinese, 2.0–2.2 per cent.

‡ Preliminary estimates.

SOURCE: India: Malenbaum's estimates based on official sources. China: W. W. Hollister, *Communist China's Gross National Product, 1950–57* (Cambridge, Mass., 1958).

for this difference, it is apparent that per capita income rose substantially more in China than in India. Both countries had high marginal rates of savings—35 per cent of the increase in income in India, 40 per cent in China—but China enjoyed the greater rise in per capita consumption, 21 per cent between 1952 and 1957, as compared to 8 per cent for India.

This relative success of the Chinese development program is in part a reflection of greater effort on the investment front. As may be seen from Table 29-5, gross investment in India rose from 9.4 per cent of gross national income in 1950 to 15.8 per cent in 1957, an average of about 14.7 per cent. Over the same period Chinese gross investment rose from 10.7 per cent of gross national income to 22.0 per cent, an average of some 17.6 per cent.[24] But when one takes into account the greater growth of Chinese output, it appears that the absolute level of Chinese gross investment in 1957 was four times what it was in 1950, while in India investment had barely doubled over the same period. It also appears that a larger share of total investment in India went into replacement and depreciation, so that the difference in net investment would be even more strikingly in China's favor.

More important than the difference in investment, however, was the difference in what was produced by investment in the two countries. China was simply more successful in raising output with a given volume of investment than India was. Professor Malenbaum made the following calculations of incremental *gross* capital-output ratios for the two countries: [25]

Period	*India*	*China*
1950–57	4.05	2.08
First Plan years	3.29	2.38
pre-Plan years	7.71	1.31
post-Plan years	4.97	....

Thus "over the period as a whole, China generated a unit of gross income flows with essentially half the gross investment that was required in India."

The Chinese victory was apparent, not only in the aggregate, but in each major sector as well. Production of food grains rose 45 per cent in India, 50 per cent in China. Expansion of rice pro-

[24] Too much weight should not be attached to the 1957 figure, since much of the investment in that year represented replenishment of inventories.

[25] Malenbaum, *India and China: Contrasts in Development Performance*, M.I.T. CIS (D/58-6), p. 15.

duction was much the same, China increasing hectarage and India raising yields. In cotton and sugar cane too, China showed the greater expansion. From 1950 to 1957, agricultural output rose by some 30 per cent in China and 15 to 20 per cent in India. A somewhat larger share of the development budget was devoted to agriculture in China than in India.

The Chinese margin of victory is wider, however, in the industrial field. In 1957 the index of industrial production (1952=100) was 144 for India and 232 for China. The more rapid Chinese expansion shows also in the figures for individual industries, with the single exception of textiles, where Indian expansion has been noteworthy. The modern industrial sector has received a considerably higher proportion of the total investment budget in China than in India.

Most significant, perhaps, is the difference in degree of structural change in the two countries. India has achieved little of the structural change which, as we have seen earlier, is almost synonymous with economic development; agriculture accounted for about half of national income in both 1957 and 1950. In China, on the other hand, agriculture's share of national income dropped from about 70 per cent in 1950 to less than 50 per cent in 1957.

According to Malenbaum, "the evidence suggests that there was in China a more careful budgeting of investible resources to meet the output targets specified in the first plans." Of course, the government sector is very much bigger in China than in India, which makes control somewhat easier; but in Malenbaum's opinion, "a mixed economy, with controls at strategic points in the allocation of foreign exchange and construction permits" should conform to a plan just about as closely as a communist one. He feels that the explanation lies less in the tightness of the controls than in the "care with which the problems of growth in an economy like India's or China's have been analyzed and in the determination of the authorities to deal with these problems." [26] In other words, India's plan was inferior to China's.

Lessons from Indian Experience

India, having a longer experience with formal development planning than any democratic country, has more to teach than most countries; the lessons of Indian experience derive from the snags into which the two Indian Five-Year Plans have run, as well as from the successes.

[26] Malenbaum, *op. cit.*, p. 43.

1. In India we see demonstrated once again the importance of entrepreneurship in both the public and the private sectors of the economy. India's success in uniting the general public behind the development plans and in bringing significant increases in per capita output in the face of tremendous obstacles reflects more than anything else the quality of Indian leadership, in the government, in the civil service, and in the business community.

2. Indian unity with respect to the necessity of preparing and executing a series of ambitious development plans also reflects, however, the efforts of the leadership group to obtain wide participation in the process. In actual fact the planning may still be done from the top down, but sincere efforts are made to encourage "planning from below," and these efforts have borne fruit in public support for the plans.

3. At the same time, ideological conflicts regarding the nature of the plan and of the planning process reflect internal political differences. Failure to carry the planning process through to completion is in part the result of compromise between these opposing views. If Indian planning is to be completely effective these conflicts must be resolved to the point where they do not inhibit the technical efficiency of the planning process.

4. The main evidence of failure to complete the planning process is the absence of firm recommendations in the Plan for the policy measures and regulations needed to implement it. Statement of targets and broad outlines of the sources of finance are not enough in what is still overwhelmingly a free private enterprise economy.

5. The selection of appropriate measures to direct and encourage the private sector along the desired development path must be based on detailed and intimate knowledge of the economic, sociological, and cultural framework. No set of general principles can provide a complete guide to development policy for a particular country. Acquisition of this knowledge may require a great deal of on the spot field research of a kind not ordinarily carried on by central government planning authorities.

6. Expansion of the scope of public investment, particularly investment in the infrastructure, is unlikely to lead to a decline in the relative size of the private sector where private enterprise is vigorous and is not deliberately hampered by public policy. On the contrary, efficient public investment is likely to have a "multiplier effect" on private investment. This relationship seems to hold even in a nominally "socialist" society.

7. Projection of past experience with respect to incremental

capital-output ratios can be dangerous, especially when past experience is limited to a period of postwar reconstruction, unusually favorable weather conditions, or other abnormal conditions.

8. In countries with the majority of the population engaged in peasant agriculture and handicrafts, there may be a conflict between maximizing output and maximizing employment; the most efficient techniques may be so much more capital-intensive than those now in use that their introduction would increase unemployment. In these conditions, the choice between maximizing output and maximizing employment becomes a matter of social policy. Before choosing the less efficient technique because it seems to provide more employment, however, all the *secondary* effects of the two technologies should be taken into account.

9. One might also glean from Indian experience a warning against gradualism. In terms of the resources in sight in 1956, the second Plan was of course fairly ambitious; in terms of what is needed to bring appreciable changes in productivity and to alter fundamentally the prognosis for future growth, however, it was clearly too modest. And if even this plan is abandoned for lack of resources, it may turn out that India will have missed her "optimum moment" for generating a take-off. A good deal of the energy of the leadership group has been directed toward the two Plans, and a good deal of popular support has been mustered for them. If now failure is admitted it may be extremely hard to mobilize the same degree of leadership and public support again.

10. Another way of saying the same thing is that India may miss her optimum moment—at least for development within a democratic framework—unless increased foreign aid is forthcoming from the West. And India may not be the only country in which the chances for true economic development are slim without substantial foreign aid and investment. Whether the aid itself is provided for public or for private investment, the actual amount of private investment will be significantly increased by foreign aid.

Indonesia

The late Hadji Agus Salim once said that the Indonesian revolution has yet to enter its economic phase. As of mid-1958, the statement was still true. Each of the governments since the establishment of the republic gave lip-service to the need for economic development, but in most cases their development plans went little further than statements that achieving increased economic welfare of the people was part of the government's program. Similarly, the official programs of the major political parties have tended to stress "social justice," "welfare," and improved distribution of the national income rather than economic development.

Since their achievement of sovereignty at the end of 1949, Indonesian leaders have been so preoccupied with reconstruction, establishing law and order, organizing government administration, and jockeying for political power that they have appeared less development-minded than their counterparts in neighboring countries. It took more than six years after the transfer of sovereignty, and over four years after the establishment of a National Planning Bureau with UN assistance, for Indonesia to produce a development plan.[27] This plan was presented in Parliament in May, 1956; but there is little to be gained by discussing its details, since it has not been implemented. The lessons of Indonesia's experience derive from its failure to prepare and execute a plan, not from the plan itself.

Political and Administrative Problems

The development plan for 1956–60 was prepared by the National Planning Bureau, to which the task of co-ordinating the planning of economic development in Indonesia is entrusted, in collaboration with various ministries. The basic plans were prepared by the various ministries. The Bureau's role has been to review, revise, and integrate these plans into a national investment budget. The Bureau also has administrative responsibilities with respect to execution of the investment budget.

The Planning Bureau was originally established directly under the Prime Minister as a regular government agency. It reported to a National Planning Board comprising the nine cabinet ministers most concerned with economic development. Its work was directed by a Director-General, who also served as Secretary to the Planning Board, with the assistance of a Deputy Director-General. The Ali Sastroamidjojo cabinet of 1955 included a Ministry of National Planning. Ir. Djuanda, the former Director-General, was appointed Minister, a post he retained after becom-

[27] For a review of some of the problems faced in preparing the plan, see Benjamin Higgins, *Indonesia's Economic Stabilization and Development* (New York, 1957).

ing Prime Minister in 1957.

The Bureau was assisted by a group of foreign experts provided to the Indonesian government through the UN. The interesting feature of the agreement between the Indonesian government and the UN was that the UN undertook to recruit and provide salaries for these experts, but the experts signed their contracts with the Indonesian government and did not report to the UN. The Bureau also had the assistance of a sizable team of American engineers, provided under an ICA contract, with similar independence of the parent agency.

Early in 1953 a Working Party on Monetary and Fiscal Policy was established within the Planning Bureau. The working party consisted of members of the Indonesian, Chinese, Dutch, British, and American commercial, industrial, and financial communities. The members were nominated by the Minister of Finance and the group met fortnightly in the offices of the Bureau, under the chairmanship of the monetary and fiscal expert. The agendas and documentation for the meetings were for the most part prepared by the Planning Bureau, although on occasion memoranda were submitted by members of the working party.

The discussions did much to dispel the mutual suspicions then prevalent between the government and private enterprise. The working party also served as a sounding board for policy proposals and served as a channel through which specialized information could flow from the business community to the government. It was contemplated at one stage that other working parties might be set up under the chairmanship of other foreign experts so as to broaden the public participation in the preparation of development plans. However, no other working parties were established; indeed the Working Party on Monetary and Fiscal Policy did not survive the change of government and the later departure of the first monetary and fiscal expert. The new government was less disposed than its predecessor to discuss policy questions with the business community, and the appointment of an Indonesian Director-General and an Indonesian deputy made direct contact of foreign experts with the business community less appropriate than before. In general, however, the process of plan preparation has not been regarded by Indonesian officials as one in which the role of the general public or special groups outside the government should be very large. This defect may be partially remedied by the recent establishment of the National Planning Board with broad regional and functional representation.

Why did it take so long after the signing of the agreement providing for foreign experts for the National Planning Bureau staff, for the Bureau to produce a complete development plan for the guidance of the Indonesian government? Part of the answer is that the Bureau's standards are high, and effective development plans cannot be turned out in a hurry, especially when there is no background of national planning to give guidance. Another part of the answer is that the Bureau has been called upon for a good deal of trouble shooting in addition to its planning function. The Director-General, in particular, is involved in current administration as well as in long-range planning.

There were also some administrative reasons. To begin with, there were delays in recruiting. Not until July, 1952, did the present writer, first of the foreign experts recruited under the agreement, arrive in Indonesia; the team was not completed until the following June. Second, the composition of the original request for nine experts reflected the government's need for assistance with certain current problems as well as for advice on longer-range development plans. For example, national income estimates were needed as a basis for both current and long-run policy: one of the experts requested was a national income specialist. The range of statistics collected and organized still reflected the concepts of a colonial administration rather than the needs of a national government; hence a general statistician was requested. Dr. Hjalmar Schacht, in his earlier report to the Indonesian government, had stressed the need for improved public administration, as a basis for economic development. A public administration expert was included in the team. As the government was aware that population pressure constituted a serious problem for Indonesia, a population expert was requested (this post ultimately being filled by the same man who served as general statistician). Since it was expected that transmigration would play a significant role in the development plan, among the specialists recruited was an expert on transmigration, with experience in administering large-scale movements of people under IRO and UNRRA. Useful as these specialists undoubtedly were, it was gradually recognized that their *expertise* was not of the sort most useful in determining priorities in a development plan. Other posts were more directly related to development planning: natural resources, agriculture, industry, labor relations and labor productivity, and money and finance.

The Bureau was later reorganized along different lines. The

monetary and fiscal expert, the population expert, and the expert on manpower training and labor relations were retained. A second expert was added in agriculture, in industry, and in natural resources. In addition, experts on power, community development, and national income were brought in on short-run assignments. Although this reorganization ultimately improved the factual base of the Bureau's work, its transitional effect was disruptive; for some time the Bureau was reduced again to four foreign experts.

A third administrative problem faced by the Bureau during the first year and a half of its existence was the lack of clear-cut and effective direction. The Bureau was then a kind of "headless monster." General direction and co-ordination were provided by the Minister of Finance, Dr. Sumitro, who had been designated by the Prime Minister as co-ordinator of the Planning Bureau. Because of the wide range of his responsibilities, however, Dr. Sumitro was unable to give continuous attention to the affairs of the Bureau. Since, in contrast to regular UN planning teams, the foreign experts were full-fledged Indonesian officials, it was considered inappropriate to have a chief of mission among them. The Indonesian research staff was headed by a research director whose relationship to the foreign experts was never clearly defined. In August, 1953, this problem was met by the appointment of two high-level administrators to the Bureau. Ir. Djuanda—for the first time out of the Indonesian Cabinet—became Director-General. Ali Budiardjo, a former Secretary General of Defense and for a few months Acting Director of the Planning Bureau, became Deputy Director-General.

A fourth administrative problem was the lack of clearly defined relationships of the Bureau to other government agencies. The Planning Board, to which the Bureau should have reported, met as such (its composition was the same as that of the Economic and Financial Council) rarely, if at all, during the first two years of the life of the Bureau. There was no clear indication of the relation of the Bureau to the various ministries represented on the Board. For a short time it seemed possible that each foreign expert might become a senior adviser to a ministry, as well as a member of a planning team, so that current economic policy as well as development planning could be co-ordinated through the Bureau, supported by the Ministry of Finance. Perhaps fortunately, this conception of the Bureau's function soon disappeared, because of the natural reluctance of several ministries to accord such a position to a foreigner. With regard to foreign aid, there was in existence a large and cumbersome "Co-ordinating Committee" (attendance at its meetings gradually crept up into the dozens), which also had loosely defined responsibilitie with regard to development planning. The relationship of the Bureau to the Co-ordinating Committee was not defined. Similarly, it was not until well along in the life of the Bureau that its responsibilities with respect to the development items in the budget were clarified. Finally, the relationship to the team of engineers provided through American bilateral technical assistance, and which was concerned with technical aspects of economic development, was also not defined.

These administrative problems have since been overcome. Unfortunately, there were more basic reasons for the delay in completion of a development plan for Indonesia and for the failure to execute the plan once completed. One problem in planning was the lack of detailed knowledge about the Indonesian resource pattern. The Netherlands East Indies government showed only limited interest in resources not being immediately exploited by Dutch capital. The resources of the Outer Islands are scarcely known, and even in Java and Sumatra, information regarding the quality and quantity of resources is incomplete. Without knowing what the resource pattern is, and consequently without knowing what is the development potential, the preparation of a development plan is obviously extremely difficult.

Planning was also complicated by interministerial rivalries, which were to some extent a reflection of interparty conflict. Acceptance of a development plan by the government would mean accepting the priorities laid down, even if it meant the expansion of activities of one ministry at the expense of others; this sort of planning was not politically possible in Indonesia.

At the root of Indonesia's failure to launch a development program, however, has been the lack of commitment on the part of the Indonesian government, and behind them the Indonesian people, to the planning and execution of a development program. There is still a lack of understanding, even among educated Indonesians, of the requirements of economic development; sovereignty and prosperity are still too directly linked in the minds of most Indonesians, and when sovereignty did not bring immediate prosperity, there was a tendency to blame either the continued presence of foreigners, or the government in power at the moment. Having won their independence, Indonesians certainly wanted higher standards of living, but most Indonesians thought "redividing the pie," rather than trying to make the "pie" bigger, would get them to that goal. In particular, they have looked to a redistribution of income as between Indonesians and foreigners (including Chinese) as a source of higher standards of living for Indonesians.

A still more fundamental problem confronts all aspects of Indonesian economic policy: the lack of resolution of the basic political conflict concerning the relationship of Indonesia to the outside world. In particular, Indonesia has not decided whether or to what extent it wishes to rely on foreign experts, foreign aid, and foreign investment in achieving its development objectives. Without such a decision, even the dimensions of the development program are hard to determine. Determining its composition is still more difficult. Priorities cannot be established independently of the scale of developmental activity, and *what* projects can be financed depends a good deal on *where* finance is sought.

Many Indonesians thought that *Merdeka* (freedom) would bring prosperity automatically. It did not; but recognition that action was needed to bring prosperity did not lead to action, because no group emerged with a program commanding enough popular support to be carried through. Indonesian political strength is divided among myriads of parties, splinter groups, and factions. Any two of the four major parties could form a stable coalition government, but no two of them have been able to agree for long, and no one of them commands a simple majority. This situation, coupled with the Indonesian tradition that action should represent unanimous opinion rather than the will of the majority, has prevented the adoption of measures to unify the country and raise its standard of living.

Even more paralyzing has been the basic ideological conflict among political leaders. True, all governments and all parties have declared in favor of "converting the colonial economy into a national economy"; but the concept of a "national economy" differed from party to party and from leader to leader. Only the Communists had a clear idea of what a "national economy" would be. All parties also had the national goal of "organizing the economy along co-operative lines," required by Article 38 of the Provisional Constitution; but this goal, too, lacked clear definition. For some leaders it meant extension to national economic policy of the principles of rice-roots village democracy—*gotong-rojong*, *kertja sama*, *ramah-tamah*, and *musjawarat desa* (mutual aid, working together, a family-like society, and government by consensus rather than majority); but what this would mean in terms of specific development projects, or monetary, fiscal, and foreign exchange policies, or decentralization of powers, was never spelled out. For other leaders, including former Vice President Hatta, the "co-operative society" was defined in the European fashion of the 1930's, as the "middle way" between Communism and unbridled monopoly capitalism. For them extension of the co-operative way to the national economy meant quite simply organizing more and bigger co-operatives.

But although there was no agreement on concrete economic and social policies there was agreement that Indonesia was not to be developed on "capitalist" lines. As ideologies, rugged individualism, free competition, private enterprise, had few enthusiastic backers. They were associated in the minds of most Indonesians with imperialism, materialism, and a ruthlessly exploitative approach to social organization. Indonesians did not want such "capitalism." So what was the economic and social system to be? No one but the Communists was quite sure. Meanwhile, it was considered necessary to avoid making decisions on particular projects and policies—such as the foreign investment, mining, and petroleum laws—lest the decisions prove inconsistent with the ultimate definition of social and economic aims.

Similarly, although all agreed that the political system was to be "democratic," they also agreed that democracy should not be construed in the ordinary Western sense. (No one but the Communists wanted a "People's Democracy.") It was to be an Indonesian democracy, rejecting, as Sukarno put it—"the principle that fifty per cent plus one is right." But what exactly did this mean? In particular, what did it mean in terms of allocation of powers among central, provincial, and local governments? No one was quite sure, and the Constituent Assembly may take years to decide. Again it was felt that no new institutions should be set up that might prejudice the final outcome.

With such confusion regarding ultimate goals, national leaders dissipated much time and energy in fruitless debate at the ideological level. Pressing economic issues drew the attention of only a handful of leaders in the agencies directly concerned. At some point, proposals for effective solution ran into an ideological or nationalist issue. Whenever it was a choice between an effective stabilization or development policy and satisfying nationalist sentiments, nationalism won.

During 1958, economic conditions in Indonesia reached their lowest ebb since the collapse of the Korean War boom early in 1952. The major contributing factor was the abortive rebellion in the Outer Islands against left-wing tendencies, corruption, and ineffective economic policy in Djakarta. Other factors were the continuing fall in prices of major exports, and the disruption of banking and transport through the government's assumption of control over certain Dutch enterprises and the departure of thousands of Dutch managers and technicians. Together these developments brought increased budget expenditures, reduced tax revenues, diminished foreign exchange earnings, further delays in the development program, and general economic deterioration.

By the end of September the Bank of Indonesia reserves were down to 7 per cent of the note circulation, as compared to the former legal ratio of 20 per cent. Imports of luxuries were cut out altogether; imports of semiluxuries and even some necessities were drastically curtailed. The black market rate for the dollar reached nine times the official rate.

Thus 1958 will go down as a black year in the economic history of the infant Indonesian republic. Yet it may also become known as the year of the turning point, the year in which the government was finally forced to be realistic and pragmatic in its approach to economic stabilization and development. For although the rebellion had unfavorable effects on the Indonesian economy in 1958, it was itself the result of the government's failure to improve economic conditions. Disappointment and dissatisfaction were particularly keen in the Outer Islands, where most of the big plantations, mines, oil fields, and refineries are located. With their abundant resources and relatively low population, the people in the Outer Islands thought they could get along very well if it were not for blunders, dishonesty, and political maneuvering in Djakarta. They wanted the central government leaders to stop jockeying for power and get on with the job of economic development. Also the Moslem parties are strongest in the Outer Islands, and it was there that deepest concern was felt over the willingness of President Sukarno and other Nationalist leaders to collaborate with the Communists. In February, 1958, the pent-up disgruntlement burst out in the form of a revolutionary government with headquarters in central Sumatra, headed by the former Governor of the Bank of Indonesia, Sjaffrudin Prawiranegara.

There is reason to hope that from the ashes of this quickly quelled rebellion the Indonesian phoenix may rise again at last. All Indonesian leaders recognize that the military defeat of the rebels does not solve the problems which gave rise to the revolt. After years of neglecting economic development for power politics, the Indonesian leadership has been forced by the rebellion to put economic stabilization and development at the top of the agenda. In a curious boomerang fashion, the very depths to which 1958 brought Indonesia improve the outlook for the future. For during 1958 Indonesian leaders learned some valuable lessons:

1. Political stability and economic development are not two separate problems. No government can "let economic development wait" while it maneuvers to keep in power.

2. Raising Indonesian incomes requires making the pie grow; redividing the pie—even redividing it between Indonesians and foreigners—is not enough.

3. Communist Parties are not easy to utilize for one's own, non-communist purposes. Both the Nationalist party and President Sukarno are considerably less enthusiastic now than they were a year ago about collaboration with the Communist Party.

4. Government by *musjarawat desa*—unanimous opinion of the village—does not work at the national level. A central government cannot merely postpone awkward decisions on which there is no unanimous agreement. Basic decisions must be made *now* if development is to start in the near future.

Hitherto the chief obstacle to effective use of foreign aid (and Indonesia has received less assistance per capita than any other country) has been its lack of development-mindedness and unwillingness to make decisions on development plans, programs, and projects when such decisions were thought to entail political risks. Now that Indonesian leaders have learned that economic stabilization and development must be given top priority and that decisions must be made, Indonesia could absorb substantial amounts of foreign aid, some under surplus commodity disposal programs to feed and clothe Java until an attack can be made on the overpopulated rural sector, and the rest for big projects in the Outer Islands.

The Indonesian government has made a good start on recovery. It has set up an Economic Stabilization Bureau and a new National Planning Board with broad regional representation. The Bank of Indonesia has been accorded new powers to fight inflation, including treasury bill reserve requirements and a "special deposit" provision not unlike the Australian one. But these measures alone will not assure development; Indonesia needs a new development plan and technical and capital assistance to carry it out. As this book goes to press, news comes through that at long last Parliament has passed the foreign investment law.

Lessons from Indonesian Experience

Lessons can be learned from both the successes and the failures of Indonesia's efforts at development planning. Some of the lessons are the obverse of those derived from Libyan experience.

1. Just as the prior undertaking of a resource survey facilitated the preparation of a plan for Libya, so the lack of precise knowledge of the quality and quantity of natural and manpower resources has been a major handicap to development planning in Indonesia. There is of course no comparison with respect to complexity of the tasks in the two countries; the very poverty and concentration of Libyan resources made it easy to survey them and easy to discern the outlines of the plan, whereas the variety of Indonesian resources and the enormous area over which they are spread make it difficult to survey them and hard to assign priorities among development projects. Nevertheless the principle is clear from the experience of both countries: to prepare a development plan, it is necessary to know what are the natural and manpower resources that can be utilized.

2. Similarly, just as the selection of the planning team in terms of development potentials facilitated planning in Libya, so the selection of a planning team in terms of current problems handicapped the Indonesian Planning Bureau in its early years. Here, too, the lesson is clear: not every expert useful to a government is a useful member of a planning team; if planning is to be effective, special knowledge of the various sectors within the economy must somehow be brought to bear in the determination of priorities for development projects. It is also helpful if the analytical framework for determining the scope and priorities of a plan can be clearly set forth. Lack of agreement among the team as to the *approach* to planning was one of the factors retarding preparation of plans in the early months of the Indonesian Planning Bureau.

3. We also see a third lesson: the need to establish clear-cut functions for a planning agency and clear-cut relationships between the planning agency and other branches of the government.

4. In Indonesia we see in different form the importance of preparing plans that are politically acceptable. An economic development plan which is incompatible with social and political

objectives is likely to fail. Although development planners may not be expert in formulating such objectives, they should endeavor to take them into account in drawing up their plans. In Indonesia thus far, little effort has been made to bring the general public into the planning process. Parliament itself has not been consulted or informed to any great extent. Thc community of professional economists, or representatives of the private enterprise sector, have as yet been accorded no clear role in planning. Instead the Planning Bureau itself has endeavored to produce a plan which will not encounter strong opposition from any quarter.

5. There are several strong points in the Indonesian plan. The very length of time devoted to its preparation has made it more solid than it might otherwise have been. The recognition that even countries of "socialist" bent cannot hope to plan the private sector in detail is a source of strength rather than weakness. Spurious planning for the private sector without providing for effective implementation of plans in that sector can only weaken a plan. By avoiding controversial issues and limiting the role of foreign experts, the Planning Bureau in Indonesia has been able to produce a plan with high degree of political acceptability. To get the same degree of acceptability for the bolder and broader plans of the future, the Bureau may find it necessary to take the public into its confidence to a greater extent in the course of plan preparation. Prime Minister Djuanda's reorganization is one step in this direction.

The Philippines

The preparation of development plans in the Philippines is the responsibility of the National Economic Council. Under Reorganization Plan No. 10, the NEC is also assigned the function of advising the government on all aspects of monetary, fiscal, foreign exchange, tariff, reparations, and other policies relating to economic development. The composition of the Council is somewhat curious. It includes two senators and two members of the house of representatives; these positions are necessarily largely political. The Governor of the Central Bank and the Chairman of the Board of the Rehabilitation Finance Corporation are members *ex officio*. There is also one representative each for industry, agriculture, and labor. Thus the NEC combines features of the United States Council of Economic Advisers and the Joint Committee on the President's Economic Report, the Board of Governors of the Federal Reserve System, and the Russian Supreme Economic Council.

The Council has a sizable secretariat, divided into three Offices: Statistical Coordination and Standards, Foreign Aid Co-ordination, and National Planning, which is concerned with the actual work of putting together a development plan. The Office of National Planning in turn is divided into six branches: agricultural resources, services (utilities), social development, trade and commerce, industrial resources, and finance.

In comparison with the planning staffs in most underdeveloped countries, the Office of National Planning is in an enviable position with respect both to numbers and to quality of its personnel. Each branch has a chief with special training and some years of experience in his field, supported by varying numbers of qualified technicians. Moreover, the NEC is able to draw on the *expertise* of the Central Bank, the Budget Commission, the Industrial Research Center, and other government agencies, although it has not always made the most of these opportunities.

The relatively large number of trained people, plus an unexplained Filipino passion for statistics, may account for the highly sophisticated methods of the Office of National Planning. All the latest devices of the development planner's craft are brought to bear in the preparation of the Philippines Five-Year Development Program. The starting point is a target increase in national income, which has been set at 6 per cent, slightly above the average of recent years. The target national income is then broken down by major sectors, using the actual structural distribution in recent years as a starting point, and providing for desired structural change within the economy during the planning period. Estimates are then made of the incremental capital-output ratio in each of these sectors. Thus the income targets, together with the sectoral capital-output ratios, provide the estimate of capital requirements.

The distribution of investment between the public and private sectors starts from the traditional distribution of investment within the country, but makes some attempt to undertake in the public sector as much investment in "impulse sectors" as can be counted upon to bring with them increases in private investment as well. A separate estimate is made, using a rather refined multiplier formula (complete with marginal propensities to consume and import and the like) of the amount of deficit-financed development spending that can be undertaken without creating an undesirable degree of inflationary pressure. Finally, in allocating foreign exchange, intermediate and long-term credit, and tax privileges, use is made of the priority formula discussed in Chapter 27. In the public sector, priorities are assigned mainly on the basis of advice from government departments and corporations, within the general framework worked out by the Council. Perhaps at some stage, the Council will decide to apply the priority formula in the public sector as well.

Although these methods are virtually beyond reproach, there are some unsatisfactory features of their application to the actual problems of the Philippines. These shortcomings reflect the political and social environment within which plans must be made rather than any deficiencies of technique among the professional planners.

The development program starts, as it should, with an analysis of the problems which the plan is designed to solve. It proceeds to a brief statement of the major objectives of the plan. The public investment program is presented in some detail, which is proper, since this is the sector over which the government has direct control. There are separate chapters on social development, finance, and public administration. The chapter on financing is brief, but this defect is perhaps inevitable in view of the wish to withhold presentation of the fiscal and foreign exchange budgets until the private sector of the plan has also been discussed. The chapter on administration has one glaring omission: it takes no account of problems of business administration, which may be as important as public administration in such an economy as the Philippines. Perhaps later versions of the plan could include some discussion of the training and recruitment of managers.

The chapter on financing private investment is in an appropriate form but varies somewhat as to substance from one section to another. The sections on tax policy, reparations, foreign aid, and foreign investment are well worked out; those on encouraging and mobilizing savings, on monetary and credit policy, on budgetary policy, and on tariffs lack positive proposals. However, the presentation in this chapter has the advantage of making it clear what the weak sections are, so that the Council can go on to direct further research efforts to these areas in subsequent versions of the program.

The inclusion of a foreign exchange budget and a fiscal budget for the whole five-year period is a strong feature of the program. Another significant feature is a separate section on "recommendations for action by the various agencies of the government."

A major problem underlying the program is the lack of adequate data on past levels of national income and of investment. A discerning reader soon discovers that what the plan really proposes is a mere extension of the status quo. It is said at one point that the rate of increase in national income has been in excess of 5 per cent since the war, and in the last year or so has been about 6 per cent; yet the target is merely a 6 per cent increase in national income. Similarly, the report now cautiously states that net investment in the recent past has been less than 10 per cent of national income. Caution with respect to statistics is admirable; but the program would be strengthened by a frank statement that the objective of economic development in the Philippines is not to accelerate the rate of increase in national income, but to sustain it in the face of increasing difficulties as the period of reconstruction recedes into the past, to distribute the fruits of economic growth more widely, and to translate the increase in national income into decreasing unemployment.

It is by no means certain that the present plan will achieve these objectives. Even with optimistic estimates of employment creation, it would take thirty years of investment at the planned level to eliminate unemployment. With more modest estimates of employment creation the planned investment would not reduce unemployment at all. Moreover, although the estimate of capital cost per job is reasonable, it is by no means pessimistic; indeed $2,000 per job would seem to be about the minimum reasonable estimate for the kind of program which is proposed.

The program as published avoids reference to the underlying estimated capital-output ratios. It is perhaps better to state the plan in general terms than to rely too much on ratio estimates of dubious validity. But there is always an implicit ratio in any development plan that gives both an investment program and an income target, and this implicit ratio is very much on the low side, about 2:1. This figure is a highly optimistic one for a program with the complexion of the one proposed in the draft plan. The second Indian Five-Year Plan has an implicit ratio of 2:2. We have seen that even this figure is much too low. Yet the Philippines plan is more heavily weighted with high-ratio projects than the Indian one.

In Chapter 2 we saw that Indonesia and the Philippines face common obstacles to economic development. In both countries, the achievement of sustained growth requires drastic structural change, involving the development of industrial exports and import-replacing industries. To reach reasonably high standards of living for the whole population, the structural change must be carried to the point of reducing substantially the proportion of employment in agriculture and shifting to more extensive and more mechanized techniques in the peasant agriculture sector. This latter form of change is more pressingly needed in Indonesia because of the limitations on further expansion of agricultural output on Java with present techniques, and the concentration of population on that island. On the other hand the problem of unemployment would seem to be more serious in the Philippines, and the social problems accompanying unbalanced growth would seem to be more severe. Indeed the Philippines problem is one of maintaining past rates of increase in income, while achieving structural change, reducing unemployment, and spreading the benefits of economic growth.

For the accomplishment of development goals, Indonesia seems more blessed by nature and the Philippines more blessed by history. Indonesia starts its planned development with a wide range of natural resources which permit balanced growth without difficulty. But it also starts with a severe lack of trained and experienced public administrators, entrepreneurs and managers, and technicians; with the hampering influence of extreme nationalism; and with the knotty problem of population pressure on Java, which is closely related to the problem of political disunity that is now occupying most of the energies of national leaders. In Indonesia the main requirement for economic development is the achievement of political unity so that the government can get on with the job.

On balance, it appears that the Philippines is in a stronger position than Indonesia for early achievement of sustained economic growth. The country is less plagued by problems of stabilization. Both the internal and external values of the currency have been kept stable for several years, and the mild inflationary pressure that has developed in the past two years is not cause for great concern. Although there is pressure on the external value of the peso, it is of a kind which is related to the long-run necessity of structural change rather than to short-run fluctuations in the foreign exchange market. Thus the Philippines authorities need not devote as much time and energy to stabilization as their counterparts in some other countries, including Indonesia. They have more freedom to concentrate on problems of economic development.

Second, because of the relatively high per capita income in

the Philippines, internal financing of the lion's share of investment requirements presents relatively little difficulty. Foreign exchange must be found to pay for the imported raw materials and equipment needed for development, but further cuts in luxury imports could provide most of that. The concentration of income and wealth presents social problems, but from the standpoint of economic development, that concentration can be converted into a source of strength. It means that high ratios of savings and investment to national income can be achieved without lowering the standard of living of the masses. In the Philippines, diverting 12 to 15 per cent of national income to public and private investment purposes, which is necessary to launch a process of sustained growth, can be accomplished without imposing hardship on any group, even in the short run.

Third, although the Philippines higher standards of literacy and education produce social problems when unaccompanied by an appropriate development program, they can become a major asset if such a program is formulated and executed. A high level of literacy is the basis for quick and widespread results in agricultural extension work, manpower training programs, and other measures designed to raise man-hour productivity. The importance attached to higher education, with some redesigning of university curricula, makes it easier to provide the flow of managers and technicians needed for relatively rapid industrialization. Moreover, perhaps because of the decades of association with the United States, Filipinos are a good deal more technology-minded than many of their neighbors; there is less resistance to technical change and more interest in new techniques than in many underdeveloped countries.

Finally, and perhaps most important, the Philippines does not as yet suffer from population pressure. The rate of population growth is high, but the base on which it takes place is still small relative to resources. Accordingly, the Philippines has been granted a "breathing spell" which many underdeveloped countries do not have, during which higher levels of productivity can be achieved so as to permit a rise in national income significantly higher than population growth.

Lessons of Experience in the Philippines

1. Perhaps the most important lesson to be learned from experience with development planning in the Philippines is that if a society is to enjoy economic growth it must "want" it, in the sense that the leadership group, in and out of government, and

the people as a whole are prepared to take the actions necessary to bring economic growth about. The Philippines, we have seen, is in a better position for a take-off than most Asian countries, starting as it does from a relatively high level of per capita income, with a good resource base, a favored position in the United States market, a relatively high level of literacy and general education, a well-trained civil service, and an unusually able and active group of indigenous entrepreneurs. Yet there is little evidence that the preparation of development plans by the government—and the five-year program discussed above is not the first plan prepared in the Philippines—has accelerated economic growth in the country. Even if carried out to the letter, they would not have accelerated growth very much, because they have been too modest. And they have not been carried out. Technical competence in the planning organization is of limited use unless the whole idea of preparing and executing an effective development program has the wholehearted support of the executive branch of government; in a democracy, it must also have the support of the legislative branch, and behind the legislature the people as a whole. Given the degree of unity in this respect that India has, the Philippines could expect very rapid advance; but this unity has not been attained, and the plans remain paper plans for the most part.

2. Some of the comments made regarding Indian planning apply also to the Philippines. The planning organization lacks sufficient detailed knowledge of the Philippines economy and of Philippines society. For an economy so regionalized as the Philippines, the whole planning procedure is excessively centralized. Moreover, the Philippines has as yet done much less than India to inculcate a process of "planning from below" which would give a sense of participation to regional and local governments and to the general public.

3. The Philippines plan illustrates the dangers of "gradualism" in a somewhat different form from those which appeared in India. A plan which implies that the elimination of unemployment will take several decades, and that the concentration of income and wealth will not be significantly reduced during that same period, cannot be expected to engender enthusiasm among the masses of the people. Indeed, with growing literacy and political consciousness, it might be asked whether such a plan can even assure political and social stability in the country.

4. Even within Manila itself, there has been too little effort to make the planning process a co-operative effort. At times even

such agencies as the Central Bank, the Budget Commission, the Industrial Research Council, the Rehabilitation Finance Corporation, and the Department of Labor—agencies with an obvious interest in the plan and with an important role to play in its implementation—have been left largely outside the planning process. Indeed even the three branches of the NEC have been less well co-ordinated than would be desirable. In addition, the supply of *expertise* available for planning purposes is so limited that efforts should be made, as in India, to use the *expertise* available from outside the government, in the universities, private banks and businesses, agricultural and labor organizations, etc.

5. Together with the discussion of the Philippines problem in Chapter 2, our review of the Philippines plan shows that the presence of an entrepreneurial group, even when combined with an extremely uneven income distribution and with as generous tax concessions for "new and essential industries" as could possibly be justified, does not guarantee a high ratio of investment to national income. We have seen that the proportion of national income directed toward net private investment is about the same in the Philippines as it is in Indonesia, where conditions would seem to be very much less favorable. This experience, together with the similar experience in other underdeveloped countries, suggests that it is not enough to have a few Schumpeterian entrepreneurs; rapid growth also requires a Schumpeterian "cluster of followers." Where demonstrated success with an innovation in the now advanced countries called forth a host of imitators, in underdeveloped countries innovation often seems to stop with the original innovator.

6. The Philippines experience provides one more example of the dangers of projecting incremental capital-output ratios based on a short period during which conditions were unusually favorable.

7. The Philippines, and India, too, demonstrate the existence of a vicious circle with respect to education. A country which is not developing will provide few employment opportunities to engineers, natural scientists, technicians, and managers; hence students tend to prefer higher education in the traditional fields of law and the humanities. The potential rate of growth is then limited by the lack of engineers, natural scientists, technicians, and managers. The vicious circle can be broken only by a plan that will simultaneously accelerate actual growth and change the educational pattern.

8. Philippines experience, especially when compared with Indo-

nesian, shows the interrelationship between stabilization and growth. Development may exert destabilizing pressure, although with appropriate timing it can be turned into a stabilizing force. But where a country is plagued with instability without rapid growth, as in Indonesia, the leadership group is able to direct less of its energies to development questions than in countries that enjoy relative economic stability, as in the Philippines.

TABLE 29-6.

Structure of Indonesian, Philippines, and Indian Development Plans

	Indonesia	Philippines	India (second Plan)
Total net investment (per cent of national income)	6	10.6	9
Public net investment (per cent of total)	55	40	60
Private net investment (per cent of total)	45	60	40
Current expenditures of central government (per cent of gross national product)	12	7.3	......
Structure of public investment (per cent):			
Agriculture	13	8.5	11.8 *
Irrigation	11	8.0	7.9
Industry and mining	25	23.0	18.5
Transport	25	25.0	28.9
Public works (and other)	....	12.0	4.3
Public utilities (power)	14	16.0	8.9
Social development	12	7.5	19.7
	100	100.0	100.0

* Includes community development.

SOURCE: Compiled from the following documents: India, *Second Five Year Plan* (New Delhi, 1956); The Philippines, *The Five-Year Economic and Social Development Program, Fiscal Years, 1957–1961* (Manila, 1957); Indonesia, *Garis-Garis Besar Rentjana Pembangunan Lima Tahun, 1956–1960* (Djakarta, 1956).

Italy

In Chapter 2, we defined the development problem in Italy as the need to raise productivity and employment in the south (*Mezzogiorno*) while, at the same time, sustaining growth in the rest of the country and solving the balance of payments problem. The problem of the south, we saw, is not merely regional; it is a problem for Italy as a whole. Dr. Rosenstein-Rodan cites four economic reasons and one social reason for giving development of the *Mezzogiorno* priority in the over-all Italian development plan: [28]

(1) Lower wages in the South are not a sufficient incentive for investment. Without a changed economic framework, the long-run flow of investment would become smaller and the bulk of it would continue to flow to the North. We might then see in the 1960's 40 million people concentrated in the North and only 10 million in the South. Expensive new housing and other not directly productive capital investment would have to be provided in the North—while the already existing social overhead capital assets in the South, which need only a slight extension, far from being increased, would not even be maintained at the present level. The over-concentration in the North might produce an economic congestion, i.e., diminishing returns (though this is far from certain). It would then be very costly to reverse the process. The end result might be an economic loss to the whole of Italy.

(2) Undeveloped land and unused manpower can be used in the South. Employing workers on the land increases income without drawing on scarce resources by using manpower which could not otherwise be used. In the process manpower will get some training while doing work it is used to.

(3) The development program in the South produces great extra-regional external economies by giving contracts to the North. An industrialization program in the North, on the other hand, could hardly use any of the Southern resources. It would thus only aggravate the existing disparity between the two areas and be ultimately checked by not creating a sufficient new effective demand.

(4) Programming requires a great deal of effort and organization besides capital. No preliminary work on investment and projects has been done for the North, while several years programming work has been accomplished for the South. While there are single projects in the North of Italy which might be directly more profitable, they are too few to provide a minimum quantum capable of generating enough momentum to create a new economic structure in Italy.

(5) Social case: without a development program in the South a social explosion would upset not only the South but the whole Italian economy.

The stagnation of the *Mezzogiorno* is reflected in the aggregate level of unemployment and the balance of payments position

[28] P. N. Rosenstein-Rodan, "Programming and Theory in Italian Practice," in *Investment Criteria and Economic Growth* (Cambridge, Mass., 1955), pp. 28–29.

of the Italian economy as a whole. As pointed out in the ten-year program ("Vanoni Plan") itself, the over-all picture with respect to growth of national income was quite impressive for the immediate pre-Plan years:[29]

. . . During the four-year period from 1951 to 1954, national income in real terms increased at an annual rate of just over 5 per cent—from 8,570 billion lire in 1950 to 10,450 billion lire in 1954 (constant prices). This rate of expansion was achieved under conditions of substantially stable prices and it is among the highest recorded in Italian economic history.

Investment was running at high levels; gross investment amounted to 21 per cent of national income, net investment to more than 14 per cent. The marginal savings rate reached 26.5 per cent of the increase in gross national income. Of this investment, public investment accounted for about 30 per cent. However, the rise in national income resulted from rising productivity rather than rising employment, and continued growth was hampered by lack of foreign exchange. Dr. Pasquale Saraceno, Secretary General of the Association for the Industrial Development of Southern Italy (SVIMEZ) points out that "the impressive postwar development, which had brought industrial production in 1954 to almost twice the pre-war level, was leaving largely unsolved the big structural problems that had characterised the Italian economic scene ever since the time—almost a century ago—of the country's political unification."[30]

The Plan

For these reasons the Italian plan is essentially employment-oriented. It begins with an estimate of the increase in the labor supply, as shown in Table 29-7. It then establishes as a target the elimination of unemployment, including disguised unemployment, during the plan period, while absorbing the current growth of the labor force. Allowing for technological displacement, frictional unemployment, and emigration, the conclusion is reached that expansion of the economy must provide four million new jobs. The required rate of growth is then projected

[29] Svimez, *Outline of Development of Income and Employment in Italy in the Ten-Year Period 1955–64*, January, 1955, p. 1.

[30] Pasquale Saraceno, "The Vanoni Plan in its Third Year: Results and Perspectives," lecture delivered to the Economic Development Institute, International Bank for Reconstruction and Development (Washington, D.C., October 27, 1937), pp. 1–2.

TABLE 29-7.

Labor Supply as Estimated for the Period 1955–64
(thousands of workers)

Additional labor supply from natural increase 1955–64		2,000
Labor supply from other sources:		
Agriculture		
Unemployment in 1954	400	
Underemployment	900 *	
	1,300	
minus frictional unemployment in 1964	250	1,050
Non-agricultural sectors		
Unemployment in 1954	1,400	
Technological unemployment	800 †	
	2,200	
minus frictional unemployment in 1964	450	1,750
		4,800
minus emigration 1955–64		800
Total labor supply 1955–64		4,000

* Including such small technological unemployment as can be foreseen in agriculture.

† Including such underemployed as are believed to exist especially in the handicraft and tertiary sectors.

SOURCE: Svimez, *Outline of Development of Income and Employment in Italy in the Ten-Year Period 1955–64* (Rome, 1955).

to various sectors of the economy by use of input-output matrices.

The planning team eschewed employment creation by retarding technological progress, pointing out that higher productivity was essential to any solution of Italy's economic problems. At the same time, the team faced squarely the possibility that in the Italian economy full employment and maximum national income may be mutually inconsistent unless and until a new labor-intensive, but nonetheless efficient, technology is discovered. Dr. Rosenstein-Rodan has put the problem in the following terms: [31]

> Under variable coefficients of production even small changes in wage-rates would lead to different factor proportions and to higher employment, without a fall in Real National Income. Under rigidly fixed coefficients of production even large changes in wage-rates may

[31] P. N. Rosenstein-Rodan, "Factor Proportions in the Italian Economy," M.I.T., CIS, December, 1953.

not lead to an appreciable increase in employment without a fall in Real National Income. Under "discontinuously variable" coefficients of production large changes in wages may be required to increase employment; the reduction in wages may, however, affect the income-and-price-elasticities of demand in such a way that the higher employment-output may represent a smaller value than the previous output-combination. . . .

The Italian economy consists presumably of three sectors: (1) a small one with fixed coefficients, (2) a large one with "discontinuously variable" coefficients, (3) a small one with variable coefficients of production. The last sector may be too small to eliminate technological unemployment although it helps to reduce it. International Trade has an effect similar to an extension of the "variable coefficients" sector; it reduces but does not eliminate the divergence between the maximum-value and the full-employment output.

There still remained the question as to the best method for eliminating unemployment and absorbing the increase in labor supply. Rosenstein-Rodan has indicated that three courses of action were considered: [32]

The *first* might be a large-scale industrialization program in the North. The advantages of increasing an existing industrial system rather than creating a new one are obvious. Many difficulties stand, however, in the way of this solution. There would be considerable uncertainty regarding markets for the newly-produced industrial product. An industrialization program in the North would mainly benefit the North and not the South, apart from some migration outlet to the North. More houses would have to be built in the North for the immigrants while existing houses can be used to a large extent in the South thus saving a proportion of capital required for development. The development of Southern Italy on the other hand would place many contracts for the industries in the North and thus benefit the North as well as the South; investment in the South produces many more extraregional external economies.

The *second* way of implementing an investment program might be an industrialization program in the South. Again, however, the same or even greater difficulties than in the North would obtain in the South. There would be uncertainty in finding proper markets for the new industrial products greater even than in the North because of the smaller size of the existing market. There would be additional difficulties in transforming Southern Italian peasants into industrial workers, a task which cannot be completely achieved within a few years.

A *third* way has been chosen: a large-scale development of agrarian

[32] *Ibid.*, pp. 27–28.

resources and social overhead capital, which is to create an additional market, a changed economic structure which would attract a flow of private capital sufficient to secure a higher standard of living in the South and a more balanced economy for Italy as a whole. The increase in output will find established markets at home and markets abroad for exports in which the comparative advantage is clearly in favor of Italy. It is a pre-industrialization program foregoing somewhat higher profits in the short run, which might be obtainable by investments elsewhere, for the sake of securing more profits in the longer run. Both the direct and indirect profits accruing from the investment must be taken into account, as well as new investment opportunities created, although the latter may only emerge after the first phase of the program has been successfully achieved.

Mere expansion, without structural change, is not enough; in the stagnant south, a discontinuous change in structure is a necessary adjunct of development, and must be provided for in the plan.[33] For this purpose, and also to provide the basic stimulus for balanced growth in the private sector, the plan includes government development projects in three "impulse sectors": agriculture, public utilities, and public works. Thus the public investment aspect of the plan involves both "sectoral planning" and "project planning."

Detailed planning in Italy is confined to public investment in those "impulse sectors" and in housing. In the rest of the economy a projection is made on the basis of a rather thorough input-output analysis (Table 29-8). This analysis, together with multiplier analysis, also yields estimates of foreign exchange requirements for the achievement of development targets. The foreign exchange drain was also one of the considerations in assigning priorities to particular projects. The other major variables in the priority formula were the ratio of value added to capital requirements and the ratio of cost of domestic factors to capital requirements (a negative weight). The heaviest weight was attached to the foreign exchange requirement because analysis proved foreign exchange to be the major limiting factor in determining the total scale of the plan. The net inflationary impact has also been calculated from household data and multiplier analysis, but the danger of inflation has proved less serious a limitation than the

[33] "The decision to develop the South of Italy by a ten-year $1.6 billion public investment program initiated a structural change which no market decision would ever have reached." P. N. Rosenstein-Rodan, "Programming in Theory and in Italian Practice," in *Investment Criteria and Economic Growth* (Cambridge, Mass., 1955), p. 26.

TABLE 29-8.

Composition of the Assumed Increase in Income 1955–64
(rounded figures)

Income	Billion lire	Percentages
Income produced by 3,200,000 additional workers in non-agricultural sectors, with average productivity of the ten-year period (Lire 900 thousand multiplied by 3.2 million)	2,900	44.2
Increase in net agricultural product	550	8.4
Income increase from better utilization of residual idle capacity	600	9.2
	4,050	61.8
National income, increasing at an annual rate of 5 per cent, is expected to rise in the ten years by	6,550	100.0
Hence increase of income to be achieved through higher productivity of workers employed in non-agricultural sectors ...	2,500	38.2

SOURCE: Svimez, *Outline of Development of Income and Employment in Italy in the Ten-Year Period 1955–64* (Rome, 1955), p. 10.

need to protect foreign exchange reserve.[34]

The housing sector is treated as the balance wheel in the economy. The three impulse sectors "are in large part closely connected with the planned process of expansion of productive capacity." For them more or less steady growth is needed. "As regards housing, by contrast, Government action is influenced up to a certain level by urgent social needs, which must be met in any event; beyond that level, the housing programme can be regarded as a further possible stimulus to the process of expansion of demand." Unlike other investment, housing does not add to productive capacity or to permanent employment. Thus it can become the basis of flexible action, to offset fluctuations in other kinds of investment in the economy.

In the field of agriculture, emphasis was placed on reclamation

[34] The multiplier analysis established the following relationships:
The marginal propensity to consume domestic goods $C = 0.45$
The marginal propensity to import $I = 0.20$
The marginal propensity to tax $T = 0.26$
The marginal propensity to save $s = 0.09$

$$\text{The multiplier } k = \frac{1}{1-c} = \frac{1}{1-0.45} = 1.8$$

and land reform. The investment program for agriculture is shown in Table 29-9. The plan also calls for 3,210 billion lire investment in provision of additional electric power, 700 billion in electrification and improvement of railroads, 450 billion for aqueducts, and 300 billion each for natural gas and telephones. The public works program includes 1,150 billion lire for roads, 790 billion for river and mountain improvement, 220 billion for schools, and 650 billion for hospitals, sewers, airports, and other works. Altogether, the program covers public investments of 11,237 billion lire.

These investments themselves were not expected to add much to permanent employment:

Table 29-9.

Breakdown of Net Investment in Agriculture, 1955–64

Type of investment	Billion lire	Per cent
Land reclamation projects	543	16
Transformation (irrigation and dry) and mountain improvement projects	1,004	29
Land reform	522	15
Mechanization	313	9
Other investment (livestock, inventories, etc.)	385	11
Facilities for produce sorting and preservation	300	9
Technical assistance and vocational training	400	11
Total	3,467	100

. . . the role of the impulse programmes consists, not so much in the direct effect on employment, as (a) in the utilisation of natural resources (agricultural and sources of power); (b) in the creation of environmental conditions and external economies essential to development; (c) in the impulse given via the multiplier to the general process of expansion.

Employment creation, then, was expected to come mainly from the private investment that would be generated by the program. The estimated capital-job ratios for three major sectors are shown in Table 29-10. Translated into dollars, they come to about $16,000 per job in heavy industry, $2,500 in small industries and handicrafts, $1,600 in tertiary activities, and $2,500 for the over-all program. These figures, of course, cannot be used in other countries without adjustment for differences in costs. However, it is likely that *capital* costs would be higher in still less developed countries than they would be in Italy. These calculations should dispel any easy optimism regarding the cost of bringing about structural change in underdeveloped economies.

The ten-year program does not include detailed recommendations for financing. Instead, sources of financing for investment in 1952–54 are presented, and a case is made for confining detailed financial plans to the first four years covered by the program.

If the goals of the Vanoni Plan were achieved, says Saraceno, the north "ought to present in 1964 the characteristics typical of a highly industrialised country with only 18 per cent of its gross income deriving from agriculture and as much as 45 per

TABLE 29-10.

Capital Directly Needed for the Creation of New Jobs

Branches	Number of jobs	Capital required per job, million lire	Total capital required, billion lire
Industries with heavy capital requirements	100,000	10.0	1,000
Other industries and the handicraft sector	1,500,000	1.5	2,200
Tertiary activities	1,600,000	1.0	1,600
Total	3,200,000	1.5	4,800

SOURCE: Svimez, *Outline of Development of Income and Employment in Italy in the Ten-Year Period 1955–64* (Rome, 1955), pp. 18, 30.

cent deriving from industrial activity." But the structural change in the south was the main goal of the Plan. "Thus, while in 1954 43 per cent of the income of the South was derived from agriculture, and 57 per cent from industrial and tertiary activities combined, in 1964—assuming that the employment aims of the 'Plan' were reached—the proportion of income derived from industry and services would have to have risen to 76 percent." [35]

Results under the Plan

In terms of over-all rates of growth, Italy's achievements under the Plan must be accounted a success; it has actually been somewhat above the target of 5 per cent per year. The over-all reduction in unemployment has also been in accordance with the Plan. However, the hoped-for reduction in the gap between the north and the south has not materialized. Rates of increase in income and employment have been about the same in the south

[35] Saraceno, *op. cit.*, p. 3.

as in the north. Considering the strength of the "backwash effects" on the south of economic development in the north, it might be regarded as a notable achievement to equalize rates of growth in the two regions, especially since the agricultural south has shared less in the world boom than the industrialized north and has suffered bad crop years. But the Italian planners are not content with this result. They had aimed at growth rates in the south double those in the north, and they are still determined to find the means of producing faster development in the south than in the north.

The balance of payments position has improved under the Plan, but the nature of this improvement is not without its worrisome features. The income-elasticity of demand for imported capital goods has proved much higher than expected, despite the high level of development of the Italian machine industries in the north. Indeed each 1 per cent increase in gross national product has brought a 2 per cent increase in industrial imports. The income elasticity of demand for imports in general has proved higher still. Under these conditions, the growth of national income in recent years might well have been accompanied by a worsening of the balance of payments position but for three developments in the world market that were no part of the Plan: the world-wide boom in investment resulted in expanded exports of Italian engineering products, which are marginal sellers in the world market, enjoying good sales in such a boom but losing their market quickly in a world recession; the Italian terms of trade improved; and there was a net inflow of foreign capital (including repatriation of Italian capital). The uncertain duration of all three of these favorable developments means that the balance of payments continues to be a problem for the Italian planners. The balance of trade by itself still shows a considerable deficit, and the need for export promotion continues.

In one respect, the difficulties that have arisen during the first years of the Vanoni Plan are similar to those that arose under the second Five-Year Plan in India; in part, they reflect the unexpected vigor of the private investment sector. It was recognized that a private investment boom in the north would not in itself solve the problems of the south. It was also recognized that it was impossible simultaneously to give the private investment boom its head, expand public investment in the "impulse sectors" through deficit finance, and maintain monetary stability. It was decided "not to hinder the spontaneous expansion of productive activity" and "to keep down the budget deficit by keeping down public expenditure." [36]

At the same time, new measures were taken to direct private investment toward the south. When the Plan was drawn up in the latter part of 1954 it had been thought that provision of the infrastructure and loan funds would be enough to attract capital to the south. By 1957 it was apparent that more powerful incentives were needed, and in July of that year a new law was passed, providing, among other things, for exemption from the proportional income tax of business profits invested in the south (up to the point where such profits reach 50 per cent of total declared profits or 50 per cent of total investment in the south by a particular enterprise). The law also provided that state-owned industrial enterprises must make at least 40 per cent of their total gross investment in the south. At time of writing, it was still too early to say for sure whether these new measures would succeed in raising growth rates in the south above those in the north. They had not done so within the first year of their operation. In correspondence with the author, Dr. Rosenstein-Rodan has expressed the view that Italy will find it difficult enough to maintain growth rates in the south as high as in the north. Italian experience illustrates very clearly how hard it is to bring about structural change in an economy where the market forces press in the opposite direction.

This account of the outcome of the Vanoni Plan during its first years also shows the need for flexibility and frequent revision of development plans, especially where the private sector is responsible for most of the production and investment. Further evidence of this need for flexibility is provided by the recasting of goals occasioned by the European Common Market. This proposal introduces an area of free trade in Europe, whereas the Plan rested on the assumption that tariff structures would remain unchanged. As Dr. Saraceno puts it, if the Common Market is to be established between 1971 and 1973, "it is necessary that the average productivity of the employed labour force in Italy should by that time have reached a level not far short of the rest of the area of the Common Market." [37] Consequently the Plan must be speeded up and capital requirements will be even higher than was originally envisaged.

[36] *Ibid.*, pp. 9–10.
[37] *Ibid.*, p. 13.

Lessons from Italian Experience

1. The need for powerful measures to counteract forces leading to disparate rates of growth in different regions and sectors of an economy, and the need for a flexible approach to development planning, are the chief lessons to be learned from Italian experience. There are also, however, some minor lessons.

2. A not unimportant lesson to be learned from Italian experience with development planning is that well-worked-out plans tend to attract foreign funds. The International Bank for Reconstruction and Development chose the Italian ten-year plan for the first major demonstration of its shift from a "project approach" to a "program approach" in its lending to underdeveloped countries. In October, 1956, the Bank lent an additional $75 million to Italy in support of its program for reconstruction of the south, with indications that total Bank support for the program would reach $300 million before the ten years were over. In making the loan to the *Cassa per il Mezzogiorno*, Eugene R. Black, then President of the Bank, said: [38]

> The Cassa program aims at nothing less than the economic and social rehabilitation of a whole region. I have myself visited the area and have retained a vivid impression of the work that is going on. Tasks of great magnitude and difficulty remain to be tackled, but much has already been accomplished and we have the fullest confidence in the ability and energy of those who are carrying it forward.

An interesting feature of the loan was the participation of the Bank of America, an American private bank with many Italian-American clients, without the IBRD's guarantee.

3. In the Italian plan, we see underlined the relationship between public and private investment. In contrast to the Indian planners, the Italian planners are counting heavily on public investment in the "impulse sectors" to generate the private investment needed to attain employment and output targets.

4. Another important lesson from Italian experience is that planning for full employment need not mean resorting to make-work projects or waste of resources. The employment target determines the *scale* of the program; it does not determine priorities. Priorities for particular projects are still determined according to their contribution to the long-run growth of per capita income. Maximizing the rate of increase in national income requires the absorption of unemployment up to the point where, with the

[38] Quoted in *The New York Times*, October 12, 1956.

given supply of capital and foreign exchange, further increases in employment would necessitate choosing more labor-intensive techniques or projects, even if they contribute less to national income than other projects or techniques that are more capital-intensive. Only at this point does a conflict arise between maximizing output and maximizing employment at a particular point of time. At this point, as we have already stated, the choice becomes a matter of social policy. Given a supply of capital and foreign exchange equal to their absorptive capacity, most underdeveloped countries can go a long way toward reducing unemployment, open and disguised (dynamic), before being confronted with this choice.

General Conclusions

Development planning experience in Libya, India, Indonesia, the Philippines, and Italy suggests several general principles.

1. To prepare an effective development plan, it is necessary to have extensive and intensive knowledge of the natural and manpower resources pattern and also of behavior patterns. The availability of information about resources and behavior helped in the preparation of plans in Libya and Italy; the lack of such information hindered planning in India and Indonesia. Knowledge of resource and behavior patterns may be somewhat more complete in the Philippines than in Indonesia, but it is still less complete than in many other countries.

2. Other current data are also useful in determining development potential in assigning priorities. The usefulness of statistical studies appears particularly clearly in the Italian case. Input-output figures, incremental capital-output ratios, estimates of leakages and multipliers, estimates of capital cost per job in various sectors or industries—all such statistics help to lend precision to a plan.

3. The importance of giving careful attention to the composition of a planning organization is borne out by experience in Libya and Indonesia, and to a lesser extent in India and Italy as well. The organization for plan preparation should reflect the component parts of the plan itself. Thus the planning team must include some experts in general economic and statistical analysis related to economic development. Planning also requires special knowledge of particular problems related to development, such as fiscal policy, monetary policy, balance of payments, and the like. Finally, the planning organization must bring to bear expert

knowledge of particular sectors and industries, such as plantations, peasant agriculture, transport and communications, small industries, and heavy industries. All this *expertise* need not be represented directly in the planning agency, if it is available in other government agencies and is made available to the planning agency regularly and systematically. The relationship between the planning team and other government agencies must be clearly defined, however, and the precise responsibility of each agency must be clearly assigned.

4. We have seen that although economic development has been a destabilizing factor in the past, it can be turned into a stabilizing force by careful attention to economic stability aspects when a development plan is prepared. Simultaneous provision for stabilization and development is most clear in the Italian and Libyan plans; but it also plays its role in the second Indian Five-Year Plan, where stepping up the pace of development was undertaken to check deflation. Various stabilization measures have been introduced during recent years in Indonesia, but the development plan itself has not been utilized in this fashion. In other words, it is not enough to avoid *de*stabilization through a development program; if well construed, the development program can be a positive stabilizing force. The need for interweaving stabilization and development makes it all the more essential that the planning team include experts in monetary and fiscal policy, balance of payments, etc.

5. A closely related point is the importance of regarding each five- or six-year plan as a phase of a longer plan. To be fully effective, the composition of each plan must reflect the development of the past five or ten years, and also the plans for later five-year periods. The broad outlines of structural change should be considered ten to twenty years in advance, and general thought should be given to the way in which priorities should change with successive five-year plans.

6. The importance of assuring public acceptance and compatibility with social and political objectives has been recognized in each of the four countries. However, experience indicates different ways of achieving such acceptability. India has gone farthest in the direction of obtaining direct public participation in the planning process and has laid most stress on bringing provincial and local governments into the planning operation. Indonesia is placing increasing stress on community development and planning by co-operatives. In Indonesia, the scope of planning may be restricted by excessive attention to political acceptability

by members of the planning organization itself. It is probably more efficient if technical experts do not themselves make political judgments, but leave such judgments to the legislative branch of the government. In the Indonesian context, this principle would mean presentation of more ambitious plans by the Economic Stabilization Bureau, leaving it to the National Planning Board to modify the plans in terms of political considerations. In Libya, the working party approach was adopted. In the Philippines, the National Economic Council secretariat might prepare draft plans based on technical considerations, leaving it to the Council to modify the plan in terms of political limitations. In the Philippines, public participation is provided by direct representation in the NEC of members of Congress; but the NEC may wish to give some attention to broadening this participation in other ways. In particular, the NEC may wish to increase the role of community development and of provincial and local governments.

7. The plan of each of these countries shows recognition of the fact that no government can make precise plans for the private sector of the economy. The planning team can design a public investment program and formulate policies to encourage and direct private investment. Otherwise, it can only indicate wishes and make forecasts of output and investment in the private sector. Formulating plans for the private sector in excessive detail can only be misleading and may pave the way for unwarranted attacks on the failure of the plan if the results diverge from targets. Although the Philippines is more insistent on the "free private enterprise" nature of its society than the governments of any of the five countries discussed here, there was a tendency at one stage of the planning process to present plans for the private sector in greater detail than in any of the other countries.

8. Although detailed targets for output, income, and employment in the private sector are meaningless in the absence of input-output projections or controls, a plan confined to the public sector alone is obviously incomplete in economies where a large proportion of total investment is undertaken by private enterprise. Structural change contrary to what the market would produce by itself is not easy to bring about in a private enterprise economy. Where structural change is the essence of development, as in all the countries discussed in this chapter, forecasts—however refined the techniques used—are not enough. The pattern of private investment must be changed, and the plan

is totally inadequate if it does not include the monetary, fiscal, foreign exchange, land-tenure, licensing, and other policies required to direct and encourage private investment along the appropriate lines. The plans should be flexible and frequently revised in the light of new developments.

9. One of the most important lessons to be derived from the experience of the five countries is the need to consider income creation and employment creation separately. In Libya, the unemployment problem arises mainly from droughts, although disguised unemployment exists most of the time. In India and Italy, it is recognized that the unemployment problem is related to the problem of factor-proportions and limited variability of technical coefficients. This problem is also important in Indonesia and the Philippines, although it seems to have attracted less attention there. The important point is that, in underdeveloped countries, increases in income may not carry with them proportionate increases in employment; rising income and rising unemployment can proceed side by side—and falling prices as well. Accordingly it is not sufficient, as it is in advanced countries, to concentrate on raising national income, with the assurance that doing so will ultimately eliminate unemployment as well. Special attention must be given to the problem of employment creation as such.

10. India, Indonesia, and the Philippines all demonstrate the importance of exercising great care in the projection of incremental capital-output ratios.

11. For each country there seems to be an "optimal moment" when economic, political, sociological, and technological factors combine to create a particularly favorable environment for a take-off into sustained growth. If this moment is missed, the re-establishment of preconditions for take-off is likely to be a long and painful job.

12. Ultimately the effectiveness of development plans depends on the whole political and ideological environment. Plans are prepared and implemented by people, and economic development will take place only if people "want" it. Leadership groups in and out of government, and the general public, too, must be prepared to make the decisions and undertake the actions essential to the process of economic growth. There are no primrose paths!

13. Sometimes the question is put: "Should investment be concentrated on accelerating growth of the growing points and leading sectors, or should investment be made in lagging sectors and regions?" The experience outlined in this chapter supports the

conclusion derived from the theoretical analysis in Part 4: the answer is "both." Concentration of investment in the expanding sectors may aggravate the problem of technological dualism. At the same time, opportunities in these sectors should not be neglected.

14. Except for Libya, all the countries discussed here can effectively use more capital assistance, and Libya can probably use still more technical assistance than it is getting. Moreover, it is questionable whether any country discussed here can really hope to achieve a take-off in the next decade or two without increased foreign aid or investment. The same, of course, is true of many other underdeveloped countries. The United States, Canada, Australia, New Zealand, the richest countries of the world today, all relied heavily on capital and skills from abroad during their periods of take-off and for a long time after. European economic history may be interpreted as a process by which different countries took turns as net importers of capital and technical skills while getting sustained economic growth under way. We have seen above that the problem confronting the now underdeveloped countries is much more complicated than that facing the now advanced countries when they were establishing preconditions for growth. "To develop or not to develop" is a question that must be answered mainly in terms of decisions and actions made by the peoples of the underdeveloped countries themselves, but foreign aid and investment may prove to be the catalyst without which the best endeavors of the underdeveloped countries will be in vain.

30 Conclusion: Proposals for Research

The major thesis of this book is the need to break out of the traditional molds of economic thought when we come to analyze the process of economic growth. Both scope and method of development economics must be different from those of equilibrium economics, and policy recommendations based on misapplication of the methods of traditional equilibrium economics are likely to take us far astray.

Our most important conclusions have already been set forth in Chapters 17 and 18. In Chapter 17, we summarized the requirements of growth theory with respect to scope and method:

1. We must learn to handle discontinuous functions.

2. We must work with multisector models, somewhere in between Keynesian macroeconomic systems and Walrasian or Leontieff general equilibrium systems.

3. We must deal with the strong possibility that cumulative movements away from equilibrium are more "normal" than a return to equilibrium after a disturbance; development is a matter of feedback mechanisms, not equilibrating adjustments.

4. Population growth, technological progress, and perhaps cultural change must be included as integral parts of the analytical system.

5. Analysis must be conducted in terms of group reactions rather than individual choice.

6. Every significant problem has to be handled in terms of a

general system rather than by a partial equilibrium analysis.

7. The process must always be put into time and analyzed in terms of model sequences and linkages.

8. We should be bold in stating hypotheses that seem to fit the facts, unless and until we find other facts or equally tenable theories, that are inconsistent with these hypotheses.

We have seen the importance of the psycho-socio-political framework in the process of growth. We have outlined the problems introduced by the "population explosion," especially when combined with "technological dualism." We have shown that expansion of international trade need not accelerate economic development and may even retard it. We have analyzed some fundamental discontinuities and demonstrated the need for a "big push" to get development started.

In Chapter 18, we indicated some of the broad implications for policy of these analytical results:

1. Current market choices are a very unreliable guide to development policy, and the more underdeveloped a country is the less useful is the marginal calculus. The calculus involved in economic development relates to the impact on total national income and its time distribution during a "crucial period" starting some years hence and ending a decade or more after that.

2. The over-all goal of development policy is eliminating poverty rather than reducing the gap between advanced and underdeveloped countries, and the polls are a better test than the market of people's willingness to pay the price of development.

3. Market forces alone are unlikely to produce economic development.

4. The present allocation of resources is no reflection of comparative advantage.

5. The planning period must extend to a couple of decades, and the current five-year-plan must be treated as part of a longer-run process.

6. Plans must be based on knowledge of the resource pattern, not only as it is but as it may be throughout the whole of the planning process.

7. A gradualist policy is likely to be self-defeating. Productivity in the agricultural as well as in the industrial sector must be raised, and doing both at once so as to maintain full employment will be expensive. Structural change is a *sine qua non* of development; no country can be truly prosperous if most gainfully occupied people are occupied in low-productivity agriculture.

8. If fertility rates do not drop as a consequence of indus-

trialization and urbanization, a positive population policy may be necessary.

The form of the recommendations in the policy chapters follows from these conclusions. We have adjured our readers to refrain from reaching conclusions on policy derived from traditional marginal analysis and urged them to think of nothing more "marginal" than the impact on the level and time distribution of national income as a whole during some "crucial period" in the future. We have stressed the need to think of incentives in very broad terms, including the effects of policy on social and cultural patterns, on sequences of decisions, on linkages forward and backward. We have indicated what the big push means in financial terms. We have shown the limitations on private savings as a means of financing development. We have suggested a tax system especially designed for the administrative and institutional conditions of underdeveloped countries. In planning economic development we have underlined the importance of what Hirschman calls strategy; one must plan in terms of a whole sequence of moves, in response to a whole sequence of reactions to our initial moves, and not in terms of the immediate impact on output of a particular good or service of a particular investment project.

One conclusion germane to Western policy emerges from the analysis: relatively few of the underdeveloped countries, particularly among those with per capita incomes below $200 per year, are likely to develop soon without substantial foreign aid. The countries clearly needing assistance include uncommitted countries of Asia and Africa: India, Indonesia, Burma, Ceylon, Egypt, and others. The outcome of the Cold War may well be determined in these countries, with their hundreds of millions of strategically located people. These countries are determined to develop, and for them aid is forthcoming from other quarters than the West. If the West does not convince them that their economic ambitions can be achieved within a democratic framework and provide them with the technical and capital assistance to do it, they are likely to try the Communist path. Once embarked on this path, can they ever turn back?

On the other hand, in order to translate such general principles into appropriate development plans and policies in particular countries at particular points of time, with as much confidence as we feel, say, in prescribing policies for checking inflation or curing unemployment in advanced countries, we need to know a good deal more than we do at this stage. The gaps that remain are bigger than those already filled. There are empty spaces in our tool kit. More serious, however, are the gaps in our empirical knowledge. Among the gaps which might be filled by a concentrated research effort, are the following:

I. Technological Data

A. Capital-output ratios, both aggregate and sectoral. It is essential to know how much investment is required for a given target increase in per capita income and how requirements vary with the composition of the development program. With increasing awareness of the importance of such data, and a consequent increase in the amount of pertinent data collected, it should be possible to improve substantially the accuracy of our ICOR estimates.

B. Capital-job ratios, both aggregate and sectoral. Since employment creation is an important objective in itself, we must know more precisely how much investment is needed to put a given number of men to work, and how this requirement varies with the composition of the development program. Here too, increasing attention to this problem should lead to a growing volume of data concerning it.

C. Factor-proportions, rates of substitution, and production functions. Our discussion of the "optimal technique," and the extent to which techniques can be adapted to factor endowments without loss of efficiency, was rather inconclusive because of the limited amount of pertinent data available. More studies of the kind being carried out by the Netherlands Economics Institute, in various underdeveloped countries, plus laboratory and pilot-plant research on new labor-intensive techniques, could provide much more information on the flexibility of factor-proportions.

D. A closely related question is: "Why do small and cottage industry programs so frequently fail? Are such industries, which by definition are smaller-scale and more labor-intensive than other known methods of producing the same commodity, inevitably inefficient? Or were the programs just badly planned and badly managed? Is it simply that some essential aspect of the production process, such as marketing, is neglected?" The United Nations has a study of these questions in process, but much more information is needed.

E. An extremely important question on which more data are needed is: "What is the potential increase in output per man-year with small-scale, labor-intensive agriculture? What can be expected from seed-selection, improvement of livestock strains, fertilizer, improved tools, simple improvements in irrigation techniques, etc.?" This question should be broken down by size of holding; what can be done with holdings as they are, with holdings double the present size, ten times the present size, a hundred times the present size? The question must also be asked, of course, in terms of the varying conditions of different underdeveloped countries.

F. A related question is, "Why do resettlement programs usually turn out to be so expensive?" How does the cost of employment creation through resettlement compare with cost of creating jobs in, say, import-replacing industries? How does the capital-output ratio of resettlement projects compare with that of import-replacing industries of various kinds?

G. More generally, what is the relationship of national income to natural resources on the one hand and human resources on the other?

II. Psycho-sociological Data

A. Demographic factors. Most important of these are the factors determining fertility rates. What makes individuals decide to limit the size of their families? What institutional arrangements are conducive to this decision? What are the requirements for making the decision effective? We must at least be able to forecast rates of population growth to determine capital requirements for economic growth. In some cases, as we have seen, it may also be necessary to control population growth, as an item of policy, if rising per capita incomes are to be assured. Demographers have of course studied these questions for a long time, but if they had money enough to finance a "forced draft" attack on the problem they could gather facts faster.

There are other demographic questions of considerable importance. What causes people to move from country to city, from agriculture to industry? How do their attitudes, values, and behavior alter when they do move? In general, do they change in a fashion conducive to acceleration of economic growth? Here again, getting the answer to these questions is largely a matter of research funds. We need a barrage of field studies in a number of underdeveloped countries at once. The work done by UNESCO on urbanization of underdeveloped countries is a start, but it is on much too small a scale.

B. Motivation and economic behavior. What makes people development-minded? What makes them technology-minded? What makes people willing or unwilling to work harder or better, or to risk capital in order to increase their incomes? What situations produce a large and growing stream of effective entrepreneurship? In general, what social, political, economic, and technical conditions produce individual behavior of a kind conducive to economic growth? How may these non-economic factors be measured?

III. Mixed Data: some of the information needed for an "optimal" development policy relates to constellations of technological, psycho-sociological, and economic data.

A. Input-output matrices. The interrelations of inputs and outputs of various industries in an economy are the outcome of both cost and demand factors and are thus the outcome of interactions between technical and psycho-sociological factors of the kind usually called "economic." If input-output matrices are to be used as a forecasting device in the preparation of development plans, both questions must be asked: Will the pattern of technical relationships remain the same when output is doubled? Will the pattern of demand remain the same when income is doubled? As mentioned above, the problem is complicated for underdeveloped countries because changes in the structure of output and consumption are an intrinsic part of the development process, and the introduction of new industries may be essential. However, as experience is gathered with the changes in input-output matrices of countries now developing, other countries will be in a better position to use input-output analysis as a forecasting device and a guide to development planning. Here again the main requirement is research funds for the purpose.

B. Linkages and model sequences. The question as to whether or not the construction of, say, a steel mill will induce others to set up an iron foundry or a bicycle factory depends partly on technical and partly on psycho-sociological considerations. Here, merely recording experience will not be enough. It will be necessary to do motivational research as well. The fact that the construction of a steel mill is followed by the establishment of an iron foundry and a bicycle factory is not incontrovertible evidence of backward and forward "linkage." It is necessary to find out why the foundry and factory were set up. The same considerations apply to model sequences of other kinds.

Filling these gaps in our knowledge will need more elaborate research projects than any yet carried out. The accumulation of knowledge can be greatly facilitated, however, if governments engaged in economic development maintain adequate records and make them available to governments of other underdeveloped countries, foreign aid agencies, and research scholars. Failures as well as successes should be recorded and studied. Information about development experience is exchanged among countries which are members of the Colombo Plan organization, and among countries within the various UN regional commissions. The information provided is not as frank and full as it should be, however, and much of the data needed to answer questions of the sort outlined above is not collected at all. Moreover, there should be no geographic limitations on the exchange of information. It might be desirable to set up within the UN, perhaps attached to the International Bank for Reconstruction and Development, a consultative committee of both underdeveloped and advanced countries, similar to the Consultative Committee of the Colombo Plan organization, but including all members of the UN.

It is clear that the research needed to improve our empirical knowledge of the development process must be interdisciplinary; economists need help both from the engineering and natural sciences and from other social sciences. So far, most of the research on non-economic factors in economic development has been undertaken—or at least organized—by economists, whose limited training leaves them inadequately equipped for the task. If psychologists, sociologists, and anthropologists are to be really useful in the field of economic development, however, they must not only be interested in its problems and have some initial understanding of the relationship of their own specialty to the others involved, but they must also be willing to undertake some revisions of their own scope and method and perhaps even of their training. For example, very few psychologists seem to share McClelland's interest in the relationship between social organization and individual motivation; if we are really to reach a position where we can generalize on these relationships, an enormous amount of research will be needed in a great many countries, with methods that will make the results comparable.

Anthropology provides a better example. If anthropologists are to be genuinely helpful to economists seeking to understand the relationship between culture and economic behavior, their scope and method must be substantially changed. To begin with, they must be interested in cultural change or dynamics, rather than in describing static societies as they are or were. They must concern themselves with societies of underdeveloped countries as a whole, and not just with primitive countries or with primitive cultures within underdeveloped countries; they must study Indonesians and Filipinos rather than the Nias tribes and Igorots. Some anthropologists, fortunately, are moving in this direction. Even more important for "consumers" of anthropological studies, however, is that anthropologists find short cuts to generalization. The traditional methods of the anthropologists confine them to intensive and prolonged study of small geographic regions. If their scientific standards are to be met, that cannot be helped. But some training in statistical method, and particularly in sampling techniques, might enable them to distinguish the strategic variables which correlate highly with everything else in a culture and thus characterize it. Thus armed, anthropologists would need less time to find out whether neighboring societies are different or the same. If they are the same, the anthropologists can move on; if they are different, more prolonged study may be necessary.

An example may help to make this point clear. The Center for International Studies at M.I.T. spent several hundred thousand dollars to send a team of social scientists (mainly sociologists and anthropologists) to an area in east central Java for two years of field work, and then to bring them back to write up their results. The whole process took more than four years. At the end of that time a good deal of information was available about economic behavior and the cultural framework in one small town and the surrounding villages. But of what use was this material for people interested in economic development principles and policies? Could we safely assume that the behavior patterns found in that tiny area were typical of east Java? Of central Java? Of Java as a whole? Of Indonesia? Of Southeast Asia? The answer was clearly no; before we could generalize from these results, similar studies would have to be made in other areas. Must we then wait many more years, and spend many more hundred thousand dollars, before the materials already gathered can be used to improve our knowledge of the development process? It seemed that it should be possible to pin down basic similarities and differences with much less time and much less money. Two anthropologists of unusual temperament, training, and interests volunteered to try. They ran into a civil war and could not carry out their research plans in full; even so, they came back with a highly useful partial answer: central Java is the same, Bali and central Sumatra are different. More of this kind of comparative follow-up should provide short cuts to generalization.

We end this book, then, not with a final conclusion but with a final plea. We enter a plea to the governments of underdeveloped countries to keep full and accurate records of their experience under their development plans, particularly records of experience related to the major gaps in our knowledge, and to make these records freely available to people who can use them in analyzing the development process. We enter a plea to organizations sponsoring research to make available increased resources for the study of economic development, especially in its technological and psycho-sociological aspects. And we enter a plea to our fellow scientists to give thought to the problems of development and to revisions in their own scope, method, and training required to permit at least some of them to give economists the help which they so badly need in this very important field.

Select Bibliography

NOTE: Articles referred to in the text are not listed here. Books referred to in the text are listed only if they have a relevance beyond the points specifically mentioned in the text.

Readers wishing a more detailed listing may consult the following specialized bibliographies:

Hazlewood, Arthur. *The Economics of Underdeveloped Areas*, London: Oxford University Press, 1954.

Meier, Gerald M., and Robert E. Baldwin. *Economic Development: Theory, History, and Policy*. New York: John Wiley & Sons, Inc., 1957. Appendices A, B, C.

Trager, Frank N. "A Selected and Annotated Bibliography on Economic Development, 1953–1957," *Economic Development and Cultural Change*, July, 1958, pp. 257–329.

PART 1

Andrews, J. Russell, and Azizali F. Mohammed. *The Economy of Pakistan*. Stanford, Calif.: Stanford University Press, 1958.

Bailey, F. G. *Caste and the Economic Frontier*. Manchester: Manchester University Press, 1957.

Gordon, Wendell. *The Economy of Latin America*. New York: Columbia University Press, 1950.

Hanson, Simon G. *Economic Development in Latin America*. Washington, D.C.: Inter-American Affairs Press, 1951.

The International Bank for Reconstruction and Development has published a number of economic surveys of underdeveloped countries through the John Hopkins University Press. Among these, the following may be mentioned as particularly interesting or readable: *The Economic Development of British Guiana*, 1953; *The Economic De-*

velopment of Ceylon, 1953; *The Economic Development of Guatemala*, 1951; *The Economic Development of Jordan*, 1957; *The Economic Development of Malaya*, 1955; *The Economic Development of Nigeria*, 1955; *The Economic Development of Syria*, 1955; *The Economy of Turkey*, 1951.

Kuznets, Simon, Wilbert Moore, and Joseph J. Spengler. *Economic Growth: Brazil, India, Japan.* Durham, N.C.: Duke University Press, 1955.

Lewis, W. Arthur. *The Theory of Economic Growth.* London: G. Allen & Unwin, Ltd., 1955.

Lockwood, William W. *The Economic Development of Japan.* Princeton, N.J.: Princeton University Press, 1954.

Schumpeter, Elizabeth B. *The Industrialization of Japan and Manchukuo.* New York: The Macmillan Company, 1940.

Shannon, Lyle W. *Underdeveloped Areas.* New York: Harper & Brothers, 1957.

Staley, Eugene. *The Future of Underdeveloped Countries.* New York: Harper & Brothers, 1957.

Vakil, Chandulal N., and C. N. Brahmanand. *Planning for an Expanding Economy.* Bombay: Vora, 1956.

Woytinsky, Wladimir S., and E. S. Woytinsky. *World Population and Production.* New York: The Twentieth Century Fund, Inc., 1953.

PART 2

Baran, Paul. *The Political Economy of Growth.* New York: Monthly Review Press, 1957.

Baumol, William. *Economic Dynamics.* New York: The Macmillan Company, 1951.

Domar, Evsey. *Essays in the Theory of Economic Growth.* New York: Oxford University Press, 1957.

Hamberg, Daniel. *Economic Growth and Instability.* New York: W. W. Norton & Company, Inc., 1956.

Keirstead, Burton. *The Theory of Economic Change.* Toronto: The Macmillan Co. of Canada, Ltd., 1948.

Meier, Gerald M., and Robert E. Baldwin. *Economic Development: Theory, History, and Policy.* New York: John Wiley & Sons, Inc., 1957. Part 1.

Robinson, Joan. *Essay on Marxian Economics.* London: Macmillan & Co., Ltd., 1942.

Schumpeter, Joseph. *History of Economic Analysis.* New York: Oxford University Press, 1954.

Sweezy, Paul. *The Theory of Capitalist Development.* New York: Oxford University Press, 1942.

PART 3

Ayres, Clarence E. *The Theory of Economic Progress.* Chapel Hill, N.C.: University of North Carolina Press, 1944.

Cairncross, Alexander K. *Home and Foreign Investment, 1870–1913.* Cambridge: Cambridge University Press, 1953.

Clark, Colin. *The Conditions of Economic Progress.* London: Macmillan & Co., Ltd., 1951.

Economic History Association. "The American West as an Underdeveloped Region," *Journal of Economic History*, XVI, No. 4 (1956), pp. 449–589.

———. "Economic Growth," *ibid.* (1947) Supplement VII.

———. "The Role of Government and Business Enterprise in the Promotion of Economic Development," *ibid.* (1950) Supplement X.

Heaton, Herbert. "Other Wests than Ours," *Journal of Economic History*, Supplement VI, 1946.

Hozelitz, B. F. (ed.). *The Progress of Underdeveloped Areas.* Chicago: University of Chicago Press, 1952.

Kuznets, Simon (ed.). *Problems in the Study of Economic Growth.* New York: National Bureau of Economic Research, Inc., 1949, especially chap. III, "Themes of Socio-Economic Growth," by Joseph J. Spengler.

Mason, Edward S. *Promoting Economic Development: United States and S. Asia.* Claremont, Calif.: 1955.

Universities–National Bureau Committee for Economic Research. *Capital Formation and Economic Growth.* Princeton, N.J.: Princeton University Press, 1955.

Williamson, Harold F. (ed.). *The Growth of the American Economy.* Englewood Cliffs, N.J.: Prentice-Hall, Inc., 1944.

Youngson, A. J. *Possibilities of Economic Progress* (in press, 1959).

PART 4

Haavelmo, Trygve. *A Study in the Theory of Economic Evolution.* Amsterdam: North Holland Publishing Co., 1954.

Johnson, Harry G. *International Trade and Economic Growth.* Cambridge, Mass.: Harvard University Press, 1958.

Kindleberger, Charles P. *Economic Development.* New York: McGraw-Hill Book Company, Inc., 1958.

Lerner, Daniel (with Lucille W. Pevsner). *The Passing of Traditional Society.* Glencoe, Ill.: Free Press, 1958.

Lewis, W. Arthur. *The Theory of Economic Growth.* London: G. Allen & Unwin, Ltd., 1955.

McClelland, David C., *et al. The Achievement Motive.* New York: Appleton-Century-Crofts, Inc., 1953.

Mead, Margaret (ed.). *Cultural Patterns and Technical Change.* Paris: UNESCO, 1953.

Moore, Wilbert E. *Industrialization and Labor.* Ithaca, N.Y.: Cornell University Press, 1951.

Myrdal, Gunnar. *Economic Theory and Underdeveloped Regions.* London: Gerald Duckworth & Co., Ltd., 1957.

Nurkse, Ragnar. *Problems of Capital Formation in Underdeveloped Countries.* Oxford: Basil Blackwell & Mott, Ltd., 1953.

Rostow, W. W. *The Process of Economic Growth.* New York: W. W. Norton & Company, Inc., 1952.

Williamson, Harold F., and John A. Buttrick. *Economic Development: Principles and Patterns.* Englewood Cliffs, N.J.: Prentice-Hall, Inc., 1954.

PART 5

Abraham, W. I. "Investment Estimates of Underdeveloped Countries: An Appraisal," *Journal of the American Statistical Association*, September, 1958, pp. 669–679.

Adler, John H., E. R. Schlesinger, and E. C. Olson. *Public Finance and Economic Development in Guatemala.* Stanford, Calif.: Stanford University Press, 1952, pp. xix, 282.

Allen, George C., and A. G. Donnithorne. *Western Enterprise in Far Eastern Economic Development: China and Japan.* London: G. Allen & Unwin, Ltd., 1954.

American Assembly. *International Stability and Progress.* New York: Columbia University Graduate School of Business, June, 1957.

Baldwin, George B. *Industrial Growth in South India: Case Studies in Economic Development.* Glencoe, Ill.: Free Press, 1959.

Belshaw, Horace. *Population Growth and Levels of Consumption.* London: G. Allen & Unwin, Ltd., 1956.

Benham, Frederic. *The Colombo Plan and Other Essays.* London and New York: Royal Institute of Foreign Affairs, 1956.

Bonne, Alfred. *Studies in Economic Development.* London: Routledge & Kegan Paul, Ltd., 1957.

Brand, W. *The Struggle for a Higher Standard of Living.* Glencoe, Ill.: Free Press, 1958.

Chandrasekhar, George. *Population and Planned Parenthood in India.* London: G. Allen & Unwin, Ltd., 1956.

Chang Kia-Ngau. *The Inflationary Spiral: The Experience in China, 1939–1950.* New York: Technology Press, M.I.T., and John Wiley & Sons, Inc., 1958.

Diamond, William. *Development Banks.* Baltimore: Johns Hopkins Press, for the Economic Development Institute, International Bank for Reconstruction and Development, 1957.

Glick, Philip M. *The Administration of Technical Assistance: Growth in the Americas.* Chicago: University of Chicago Press, 1957.

Hagen, Everett E. *The Economic Development of Burma.* Washington, D.C.: National Planning Association, 1956.

Hicks, J. R., and U. K. Hicks. *Report on Finance and Taxation in Jamaica.* Kingston, Jamaica: Government Printer, 1955.

Higgins, Benjamin. *Indonesia's Economic Stabilization and Development.* New York: Institute of Pacific Relations, 1957.

Higgins, Benjamin, and Wilfred Malenbaum. *Financing Economic Development.* New York: Carnegie Endowment for International Peace, 1955.

Iversen, Carl. *A Report on Monetary Policy in Iraq.* Copenhagen: Ejnar Munksgaard, 1954.

Keenleyside, H. C. "Administrative Problems of Technical Assistance Administration," *Canadian Journal of Economics and Political Science,* August, 1952, pp. 345–357.

Li, Choh-Ming. *Economic Development of Communist China: An Appraisal of the Five Years of Industrialization.* Berkeley, Calif.: University of California Press, 1958.

Millikan, Max, and W. W. Rostow. *A Proposal: Key to an Effective Foreign Policy.* New York: Harper & Brothers, 1957.

Nurkse, Ragnar, *et al.* "The Quest for a Stabilization Policy in Primary Producing Countries," *Kyklos,* XI, No. 2, 1958.

Rosen, George. *Industrial Change in India: Industrial Growth, Capital Requirements, and Technological Change, 1937–1955.* Glencoe, Ill.: Free Press, 1958.

Rostow, W. W., *et al. The Prospects for Communist China.* New York: John Wiley & Sons, Inc., 1954.

Russell, Sir John. *World Populations and World Food Supplies.* London: G. Allen & Unwin, Ltd., 1957.

Schlesinger, Eugene R. *Multiple Exchange Rates and Economic Development.* Princeton, N.J.: Princeton University Press, 1952, pp. i, 76.

Schultz, Theodore W. *The Economic Organization of Agriculture.* New York: McGraw-Hill Book Company, Inc., 1953.

Tsuru, S. *Essays on the Japanese Economy.* Tokyo: Kinokumiya Bookstore, Tokyo, 1958.

United Nations Department of Economic Affairs. *Domestic Financing of Economic Development.* New York: 1950, pp. vi, 231.

United Nations Economic Commission for Asia and the Far East.

Mobilization of Domestic Capital in Certain Countries of Asia and the Far East. Bangkok: 1951, pp. xii, 239.

———. *Mobilization of Domestic Capital.* Bangkok: 1953.

Wald, Haskell P., and J. N. Froomkin (eds.). *Agricultural Taxation and Economic Development.* Cambridge, Mass.: Harvard University Printing Office, 1954.

Wallich, Henry C., and J. H. Adler. *Public Finance in a Developing Country: El Salvador.* Cambridge, Mass.: Harvard University Press, 1951.

Wolf, Charles, and S. C. Sufrin. *Capital Formation and Foreign Investment in Underdeveloped Areas.* Syracuse, N.Y.: Syracuse University Press, 1955.

Index